COMPILATION OF SELECTED UNITED STATES COAST GUARD AND MARITIME TRANSPORTATION RELATED LAWS

VOLUME 3

Updated through the 118th Congress.

Prepared By M. TWINCHEK

2025

Forward

This Compilation of Selected United States Coast Guard and Maritime Transportation Related Laws is a resource for those interested in U.S. laws governing the Coast Guard. This compilation includes laws governing United States Coast Guard and its establishment; the Coast Guard Academy; water pollution; lifesaving; ports and waterways; merchant marines; and other aspects of the United States Coast Guard.

The materials included comes from publicly available, open source information, prepared for the public by the Office of the Legislative Counsel of the U.S. House of Representatives and the Office of the Law Revision Counsel.

Items listed as a Statute Compilation do not appear in the U.S. Code or that have been classified to a title of the U.S. Code that has not been enacted into positive law. Each Statute Compilation incorporates the amendments made to the underlying statute since it was originally enacted and are current as of the date noted.

This compilation is not an official document and should not be cited as evidence of any law. The official version of Federal law is found in the United States Statutes at Large and in the U.S. Code, the legal effect of which is established in sections 112 and 204, respectively, of title 1, United States Code.

A special thanks is extended to the Office of Law Revision Counsel and the House Office of the Legislative Counsel for providing the U.S. Code and statute compilations; and to the Government Publications Office for hosting and making these available for use to the public. An additional thank you is offered to the staff of the House and Senate Committees who were gracious in responding to inquiries and providing background information on the legislation included.

Questions and comments may be directed to:

M. Twinchek

Email: mtwinchek@outlook.com

Contents

HOMELAND SECURITY ACT OF 2002

SEC. 888

PUBLIC LAW 107-296
AS AMENDED THROUGH P.L. 118-186

SECTION 888 of the HOMELAND SECURITY ACT OF 2002

[Public Law 107–296; Approved November 25, 2002]

[As Amended Through P.L. 118–186, Enacted December 23, 2024]

AN ACT To establish the Department of Homeland Security, and for other purposes.

Be it enacted by the Senate and House of Representatives of the United States of America in Congress assembled,

SECTION 1. SHORT TITLE; TABLE OF CONTENTS.

(a) [6 U.S.C. 101 note] SHORT TITLE.—This Act may be cited as the "Homeland Security Act of 2002".

(b) TABLE OF CONTENTS.—The table of contents for this Act is as follows:

* * * * * * *

TITLE VIII—COORDINATION WITH NON-FEDERAL ENTITIES; INSPECTOR GENERAL; UNITED STATES SECRET

SERVICE; COAST GUARD; GENERAL PROVISIONS

* * * * * * *

Subtitle H—Miscellaneous Provisions

* * * * * * *

SEC. 888. [6 U.S.C. 468] PRESERVING COAST GUARD MISSION PERFORMANCE.

(a) DEFINITIONS.—In this section:

(1) NON-HOMELAND SECURITY MISSIONS.—The term "non-homeland security missions" means the following missions of the Coast Guard:

(A) Marine safety.

(B) Search and rescue.

(C) Aids to navigation.

(D) Living marine resources (fisheries law enforcement).

(E) Marine environmental protection.

(F) Ice operations.

(2) HOMELAND SECURITY MISSIONS.—The term "homeland security missions" means the following missions of the Coast Guard:

(A) Ports, waterways and coastal security.

(B) Drug interdiction.

(C) Migrant interdiction.

(D) Defense readiness.

(E) Other law enforcement.

(b) TRANSFER.—There are transferred to the Department the authorities, functions, personnel, and assets of the Coast Guard, which shall be maintained as a distinct entity within the Department, including the authorities and functions of the Secretary of Transportation relating thereto.

(c) MAINTENANCE OF STATUS OF FUNCTIONS AND

ASSETS.—Notwithstanding any other provision of this Act, the authorities, functions, and capabilities of the Coast Guard to perform its missions shall be maintained intact and without significant reduction after the transfer of the Coast Guard to the Department, except as specified in subsequent Acts.

(d) CERTAIN TRANSFERS PROHIBITED.—No mission, function, or asset (including for purposes of this subsection any ship, aircraft, or helicopter) of the Coast Guard may be diverted to the principal and continuing use of any other organization, unit, or entity of the Department, except for details or assignments that do not reduce the Coast Guard's capability to perform its missions.

(e) CHANGES TO MISSIONS.—

(1) PROHIBITION.—The Secretary may not substantially or significantly reduce the missions of the Coast Guard or the Coast Guard's capability to perform those missions, except as specified in subsequent Acts.

(2) WAIVER.—The Secretary may waive the restrictions under paragraph (1) for a period of not to exceed 90 days upon a declaration and certification by the Secretary to Congress that a clear, compelling, and immediate need exists for such a waiver. A certification under this paragraph shall include a detailed justification for the declaration and certification, including the reasons and specific information that demonstrate that the Nation and the Coast Guard cannot respond effectively if the restrictions under paragraph (1) are not waived.

(f) DIRECT REPORTING TO SECRETARY.—Upon the transfer of the Coast Guard to the Department, the Commandant shall report directly to the Secretary without being required to report through any other official of the Department.

(g) OPERATION AS A SERVICE IN THE NAVY.—None of the conditions and restrictions in this section shall apply when the Coast Guard operates as a service in the Navy under section 3 of title 14, United States Code.

* * * * * * *

DINGELL-JOHNSON SPORT FISH RESTORATION ACT

CHAPTER 658, APPROVED AUGUST 9, 1950, 64 STAT. 430

AS AMENDED THROUGH P.L. 117-286

DINGELL-JOHNSON SPORT FISH RESTORATION ACT

[Chapter 658, Approved Aug. 9, 1950, 64 Stat. 430]

[As Amended Through P.L. 117–286, Enacted December 27, 2022]

AN ACT To provide that the United States shall aid the States in fish restoration and management projects, and for other purposes.

Be it enacted by the Senate and House of Representatives of the United States of America in Congress assembled,

[16 U.S.C. 777] That (a) the Secretary of the Interior[1] is authorized and directed to cooperate with the States through their respective State fish and game departments in fish restoration and management projects as hereinafter set forth: No money apportioned under this Act to any State, except as hereinafter provided, shall be expended therein until its legislature, or other State agency authorized by the State constitution to make laws governing the conservation of fish, shall have assented to the provisions of this Act and shall have passed laws for the conservation of fish, which shall include a prohibition against the diversion of license fees paid by fishermen for any other purpose than the administration of said State fish and game department, except that, until the final adjournment of the first regular session of the legislature held after passage of this Act, the assent of the governor of the State shall be sufficient. The Secretary of the interior and the State fish and game department of each State accepting the benefits of this Act shall agree upon the fish restoration and management projects to be aided in such State under the terms of this Act, and all projects shall conform to the standards fixed by the Secretary of the Interior.

---

[1] Transfer of functions to Secretary of Commerce from Secretary of the Interior in view of: creation of National Oceanic and Atmospheric Administration in Department of Commerce and Office of Administrator of such Administration;

abolition of Bureau of Commercial Fisheries in Department of the Interior and Office of Director of such Bureau; transfers of functions, including functions formerly vested by law in Secretary of the Interior or Department of the Interior which were administered through Bureau of Commercial Fisheries or were primarily related to such Bureau, exclusive of certain enumerated functions with respect to Great Lakes fishery research, Missouri River Reservoir research, Gulf-Breeze Biological Laboratory, and Trans-Alaska pipeline investigations; and transfer of marine sport fish program of Bureau of Sport Fisheries and Wildlife by Reorg. Plan No. 4 of 1970, eff. Oct. 3, 1970, 35 F.R. 15627, 84 Stat. 2090, set out in the Appendix to Title 5, Government Organization and Employees.

(b) ALLOCATION OF AMOUNTS BY COASTAL STATES BETWEEN MARINE FISH PROJECTS AND FRESHWATER FISH PROJECTS.—

(1) IN GENERAL.—Subject to paragraph (2), each coastal State, to the extent practicable, shall equitably allocate amounts apportioned to such State under this Act between marine fish projects and freshwater fish projects in the same proportion as the estimated number of resident marine anglers and the estimated number of resident freshwater anglers, respectively, bear to the estimated number of all resident anglers in that State.

(2) PRESERVATION OF FRESHWATER PROJECT ALLOCATION AT 1988 LEVEL.—(A) Subject to subparagraph (B), the amount allocated by a State pursuant to this subsection to freshwater fish projects for each fiscal year shall not be less than the amount allocated by such State to such projects for fiscal year 1988.

(B) Subparagraph (A) shall not apply to a State with respect to any fiscal year for which the amount apportioned to the State under this Act is less than the amount apportioned to the State under this Act for fiscal year 1988.

(3) COASTAL STATE DEFINED.—As used in this subsection, the term "coastal State" means any one of the States of Alabama, Alaska, California, Connecticut, Delaware, Florida, Georgia, Hawaii, Louisiana, Maine, Maryland, Massachusetts, Mississippi, New Hampshire, New Jersey, New York, North Carolina, Oregon, Rhode Island, South Carolina, Texas, Virginia, and Washington. The term also includes the Commonwealth of Puerto Rico, the United States Virgin Islands, Guam, American Samoa, and the Commonwealth of the Northern Mariana Islands.

SEC. 2. **[16 U.S.C. 777a]** For purposes of this Act—

(1) the term "fish restoration and management projects" shall be construed to mean projects designed for the restoration and management of all species of fish which have material value in connection with sport or recreation in the marine and/or fresh waters of the United States and include—

(A) such research into problems of fish management and culture as may be necessary to efficient administration affecting fish resources;

(B) the acquisition of such facts as are necessary to guide and direct the regulation of fishing by law, including the extent of the fish population, the drain on the fish supply from fishing and/or natural causes, the necessity of legal regulation of fishing, and the effects of any measures of regulation that are applied;

(C) the formulation and adoption of plans of restocking waters with food and game fishes according to natural areas or districts to which such plans are applicable, together with the acquisition of such facts as are necessary to the formulation, execution, and testing the efficacy of such plans;

(D) the selection, restoration, rehabilitation, and improvement of areas of water or land adaptable as hatching, feeding, resting, or breeding places for fish, including acquisition by purchase, condemnation, lease, or gift of such areas or estates or interests therein as are suitable or capable of being made suitable therefor, and the construction thereon or therein of such works as may be necessary to make them available for such purposes, and such preliminary or incidental costs and expenses as may be incurred in and about such works; the term "State fish and game department" shall be construed to mean and include any department or division of department of another name, or commission, or official or officials, of a State empowered under its laws to exercise the functions ordinarily exercised by a State fish and game department;

(2) the term "outreach and communications program" means a program to improve communications with anglers, boaters, and the general public regarding angling and boating opportunities, to reduce barriers to participation in these

activities, to advance adoption of sound fishing and boating practices, to promote conservation and the responsible use of the Nation's aquatic resources, and to further safety in fishing and boating; and

(3) the term "aquatic resource education program" means a program designed to enhance the public's understanding of aquatic resources and sportfishing, and to promote the development of responsible attitudes and ethics toward the aquatic environment.

SEC. 3. **[16 U.S.C. 777b]** To carry out the provisions of this Act for fiscal years after September 30, 1984, there are authorized to be appropriated from the Sport Fish Restoration and Boating Trust Fund established by section 9504(a) of the Internal Revenue Code of 1986 the amounts paid, transferred, or otherwise credited to that Trust Fund, except as provided in section 9504(c) of the Internal Revenue Code of 1986.[2] For purposes of the provision of the Act of August 31, 1951, which refers to this section, such amounts shall be treated as the amounts that are equal to the revenues described in this section. The appropriation made under the provisions of this section for each fiscal year shall continue available during succeeding fiscal years. So much of such appropriation apportioned to any State for any fiscal year as remains unexpended at the close thereof is authorized to be made available for expenditure in that State until the close of the succeeding fiscal year. Any amount apportioned to any State under the provisions of this Act which is unexpended or unobligated at the end of the period during which it is available for expenditure on any project is authorized to be made available for expenditure by the Secretary of the Interior to supplement the 58.012 percent of the balance of each annual appropriation to be apportioned among the States, as provided for in section 4(c).

---

[2] The Act of August 31, 1951 (Chapter 375; 65 Stat. 261) in title I under the heading Fish and Wildlife Service, provides:

FEDERAL AID IN RESTORTATION AND MANAGEMENT

For carrying out the provisions of the Act of August 9, 1950 (Public Law 681), amounts equal to the revenues described in section 3 of said Act and credited during the next preceding fiscal year and each fiscal year thereafter, to remain available until expended.

SEC. 4. **[16 U.S.C. 777c]** (a) IN GENERAL.—For each fiscal year through fiscal year 2026, the balance of each annual appropriation made in accordance with the provisions of section 3 remaining after the distributions for administrative expenses and other purposes under subsection (b) and for activities under section 14(e) shall be distributed as follows:

[3] Section 34002(1) of division C of Public Law 112–141 amended section 4(a) of the Federal Aid in Fish Restoration Act (16 U.S.C. 777c), which is the commonly referred to Act name for the Dingell-Johnson Sport Fish Restoration Act.

(1) COASTAL WETLANDS.—An amount equal to 18.673 percent to the Secretary of the Interior for distribution as provided in the Coastal Wetlands Planning,[4] Protection, and Restoration Act (16 U.S.C. 3951 et seq.).

[4] Transfer of functions to Secretary of Commerce from Secretary of the Interior by Reorg. Plan No. 4 of 1970, eff. Oct. 3, 1970, 35 F.R. 15627, 84 Stat. 2090, see note set out under section 777 of this title.

(2) BOATING SAFETY.—An amount equal to 17.315 percent to the Secretary of the department in which the Coast Guard is operating for State recreational boating safety programs under section 13107 of title 46, United States Code.

(3) BOATING INFRASTRUCTURE IMPROVEMENT.—

(A) IN GENERAL.—An amount equal to 4 percent to the Secretary of the Interior for qualified projects under section 5604(c) of the Clean Vessel Act of 1992 (33 U.S.C. 1322 note) and section 7404(d) of the Sportfishing and Boating Safety Act of 1998 (16 U.S.C. 777g–1(d)).

(B) LIMITATION.—Not more than 75 percent of the amount under subparagraph (A) shall be available for projects under either of the sections referred to in subparagraph (A).

(4) NATIONAL OUTREACH AND COMMUNICATIONS.—An amount equal to 2.0 percent to the Secretary of the Interior for the National Outreach and Communications Program under section 8(d) of this Act. Such amounts shall remain available for 3 fiscal years, after which any portion thereof that is unobligated by the Secretary for that program may be expended by the Secretary under subsection (c) of this section.

(b) SET-ASIDE FOR EXPENSES FOR ADMINISTRATION OF THE

DINGELL-JOHNSON SPORT FISH RESTORATION ACT.—

(1) IN GENERAL.—

(A)[5] SET-ASIDE FOR ADMINISTRATION.—From the annual appropriation made in accordance with section 3, for each fiscal year through fiscal year 2026, the Secretary of the Interior may use no more than the amount specified in subparagraph (B) for the fiscal year for expenses for administration incurred in the implementation of this Act, in accordance with this section and section 9. The amount specified in subparagraph (B) for a fiscal year may not be included in the amount of the annual appropriation distributed under subsection (a) for the fiscal year.

[5] Section 34002(2) of division C of Public Law 112–141 provides for an amendment to section 4(b)(1)(A) of the Federal Aid in Fish Restoration Act (16 U.S.C. 777c), which is a popular name for the Dingell-Johnson Sport Fish Restoration Act.

(B) AVAILABLE AMOUNTS.—The available amount referred to in subparagraph (A) is—

(i) for the fiscal year that includes November 15, 2021, the product obtained by multiplying—

(I) $12,786,434; and

(II) the change, relative to the preceding fiscal year, in the Consumer Price Index for All Urban Consumers published by the Department of Labor; and

(ii) for each fiscal year thereafter, the sum obtained by adding—

(I) the available amount specified in this subparagraph for the preceding fiscal year; and

(II) the product obtained by multiplying—

(aa) the available amount specified in this subparagraph for the preceding fiscal year; and

(bb) the change, relative to the preceding fiscal year, in the Consumer Price Index for All Urban Consumers published by the Department of Labor.

(2) SET-ASIDE FOR COAST GUARD ADMINISTRATION.—

(A) IN GENERAL.—From the annual appropriation made in accordance with section 3, for each of fiscal years 2022 through 2026, the Secretary of the department in which the Coast Guard is operating may use no more than the amount specified in subparagraph (B) for the fiscal year for the purposes set forth in section 13107(c) of title 46, United States Code. The amount specified in subparagraph (B) for a fiscal year may not be included in the amount of the annual appropriation distributed under subsection (a) for the fiscal year.

(B) AVAILABLE AMOUNTS.—The available amount referred to in subparagraph (A) is—

(i) for fiscal year 2022, $12,786,434; and

(ii) for fiscal year 2023 and each fiscal year thereafter, the sum obtained by adding—

(I) the available amount specified in this subparagraph for the preceding fiscal year; and

(II) the product obtained by multiplying—

(aa) the available amount specified in this subparagraph for the preceding fiscal year; and

(bb) the change, relative to the preceding fiscal year, in the Consumer Price Index for All Urban Consumers published by the Department of Labor.

(3) PERIOD OF AVAILABILITY; APPORTIONMENT OF UNOBLIGATED AMOUNTS.—

(A) PERIOD OF AVAILABILITY.—For each fiscal year, the available amount under paragraph (1) shall remain available for obligation for use under that paragraph until the end of the subsequent fiscal year.

(B) APPORTIONMENT OF UNOBLIGATED AMOUNTS.—Not later than 60 days after the end of a fiscal year, the Secretary of the Interior shall apportion among the States any of the available amount under paragraph (1) that remains unobligated at the end of the fiscal year, on the same basis and in the same manner as other amounts made available under this Act are apportioned among the States under subsection (c) for the fiscal year.

(c)(1) The Secretary, after the distribution, transfer, use and deduction under subsection (b), and after deducting amounts used for activities under section 14(e), shall apportion 58.012 percent of the balance of each such annual appropriation among the several States in the following manner: 40 percent in the ratio which the area of each State including coastal and Great Lakes waters (as determined by the Secretary of the Interior) bears to the total area of all the States, and 60 percent in the ratio which the number of persons holding paid licenses to fish for sport or recreation in the State in the second fiscal year preceding the fiscal year for which such apportionment is made, as certified to said Secretary by the State fish and game departments, bears to the number of such persons in all the States. Such apportionments shall be adjusted equitably so that no State shall receive less than 1 percent nor more than 5 percent of the total amount apportioned. Where the apportionment to any State under this section is less than $4,500 annually, the Secretary of the Interior may allocate not more than $4,500 of said appropriation to said State to carry out the purposes of this Act when said State certifies to the Secretary of the Interior that it has set aside not less than $1,500 from its fish-and-game funds or has made, through its legislature, an appropriation in this amount for said purposes.

(2) The Secretary shall deduct from the amount to be apportioned under paragraph (1) the amounts used for grants under section 14(a).

(d) So much of any sum not allocated under the provisions of this section for any fiscal year is hereby authorized to be made available for expenditure to carry out the purposes of this Act until the close of the succeeding fiscal year. The term fiscal year as used in this section shall be a period of twelve consecutive months from October 1 through the succeeding September 30, except that the period for enumeration of persons holding licenses to fish shall be a State's fiscal or license year.

(e) EXPENSES FOR ADMINISTRATION OF CERTAIN PROGRAMS.—

(1) IN GENERAL.—For each fiscal year, of the amounts appropriated under section 3, the Secretary of the Interior shall use only funds authorized for use under paragraphs (1), (3), (4), and (5) of subsection (a) to pay the expenses for administration

incurred in carrying out the provisions of law referred to in those paragraphs, respectively.

(2) MAXIMUM AMOUNT.—For each fiscal year, the Secretary of the Interior may use not more than $1,300,000 in accordance with paragraph (1).

(f) TRANSFER OF CERTAIN FUNDS.—Amounts available under paragraphs (3) and (4) of subsection (a) that are unobligated by the Secretary of the Interior after 3 fiscal years shall be transferred to the Secretary of the department in which the Coast Guard is operating and shall be expended for State recreational boating safety programs under section 13107(a) of title 46, United States Code.

SEC. 5. **[16 U.S.C. 777d]** For each fiscal year beginning with the fiscal year ending June 30, 1951, the Secretary of the Interior shall certify, at the time at which a deduction or apportionment is made, to the Secretary of the Treasury, and to each State fish and game department, the sum which he has estimated to be deducted for administering this Act and the sum which he has apportioned to each State for such fiscal year.

SEC. 6. **[16 U.S.C. 777e]** (a) Any State desiring to avail itself of the benefits of this Act shall, by its State fish and game department, submit programs or projects for fish restoration in either of the following two ways:

(1) The State shall prepare and submit to the Secretary of the Interior a comprehensive fish and wildlife resource management plan which shall insure the perpetuation of these resources for the economic, scientific, and recreational enrichment of the people. Such plan shall be for a period of not less than five years and be based on projections of desires and needs of the people for a period of not less than fifteen years. It shall include provisions for updating at intervals of not more than three years and be provided in a format as may be required by the Secretary of the Interior. If the Secretary of the Interior finds that such plans conform to standards established by him and approves such plans, he may finance up to 75 per centum of the cost of implementing segments of those plans meeting the purposes of this Act from funds apportioned under this Act upon this approval of an annual agreement submitted to him.

(2) A State may elect to avail itself of the benefits of this Act by its State fish and game department submitting to the Secretary of the Interior full and detailed statements of any fish restoration and management project proposed for that State. If the Secretary of the Interior finds that such project meets with the standards set by him and approves said project, the State fish and game department shall furnish to him such surveys, plans, specifications, and estimates therefor as he may require. If the Secretary of the interior approves the plans, specifications, and estimates for the project, he shall notify the State fish and game department and immediately set aside so much of said appropriation as represents the share of the United States payable under this Act on account of such project, which sum so set aside shall not exceed 75 per centum of the total estimated cost thereof.

The Secretary of the Interior shall approve only such comprehensive plans or projects as may be substantial in character and design and the expenditure of funds hereby authorized shall be applied only to such approved comprehensive fishery plan or projects and if otherwise applied they shall be replaced by the State before it may participate in any further apportionment under this Act. No payment of any money apportioned under this Act shall be made on any comprehensive fishery plan or project until an agreement to participate therein shall have been submitted to and approved by the Secretary of the Interior.

(b) If the State elects to avail itself of the benefits of this Act by preparing a comprehensive fish and wildlife plan under option (1) of subsection (a) of this section, then the term "project" may be defined for the purpose of this Act as a fishery program, all other definitions notwithstanding.

(c) Administrative costs in the form of overhead or indirect costs for services provided by State central service activities outside of the State fish and game department charged against programs or projects supported by funds made available under this Act shall not exceed in any one fiscal year 3 per centum of the annual apportionment to the State.

(d) The Secretary of the Interior may enter into agreements to finance up to 75 per centum of the initial costs of the acquisition of lands or interests therein and the construction of structures or facilities from appropriations currently available for the purposes of this Act; and to agree to finance up to 75 per centum of the remaining costs over such a period of time as the Secretary may consider necessary. The liability of the United States in any such agreement is contingent upon the continued availability of funds for the purposes of this Act.

SEC. 7. **[16 U.S.C. 777f]** (a) When the Secretary of the Interior shall find that any project approved by him has been completed or, if involving research relating to fish, is being conducted, in compliance with said plans and specifications, he shall cause to be paid to the proper authority of said State the amount set aside for said project. The Secretary of the Interior may, in his discretion, from time to time, make payments on said project as the same progresses; but these payments, including previous payments, if any, shall not be more than the United States' pro rata share of the project in conformity with said plans and specifications. If a State has elected to avail itself of the benefits of this Act by preparing a comprehensive fish and wildlife plan as provided for under option (1) of subsection (a) of section 6 of this Act, and this plan has been approved by the Secretary of the Interior, then the Secretary may, in his discretion, and under such rules and regulations, as he may prescribe, advance funds to the State for financing the United States' pro rata share agreed upon between the State fish and game department and the Secretary.

(b) Any construction work and labor in each State shall be performed in accordance with its laws and under the direct supervision of the State fish and game department, subject to the inspection and approval of the Secretary of the Interior and in accordance with the rules and regulations made pursuant to this Act. The Secretary of the Interior and the State fish and game department of each State may jointly determine at what times and in what amounts payments shall be made under this Act. Such payments shall be made against the said appropriation to such official or officials, or depository, as may be designated by the State fish and game department and authorized under the laws of the State to receive public funds of the State.

SEC. 8. **[16 U.S.C. 777g]** (a) To maintain fish-restoration and management projects established under the provisions of this Act shall be the duty of the States according to their respective laws.

Beginning July 1, 1953, maintenance of projects heretofore completed under the provisions of this Act may be considered as projects under this Act. Title to any real or personal property acquired by any State, and to improvements placed on State-owned lands through the use of funds paid to the State under the provisions of this Act, shall be vested in such State.

(b)(1) Each State shall allocate 15 percent of the funds apportioned to it for each fiscal year under section 4 of this Act for the payment of up to 75 per centum of the costs of the acquisition, development, renovation, or improvement of facilities (and auxiliary facilities necessary to insure the safe use of such facilities) that create, or add to, public access to the waters of the United States to improve the suitability of such waters for recreational boating purposes. Notwithstanding this provision, States within a United States Fish and Wildlife Service Administrative Region may allocate more or less than 15 percent in a fiscal year, provided that the total regional allocation averages 15 percent over a 5 year period.

(2) So much of the funds that are allocated by a State under paragraph (1) in any fiscal year that remained unexpended or unobligated at the close of such year are authorized to be made available for the purposes described in paragraph (1) during the succeeding four fiscal years, but any portion of such funds that remain unexpended or unobligated at the close of such period are authorized to be made available for expenditure by the Secretary of the Interior to supplement the 58.012 percent of the balance of each annual appropriation to be apportioned among the States under section 4(c).

(c) Each State may use not to exceed 15 percent of the funds apportioned to it under section 4 of this Act to pay up to 75 per centum of the costs of an aquatic resource education and outreach and communications program for the purpose of increasing public understanding of the Nation's water resources and associated aquatic life forms. The non-Federal share of such costs may not be derived from other Federal grant programs. The Secretary shall issue not later than the one hundred and twentieth day after the effective date of this subsection such regulations as he deems advisable regarding the criteria for such programs.

(d) NATIONAL OUTREACH AND COMMUNICATIONS PROGRAM.—

(1) IMPLEMENTATION.—Within 1 year after the date of

enactment of the Sportfishing and Boating Safety Act of 1998, the Secretary of the Interior shall develop and implement, in cooperation and consultation with the Sport Fishing and Boating Partnership Council, a national plan for outreach and communications.

(2) CONTENT.—The plan shall provide—

(A) guidance, including guidance on the development of an administrative process and funding priorities, for outreach and communications programs; and

(B) for the establishment of a national program.

(3) SECRETARY MAY MATCH OR FUND PROGRAMS.—Under the plan, the Secretary may obligate amounts available under subsection (a)(5) or subsection (b) of section 4 of this Act—

(A) to make grants to any State or private entity to pay all or any portion of the cost of carrying out any outreach and communications program under the plan; or

(B) to fund contracts with States or private entities to carry out such a program.

(4) REVIEW.—The plan shall be reviewed periodically, but not less frequently than once every 3 years.

(e) STATE OUTREACH AND COMMUNICATIONS PROGRAM.—Within 12 months after the completion of the national plan under subsection (d)(1), a State shall develop a plan for an outreach and communications program and submit it to the Secretary. In developing the plan, a State shall—

(1) review the national plan developed under subsection (d);

(2) consult with anglers, boaters, the sportfishing and boating industries, and the general public; and

(3) establish priorities for the State outreach and communications program proposed for implementation.

(f) PUMPOUT STATIONS AND WASTE RECEPTION FACILITIES.—Amounts apportioned to States under section 4 of this Act may be used to pay not more than 75 percent of the costs of constructing, renovating, operating, or maintaining pumpout stations and waste reception facilities (as those terms are defined in the Clean Vessel Act of 1992).

(g) SURVEYS.—

(1) NATIONAL FRAMEWORK.—Within 6 months after the date of enactment of the Sportfishing and Boating Safety Act of 1998, the Secretary, in consultation with the States, shall adopt a national framework for a public boat access needs assessment which may be used by States to conduct surveys to determine the adequacy, number, location, and quality of facilities providing access to recreational waters for all sizes of recreational boats.

(2) STATE SURVEYS.—Within 18 months after such date of enactment, each State that agrees to conduct a public boat access needs survey following the recommended national framework shall report its findings to the Secretary for use in the development of a comprehensive national assessment of recreational boat access needs and facilities.

(3) EXCEPTION.—Paragraph (2) does not apply to a State if, within 18 months after such date of enactment, the Secretary certifies that the State has developed and is implementing a plan that ensures there are and will be public boat access adequate to meet the needs of recreational boaters on its waters.

(4) FUNDING.—A State that conducts a public boat access needs survey under paragraph (2) may fund the costs of conducting that assessment out of amounts allocated to it as funding dedicated to motorboat access to recreational waters under subsection (b)(1) of this section.

SEC. 9. [16 U.S.C. 777h] REQUIREMENTS AND RESTRICTIONS CONCERNING USE OF AMOUNTS FOR EXPENSES FOR ADMINISTRATION.

(a) AUTHORIZED EXPENSES FOR ADMINISTRATION.—Except as provided in subsection (b), the Secretary of the Interior may use available amounts under section 4(b) only for expenses for administration that directly support the implementation of this Act that consist of—

(1) personnel costs of employees for the work hours of each employee spent directly administering this Act, as those hours are certified by the supervisor of the employee;

(2) support costs directly associated with personnel costs authorized under paragraph (1), excluding costs associated with staffing and operation of regional offices of the United

States Fish and Wildlife Service and the Department of the Interior other than for the purposes of this Act;

(3) costs of determining under section 6(a) whether State comprehensive plans and projects are substantial in character and design;

(4) overhead costs, including the costs of general administrative services, that are directly attributable to administration of this Act and are based on—

(A) actual costs, as determined by a direct cost allocation methodology approved by the Director of the Office of Management and Budget for use by Federal agencies; and

(B) in the case of costs that are not determinable under subparagraph (A), an amount per employee authorized under paragraph (1) that does not exceed the amount charged or assessed for costs per full-time equivalent employee for any other division or program of the United States Fish and Wildlife Service;

(5) costs incurred in auditing, every 5 years, the wildlife and sport fish activities of each State fish and game department and the use of funds under section 6 by each State fish and game department;

(6) costs of audits under subsection (d);

(7) costs of necessary training of Federal and State personnel who administer this Act to improve administration of this Act;

(8) costs of travel to States, territories, and Canada by personnel who—

(A) administer this Act for purposes directly related to administration of State programs or projects; or

(B) administer grants under section 6 or 14;

(9) costs of travel outside the United States (except travel to Canada), by personnel who administer this Act , for purposes that directly relate to administration of this Act and that are approved directly by the Assistant Secretary for Fish and Wildlife and Parks;

(10) relocation expenses for personnel who, after relocation, will administer this Act on a full-time or part-time basis for at

least 1 year, as certified by the Director of the United States Fish and Wildlife Service at the time at which the relocation expenses are incurred, subject to the condition that the percentage of the relocation expenses paid with funds made available pursuant to this Act may not exceed the percentage of the work hours of the employee that are spent administering this Act; and

(11) costs to audit, evaluate, approve, disapprove, and advise concerning grants under sections 6 and 14.

(b) REPORTING OF OTHER USES.—

(1) IN GENERAL.—Subject to paragraph (2), if the Secretary of the Interior determines that available amounts under section 4(b) should be used for an expense for administration other than an expense for administration described in subsection (a), the Secretary—

(A) shall submit to the Committee on Environment and Public Works of the Senate and the Committee on Resources of the House of Representatives a report describing the expense for administration and stating the amount of the expense; and

(B) may use any such available amounts for the expense for administration only after the end of the 30-day period beginning on the date of submission of the report under subparagraph (A).

(2) MAXIMUM AMOUNT.—For any fiscal year, the Secretary of the Interior may use under paragraph (1) not more than $25,000.

(c) RESTRICTION ON USE TO SUPPLEMENT GENERAL APPROPRIATIONS.—The Secretary of the Interior shall not use available amounts under subsection (b) to supplement the funding of any function for which general appropriations are made for the United States Fish and Wildlife Service or any other entity of the Department of the Interior.

(d) AUDIT REQUIREMENT.—

(1) IN GENERAL.—The Inspector General of the Department of the Interior shall procure the performance of biennial audits, in accordance with generally accepted accounting principles, of expenditures and obligations of amounts used by the Secretary of the Interior for expenses for administration incurred in

implementation of this Act.

(2) AUDITOR.—

(A) IN GENERAL.—An audit under this subsection shall be performed under a contract that is awarded under competitive procedures (as defined in section 4 of the Office of Federal Procurement Policy Act (41 U.S.C. 403)) by a person or entity that is not associated in any way with the Department of the Interior (except by way of a contract for the performance of an audit or other review).

(B) SUPERVISION OF AUDITOR.—The auditor selected under subparagraph (A) shall report to, and be supervised by, the Inspector General of the Department of the Interior, except that the auditor shall submit a copy of the biennial audit findings to the Secretary of the Interior at the time at which the findings are submitted to the Inspector General of the Department of the Interior.

(3) REPORT TO CONGRESS.—The Inspector General of the Department of the Interior shall promptly submit to the Committee on Resources of the House of Representatives and the Committee on Environment and Public Works of the Senate—

(A) a report on the results of each audit under this subsection; and

(B) a copy of each audit under this subsection.

SEC. 10. **[16 U.S.C. 777i]** The Secretary of the Interior is authorized to make rules and regulations for carrying out the provisions of this Act.

[Sec. 11.Repealed, Public Law 89–348 (79 Stat. 1311).]

SEC. 12. **[16 U.S.C. 777k]** The Secretary of the Interior is authorized to cooperate with the Secretary of Agriculture of Puerto Rico, the Mayor of the District of Columbia, the Governor of Guam, the Governor of American Samoa, the Governor of the Commonwealth of the Northern Mariana Islands, and the Governor of the Virgin Islands, in the conduct of fish restoration and management projects as defined in section 2 of this Act, upon such terms and conditions as he shall deem fair, just, and equitable, and is authorized to apportion to Puerto Rico, the District of Columbia, Guam, American Samoa, the Commonwealth of the Northern

Mariana Islands, and the Virgin Islands, out of money available for apportionment under this Act, such sums as he shall determine, not exceeding for Puerto Rico 1 per centum, for the District of Columbia one-third of 1 per centum, for Guam one-third of 1 per centum, for American Samoa one-third of 1 per centum, for the Commonwealth of the Northern Mariana Islands one-third of 1 per centum, and for the Virgin Islands one-third of 1 per centum of the total amount apportioned in any one year, but the Secretary shall in no event require any of said cooperating agencies to pay an amount which will exceed 25 per centum of the cost of any project. Any unexpended or unobligated balance of any apportionment made pursuant to this section shall be made available for expenditure in Puerto Rico, the District of Columbia, Guam, the Commonwealth of the Northern Mariana Islands, or the Virgin Islands, as the case may be, in the succeeding year, on any approved projects, and if unexpended or unobligated at the end of such year is authorized to be made available for expenditure by the Secretary of the Interior to supplement the 58.012 percent of the balance of each annual appropriation to be apportioned among the States under section 4(c) of this Act.

SEC. 13. [16 U.S.C. 777l] STATE USE OF CONTRIBUTIONS.

A State may use contributions of funds, real property, materials, and services to carry out an activity under this Act in lieu of payment by the State of the State share of the cost of such activity. Such a State share shall be considered to be paid in an amount equal to the fair market value of any contribution so used.

SEC. 14. [16 U.S.C. 777m] MULTISTATE CONSERVATION GRANT PROGRAM.

(a) IN GENERAL.—

(1) AMOUNT FOR GRANTS.—Not more than $3,000,000 shall be distributed to the Secretary of the Interior for making multistate conservation project grants in accordance with this section.

(2) PERIOD OF AVAILABILITY; APPORTIONMENT.—

(A) PERIOD OF AVAILABILITY.—Amounts made available under paragraph (1) shall remain available for making grants only for the first fiscal year for which the amount is made available and the following fiscal year.

(B) APPORTIONMENT.—At the end of the period of availability under subparagraph (A), the Secretary of the Interior shall apportion any amounts that remain available among the States in the manner specified in section 4(c) for use by the States in the same manner as funds apportioned under section 4(c).

(b) SELECTION OF PROJECTS.—

(1) STATES OR ENTITIES TO BE BENEFITED.—A project shall not be eligible for a grant under this section unless the project will benefit—

(A) at least 26 States;

(B) a majority of the States in a region of the United States Fish and Wildlife Service; or

(C) a regional association of State fish and game departments.

(2) USE OF SUBMITTED PRIORITY LIST OF PROJECTS.—The Secretary of the Interior may make grants under this section only for projects identified on a priority list of sport fish restoration projects described in paragraph (3).

(3) PRIORITY LIST OF PROJECTS.—A priority list referred to in paragraph (2) is a priority list of sport fish restoration projects that the International Association of Fish and Wildlife Agencies—

(A) prepares through a committee comprised of the heads of State fish and game departments (or their designees), in consultation with—

(i) nongovernmental organizations that represent conservation organizations;

(ii) sportsmen organizations; and

(iii) industries that fund the sport fish restoration programs under this Act;

(B) approves by vote of a majority of the heads of State fish and game departments (or their designees); and

(C) not later than October 1 of each fiscal year, submits to the Assistant Director for Wildlife and Sport Fish Restoration Programs.

(4) PUBLICATION.—The Assistant Director for Wildlife and Sport Fish Restoration Programs shall publish in the Federal

Register each priority list submitted under paragraph (3)(C).

(c) ELIGIBLE GRANTEES.—

(1) IN GENERAL.—The Secretary of the Interior may make a grant under this section only to—

(A) a State or group of States;

(B) the United States Fish and Wildlife Service, or a State or group of States, for the purpose of carrying out the National Survey of Fishing, Hunting, and Wildlife-Associated Recreation; and

(C) subject to paragraph (2), a nongovernmental organization.

(2) NONGOVERNMENTAL ORGANIZATIONS.—

(A) IN GENERAL.—Any nongovernmental organization that applies for a grant under this section shall submit with the application to the International Association of Fish and Wildlife Agencies a certification that the organization—

(i) will not use the grant funds to fund, in whole or in part, any activity of the organization that promotes or encourages opposition to the regulated taking of fish; and

(ii) will use the grant funds in compliance with subsection (d).

(B) PENALTIES FOR CERTAIN ACTIVITIES.—Any nongovernmental organization that is found to use grant funds in violation of subparagraph (A) shall return all funds received under this section and be subject to any other applicable penalties under law.

(d) USE OF GRANTS.—A grant under this section shall not be used, in whole or in part, for an activity, project, or program that promotes or encourages opposition to the regulated taking of fish.

(e) FUNDING FOR OTHER ACTIVITIES.—Not more than $1,200,000 of each annual appropriation made in accordance with the provisions of section 3 shall be distributed to the Secretary of the Interior for use as follows:

(1) $200,000 shall be made available for each of—

(A) the Atlantic States Marine Fisheries Commission;

(B) the Gulf States Marine Fisheries Commission;

(C) the Pacific States Marine Fisheries Commission; and

(D) the Great Lakes Fisheries Commission.

(2) $400,000 shall be made available for the Sport Fishing and Boating Partnership Council established by the United States Fish and Wildlife Service.

(3) A portion, as determined by the Sport Fishing and Boating Partnership Council, of funds disbursed for the purposes described in paragraph (2) but remaining unobligated as of October 1, 2021, shall be used to study the impact of derelict vessels and identify recyclable solutions for recreational vessels.

(f) NONAPPLICABILITY OF CHAPTER 10 OF TITLE 5, UNITED STATES CODE.—Chapter 10 of title 5, United States Code, shall not apply to any activity carried out under this section.

SEC. 15. [16 U.S.C. 777 note] SHORT TITLE.

This Act may be cited as the "Dingell-Johnson Sport Fish Restoration Act".

26 U.S.C. –Internal Revenue Code

Sec. 9504. Sport Fish Restoration and Boating Trust Fund

TITLE 26—INTERNAL REVENUE CODE

(Aug. 16, 1954, ch. 736, 68A Stat. 3; Pub. L. 99–514, §2, Oct. 22, 1986, 100 Stat. 2095.)

INTERNAL REVENUE TITLE

Subtitle

* * * * * * *

I. Trust Fund Code.

* * * * * * *

K. Group health plan requirements.

* * * * * * *

Subtitle I—Trust Fund Code

§9500. Short title

This subtitle may be cited as the "Trust Fund Code of 1981".

(Added Pub. L. 97–119, title I, §103(a), Dec. 29, 1981, 95 Stat. 1636.)

CHAPTER 98—TRUST FUND CODE

Subchapter		Sec.[1]
A.	Establishment of Trust Funds	9501
B.	General provisions	9601

[1] *Section numbers editorially supplied.*

Subchapter A—Establishment of Trust Funds

Sec.

* * * * * * *

9504. Sport Fish Restoration and Boating Trust Fund.

* * * * * * *

§9504. Sport Fish Restoration and Boating Trust Fund

(a) Creation of Trust Fund

There is hereby established in the Treasury of the United States a trust fund to be known as the "Sport Fish Restoration and Boating Trust Fund". Such Trust Fund shall consist of such amounts as may be appropriated, credited, or paid to it as provided in this section, section 9503(c)(3), section 9503(c)(4), or section 9602(b).

(b) Sport Fish Restoration and Boating Trust Fund

(1) Transfer of certain taxes to Trust Fund

There is hereby appropriated to the Sport Fish Restoration and Boating Trust Fund amounts equivalent to the following amounts received in the Treasury on or after October 1, 1984—

(A) the taxes imposed by section 4161(a) (relating to sport fishing equipment), and

(B) the import duties imposed on fishing tackle under heading 9507 of the Harmonized Tariff Schedule of the United States (19 U.S.C. 1202) and on yachts and pleasure craft under chapter 89 of the Harmonized Tariff Schedule of the United States.

(2) Expenditures from Trust Fund

Amounts in the Sport Fish Restoration and Boating Trust Fund shall be available, as provided by appropriation Acts, for making expenditures—

(A) to carry out the purposes of the Dingell-Johnson Sport Fish Restoration Act (as in effect on the date of the enactment of the Infrastructure Investment and Jobs Act),

(B) to carry out the purposes of section 7404(d) of the Transportation Equity Act for the 21st Century (as in effect on the date of the enactment of the Infrastructure Investment and Jobs Act), and

(C) to carry out the purposes of the Coastal Wetlands Planning, Protection and Restoration Act (as in effect on the date of the enactment of the Infrastructure Investment and Jobs Act).

Amounts transferred to such account under section 9503(c)(4) may be used only for making expenditures described in subparagraph (C) of this paragraph.

(c) Expenditures from Boat Safety Account

Amounts remaining in the Boat Safety Account on October 1, 2005, and amounts thereafter credited to the Account under section 9602(b), shall be available, without further appropriation, for making expenditures before October 1, 2010, to carry out the purposes of section 15 [1] of the Dingell-Johnson Sport Fish Restoration Act (as in effect on the date of the enactment of the Safe, Accountable, Flexible, Efficient Transportation Equity Act: A

Legacy for Users). For purposes of section 9602, the Boat Safety Account shall be treated as a Trust Fund established by this subchapter.

(d) Limitation on transfers to Trust Fund

(1) In general

Except as provided in paragraph (2), no amount may be appropriated or paid to the Sport Fish Restoration and Boating Trust Fund on and after the date of any expenditure from such Trust Fund which is not permitted by this section. The determination of whether an expenditure is so permitted shall be made without regard to—

(A) any provision of law which is not contained or referenced in this title or in a revenue Act, and

(B) whether such provision of law is a subsequently enacted provision or directly or indirectly seeks to waive the application of this subsection.

(2) Exception for prior obligations

Paragraph (1) shall not apply to any expenditure to liquidate any contract entered into (or for any amount otherwise obligated) before October 1, 2026, in accordance with the provisions of this section.

(e) Cross reference

For provision transferring motorboat fuels taxes to Sport Fish Restoration and Boating Trust Fund, see section 9503(c)(3).

ACT OF MARCH 23, 1906
BRIDGE ACT OF 1906

CHAPTER 1130; 34 STAT. 84
AMENDED THROUGH P.L. 115-232

ACT OF MARCH 23, 1906

[Chapter 1130; 34 Stat. 84] [Popularly known as the "Bridge Act of 1906" or the "General Bridge Act of 1906"]

[As Amended Through P.L. 115–232, Enacted August 13, 2018]

An Act To regulate the construction of bridges over navigable waters.

Be it enacted by the Senate and House of Representatives of the United States of America in Congress assembled,

[33 U.S.C. 491] That when, hereafter, authority is granted by Congress to any persons to construct and maintain a bridge across or over any of the navigable waters of the United States, such bridge shall not be built or commenced until the plans and specifications for its construction, together with such drawings of the proposed construction and such map of the proposed location as may be required for a full understanding of the subject, have been submitted to the Secretary of the department in which the Coast Guard is operating for the Secretary's approval, nor until the Secretary shall have approved such plans and specifications and the location of such bridge and accessory works; and when the plans for any bridge to be constructed under the provisions of this Act have been approved by the Secretary it shall not be lawful to deviate from such plans, either before or after completion of the structure, unless the modification of such plans has previously been submitted to and received the approval of the Secretary. This section shall not apply to any bridge over waters which are not subject to the ebb and flow of the tide and which are not used and are not susceptible to use in their natural condition or by reasonable improvement as a means to transport interstate or foreign commerce.

SEC. 2. **[33 U.S.C. 492]** That any bridge built in accordance with the provisions of this Act shall be a lawful structure and shall be recognized and known as a post route, upon which no higher charge shall be made for the transmission over the same of the mails, the troops, and the munitions of war of the United States than the rate per mile paid for the transportation over any railroad, street railway, or public highway leading to said bridge; and the United States shall have the right to construct, maintain, and repair, without any charge therefor, telegraph and telephone lines across and upon said bridge and its approaches; and equal privileges in the use of said bridge and its approaches shall be granted to all telegraph and telephone companies.

SEC. 3. **[33 U.S.C. 493]** That all railroad companies desiring the use of any railroad bridge built in accordance with the provisions of this Act shall be entitled to equal rights and privileges relative to the passage of railway trains or cars over the same and over the approaches thereto upon payment of a reasonable compensation for such use; and in case of any disagreement between the parties in regard to the terms of such use or the sums to be paid all matters at issue shall be determined by the Secretary of Transportation upon hearing the allegations and proofs submitted to him.

SEC. 4. **[33 U.S.C. 494]** That no bridge erected or maintained under the provisions of this Act shall at any time unreasonably obstruct the free navigation of the waters over which it is constructed, and if any bridge erected in accordance with the provisions of this Act shall, in the opinion of the Secretary of the department in which the Coast Guard is operating, at any time unreasonably obstruct such navigation, either on account of insufficient height, width of span, or otherwise, or if there be difficulty in passing the draw opening or the drawspan of such bridge by rafts, steamboats, or other water craft, it shall be the duty of the Secretary of the department in which the Coast Guard is operating, after giving the parties interested reasonable opportunity to be heard, to notify the persons owning or controlling such bridge to so alter the same as to render navigation through or under it reasonably free, easy, and unobstructed, stating in such notice the changes required to be made, and prescribing in each case a reasonable time in which to make such changes, and if at the end of the time so specified the changes so required have not been made, the persons owning or controlling such bridge shall be deemed guilty of a violation of this Act; and all such alterations shall be made and all such obstructions shall be removed at the expense of the persons owning or operating said bridge. The persons owning or operating any such bridge shall maintain, at their own expense, such lights and other signals thereon as the Secretary of Commerce and Labor shall prescribe. If the bridge shall be constructed with a draw, then the draw shall be opened promptly by the persons owning or operating such bridge upon reasonable signal for the passage of boats and other water craft.

SEC. 5. **[33 U.S.C. 495]** (a) That any persons who shall willfully fail or refuse to comply with the lawful order of the Secretary of the department in which the Coast Guard is operating or the Chief of Engineers, made in accordance with the provisions of this Act, shall be deemed guilty of a misdemeanor and on conviction thereof shall be punished in any court of competent jurisdiction by a fine not exceeding five thousand dollars, and every month such persons shall remain in default shall be deemed a new offense and subject such persons to additional penalties therefor; and in addition to the penalties above described the Secretary of the department in which the Coast Guard is operating and the Chief of Engineers may, upon refusal of the persons owning or controlling any such bridge and accessory works to comply with any lawful order issued by the Secretary of the department in which the Coast Guard is operating or Chief of Engineers in regard thereto, cause the removal of such bridge and accessory works at the expense of the persons owning or controlling such bridge, and suit for such expense may be brought in the name of the United States against such persons, and recovery had for such expense in any court of competent jurisdiction; and the removal of any structures erected or maintained in violation of the provisions of this Act or the order or direction of the Secretary of the department in which the Coast Guard is operating or Chief of Engineers made in pursuance thereof may be enforced by injunction, mandamus, or other summary process, upon application to the circuit court in the district in which such structure may, in whole or in part, exist, and proper proceedings to this end may be instituted under the direction of the Attorney-General of the United States at the request of the Secretary of the department in which the Coast Guard is operating; and in case of any litigation arising from any obstruction or alleged obstruction to navigation created by the construction of any bridge under this Act, the cause or question arising may be tried before the circuit court of the United States in any district which any portion of said obstruction or bridge touches.

(b) Whoever violates any provision of this Act, or any order issued under this Act, shall be liable to a civil penalty of not more than $25,000 for a violation occurring in 2008 and any year thereafter. Each day a violation continues shall be deemed a separate offense. No penalty may be assessed under this subsection until the person charged is given notice and an opportunity for a hearing on the charge. The Secretary of the department in which the Coast Guard is operating may assess and collect any civil penalty incurred under this subsection and, in his discretion, may remit, mitigate, or compromise any penalty until the matter is referred to the Attorney General. If a person against whom a civil penalty is assessed under this subsection fails to pay that penalty, an action may be commenced in the district court of the United States for any district in which the violation occurs for such penalty.

SEC. 6. **[33 U.S.C. 496]** That whenever Congress shall hereafter by law authorize the construction of any bridge over or across any of the navigable waters of the United States, and no time for the commencement and completion of such bridge is named in said Act, the authority thereby granted shall cease and be null and void unless the actual construction of the bridge authorized in such Act be commenced within one year and completed within three years from the date of the passage of such Act.

SEC. 7. **[33 U.S.C. 497]** That the word "persons" as used in this Act shall be construed to import both the singular and the plural, as the case demands, and shall include municipalities, quasi municipal corporations, corporations, companies, and associations.

SEC. 8. **[33 U.S.C. 498]** That the right to alter, amend, or repeal this Act is hereby expressly reserved as to any and all bridges which may be built in accordance with the provisions of this Act, and the United States shall incur no liability for the alteration, amendment, or repeal thereof to the owner or owners or any other persons interested in any bridge which shall have been constructed in accordance with its provisions.

Act of June 21, 1940
"Truman-Hobbs Act"

Chapt. 409, 76 Sate. 497
As amended through P.L. 116-283

ACT OF JUNE 21, 1940

[Chapter 409, 76 Stat. 497] [Popularly known as the "Truman-Hobbs Act"]

[As Amended Through P.L. 116–283, Enacted January 1, 2021]

AN ACT To provide for the alteration of certain bridges over navigable waters of the United States, for the apportionment of the cost of such alterations between the United States and the owners of such bridges, and for other purposes.

Be it enacted by the Senate and House of Representatives of the United States of America in Congress assembled,

DEFINITIONS

SECTION 1. **[33 U.S.C. 511]** When used in this Act, unless the context indicates otherwise—

The term "alteration" includes changes of any kind, reconstruction, or removal in whole or in part.

The term "bridge" means a lawful bridge over navigable waters of the United States, including approaches, fenders, and appurtenances thereto, which is used and operated for the purpose of carrying railroad traffic, or both railroad and highway traffic, or if a State, county, municipality, or other political subdivision is the owner or joint owner thereof, which is used and operated for the purpose of carrying highway traffic.

The term "bridge owner" means any State, county, municipality, or other political subdivision, or any corporation, association, partnership, or individual owning, or jointly owning, any bridge, and, when any bridge shall be in the possession or under the control of any trustee, receiver, trustee in a case under title 11 of the United States Code, or lessee, such term shall include both the owner of the legal title and the person or the entity in possession or control of such bridge.

The term "Secretary" means the Secretary of the department in which the Coast Guard is operating.

The term "United States", when used in a geographical sense, includes the Territories and possessions of the United States.

OBSTRUCTION OF NAVIGATION

SEC. 2. **[33 U.S.C. 512]** No bridge shall at any time unreasonably obstruct the free navigation of any navigable waters of the United States.

NOTICE, HEARINGS, AND FINDINGS

SEC. 3. **[33 U.S.C. 513]** Whenever any bridge shall, in the opinion of the Secretary, at any time unreasonably obstruct such navigation, it shall be the duty of the Secretary, after notice to interested parties, to hold a hearing at which the bridge owner, those interested in water navigation thereunder or therethrough, those interested in either railroad or highway traffic thereover, and any other party or parties in interest shall have full opportunity to offer evidence and be heard as to whether any alteration of such bridge is needed, and if so what alterations are needed, having due regard to the necessity of free and unobstructed water navigation and to the necessities of the rail or highway traffic. If, upon such hearing, the Secretary determines that any alterations of such bridge are necessary in order to render navigation through or under it reasonably free, easy, and unobstructed, having due regard also for the necessities of rail or highway traffic thereover, he shall so find and shall issue and cause to be served upon interested parties an order requiring such alterations of such bridge as he finds to be reasonably necessary for the purposes of navigation.

SUBMISSION AND APPROVAL OF GENERAL PLANS AND SPECIFICATIONS

SEC. 4. **[33 U.S.C. 514]** After the service of an order under this Act, it shall be the duty of the bridge owner to prepare and submit to the Secretary of the department in which the Coast Guard is operating, within a reasonable time as prescribed by the Secretary, general plans and specifications to provide for the alteration of such bridge in accordance with such order, and for such additional alteration of such bridge as the bridge owner may desire to meet the necessities of railroad or highway traffic, or both. The Secretary may approve or reject such general plans and specifications, in whole or in part, and may require the submission of new or additional plans and specifications, but when the Secretary shall have approved general plans and specifications, they shall be final and binding upon all parties unless changes therein be afterward approved by the Secretary and the bridge owner.

CONTRACTS FOR PROJECT; GUARANTY OF COST

SEC. 5. **[33 U.S.C. 515]** After approval of such general plans and specifications by the Secretary, and after notification of such approval, the bridge owner shall, in such manner and within such times as the Secretary may prescribe, take bids for the alteration of such bridge in accordance with such general plans and specifications. All bids, including any bid for all or part of the project submitted by the bridge owner, shall be submitted to the Secretary, together with a recommendation by the bridge owner as to the most competent bid or bids, and at the same time the bridge owner shall submit to the Secretary a written guaranty that the total cost of the project, including the cost of such work as is to be performed by the bridge owner and not included in the work to be performed by contract, shall not exceed the sum stated in said guaranty. The Secretary may direct the bridge owner to reject all bids and to take new bids, or may authorize the bridge owner to proceed with the project, by contract, or partly by contract and partly by the bridge owner, or wholly by the bridge owner. Upon such authorization and fixing of the proportionate shares of the cost as provided in section 6, the bridge owner shall, within a reasonable time to be prescribed by the Secretary, proceed with the work of alteration; and the cost thereof shall be borne by the United States and by the bridge owner, as hereinafter provided: *Provided,* That where funds have been appropriated for part only of a project, the bridge owner may take bids for part only of the work. In the event the bridge owner proceeds with the alteration through the taking of successive partial bids, the bridge owner shall, if required by the Secretary, submit a revised guaranty of cost after bids are accepted for successive parts of the work..[1]

[1] So in law. Section 1(b) of P.L. 85–640 (72 Stat. 595) added after the word "provided" the following: ": *Provided,* That where funds have been appropriated for part only of a project, the bridge owner may take bids for part only of the work. In the event the bridge owner proceeds with the alteration through the taking of successive partial bids, the bridge owner shall, if required by the

Secretary, submit a revised guaranty of cost after bids are accepted for successive parts of the work.". The amendment did not strike the period after the word "provided".

APPORTIONMENT OF COST

SEC. 6. **[33 U.S.C. 516]** At the time the Secretary shall authorize the bridge owner to proceed with the project, as provided in section 5, and after an opportunity to the bridge owner to be heard thereon, the Secretary shall determine and issue an order specifying the proportionate shares of the total cost of the project to be borne by the United States and by the bridge owner. Such apportionment shall be made on the following basis: The bridge owner shall bear such part of the cost as is attributable to the direct and special benefits which will accrue to the bridge owner as a result of the alteration, including the expectable savings in repair or maintenance costs; and that part of the cost attributable to the requirements of traffic by railroad or highway, or both, including any expenditure for increased carrying capacity of the bridge, and including such proportion of the actual capital cost of the old bridge or of such part of the old bridge as may be altered or changed or rebuilt, as the used service life of the whole or a part, as the case may be, bears to the total estimated service life of the whole or such part: *Provided further,* That in the event the alteration or relocation of any bridge may be desirable for the reason that the bridge unreasonably obstructs navigation, but also for some other reason, the Secretary may require equitable contribution from any interested person, firm, association, corporation, municipality, county, or State desiring such alteration or relocation for such other reason, as a condition precedent to the making of an order for such alteration or relocation. The United States shall bear the balance of the cost, including that part attributable to the necessities of navigation: *And provided further,* That where the bridge owner proceeds with the alteration on a successive partial bid basis the Secretary is authorized to issue an order of apportionment of cost for the entire alteration based on the accepted bid for the first part of the alteration and an estimate of cost for the remainder of the work. The Secretary is authorized to revise the order of apportionment of cost, to the extent he deems reasonable and proper, to meet any changed conditions..[2]

[2] So in law. Section 1(c) of P.L. 85–640 (72 Stat. 595) added after the word

"navigation" the following: ": *And provided further,* That where the bridge owner proceeds with the alteration on a successive partial bid basis the Secretary is authorized to issue an order of apportionment of cost for the entire alteration based on the accepted bid for the first part of the alteration and an estimate of cost for the remainder of the work. The Secretary is authorized to revise the order of apportionment of cost, to the extent he deems reasonable and proper, to meet any changed conditions.". The amendment did not strike the period after the word "navigation".

PAYMENT OF SHARE OF THE UNITED STATES

SEC. 7. **[33 U.S.C. 517]** Following service of the order requiring alteration of the bridge, the Secretary of the department in which the Coast Guard is operating may make partial payments as the work progresses to the extent that funds have been appropriated. The total payments out of Federal funds shall not exceed the proportionate share of the United States of the total cost of the project paid or incurred by the bridge owner, and, if such total cost exceeds the cost guaranteed by the bridge owner, shall not exceed the proportionate share of the United States of such guaranteed cost, except that if the cost of the work exceeds the guaranteed cost by reason of emergencies, conditions beyond the control of the owner, or unforeseen or undetermined conditions, the Secretary of the department in which the Coast Guard is operating may, after full review of all the circumstances, provide for additional payments by the United States to help defray such excess cost to the extent he deems to be reasonable and proper, and shall certify such additional payments to the Secretary of the Treasury for payment. All payments to any bridge owner herein provided for shall be made by the Secretary of the Treasury through the Division of Disbursement upon certifications of the Secretary of the department in which the Coast Guard is operating.

APPROPRIATION AUTHORIZED

SEC. 8. **[33 U.S.C. 518]** There are hereby authorized to be appropriated such sums as may be necessary to carry out the provisions of this Act.

FAILURE TO COMPLY WITH ORDERS; PENALTIES; REMOVAL OF BRIDGE

SEC. 9. **[33 U.S.C. 519]** Any bridge owner who shall willfully fail or refuse to comply with any lawful order of the Secretary, made in accordance with the provisions of this Act, shall be deemed guilty of a misdemeanor and on conviction thereof shall be punished in any court of competent jurisdiction by a fine not exceeding $5,000, and every month such bridge owner shall remain in default shall be deemed a new offense and subject such bridge owner to additional penalties therefor. In addition to the penalties above prescribed the Secretary may, upon the failure or refusal of any bridge owner to comply with any lawful order issued by the Secretary in regard thereto, cause the removal of any such bridge and accessory works at the expense of the bridge owner; and suit for such expense may be brought in the name of the United States against such bridge owner and recovery had for such expense in any court of competent jurisdiction. The removal of any bridge erected or maintained in violation of the provisions of this Act or the order or direction of the Secretary made in pursuance thereof, and compliance with any order of the Secretary made with respect to any bridge in accordance with the provisions of this Act, may be enforced by injunction, mandamus, or other summary process upon application to the district court of any district in which such bridge may, in whole or in part, exist, and proper proceedings to this end may be instituted under the direction of the Attorney General of the United States at the request of the Secretary.

REVIEW OF FINDINGS AND ORDERS

SEC. 10. **[33 U.S.C. 520]** Any order made or issued under section 6 of this Act may be reviewed by the circuit court of appeals for any judicial circuit in which the bridge in question is wholly or partly located, if a petition for such review is filed within three months after the date such order is issued. The judgment of any such court shall be final except that it shall be subject to review by the Supreme Court of the United States upon certification or certiorari, in the manner provided in sections 239 and 240 of the Judicial Code, as amended. The review by such Court shall be limited to questions of law, and the findings of fact by the Secretary, if supported by substantial evidence, shall be conclusive. Upon such review, such Court shall have power to affirm or, if the order is not in accordance with law, to modify or to reverse the order, with or without remanding the case for a rehearing as justice may require. Proceedings under this section shall not operate as a stay of any order of the Secretary issued under provisions of this Act other than section 6, or relieve any bridge owner of any liability or penalty under such provisions.

REGULATIONS AND ORDERS

SEC. 11. **[33 U.S.C. 521]** The Secretary is authorized to prescribe such rules and regulations, and to make and issue such orders, as may be necessary or appropriate for carrying out the provisions of this Act.

[Section 12 was struck by section 8507(b) of Public Law 116-283.]

RELOCATION OF BRIDGES

SEC. 13. **[33 U.S.C. 523]** If the owner of any bridge and the Secretary shall agree that in order to remove an obstruction to navigation, or for any other purpose, a relocation of such bridge or the construction of a new bridge upon a new location would be preferable to an alteration of the existing bridge, such relocation or new construction may be carried out at such new site and upon such terms as may be acceptable to the bridge owner and the Secretary, and the cost of such relocation or new construction, including also any expense of changes in and additions to rights-of-way, stations, tracks, spurs, sidings, switches, signals, and other railroad facilities and property, and relocation of shippers required for railroad connection with the bridge at the new site, shall be apportioned as between the bridge owner and the United States in the manner which is provided for in section 6 hereof in the case of an alteration and the share of the United States paid from the appropriation authorized in section 8 hereof: *Provided,* That nothing in this section shall be construed as requiring the United States to pay any part of the expense of building any bridge across a navigable stream which the Secretary of the department in which the Coast Guard is operating shall not find to be, in fact, a relocation of an existing bridge.

Coast Guard Authorization Act of 1998

Public Law 105-383
Amended through P.L. 117-144

Coast Guard and Maritime Transportation Act of 2006

Public Law 109-241
As amended through P.L. 116-283

Coast Guard and Maritime Transportation Act of 2006

[(Public Law 109–241)]

[As Amended Through P.L. 116–283, Enacted January 1, 2021]

AN ACT To authorize appropriations for the Coast Guard for fiscal year 2006, to make technical corrections to various laws administered by the Coast Guard, and for other purposes.

Be it enacted by the Senate and House of Representatives of the United States of America in Congress assembled,

* * * * * * *

TITLE IV—MISCELLANEOUS

* * * * * * *

SEC. 421. [46 U.S.C. 8103 note] DISTANT WATER TUNA FLEET.

(a) MANNING REQUIREMENTS.—

(1) IN GENERAL.—Notwithstanding section 8103(a) of title 46, United States Code, United States purse seine fishing vessels fishing exclusively for highly migratory species in the treaty area under a fishing license issued pursuant to the 1987 Treaty on Fisheries Between the Governments of Certain Pacific Islands States and the Government of the United States of America, or transiting to or from the treaty area exclusively for such purpose, may engage foreign citizens to meet the manning requirement (except for the master) until the date of expiration of this section if, after timely notice of a vacancy to meet the manning requirement, no United States citizen personnel are readily available to fill such vacancy.

(2) DEFINITION.—In this subsection, the term "treaty area"

has the meaning given the term in the Treaty on Fisheries Between the Governments of Certain Pacific Island States and the Government of the United States of America as in effect on the date of the enactment of the Coast Guard and Maritime Transportation Act of 2006 (Public Law 109–241).

(b) LICENSING RESTRICTIONS.—

(1) IN GENERAL.—Subsection (a) only applies to a foreign citizen who holds a credential that is equivalent to the credential issued by the Coast Guard to a United States citizen for the position, with respect to requirements for experience, training, and other qualifications.

(2) TREATMENT OF CREDENTIAL.—An equivalent credential under paragraph (1) shall be considered as meeting the requirements of section 8304 of title 46, United States Code, but only while a person holding the credential is in the service of the vessel to which this section applies.

(c) EXPIRATION.—This section expires on the date the Treaty on Fisheries Between the Governments of Certain Pacific Island States and the Government of the United States of America ceases to have effect for any party under Article 13.6 of such treaty, as in effect on the date of enactment of the Coast Guard Authorization Act of 2020.

(d) REPORTS.—On March 1, 2007, and annually thereafter until the date of expiration of this section, the Coast Guard and the National Marine Fisheries Service shall submit a report to the Committee on Commerce, Science, and Transportation of the Senate and the Committees on Transportation and Infrastructure and Resources of the House of Representatives, providing the following information on the United States purse seine fleet referred to in subsection (a):

(1) The number and identity of vessels in the fleet using foreign citizens to meet manning requirements pursuant to this section and any marine casualties involving such vessel.

(2) The number of vessels in the fishery under United States flag as of January 1 of the year in which the report is submitted, the percentage ownership or control of such vessels by non-United States citizens, and the nationality of such ownership or control.

(3) Description of any transfers or sales of United States flag vessels in the previous calendar year, and the disposition of

such vessel, including whether the vessel was scrapped or sold, and, if sold, the nationality of the new owner and location of any fishery to which the vessel will be transferred.

(4) Landings of tuna by vessels under flag in the 2 previous calendar years, including an assessment of landing trends, and a description of landing percentages and totals—

(A) delivered to American Samoa and any other port in a State or territory of the United States; and

(B) delivered to ports outside of a State or territory of the United States, including the identity of the port.

(5) An evaluation of capacity and trends in the purse seine fleet fishing in the area covered by the South Pacific Regional Fisheries Treaty, and any transfer of capacity from such fleet or area to other fisheries, including those governed under the Western and Central Pacific Fisheries Convention and the Inter-American Tropical Tuna Convention.

* * * * * * *

COAST GUARD AUTHORIZATION ACT OF 2010

PUBLIC LAW 111-281

AS AMENDED THROUGH P.L. 116-283

Coast Guard Authorization Act of 2010

[(Public Law 111–281)]

[As Amended Through P.L. 116–283, Enacted January 1, 2021]

AN ACT To authorize appropriations for the Coast Guard for fiscal year 2011, and for other purposes.

Be it enacted by the Senate and House of Representatives of the United States of America in Congress assembled,

SECTION 1. SHORT TITLE; TABLE OF CONTENTS.

(a) SHORT TITLE.—This Act may be cited as the "Coast Guard Authorization Act of 2010".

* * * * * * *

TITLE IV—ACQUISITION REFORM

SEC. 401. CHIEF ACQUISITION OFFICER.

(a) IN GENERAL.—Chapter 3 of title 14, United States Code, is further amended by adding at the end the following:

"SEC. 56. Chief Acquisition Officer

"(a) IN GENERAL.—There shall be in the Coast Guard a Chief Acquisition Officer selected by the Commandant who shall be a Rear Admiral or civilian from the Senior Executive Service (career reserved) and who meets the qualifications set forth under subsection (b). The Chief Acquisition Officer shall serve at the Assistant Commandant level and have acquisition management as that individual's primary duty.

"(b) QUALIFICATIONS.—

"(1) The Chief Acquisition Officer and any flag officer serving in the Acquisition Directorate shall be an acquisition professional with a Level III acquisition management certification and must have at least 10 years experience in an acquisition position, of which at least 4 years were spent as—

“(A) the program executive officer;

“(B) the program manager of a Level 1 or Level 2 acquisition project or program;

“(C) the deputy program manager of a Level 1 or Level 2 acquisition;

“(D) the project manager of a Level 1 or Level 2 acquisition; or

“(E) any other acquisition position of significant responsibility in which the primary duties are supervisory or management duties.

“(2) The Commandant shall periodically publish a list of the positions designated under paragraph (1).

“(3) In this subsection each of the terms ‘Level 1 acquisition’ and ‘Level 2 acquisition’ has the meaning that term has in chapter 15 of this title.

“(c) FUNCTIONS OF THE CHIEF ACQUISITION OFFICER.—The functions of the Chief Acquisition Officer include—

“(1) monitoring the performance of acquisition projects and programs on the basis of applicable performance measurements and advising the Commandant, through the chain of command, regarding the appropriate business strategy to achieve the missions of the Coast Guard;

“(2) maximizing the use of full and open competition at the prime contract and subcontract levels in the acquisition of property, capabilities, assets, and services by the Coast Guard by establishing policies, procedures, and practices that ensure that the Coast Guard receives a sufficient number of sealed bids or competitive proposals from responsible sources to fulfill the Government’s requirements, including performance and delivery schedules, at the lowest cost or best value considering the nature of the property, capability, asset, or service procured;

“(3) making acquisition decisions in concurrence with the technical authority, or technical authorities, of the Coast Guard, as designated by the Commandant, consistent with all other applicable laws and decisions establishing procedures within the Coast Guard;

"(4) ensuring the use of detailed performance specifications in instances in which performance-based contracting is used;

"(5) managing the direction of acquisition policy for the Coast Guard, including implementation of the unique acquisition policies, regulations, and standards of the Coast Guard;

"(6) developing and maintaining an acquisition career management program in the Coast Guard to ensure that there is an adequate acquisition workforce;

"(7) assessing the requirements established for Coast Guard personnel regarding knowledge and skill in acquisition resources and management and the adequacy of such requirements for facilitating the achievement of the performance goals established for acquisition management;

"(8) developing strategies and specific plans for hiring, training, and professional development; and

"(9) reporting to the Commandant, through the chain of command, on the progress made in improving acquisition management capability."

(b) CLERICAL AMENDMENT.—The table of contents for chapter 3 of title 14, United States Code, is amended by adding at the end the following:

"56. Chief Acquisition Officer."

(c) [14 U.S.C. 308 note] SELECTION DEADLINE.—As soon as practicable after the date of enactment of this Act, but no later than October 1, 2011, the Commandant of the Coast Guard shall select a Chief Acquisition Officer under section 56 of title 14, United States Code, as amended by this section.

(d) [14 U.S.C. 308 note] SPECIAL RATE SUPPLEMENTS.—

(1) REQUIREMENT TO ESTABLISH.—Not later than 1 year after the date of enactment of this Act and in accordance with section 9701.333 of title 5, Code of Federal Regulations, the Commandant of the Coast Guard shall establish special rate supplements that provide higher pay levels for employees necessary to carry out the amendment made by this section.

(2) SUBJECT TO APPROPRIATIONS.—The requirement under paragraph (1) is subject to the availability of appropriations.

* * * * * * *

TITLE IX—MISCELLANEOUS PROVISIONS

* * * * * * *

SEC. 914. [14 U.S.C. 501 note] CONVEYANCE OF COAST GUARD VESSELS FOR PUBLIC PURPOSES.

(a) IN GENERAL.—Whenever the transfer of ownership of a Coast Guard vessel or aircraft to an eligible entity for use for educational, cultural, historical, charitable, recreational, or other public purposes is authorized by law or declared excess by the Commandant, the Coast Guard shall transfer the vessel or aircraft to the General Services Administration for conveyance to the eligible entity.

(b) CONDITIONS OF CONVEYANCE.—The General Services Administration may not convey a vessel or aircraft to an eligible entity as authorized by law unless the eligible entity agrees—

(1) to provide the documentation needed by the General Services Administration to process a request for aircraft or vessels under section 102.37.225 of title 41, Code of Federal Regulations;

(2) to comply with the special terms, conditions, and restrictions imposed on aircraft and vessels under section 102.37.460 of such title;

(3) to make the vessel available to the United States Government if it is needed for use by the Commandant of the Coast Guard in time of war or a national emergency; and

(4) to hold the United States Government harmless for any claims arising from exposure to hazardous materials, including asbestos and polychlorinated biphenyls, that occurs after conveyance of the vessel, except for claims arising from use of the vessel by the United States Government under paragraph (3).

(c) OTHER OBLIGATIONS UNAFFECTED.—Nothing in this section

amends or affects any obligation of the Coast Guard or any other person under the Toxic Substances Control Act (15 U.S.C. 2601 et seq.) or any other law regarding use or disposal of hazardous materials including asbestos and polychlorinated biphenyls.

(d) ELIGIBLE ENTITY DEFINED.—In this section, the term "eligible entity" means a State or local government, nonprofit corporation, educational agency, community development organization, or other entity that agrees to comply with the conditions established under this section.

* * * * * * *

AMERICAS CUP ACT OF 2011

PUBLIC LAW 112-217
AS AMENDED THROUGH P.L. 116-283

America's Cup Act of 2011

[(Public Law 112–61)]

[As Amended Through P.L. 116–283, Enacted January 1, 2021]

AN ACT To facilitate the hosting in the United States of the 34th America's Cup by authorizing certain eligible vessels to participate in activities related to the competition, and for other purposes.

Be it enacted by the Senate and House of Representatives of the United States of America in Congress assembled,

SECTION 1. SHORT TITLE.

This Act may be cited as the "America's Cup Act of 2011".

SEC. 2. DEFINITIONS.

In this Act:

(1) 34TH AMERICA'S CUP.—The term "34th America's Cup"—

(A) means the sailing competitions, commencing in 2011, to be held in the United States in response to the challenge to the defending team from the United States, in accordance with the terms of the America's Cup governing Deed of Gift, dated October 24, 1887; and

(B) if a United States yacht club successfully defends the America's Cup, includes additional sailing competitions conducted by America's Cup Race Management during the 1-year period beginning on the last date of such defense.

(2) AMERICA'S CUP RACE MANAGEMENT.—The term "America's Cup Race Management" means the entity established to provide for independent, professional, and neutral race management of the America's Cup sailing competitions.

(3) ELIGIBILITY CERTIFICATION.—The term "Eligibility Certification" means a certification issued under section 4.

(4) ELIGIBLE VESSEL.—The term "eligible vessel" means a competing vessel or supporting vessel of any registry that—

(A) is recognized by America's Cup Race Management as an official competing vessel, or supporting vessel of, the 34th America's Cup, as evidenced in writing to the Administrator of the Maritime Administration of the Department of Transportation;

(B) transports not more than 25 individuals, in addition to the crew;

(C) is not a ferry (as defined under section 2101(10b) of title 46, United States Code);

(D) does not transport individuals in point-to-point service for hire; and

(E) does not transport merchandise between ports in the United States.

(5) SUPPORTING VESSEL.—The term "supporting vessel" means a vessel that is operating in support of the 34th America's Cup by—

(A) positioning a competing vessel on the race course;

(B) transporting equipment and supplies utilized for the staging, operations, or broadcast of the competition; or

(C) transporting individuals who—

(i) have not purchased tickets or directly paid for their passage; and

(ii) who are engaged in the staging, operations, or broadcast of the competition, race team personnel, members of the media, or event sponsors.

SEC. 3. AUTHORIZATION OF ELIGIBLE VESSELS.

Notwithstanding sections 55102, 55103, and 55111 of title 46, United States Code, an eligible vessel, operating only in preparation for, or in connection with, the 34th America's Cup competition, may position competing vessels and may transport individuals and equipment and supplies utilized for the staging, operations, or broadcast of the competition from and around the ports in the United States.

SEC. 4. CERTIFICATION.

(a) REQUIREMENT.—A vessel may not operate under section 3 unless the vessel has received an Eligibility Certification.

(b) ISSUANCE.—The Administrator of the Maritime Administration of the Department of Transportation is authorized to issue an Eligibility Certification with respect to any vessel that the Administrator determines, in his or her sole discretion, meets the requirements set forth in section 2(4).

SEC. 5. ENFORCEMENT.

Notwithstanding sections 55102, 55103, and 55111 of title 46, United States Code, an Eligibility Certification shall be conclusive evidence to the Secretary of the Department of Homeland Security of the qualification of the vessel for which it has been issued to participate in the 34th America's Cup as a competing vessel or a supporting vessel.

SEC. 6. PENALTY.

Any vessel participating in the 34th America's Cup as a competing vessel or supporting vessel that has not received an Eligibility Certification or is not in compliance with section 12112 of title 46, United States Code, shall be subject to the applicable penalties provided in chapters 121 and 551 of title 46, United States Code.

SEC. 7. WAIVERS.

(a) IN GENERAL.—Notwithstanding sections 12112 and 12132 and chapter 551 of title 46, United States Code, the Secretary of the department in which the Coast Guard is operating may issue a certificate of documentation with a coastwise endorsement for each of the following vessels:

(1) M/V GEYSIR (United States official number 622178).

(2) OCEAN VERITAS (IMO number 7366805).

(3) LUNA (United States official number 280133).

(b) DOCUMENTATION OF LNG TANKERS.—

(1) IN GENERAL.—Notwithstanding sections 12112 and 12132 and chapter 551 of title 46, United States Code, the Secretary of the department in which the Coast Guard is operating may issue a certificate of documentation with a coastwise endorsement for each of the following vessels:

(A) LNG GEMINI (United States official number 595752).

(B) LNG LEO (United States official number 595753).

(C) LNG VIRGO (United States official number 595755).

(2) LIMITATION ON OWNERSHIP.—The Secretary of the department in which the Coast Guard is operating may only issue a certificate of documentation with a coastwise endorsement to a vessel designated in paragraph (1) if the owner of the vessel is an individual or individuals who are citizens of the United States, or is an entity deemed to be such a citizen under section 50501 of title 46, United States Code.

(3) LIMITATION ON REPAIR AND MODIFICATION.—

(A) REQUIREMENT.—Any qualified work shall be performed at a shipyard facility located in the United States.

(B) EXCEPTIONS.—The requirement in subparagraph (A) does not apply to any qualified work—

(i) for which the owner or operator enters into a binding agreement no later than 1 year after the date of enactment of the Elijah E. Cummings Coast Guard Authorization Act of 2020; or

(ii) necessary for the safe towage of the vessel from outside the United States to a shipyard facility in the United States for completion of the qualified work.

(C) DEFINITION.—In this paragraph, qualified work means repair and modification necessary for the issuance of a certificate of inspection issued as a result of the waiver for which a coastwise endorsement is issued under paragraph (1).

(4) LIMITATION ON OPERATION.—Coastwise trade authorized under paragraph (1) shall be limited to carriage of natural gas, as that term is defined in section 3(13) of the Deepwater Port Act of 1974 (33 U.S.C. 1502(13)).

(5) TERMINATION OF EFFECTIVENESS OF ENDORSEMENTS.—The coastwise endorsement issued under paragraph (1) for a vessel shall expire on the date of the sale of the vessel by the owner to a person who is not related by

ownership or control to such owner, unless prior to any such sale the vessel has been operated in a coastwise trade for not less than 1 year after the date of enactment of the Elijah E. Cummings Coast Guard Authorization Act of 2020 and prior to sale of vessel.

(c) OPERATION OF A DRY DOCK.—A vessel transported in Dry Dock #2 (State of Alaska registration AIDEA FDD-2) is not merchandise for purposes of section 55102 of title 46, United States Code, if, during such transportation, Dry Dock #2 remains connected by a utility or other connecting line to pierside moorage located in Ketchikan, Alaska.

Coast Guard and Maritime Transportation Act of 2012

Public Law 112-213

As amended through P.L. 116-283

Coast Guard and Maritime Transportation Act of 2012

[(Public Law 112–213)]

[As Amended Through P.L. 116–283, Enacted January 1, 2021]

AN ACT To authorize appropriations for the Coast Guard for fiscal years 2013 through 2014, and for other purposes.

Be it enacted by the Senate and House of Representatives of the United States of America in Congress assembled,

SECTION 1. SHORT TITLE; TABLE OF CONTENTS.

(a) SHORT TITLE.—This Act may be cited as the "Coast Guard and Maritime Transportation Act of 2012".

(b) TABLE OF CONTENTS.—The table of contents for this Act is as follows:

[1] Section 8111(c)(2) of Public Law 116–283 provides for a repeal of section 222 without including a conforming amendment to strike such item for section 222 in the table of sections.

TITLE III—SHIPPING AND NAVIGATION

TITLE IV—MARITIME ADMINISTRATION AUTHORIZATION

TITLE I—AUTHORIZATION

SEC. 101. AUTHORIZATION OF APPROPRIATIONS.

Funds are authorized to be appropriated for each of fiscal years

2013 and 2014 for necessary expenses of the Coast Guard as follows:

(1) For the operation and maintenance of the Coast Guard—

(A) $6,882,645,000 for fiscal year 2013; and

(B) $6,981,036,000 for fiscal year 2014;

of which $24,500,000 is authorized each fiscal year to be derived from the Oil Spill Liability Trust Fund to carry out the purposes of section 1012(a)(5) of the Oil Pollution Act of 1990 (33 U.S.C. 2712(a)(5)).

(2) For the acquisition, construction, rebuilding, and improvement of aids to navigation, shore and offshore facilities, vessels, and aircraft, including equipment related thereto—

(A) $1,545,312,000 for fiscal year 2013; and

(B) $1,546,448,000 for fiscal year 2014;

to remain available until expended and of which $20,000,000 is authorized each fiscal year to be derived from the Oil Spill Liability Trust Fund to carry out the purposes of section 1012(a)(5) of the Oil Pollution Act of 1990 (33 U.S.C. 2712(a)(5)).

(3) For the Coast Guard Reserve program, including personnel and training costs, equipment, and services—

(A) $138,111,000 for fiscal year 2013; and

(B) $140,016,000 for fiscal year 2014.

(4) For environmental compliance and restoration of Coast Guard vessels, aircraft, and facilities (other than parts and equipment associated with operation and maintenance)—

(A) $16,699,000 for fiscal year 2013; and

(B) $16,701,000 for fiscal year 2014;

to remain available until expended.

(5) To the Commandant of the Coast Guard for research, development, test, and evaluation of technologies, materials, and human factors directly related to improving the performance of the Coast Guard's mission with respect to search and rescue, aids to navigation, marine safety, marine environmental protection, enforcement of laws and treaties, ice operations, oceanographic research, and defense readiness—

(A) $19,848,000 for fiscal year 2013; and

(B) $19,890,000 for fiscal year 2014.

(6) For alteration or removal of bridges over navigable waters of the United States constituting obstructions to navigation, and for personnel and administrative costs associated with the Alteration of Bridges Program—

(A) $16,000,000 for fiscal year 2013; and

(B) $16,000,000 for fiscal year 2014.

SEC. 102. AUTHORIZED LEVELS OF MILITARY STRENGTH AND TRAINING.

(a) ACTIVE DUTY STRENGTH.—The Coast Guard is authorized an end-of-year strength for active duty personnel of 47,000 for each of fiscal years 2013 and 2014.

(b) MILITARY TRAINING STUDENT LOADS.—The Coast Guard is authorized average military training student loads for each of fiscal years 2013 and 2014 as follows:

(1) For recruit and special training, 2,500 student years.

(2) For flight training, 165 student years.

(3) For professional training in military and civilian institutions, 350 student years.

(4) For officer acquisition, 1,200 student years.

TITLE II—COAST GUARD

SEC. 201. INTERFERENCE WITH COAST GUARD TRANSMISSIONS.

Section 88 of title 14, United States Code, is amended by adding at the end the following:

"(e) An individual who knowingly and willfully operates a device with the intention of interfering with the broadcast or reception of a radio, microwave, or other signal (including a signal from a global positioning system) transmitted, retransmitted, or augmented by the Coast Guard for the purpose of maritime safety is—

"(1) guilty of a class E felony; and

"(2) subject to a civil penalty of not more than $1,000 per day for each violation."

SEC. 202. COAST GUARD AUTHORITY TO OPERATE AND

MAINTAIN COAST GUARD ASSETS.

Section 93 of title 14, United States Code, is amended by adding at the end the following:

"(e) OPERATION AND MAINTENANCE OF COAST GUARD ASSETS AND FACILITIES. All authority, including programmatic budget authority, for the operation and maintenance of Coast Guard vessels, aircraft, systems, aids to navigation, infrastructure, and other assets or facilities shall be allocated to and vested in the Coast Guard and the department in which the Coast Guard is operating."

SEC. 203. LIMITATION ON EXPENDITURES.

Section 149(d) of title 14, United States Code, is amended by adding at the end the following:

"(3) The amount of funds used under this subsection may not exceed $100,000 in any fiscal year."

SEC. 204. ACADEMY PAY, ALLOWANCES, AND EMOLUMENTS.

Section 195 of title 14, United States Code, is amended—

(1) by striking "person" each place it appears and inserting "foreign national"; and

(2) by striking "pay and allowances" each place it appears and inserting "pay, allowances, and emoluments".

SEC. 205. POLICY ON SEXUAL HARASSMENT AND SEXUAL VIOLENCE.

(a) ESTABLISHMENT.—Chapter 9 of title 14, United States Code, is amended by adding at the end the following:

"SEC. 200. Policy on sexual harassment and sexual violence

"(a) REQUIRED POLICY. The Commandant of the Coast Guard shall direct the Superintendent of the Coast Guard Academy to prescribe a policy on sexual harassment and sexual violence applicable to the cadets and other personnel of the Academy.

"(b) MATTERS TO BE SPECIFIED IN POLICY. The policy on sexual harassment and sexual violence under this section shall include specification of the following:

"(1) Programs to promote awareness of the incidence of rape, acquaintance rape, and other sexual offenses of a criminal nature that involve cadets or other Academy personnel.

"(2) Information about how the Coast Guard and the

Academy will protect the confidentiality of victims of sexual harassment or sexual violence, including how any records, statistics, or reports intended for public release will be formatted such that the confidentiality of victims is not jeopardized.

"(3) Procedures that cadets and other Academy personnel should follow in the case of an occurrence of sexual harassment or sexual violence, including—

"(A) if the victim chooses to report an occurrence of sexual harassment or sexual violence, a specification of the person or persons to whom the alleged offense should be reported and options for confidential reporting, including written information to be given to victims that explains how the Coast Guard and the Academy will protect the confidentiality of victims;

"(B) a specification of any other person whom the victim should contact; and

"(C) procedures on the preservation of evidence potentially necessary for proof of criminal sexual assault.

"(4) Procedures for disciplinary action in cases of criminal sexual assault involving a cadet or other Academy personnel.

"(5) Sanctions authorized to be imposed in a substantiated case of sexual harassment or sexual violence involving a cadet or other Academy personnel, including with respect to rape, acquaintance rape, or other criminal sexual offense, whether forcible or nonforcible.

"(6) Required training on the policy for all cadets and other Academy personnel who process allegations of sexual harassment or sexual violence involving a cadet or other Academy personnel.

"(c) ASSESSMENT.

"(1) IN GENERAL. The Commandant shall direct the Superintendent to conduct at the Academy during each Academy program year an assessment to determine the effectiveness of the policies of the Academy with respect to sexual harassment and sexual violence involving cadets or other Academy personnel.

"(2) BIENNIAL SURVEY. For the assessment at the Academy under paragraph (1) with respect to an Academy program year that begins in an odd-numbered calendar year, the Superintendent shall conduct a survey of cadets and other Academy personnel—

"(A) to measure—

"(i) the incidence, during that program year, of sexual harassment and sexual violence events, on or off the Academy reservation, that have been reported to an official of the Academy; and

"(ii) the incidence, during that program year, of sexual harassment and sexual violence events, on or off the Academy reservation, that have not been reported to an official of the Academy; and

"(B) to assess the perceptions of the cadets and other Academy personnel with respect to—

"(i) the Academy's policies, training, and procedures on sexual harassment and sexual violence involving cadets or other Academy personnel;

"(ii) the enforcement of such policies;

"(iii) the incidence of sexual harassment and sexual violence involving cadets or other Academy personnel; and

"(iv) any other issues relating to sexual harassment and sexual violence involving cadets or other Academy personnel.

"(d) REPORT.

"(1) IN GENERAL. The Commandant shall direct the Superintendent to submit to the Commandant a report on sexual harassment and sexual violence involving cadets or other Academy personnel for each Academy program year.

"(2) REPORT SPECIFICATIONS. Each report under paragraph (1) shall include, for the Academy program year covered by the report, the following:

"(A) The number of sexual assaults, rapes, and other sexual offenses involving cadets or other Academy personnel that have been reported to Academy officials during the Academy program year and, of those reported cases, the number that have been substantiated.

"(B) A plan for the actions that are to be taken in

the following Academy program year regarding prevention of and response to sexual harassment and sexual violence involving cadets or other Academy personnel.

"(3) BIENNIAL SURVEY. Each report under paragraph (1) for an Academy program year that begins in an odd-numbered calendar year shall include the results of the survey conducted in that Academy program year under subsection (c)(2).

"(4) TRANSMISSION OF REPORT. The Commandant shall transmit each report received by the Commandant under this subsection, together with the Commandant's comments on the report, to—

"(A) the Committee on Commerce, Science, and Transportation of the Senate; and

"(B) the Committee on Transportation and Infrastructure of the House of Representatives.

"(5) FOCUS GROUPS.

"(A) IN GENERAL. For each Academy program year with respect to which the Superintendent is not required to conduct a survey at the Academy under subsection (c)(2), the Commandant shall require focus groups to be conducted at the Academy for the purposes of ascertaining information relating to sexual assault and sexual harassment issues at the Academy.

"(B) INCLUSION IN REPORTS. Information derived from a focus group under subparagraph (A) shall be included in the next transmitted Commandant's report under this subsection.

"(e) VICTIM CONFIDENTIALITY. To the extent that information collected under the authority of this section is reported or otherwise made available to the public, such information shall be provided in a form that is consistent with applicable privacy protections under Federal law and does not jeopardize the confidentiality of victims."

(b) CLERICAL AMENDMENT.—The analysis for chapter 9 of title 14, United States Code, is amended by inserting after the item relating to section 199 the following:

"200. Policy on sexual harassment and sexual violence.".

SEC. 206. APPOINTMENTS OF PERMANENT COMMISSIONED OFFICERS.

Section 211 of title 14, United States Code, is amended by adding at the end the following:

"(d) For the purposes of this section, the term 'original', with respect to the appointment of a member of the Coast Guard, refers to that member's most recent appointment in the Coast Guard that is neither a promotion nor a demotion."

SEC. 207. SELECTION BOARDS; OATH OF MEMBERS.

Section 254 of title 14, United States Code, is amended to read as follows:

"SEC. 254. Selection boards; oath of members

"Each member of a selection board shall swear—

"(1) that the member will, without prejudice or partiality, and having in view both the special fitness of officers and the efficiency of the Coast Guard, perform the duties imposed upon the member; and

"(2) an oath in accordance with section 635."

SEC. 208. SPECIAL SELECTION BOARDS; CORRECTION OF ERRORS.

(a) IN GENERAL.—Chapter 11 of title 14, United States Code, is amended by inserting after section 262 the following:

"SEC. 263. Special selection boards; correction of errors

"(a) OFFICERS NOT CONSIDERED DUE TO ADMINISTRATIVE ERROR.

"(1) IN GENERAL. If the Secretary determines that as the result of an administrative error—

"(A) an officer or former officer was not considered for selection for promotion by a selection board convened under section 251; or

"(B) the name of an officer or former officer was not placed on an all-fully-qualified-officers list;

the Secretary shall convene a special selection board to determine whether such officer or former officer should be recommended for promotion and such officer or former officer shall not be considered to have failed of selection for promotion prior to the consideration of the special selection board.

"(2) EFFECT OF FAILURE TO RECOMMEND FOR PROMOTION.

If a special selection board convened under paragraph (1) does not recommend for promotion an officer or former officer, whose grade is below the grade of captain and whose name was referred to that board for consideration, the officer or former officer shall be considered to have failed of selection for promotion.

"(b) OFFICERS CONSIDERED BUT NOT SELECTED; MATERIAL ERROR.

"(1) IN GENERAL. In the case of an officer or former officer who was eligible for promotion, was considered for selection for promotion by a selection board convened under section 251, and was not selected for promotion by that board, the Secretary may convene a special selection board to determine whether the officer or former officer should be recommended for promotion, if the Secretary determines that—

"(A) an action of the selection board that considered the officer or former officer—

"(i) was contrary to law in a matter material to the decision of the board; or

"(ii) involved material error of fact or material administrative error; or

"(B) the selection board that considered the officer or former officer did not have before it for consideration material information.

"(2) EFFECT OF FAILURE TO RECOMMEND FOR PROMOTION. If a special selection board convened under paragraph (1) does not recommend for promotion an officer or former officer, whose grade is that of commander or below and whose name was referred to that board for consideration, the officer or former officer shall be considered—

"(A) to have failed of selection for promotion with respect to the board that considered the officer or former officer prior to the consideration of the special selection board; and

"(B) to incur no additional failure of selection for promotion as a result of the action of the special selection board.

"(c) REQUIREMENTS FOR SPECIAL SELECTION BOARDS. Each special selection board convened under this section shall—

"(1) be composed in accordance with section 252 and the members of the board shall be required to swear the oaths described in section 254;

"(2) consider the record of an applicable officer or former officer as that record, if corrected, would have appeared to the selection board that should have considered or did consider the officer or former officer prior to the consideration of the special selection board and that record shall be compared with a sampling of the records of—

"(A) those officers of the same grade who were recommended for promotion by such prior selection board; and

"(B) those officers of the same grade who were not recommended for promotion by such prior selection board; and

"(3) submit to the Secretary a written report in a manner consistent with sections 260 and 261.

"(d) APPOINTMENT OF OFFICERS RECOMMENDED FOR PROMOTION.

"(1) IN GENERAL. An officer or former officer whose name is placed on a promotion list as a result of the recommendation of a special selection board convened under this section shall be appointed, as soon as practicable, to the next higher grade in accordance with the law and policies that would have been applicable to the officer or former officer had the officer or former officer been recommended for promotion by the selection board that should have considered or did consider the officer or former officer prior to the consideration of the special selection board.

"(2) EFFECT. An officer or former officer who is promoted to the next higher grade as a result of the recommendation of a special selection board convened under this section shall have, upon such promotion, the same date of rank, the same effective date for the pay and allowances of that grade, and the same position on the active duty promotion list as the officer or former officer would have had if the officer or former officer had been recommended for promotion to that grade by the selection board that should have considered or did consider the officer or former officer prior to the consideration of the special selection board.

"(3) RECORD CORRECTION. If the report of a special selection board convened under this section, as approved by the President, recommends for promotion to the next higher grade an officer not eligible for promotion or a former officer whose name was referred to the board for consideration, the Secretary may act under section 1552 of title 10 to correct the military record of the officer or former officer to correct an error or remove an injustice resulting from the officer or former officer not being selected for promotion by the selection board that should have considered or did consider the officer or former officer prior to the consideration of the special selection board.

"(e) APPLICATION PROCESS AND TIME LIMITS. The Secretary shall issue regulations regarding the process by which an officer or former officer may apply to have a matter considered by a special selection board convened under this section, including time limits related to such applications.

"(f) LIMITATION OF OTHER JURISDICTION. No official or court of the United States shall have authority or jurisdiction over any claim based in any way on the failure of an officer or former officer to be selected for promotion by a selection board convened under section 251, until—

"(1) the claim has been referred to a special selection board convened under this section and acted upon by that board; or

"(2) the claim has been rejected by the Secretary without consideration by a special selection board convened under this section.

"(g) JUDICIAL REVIEW.

"(1) IN GENERAL. A court of the United States may review—

"(A) a decision of the Secretary not to convene a special selection board under this section to determine if the court finds that the decision of the Secretary was arbitrary or capricious, not based on substantial evidence, or otherwise contrary to law; and

"(B) an action of a special selection board under this section to determine if the court finds that the action of the special selection board was contrary to law or involved material error of fact or material administrative error.

"(2) REMAND AND RECONSIDERATION. If, with respect to a

review under paragraph (1), a court makes a finding described in subparagraph (A) or (B) of that paragraph, the court shall remand the case to the Secretary and the Secretary shall provide the applicable officer or former officer consideration by a new special selection board convened under this section.

"(h) DESIGNATION OF BOARDS. The Secretary may designate a selection board convened under section 251 as a special selection board convened under this section. A selection board so designated may function in the capacity of a selection board convened under section 251 and a special selection board convened under this section."

(b) SELECTION BOARDS; SUBMISSION OF REPORTS.—Section 261(d) of title 14, United States Code, is amended by striking "selection board" and inserting "selection board, including a special selection board convened under section 263,".

(c) FAILURE OF SELECTION FOR PROMOTION.—Section 262 of title 14, United States Code, is amended to read as follows:

"SEC. 262. Failure of selection for promotion

"An officer, other than an officer serving in the grade of captain, who is, or is senior to, the junior officer in the promotion zone established for his grade under section 256 of this title, fails of selection if he is not selected for promotion by the selection board which considered him, or if having been recommended for promotion by the board, his name is thereafter removed from the report of the board by the President."

(d) CLERICAL AMENDMENT.—The analysis for chapter 11 of title 14, United States Code, is amended by inserting after the item relating to section 262 the following:

"263. Special selection boards; correction of errors.".

(e) APPLICABILITY; RULE OF CONSTRUCTION.—

(1) [14 U.S.C. 261 note] APPLICABILITY.—The amendments made by this section shall take effect on the date of enactment of this Act and the Secretary may convene a special selection board on or after that date under section 263 of title 14, United States Code, with respect to any error or other action for which such a board may be convened if that error or other action occurred on or after the date that is 1 year before the date of enactment of this Act.

(2) [14 U.S.C. 271 note] RULE OF CONSTRUCTION.—Sections

271, 272, and 273 of title 14, United States Code, apply to the activities of—

(A) a selection board convened under section 251 of such title; and

(B) a special selection board convened under section 263 of such title.

SEC. 209. PROHIBITION OF CERTAIN INVOLUNTARY ADMINISTRATIVE SEPARATIONS.

(a) IN GENERAL.—Chapter 11 of title 14, United States Code, as amended by this Act, is further amended by inserting after section 426 the following:

"SEC. 427. Prohibition of certain involuntary administrative separations

"(a) IN GENERAL. Except as provided in subsection (b), the Secretary may not authorize the involuntary administrative separation of a covered individual based on a determination that the covered individual is unsuitable for deployment or other assignment due to a medical condition of the covered individual considered by a Physical Evaluation Board during an evaluation of the covered individual that resulted in the covered individual being determined to be fit for duty.

"(b) REEVALUATION.

"(1) IN GENERAL. The Secretary may require a Physical Evaluation Board to reevaluate any covered individual if the Secretary determines there is reason to believe that a medical condition of the covered individual considered by a Physical Evaluation Board during an evaluation of the covered individual renders the covered individual unsuitable for continued duty.

"(2) RETIREMENTS AND SEPARATIONS. A covered individual who is determined, based on a reevaluation under paragraph (1), to be unfit to perform the duties of the covered individual's office, grade, rank, or rating may be retired or separated for physical disability under this chapter.

"(c) COVERED INDIVIDUAL DEFINED. In this section, the term 'covered individual' means any member of the Coast Guard who has been determined by a Physical Evaluation Board, pursuant to a physical evaluation by that board, to be fit for duty."

(b) CLERICAL AMENDMENT.—The analysis for chapter 11 of title 14, United States Code, as amended by this Act, is further amended by inserting after the item relating to section 426 the following:

"427. Prohibition of certain involuntary administrative separations.".

SEC. 210. MAJOR ACQUISITIONS.

(a) IN GENERAL.—Subchapter I of chapter 15 of title 14, United States Code, is amended by adding at the end the following:

"SEC. 569a. Major acquisitions

"(a) IN GENERAL. In conjunction with the transmittal by the President to Congress of the budget of the United States for fiscal year 2014 and biennially thereafter, the Secretary shall submit to the Committee on Commerce, Science, and Transportation of the Senate and the Committee on Transportation and Infrastructure of the House of Representatives a report on the status of all major acquisition programs.

"(b) INFORMATION TO BE INCLUDED. Each report under subsection (a) shall include for each major acquisition program—

"(1) a statement of the Coast Guard's mission needs and performance goals relating to such program, including a justification for any change to those needs and goals subsequent to a report previously submitted under this section;

"(2) a justification explaining how the projected number and capabilities of assets acquired under such program meet applicable mission needs and performance goals;

"(3) an identification of any and all mission hour gaps, accompanied by an explanation of how and when the Coast Guard will close those gaps;

"(4) an identification of any changes with respect to such program, including—

"(A) any changes to the timeline for the acquisition of each new asset and the phaseout of legacy assets; and

"(B) any changes to—

"(i) the costs of new assets or legacy assets for that fiscal year or future fiscal years; or

"(ii) the total acquisition cost;

"(5) a justification explaining how any change to such program fulfills the mission needs and performance goals of the

Coast Guard;

"(6) a description of how the Coast Guard is planning for the integration of each new asset acquired under such program into the Coast Guard, including needs related to shore-based infrastructure and human resources;

"(7) an identification of how funds in the applicable fiscal year's budget request will be allocated, including information on the purchase of specific assets;

"(8) a projection of the remaining operational lifespan and life-cycle cost of each legacy asset that also identifies any anticipated resource gaps;

"(9) a detailed explanation of how the costs of legacy assets are being accounted for within such program; and

"(10) an annual performance comparison of new assets to legacy assets.

"(c) ADEQUACY OF ACQUISITION WORKFORCE. Each report under subsection (a) shall—

"(1) include information on the scope of the acquisition activities to be performed in the next fiscal year and on the adequacy of the current acquisition workforce to meet that anticipated workload;

"(2) specify the number of officers, members, and employees of the Coast Guard currently and planned to be assigned to each position designated under section 562(c) of this subchapter; and

"(3) identify positions that are or will be understaffed and actions that will be taken to correct such understaffing.

"(d) CUTTERS NOT MAINTAINED IN CLASS. Each report under subsection (a) shall identify which, if any, Coast Guard cutters that have been issued a certificate of classification by the American Bureau of Shipping have not been maintained in class, with an explanation detailing the reasons why the cutters have not been maintained in class.

"(e) MAJOR ACQUISITION PROGRAM DEFINED. In this section, the term 'major acquisition program' means an ongoing acquisition undertaken by the Coast Guard with a life-cycle cost estimate greater than or equal to $300,000,000."

(b) CLERICAL AMENDMENT.—The analysis for chapter 15 of title 14, United States Code, is amended by inserting after the item relating to section 569 the following:

"569a. Major acquisitions.".

(c) REPEALS.—

(1) Section 408(a) of the Coast Guard and Maritime Transportation Act of 2006 (14 U.S.C. 663 note) is repealed.

(2) Title 14, United States Code, is amended—

(A) in section 562, by repealing subsection (e); and

(B) in section 573(c)(3), by repealing subparagraph (B).

SEC. 211. ADVANCE PROCUREMENT FUNDING.

(a) IN GENERAL.—Subchapter II of chapter 15 of title 14, United States Code, is amended by adding at the end the following:

"SEC. 577. Advance procurement funding

"(a) IN GENERAL. With respect to any Coast Guard vessel for which amounts are appropriated and any amounts otherwise made available for vessels for the Coast Guard in any fiscal year, the Commandant of the Coast Guard may enter into a contract or place an order, in advance of a contract or order for construction of a vessel, for—

"(1) materials, parts, components, and labor for the vessel;

"(2) the advance construction of parts or components for the vessel;

"(3) protection and storage of materials, parts, or components for the vessel; and

"(4) production planning, design, and other related support services that reduce the overall procurement lead time of the vessel.

"(b) USE OF MATERIALS, PARTS, AND COMPONENTS MANUFACTURED IN THE UNITED STATES. In entering into contracts and placing orders under subsection (a), the Commandant may give priority to persons that manufacture materials, parts, and components in the United States."

(b) CLERICAL AMENDMENT.—The analysis for chapter 15 of title 14, United States Code, as amended by this Act, is further amended by inserting after the item relating to section 576 the following:

"577. Advance procurement funding.".

SEC. 212. MINOR CONSTRUCTION.

(a) IN GENERAL.—Section 656 of title 14, United States Code, is amended by adding at the end the following:

"(d) MINOR CONSTRUCTION AND IMPROVEMENT.

"(1) IN GENERAL. Subject to the reporting requirements set forth in paragraph (2), each fiscal year the Secretary may expend from amounts made available for the operating expenses of the Coast Guard not more than $1,500,000 for minor construction and improvement projects at any location.

"(2) REPORTING REQUIREMENTS. Not later than 90 days after the end of each fiscal year, the Secretary shall submit to the Committee on Commerce, Science, and Transportation of the Senate and the Committee on Transportation and Infrastructure of the House of Representatives a report on each project undertaken during the course of the preceding fiscal year for which the amount expended under paragraph (1) exceeded $500,000."

(b) CLERICAL AMENDMENTS.—

(1) HEADING.—Section 656 of title 14, United States Code, as amended by this Act, is further amended by striking the section designation and heading and inserting the following:

"SEC. 656. Use of certain appropriated funds"

(2) ANALYSIS.—The analysis for chapter 17 of title 14, United States Code, is amended by striking the item relating to section 656 and inserting the following:

"656. Use of certain appropriated funds.".

SEC. 213. CAPITAL INVESTMENT PLAN AND ANNUAL LIST OF PROJECTS TO CONGRESS.

(a) CAPITAL INVESTMENT PLAN.—Section 663 of title 14, United States Code, is amended to read as follows:

"SEC. 663. Capital investment plan

"(a) IN GENERAL. On the date on which the President submits to Congress a budget pursuant to section 1105 of title 31, the Commandant of the Coast Guard shall submit to the Committee on Transportation and Infrastructure of the House of Representatives and the Committee on Commerce, Science, and Transportation of the Senate—

"(1) a capital investment plan for the Coast Guard that identifies for each capital asset for which appropriations are proposed in that budget—

"(A) the proposed appropriations included in the budget;

"(B) the total estimated cost of completion;

"(C) projected funding levels for each fiscal year for the next 5 fiscal years or until project completion, whichever is earlier;

"(D) an estimated completion date at the projected funding levels; and

"(E) an acquisition program baseline, as applicable; and

"(2) a list of each unfunded priority for the Coast Guard.

"(b) UNFUNDED PRIORITY DEFINED. In this section, the term 'unfunded priority' means a program or mission requirement that—

"(1) has not been selected for funding in the applicable proposed budget;

"(2) is necessary to fulfill a requirement associated with an operational need; and

"(3) the Commandant would have recommended for inclusion in the applicable proposed budget had additional resources been available or had the requirement emerged before the budget was submitted."

(b) ANNUAL LIST OF PROJECTS TO CONGRESS.—Section 693 of title 14, United States Code, is amended to read as follows:

"SEC. 693. Annual list of projects to Congress

"The Commandant of the Coast Guard shall submit to the Committee on Transportation and Infrastructure of the House of Representatives and the Committee on Commerce, Science, and Transportation of the Senate a prioritized list of projects eligible for environmental compliance and restoration funding for each fiscal year concurrent with the President's budget submission for that fiscal year."

(c) CLERICAL AND CONFORMING AMENDMENTS.—

(1) ANALYSIS FOR CHAPTER 17.—The analysis for chapter 17 of title 14, United States Code, as amended by this Act, is further amended by striking the item relating to section 663 and inserting the following:

"663. Capital investment plan.".

(2) ANALYSIS FOR CHAPTER 19.—The analysis for chapter 19 of title 14, United States Code, is amended by striking the item relating to section 693 and inserting the following:

"693. Annual list of projects to Congress.".

(3) COAST GUARD AUTHORIZATION ACT OF 2010.—Section 918 of the Coast Guard Authorization Act of 2010 (14 U.S.C. 663 note), and the item relating to that section in the table of contents in section 1(b) of that Act, are repealed.

SEC. 214. AIRCRAFT ACCIDENT INVESTIGATIONS.

(a) IN GENERAL.—Chapter 17 of title 14, United States Code, is amended by adding at the end the following:

"SEC. 678. Aircraft accident investigations

"(a) IN GENERAL. Whenever the Commandant of the Coast Guard conducts an accident investigation of an accident involving an aircraft under the jurisdiction of the Commandant, the records and report of the investigation shall be treated in accordance with this section.

"(b) PUBLIC DISCLOSURE OF CERTAIN ACCIDENT INVESTIGATION INFORMATION.

"(1) IN GENERAL. Subject to paragraph (2), the Commandant, upon request, shall publicly disclose unclassified tapes, scientific reports, and other factual information pertinent to an aircraft accident investigation.

"(2) CONDITIONS. The Commandant shall only disclose information requested pursuant to paragraph (1) if the Commandant determines—

"(A) that such tapes, reports, or other information would be included within and releasable with the final accident investigation report; and

"(B) that release of such tapes, reports, or other information—

"(i) would not undermine the ability of accident or safety investigators to continue to conduct the investigation; and

"(ii) would not compromise national security.

"(3) RESTRICTION. A disclosure under paragraph (1) may not be made by or through officials with responsibility for, or who are conducting, a safety investigation with respect to the accident.

"(c) OPINIONS REGARDING CAUSATION OF ACCIDENT. Following an aircraft accident referred to in subsection (a)—

"(1) if the evidence surrounding the accident is sufficient for the investigators who conduct the accident investigation to come to an opinion as to the cause or causes of the accident, the final report of the accident investigation shall set forth the opinion of the investigators as to the cause or causes of the accident; and

"(2) if the evidence surrounding the accident is not sufficient for the investigators to come to an opinion as to the cause or causes of the accident, the final report of the accident investigation shall include a description of those factors, if any, that, in the opinion of the investigators, substantially contributed to or caused the accident.

"(d) USE OF INFORMATION IN CIVIL OR CRIMINAL PROCEEDINGS. For purposes of any civil or criminal proceeding arising from an aircraft accident referred to in subsection (a), any opinion of the accident investigators as to the cause of, or the factors contributing to, the accident set forth in the accident investigation report may not be considered as evidence in such proceeding, nor may such report be considered an admission of liability by the United States or by any person referred to in such report.

"(e) DEFINITIONS. For purposes of this section—

"(1) the term 'accident investigation' means any form of investigation by Coast Guard personnel of an aircraft accident referred to in subsection (a), other than a safety investigation; and

"(2) the term 'safety investigation' means an investigation by Coast Guard personnel of an aircraft accident referred to in subsection (a) that is conducted solely to determine the cause of the accident and to obtain information that may prevent the occurrence of similar accidents."

(b) CLERICAL AMENDMENT.—The analysis for chapter 17 of title 14, United States Code, as amended by this Act, is further amended by adding at the end the following:

"678. Aircraft accident investigations.".

SEC. 215. COAST GUARD AUXILIARY ENROLLMENT ELIGIBILITY.

(a) IN GENERAL.—Section 823 of title 14, United States Code, is amended to read as follows:

"SEC. 823. Eligibility; enrollments

"The Auxiliary shall be composed of nationals of the United States, as defined in section 101(a)(22) of the Immigration and Nationality Act (8 U.S.C. 1101(a)(22)), and aliens lawfully admitted for permanent residence, as defined in section 101(a)(20) of the Immigration and Nationality Act (8 U.S.C. 1101(a)(20))—

"(1) who—

"(A) are owners, sole or part, of motorboats, yachts, aircraft, or radio stations; or

"(B) by reason of their special training or experience are deemed by the Commandant to be qualified for duty in the Auxiliary; and

"(2) who may be enrolled therein pursuant to applicable regulations."

(b) CLERICAL AMENDMENT.—The analysis for chapter 23 of title 14, United States Code, is amended by striking the item relating to section 823 and inserting the following:

"823. Eligibility; enrollments.".

SEC. 216. REPEALS.

(a) DISTRICT OMBUDSMEN.—Section 55 of title 14, United States Code, and the item relating to such section in the analysis for chapter 3 of such title, are repealed.

(b) COOPERATION WITH RESPECT TO AIDS TO AIR NAVIGATION.—Section 82 of title 14, United States Code, and the item relating to such section in the analysis for chapter 5 of such title, are repealed.

(c) OCEAN STATIONS.—Section 90 of title 14, United States Code, and the item relating to such section in the analysis for chapter 5 of such title, are repealed.

(d) DETAIL OF MEMBERS TO ASSIST FOREIGN GOVERNMENTS.—Section 149(a) of title 14, United States Code, is amended by striking the second and third sentences.

(e) ADVISORY COMMITTEE.—Section 193 of title 14, United States Code, and the item relating to such section in the analysis for chapter 9 of such title, are repealed.

(f) HISTORY FELLOWSHIPS.—Section 198 of title 14, United

States Code, and the item relating to such section in the analysis for chapter 9 of such title, are repealed.

SEC. 217. TECHNICAL CORRECTIONS TO TITLE 14.

Title 14, United States Code, as amended by this Act, is further amended—

(1) by amending chapter 1 to read as follows:

"Chapter 1—ESTABLISHMENT AND DUTIES

"SEC. 1. Establishment of Coast Guard

The Coast Guard, established January 28, 1915, shall be a military service and a branch of the armed forces of the United States at all times.

"SEC. 2. Primary duties

The Coast Guard shall—

"(1) enforce or assist in the enforcement of all applicable Federal laws on, under, and over the high seas and waters subject to the jurisdiction of the United States;

"(2) engage in maritime air surveillance or interdiction to enforce or assist in the enforcement of the laws of the United States;

"(3) administer laws and promulgate and enforce regulations for the promotion of safety of life and property on and under the high seas and waters subject to the jurisdiction of the United States, covering all matters not specifically delegated by law to some other executive department;

"(4) develop, establish, maintain, and operate, with due regard to the requirements of national defense, aids to maritime navigation, icebreaking facilities, and rescue facilities for the promotion of safety on, under, and over the high seas and waters subject to the jurisdiction of the United States;

"(5) pursuant to international agreements, develop, establish, maintain, and operate icebreaking facilities on, under, and over waters other than the high seas and waters subject to the jurisdiction of the United States;

"(6) engage in oceanographic research of the high seas and in waters subject to the jurisdiction of the United States; and

"(7) maintain a state of readiness to function as a specialized service in the Navy in time of war, including the fulfillment of Maritime Defense Zone command responsibilities.

"SEC. 3. Department in which the Coast Guard operates

"(a) IN GENERAL. The Coast Guard shall be a service in the Department of Homeland Security, except when operating as a service in the Navy.

"(b) TRANSFERS. Upon the declaration of war if Congress so directs in the declaration or when the President directs, the Coast Guard shall operate as a service in the Navy, and shall so continue until the President, by Executive order, transfers the Coast Guard back to the Department of Homeland Security. While operating as a service in the Navy, the Coast Guard shall be subject to the orders of the Secretary of the Navy, who may order changes in Coast Guard operations to render them uniform, to the extent such Secretary deems advisable, with Navy operations.

"(c) OPERATION AS A SERVICE IN THE NAVY. Whenever the Coast Guard operates as a service in the Navy—

"(1) applicable appropriations of the Navy Department shall be available for the expense of the Coast Guard;

"(2) applicable appropriations of the Coast Guard shall be available for transfer to the Navy Department;

"(3) precedence between commissioned officers of corresponding grades in the Coast Guard and the Navy shall be determined by the date of rank stated by their commissions in those grades;

"(4) personnel of the Coast Guard shall be eligible to

receive gratuities, medals, and other insignia of honor on the same basis as personnel in the naval service or serving in any capacity with the Navy; and

"(5) the Secretary may place on furlough any officer of the Coast Guard and officers on furlough shall receive one half of the pay to which they would be entitled if on leave of absence, but officers of the Coast Guard Reserve shall not be so placed on furlough.

"SEC. 4. Secretary defined

In this title, the term 'Secretary' means the Secretary of the respective department in which the Coast Guard is operating."

(2) in section 95(c), by striking "of Homeland Security";

(3) in section 259(c)(1), by striking "After selecting" and inserting "In selecting";

(4) in section 286a(d), by striking "severance pay" each place it appears and inserting "separation pay";

(5) in the second sentence of section 290(a), by striking "in the grade of vice admiral" and inserting "in or above the grade of vice admiral";

(6) in section 516(a), by striking "of Homeland Security";

(7) by amending section 564 to read as follows:

"SEC. 564. Prohibition on use of lead systems integrators

"(a) IN GENERAL.

"(1) USE OF LEAD SYSTEMS INTEGRATOR. The Commandant may not use a private sector entity as a lead systems integrator.

"(2) FULL AND OPEN COMPETITION. The Commandant shall use full and open competition for any acquisition contract unless otherwise excepted in accordance with Federal acquisition laws and regulations promulgated under those laws, including the Federal Acquisition Regulation.

"(3) NO EFFECT ON SMALL BUSINESS ACT. Nothing in this subsection shall be construed to supersede or otherwise affect the authorities provided by and under the Small Business Act (15 U.S.C. 631 et seq.).

"(b) LIMITATION ON FINANCIAL INTEREST IN

SUBCONTRACTORS. Neither an entity performing lead systems integrator functions for a Coast Guard acquisition nor a Tier 1 subcontractor for any acquisition may have a financial interest in a subcontractor below the Tier 1 subcontractor level unless—

"(1) the subcontractor was selected by the prime contractor through full and open competition for such procurement;

"(2) the procurement was awarded by an entity performing lead systems integrator functions or a subcontractor through full and open competition;

"(3) the procurement was awarded by a subcontractor through a process over which the entity performing lead systems integrator functions or a Tier 1 subcontractor exercised no control; or

"(4) the Commandant has determined that the procurement was awarded in a manner consistent with Federal acquisition laws and regulations promulgated under those laws, including the Federal Acquisition Regulation."

(8) in section 569(a), by striking "and annually thereafter,";

(9) in the analysis for chapter 17—

(A) by striking the item relating to section 669 and inserting the following:

"669. Telephone installation and charges."; and

(B) by striking the item relating to section 674 and inserting the following:

"674. Small boat station rescue capability.";

(10) in section 666(a), by striking "of Homeland Security" and inserting "of the department in which the Coast Guard is operating";

(11) in section 673(a)(3), by striking "of Homeland Security (when the Coast Guard is not operating as a service in the Navy)";

(12) in section 674, by striking "of Homeland Security";

(13) in section 675(a), by striking "Secretary" and all that follows through "may not" and inserting "Secretary may not"; and

(14) in the first sentence of section 740(d), by striking "that

appointment" and inserting "that appointment to the Reserve".

SEC. 218. ACQUISITION WORKFORCE EXPEDITED HIRING AUTHORITY.

Section 404 of the Coast Guard Authorization Act of 2010 (Public Law 111-281; 124 Stat. 2950) is amended—

(1) in subsection (a)(1), by striking "as shortage category positions;" and inserting "as positions for which there exists a shortage of candidates or there is a critical hiring need;";

(2) in subsection (b)—

(A) by striking "paragraph" and inserting "section"; and

(B) by striking "2012." and inserting "2015."; and

(3) in subsection (c), by striking "section 562(d) of title 14, United States Code, as added by this title," and inserting "section 569a of title 14, United States Code,".

SEC. 219. [10 U.S.C. 1293 note] RENEWAL OF TEMPORARY EARLY RETIREMENT AUTHORITY.

For fiscal years 2019 through 2025—

(1) notwithstanding subsection (c)(1) of section 4403 of the National Defense Authorization Act for Fiscal Year 1993 (10 U.S.C. 1293 note), such section shall apply to the Coast Guard in the same manner and to the same extent it applies to the Department of Defense, except that—

(A) the Secretary of Homeland Security shall implement such section with respect to the Coast Guard and, for purposes of that implementation, shall apply the applicable provisions of title 14, United States Code, relating to retirement of Coast Guard personnel; and

(B) the total number of commissioned officers who retire pursuant to this section may not exceed 200, and the total number of enlisted members who retire pursuant to this section may not exceed 300; and

(2) only appropriations available for necessary expenses for the operation and maintenance of the Coast Guard shall be expended for the retired pay of personnel who retire pursuant to this section.

SEC. 220. RESPONSE BOAT-MEDIUM PROCUREMENT.

(a) REQUIREMENT TO FULFILL APPROVED PROGRAM OF RECORD.—Except as provided in subsection (b), the Commandant of the Coast Guard shall maintain the schedule and requirements for the total acquisition of 180 boats as specified in the approved program of record for the Response Boat-Medium acquisition program in effect on June 1, 2012.

(b) APPLICABILITY.—Subsection (a) shall not apply on and after the date on which the Commandant submits to the Committee on Transportation and Infrastructure of the House of Representatives and the Committee on Commerce, Science, and Transportation of the Senate such documentation as the Coast Guard Major Systems Acquisition Manual requires to justify reducing the approved program of record for Response Boat-Medium to a total acquisition of less than 180 boats.

SEC. 221. [14 U.S.C. 573 note] NATIONAL SECURITY CUTTERS. [Subsections (a) and (b) were repealed by sections 311(d)(2) and 818(b)(1) (respectively) of Public Law 115–282.]

TITLE III—SHIPPING AND NAVIGATION

SEC. 301. IDENTIFICATION OF ACTIONS TO ENABLE QUALIFIED UNITED STATES FLAG CAPACITY TO MEET NATIONAL DEFENSE REQUIREMENTS.

Section 501(b) of title 46, United States Code, is amended—

(1) by striking "When the head" and inserting the following:

"(1) IN GENERAL. When the head"

; and

(2) by adding at the end the following:

"(2) DETERMINATIONS. The Maritime Administrator shall—

"(A) for each determination referred to in paragraph (1), identify any actions that could be taken to enable qualified United States flag capacity to meet national defense requirements;

"(B) provide notice of each such determination to the Secretary of Transportation and the head of the agency referred to in paragraph (1) for which the determination is made; and

"(C) publish each such determination on the Internet Web site of the Department of Transportation not later than 48 hours after notice of the determination is provided to the Secretary of Transportation.

"(3) NOTICE TO CONGRESS.

"(A) IN GENERAL. The head of an agency referred to in paragraph (1) shall notify the Committee on Transportation and Infrastructure of the House of Representatives and the Committee on Commerce, Science, and Transportation of the Senate—

"(i) of any request for a waiver of the navigation or vessel-inspection laws under this section not later than 48 hours after receiving such a request; and

"(ii) of the issuance of any such waiver not later than 48 hours after such issuance.

"(B) CONTENTS. Such head of an agency shall include in each notification under subparagraph (A)(ii) an explanation of—

"(i) the reasons the waiver is necessary; and

"(ii) the reasons actions referred to in paragraph (2)(A) are not feasible."

SEC. 302. LIMITATION OF LIABILITY FOR NON-FEDERAL VESSEL TRAFFIC SERVICE OPERATORS.

(a) IN GENERAL.—Section 2307 of title 46, United States Code, is amended—

(1) by striking the section designation and heading and inserting the following:

"SEC. 2307. Limitation of liability for Coast Guard Vessel Traffic Service pilots and non-Federal vessel traffic service operators"

(2) by striking "Any pilot" and inserting the following:

"(a) COAST GUARD VESSEL TRAFFIC SERVICE PILOTS. Any pilot"

; and

(3) by adding at the end the following:

"(b) NON-FEDERAL VESSEL TRAFFIC SERVICE OPERATORS. An entity operating a non-Federal vessel traffic information service or advisory service pursuant to a duly executed written agreement with the Coast Guard, and any pilot acting on behalf of such entity, is not liable for damages caused by or related to information, advice, or communication assistance provided by such entity or pilot while so operating or acting unless the acts or omissions of such entity or pilot constitute gross negligence or willful misconduct."

(b) CLERICAL AMENDMENT.—The analysis for chapter 23 of title 46, United States Code, is amended by striking the item relating to section 2307 and inserting the following:

"2307. Limitation of liability for Coast Guard Vessel Traffic Service pilots and non-Federal vessel traffic service operators.".

SEC. 303. SURVIVAL CRAFT.

Section 3104 of title 46, United States Code, is amended—

(1) in subsection (b) by striking "January 1, 2015" and inserting "the date that is 30 months after the date on which the report described in subsection (c) is submitted"; and

(2) by adding at the end the following:

"(c) REPORT. Not later than 180 days after the date of enactment of this subsection, the Commandant of the Coast Guard shall submit to the Committee on Transportation and Infrastructure of the House of Representatives and the Committee on Commerce, Science, and Transportation of the Senate a report on the carriage of survival craft that ensures no part of an individual is immersed in water, which shall include—

"(1) the number of casualties, by vessel type and area of operation, as the result of immersion in water reported to the Coast Guard for each of fiscal years 1991 through 2011;

"(2) the effect the carriage of such survival craft has on—

"(A) vessel safety, including stability and safe navigation; and

"(B) survivability of individuals, including persons with disabilities, children, and the elderly;

"(3) the efficacy of alternative safety systems, devices, or measures;

"(4) the cost and cost effectiveness of requiring the carriage of such survival craft on vessels; and

"(5) the number of small businesses and nonprofit entities that would be affected by requiring the carriage of such survival craft on vessels."

SEC. 304. CLASSIFICATION SOCIETIES.

Section 3316 of title 46, United States Code, is amended—

(1) in subsection (b)(2)—

(A) by striking "and" at the end of subparagraph (A);

(B) by striking the period at the end of subparagraph (B) and inserting "; and"; and

(C) by adding at the end the following:

"(C) if the Secretary of State determines that the foreign classification society does not provide comparable services in or for a state sponsor of terrorism."

(2) in subsection (d)(2)—

(A) by striking "and" at the end of subparagraph (A);

(B) by striking the period at the end of subparagraph (B) and inserting "; and"; and

(C) by adding at the end the following:

"(C) the Secretary of State determines that the foreign classification society does not provide comparable services in or for a state sponsor of terrorism."

; and

(3) by adding at the end the following:

"(e) The Secretary shall revoke a delegation made to a classification society under subsection (b) or (d) if the Secretary of State determines that the classification society provides comparable services in or for a state sponsor of terrorism.

"(f) In this section, the term 'state sponsor of terrorism' means any country the government of which the Secretary of State has determined has repeatedly provided support for acts of international terrorism pursuant to section 6(j) of the Export Administration Act of 1979 (as continued in effect under the International Emergency Economic Powers Act), section 620A of the Foreign Assistance Act of 1961, section 40 of the Arms Export Control Act, or any other provision of law."

SEC. 305. DOCKSIDE EXAMINATIONS.

(a) IN GENERAL.—Section 4502(f) of title 46, United States Code, is amended—

(1) in paragraph (1), by striking "and" at the end;

(2) in paragraph (2)—

(A) by striking "at least once every 2 years" and inserting "at least once every 5 years"; and

(B) by striking the period at the end and inserting "; and"; and

(3) by adding at the end the following:

"(3) shall complete the first dockside examination of a vessel under this subsection not later than October 15, 2015."

(b) DATABASE.—Section 4502(g)(4) of title 46, United States Code, is amended by striking "a publicly accessible" and inserting "an".

(c) CERTIFICATION.—Section 4503 of title 46, United States Code, is amended—

(1) in subsection (c), by striking "July 1, 2012." and inserting "July 1, 2013.";

(2) in subsection (d)—

(A) in paragraph (1)(B), by striking "July 1, 2012;" and inserting "July 1, 2013;"; and

(B) in paragraph (2)—

(i) by striking "July 1, 2012," each place it appears and inserting "July 1, 2013,"; and

(ii) by striking "substantial change to the dimension of or type of vessel" and inserting "major conversion"; and

(3) by adding at the end the following:

"(e) For the purposes of this section, the term 'built' means, with respect to a vessel, that the vessel's construction has reached any of the following stages:

"(1) The vessel's keel is laid.

"(2) Construction identifiable with the vessel has begun and assembly of that vessel has commenced comprising of at least 50 metric tons or one percent of the estimated mass of all structural material, whichever is less."

(d) CONFORMING AMENDMENTS.—Chapter 51 of title 46, United States Code, is amended—

(1) in section 5102(b)(3), by striking "July 1, 2012." and inserting "July 1, 2013."; and

(2) in section 5103(c)—

(A) by striking "July 1, 2012," each place it appears and inserting "July 1, 2013,"; and

(B) by striking "substantial change to the dimension of or type of the vessel" and inserting "major conversion".

SEC. 306. AUTHORITY TO EXTEND THE DURATION OF MEDICAL CERTIFICATES.

(a) IN GENERAL.—Chapter 75 of title 46, United States Code, is amended by adding at the end the following:

"SEC. 7508. Authority to extend the duration of medical certificates

"(a) GRANTING OF EXTENSIONS. Notwithstanding any other provision of law, the Secretary may extend for not more than one year a medical certificate issued to an individual holding a license, merchant mariner's document, or certificate of registry issued under chapter 71 or 73 if the Secretary determines that the extension is required to enable the Coast Guard to eliminate a backlog in processing applications for medical certificates or is in response to a national emergency or natural disaster.

"(b) MANNER OF EXTENSION. An extension under this section may be granted to individual seamen or a specifically identified group of seamen."

(b) CLERICAL AMENDMENT.—The analysis for chapter 75 of title 46, United States Code, is amended by adding at the end the following:

"7508. Authority to extend the duration of medical certificates.".

SEC. 307. CLARIFICATION OF RESTRICTIONS ON AMERICAN FISHERIES ACT VESSELS.

Section 12113(d)(2) of title 46, United States Code, is amended—

(1) in subparagraph (B)—

(A) by striking "that the regional" and inserting the following:"that—

"(i) the regional"

(B) by striking the semicolon and inserting "; and"; and

(C) by adding at the end the following:

"(ii) in the case of a vessel listed in paragraphs (1) through (20) of section 208(e) of the American Fisheries Act (title II of division C of Public Law 105-277; 112 Stat. 2681-625 et seq.), the vessel is neither participating in nor eligible to participate in the non-AFA trawl catcher processor subsector (as that term is defined under section 219(a)(7) of the Department of Commerce and Related Agencies Appropriations Act, 2005 (Public Law 108-447; 118 Stat. 2887));"

; and

(2) by amending subparagraph (C) to read as follows:

"(C) the vessel—

"(i) is either a rebuilt vessel or replacement vessel under section 208(g) of the American Fisheries Act (title II of division C of Public Law 105-277; 112 Stat. 2681-627);

"(ii) is eligible for a fishery endorsement under this section; and

"(iii) in the case of a vessel listed in paragraphs (1) through (20) of section 208(e) of the American Fisheries Act (title II of division C of Public Law 105-277; 112 Stat. 2681-625 et seq.), is neither participating in nor eligible to participate in the non-AFA trawl catcher processor subsector (as that term is defined under section 219(a)(7) of the Department of Commerce and Related Agencies Appropriations Act, 2005 (Public Law 108-447; 118 Stat. 2887); or"

SEC. 308. INVESTIGATIONS BY SECRETARY.

(a) IN GENERAL.—Chapter 121 of title 46, United States Code, is amended by inserting after section 12139 the following:

"SEC. 12140. Investigations by Secretary

"(a) IN GENERAL. The Secretary may conduct investigations and inspections regarding compliance with this chapter and regulations prescribed under this chapter.

"(b) AUTHORITY TO OBTAIN EVIDENCE.

"(1) IN GENERAL. For the purposes of any investigation conducted under this section, the Secretary may issue a subpoena to require the attendance of a witness or the production of documents or other evidence relevant to the matter under investigation if—

"(A) before the issuance of the subpoena, the Secretary requests a determination by the Attorney General as to whether the subpoena—

"(i) is reasonable; and

"(ii) will interfere with a criminal investigation; and

"(B) the Attorney General—

"(i) determines that the subpoena is reasonable and will not interfere with a criminal investigation; or

"(ii) fails to make a determination with respect to the subpoena before the date that is 30 days after the date on which the Secretary makes a request under subparagraph (A) with respect to the subpoena.

"(2) ENFORCEMENT. In the case of a refusal to obey a subpoena issued to any person under this section, the Secretary may invoke the aid of the appropriate district court of the United States to compel compliance."

(b) CLERICAL AMENDMENT.—The analysis for chapter 121 of title 46, United States Code, is amended by inserting after the item relating to section 12139 the following:

"12140. Investigations by Secretary.".

SEC. 309. PENALTIES.

Section 12151(a) of title 46, United States Code, is amended—

(1) by striking "A person that violates" and inserting the

following:

"(1) CIVIL PENALTIES. Except as provided in paragraph (2), a person that violates"

(2) by striking "$10,000" and inserting "$15,000"; and

(3) by adding at the end the following:

"(2) ACTIVITIES INVOLVING MOBILE OFFSHORE DRILLING UNITS. A person that violates section 12111(d) or a regulation prescribed under that section is liable to the United States Government for a civil penalty in an amount that is $25,000 or twice the charter rate of the vessel involved in the violation (as determined by the Secretary), whichever is greater. Each day of a continuing violation is a separate violation."

SEC. 310. UNITED STATES COMMITTEE ON THE MARINE TRANSPORTATION SYSTEM.

(a) IN GENERAL.—Chapter 555 of title 46, United States Code, is amended by adding at the end the following:

"SEC. 55502. United States Committee on the Marine Transportation System

"(a) ESTABLISHMENT. There is established a United States Committee on the Marine Transportation System (in this section referred to as the 'Committee').

"(b) PURPOSE. The Committee shall serve as a Federal interagency coordinating committee for the purpose of—

"(1) assessing the adequacy of the marine transportation system (including ports, waterways, channels, and their intermodal connections);

"(2) promoting the integration of the marine transportation system with other modes of transportation and other uses of the marine environment; and

"(3) coordinating, improving the coordination of, and making recommendations with regard to Federal policies that impact the marine transportation system.

"(c) MEMBERSHIP.

"(1) IN GENERAL. The Committee shall consist of—

"(A) the Secretary of Transportation;

"(B) the Secretary of Defense;

"(C) the Secretary of Homeland Security;

"(D) the Secretary of Commerce;

"(E) the Secretary of the Treasury;

"(F) the Secretary of State;

"(G) the Secretary of the Interior;

"(H) the Secretary of Agriculture;

"(I) the Attorney General;

"(J) the Secretary of Labor;

"(K) the Secretary of Energy;

"(L) the Administrator of the Environmental Protection Agency;

"(M) the Chairman of the Federal Maritime Commission;

"(N) the Chairman of the Joint Chiefs of Staff; and

"(O) the head of any other Federal agency who a majority of the voting members of the Committee determines can further the purpose and activities of the Committee.

"(2) NONVOTING MEMBERS. The Committee may include as many nonvoting members as a majority of the voting members of the Committee determines is appropriate to further the purpose and activities of the Committee.

"(d) SUPPORT.

"(1) COORDINATING BOARD.

"(A) IN GENERAL. There is hereby established, within the Committee, a Coordinating Board. Each member of the Committee may select a senior level representative to serve on such Board. The Board shall assist the Committee in carrying out its purpose and activities.

"(B) CHAIR. There shall be a Chair of the Coordinating Board. The Chair of the Coordinating Board shall rotate each year among the Secretary of Transportation, the Secretary of Defense, the Secretary of Homeland Security, and the Secretary of Commerce. The order of rotation shall be determined by a majority of the voting members of the Committee.

"(2) EXECUTIVE DIRECTOR. The Secretary of Transportation, in consultation with the Secretary of Defense, the Secretary of Homeland Security, and the Secretary of Commerce, shall appoint an Executive Director of the Committee.

"(3) TRANSFERS. Notwithstanding any other provision of law, the head of a Federal department or agency who is a member of the Committee may—

"(A) provide, on a reimbursable or nonreimbursable basis, facilities, equipment, services, personnel, and other support services to carry out the activities of the Committee; and

"(B) transfer funds to another Federal department or agency in order to carry out the activities of the Committee.

"(e) MARINE TRANSPORTATION SYSTEM ASSESSMENT AND STRATEGY. Not later than one year after the date of enactment of this Act and every 5 years thereafter, the Committee shall provide to the Committee on Commerce, Science, and Transportation and the Committee on Environment and Public Works of the Senate and the Committee on Transportation and Infrastructure of the House of Representatives a report that includes—

"(1) steps taken to implement actions recommended in the document titled 'National Strategy for the Marine Transportation System: A Framework for Action' and dated July 2008;

"(2) an assessment of the condition of the marine transportation system;

"(3) a discussion of the challenges the marine transportation system faces in meeting user demand, including estimates of investment levels required to ensure system infrastructure meets such demand;

"(4) a plan, with recommended actions, for improving the marine transportation system to meet current and future challenges; and

"(5) steps taken to implement actions recommended in previous reports required under this subsection.

"(f) CONSULTATION. In carrying out its purpose and activities, the Committee may consult with marine transportation system-related advisory committees, interested parties, and the public."

(b) CLERICAL AMENDMENT.—The analysis for chapter 555 of title 46, United States Code, is amended by adding at the end the following:

"55502. United States Committee on the Marine Transportation System.".

SEC. 311. TECHNICAL CORRECTION TO TITLE 46.

Section 7507(a) of title 46, United States Code, is amended by striking "73" each place it appears and inserting "71".

SEC. 312. DEEPWATER PORTS.

Section 3(9)(A) of the Deepwater Port Act of 1974 (33 U.S.C. 1502(9)(A)) is amended by inserting "or from" before "any State".

TITLE IV—MARITIME ADMINISTRATION AUTHORIZATION

SEC. 401. SHORT TITLE.

This title may be cited as the "Maritime Administration Authorization Act for Fiscal Year 2013".

SEC. 402. AUTHORIZATION OF APPROPRIATIONS FOR NATIONAL SECURITY ASPECTS OF THE MERCHANT MARINE FOR FISCAL YEAR 2013.

Funds are hereby authorized to be appropriated for fiscal year 2013, to be available without fiscal year limitation if so provided in appropriations Acts, for the use of the Department of Transportation for Maritime Administration programs associated with maintaining national security aspects of the merchant marine, as follows:

(1) For expenses necessary for operations of the United States Merchant Marine Academy, $77,253,000, of which—

(A) $67,253,000 shall remain available until expended for Academy operations; and

(B) $10,000,000 shall remain available until expended for capital asset management at the Academy.

(2) For expenses necessary to support the State maritime academies, $16,045,000, of which—

(A) $2,400,000 shall remain available until expended for student incentive payments;

(B) $2,545,000 shall remain available until expended

for direct payments to such academies; and

(C) $11,100,000 shall remain available until expended for maintenance and repair of State maritime academy training vessels.

(3) For expenses necessary to dispose of vessels in the National Defense Reserve Fleet, $12,717,000, to remain available until expended.

(4) For expenses to maintain and preserve a United States-flag merchant marine to serve the national security needs of the United States under chapter 531 of title 46, United States Code, $186,000,000.

(5) For the cost (as defined in section 502(5) of the Federal Credit Reform Act of 1990 (2 U.S.C. 661a(5))) of loan guarantees under the program authorized by chapter 537 of title 46, United States Code, $3,750,000, all of which shall remain available until expended for administrative expenses of the program.

SEC. 403. MARITIME ENVIRONMENTAL AND TECHNICAL ASSISTANCE.

(a) IN GENERAL.—Chapter 503 of title 46, United States Code, is amended by adding at the end the following:

"SEC. 50307. Maritime environmental and technical assistance program

"(a) IN GENERAL. The Secretary of Transportation may engage in the environmental study, research, development, assessment, and deployment of emerging marine technologies and practices related to the marine transportation system through the use of public vessels under the control of the Maritime Administration or private vessels under United States registry, and through partnerships and cooperative efforts with academic, public, private, and nongovernmental entities and facilities.

"(b) COMPONENTS. Under this section, the Secretary of Transportation may—

"(1) identify, study, evaluate, test, demonstrate, or improve emerging marine technologies and practices that are likely to achieve environmental improvements by—

"(A) reducing air emissions, water emissions, or other ship discharges;

"(B) increasing fuel economy or the use of alternative fuels and alternative energy (including the use of shore power); or

"(C) controlling aquatic invasive species; and

"(2) coordinate with the Environmental Protection Agency, the Coast Guard, and other Federal, State, local, or tribal agencies, as appropriate.

"(c) COORDINATION. Coordination under subsection (b)(2) may include—

"(1) activities that are associated with the development or approval of validation and testing regimes; and

"(2) certification or validation of emerging technologies or practices that demonstrate significant environmental benefits.

"(d) ASSISTANCE. The Secretary of Transportation may accept gifts, or enter into cooperative agreements, contracts, or other agreements with academic, public, private, and nongovernmental entities and facilities to carry out the activities authorized under subsection (a)."

(b) CONFORMING AMENDMENT.—The analysis for chapter 503 of title 46, United States Code, is amended by inserting after the item relating to section 50306 the following:

"50307. Maritime environmental and technical assistance program.".

SEC. 404. PROPERTY FOR INSTRUCTIONAL PURPOSES.

Section 51103(b) of title 46, United States Code, is amended—

(1) in the subsection heading, by striking "Surplus";

(2) by amending paragraph (1) to read as follows:

"(1) IN GENERAL. The Secretary may cooperate with and assist the institutions named in paragraph (2) by making vessels, fuel, shipboard equipment, and other marine equipment, owned by the United States Government and determined by the entity having custody and control of such property to be excess or surplus, available to those institutions for instructional purposes, by gift, loan, sale, lease, or charter on terms and conditions the Secretary considers appropriate. The consent of the Secretary of the Navy shall be obtained with respect to any property from National Defense Reserve Fleet vessels, if such vessels are either Ready Reserve Force vessels or other National Defense Reserve Fleet vessels determined to be of sufficient value to the Navy to warrant their further preservation and retention."

; and

(3) in paragraph (2)(C), by inserting "or a training institution that is an instrumentality of a State, the District of Columbia, a territory or possession of the United States, or a unit of local government thereof" after "a nonprofit training institution".

SEC. 405. SHORT SEA TRANSPORTATION.

(a) PURPOSE.—Section 55601 of title 46, United States Code, is amended—

(1) in subsection (a), by striking "landside congestion." and inserting "landside congestion or to promote short sea transportation.";

(2) in subsection (c), by striking "coastal corridors" and inserting "coastal corridors or to promote short sea transportation";

(3) in subsection (d), by striking "that the project may" and all that follows through the end of the subsection and inserting"that the project uses documented vessels and—

"(1) mitigates landside congestion; or

"(2) promotes short sea transportation."

; and

(4) in subsection (f), by striking "shall" each place it appears and inserting "may".

(b) DOCUMENTATION.—Section 55605 is amended in the matter preceding paragraph (1) by striking "by vessel" and inserting "by a documented vessel".

SEC. 406. LIMITATION OF NATIONAL DEFENSE RESERVE FLEET VESSELS TO THOSE OVER 1,500 GROSS TONS.

Section 57101(a) of title 46, United States Code, is amended by inserting "of 1,500 gross tons or more or such other vessels as the Secretary of Transportation determines are appropriate" after "Administration".

SEC. 407. TRANSFER OF VESSELS TO THE NATIONAL DEFENSE

RESERVE FLEET.

Section 57101 of title 46, United States Code, is amended by adding at the end the following:

"(c) AUTHORITY OF FEDERAL ENTITIES TO TRANSFER VESSELS. All Federal entities are authorized to transfer vessels to the National Defense Reserve Fleet without reimbursement subject to the approval of the Secretary of Transportation and the Secretary of the Navy with respect to Ready Reserve Force vessels and the Secretary of Transportation with respect to all other vessels."

SEC. 408. CLARIFICATION OF HEADING.

(a) IN GENERAL.—The section designation and heading for section 57103 of title 46, United States Code, is amended to read as follows:

"SEC. 57103. Donation of nonretention vessels in the National Defense Reserve Fleet"

(b) CLERICAL AMENDMENT.—The analysis for chapter 571 of title 46, United States Code, is amended by striking the item relating to section 57103 and inserting the following:

"57103. Donation of nonretention vessels in the National Defense Reserve Fleet.".

SEC. 409. MISSION OF THE MARITIME ADMINISTRATION.

Section 109(a) of title 49, United States Code, is amended—

(1) in the subsection heading by striking "Organization" and inserting "Organization and Mission"; and

(2) by adding at the end the following: "The mission of the Maritime Administration is to foster, promote, and develop the merchant maritime industry of the United States.".

SEC. 410. AMENDMENTS RELATING TO THE NATIONAL DEFENSE RESERVE FLEET.

Subparagraphs (B), (C), and (D) of section 11(c)(1) of the Merchant Ship Sales Act of 1946 (50 U.S.C. App. 1744(c)(1)) are amended to read as follows:

"(B) activate and conduct sea trials on each vessel at a frequency that is considered by the Secretary to be necessary;

"(C) maintain and adequately crew, as necessary, in an enhanced readiness status those vessels that are scheduled to be activated in 5 or less days;

"(D) locate those vessels that are scheduled to be activated near embarkation ports specified for those vessels; and"

SEC. 411. REQUIREMENT FOR BARGE DESIGN.

Not later than 270 days after the date of enactment of this Act, the Administrator of the Maritime Administration shall complete the design for a containerized, articulated barge, as identified in the dual-use vessel study carried out by the Administrator and the Secretary of Defense, that is able to utilize roll-on/roll-off or load-on/load-off technology in marine highway maritime commerce.

SEC. 412. CONTAINER-ON-BARGE TRANSPORTATION.

(a) ASSESSMENT.—The Administrator of the Maritime Administration shall assess the potential for using container-on-barge transportation in short sea transportation (as such term is defined in section 55605 of title 46, United States Code).

(b) FACTORS.—In conducting the assessment under subsection (a), the Administrator shall consider—

(1) the environmental benefits of increasing container-on-barge movements in short sea transportation;

(2) the regional differences in the use of short sea transportation;

(3) the existing programs established at coastal and Great Lakes ports for establishing awareness of deep sea shipping operations;

(4) the mechanisms necessary to ensure that implementation of a plan under subsection (c) will not be inconsistent with antitrust laws; and

(5) the potential frequency of container-on-barge service at short sea transportation ports.

(c) RECOMMENDATIONS.—The assessment under subsection (a) may include recommendations for a plan to increase awareness of the potential for use of container-on-barge transportation.

(d) DEADLINE.—Not later than 180 days after the date of enactment of this Act, the Administrator shall submit the assessment required under this section to the Committee on Commerce, Science, and Transportation of the Senate and the Committee on Transportation and Infrastructure of the House of Representatives.

SEC. 413. DEPARTMENT OF DEFENSE NATIONAL STRATEGIC PORTS STUDY AND COMPTROLLER GENERAL STUDIES AND REPORTS ON STRATEGIC PORTS.

(a) SENSE OF CONGRESS ON COMPLETION OF DOD REPORT.—It is the sense of Congress that the Secretary of Defense should expedite completion of the study of strategic ports in the United States called for in the conference report to accompany the National Defense Authorization Act for Fiscal Year 2012 (Conference Report 112-329) so that it can be submitted to Congress before July 1, 2013.

(b) SUBMISSION OF REPORT TO COMPTROLLER GENERAL.—In addition to submitting the report referred to in subsection (a) to Congress, the Secretary of Defense shall submit the report to the Comptroller General of the United States for consideration under subsection (c).

(c) COMPTROLLER GENERAL STUDIES AND REPORTS ON STRATEGIC PORTS.—

(1) COMPTROLLER GENERAL REVIEW.—Not later than 90 days after receipt of the report referred to in subsection (a), the Comptroller General shall conduct an assessment of the report and submit to the Committee on Armed Services of the House of Representatives and the Committee on Armed Services of the Senate a report of such assessment.

(2) COMPTROLLER GENERAL STUDY AND REPORT.—Not later than 270 days after the date of enactment of this Act, the Comptroller General shall conduct a study of the Department of Defense's programs and efforts related to the state of strategic ports with respect to the Department's operational and readiness requirements, and report to the Committee on Armed Services of the House of Representatives and the Committee on Armed Services of the Senate on the findings of such study. The report may include an assessment of—

(A) the extent to which the facilities at strategic ports meet the Department of Defense's requirements;

(B) the extent to which the Department has identified gaps in the ability of existing strategic ports to meet its needs and identified and undertaken efforts to address any gaps; and

(C) the Department's ability to oversee, coordinate, and provide security for military deployments through strategic ports.

(d) STRATEGIC PORT DEFINED.—In this section, the term "strategic port" means a United States port designated by the Secretary of Defense as a significant transportation hub important to the readiness and cargo throughput capacity of the Department of Defense.

SEC. 414. MARITIME WORKFORCE STUDY.

(a) TRAINING STUDY.—The Comptroller General of the United States shall conduct a study on the training needs of the maritime workforce.

(b) STUDY COMPONENTS.—The study shall—

(1) analyze the impact of maritime training requirements imposed by domestic and international regulations and conventions, companies, and government agencies that charter or operate vessels;

(2) evaluate the ability of the United States maritime training infrastructure to meet the needs of the maritime industry;

(3) identify trends in maritime training;

(4) compare the training needs of United States mariners with the vocational training and educational assistance programs available from Federal agencies to evaluate the ability of Federal programs to meet the training needs of United States mariners;

(5) include recommendations to enhance the capabilities of the United States maritime training infrastructure; and

(6) include recommendations to assist United States mariners and those entering the maritime profession to achieve the required training.

(c) FINAL REPORT.—Not later than 1 year after the date of enactment of this Act, the Comptroller General shall submit a report on the results of the study to the Committee on Commerce, Science, and Transportation and the Committee on Armed Services of the Senate and the Committee on Transportation and Infrastructure and the Committee on Armed Services of the House of Representatives.

SEC. 415. MARITIME ADMINISTRATION VESSEL RECYCLING

CONTRACT AWARD PRACTICES.

(a) ASSESSMENT.—The Comptroller General of the United States shall conduct an assessment of the source selection procedures and practices used to award the Maritime Administration's National Defense Reserve Fleet vessel recycling contracts.

(b) CONTENTS.—The assessment under subsection (a) shall include a review of—

(1) whether the Maritime Administration's contract source selection procedures and practices are consistent with law, including the Federal Acquisition Regulation, and Federal best practices associated with making source selection decisions;

(2) the process, procedures, and practices used for the Maritime Administration's qualification of vessel recycling facilities; and

(3) any other aspect of the Maritime Administration's vessel recycling process that the Comptroller General deems appropriate to review.

(c) FINDINGS.—Not later than one year after the date of enactment of this Act, the Comptroller General shall report the findings of the assessment under subsection (a) to the Committee on Commerce, Science, and Transportation and the Committee on Armed Services of the Senate and the Committee on Transportation and Infrastructure and the Committee on Armed Services of the House of Representatives.

TITLE V—PIRACY

SEC. 501. [46 U.S.C. 101 note] SHORT TITLE.

This title may be cited as the "Piracy Suppression Act of 2012".

SEC. 502. TRAINING FOR USE OF FORCE AGAINST PIRACY.

(a) IN GENERAL.—Chapter 517 of title 46, United States Code, is amended by adding at the end the following:

"SEC. 51705. Training for use of force against piracy

"The Secretary of Transportation, in consultation with the Secretary of Defense and the Secretary of the department in which the Coast Guard is operating, shall certify a training curriculum for United States mariners on the use of force against pirates. The curriculum shall include—

"(1) information on waters designated as high-risk waters by the Commandant of the Coast Guard;

"(2) information on current threats and patterns of attack by pirates;

"(3) tactics for defense of a vessel, including instruction on the types, use, and limitations of security equipment;

"(4) standard rules for the use of force for self-defense as developed by the Secretary of the department in which the Coast Guard is operating under section 912(c) of the Coast Guard Authorization Act of 2010 (Public Law 111-281; 46 U.S.C. 8107 note), including instruction on firearm safety for crewmembers of vessels carrying cargo under section 55305 of this title; and

"(5) procedures to follow to improve crewmember survivability if captured and taken hostage by pirates."

(b) **[46 U.S.C. 51705 note]** DEADLINE.—The Secretary of Transportation shall certify the curriculum required under the amendment made by subsection (a) not later than 270 days after the date of enactment of this Act.

(c) CLERICAL AMENDMENT.—The analysis for chapter 517 of title 46, United States Code, is amended by adding at the end the following:

"51705. Training program for use of force against piracy.".

SEC. 503. SECURITY OF GOVERNMENT-IMPELLED CARGO.

Section 55305 of title 46, United States Code, is amended by adding at the end the following:

"(e) SECURITY OF GOVERNMENT-IMPELLED CARGO.

"(1) In order to ensure the safety of vessels and crewmembers transporting equipment, materials, or commodities under this section, the Secretary of Transportation shall direct each department or agency (except the Department of Defense), when responsible for the carriage of such equipment, materials, or commodities, to provide armed personnel aboard vessels of the United States carrying such equipment, materials, or commodities if the vessels are transiting high-risk waters.

"(2) The Secretary of Transportation shall direct each

department or agency responsible to provide armed personnel under paragraph (1) to reimburse, subject to the availability of appropriations, the owners or operators of applicable vessels for the cost of providing armed personnel.

"(3) In this subsection, the term 'high-risk waters' means waters so designated by the Commandant of the Coast Guard in the Port Security Advisory in effect on the date on which an applicable voyage begins."

SEC. 504. ACTIONS TAKEN TO PROTECT FOREIGN-FLAGGED VESSELS FROM PIRACY.

Not later than 180 days after the date of enactment of this Act, the Secretary of Defense, in consultation with the Secretary of the department in which the Coast Guard is operating, shall provide to the Committee on Armed Services and the Committee on Transportation and Infrastructure of the House of Representatives and the Committee on Armed Services and the Committee on Commerce, Science, and Transportation of the Senate a report on actions taken by the Secretary of Defense to protect foreign-flagged vessels from acts of piracy on the high seas. The report shall include—

(1) the total number of incidents for each of the fiscal years 2009 through 2012 in which a member of the armed services or an asset under the control of the Secretary of Defense was used to interdict or defend against an act of piracy directed against any vessel not documented under the laws of the United States; and

(2) the estimated cost for each of the fiscal years 2009 through 2012 for such incidents.

TITLE VI—MARINE DEBRIS

SEC. 601. SHORT TITLE.

This title may be cited as the "Marine Debris Act Amendments of 2012".

SEC. 602. SHORT TITLE AMENDMENT; REFERENCES.

(a) SHORT TITLE AMENDMENT.—Section 1 of the Marine Debris Research, Prevention, and Reduction Act (33 U.S.C. 1951 note) is amended by striking "Research, Prevention, and Reduction".

(b) REFERENCES.—Except as otherwise expressly provided, whenever in this title an amendment is expressed as an amendment to a section or other provision, the reference shall be considered to be made to a section or other provision of the Marine Debris Act (33 U.S.C. 1951 et seq.), as so retitled by subsection (a) of this section.

SEC. 603. PURPOSE.

Section 2 (33 U.S.C. 1951) is amended to read as follows:

"SEC. 2. PURPOSE

"The purpose of this Act is to address the adverse impacts of marine debris on the United States economy, the marine environment, and navigation safety through the identification, determination of sources, assessment, prevention, reduction, and removal of marine debris."

SEC. 604. NOAA MARINE DEBRIS PROGRAM.

(a) NAME OF PROGRAM.—Section 3 (33 U.S.C. 1952) is amended—

(1) in the section heading by striking "prevention and removal"; and

(2) in subsection (a)—

(A) by striking "Prevention and Removal Program to reduce and prevent the occurrence and" and inserting "Program to identify, determine sources of, assess, prevent, reduce, and remove marine debris and address the";

(B) by inserting "the economy of the United States," after "marine debris on"; and

(C) by inserting a comma after "environment".

(b) PROGRAM COMPONENTS.—Section 3(b) (33 U.S.C. 1952(b)) is amended to read as follows:

"(b) PROGRAM COMPONENTS. The Administrator, acting through the Program and subject to the availability of appropriations, shall—

"(1) identify, determine sources of, assess, prevent, reduce, and remove marine debris, with a focus on marine debris posing a threat to living marine resources and navigation safety;

"(2) provide national and regional coordination to assist States, Indian tribes, and regional organizations in the identification, determination of sources, assessment, prevention, reduction, and removal of marine debris;

"(3) undertake efforts to reduce the adverse impacts of lost and discarded fishing gear on living marine resources and navigation safety, including—

"(A) research and development of alternatives to gear posing threats to the marine environment and methods for marking gear used in certain fisheries to enhance the tracking, recovery, and identification of lost and discarded gear; and

"(B) the development of effective nonregulatory measures and incentives to cooperatively reduce the volume of lost and discarded fishing gear and to aid in gear recovery;

"(4) undertake outreach and education activities for the public and other stakeholders on sources of marine debris, threats associated with marine debris, and approaches to identifying, determining sources of, assessing, preventing, reducing, and removing marine debris and its adverse impacts on the United States economy, the marine environment, and navigation safety, including outreach and education activities through public-private initiatives; and

"(5) develop, in consultation with the Interagency Committee, interagency plans for the timely response to events determined by the Administrator to be severe marine debris events, including plans to—

"(A) coordinate across agencies and with relevant State, tribal, and local governments to ensure adequate, timely, and efficient response;

"(B) assess the composition, volume, and trajectory of marine debris associated with a severe marine debris event; and

"(C) estimate the potential impacts of a severe marine debris event, including economic impacts on human health, navigation safety, natural resources, tourism, and livestock, including aquaculture."

(c) GRANT CRITERIA AND GUIDELINES.—Section 3(c) (33 U.S.C. 1952(c)) is amended—

(1) in paragraph (1), by striking "section 2(1)" and inserting "section 2";

(2) by striking paragraph (5); and

(3) by redesignating paragraphs (6) and (7) as paragraphs (5) and (6), respectively.

(d) REPEAL.—Section 2204 of the Marine Plastic Pollution Research and Control Act of 1987 (33 U.S.C. 1915), and the item relating to that section in the table of contents contained in section 2 of the United States-Japan Fishery Agreement Approval Act of 1987, are repealed.

SEC. 605. REPEAL OF OBSOLETE PROVISIONS.

Section 4 (33 U.S.C. 1953) is amended—

(1) by striking "(a) Strategy.—"; and

(2) by striking subsections (b) and (c).

SEC. 606. COORDINATION.

(a) INTERAGENCY MARINE DEBRIS COORDINATING COMMITTEE.—

(1) IN GENERAL.—Section 2203 of the Marine Plastic Pollution Research and Control Act of 1987 (33 U.S.C. 1914) is redesignated and moved to replace and appear as section 5 of the Marine Debris Act (33 U.S.C. 1954), as so retitled by section 602(a) of this title.

(2) CONFORMING AMENDMENT.—Section 5 of the Marine Debris Act (33 U.S.C. 1954), as amended by paragraph (1) of this subsection, is further amended in subsection (d)(2)—

(A) by striking "this Act" and inserting "the Marine Plastic Pollution Research and Control Act of 1987"; and

(B) by inserting "of the Marine Plastic Pollution Research and Control Act of 1987" after "section 2201".

(3) CLERICAL AMENDMENT.—The item relating to section 2203 in the table of contents contained in section 2 of the United States-Japan Fishery Agreement Approval Act of 1987 is repealed.

(b) BIENNIAL PROGRESS REPORTS.—Section 5(c)(2) of the Marine Debris Research, Prevention, and Reduction Act (33 U.S.C. 1954(c)(2)), as in effect immediately before the enactment of this Act—

(1) is redesignated and moved to appear as subsection (e) at the end of section 5 of the Marine Debris Act, as amended by

subsection (a) of this section; and

(2) is amended—

(A) by striking "Annual progress reports.—" and all that follows through "thereafter" and inserting "Biennial Progress Reports.—Biennially";

(B) by striking "Interagency" each place it appears;

(C) by striking "chairperson" and inserting "Chairperson";

(D) by inserting "Natural" before "Resources";

(E) by redesignating subparagraphs (A) through (E) as paragraphs (1) through (5), respectively; and

(F) by moving all text 2 ems to the left.

SEC. 607. CONFIDENTIALITY OF SUBMITTED INFORMATION.

Section 6(2) (33 U.S.C. 1955(2)) is amended by striking "by the fishing industry".

SEC. 608. DEFINITIONS.

Section 7 (33 U.S.C. 1956) is amended—

(1) in paragraph (2), by striking "2203 of the Marine Plastic Pollution Research and Control Act of 1987 (33 U.S.C. 1914)" and inserting "5 of this Act"

(2) by striking paragraph (3) and inserting the following:

"(3) MARINE DEBRIS. The term "'marine debris"' means any persistent solid material that is manufactured or processed and directly or indirectly, intentionally or unintentionally, disposed of or abandoned into the marine environment or the Great Lakes."

(3) by striking paragraph (5);

(4) by redesignating paragraph (7) as paragraph (5);

(5) in paragraph (5), as redesignated by paragraph (4) of this section, by striking "Prevention and Removal"

(6) by striking paragraph (6) and inserting the following:

"(6) SEVERE MARINE DEBRIS EVENT. The term "'severe marine debris event"' means atypically large amounts of marine debris caused by a natural disaster, including a tsunami, flood, landslide, or hurricane, or other source."

; and

(7) by redesignating paragraph (8) as paragraph (7).

SEC. 609. SEVERE MARINE DEBRIS EVENT DETERMINATION.

(a) IN GENERAL.—The Administrator of the National Oceanic and Atmospheric Administration shall determine whether the March 2011, Tohoku earthquake and subsequent tsunami and the October 2012, hurricane Sandy each caused a severe marine debris event (as that term is defined in section 7(6) of the Marine Debris Act (33 U.S.C. 1956(6)), as amended by this Act).

(b) DEADLINE.—Not later than 30 days after the date of enactment of this Act, the Administrator shall provide the determination required under subsection (a) to the Committee on Commerce, Science, and Transportation of the Senate and the Committee on Transportation and Infrastructure and the Committee on Natural Resources of the House of Representatives.

TITLE VII—MISCELLANEOUS

SEC. 701. [46 U.S.C. 8103 note] DISTANT WATER TUNA FLEET.

Section 421 of the Coast Guard and Maritime Transportation Act of 2006 (Public Law 109-241; 120 Stat. 547) is amended—

(1) by striking subsection (b) and inserting the following:

"(b) LICENSING RESTRICTIONS.

"(1) IN GENERAL. Subsection (a) only applies to a foreign citizen who holds a credential that is equivalent to the credential issued by the Coast Guard to a United States citizen for the position, with respect to requirements for experience, training, and other qualifications.

"(2) TREATMENT OF CREDENTIAL. An equivalent credential under paragraph (1) shall be considered as meeting the requirements of section 8304 of title 46, United States Code, but only while a person holding the credential is in the service of the vessel to which this section applies."

(2) in subsection (c) by inserting "or Guam" before the period at the end; and

(3) in subsection (d) by striking "on December 31, 2012" and inserting "on the date the Treaty on Fisheries Between the Governments of Certain Pacific Island States and the

Government of the United States of America ceases to have effect for any party under Article 12.6 or 12.7 of such treaty, as in effect on the date of enactment of the Coast Guard and Maritime Transportation Act of 2012".

SEC. 702. TECHNICAL CORRECTIONS.

(a) STUDY OF BRIDGES.—Section 905 of the Coast Guard Authorization Act of 2010 (Public Law 111-281; 33 U.S.C. 494a) is amended to read as follows:

"SEC. 905. STUDY OF BRIDGES OVER NAVIGABLE WATERS

"The Commandant of the Coast Guard shall submit to the Committee on Commerce, Science, and Transportation of the Senate and the Committee on Transportation and Infrastructure of the House of Representatives a comprehensive study on the construction or alteration of any bridge, drawbridge, or causeway over the navigable waters of the United States with a channel depth of 25 feet or greater that may impede or obstruct future navigation to or from port facilities and for which a permit under the Act of March 23, 1906 (33 U.S.C. 491 et seq.), popularly known as the Bridge Act of 1906, was requested during the period beginning on January 1, 2006, and ending on August 3, 2011."

(b) WAIVER.—Section 7(c) of the America's Cup Act of 2011 (125 Stat. 755) is amended by inserting "located in Ketchikan, Alaska" after "moorage".

SEC. 703. EXTENSION OF MORATORIUM.

Section 2(a) of Public Law 110-299 (33 U.S.C. 1342 note) is amended by striking "2013" and inserting "2014".

SEC. 704. NOTICE OF ARRIVAL.

The regulations required under section 109(a) of the Security and Accountability For Every Port Act of 2006 (33 U.S.C. 1223 note) dealing with notice of arrival requirements for foreign vessels on the Outer Continental Shelf shall not apply to a vessel documented under section 12105 of title 46, United States Code, unless the vessel arrives from a foreign port or place.

SEC. 705. WAIVERS.

(a) TEXAS STAR CASINO.—

(1) IN GENERAL.—Notwithstanding section 12113(a)(4) of

title 46, United States Code, the Secretary of the department in which the Coast Guard is operating may issue a certificate of documentation with a fishery endorsement for the Texas Star Casino (IMO number 7722047).

(2) RESTRICTION.—Notwithstanding section 12113(b)(1) of title 46, United States Code, a fishery endorsement issued under paragraph (1) is not valid for any fishery for which a fishery management plan has been approved by the Secretary of Commerce pursuant to section 304 of the Magnuson-Stevens Fishery Conservation and Management Act (16 U.S.C. 1854) before the date of enactment of this Act.

(b) RANGER III.—Section 3703a of title 46, United States Code, does not apply to the passenger vessel Ranger III (United States official number 277361), during any period that the vessel is owned and operated by the National Park Service.

SEC. 706. NATIONAL RESPONSE CENTER NOTIFICATION REQUIREMENTS.

The Ohio River Valley Water Sanitation Commission, established pursuant to the Ohio River Valley Water Sanitation Compact consented to and approved by Congress in the Act of July 11, 1940 (54 Stat. 752), is deemed a Government agency for purposes of the notification requirements of section 103 of the Comprehensive Environmental Response, Compensation, and Liability Act of 1980 (42 U.S.C. 9603). The National Response Center shall convey notification, including complete and unredacted incident reports, expeditiously to the Commission regarding each release in or affecting the Ohio River Basin for which notification to all appropriate Government agencies is required.

SEC. 707. VESSEL DETERMINATIONS.

The vessel with United States official number 981472 and the vessel with United States official number 988333 shall each be deemed to be a new vessel effective on the date of delivery after January 1, 2008, from a privately owned United States shipyard if no encumbrances are on record with the Coast Guard at the time of the issuance of the new vessel certificate of documentation for each vessel.

SEC. 708. MILLE LACS LAKE, MINNESOTA.

The waters of Mille Lacs Lake, Minnesota, are not waters

subject to the jurisdiction of the United States for the purposes of section 2 of title 14, United States Code.

SEC. 709. [46 U.S.C. 70105 note] TRANSPORTATION WORKER IDENTIFICATION CREDENTIAL PROCESS REFORM.

Not later than 270 days after the date of enactment of this Act, the Secretary of Homeland Security shall reform the process for Transportation Worker Identification Credential enrollment, activation, issuance, and renewal to require, in total, not more than one in-person visit to a designated enrollment center except in cases in which there are extenuating circumstances, as determined by the Secretary, requiring more than one such in-person visit.

SEC. 710. INVESTMENT AMOUNT.

Not later than 30 days after the date of enactment of this Act, the Secretary of the Treasury shall increase the $22,500,000 invested in income-producing securities for purposes of section 5006(b) of the Oil Pollution Act of 1990 (33 U.S.C. 2736(b)) by $12,851,340.

SEC. 711. [46 U.S.C. 70101 note] INTEGRATED CROSS-BORDER MARITIME LAW ENFORCEMENT OPERATIONS BETWEEN THE UNITED STATES AND CANADA.

(a) AUTHORIZATION.—The Secretary of Homeland Security, acting through the Commandant of the Coast Guard, may establish an Integrated Cross-Border Maritime Law Enforcement Operations Program to coordinate the maritime security operations of the United States and Canada (in this section referred to as the "Program").

(b) PURPOSE.—The Secretary, acting through the Commandant, shall administer the Program in a manner that results in a cooperative approach between the United States and Canada to strengthen border security and detect, prevent, suppress, investigate, and respond to terrorism and violations of law related to border security.

(c) TRAINING.—The Secretary, acting through the Commandant and in consultation with the Secretary of State, may—

(1) establish, as an element of the Program, a training program for individuals who will serve as maritime law enforcement officers; and

(2) conduct training jointly with Canada to enhance border security, including training—

(A) on the detection and apprehension of suspected terrorists and individuals attempting to unlawfully cross or unlawfully use the international maritime border between the United States and Canada;

(B) on the integration, analysis, and dissemination of port security information by and between the United States and Canada;

(C) on policy, regulatory, and legal considerations related to the Program;

(D) on the use of force in maritime security;

(E) on operational procedures and protection of sensitive information; and

(F) on preparedness and response to maritime terrorist incidents.

(d) COORDINATION.—The Secretary, acting through the Commandant, shall coordinate the Program with other similar border security and antiterrorism programs within the Department of Homeland Security.

(e) MEMORANDA OF AGREEMENT.—The Secretary may enter into any memorandum of agreement necessary to carry out the Program.

SEC. 712. BRIDGE PERMITS.

(a) [33 U.S.C. 491 note] IN GENERAL.—For the purposes of reviewing a permit application pursuant to section 9 of the Act of March 3, 1899, popularly known as the Rivers and Harbors Appropriation Act of 1899 (33 U.S.C. 401), the Act of March 23, 1906, popularly known as the Bridge Act of 1906 (33 U.S.C. 491 et seq.), the Act of June 21, 1940, popularly known as the Truman-Hobbs Act (33 U.S.C. 511 et seq.), or the General Bridge Act of 1946 (33 U.S.C. 525 et seq.), the Secretary of the department in which the Coast Guard is operating may—

(1) accept voluntary services from one or more owners of a bridge; and

(2) accept and credit to Coast Guard operating expenses any amounts received from one or more owners of a bridge.

(b) EXPEDITED PROCESS.—The Secretary of the department in

which the Coast Guard is operating shall complete, on an expeditious basis and using the shortest existing applicable process, determinations on any required approval for issuance of any permits under the jurisdiction of such department related to the construction or alteration of a bridge over the Kill Van Kull consistent with Executive Order No. 13604 (March 22, 2012) and the Administration's objectives for the project.

SEC. 713. TONNAGE OF AQUEOS ACADIAN.

The Secretary of the department in which the Coast Guard is operating may consider the tonnage measurements for the vessel Aqueos Acadian (United States official number 553645) recorded on the certificate of inspection for the vessel issued on September 8, 2011, to be valid until May 2, 2014, if the vessel and the use of its space is not changed after November 16, 2012, in a way that substantially affects the tonnage of the vessel.

SEC. 714. NAVIGABILITY DETERMINATION.

(a) IN GENERAL.—Not later than 180 days after the date of enactment of this Act, the Commandant of the Coast Guard shall submit to the Committee on Transportation and Infrastructure of the House of Representatives and the Committee on Commerce, Science, and Transportation of the Senate an assessment of the impact of additional regulatory requirements imposed on passenger vessels operating on the Ringo Cocke Canal in Louisiana as a result of the covered navigability determination.

(b) RESTRICTION.—Before the date that is 180 days after the date on which the assessment required under subsection (a) is submitted, the Commandant may not enforce any regulatory requirements imposed on passenger vessels operating on the Ringo Cocke Canal in Louisiana that are a result of the covered navigability determination.

(c) COVERED NAVIGABILITY DETERMINATION DEFINED.—In this section, the term "covered navigability determination" means the Coast Guard's Navigability Determination for Ringo Cocke Canal, Louisiana, dated March 25, 2010.

SEC. 715. COAST GUARD HOUSING.

Not later than 30 days after the date of enactment of this Act, the Commandant of the Coast Guard shall submit to the Committee on Commerce, Science, and Transportation of the Senate and the

Committee on Transportation and Infrastructure of the House of Representatives the Coast Guard's National Housing Assessment and any analysis conducted by the Coast Guard of such assessment.

SEC. 716. ASSESSMENT OF NEEDS FOR ADDITIONAL COAST GUARD PRESENCE IN HIGH-LATITUDE REGIONS.

Not later than 180 days after the date of enactment of this Act, the Secretary of the department in which the Coast Guard is operating shall submit to the Committee on Commerce, Science, and Transportation of the Senate and the Committee on Transportation and Infrastructure of the House of Representatives an assessment of the need for additional Coast Guard prevention and response capability in the high-latitude regions. The assessment shall address needs for all Coast Guard mission areas, including search and rescue, marine pollution response and prevention, fisheries enforcement, and maritime commerce. The Secretary shall include in the assessment—

(1) an analysis of the high-latitude operating capabilities of all current Coast Guard assets other than icebreakers, including assets acquired under the Deepwater program;

(2) an analysis of projected needs for Coast Guard operations in the high-latitude regions; and

(3) an analysis of shore infrastructure, personnel, logistics, communications, and resources requirements to support Coast Guard operations in the high-latitude regions, including forward operating bases and existing infrastructure in the furthest north locations that are ice free, or nearly ice free, year round.

SEC. 717. POTENTIAL PLACE OF REFUGE.

(a) CONSULTATION.—Not later than 1 year after the date of enactment of this Act, the Commandant of the Coast Guard shall consult with appropriate Federal agencies and with State and local interests to determine what improvements, if any, are necessary to designate existing ice-free facilities or infrastructure in the Central Bering Sea as a fully functional, year-round Potential Place of Refuge.

(b) PURPOSES.—The purposes of the consultation under subsection (a) shall be to enhance safety of human life at sea and protect the marine environment in the Central Bering Sea.

(c) DEADLINE FOR SUBMISSION.—Not later than 90 days after making the determination under subsection (a), the Commandant shall inform the Committee on Commerce, Science, and Transportation of the Senate and the Committee on Transportation and Infrastructure of the House of Representatives in writing of the findings under subsection (a).

SEC. 718. MERCHANT MARINER MEDICAL EVALUATION PROGRAM.

(a) IN GENERAL.—Not later than 180 days after the date of enactment of this Act, the Commandant of the Coast Guard shall submit to the Committee on Transportation and Infrastructure of the House of Representatives and the Committee on Commerce, Science, and Transportation of the Senate an assessment of the Coast Guard National Maritime Center's merchant mariner medical evaluation program and alternatives to the program.

(b) CONTENTS.—The assessment required under subsection (a) shall include the following:

(1) An overview of the adequacy of the program for making medical certification determinations for issuance of merchant mariners' documents.

(2) An analysis of how a system similar to the Federal Motor Carrier Safety Administration's National Registry of Certified Medical Examiners program, and the Federal Aviation Administration's Designated Aviation Medical Examiners program, could be applied by the Coast Guard in making medical fitness determinations for issuance of merchant mariners' documents.

(3) An explanation of how the amendments to the International Convention on Standards of Training, Certification and Watchkeeping for Seafarers, 1978, that entered into force on January 1, 2012, required changes to the Coast Guard's merchant mariner medical evaluation program.

SEC. 719. DETERMINATIONS.

Not later than 270 days after the date of enactment of this Act, the Secretary of the department in which the Coast Guard is operating shall provide to the Committee on Transportation and Infrastructure of the House of Representatives and the Committee on Commerce, Science, and Transportation of the Senate an assessment of—

(1) the loss of United States shipyard jobs and industrial base expertise as a result of rebuild, conversion, and double-hull work on United States-flag vessels eligible to engage in the coastwise trade being performed in foreign shipyards;

(2) enforcement of the Coast Guard's foreign rebuild determination regulations; and

(3) recommendations for improving transparency in the Coast Guard's foreign rebuild determination process.

SEC. 720. IMPEDIMENTS TO THE UNITED STATES-FLAG REGISTRY.

(a) ASSESSMENT.—Not later than 180 days after the date of enactment of this Act, the Commandant of the Coast Guard shall submit to the Committee on Transportation and Infrastructure of the House of Representatives and the Committee on Commerce, Science, and Transportation of the Senate an assessment of factors under the authority of the Coast Guard that impact the ability of vessels documented in the United States to effectively compete in international transportation markets.

(b) CONTENT.—The assessment under subsection (a) shall include—

(1) a review of differences between Coast Guard policies and regulations governing the inspection of vessels documented in the United States and International Maritime Organization policies and regulations governing the inspection of vessels not documented in the United States;

(2) a statement on the impact such differences have on operating costs for vessels documented in the United States; and

(3) recommendations on whether to harmonize any such differences.

(c) CONSULTATION.—In preparing the assessment under subsection (a), the Commandant may consider the views of representatives of the owners or operators of vessels documented in the United States and the organizations representing the employees employed on such vessels.

SEC. 721. ARCTIC DEEPWATER SEAPORT.

(a) STUDY.—The Commandant of the Coast Guard, in consultation with the Commanding General of the Army Corps of Engineers, the Maritime Administrator, and the Chief of Naval Operations, shall conduct a study on the feasibility of establishing a deepwater seaport in the Arctic to protect and advance strategic United States interests within the Arctic region.

(b) SCOPE.—The study under subsection (a) shall include an analysis of—

(1) the capability provided by a deepwater seaport that—

(A) is in the Arctic (as that term is defined in the section 112 of the Arctic Research and Policy Act of 1984 (15 U.S.C. 4111)); and

(B) has a depth of not less than 34 feet;

(2) the potential and optimum locations for such deepwater seaport;

(3) the resources needed to establish such deepwater seaport;

(4) the timeframe needed to establish such deepwater seaport;

(5) the infrastructure required to support such deepwater seaport; and

(6) any other issues the Secretary considers necessary to complete the study.

(c) DEADLINE FOR SUBMISSION OF FINDINGS.—Not later than 1 year after the date of enactment of this Act, the Commandant shall submit the findings of the study under subsection (a) to the Committee on Commerce, Science, and Transportation of the Senate and the Committee on Transportation and Infrastructure of the House of Representatives.

SEC. 722. RISK ASSESSMENT OF TRANSPORTING CANADIAN OIL SANDS.

(a) IN GENERAL.—The Commandant of the Coast Guard shall assess the increased vessel traffic in the Salish Sea (including Puget Sound, the Strait of Georgia, Haro Strait, Rosario Strait, and the Strait of Juan de Fuca), that may occur from the transport of Canadian oil sands oil.

(b) SCOPE.—The assessment required under subsection (a)

shall, at a minimum, consider—

(1) the extent to which vessel (including barge, tanker, and supertanker) traffic may increase due to Canadian oil sands development;

(2) whether the transport of oil from Canadian oil sands within the Salish Sea is likely to require navigation through United States territorial waters;

(3) the rules or regulations that restrict supertanker traffic in United States waters, including an assessment of whether there are methods to bypass those rules or regulations in such waters and adjacent Canadian waters;

(4) the rules or regulations that restrict the amount of oil transported in tankers or barges in United States waters, including an assessment of whether there are methods to bypass those rules or regulations in such waters and adjacent Canadian waters;

(5) the spill response capability throughout the shared waters of the United States and Canada, including oil spill response planning requirements for vessels bound for one nation transiting through the waters of the other nation;

(6) the vessel emergency response towing capability at the entrance to the Strait of Juan de Fuca;

(7) the agreement between the United States and Canada that outlines requirements for laden tank vessels to be escorted by tug boats;

(8) whether oil extracted from oil sands has different properties from other types of oil, including toxicity and other properties, that may require different maritime clean up technologies;

(9) a risk assessment of the increasing supertanker, tanker, and barge traffic associated with Canadian oil sands development or expected to be associated with Canadian oil sands development; and

(10) the potential costs and benefits to the United States public and the private sector of maritime transportation of oil sands products.

(c) CONSULTATION REQUIREMENT.—In conducting the assessment required under this section, the Commandant shall consult with the State of Washington, affected tribal governments, and industry, including vessel operators, oil sands producers, and spill response experts. The Commandant may consult with the Secretary of State.

(d) DEADLINE FOR SUBMISSION.—Not later than 180 days after the date of enactment of this Act, the Commandant shall submit the assessment required under this section to the Committee on Commerce, Science, and Transportation of the Senate and the Committee on Transportation and Infrastructure of the House of Representatives.

Coast Guard Headquarters Building Designation

14 USC 1 note

TITLE 14—COAST GUARD

This title was enacted by act Aug. 4, 1949, ch. 393, §1, 63 Stat. 495

SUBTITLE I—ESTABLISHMENT, POWERS, DUTIES, AND ADMINISTRATION

* * * * * * *

CHAPTER 1—ESTABLISHMENT AND DUTIES

* * * * * * *

§101. Establishment of Coast Guard

The Coast Guard, established January 28, 1915, shall be a military service and a branch of the armed forces of the United States at all times.

(Aug. 4, 1949, ch. 393, 63 Stat. 496, §1; Pub. L. 94–546, §1(1), Oct. 18, 1976, 90 Stat. 2519; Pub. L. 107–296, title XVII, §1704(a), Nov. 25, 2002, 116 Stat. 2314; Pub. L. 112–213, title II, §217(1), Dec. 20, 2012, 126 Stat. 1555; renumbered §101, Pub. L. 115–282, title I, §103(b), Dec. 4, 2018, 132 Stat. 4195.)

Designation of Coast Guard Headquarters Building

Pub. L. 113–31, Aug. 9, 2013, 127 Stat. 511, provided that:

"SECTION 1. DESIGNATION.

"The headquarters building of the Coast Guard on the campus located at 2701 Martin Luther King, Jr., Avenue Southeast in the District of Columbia shall be known and designated as the 'Douglas A. Munro Coast Guard Headquarters Building'.

"SEC. 2. REFERENCES.

"Any reference in a law, map, regulation, document, paper, or other record of the United States to the building referred to in section 1 shall be deemed to be a reference to the 'Douglas A. Munro Coast Guard Headquarters Building'."

HOWARD COBLE COAST GUARD AND MARITIME TRANSPORTATION ACT OF 2014

PUBLIC LAW 113-283

AS AMENDED THROUGH P.L. 116-283

Howard Coble Coast Guard and Maritime Transportation Act of 2014

[(Public Law 113–281)]

[As Amended Through P.L. 116–283, Enacted January 1, 2021]

AN ACT To authorize appropriations for the Coast Guard for fiscal year 2015, and for other purposes.

Be it enacted by the Senate and House of Representatives of the United States of America in Congress assembled,

SECTION 1. [14 U.S.C. 1 note] SHORT TITLE.

This Act may be cited as the "Howard Coble Coast Guard and Maritime Transportation Act of 2014".

SEC. 2. TABLE OF CONTENTS.

The table of contents for this Act is the following:

[1] Section 8111(c)(3) of Public Law 116–283 provides for a repeal of section 222 without including a conforming amendment to strike such item for section 222 in the table of sections.

TITLE I—AUTHORIZATION

SEC. 101. AUTHORIZATION OF APPROPRIATIONS.

Funds are authorized to be appropriated for fiscal year 2015 for necessary expenses of the Coast Guard as follows:

(1) For the operation and maintenance of the Coast Guard, $6,981,036,000.

(2) For the acquisition, construction, rebuilding, and improvement of aids to navigation, shore and offshore facilities, vessels, and aircraft, including equipment related thereto, $1,546,448,000, to remain available until expended.

(3) For the Coast Guard Reserve program, including personnel and training costs, equipment, and services, $140,016,000.

(4) For environmental compliance and restoration of Coast

Guard vessels, aircraft, and facilities (other than parts and equipment associated with operation and maintenance), $16,701,000, to remain available until expended.

(5) To the Commandant of the Coast Guard for research, development, test, and evaluation of technologies, materials, and human factors directly related to improving the performance of the Coast Guard's mission with respect to search and rescue, aids to navigation, marine safety, marine environmental protection, enforcement of laws and treaties, ice operations, oceanographic research, and defense readiness, $19,890,000.

(6) For alteration or removal of bridges over navigable waters of the United States constituting obstructions to navigation, and for personnel and administrative costs associated with the Alteration of Bridges Program, $16,000,000.

SEC. 102. AUTHORIZED LEVELS OF MILITARY STRENGTH AND TRAINING.

(a) ACTIVE DUTY STRENGTH.—The Coast Guard is authorized an end-of-year strength for active duty personnel of 43,000 for fiscal year 2015.

(b) MILITARY TRAINING STUDENT LOADS.—The Coast Guard is authorized average military training student loads for fiscal year 2015 as follows:

(1) For recruit and special training, 2,500 student years.

(2) For flight training, 165 student years.

(3) For professional training in military and civilian institutions, 350 student years.

(4) For officer acquisition, 1,200 student years.

TITLE II—COAST GUARD

SEC. 201. [14 U.S.C. 42] COMMISSIONED OFFICERS.

Section 42(a) of title 14, United States Code, is amended by striking "7,200" and inserting "6,900".

SEC. 202. COMMANDANT; APPOINTMENT.

Section 44 of title 14, United States Code, is amended by

inserting after the first sentence the following: "The term of an appointment, and any reappointment, shall begin on June 1 of the appropriate year and end on May 31 of the appropriate year, except that, in the event of death, retirement, resignation, or reassignment, or when the needs of the Service demand, the Secretary may alter the date on which a term begins or ends if the alteration does not result in the term exceeding a period of 4 years.".

SEC. 203. PREVENTION AND RESPONSE WORKFORCES.

Section 57 of title 14, United States Code, is amended—

(1) in subsection (b)—

(A) in paragraph (2) by striking "or" at the end;

(B) in paragraph (3) by striking the period at the end and inserting a semicolon; and

(C) by adding at the end the following:

"(4) waterways operations manager shall have knowledge, skill, and practical experience with respect to marine transportation system management; or

"(5) port and facility safety and security specialist shall have knowledge, skill, and practical experience with respect to the safety, security, and environmental protection responsibilities associated with maritime ports and facilities."

(2) in subsection (c) by striking "or marine safety engineer" and inserting "marine safety engineer, waterways operations manager, or port and facility safety and security specialist"; and

(3) in subsection (f)(2) by striking "investigator or marine safety engineer." and inserting "investigator, marine safety engineer, waterways operations manager, or port and facility safety and security specialist.".

SEC. 204. [14 U.S.C. 58] CENTERS OF EXPERTISE.

Section 58(b) of title 14, United States Code, is amended to read as follows:

"(b) MISSIONS.—Any center established under subsection (a) shall—

"(1) promote, facilitate, and conduct—

"(A) education;

"(B) training; and

"(C) activities authorized under section 93(a)(4);

"(2) be a repository of information on operations, practices, and resources related to the mission for which the center was established; and

"(3) perform and support the mission for which the center was established."

SEC. 205. PENALTIES.

(a) AIDS TO NAVIGATION AND FALSE DISTRESS MESSAGES.—Chapter 5 of title 14, United States Code, is amended—

(1) in section 83 by striking "$100" and inserting "$1,500";

(2) in section 84 by striking "$500" and inserting "$1,500";

(3) in section 85 by striking "$100" and inserting "$1,500"; and

(4) in section 88(c)(2) by striking "$5,000" and inserting "$10,000".

(b) UNAUTHORIZED USE OF WORDS "COAST GUARD".—Section 639 of title 14, United States Code, is amended by striking "$1,000" and inserting "$10,000".

SEC. 206. AGREEMENTS.

(a) IN GENERAL.—Section 93(a)(4) of title 14, United States Code, is amended—

(1) by striking ", investigate" and inserting "and investigate"; and

(2) by striking ", and cooperate and coordinate such activities with other Government agencies and with private agencies".

(b) AUTHORITY.—Chapter 5 of title 14, United States Code, as amended by this Act, is further amended by adding at the end the following:

"SEC. 102. [14 U.S.C. 102] Agreements

"(a) IN GENERAL.—In carrying out section 93(a)(4), the Commandant may—

"(1) enter into cooperative agreements, contracts, and other agreements with—

"(A) Federal entities;

"(B) other public or private entities in the United States, including academic entities; and

"(C) foreign governments with the concurrence of the Secretary of State; and

"(2) impose on and collect from an entity subject to an agreement or contract under paragraph (1) a fee to assist with expenses incurred in carrying out such section.

"(b) DEPOSIT AND USE OF FEES.—Fees collected under this section shall be deposited in the general fund of the Treasury as offsetting receipts. The fees may be used, to the extent provided in advance in an appropriation law, only to carry out activities under section 93(a)(4)."

(c) CLERICAL AMENDMENT.—The analysis for such chapter is amended by adding at the end the following:

"102. Agreements.".

SEC. 207. [14 U.S.C. 93] TUITION ASSISTANCE PROGRAM COVERAGE OF TEXTBOOKS AND OTHER EDUCATIONAL MATERIALS.

Section 93(a)(7) of title 14, United States Code, is amended by inserting "and the textbooks, manuals, and other materials required as part of such training or course of instruction" after "correspondence courses".

SEC. 208. COAST GUARD HOUSING.

(a) COMMANDANT; GENERAL POWERS.—Section 93(a)(13) of title 14, United States Code, is amended by striking "the Treasury" and inserting "the fund established under section 687".

(b) LIGHTHOUSE PROPERTY.—Section 672a(b) of title 14, United States Code, is amended by striking "the Treasury" and inserting "the fund established under section 687".

(c) CONFORMING AMENDMENT.—Section 687(b) of title 14, United States Code, is amended by adding at the end the following:

"(4) Monies received under section 93(a)(13).

"(5) Amounts received under section 672a(b)."

SEC. 209. LEASE AUTHORITY.

Section 93 of title 14, United States Code, is amended by adding at the end the following:

"(f) LEASING OF TIDELANDS AND SUBMERGED LANDS.—

"(1) AUTHORITY.—The Commandant may lease under subsection (a)(13) submerged lands and tidelands under the control of the Coast Guard without regard to the limitation under that subsection with respect to lease duration.

"(2) LIMITATION.—The Commandant may lease submerged lands and tidelands under paragraph (1) only if—

"(A) lease payments are—

"(i) received exclusively in the form of cash;

"(ii) equal to the fair market value of the use of the leased submerged lands or tidelands for the period during which such lands are leased, as determined by the Commandant; and

"(iii) deposited in the fund established under section 687; and

"(B) the lease does not provide authority to or commit the Coast Guard to use or support any improvements to such submerged lands or tidelands, or obtain goods or services from the lessee."

SEC. 210. NOTIFICATION OF CERTAIN DETERMINATIONS.

(a) IN GENERAL.—Chapter 5 of title 14, United States Code, as amended by this Act, is further amended by adding at the end the following:

"SEC. 103. [14 U.S.C. 103] Notification of certain determinations

"(a) IN GENERAL.—At least 90 days prior to making a final determination that a waterway, or a portion thereof, is navigable for purposes of the jurisdiction of the Coast Guard, the Commandant shall provide notification regarding the proposed determination to—

"(1) the Governor of each State in which such waterway, or portion thereof, is located;

"(2) the public; and

"(3) the Committee on Commerce, Science, and Transportation of the Senate and the Committee on Transportation and Infrastructure of the House of Representatives.

"(b) CONTENT REQUIREMENT.—Each notification provided under subsection (a) to an entity specified in paragraph (3) of that subsection shall include—

"(1) an analysis of whether vessels operating on the waterway, or portion thereof, subject to the proposed determination are subject to inspection or similar regulation by State or local officials;

"(2) an analysis of whether operators of commercial vessels on such waterway, or portion thereof, are subject to licensing or similar regulation by State or local officials; and

"(3) an estimate of the annual costs that the Coast Guard may incur in conducting operations on such waterway, or portion thereof."

(b) CLERICAL AMENDMENT.—The analysis for such chapter, as amended by this Act, is further amended by adding at the end the following:

"103. Notification of certain determinations.".

SEC. 211. ANNUAL BOARD OF VISITORS.

Section 194 of title 14, United States Code, is amended to read as follows:

"SEC. 194. [14 U.S.C. 194] Annual Board of Visitors

"(a) IN GENERAL.—A Board of Visitors to the Coast Guard Academy is established to review and make recommendations on the operation of the Academy.

"(b) MEMBERSHIP.—

"(1) IN GENERAL.—The membership of the Board shall consist of the following:

"(A) The chairman of the Committee on Commerce, Science, and Transportation of the Senate, or the chairman's designee.

"(B) The chairman of the Committee on Transportation and Infrastructure of the House of Representatives, or the chairman's designee.

"(C) 3 Members of the Senate designated by the Vice President.

"(D) 4 Members of the House of Representatives designated by the Speaker of the House of Representatives.

"(E) 6 individuals designated by the President.

"(2) LENGTH OF SERVICE.—

"(A) MEMBERS OF CONGRESS.—A Member of Congress designated under subparagraph (C) or (D) of paragraph (1) as a member of the Board shall be designated as a member in the First Session of a Congress and serve for the duration of that Congress.

"(B) INDIVIDUALS DESIGNATED BY THE PRESIDENT.—Each individual designated by the President under subparagraph (E) of paragraph (1) shall serve as a member of the Board for 3 years, except that any such member whose term of office has expired shall continue to serve until a successor is appointed.

"(3) DEATH OR RESIGNATION OF A MEMBER.—If a member of the Board dies or resigns, a successor shall be designated for any unexpired portion of the term of the member by the official who designated the member.

"(c) ACADEMY VISITS.—

"(1) ANNUAL VISIT.—The Board shall visit the Academy annually to review the operation of the Academy.

"(2) ADDITIONAL VISITS.—With the approval of the Secretary, the Board or individual members of the Board may make other visits to the Academy in connection with the duties of the Board or to consult with the Superintendent of the Academy.

"(d) SCOPE OF REVIEW.—The Board shall review, with respect to the Academy—

"(1) the state of morale and discipline;

"(2) the curriculum;

"(3) instruction;

"(4) physical equipment;

"(5) fiscal affairs; and

"(6) other matters relating to the Academy that the Board determines appropriate.

"(e) REPORT.—Not later than 60 days after the date of an annual visit of the Board under subsection (c)(1), the Board shall submit to the Secretary, the Committee on Commerce, Science, and

Transportation of the Senate, and the Committee on Transportation and Infrastructure of the House of Representatives a report on the actions of the Board during such visit and the recommendations of the Board pertaining to the Academy.

"(f) ADVISORS.—If approved by the Secretary, the Board may consult with advisors in carrying out this section.

"(g) REIMBURSEMENT.—Each member of the Board and each adviser consulted by the Board under subsection (f) shall be reimbursed, to the extent permitted by law, by the Coast Guard for actual expenses incurred while engaged in duties as a member or adviser."

SEC. 212. FLAG OFFICERS.

(a) IN GENERAL.—Title 14, United States Code, is amended by inserting after section 295 the following:

"SEC. 296. [14 U.S.C. 296] Flag officers

"During any period in which the Coast Guard is not operating as a service in the Navy, section 1216(d) of title 10 does not apply with respect to flag officers of the Coast Guard."

(b) CLERICAL AMENDMENT.—The analysis for chapter 11 of title 14, United States Code, is amended by inserting after the item relating to section 295 the following:

"296. Flag officers.".

SEC. 213. REPEAL OF LIMITATION ON MEDALS OF HONOR.

Section 494 of title 14, United States Code, is amended by striking "medal of honor," each place it appears.

SEC. 214. COAST GUARD FAMILY SUPPORT AND CHILD CARE.

(a) IN GENERAL.—Title 14, United States Code, as amended by this Act, is further amended by inserting after chapter 13 the following:

"CHAPTER 14—COAST GUARD FAMILY SUPPORT AND CHILD CARE

""subchapter i— general provisions

"Sec.

"531. Work-life policies and programs.

"532. Surveys of Coast Guard families.

SUBCHAPTER "Subchapter I—GENERAL PROVISIONS

"SEC. 531. [14 U.S.C. 531] Work-life policies and programs

"The Commandant is authorized—

"(1) to establish an office for the purpose of developing, promulgating, and coordinating policies, programs, and activities related to the families of Coast Guard members;

"(2) to implement and oversee policies, programs, and activities described in paragraph (1) as the Commandant considers necessary; and

"(3) to perform such other duties as the Commandant considers necessary.

"SEC. 532. [14 U.S.C. 532] Surveys of Coast Guard families

"(a) AUTHORITY.—The Commandant, in order to determine the effectiveness of Federal policies, programs, and activities related to the families of Coast Guard members, may survey—

"(1) any Coast Guard member;

"(2) any retired Coast Guard member;

"(3) the immediate family of any Coast Guard member or retired Coast Guard member; and

"(4) any survivor of a deceased Coast Guard member.

"(b) VOLUNTARY PARTICIPATION.—Participation in any survey conducted under subsection (a) shall be voluntary.

"(c) FEDERAL RECORDKEEPING.—Each person surveyed under subsection (a) shall be considered an employee of the United States for purposes of section 3502(3)(A)(i) of title 44.

SUBCHAPTER "Subchapter II—COAST GUARD FAMILY SUPPORT

"SEC. 542. [14 U.S.C. 542] Education and training opportunities for Coast Guard spouses

"(a) TUITION ASSISTANCE.—The Commandant may provide, subject to the availability of appropriations, tuition assistance to an eligible spouse to facilitate the acquisition of—

"(1) education and training required for a degree or credential at an accredited college, university, or technical school in the United States that expands employment and portable career opportunities for the spouse; or

"(2) education prerequisites and a professional license or credential required, by a government or government-sanctioned licensing body, for an occupation that expands employment and portable career opportunities for the spouse.

"(b) DEFINITIONS.—In this section, the following definitions apply:

"(1) ELIGIBLE SPOUSE.—

"(A) IN GENERAL.—The term 'eligible spouse' means the spouse of a member of the Coast Guard who is serving on active duty and includes a spouse who receives transitional compensation under section 1059 of title 10.

"(B) EXCLUSION.—The term 'eligible spouse' does not include a person who—

"(i) is married to, but legally separated from, a member of the Coast Guard under a court order or statute of any State or territorial possession of the United States; or

"(ii) is eligible for tuition assistance as a member of the Armed Forces.

"(2) PORTABLE CAREER.—The term 'portable career' includes an occupation that requires education, training, or both that results in a credential that is recognized by an industry, profession, or specific type of business.

"SEC. 543. [14 U.S.C. 543] Youth sponsorship initiatives

"(a) IN GENERAL.—The Commandant is authorized to establish,

within any Coast Guard unit, an initiative to help integrate into new surroundings the dependent children of members of the Coast Guard who received permanent change of station orders.

"(b) DESCRIPTION OF INITIATIVE.—An initiative established under subsection (a) shall—

"(1) provide for the involvement of a dependent child of a member of the Coast Guard in the dependent child's new Coast Guard community; and

"(2) primarily focus on preteen and teenaged children.

"(c) AUTHORITY.—In carrying out an initiative under subsection (a), the Commandant may—

"(1) provide to a dependent child of a member of the Coast Guard information on youth programs and activities available in the dependent child's new Coast Guard community; and

"(2) enter into agreements with nonprofit entities to provide youth programs and activities to such child.

SUBCHAPTER "Subchapter III—COAST GUARD CHILD CARE

"SEC. 551. [14 U.S.C. 551] Definitions

"In this subchapter, the following definitions apply:

"(1) CHILD ABUSE AND NEGLECT.—The term '"child abuse and neglect"' has the meaning given that term in section 3 of the Child Abuse Prevention and Treatment Act (42 U.S.C. 5101 note).

"(2) CHILD DEVELOPMENT CENTER EMPLOYEE.—The term '"child development center employee"' means a civilian employee of the Coast Guard who is employed to work in a Coast Guard child development center without regard to whether the employee is paid from appropriated or nonappropriated funds.

"(3) COAST GUARD CHILD DEVELOPMENT CENTER.—The term '"Coast Guard child development center"' means a facility on Coast Guard property or on property under the jurisdiction of the commander of a Coast Guard unit at which child care services are provided for members of the Coast Guard.

"(4) COMPETITIVE SERVICE POSITION.—The term

"'competitive service position'" means a position in the competitive service (as defined in section 2102 of title 5).

"(5) FAMILY HOME DAYCARE.—The term "'family home daycare'" means home-based child care services provided for a member of the Coast Guard by an individual who—

"(A) is certified by the Commandant as qualified to provide home-based child care services; and

"(B) provides home-based child care services on a regular basis in exchange for monetary compensation.

"SEC. 553. [14 U.S.C. 553] Child development center standards and inspections

"(a) STANDARDS.—The Commandant shall require each Coast Guard child development center to meet standards that the Commandant considers appropriate to ensure the health, safety, and welfare of the children and employees at the center.

"(b) INSPECTIONS.—The Commandant shall provide for regular and unannounced inspections of each Coast Guard child development center to ensure compliance with this section.

"(c) NATIONAL REPORTING.—

"(1) IN GENERAL.—The Commandant shall maintain and publicize a means by which an individual can report, with respect to a Coast Guard child development center or a family home daycare—

"(A) any suspected violation of—

"(i) standards established under subsection (a); or

"(ii) any other applicable law or standard;

"(B) suspected child abuse or neglect; or

"(C) any other deficiency.

"(2) ANONYMOUS REPORTING.—The Commandant shall ensure that an individual making a report pursuant to paragraph (1) may do so anonymously if so desired by the individual.

"(3) PROCEDURES.—The Commandant shall establish procedures for investigating reports made pursuant to paragraph (1).

"SEC. 554. [14 U.S.C. 554] Child development center employees

"(a) TRAINING.—

"(1) IN GENERAL.—The Commandant shall establish a training program for Coast Guard child development center employees and satisfactory completion of the training program shall be a condition of employment for each employee of a Coast Guard child development center.

"(2) TIMING FOR NEW HIRES.—The Commandant shall require each employee of a Coast Guard child development center to complete the training program established under paragraph (1) not later than 6 months after the date on which the employee is hired.

"(3) MINIMUM REQUIREMENTS.—The training program established under paragraph (1) shall include, at a minimum, instruction with respect to—

"(A) early childhood development;

"(B) activities and disciplinary techniques appropriate to children of different ages;

"(C) child abuse and neglect prevention and detection; and

"(D) cardiopulmonary resuscitation and other emergency medical procedures.

"(4) USE OF DEPARTMENT OF DEFENSE PROGRAMS.—The Commandant may use Department of Defense training programs, on a reimbursable or nonreimbursable basis, for purposes of this subsection.

"(b) TRAINING AND CURRICULUM SPECIALISTS.—

"(1) SPECIALIST REQUIRED.—The Commandant shall require that at least 1 employee at each Coast Guard child development center be a specialist in training and curriculum development with appropriate credentials and experience.

"(2) DUTIES.—The duties of the specialist described in paragraph (1) shall include—

"(A) special teaching activities;

"(B) daily oversight and instruction of other child care employees;

"(C) daily assistance in the preparation of lesson plans;

"(D) assisting with child abuse and neglect prevention

and detection; and

"(E) advising the director of the center on the performance of the other child care employees.

"(3) COMPETITIVE SERVICE.—Each specialist described in paragraph (1) shall be an employee in a competitive service position.

"SEC. 555. [14 U.S.C. 555] Parent partnerships with child development centers

"(a) PARENT BOARDS.—

"(1) FORMATION.—The Commandant shall require that there be formed at each Coast Guard child development center a board of parents, to be composed of parents of children attending the center.

"(2) FUNCTIONS.—Each board of parents formed under paragraph (1) shall—

"(A) meet periodically with the staff of the center at which the board is formed and the commander of the unit served by the center, for the purpose of discussing problems and concerns; and

"(B) be responsible, together with the staff of the center, for coordinating any parent participation initiative established under subsection (b).

"(3) FACA.—The Federal Advisory Committee Act (5 U.S.C. App.) does not apply to a board of parents formed under paragraph (1).

"(b) PARENT PARTICIPATION INITIATIVE.—The Commandant is authorized to establish a parent participation initiative at each Coast Guard child development center to encourage and facilitate parent participation in educational and related activities at the center."

(b) TRANSFER OF PROVISIONS.—

(1) IN GENERAL.—

(A) [14 U.S.C. 541] REIMBURSEMENT FOR ADOPTION EXPENSES.—Section 514 of title 14, United States Code, is redesignated as section 541 and transferred to appear before section 542 of such title, as added by subsection (a) of this section.

(B) [14 U.S.C. 552] CHILD DEVELOPMENT SERVICES.—Section 515 of title 14, United States Code—

(i) is redesignated as section 552 and transferred to appear after section 551 of such title, as added by subsection (a) of this section; and

(ii) is amended—

(I) in subsection (b)(2)(B) by inserting "and whether a family is participating in an initiative established under section 555(b)" after "family income";

(II) by striking subsections (c) and (e); and

(III) by redesignating subsection (d) as subsection (c).

(C) [14 U.S.C. 657] DEPENDENT SCHOOL CHILDREN.—Section 657 of title 14, United States Code—

(i) is redesignated as section 544 and transferred to appear after section 543 of such title, as added by subsection (a) of this section; and

(ii) is amended in subsection (a) by striking "Except as otherwise" and all that follows through "the Secretary may" and inserting "The Secretary may".

(2) CONFORMING AMENDMENTS.—

(A) PART I.—The analysis for part I of title 14, United States Code, is amended by inserting after the item relating to chapter 13 the following:

"14. Coast Guard Family Support and Child Care531".

(B) CHAPTER 13.—The analysis for chapter 13 of title 14, United States Code, is amended—

(i) by striking the item relating to section 514; and

(ii) by striking the item relating to section 515.

(C) CHAPTER 14.—The analysis for chapter 14 of title 14, United States Code, as added by subsection (a) of this section, is amended by inserting—

(i) before the item relating to section 542 the following:

"541. Reimbursement for adoption expenses.";

(ii) after the item relating to section 551 the

following:

"552. Child development services."; and

(iii) after the item relating to section 543 the following:

"544. Dependent school children.".

(D) CHAPTER 17.—The analysis for chapter 17 of title 14, United States Code, is amended by striking the item relating to section 657.

(c) COMMANDANT; GENERAL POWERS.—Section 93(a)(7) of title 14, United States Code, as amended by this Act, is further amended by inserting ", and to eligible spouses as defined under section 542," after "Coast Guard".

(d) SENSE OF CONGRESS.—

(1) IN GENERAL.—It is the sense of Congress that the amount of funds appropriated for a fiscal year for operating expenses related to Coast Guard child development services should not be less than the amount of the child development center fee receipts estimated to be collected by the Coast Guard during that fiscal year.

(2) CHILD DEVELOPMENT CENTER FEE RECEIPTS DEFINED.—In this subsection, the term "child development center fee receipts" means fees paid by members of the Coast Guard for child care services provided at Coast Guard child development centers.

SEC. 215. MISSION NEED STATEMENT.

(a) IN GENERAL.—Section 569 of title 14, United States Code, is amended to read as follows:

"SEC. 569. [14 U.S.C. 569] Mission need statement

"(a) IN GENERAL.—On the date on which the President submits to Congress a budget for fiscal year 2016 under section 1105 of title 31, on the date on which the President submits to Congress a budget for fiscal year 2019 under such section, and every 4 years thereafter, the Commandant shall submit to the Committee on Transportation and Infrastructure of the House of Representatives and the Committee on Commerce, Science, and Transportation of the Senate an integrated major acquisition mission need statement.

"(b) DEFINITIONS.—In this section, the following definitions apply:

"(1) INTEGRATED MAJOR ACQUISITION MISSION NEED STATEMENT.—The term 'integrated major acquisition mission need statement' means a document that—

"(A) identifies current and projected gaps in Coast Guard mission capabilities using mission hour targets;

"(B) explains how each major acquisition program addresses gaps identified under subparagraph (A) if funded at the levels provided for such program in the most recently submitted capital investment plan; and

"(C) describes the missions the Coast Guard will not be able to achieve, by fiscal year, for each gap identified under subparagraph (A).

"(2) MAJOR ACQUISITION PROGRAM.—The term 'major acquisition program' has the meaning given that term in section 569a(e).

"(3) CAPITAL INVESTMENT PLAN.—The term 'capital investment plan' means the plan required under section 663(a)(1)."

(b) CLERICAL AMENDMENT.—The analysis for chapter 15 of title 14, United States Code, is amended by striking the item relating to section 569 and inserting the following:

"569. Mission need statement.".

SEC. 216. TRANSMISSION OF ANNUAL COAST GUARD AUTHORIZATION REQUEST.

(a) IN GENERAL.—Title 14, United States Code, as amended by this Act, is further amended by inserting after section 662 the following:

"SEC. 662a. [14 U.S.C. 662a] Transmission of annual Coast Guard authorization request

"(a) IN GENERAL.—Not later than 30 days after the date on which the President submits to Congress a budget for a fiscal year pursuant to section 1105 of title 31, the Secretary shall submit to the Committee on Transportation and Infrastructure of the House of Representatives and the Committee on Commerce, Science, and Transportation of the Senate a Coast Guard authorization request with respect to such fiscal year.

"(b) COAST GUARD AUTHORIZATION REQUEST DEFINED.—In this section, the term 'Coast Guard authorization request' means a proposal for legislation that, with respect to the Coast Guard for the relevant fiscal year—

"(1) recommends end strengths for personnel for that fiscal year, as described in section 661;

"(2) recommends authorizations of appropriations for that fiscal year, including with respect to matters described in section 662; and

"(3) addresses any other matter that the Secretary determines is appropriate for inclusion in a Coast Guard authorization bill."

(b) CLERICAL AMENDMENT.—The analysis for chapter 17 of title 14, United States Code, as amended by this Act, is further amended by inserting after the item relating to section 662 the following:

"662a. Transmission of annual Coast Guard authorization request.".

SEC. 217. INVENTORY OF REAL PROPERTY.

(a) IN GENERAL.—Chapter 17 of title 14, United States Code, is amended by adding at the end the following:

"SEC. 679. [14 U.S.C. 679] Inventory of real property

"(a) IN GENERAL.—Not later than September 30, 2015, the Commandant shall establish an inventory of all real property, including submerged lands, under the control of the Coast Guard, which shall include—

"(1) the size, the location, and any other appropriate description of each unit of such property;

"(2) an assessment of the physical condition of each unit of such property, excluding lands;

"(3) a determination of whether each unit of such property should be—

"(A) retained to fulfill a current or projected Coast Guard mission requirement; or

"(B) subject to divestiture; and

"(4) other information the Commandant considers appropriate.

"(b) INVENTORY MAINTENANCE.—The Commandant shall—

"(1) maintain the inventory required under subsection (a) on an ongoing basis; and

"(2) update information on each unit of real property

included in such inventory not later than 30 days after any change relating to the control of such property.

"(c) RECOMMENDATIONS TO CONGRESS.—Not later than March 30, 2016, and every 5 years thereafter, the Commandant shall submit to the Committee on Transportation and Infrastructure of the House of Representatives and the Committee on Commerce, Science, and Transportation of the Senate a report that includes—

"(1) a list of all real property under the control of the Coast Guard and the location of such property by property type;

"(2) recommendations for divestiture with respect to any units of such property; and

"(3) recommendations for consolidating any units of such property, including—

"(A) an estimate of the costs or savings associated with each recommended consolidation; and

"(B) a discussion of the impact that such consolidation would have on Coast Guard mission effectiveness."

(b) CLERICAL AMENDMENT.—The analysis for such chapter, as amended by this Act, is further amended by adding at the end the following:

"679. Inventory of real property.".

SEC. 218. RETIRED SERVICE MEMBERS AND DEPENDENTS SERVING ON ADVISORY COMMITTEES.

(a) IN GENERAL.—Chapter 17 of title 14, United States Code, as amended by this Act, is further amended by adding at the end the following:

"SEC. 680. [14 U.S.C. 680] Retired service members and dependents serving on advisory committees

"A committee that—

"(1) advises or assists the Coast Guard with respect to a function that affects a member of the Coast Guard or a dependent of such a member; and

"(2) includes in its membership a retired Coast Guard member or a dependent of such a retired member;

shall not be considered an advisory committee under the Federal Advisory Committee Act (5 U.S.C. App.) solely because of such membership."

(b) CLERICAL AMENDMENT.—The analysis for such chapter, as amended by this Act, is further amended by inserting after the item relating to section 679 the following:

"680. Retired service members and dependents serving on advisory committees.".

SEC. 219. [14 U.S.C. 712] ACTIVE DUTY FOR EMERGENCY AUGMENTATION OF REGULAR FORCES.

Section 712(a) of title 14, United States Code, is amended by striking "not more than 60 days in any 4-month period and".

SEC. 220. ACQUISITION WORKFORCE EXPEDITED HIRING AUTHORITY.

Section 404(b) of the Coast Guard Authorization Act of 2010 (Public Law 111-281; 124 Stat. 2951) is amended by striking "2015" and inserting "2017".

SEC. 221. COAST GUARD ADMINISTRATIVE SAVINGS.

(a) ELIMINATION OF OUTDATED AND DUPLICATIVE REPORTS.—

(1) MARINE INDUSTRY TRAINING.—Section 59 of title 14, United States Code, is amended—

(A) by striking "(a) In General.—The Commandant" and inserting "The Commandant"; and

(B) by striking subsection (b).

(2) OPERATIONS AND EXPENDITURES.—Section 651 of title 14, United States Code, and the item relating to such section in the analysis for chapter 17 of such title, are repealed.

(3) DRUG INTERDICTION.—Section 103 of the Coast Guard Authorization Act of 1996 (14 U.S.C. 89 note), and the item relating to that section in the table of contents in section 2 of that Act, are repealed.

(4) NATIONAL DEFENSE.—Section 426 of the Maritime Transportation Security Act of 2002 (14 U.S.C. 2 note), and the item relating to that section in the table of contents in section 1(b) of that Act, are repealed.

(5) LIVING MARINE RESOURCES.—Section 4(b) of the Cruise Vessel Security and Safety Act of 2010 (16 U.S.C. 1828 note) is amended by adding at the end the following: "No report shall be required under this subsection, including that no report shall be required under section 224 of the Coast Guard and Maritime Transportation Act of 2004 or section 804 of the Coast Guard

and Maritime Transportation Act of 2006, for fiscal years beginning after fiscal year 2014.".

(b) CONSOLIDATION AND REFORM OF REPORTING REQUIREMENTS.—

(1) MARINE SAFETY.—

(A) IN GENERAL.—Section 2116(d)(2)(B) of title 46, United States Code, is amended to read as follows:

"(B) on the program's mission performance in achieving numerical measurable goals established under subsection (b), including—

"(i) the number of civilian and military Coast Guard personnel assigned to marine safety positions; and

"(ii) an identification of marine safety positions that are understaffed to meet the workload required to accomplish each activity included in the strategy and plans under subsection (a); and"

(B) CONFORMING AMENDMENT.—Section 57 of title 14, United States Code, as amended by this Act, is further amended—

(i) by striking subsection (e); and

(ii) by redesignating subsections (f), (g), and (h) as subsections (e), (f), and (g) respectively.

(2) [14 U.S.C. 656] MINOR CONSTRUCTION.—Section 656(d)(2) of title 14, United States Code, is amended to read as follows:

"(2) REPORT.—Not later than the date on which the President submits to Congress a budget under section 1105 of title 31 each year, the Secretary shall submit to the Committee on Transportation and Infrastructure of the House of Representatives and the Committee on Commerce, Science, and Transportation of the Senate a report describing each project carried out under paragraph (1), in the most recently concluded fiscal year, for which the amount expended under such paragraph for such project was more than $1,000,000. If no such project was carried out during a fiscal year, no report under this paragraph shall be required with respect to that fiscal year."

SEC. 222. TECHNICAL CORRECTIONS TO TITLE 14.

Title 14, United States Code, as amended by this Act, is further amended—

(1) in section 93(b)(1) by striking "Notwithstanding subsection (a)(14)" and inserting "Notwithstanding subsection (a)(13)"; and

(2) in section 197(b) by striking "of Homeland Security".

[Section 223 was repealed by section 311(d)(1) of Public Law 115–282.]

SEC. 224. MAINTAINING MEDIUM ENDURANCE CUTTER MISSION CAPABILITY.

Not later than 120 days after the date of enactment of this Act, the Secretary of the department in which the Coast Guard is operating shall submit to the Committee on Transportation and Infrastructure of the House of Representatives and the Committee on Commerce, Science, and Transportation of the Senate a report that includes—

(1) a schedule and plan for decommissioning, not later than September 30, 2029, each of the 210-foot, Reliance-Class Cutters operated by the Coast Guard on the date of enactment of this Act;

(2) a schedule and plan for enhancing the maintenance or extending the service life of each of the 270-foot, Famous-Class Cutters operated by the Coast Guard on the date of enactment of this Act—

(A) to maintain the capability of the Coast Guard to carry out sea-going missions with respect to such Cutters at the level of capability existing on September 30, 2013; and

(B) for the period beginning on the date of enactment of this Act and ending on the date on which the final Offshore Patrol Cutter is scheduled to be commissioned under paragraph (4);

(3) an identification of the number of Offshore Patrol Cutters capable of sea state 5 operations that, if 8 National Security Cutters are commissioned, are necessary to return the

sea state 5 operating capability of the Coast Guard to the level of capability that existed prior to the decommissioning of the first High Endurance Cutter in fiscal year 2011;

(4) a schedule and plan for commissioning the number of Offshore Patrol Cutters identified under paragraph (3); and

(5) a schedule and plan for commissioning, not later than September 30, 2034, a number of Offshore Patrol Cutters not capable of sea state 5 operations that is equal to—

(A) 25; less

(B) the number of Offshore Patrol Cutters identified under paragraph (3).

SEC. 225. AVIATION CAPABILITY.

The Secretary of the department in which the Coast Guard is operating may—

(1) request and accept through a direct military-to-military transfer under section 2571 of title 10, United States Code, such H-60 helicopters as may be necessary to establish a year-round operational capability in the Coast Guard's Ninth District; and

(2) use funds provided under section 101 of this Act to convert such helicopters to Coast Guard MH-60T configuration.

SEC. 226. GAPS IN WRITINGS ON COAST GUARD HISTORY.

Not later than 1 year after the date of enactment of this Act, the Commandant of the Coast Guard shall submit to the Committee on Commerce, Science, and Transportation of the Senate and the Committee on Transportation and Infrastructure of the House of Representatives a report on any gaps that exist in writings on the history of the Coast Guard. The report shall address, at a minimum, operations, broad topics, and biographies with respect to the Coast Guard.

SEC. 227. OFFICER EVALUATION REPORTS.

(a) ASSESSMENT REQUIRED.—Not later than 180 days after the date of enactment of this Act, the Commandant of the Coast Guard shall provide to the Committee on Commerce, Science, and Transportation of the Senate and the Committee on Transportation and Infrastructure of the House of Representatives a written assessment of the Coast Guard's officer evaluation reporting system.

(b) CONTENTS OF ASSESSMENT.—The assessment required under subsection (a) shall include, at a minimum, an analysis of—

(1) the extent to which the Coast Guard's officer evaluation reports differ in length, form, and content from the officer fitness reports used by the Navy and other branches of the Armed Forces;

(2) the extent to which differences determined pursuant to paragraph (1) are the result of inherent differences between—

(A) the Coast Guard and the Navy; and

(B) the Coast Guard and other branches of the Armed Forces;

(3) the feasibility of more closely aligning and conforming the Coast Guard's officer evaluation reports with the officer fitness reports of the Navy and other branches of the Armed Forces; and

(4) the costs and benefits of the alignment and conformity described in paragraph (3), including with respect to—

(A) Coast Guard administrative efficiency;

(B) fairness and equity for Coast Guard officers; and

(C) carrying out the Coast Guard's statutory mission of defense readiness, including when operating as a service in the Navy.

SEC. 228. [14 U.S.C. 81] IMPROVED SAFETY INFORMATION FOR VESSELS.

Not later than 1 year after the date of enactment of this Act, the Secretary of the department in which the Coast Guard is operating shall establish a process that allows an operator of a marine exchange or other non-Federal vessel traffic information service to use the automatic identification system to transmit weather, ice, and other important navigation safety information to vessels.

[Section 229 was repealed by section 610(a)(3)(A) of Public Law 114–120.]

SEC. 230. ANALYSIS OF RESOURCE DEFICIENCIES WITH RESPECT TO MARITIME BORDER SECURITY.

(a) IN GENERAL.—Not later than 120 days after the date of enactment of this Act, the Commandant of the Coast Guard shall provide to the Committee on Commerce, Science, and

Transportation of the Senate and the Committee on Transportation and Infrastructure and the Committee on Homeland Security of the House of Representatives a report describing any Coast Guard resource deficiencies related to—

(1) securing maritime borders with respect to the Great Lakes and the coastal areas of the Southeastern and Southwestern United States, including with respect to Florida, California, Puerto Rico, and the United States Virgin Islands;

(2) patrolling and monitoring maritime approaches to the areas described in paragraph (1); and

(3) patrolling and monitoring relevant portions of the Western Hemisphere Drug Transit Zone.

(b) SCOPE.—In preparing the report under subsection (a), the Commandant shall consider, at a minimum—

(1) the Coast Guard's statutory missions with respect to migrant interdiction, drug interdiction, defense readiness, living marine resources, and ports, waterways, and coastal security;

(2) whether Coast Guard missions are being executed to meet national performance targets set under the National Drug Control Strategy;

(3) the number and types of cutters and other vessels required to effectively execute Coast Guard missions;

(4) the number and types of aircraft, including unmanned aircraft, required to effectively execute Coast Guard missions;

(5) the number of assets that require upgraded sensor and communications systems to effectively execute Coast Guard missions;

(6) the Deployable Specialized Forces required to effectively execute Coast Guard missions; and

(7) whether additional shoreside facilities are required to accommodate Coast Guard personnel and assets in support of Coast Guard missions.

SEC. 231. MODERNIZATION OF NATIONAL DISTRESS AND RESPONSE SYSTEM.

(a) REPORT.—Not later than 60 days after the date of enactment of this Act, the Secretary of the department in which the Coast

Guard is operating shall submit to the Committee on Transportation and Infrastructure of the House of Representatives and the Committee on Commerce, Science, and Transportation of the Senate a report on the implementation of the Rescue 21 project in Alaska and in Coast Guard sectors Upper Mississippi River, Lower Mississippi River, and Ohio River Valley.

(b) CONTENTS.—The report required under subsection (a) shall—

(1) describe what improvements are being made to the distress response system in the areas specified in subsection (a), including information on which areas will receive digital selective calling and direction finding capability;

(2) describe the impediments to installing digital selective calling and direction finding capability in areas where such technology will not be installed;

(3) identify locations in the areas specified in subsection (a) where communication gaps will continue to present a risk to mariners after completion of the Rescue 21 project;

(4) include a list of all reported marine accidents, casualties, and fatalities occurring in the locations identified under paragraph (3) since 1990; and

(5) provide an estimate of the costs associated with installing the technology necessary to close communication gaps in the locations identified under paragraph (3).

SEC. 232. REPORT RECONCILING MAINTENANCE AND OPERATIONAL PRIORITIES ON THE MISSOURI RIVER.

Not later than 1 year after the date of enactment of this Act, the Commandant of the Coast Guard shall submit to the Committee on Commerce, Science, and Transportation of the Senate and the Committee on Transportation and Infrastructure of the House of Representatives a report that outlines a course of action to reconcile general maintenance priorities for cutters with operational priorities on the Missouri River.

SEC. 233. MARITIME SEARCH AND RESCUE ASSISTANCE POLICY ASSESSMENT.

(a) IN GENERAL.—The Commandant of the Coast Guard shall assess the Maritime Search and Rescue Assistance Policy as it relates to State and local responders.

(b) SCOPE.—The assessment under subsection (a) shall consider, at a minimum—

(1) the extent to which Coast Guard search and rescue coordinators have entered into domestic search and rescue agreements with State and local responders under the National Search and Rescue Plan;

(2) whether the domestic search and rescue agreements include the Maritime Search and Rescue Assistance Policy; and

(3) the extent to which Coast Guard sectors coordinate with 911 emergency centers, including ensuring the dissemination of appropriate maritime distress check-sheets.

(c) REPORT.—Not later than 180 days after the date of enactment of this Act, the Commandant of the Coast Guard shall submit a report on the assessment under subsection (a) to the Committee on Commerce, Science, and Transportation of the Senate and the Committee on Transportation and Infrastructure of the House of Representatives.

TITLE III—SHIPPING AND NAVIGATION

SEC. 301. REPEAL.

Chapter 555 of title 46, United States Code, is amended—

(1) [46 U.S.C. 55501] by repealing section 55501;

(2) by redesignating section 55502 as section 55501; and

(3) in the analysis by striking the items relating to sections 55501 and 55502 and inserting the following:

"55501. United States Committee on the Marine Transportation System.".

SEC. 302. DONATION OF HISTORICAL PROPERTY.

Section 51103 of title 46, United States Code, is amended by adding at the end the following:

"(e) DONATION FOR HISTORICAL PURPOSES.—

"(1) IN GENERAL.—The Secretary may convey the right, title, and interest of the United States Government in any property administered by the Maritime Administration, except real estate or vessels, if—

"(A) the Secretary determines that such property is not needed by the Maritime Administration; and

"(B) the recipient—

"(i) is a nonprofit organization, a State, or a political subdivision of a State;

"(ii) agrees to hold the Government harmless for any claims arising from exposure to hazardous materials, including asbestos, polychlorinated biphenyls, or lead paint, after conveyance of the property;

"(iii) provides a description and explanation of the intended use of the property to the Secretary for approval;

"(iv) has provided to the Secretary proof, as determined by the Secretary, of resources sufficient to accomplish the intended use provided under clause (iii) and to maintain the property;

"(v) agrees that when the recipient no longer requires the property, the recipient shall—

"(I) return the property to the Secretary, at the recipient's expense and in the same condition as received except for ordinary wear and tear; or

"(II) subject to the approval of the Secretary, retain, sell, or otherwise dispose of the property in a manner consistent with applicable law; and

"(vi) agrees to any additional terms the Secretary considers appropriate.

"(2) REVERSION.—The Secretary shall include in any conveyance under this subsection terms under which all right, title, and interest conveyed by the Secretary shall revert to the Government if the Secretary determines the property has been used other than as approved by the Secretary under paragraph (1)(B)(iii)."

SEC. 303. [46 U.S.C. 54101] SMALL SHIPYARDS.

Section 54101(i) of title 46, United States Code, is amended by striking "2009 through 2013" and inserting "2015 through 2017".

SEC. 304. DRUG TESTING REPORTING.

Section 7706 of title 46, United States Code, is amended—

(1) in subsection (a), by inserting "an applicant for employment by a Federal agency," after "Federal agency,"; and

(2) in subsection (c), by—

(A) inserting "or an applicant for employment by a Federal agency" after "an employee"; and

(B) striking "the employee." and inserting "the employee or the applicant.".

SEC. 305. OPPORTUNITIES FOR SEA SERVICE VETERANS.

(a) ENDORSEMENTS FOR VETERANS.—Section 7101 of title 46, United States Code, is amended by adding at the end the following:

"(j) The Secretary may issue a license under this section in a class under subsection (c) to an applicant that—

"(1) has at least 3 months of qualifying service on vessels of the uniformed services (as that term is defined in section 101(a) of title 10) of appropriate tonnage or horsepower within the 7-year period immediately preceding the date of application; and

"(2) satisfies all other requirements for such a license."

(b) SEA SERVICE LETTERS.—

(1) IN GENERAL.—Title 14, United States Code, is amended by inserting after section 427 the following:

"SEC. 428. [14 U.S.C. 428] Sea service letters

"(a) IN GENERAL.—The Secretary shall provide a sea service letter to a member or former member of the Coast Guard who—

"(1) accumulated sea service on a vessel of the armed forces (as such term is defined in section 101(a) of title 10); and

"(2) requests such letter.

"(b) DEADLINE.—Not later than 30 days after receiving a request for a sea service letter from a member or former member of the Coast Guard under subsection (a), the Secretary shall provide such letter to such member or former member if such member or former member satisfies the requirement under subsection (a)(1)."

(2) CLERICAL AMENDMENT.—The analysis for chapter 11 of title 14, United States Code, is amended by inserting after the item relating to section 427 the following:

"428. Sea service letters.".

(c) [46 U.S.C. 7302 note] CREDITING OF UNITED STATES ARMED FORCES SERVICE, TRAINING, AND QUALIFICATIONS.—

(1) MAXIMIZING CREDITABILITY.—The Secretary of the department in which the Coast Guard is operating, in implementing United States merchant mariner license, certification, and document laws and the International Convention on Standards of Training, Certification and Watchkeeping for Seafarers, 1978, shall maximize the extent to which United States Armed Forces service, training, and qualifications are creditable toward meeting the requirements of such laws and such Convention.

(2) NOTIFICATION.—Not later than 90 days after the date of enactment of this Act, the Secretary shall notify the Committee on Transportation and Infrastructure of the House of Representatives and the Committee on Commerce, Science, and Transportation of the Senate on the steps taken to implement this subsection.

(d) [46 U.S.C. 7301 note] MERCHANT MARINE POST-SERVICE CAREER OPPORTUNITIES.—Not later than 180 days after the date of enactment of this Act, the Commandant of the Coast Guard shall take steps to promote better awareness, on an ongoing basis, among Coast Guard personnel regarding post-service use of Coast Guard training, education, and practical experience in satisfaction of requirements for merchant mariner credentials under section 11.213 of title 46, Code of Federal Regulations.

SEC. 306. CLARIFICATION OF HIGH-RISK WATERS.

Section 55305(e) of title 46, United States Code, is amended—

(1) in paragraph (1)—

(A) by striking "provide armed personnel aboard" and inserting "reimburse, subject to the availability of appropriations, the owners or operators of"; and

(B) by inserting "for the cost of providing armed personnel aboard such vessels" before "if"; and

(2) by striking paragraphs (2) and (3) and inserting the following:

"(2) In this subsection, the term 'high-risk waters' means waters so designated by the Commandant of the Coast Guard in the maritime security directive issued by the Commandant and in effect on the date on which an applicable voyage begins, if the Secretary of Transportation—

"(A) determines that an act of piracy occurred in the 12-month period preceding the date the voyage begins; or

"(B) in such period, issued an advisory warning that an act of piracy is possible in such waters."

SEC. 307. TECHNICAL CORRECTIONS.

(a) [46 U.S.C. 2116] TITLE 46.—Section 2116(b)(1)(D) of title 46, United States Code, is amended by striking "section 93(c)" and inserting "section 93(c) of title 14".

(b) COAST GUARD AND MARITIME TRANSPORTATION ACT OF 2006.—Section 304(a) of the Coast Guard and Maritime Transportation Act of 2006 (Public Law 109-241; 33 U.S.C. 1503 note) is amended by inserting "and from" before "the United States".

(c) DEEPWATER PORT ACT OF 1974.—Section 4(i) of the Deepwater Port Act of 1974 (33 U.S.C. 1503(i)) is amended by inserting "or that will supply" after "be supplied with".

SEC. 308. REPORT.

Not later than 1 year after the date of the enactment of this Act, the Comptroller General of the United States shall submit to the Committee on Transportation and Infrastructure of the House of Representatives and the Committee on Commerce, Science, and Transportation of the Senate a report on the number of jobs, including vessel construction and vessel operating jobs, that would be created in the United States maritime industry each year in 2015 through 2025 if liquified natural gas exported from the United States were required to be carried—

(1) before December 31, 2018, on vessels documented under the laws of the United States; and

(2) on and after such date, on vessels documented under the laws of the United States and constructed in the United States.

SEC. 309. FISHING SAFETY GRANT PROGRAMS.

(a) FISHING SAFETY TRAINING GRANT PROGRAM.—Section 4502(i)(4) of title 46, United States Code, is amended by striking "2010 through 2014" and inserting "2015 through 2017".

(b) FISHING SAFETY RESEARCH GRANT PROGRAM.—Section 4502(j)(4) of title 46, United States Code, is amended by striking “2010 through 2014” and inserting “2015 through 2017”.

SEC. 310. ESTABLISHMENT OF MERCHANT MARINE PERSONNEL ADVISORY COMMITTEE.

(a) ESTABLISHMENT.—Chapter 81 of title 46, United States Code, is amended by adding at the end the following:

“SEC. 8108. [46 U.S.C. 8108] Merchant Marine Personnel Advisory Committee

“(a) ESTABLISHMENT.—The Secretary shall establish a Merchant Marine Personnel Advisory Committee (in this section referred to as ‘the Committee’). The Committee—

“(1) shall act solely in an advisory capacity to the Secretary through the Commandant of the Coast Guard on matters relating to personnel in the United States merchant marine, including training, qualifications, certification, documentation, and fitness standards, and other matters as assigned by the Commandant;

“(2) shall review and comment on proposed Coast Guard regulations and policies relating to personnel in the United States merchant marine, including training, qualifications, certification, documentation, and fitness standards;

“(3) may be given special assignments by the Secretary and may conduct studies, inquiries, workshops, and fact finding in consultation with individuals and groups in the private sector and with State or local governments;

“(4) shall advise, consult with, and make recommendations reflecting its independent judgment to the Secretary;

“(5) shall meet not less than twice each year; and

“(6) may make available to Congress recommendations that the Committee makes to the Secretary.

“(b) MEMBERSHIP.—

“(1) IN GENERAL.—The Committee shall consist of not more than 19 members who are appointed by and serve terms of a duration determined by the Secretary. Before filling a position on the Committee, the Secretary shall publish a notice in the Federal Register soliciting nominations for membership on the

Committee.

"(2) REQUIRED MEMBERS.—Subject to paragraph (3), the Secretary shall appoint as members of the Committee—

"(A) 9 United States citizens with active licenses or certificates issued under chapter 71 or merchant mariner documents issued under chapter 73, including—

"(i) 3 deck officers who represent the viewpoint of merchant marine deck officers, of whom—

"(I) 2 shall be licensed for oceans any gross tons;

"(II) 1 shall be licensed for inland river route with a limited or unlimited tonnage;

"(III) 2 shall have a master's license or a master of towing vessels license;

"(IV) 1 shall have significant tanker experience; and

"(V) to the extent practicable—

"(aa) 1 shall represent the viewpoint of labor; and

"(bb) another shall represent a management perspective;

"(ii) 3 engineering officers who represent the viewpoint of merchant marine engineering officers, of whom—

"(I) 2 shall be licensed as chief engineer any horsepower;

"(II) 1 shall be licensed as either a limited chief engineer or a designated duty engineer; and

"(III) to the extent practicable—

"(aa) 1 shall represent a labor viewpoint; and

"(bb) another shall represent a management perspective;

"(iii) 2 unlicensed seamen, of whom—

"(I) 1 shall represent the viewpoint of able-bodied seamen; and

"(II) another shall represent the viewpoint of qualified members of the engine department; and

"(iv) 1 pilot who represents the viewpoint of merchant marine pilots;

"(B) 6 marine educators, including—

"(i) 3 marine educators who represent the viewpoint of maritime academies, including—

"(I) 2 who represent the viewpoint of State maritime academies and are jointly recommended by such State maritime academies; and

"(II) 1 who represents either the viewpoint of the State maritime academies or the United States Merchant Marine Academy; and

"(ii) 3 marine educators who represent the viewpoint of other maritime training institutions, 1 of whom shall represent the viewpoint of the small vessel industry;

"(C) 2 individuals who represent the viewpoint of shipping companies employed in ship operation management; and

"(D) 2 members who are appointed from the general public.

"(3) CONSULTATION.—The Secretary shall consult with the Secretary of Transportation in making an appointment under paragraph (2)(B)(i)(II).

"(c) CHAIRMAN AND VICE CHAIRMAN.—The Secretary shall designate one member of the Committee as the Chairman and one member of the Committee as the Vice Chairman. The Vice Chairman shall act as Chairman in the absence or incapacity of the Chairman, or in the event of a vacancy in the office of the Chairman.

"(d) SUBCOMMITTEES.—The Committee may establish and disestablish subcommittees and working groups for any purpose consistent with this section, subject to conditions imposed by the Committee. Members of the Committee and additional persons drawn from the general public may be assigned to such subcommittees and working groups. Only Committee members may chair subcommittee or working groups.

"(e) TERMINATION.—The Committee shall terminate on

September 30, 2020."

(b) CLERICAL AMENDMENT.—The analysis for such chapter is amended by adding at the end the following:

"8108. Merchant Marine Personnel Advisory Committee.".

SEC. 311. TRAVEL AND SUBSISTENCE.

(a) [46 U.S.C. 2110] TITLE 46, UNITED STATES CODE.—Section 2110 of title 46, United States Code, is amended—

(1) by amending subsection (b) to read as follows:

"(b)(1) In addition to the collection of fees and charges established under subsection (a), in providing a service or thing of value under this subtitle the Secretary may accept in-kind transportation, travel, and subsistence.

"(2) The value of in-kind transportation, travel, and subsistence accepted under this paragraph may not exceed applicable per diem rates set forth in regulations prescribed under section 464 of title 37."

; and

(2) in subsection (c), by striking "subsections (a) and (b)," and inserting "subsection (a),".

(b) [14 U.S.C. 664] TITLE 14, UNITED STATES CODE.—Section 664 of title 14, United States Code, is amended by redesignating subsections (e) though (g) as subsections (f) through (h), respectively, and by inserting after subsection (d) the following:

"(e)(1) In addition to the collection of fees and charges established under this section, in the provision of a service or thing of value by the Coast Guard the Secretary may accept in-kind transportation, travel, and subsistence.

"(2) The value of in-kind transportation, travel, and subsistence accepted under this paragraph may not exceed applicable per diem rates set forth in regulations prescribed under section 464 of title 37."

(c) [14 U.S.C. 664 note] LIMITATION.—The Secretary of the Department in which the Coast Guard is operating may not accept in-kind transportation, travel, or subsistence under section 664(e) of title 14, United States Code, or section 2110(d)(4) of title 46, United States Code, as amended by this section, until the Commandant of the Coast Guard—

(1) amends the Standards of Ethical Conduct for members

and employees of the Coast Guard to include regulations governing the acceptance of in-kind reimbursements; and

(2) notifies the Committee on Commerce, Science, and Transportation of the Senate and the Committee on Transportation and Infrastructure of the House of Representatives of the amendments made under paragraph (1).

SEC. 312. PROMPT INTERGOVERNMENTAL NOTICE OF MARINE CASUALTIES.

Section 6101 of title 46, United States Code, is amended—

(1) by inserting after subsection (b) the following:

"(c) NOTICE TO STATE AND TRIBAL GOVERNMENTS.—Not later than 24 hours after receiving a notice of a major marine casualty under this section, the Secretary shall notify each State or federally recognized Indian tribe that is, or may reasonably be expected to be, affected by such marine casualty."

(2) in subsection (h)—

(A) by striking "(1)"; and

(B) by redesignating subsection (h)(2) as subsection (i) of section 6101, and in such subsection—

(i) by striking "paragraph," and inserting "section,"; and

(ii) by redesignating subparagraphs (A) through (D) as paragraphs (1) through (4); and

(3) by redesignating the last subsection as subsection (j).

SEC. 313. AREA CONTINGENCY PLANS.

Section 311(j)(4) of the Federal Water Pollution Control Act (33 U.S.C. 1321(j)(4)) is amended—

(1) in subparagraph (A), by striking "qualified personnel of Federal, State, and local agencies." and inserting"qualified—

"(i) personnel of Federal, State, and local agencies; and

"(ii) members of federally recognized Indian tribes, where applicable."

(2) in subparagraph (B)(ii)—

(A) by striking "and local" and inserting ", local, and tribal"; and

(B) by striking "wildlife;" and inserting "wildlife,

including advance planning with respect to the closing and reopening of fishing areas following a discharge;";

(3) in subparagraph (B)(iii), by striking "and local" and inserting ", local, and tribal"; and

(4) in subparagraph (C)—

(A) in clause (iv), by striking "and Federal, State, and local agencies" and inserting ", Federal, State, and local agencies, and tribal governments";

(B) by redesignating clauses (vii) and (viii) as clauses (viii) and (ix), respectively; and

(C) by inserting after clause (vi) the following:

"(vii) include a framework for advance planning and decisionmaking with respect to the closing and reopening of fishing areas following a discharge, including protocols and standards for the closing and reopening of fishing areas;"

SEC. 314. INTERNATIONAL ICE PATROL REFORM.

(a) IN GENERAL.—Chapter 803 of title 46, United States Code, is amended—

(1) **[46 U.S.C. 80301]** in section 80301, by adding at the end the following:

"(c) PAYMENTS.—Payments received pursuant to subsection (b)(1) shall be credited to the appropriation for operating expenses of the Coast Guard."

(2) in section 80302—

(A) in subsection (b), by striking "An ice patrol vessel" and inserting "The ice patrol";

(B) in subsection (c)(1), by striking "An ice patrol vessel" and inserting "The ice patrol"; and

(C) in the first sentence of subsection (d), by striking "vessels" and inserting "aircraft"; and

(3) by adding at the end the following:

"SEC. 80304. Limitation on ice patrol data

"Notwithstanding sections 80301 and 80302, data collected by an ice patrol conducted by the Coast Guard under this chapter may not be disseminated to a vessel unless such vessel is—

"(1) documented under the laws of the United States; or

"(2) documented under the laws of a foreign country that made the payment or contribution required under section 80301(b) for the year preceding the year in which the data is collected."

(b) CLERICAL AMENDMENT.—The analysis for such chapter is amended by adding at the end the following:

"80304. Limitation on ice patrol data.".

(c) [46 U.S.C. 80301 note] EFFECTIVE DATE.—This section shall take effect on January 1, 2017.

SEC. 315. [46 U.S.C. 3316] OFFSHORE SUPPLY VESSEL THIRD-PARTY INSPECTION.

Section 3316 of title 46, United States Code, is amended by redesignating subsection (f) as subsection (g), and by inserting after subsection (e) the following:

"(f)(1) Upon request of an owner or operator of an offshore supply vessel, the Secretary shall delegate the authorities set forth in paragraph (1) of subsection (b) with respect to such vessel to a classification society to which a delegation is authorized under that paragraph. A delegation by the Secretary under this subsection shall be used for any vessel inspection and examination function carried out by the Secretary, including the issuance of certificates of inspection and all other related documents.

"(2) If the Secretary determines that a certificate of inspection or related document issued under authority delegated under paragraph (1) of this subsection with respect to a vessel has reduced the operational safety of that vessel, the Secretary may terminate the certificate or document, respectively.

"(3) Not later than 2 years after the date of the enactment of the Howard Coble Coast Guard and Maritime Transportation Act of 2014, and for each year of the subsequent 2-year period, the Secretary shall provide to the Committee on Transportation and Infrastructure of the House of Representatives and the Committee on Commerce, Science, and Transportation of the Senate a report describing—

"(A) the number of vessels for which a delegation was made under paragraph (1);

"(B) any savings in personnel and operational costs incurred by the Coast Guard that resulted from the delegations; and

"(C) based on measurable marine casualty and other data, any impacts of the delegations on the operational safety of vessels for which the delegations were made, and on the crew on those vessels."

SEC. 316. WATCHES.

Section 8104 of title 46, United States Code, is amended—

(1) in subsection (d), by striking "coal passers, firemen, oilers, and water tenders" and inserting "and oilers"; and

(2) in subsection (g)(1), by striking "(except the coal passers, firemen, oilers, and water tenders)".

SEC. 317. [33 U.S.C. 1321 note] COAST GUARD RESPONSE PLAN REQUIREMENTS.

(a) VESSEL RESPONSE PLAN CONTENTS.—The Secretary of the department in which the Coast Guard is operating shall require that each vessel response plan prepared for a mobile offshore drilling unit includes information from the facility response plan prepared for the mobile offshore drilling unit regarding the planned response to a worst case discharge, and to a threat of such a discharge.

(b) DEFINITIONS.—In this section:

(1) MOBILE OFFSHORE DRILLING UNIT.—The term "mobile offshore drilling unit" has the meaning given that term in section 1001 of the Oil Pollution Act of 1990 (33 U.S.C. 2701).

(2) RESPONSE PLAN.—The term "response plan" means a response plan prepared under section 311(j) of the Federal Water Pollution Control Act (33 U.S.C. 1321(j)).

(3) WORST CASE DISCHARGE.—The term "worst case discharge" has the meaning given that term under section 311(a) of the Federal Water Pollution Control Act (33 U.S.C. 1321(a)).

(c) RULE OF CONSTRUCTION.—Nothing in this section shall be construed to require the Coast Guard to review or approve a facility response plan for a mobile offshore drilling unit.

SEC. 318. REGIONAL CITIZENS' ADVISORY COUNCIL.

Section 5002(k)(3) of the Oil Pollution Act of 1990 (33 U.S.C. 2732(k)(3)) is amended by striking "not more than $1,000,000" and inserting "not less than $1,400,000".

SEC. 319. UNINSPECTED PASSENGER VESSELS IN THE UNITED STATES VIRGIN ISLANDS.

(a) **[46 U.S.C. 4105]** IN GENERAL.—Section 4105 of title 46, United States Code, is amended—

(1) by redesignating subsection (b) as subsection (c); and

(2) by inserting after subsection (a) the following:

"(b)(1) In applying this title with respect to an uninspected vessel of less than 24 meters overall in length that carries passengers to or from a port in the United States Virgin Islands, the Secretary shall substitute '12 passengers' for '6 passengers' each place it appears in section 2101(42) if the Secretary determines that the vessel complies with, as applicable to the vessel—

"(A) the Code of Practice for the Safety of Small Commercial Motor Vessels (commonly referred to as the 'Yellow Code'), as published by the U.K. Maritime and Coastguard Agency and in effect on January 1, 2014; or

"(B) the Code of Practice for the Safety of Small Commercial Sailing Vessels (commonly referred to as the 'Blue Code'), as published by such agency and in effect on such date.

"(2) If the Secretary establishes standards to carry out this subsection—

"(A) such standards shall be identical to those established in the Codes of Practice referred to in paragraph (1); and

"(B) on any dates before the date on which such standards are in effect, the Codes of Practice referred to in paragraph (1) shall apply with respect to the vessels referred to in paragraph (1)."

(b) TECHNICAL CORRECTION.—Section 4105(c) of title 46, United States Code, as redesignated by subsection (a)(1) of this section, is amended by striking "Within twenty-four months of the date of enactment of this subsection, the" and inserting "The".

SEC. 320. TREATMENT OF ABANDONED SEAFARERS.

(a) IN GENERAL.—Chapter 111 of title 46, United States Code, is amended by adding at the end the following:

"SEC. 11113. [46 U.S.C. 11113] Treatment of abandoned seafarers

"(a) ABANDONED SEAFARERS FUND.—

"(1) ESTABLISHMENT.—There is established in the Treasury a separate account to be known as the Abandoned Seafarers Fund.

"(2) AUTHORIZED USES.—Amounts in the Fund may be appropriated to the Secretary for use—

"(A) to pay necessary support of a seafarer—

"(i) who—

"(I) was paroled into the United States under section 212(d)(5) of the Immigration and Nationality Act (8 U.S.C. 1182(d)(5)), or for whom the Secretary has requested parole under such section; and

"(II) is involved in an investigation, reporting, documentation, or adjudication of any matter that is related to the administration or enforcement of law by the Coast Guard; or

"(ii) who—

"(I) is physically present in the United States;

"(II) the Secretary determines was abandoned in the United States; and

"(III) has not applied for asylum under the Immigration and Nationality Act (8 U.S.C. 1101 et seq.); and

"(B) to reimburse a vessel owner or operator for the costs of necessary support of a seafarer who has been paroled into the United States to facilitate an investigation, reporting, documentation, or adjudication of any matter that is related to the administration or enforcement of law by the Coast Guard, if—

"(i) the vessel owner or operator is not convicted of a criminal offense related to such matter; or

"(ii) the Secretary determines that reimbursement is appropriate.

"(3) CREDITING OF AMOUNTS TO FUND.—

"(A) IN GENERAL.—Except as provided in subparagraph (B), there shall be credited to the Fund the following:

"(i) Penalties deposited in the Fund under section 9 of the Act to Prevent Pollution from Ships (33 U.S.C. 1908).

"(ii) Amounts reimbursed or recovered under subsection (c).

"(B) LIMITATION.—Amounts may be credited to the Fund under subparagraph (A) only if the unobligated balance of the Fund is less than $5,000,000.

"(4) REPORT REQUIRED.—On the date on which the President submits each budget for a fiscal year pursuant to section 1105 of title 31, the Secretary shall submit to the Committee on Transportation and Infrastructure of the House of Representatives and the Committee on Commerce, Science, and Transportation of the Senate a report that describes—

"(A) the amounts credited to the Fund under paragraph (2) for the preceding fiscal year; and

"(B) amounts in the Fund that were expended for the preceding fiscal year.

"(b) LIMITATION.—Nothing in this section shall be construed—

"(1) to create a private right of action or any other right, benefit, or entitlement to necessary support for any person; or

"(2) to compel the Secretary to pay or reimburse the cost of necessary support.

"(c) REIMBURSEMENT; RECOVERY.—

"(1) IN GENERAL.—A vessel owner or operator shall reimburse the Fund an amount equal to the total amount paid from the Fund for necessary support of a seafarer, if—

"(A) the vessel owner or operator—

"(i) during the course of an investigation,

reporting, documentation, or adjudication of any matter under this Act that the Coast Guard referred to a United States attorney or the Attorney General, fails to provide necessary support of a seafarer who was paroled into the United States to facilitate the investigation, reporting, documentation, or adjudication; and

"(ii) subsequently is—

"(I) convicted of a criminal offense related to such matter; or

"(II) required to reimburse the Fund pursuant to a court order or negotiated settlement related to such matter; or

"(B) the vessel owner or operator abandons a seafarer in the United States, as determined by the Secretary based on substantial evidence.

"(2) ENFORCEMENT.—If a vessel owner or operator fails to reimburse the Fund under paragraph (1) within 60 days after receiving a written, itemized description of reimbursable expenses and a demand for payment, the Secretary may—

"(A) proceed in rem against the vessel on which the seafarer served in the Federal district court for the district in which the vessel is found; and

"(B) withhold or revoke the clearance required under section 60105 for the vessel and any other vessel operated by the same operator (as that term is defined in section 2(9)(a) of the Act to Prevent Pollution from Ships (33 U.S.C. 1901(9)(a)) as the vessel on which the seafarer served.

"(3) OBTAINING CLEARANCE.—A vessel may obtain clearance from the Secretary after it is withheld or revoked under paragraph (2)(B) if the vessel owner or operator—

"(A) reimburses the Fund the amount required under paragraph (1); or

"(B) provides a bond, or other evidence of financial responsibility, sufficient to meet the amount required to be reimbursed under paragraph (1).

"(4) NOTIFICATION REQUIRED.—The Secretary shall notify the vessel at least 72 hours before taking any action under paragraph (2)(B).

"(d) DEFINITIONS.—In this section:

"(1) ABANDONS; ABANDONED.—Each of the terms 'abandons' and 'abandoned' means—

"(A) a vessel owner's or operator's unilateral severance of ties with a seafarer; or

"(B) a vessel owner's or operator's failure to provide necessary support of a seafarer.

"(2) FUND.—The term 'Fund' means the Abandoned Seafarers Fund established under this section.

"(3) NECESSARY SUPPORT.—The term 'necessary support' means normal wages and expenses the Secretary considers reasonable for lodging, subsistence, clothing, medical care (including hospitalization), repatriation, and any other support the Secretary considers to be appropriate.

"(4) SEAFARER.—The term 'seafarer' means an alien crew member who is employed or engaged in any capacity on board a vessel subject to the jurisdiction of the United States.

"(5) VESSEL SUBJECT TO THE JURISDICTION OF THE UNITED STATES.—The term 'vessel subject to the jurisdiction of the United States' has the meaning given that term in section 70502(c), except that it does not include a vessel that is—

"(A) owned, or operated under a bareboat charter, by the United States, a State or political subdivision thereof, or a foreign nation; and

"(B) not engaged in commerce."

(b) CLERICAL AMENDMENT.—The analysis for such chapter is amended by adding at the end the following:

"11113. Treatment of abandoned seafarers.".

(c) CONFORMING AMENDMENT.—Section 9 of the Act to Prevent Pollution from Ships (33 U.S.C. 1908) is amended by adding at the end the following:

"(g) Any penalty collected under subsection (a) or (b) that is not paid under that subsection to the person giving information leading to the conviction or assessment of such penalties shall be deposited in the Abandoned Seafarers Fund established under section 11113 of title 46, United States Code."

SEC. 321. WEBSITE.

(a) [46 U.S.C. 3507] REPORTS TO SECRETARY OF TRANSPORTATION; INCIDENTS AND DETAILS.—Section 3507(g)(3)(A) of title 46, United States Code, is amended—

(1) in clause (ii) by striking "the incident to an Internet based portal maintained by the Secretary" and inserting "each incident specified in clause (i) to the Internet website maintained by the Secretary of Transportation under paragraph (4)(A)"; and

(2) in clause (iii) by striking "based portal maintained by the Secretary" and inserting "website maintained by the Secretary of Transportation under paragraph (4)(A)".

(b) AVAILABILITY OF INCIDENT DATA ON INTERNET.—Section 3507(g)(4) of title 46, United States Code, is amended—

(1) by striking subparagraph (A) and inserting the following:

"(A) WEBSITE.—

"(i) IN GENERAL.—The Secretary of Transportation shall maintain a statistical compilation of all incidents on board a cruise vessel specified in paragraph (3)(A)(i) on an Internet website that provides a numerical accounting of the missing persons and alleged crimes reported under that paragraph without regard to the investigative status of the incident.

"(ii) UPDATES AND OTHER REQUIREMENTS.—The compilation under clause (i) shall—

"(I) be updated not less frequently than quarterly;

"(II) be able to be sorted by cruise line;

"(III) identify each cruise line by name;

"(IV) identify each crime or alleged crime committed or allegedly committed by a passenger or crewmember;

"(V) identify the number of individuals alleged overboard; and

"(VI) include the approximate number of passengers and crew carried by each cruise line during each quarterly reporting period.

"(iii) USER-FRIENDLY FORMAT.—The Secretary of Transportation shall ensure that the compilation, data, and any other information provided on the Internet website maintained under this subparagraph are in a user-friendly format. The Secretary shall, to the greatest extent practicable, use existing commercial off the shelf technology to transfer and establish the website, and shall not independently develop software, or acquire new hardware in operating the site."

; and

(2) in subparagraph (B) by striking "Secretary" and inserting "Secretary of Transportation".

SEC. 322. COAST GUARD REGULATIONS.

(a) IN GENERAL.—Not later than 1 year after the date of the enactment of this Act, the Secretary of the department in which the Coast Guard is operating shall submit to the Committee on Commerce, Science, and Transportation of the Senate and the Committee on Transportation and Infrastructure of the House of Representatives an analysis of the Coast Guard's proposed promulgation of safety and environmental management system requirements for vessels engaged in Outer Continental Shelf activities. The analysis shall include—

(1) a discussion of any new operational, management, design and construction, financial, and other mandates that would be imposed on vessel owners and operators;

(2) an estimate of all associated direct and indirect operational, management, personnel, training, vessel design and construction, record keeping, and other costs;

(3) an identification and justification of any of such proposed requirements that exceed those in international conventions applicable to the design, construction, operation, and management of vessels engaging in United States Outer Continental Shelf activities; and

(4) an identification of exemptions to the proposed requirements, that are based upon vessel classification, tonnage, offshore activity or function, alternative certifications, or any other appropriate criteria.

(b) LIMITATION.—The Secretary may not issue proposed regulations relating to safety and environmental management system requirements for vessels on the United States Outer Continental Shelf for which noticed was published on September 10, 2013 (78 Fed. Reg. 55230) earlier than 6 months after the submittal of the analysis required by subsection (a).

TITLE IV—FEDERAL MARITIME COMMISSION

SEC. 401. AUTHORIZATION OF APPROPRIATIONS.

There is authorized to be appropriated to the Federal Maritime Commission $24,700,000 for fiscal year 2015.

SEC. 402. AWARD OF REPARATIONS.

Section 41305 of title 46, United States Code, is amended—

(1) in subsection (b), by striking ", plus reasonable attorney fees"; and

(2) by adding at the end the following:

"(e) ATTORNEY FEES.—In any action brought under section 41301, the prevailing party may be awarded reasonable attorney fees."

SEC. 403. TERMS OF COMMISSIONERS.

(a) IN GENERAL.—Section 301(b) of title 46, United States Code, is amended—

(1) by amending paragraph (2) to read as follows:

"(2) TERMS.—The term of each Commissioner is 5 years. When the term of a Commissioner ends, the Commissioner may continue to serve until a successor is appointed and qualified, but for a period not to exceed one year. Except as provided in paragraph (3), no individual may serve more than 2 terms."

; and

(2) by redesignating paragraph (3) as paragraph (5), and inserting after paragraph (2) the following:

"(3) VACANCIES.—A vacancy shall be filled in the same manner as the original appointment. An individual appointed to fill a vacancy is appointed only for the unexpired term of the individual being succeeded. An individual appointed to fill a vacancy may serve 2 terms in addition to the remainder of the term for which the predecessor of that individual was appointed.

"(4) CONFLICTS OF INTEREST.—

"(A) LIMITATION ON RELATIONSHIPS WITH REGULATED ENTITIES.—A Commissioner may not have a pecuniary interest in, hold an official relation to, or own stocks or bonds of any entity the Commission regulates under chapter 401 of this title.

"(B) LIMITATION ON OTHER ACTIVITIES.—A Commissioner may not engage in another business, vocation, or employment."

(b) [46 U.S.C. 301 note] APPLICABILITY.—The amendment made by subsection (a)(1) does not apply with respect to a Commissioner of the Federal Maritime Commission appointed and confirmed by the Senate before the date of the enactment of this Act.

TITLE V—ARCTIC MARITIME TRANSPORTATION

SEC. 501. ARCTIC MARITIME TRANSPORTATION.

(a) ARCTIC MARITIME TRANSPORTATION.—Chapter 5 of title 14, United States Code, is amended by inserting after section 89 the following:

"SEC. 90. [14 U.S.C. 90] Arctic maritime transportation

"(a) PURPOSE.—The purpose of this section is to ensure safe and secure maritime shipping in the Arctic including the availability of aids to navigation, vessel escorts, spill response capability, and maritime search and rescue in the Arctic.

"(b) INTERNATIONAL MARITIME ORGANIZATION AGREEMENTS.—To carry out the purpose of this section, the Secretary is encouraged to enter into negotiations through the International Maritime Organization to conclude and execute agreements to promote coordinated action among the United States, Russia, Canada, Iceland, Norway, and Denmark and other seafaring and Arctic nations to ensure, in the Arctic—

"(1) placement and maintenance of aids to navigation;

"(2) appropriate marine safety, tug, and salvage capabilities;

"(3) oil spill prevention and response capability;

"(4) maritime domain awareness, including long-range vessel tracking; and

"(5) search and rescue.

"(c) COORDINATION BY COMMITTEE ON THE MARITIME TRANSPORTATION SYSTEM.—The Committee on the Maritime Transportation System established under section 55501 of title 46, United States Code, shall coordinate the establishment of domestic transportation policies in the Arctic necessary to carry out the purpose of this section.

"(d) AGREEMENTS AND CONTRACTS.—The Secretary may, subject to the availability of appropriations, enter into cooperative agreements, contracts, or other agreements with, or make grants to, individuals and governments to carry out the purpose of this section or any agreements established under subsection (b).

"(e) ICEBREAKING.—The Secretary shall promote safe maritime navigation by means of icebreaking where necessary, feasible, and effective to carry out the purposes of this section.

"(f) ARCTIC DEFINITION.—In this section, the term 'Arctic'? has the meaning given such term in section 112 of the Arctic Research and Policy Act of 1984 (15 U.S.C. 4111)."

(b) CLERICAL AMENDMENT.—The analysis for such chapter is amended by inserting after the item relating to section 89 the following:

"90. Arctic maritime transportation".

(c) CONFORMING AMENDMENT.—Section 307 of the Coast Guard Authorization Act of 2010 (Public Law 111-281; 14 U.S.C. 92 note) is repealed.

SEC. 502. ARCTIC MARITIME DOMAIN AWARENESS.

(a) IN GENERAL.—Chapter 7 of title 14, United States Code, is amended by adding at the end the following:

"SEC. 154. [14 U.S.C. 154] Arctic maritime domain awareness

"(a) IN GENERAL.—The Commandant shall improve maritime domain awareness in the Arctic—

"(1) by promoting interagency cooperation and

coordination;

"(2) by employing joint, interagency, and international capabilities; and

"(3) by facilitating the sharing of information, intelligence, and data related to the Arctic maritime domain between the Coast Guard and departments and agencies listed in subsection (b).

"(b) COORDINATION.—The Commandant shall seek to coordinate the collection, sharing, and use of information, intelligence, and data related to the Arctic maritime domain between the Coast Guard and the following:

"(1) The Department of Homeland Security.

"(2) The Department of Defense.

"(3) The Department of Transportation.

"(4) The Department of State.

"(5) The Department of the Interior.

"(6) The National Aeronautics and Space Administration.

"(7) The National Oceanic and Atmospheric Administration.

"(8) The Environmental Protection Agency.

"(9) The National Science Foundation.

"(10) The Arctic Research Commission.

"(11) Any Federal agency or commission or State the Commandant determines is appropriate.

"(c) COOPERATION.—The Commandant and the head of a department or agency listed in subsection (b) may by agreement, on a reimbursable basis or otherwise, share personnel, services, equipment, and facilities to carry out the requirements of this section.

"(d) 5-YEAR STRATEGIC PLAN.—Not later than January 1, 2016 and every 5 years thereafter, the Commandant shall submit to the Committee on Commerce, Science, and Transportation of the Senate and the Committee on Transportation and Infrastructure of the House of Representatives a 5-year strategic plan to guide interagency and international intergovernmental cooperation and coordination for the purpose of improving maritime domain awareness in the Arctic.

"(e) DEFINITIONS.—In this section the term 'Arctic' has the meaning given that term in section 112 of the Arctic Research and Policy Act of 1984 (15 U.S.C. 4111)."

(b) CLERICAL AMENDMENT.—The analysis for such chapter is amended by inserting after the item relating to section 153 the following:

"154. Arctic maritime domain awareness.".

SEC. 503. IMO POLAR CODE NEGOTIATIONS.

Not later than 30 days after the date of the enactment of this Act, and thereafter with the submission of the budget proposal submitted for each of fiscal years 2016, 2017, and 2018 under section 1105 of title 31, United States Code, the Secretary of the department in which the Coast Guard is operating shall submit to the Committee on Transportation and Infrastructure of the House of Representatives and the Committee on Commerce, Science, and Transportation of the Senate, a report on—

(1) the status of the negotiations at the International Maritime Organization regarding the establishment of a draft international code of safety for ships operating in polar waters, popularly known as the Polar Code, and any amendments proposed by such a code to be made to the International Convention for the Safety of Life at Sea and the International Convention for the Prevention of Pollution from Ships;

(2) the coming into effect of such a code and such amendments for nations that are parties to those conventions;

(3) impacts, for coastal communities located in the Arctic (as that term is defined in the section 112 of the Arctic Research and Policy Act of 1984 (15 U.S.C. 4111)) of such a code or such amendments, on—

(A) the costs of delivering fuel and freight; and

(B) the safety of maritime transportation; and

(4) actions the Secretary must take to implement the requirements of such a code and such amendments.

SEC. 504. FORWARD OPERATING FACILITIES.

The Secretary of the department in which the Coast Guard is operating may construct facilities in the Arctic (as that term is defined in section 112 of the Arctic Research and Policy Act of 1984 (15 U.S.C. 4111). The facilities shall—

(1) support aircraft maintenance, including exhaust ventilation, heat, an engine wash system, fuel, ground support services, and electrical power;

(2) provide shelter for both current helicopter assets and those projected to be located at Air Station Kodiak, Alaska, for at least 20 years; and

(3) include accommodations for personnel.

SEC. 506. ICEBREAKING IN POLAR REGIONS.

(a) IN GENERAL.—Chapter 5 of title 14, United States Code, is amended by inserting after section 86 the following:

"SEC. 87. [14 U.S.C. 87] Icebreaking in polar regions

"The President shall facilitate planning for the design, procurement, maintenance, deployment, and operation of icebreakers as needed to support the statutory missions of the Coast Guard in the polar regions by allocating all funds to support icebreaking operations in such regions, except for recurring incremental costs associated with specific projects, to the Coast Guard."

(b) CLERICAL AMENDMENT.—The analysis for such chapter is amended by inserting after the item relating to section 86 the following:

"87. Icebreaking in polar regions.".

TITLE VI—MISCELLANEOUS

SEC. 601. DISTANT WATER TUNA FLEET.

Section 421 of the Coast Guard and Maritime Transportation Act of 2006 (46 U.S.C. 8103 note) is amended—

(1) by striking subsections (c) and (e); and

(2) by redesignating subsections (d) and (f) as subsections (c) and (d), respectively.

SEC. 602. EXTENSION OF MORATORIUM.

Section 2(a) of Public Law 110-299 (33 U.S.C. 1342 note) is amended by striking "2014" and inserting "2017".

SEC. 603. NATIONAL MARITIME STRATEGY.

(a) IN GENERAL.—Not later than 18 months after the date of the enactment of the John S. McCain National Defense Authorization

Act for Fiscal Year 2019, the Secretary of Transportation, in consultation with the Secretary of the department in which the Coast Guard is operating, shall submit to the Committee on Transportation and Infrastructure of the House of Representatives and the Committee on Commerce, Science, and Transportation of the Senate a national maritime strategy.

(b) CONTENTS.—The strategy required under subsection (a) shall—

(1) identify—

(A) Federal regulations and policies that reduce the competitiveness of United States flag vessels in international transportation markets; and

(B) the impact of reduced cargo flow due to reductions in the number of members of the United States Armed Forces stationed or deployed outside of the United States; and

(2) include recommendations to—

(A) make United States flag vessels more competitive in shipping routes between United States and foreign ports;

(B) increase the use of United States flag vessels to carry cargo imported to and exported from the United States;

(C) ensure compliance by Federal agencies with chapter 553 of title 46, United States Code;

(D) increase the use of third-party inspection and certification authorities to inspect and certify vessels;

(E) increase the use of short sea transportation routes, including routes designated under section 55601(c) of title 46, United States Code, to enhance intermodal freight movements; and

(F) enhance United States shipbuilding capability.

SEC. 604. WAIVERS.

(a) "JOHN CRAIG".—

(1) IN GENERAL.—Section 8902 of title 46, United States Code, shall not apply to the vessel *John Craig* (United States official number D1110613) when such vessel is operating on

the portion of the Kentucky River, Kentucky, located at approximately mile point 158, in Pool Number 9, between Lock and Dam Number 9 and Lock and Dam Number 10.

(2) APPLICATION.—Paragraph (1) shall apply on and after the date on which the Secretary of the department in which the Coast Guard is operating determines that a licensing requirement has been established under Kentucky State law that applies to an operator of the vessel *John Craig*

(b) "F/V WESTERN CHALLENGER".—Notwithstanding section 12132 of title 46, United States Code, the Secretary of the department in which the Coast Guard is operating may issue a certificate of documentation with a coastwise endorsement and fishery endorsement for the *F/V Western Challenger* (IMO number 5388108).

SEC. 605. COMPETITION BY UNITED STATES FLAG VESSELS.

(a) IN GENERAL.—The Commandant of the Coast Guard shall enter into an arrangement with the National Academy of Sciences to conduct an assessment of authorities under subtitle II of title 46, United States Code, that have been delegated to the Coast Guard and that impact the ability of vessels documented under the laws of the United States to effectively compete in international transportation markets.

(b) REVIEW OF DIFFERENCES WITH IMO STANDARDS.—The assessment under subsection (a) shall include a review of differences between United States laws, policies, regulations, and guidance governing the inspection of vessels documented under the laws of the United States and standards set by the International Maritime Organization governing the inspection of vessels.

(c) DEADLINE.—Not later than 180 days after the date on which the Commandant enters into an arrangement with the National Academy of Sciences under subsection (a), the Commandant shall submit to the Committee on Transportation and Infrastructure of the House of Representatives and the Committee on Commerce, Science, and Transportation of the Senate the assessment required under such subsection.

SEC. 606. VESSEL REQUIREMENTS FOR NOTICES OF ARRIVAL AND DEPARTURE AND AUTOMATIC IDENTIFICATION SYSTEM.

Not later than 30 days after the date of the enactment of this

Act, the Secretary of the department in which the Coast Guard is operating shall notify the Committee on Transportation and Infrastructure of the House of Representatives and the Committee on Commerce, Science, and Transportation of the Senate of the status of the final rule that relates to the notice of proposed rulemaking titled "Vessel Requirements for Notices of Arrival and Departure, and Automatic Identification System" and published in the Federal Register on December 16, 2008 (73 Fed. Reg. 76295).

SEC. 607. CONVEYANCE OF COAST GUARD PROPERTY IN ROCHESTER, NEW YORK.

(a) CONVEYANCE AUTHORIZED.—The Commandant of the Coast Guard is authorized to convey, at fair market value, all right, title, and interest of the United States in and to a parcel of real property, consisting of approximately 0.2 acres, that is under the administrative control of the Coast Guard and located at 527 River Street in Rochester, New York.

(b) RIGHT OF FIRST REFUSAL.—The City of Rochester, New York, shall have the right of first refusal with respect to the purchase, at fair market value, of the real property described in subsection (a).

(c) SURVEY.—The exact acreage and legal description of the property described in subsection (a) shall be determined by a survey satisfactory to the Commandant.

(d) FAIR MARKET VALUE.—The fair market value of the property described in subsection (a) shall—

(1) be determined by appraisal; and

(2) be subject to the approval of the Commandant.

(e) COSTS OF CONVEYANCE.—The responsibility for all reasonable and necessary costs, including real estate transaction and environmental documentation costs, associated with a conveyance under subsection (a) shall be determined by the Commandant and the purchaser.

(f) ADDITIONAL TERMS AND CONDITIONS.—The Commandant may require such additional terms and conditions in connection with a conveyance under subsection (a) as the Commandant considers appropriate and reasonable to protect the interests of the United States.

(g) DEPOSIT OF PROCEEDS.—Any proceeds from a conveyance

under subsection (a) shall be deposited in the fund established under section 687 of title 14, United States Code.

SEC. 608. CONVEYANCE OF CERTAIN PROPERTY IN GIG HARBOR, WASHINGTON.

(a) DEFINITIONS.—In this section, the following definitions apply:

(1) CITY.—The term "City" means the city of Gig Harbor, Washington.

(2) PROPERTY.—The term "Property" means the parcel of real property, together with any improvements thereon, consisting of approximately 0.86 acres of fast lands commonly identified as tract 65 of lot 1 of section 8, township 21 north, range 2 east, Willamette Meridian, on the north side of the entrance of Gig Harbor, narrows of Puget Sound, Washington.

(3) SECRETARY.—The term "Secretary" means the Secretary of the Interior.

(b) CONVEYANCE.—

(1) AUTHORITY TO CONVEY.—Not later than 30 days after the date on which the Secretary of the department in which the Coast Guard is operating relinquishes the reservation of the Property for lighthouse purposes, at the request of the City and subject to the requirements of this section, the Secretary shall convey to the City all right, title, and interest of the United States in and to the Property, notwithstanding the land use planning requirements of sections 202 and 203 of the Federal Land Policy and Management Act of 1976 (43 U.S.C. 1712, 1713).

(2) TERMS OF CONVEYANCE.—A conveyance made under paragraph (1) shall be made—

(A) subject to valid existing rights;

(B) at the fair market value as described in subsection (c); and

(C) subject to any other condition that the Secretary may consider appropriate to protect the interests of the United States.

(3) COSTS.—The City shall pay any transaction or administrative costs associated with a conveyance under

paragraph (1), including the costs of the appraisal, title searches, maps, and boundary and cadastral surveys.

(4) CONVEYANCE IS NOT A MAJOR FEDERAL ACTION.—A conveyance under paragraph (1) shall not be considered a major Federal action for purposes of section 102(2) of the National Environmental Policy Act of 1969 (42 U.S.C. 4332(2)).

(c) FAIR MARKET VALUE.—

(1) DETERMINATION.—The fair market value of the Property shall be—

(A) determined by an appraisal conducted by an independent appraiser selected by the Secretary; and

(B) approved by the Secretary in accordance with paragraph (3).

(2) REQUIREMENTS.—An appraisal conducted under paragraph (1) shall—

(A) be conducted in accordance with nationally recognized appraisal standards, including—

(i) the Uniform Appraisal Standards for Federal Land Acquisitions; and

(ii) the Uniform Standards of Professional Appraisal Practice; and

(B) shall reflect the equitable considerations described in paragraph (3).

(3) EQUITABLE CONSIDERATIONS.—In approving the fair market value of the Property under this subsection, the Secretary shall take into consideration matters of equity and fairness, including the City's past and current lease of the Property, any maintenance or improvements by the City to the Property, and such other factors as the Secretary considers appropriate.

(d) REVOCATION; REVERSION.—Effective on and after the date on which a conveyance of the Property is made under subsection (b)(1)—

(1) Executive Order 3528, dated August 9, 1921, is revoked; and

(2) the use of the tide and shore lands belonging to the State of Washington and adjoining and bordering the Property, that were granted to the Government of the United States

pursuant to the Act of the Legislature, State of Washington, approved March 13, 1909, the same being chapter 110 of the Session Laws of 1909, shall revert to the State of Washington.

SEC. 609. VESSEL DETERMINATION.

The vessel assigned United States official number 1205366 is deemed a new vessel effective on the date of delivery of the vessel after January 1, 2012, from a privately owned United States shipyard, if no encumbrances are on record with the Coast Guard at the time of the issuance of the new certificate of documentation for the vessel.

SEC. 610. SAFE VESSEL OPERATION IN THE GREAT LAKES.

The Secretary of the department in which the Coast Guard is operating and the Administrator of the Environmental Protection Agency may not prohibit a vessel operating within the boundaries of any national marine sanctuary that preserves shipwrecks or maritime heritage in the Great Lakes from taking up or discharging ballast water to allow for safe and efficient vessel operation if the uptake or discharge meets all Federal and State ballast water management requirements that would apply if the area were not a marine sanctuary, unless the designation documents for such sanctuary do not allow taking up or discharging ballast water in such sanctuary.

SEC. 611. PARKING FACILITIES.

(a) ALLOCATION AND ASSIGNMENT.—

(1) IN GENERAL.—Subject to the requirements of this section, the Administrator of General Services, in coordination with the Commandant of the Coast Guard, shall allocate and assign the spaces in parking facilities at the Department of Homeland Security St. Elizabeths Campus to allow any member or employee of the Coast Guard, who is assigned to the Campus, to use such spaces.

(2) TIMING.—In carrying out paragraph (1), and in addition to the parking spaces allocated and assigned to Coast Guard members and employees in fiscal year 2014, the Administrator shall allocate and assign not less than—

(A) 300 parking spaces not later than September 30, 2015;

(B) 700 parking spaces not later than September 30, 2016; and

(C) 1,042 parking spaces not later than September 30, 2017.

(3)[1] REIMBURSEMENT.—Through September 30, 2017, additional parking made available under paragraph (2) shall be made available at no cost to the Coast Guard or members and employees of the Coast Guard.

[1] Margin for paragraph (3) is so in law. Probably should be moved to the right in order to conform with margins of paragraphs (1) and (2).

(b) TRANSPORTATION MANAGEMENT REPORT.—Not later than 1 year after the date of the enactment of this Act, and each fiscal year thereafter in which spaces are allocated and assigned under subsection (a)(2), the Administrator shall provide to the Committee on Commerce, Science, and Transportation of the Senate and the Committee on Transportation and Infrastructure of the House of Representatives a report on—

(1) the impact of assigning and allocating parking spaces under subsection (a) on the congestion of roads connecting the St. Elizabeths Campus to the portions of Suitland Parkway and I-295 located in the Anacostia section of the District of Columbia; and

(2) progress made toward completion of essential transportation improvements identified in the Transportation Management Program for the St. Elizabeths Campus.

(c) REALLOCATION.—Notwithstanding subsection (a), the Administrator may revise the allocation and assignment of spaces to members and employees of the Coast Guard made under subsection (a) as necessary to accommodate employees of the Department of Homeland Security, other than the Coast Guard, when such employees are assigned to the St. Elizabeths Campus.

Coast Guard Authorization Act of 2016

Public Law 114-120

As amended through P.L. 117-263

Coast Guard Authorization Act of 2016

[(Public Law 114–120)]

[As Amended Through P.L. 117–263, Enacted December 23, 2022]

AN ACT To authorize appropriations for the Coast Guard for fiscal years 2016 and 2017, and for other purposes.

Be it enacted by the Senate and House of Representatives of the United States of America in Congress assembled,

SECTION 1. SHORT TITLE.

This Act may be cited as the "Coast Guard Authorization Act of 2016".[1]

[1] Section 3503(a) of P.L. 114–328 provides for an amendment to the Coast Guard Authorization Act of 2015 by striking "Coast Guard Authorization Act of 2015" each place it appears (including in quoted material) and inserting "Coast Guard Authorization Act of 2016".

SEC. 2. TABLE OF CONTENTS.

The table of contents for this Act is as follows:

TITLE I—AUTHORIZATIONS

SEC. 101. AUTHORIZATIONS.

(a) IN GENERAL.—Title 14, United States Code, is amended by adding at the end the following:

"PART III—COAST GUARD AUTHORIZATIONS AND REPORTS TO CONGRESS

"Chap. Sec.

"CHAPTER 27—AUTHORIZATIONS

"§ 2702. [14 U.S.C. 2702] Authorization of appropriations

"Funds are authorized to be appropriated for each of fiscal years 2016 and 2017 for necessary expenses of the Coast Guard as follows:

"(1) For the operation and maintenance of the Coast Guard, not otherwise provided for—

"(A) $6,981,036,000 for fiscal year 2016; and

"(B) $6,981,036,000 for fiscal year 2017.

"(2) For the acquisition, construction, renovation, and improvement of aids to navigation, shore facilities, vessels, and aircraft, including equipment related thereto, and for maintenance, rehabilitation, lease, and operation of facilities and equipment—

"(A) $1,945,000,000 for fiscal year 2016; and

"(B) $1,945,000,000 for fiscal year 2017.

"(3) For the Coast Guard Reserve program, including operations and maintenance of the program, personnel and training costs, equipment, and services—

"(A) $140,016,000 for fiscal year 2016; and

"(B) $140,016,000 for fiscal year 2017.

"(4) For the environmental compliance and restoration functions of the Coast Guard under chapter 19 of this title—

"(A) $16,701,000 for fiscal year 2016; and

"(B) $16,701,000 for fiscal year 2017.

"(5) To the Commandant of the Coast Guard for research, development, test, and evaluation of technologies, materials, and human factors directly related to improving the performance of the Coast Guard's mission with respect to search and rescue, aids to navigation, marine safety, marine environmental protection, enforcement of laws and treaties, ice operations, oceanographic research, and defense readiness, and for maintenance, rehabilitation, lease, and operation of facilities and equipment—

"(A) $19,890,000 for fiscal year 2016; and

"(B) $19,890,000 for fiscal year 2017.

"§ 2704. [14 U.S.C. 2704] Authorized levels of military strength and training

"(a) ACTIVE DUTY STRENGTH.—The Coast Guard is authorized an end-of-year strength for active duty personnel of 43,000 for each of fiscal years 2016 and 2017.

"(b) MILITARY TRAINING STUDENT LOADS.—The Coast Guard is authorized average military training student loads for each of fiscal years 2016 and 2017 as follows:

"(1) For recruit and special training, 2,500 student years.

"(2) For flight training, 165 student years.

"(3) For professional training in military and civilian institutions, 350 student years.

"(4) For officer acquisition, 1,200 student years.

"CHAPTER 29—REPORTS

"§ 2904. [14 U.S.C. 2904] Manpower requirements plan

"(a) IN GENERAL.—On the date on which the President submits to the Congress a budget for fiscal year 2017 under section 1105 of title 31, on the date on which the President submits to the Congress a budget for fiscal year 2019 under such section, and every 4 years thereafter, the Commandant shall submit to the Committee on Transportation and Infrastructure of the House of Representatives and the Committee on Commerce, Science, and Transportation of the Senate a manpower requirements plan.

"(b) SCOPE.—A manpower requirements plan submitted under subsection (a) shall include for each mission of the Coast Guard—

"(1) an assessment of all projected mission requirements for the upcoming fiscal year and for each of the 3 fiscal years thereafter;

"(2) the number of active duty, reserve, and civilian personnel assigned or available to fulfill such mission requirements—

"(A) currently; and

"(B) as projected for the upcoming fiscal year and each of the 3 fiscal years thereafter;

"(3) the number of active duty, reserve, and civilian personnel required to fulfill such mission requirements—

"(A) currently; and

"(B) as projected for the upcoming fiscal year and each of the 3 fiscal years thereafter;

"(4) an identification of any capability gaps between mission requirements and mission performance caused by deficiencies in the numbers of personnel available—

"(A) currently; and

"(B) as projected for the upcoming fiscal year and each of the 3 fiscal years thereafter; and

"(5) an identification of the actions the Commandant will take to address capability gaps identified under paragraph (4).

"(c) CONSIDERATION.—In composing a manpower requirements plan for submission under subsection (a), the Commandant shall consider—

"(1) the marine safety strategy required under section 2116 of title 46;

"(2) information on the adequacy of the acquisition workforce included in the most recent report under section 2903 of this title; and

"(3) any other Federal strategic planning effort the Commandant considers appropriate."

(b) REQUIREMENT FOR PRIOR AUTHORIZATION OF APPROPRIATIONS.—Section 662 of title 14, United States Code, is amended—

(1) [14 U.S.C. 2701] by redesignating such section as section 2701;

(2) by transferring such section to appear before section 2702 of such title (as added by subsection (a) of this section); and

(3) by striking paragraphs (1) through (5) and inserting the following:

"(1) For the operation and maintenance of the Coast Guard, not otherwise provided for.

"(2) For the acquisition, construction, renovation, and improvement of aids to navigation, shore facilities, vessels, and aircraft, including equipment related thereto, and for maintenance, rehabilitation, lease, and operation of facilities and equipment.

"(3) For the Coast Guard Reserve program, including operations and maintenance of the program, personnel and training costs, equipment, and services.

"(4) For the environmental compliance and restoration functions of the Coast Guard under chapter 19 of this title.

"(5) For research, development, test, and evaluation of technologies, materials, and human factors directly related to improving the performance of the Coast Guard.

"(6) For alteration or removal of bridges over navigable waters of the United States constituting obstructions to navigation, and for personnel and administrative costs associated with the Alteration of Bridges Program."

(c) AUTHORIZATION OF PERSONNEL END STRENGTHS.—Section 661 of title 14, United States Code, is amended—

(1) [14 U.S.C. 2703] by redesignating such section as section 2703; and

(2) by transferring such section to appear before section 2704 of such title (as added by subsection (a) of this section).

(d) REPORTS.—

(1) TRANSMISSION OF ANNUAL COAST GUARD AUTHORIZATION REQUEST.—Section 662a of title 14, United States Code, is amended—

(A) [14 U.S.C. 2901] by redesignating such section as section 2901;

(B) by transferring such section to appear before section 2904 of such title (as added by subsection (a) of this section); and

(C) in subsection (b)—

(i) in paragraph (1) by striking "described in section 661" and inserting "described in section 2703"; and

(ii) in paragraph (2) by striking "described in section 662" and inserting "described in section 2701".

(2) CAPITAL INVESTMENT PLAN.—Section 663 of title 14, United States Code, is amended—

(A) [14 U.S.C. 2902] by redesignating such section as section 2902; and

(B) by transferring such section to appear after section 2901 of such title (as so redesignated and transferred by paragraph (1) of this subsection).

(3) MAJOR ACQUISITIONS.—Section 569a of title 14, United States Code, is amended—

(A) [14 U.S.C. 2903] by redesignating such section as section 2903;

(B) by transferring such section to appear after section 2902 of such title (as so redesignated and transferred by paragraph (2) of this subsection); and

(C) in subsection (c)(2) by striking "of this subchapter".

(e) ICEBREAKERS.—

(1) ICEBREAKING ON THE GREAT LAKES.—For fiscal years 2016 and 2017, the Commandant of the Coast Guard may use funds made available pursuant to section 2702(2) of title 14, United States Code (as added by subsection (a) of this section) for the selection of a design for and the construction of an icebreaker that is capable of buoy tending to enhance icebreaking capacity on the Great Lakes.

(2) POLAR ICEBREAKING.—Of the amounts authorized to be appropriated under section 2702(2) of title 14, United States Code, as amended by subsection (a), there is authorized to be appropriated to the Coast Guard $4,000,000 for fiscal year 2016 and $10,000,000 for fiscal year 2017 for preacquisition activities for a new polar icebreaker, including initial specification development and feasibility studies.

(f) [14 U.S.C. 569 note] ADDITIONAL SUBMISSIONS.—The Commandant of the Coast Guard shall submit to the Committee on Homeland Security of the House of Representatives—

(1) each plan required under section 2904 of title 14, United States Code, as added by subsection (a) of this section;

(2) each plan required under section 2903(e) of title 14, United States Code, as added by section 206 of this Act;

(3) each plan required under section 2902 of title 14, United States Code, as redesignated by subsection (d) of this section; and

(4) each mission need statement required under section 569 of title 14, United States Code.

SEC. 102. CONFORMING AMENDMENTS.

(a) **[14 U.S.C. 1]** ANALYSIS FOR TITLE 14.—The analysis for title 14, United States Code, is amended by adding after the item relating to part II the following:

"**III. Coast Guard Authorizations and Reports to Congress 2701**".

(b) **[14 U.S.C. 561]** ANALYSIS FOR CHAPTER 15.—The analysis for chapter 15 of title 14, United States Code, is amended by striking the item relating to section 569a.

(c) **[14 U.S.C. 631]** ANALYSIS FOR CHAPTER 17.—The analysis for chapter 17 of title 14, United States Code, is amended by striking the items relating to sections 661, 662, 662a, and 663.

(d) **[14 U.S.C. 2701]** ANALYSIS FOR CHAPTER 27.—The analysis for chapter 27 of title 14, United States Code, as added by section 101(a) of this Act, is amended by inserting—

(1) before the item relating to section 2702 the following:

"2701. Requirement for prior authorization of appropriations.";

and

(2) before the item relating to section 2704 the following:

"2703. Authorization of personnel end strengths.".

(e) **[14 U.S.C. 2901]** ANALYSIS FOR CHAPTER 29.—The analysis for chapter 29 of title 14, United States Code, as added by section 101(a) of this Act, is amended by inserting before the item relating to section 2904 the following:

"2901. Transmission of annual Coast Guard authorization request."2902. Capital investment plan."2903. Major acquisitions.".

(f) MISSION NEED STATEMENT.—Section 569(b) of title 14, United States Code, is amended—

(1) in paragraph (2) by striking "in section 569a(e)" and inserting "in section 2903"; and

(2) in paragraph (3) by striking "under section 663(a)(1)" and inserting "under section 2902(a)(1)".

TITLE II—COAST GUARD

SEC. 201. VICE COMMANDANT.

(a) GRADES AND RATINGS.—Section 41 of title 14, United States Code, is amended by striking "an admiral," and inserting "admirals (two);".

(b) VICE COMMANDANT; APPOINTMENT.—Section 47 of title 14, United States Code, is amended by striking "vice admiral" and inserting "admiral".

(c) CONFORMING AMENDMENT.—Section 51 of title 14, United States Code, is amended—

(1) in subsection (a) by inserting "admiral or" before "vice admiral,";

(2) in subsection (b) by inserting "admiral or" before "vice admiral," each place it appears; and

(3) in subsection (c) by inserting "admiral or" before "vice admiral,".

SEC. 202. VICE ADMIRALS.

Section 50 of title 14, United States Code, is amended—

(1) in subsection (a)—

(A) by striking paragraph (1) and inserting the following:

"(1) The President may—

"(A) designate, within the Coast Guard, no more than five positions of importance and responsibility that shall be held by officers who, while so serving—

"(i) shall have the grade of vice admiral, with the pay and allowances of that grade; and

"(ii) shall perform such duties as the Commandant may prescribe, except that if the President designates five such positions, one position shall be the Chief of Staff of the Coast

Guard; and

"(B) designate, within the executive branch, other than within the Coast Guard or the National Oceanic and Atmospheric Administration, positions of importance and responsibility that shall be held by officers who, while so serving, shall have the grade of vice admiral, with the pay and allowances of that grade."

; and

(B) in paragraph (3)(A) by striking "under paragraph (1)" and inserting "under paragraph (1)(A)"; and

(2) in subsection (b)(2)—

(A) in subparagraph (B) by striking "and" at the end;

(B) by redesignating subparagraph (C) as subparagraph (D); and

(C) by inserting after subparagraph (B) the following:

"(C) at the discretion of the Secretary, while awaiting orders after being relieved from the position, beginning on the day the officer is relieved from the position, but not for more than 60 days; and"

SEC. 203. COAST GUARD REMISSION OF INDEBTEDNESS.

(a) EXPANSION OF AUTHORITY TO REMIT INDEBTEDNESS.—Section 461 of title 14, United States Code, is amended to read as follows:

"SEC. 461. Remission of indebtedness

"The Secretary may have remitted or cancelled any part of a person's indebtedness to the United States or any instrumentality of the United States if—

"(1) the indebtedness was incurred while the person served on active duty as a member of the Coast Guard; and

"(2) the Secretary determines that remitting or cancelling the indebtedness is in the best interest of the United States."

(b) CLERICAL AMENDMENT.—The analysis for chapter 13 of title 14, United States Code, is amended by striking the item relating to section 461 and inserting the following:

"461. Remission of indebtedness.".

SEC. 204. ACQUISITION REFORM.

(a) MINIMUM PERFORMANCE STANDARDS.—Section 572(d)(3) of title 14, United States Code, is amended—

(1) by redesignating subparagraphs (C) through (H) as subparagraphs (E) through (J), respectively;

(2) by redesignating subparagraph (B) as subparagraph (C);

(3) by inserting after subparagraph (A) the following:

"(B) the performance data to be used to determine whether the key performance parameters have been resolved;"

; and

(4) by inserting after subparagraph (C), as redesignated by paragraph (2) of this subsection, the following:

"(D) the results during test and evaluation that will be required to demonstrate that a capability, asset, or subsystem meets performance requirements;"

(b) CAPITAL INVESTMENT PLAN.—Section 2902 of title 14, United States Code, as redesignated and otherwise amended by this Act, is further amended—

(1) in subsection (a)(1)—

(A) in subparagraph (B), by striking "completion;" and inserting "completion based on the proposed appropriations included in the budget;"; and

(B) in subparagraph (D), by striking "at the projected funding levels;" and inserting "based on the proposed appropriations included in the budget;"; and

(2) by redesignating subsection (b) as subsection (c), and inserting after subsection (a) the following:

"(b) NEW CAPITAL ASSETS.—In the fiscal year following each fiscal year for which appropriations are enacted for a new capital asset, the report submitted under subsection (a) shall include—

"(1) an estimated life-cycle cost estimate for the new capital asset;

"(2) an assessment of the impact the new capital asset will have on—

"(A) delivery dates for each capital asset;

"(B) estimated completion dates for each capital asset;

"(C) the total estimated cost to complete each capital asset; and

"(D) other planned construction or improvement projects; and

"(3) recommended funding levels for each capital asset necessary to meet the estimated completion dates and total estimated costs included in the such asset's approved acquisition program baseline."

; and

(3) by amending subsection (c), as so redesignated, to read as follows:

"(c) **[14 U.S.C. 93 note]** DEFINITIONS.—In this section—

"(1) the term 'unfunded priority' means a program or mission requirement that—

"(A) has not been selected for funding in the applicable proposed budget;

"(B) is necessary to fulfill a requirement associated with an operational need; and

"(C) the Commandant would have recommended for inclusion in the applicable proposed budget had additional resources been available or had the requirement emerged before the budget was submitted; and

"(2) the term 'new capital asset' means—

"(A) an acquisition program that does not have an approved acquisition program baseline; or

"(B) the acquisition of a capital asset in excess of the number included in the approved acquisition program baseline."

(c) DAYS AWAY FROM HOMEPORT.—Not later than 1 year after the date of the enactment of this Act, the Commandant of the Coast Guard shall—

(2)[1] notify the Committee on Transportation and Infrastructure of the House of Representatives and the

Committee on Commerce, Science, and Transportation of the Senate of the standard implemented under paragraph (1).

[1] Paragraph (1) of subsection (c) was repealed by section 818(b)(2) of Public Law 115–282.

(d) FIXED WING AIRCRAFT FLEET MIX ANALYSIS.—Not later than September 30, 2016, the Commandant of the Coast Guard shall submit to the Committee on Transportation and Infrastructure of the House of Representatives and the Committee on Commerce, Science, and Transportation of the Senate a revised fleet mix analysis of Coast Guard fixed wing aircraft.

(e) LONG-TERM MAJOR ACQUISITIONS PLAN.—Section 2903 of title 14, United States Code, as redesignated and otherwise amended by this Act, is further amended—

(1) by redesignating subsection (e) as subsection (g); and

(2) by inserting after subsection (d) the following:

"(e) LONG-TERM MAJOR ACQUISITIONS PLAN.—Each report under subsection (a) shall include a plan that describes for the upcoming fiscal year, and for each of the 20 fiscal years thereafter—

"(1) the numbers and types of cutters and aircraft to be decommissioned;

"(2) the numbers and types of cutters and aircraft to be acquired to—

"(A) replace the cutters and aircraft identified under paragraph (1); or

"(B) address an identified capability gap; and

"(3) the estimated level of funding in each fiscal year required to—

"(A) acquire the cutters and aircraft identified under paragraph (2);

"(B) acquire related command, control, communications, computer, intelligence, surveillance, and reconnaissance systems; and

"(C) acquire, construct, or renovate shoreside infrastructure.

"(f) QUARTERLY UPDATES ON RISKS OF PROGRAMS.—

"(1) IN GENERAL.—Not later than 15 days after the end of each fiscal year quarter, the Commandant of the Coast Guard shall submit to the committees of Congress specified in subsection (a) an update setting forth a current assessment of the risks associated with all current major acquisition programs.

"(2) ELEMENTS.—Each update under this subsection shall set forth, for each current major acquisition program, the following:

"(A) The top five current risks to such program.

"(B) Any failure of such program to demonstrate a key performance parameter or threshold during operational test and evaluation conducted during the fiscal year quarter preceding such update.

"(C) Whether there has been any decision during such fiscal year quarter to order full-rate production before all key performance parameters or thresholds are met.

"(D) Whether there has been any breach of major acquisition program cost (as defined by the Major Systems Acquisition Manual) during such fiscal year quarter.

"(E) Whether there has been any breach of major acquisition program schedule (as so defined) during such fiscal year quarter."

SEC. 205. AUXILIARY JURISDICTION.

(a) IN GENERAL.—Section 822 of title 14, United States Code, is amended—

(1) by striking "The purpose" and inserting the following:

"(a) IN GENERAL.—The purpose"

; and

(2) by adding at the end the following:

"(b) LIMITATION.—The Auxiliary may conduct a patrol of a waterway, or a portion thereof, only if—

"(1) the Commandant has determined such waterway, or portion thereof, is navigable for purposes of the jurisdiction of the Coast Guard; or

"(2) a State or other proper authority has requested such patrol pursuant to section 141 of this title or section 13109 of title 46."

(b) NOTIFICATION.—The Commandant of the Coast Guard shall—

(1) review the waterways patrolled by the Coast Guard Auxiliary in the most recently completed fiscal year to determine whether such waterways are eligible or ineligible for patrol under section 822(b) of title 14, United States Code (as added by subsection (a)); and

(2) not later than 180 days after the date of the enactment of this Act, provide to the Committee on Transportation and Infrastructure of the House of Representatives and the Committee on Commerce, Science, and Transportation of the Senate a written notification of—

(A) any waterways determined ineligible for patrol under paragraph (1); and

(B) the actions taken by the Commandant to ensure Auxiliary patrols do not occur on such waterways.

SEC. 206. COAST GUARD COMMUNITIES.

Section 409 of the Coast Guard Authorization Act of 1998 (14 U.S.C. 639 note) is amended in the second sentence by striking "90 days" and inserting "30 days".

SEC. 207. POLAR ICEBREAKERS. **[**Subsection (a) was repealed by section 311(d)(3) of Public Law 115–282.**]**

(b) "POLAR SEA" MATERIEL CONDITION ASSESSMENT AND SERVICE LIFE EXTENSION.—Section 222 of the Coast Guard and Maritime Transportation Act of 2012 (Public Law 112-213; 126 Stat. 1560) is amended—

(1) by amending subsection (a) to read as follows:

"(a) IN GENERAL.—Not later than 1 year after the date of the enactment of the Coast Guard Authorization Act of 2016, the Secretary of the department in which the Coast Guard is operating shall—

"(1) complete a materiel condition assessment with respect to the Polar Sea;

"(2) make a determination of whether it is cost effective

to reactivate the Polar Sea compared with other options to provide icebreaking services as part of a strategy to maintain polar icebreaking services; and

"(3) submit to the Committee on Transportation and Infrastructure and the Committee on Science, Space, and Technology of the House of Representatives and the Committee on Commerce, Science, and Transportation of the Senate—

"(A) the assessment required under paragraph (1); and

"(B) written notification of the determination required under paragraph (2)."

(2) in subsection (b) by striking "analysis" and inserting "written notification";

(3) by striking subsection (c);

(4) by redesignating subsections (d) through (h) as subsections (c) through (g), respectively;

(5) in subsection (c) (as redesignated by paragraph (4) of this section)—

(A) in paragraph (1)—

(i) in subparagraph (A) by striking "based on the analysis required"; and

(ii) in subparagraph (C) by striking "analysis" and inserting "written notification";

(B) in paragraph (2)—

(i) by striking "analysis" each place it appears and inserting "written notification";

(ii) by striking "subsection (a)" and inserting "subsection (a)(3)(B)";

(iii) by striking "subsection (c)" each place it appears and inserting "that subsection"; and

(iv) by striking "under subsection (a)(5)"; and

(C) in paragraph (3)—

(i) by striking "in the analysis submitted under this section";

(ii) by striking "(a)(5)" and inserting "(a)";

(iii) by striking "then" and all that follows through "(A)" and inserting "then";

(iv) by striking "; or" and inserting a period; and

(v) by striking subparagraph (B); and

(6) in subsection (d) (as redesignated by paragraph (4) of this subsection) by striking "in subsection (d)" and inserting "in subsection (c)".

SEC. 208. AIR FACILITY CLOSURES.

(a) IN GENERAL.—Chapter 17 of title 14, United States Code, is amended by inserting after section 676 the following:

"SEC. 676a. [14 U.S.C. 676a] Air facility closures

"(a) PROHIBITION.—

"(1) IN GENERAL.—The Coast Guard may not—

"(A) close a Coast Guard air facility that was in operation on November 30, 2014; or

"(B) retire, transfer, relocate, or deploy an aviation asset from an air facility described in subparagraph (A) for the purpose of closing such facility.

"(2) SUNSET.—Paragraph (1) shall have no force or effect beginning on the later of—

"(A) January 1, 2018; or

"(B) the date on which the Secretary submits to the Committee on Transportation and Infrastructure of the House of Representatives, and to the Committee on Commerce, Science, and Transportation of the Senate, rotary wing strategic plans prepared in accordance with section 208(b) of the Coast Guard Authorization Act of 2016.

"(b) CLOSURES.—

"(1) IN GENERAL.—Beginning on January 1, 2018, the Secretary may not close a Coast Guard air facility, except as specified by this section.

"(2) DETERMINATIONS.—The Secretary may not propose closing or terminating operations at a Coast Guard air facility unless the Secretary determines that—

"(A) remaining search and rescue capabilities maintain

the safety of the maritime public in the area of the air facility;

"(B) regional or local prevailing weather and marine conditions, including water temperatures or unusual tide and current conditions, do not require continued operation of the air facility; and

"(C) Coast Guard search and rescue standards related to search and response times are met.

"(3) PUBLIC NOTICE AND COMMENT.—Prior to closing an air facility, the Secretary shall provide opportunities for public comment, including the convening of public meetings in communities in the area of responsibility of the air facility with regard to the proposed closure or cessation of operations at the air facility.

"(4) NOTICE TO CONGRESS.—Prior to closure, cessation of operations, or any significant reduction in personnel and use of a Coast Guard air facility that is in operation on or after December 31, 2015, the Secretary shall—

"(A) submit to the Congress a proposal for such closure, cessation, or reduction in operations along with the budget of the President submitted to Congress under section 1105(a) of title 31 for the fiscal year in which the action will be carried out; and

"(B) not later than 7 days after the date a proposal for an air facility is submitted pursuant to subparagraph (A), provide written notice of such proposal to each of the following:

"(i) Each member of the House of Representatives who represents a district in which the air facility is located.

"(ii) Each member of the Senate who represents a State in which the air facility is located.

"(iii) Each member of the House of Representatives who represents a district in which assets of the air facility conduct search and rescue operations.

"(iv) Each member of the Senate who represents a State in which assets of the air facility conduct search and rescue operations.

"(v) The Committee on Appropriations of the House of Representatives.

"(vi) The Committee on Transportation and Infrastructure of the House of Representatives.

"(vii) The Committee on Appropriations of the Senate.

"(viii) The Committee on Commerce, Science, and Transportation of the Senate.

"(c) OPERATIONAL FLEXIBILITY.—The Secretary may implement any reasonable management efficiencies within the air station and air facility network, such as modifying the operational posture of units or reallocating resources as necessary to ensure the safety of the maritime public nationwide."

(b) ROTARY WING STRATEGIC PLANS.—

(1) IN GENERAL.—The Secretary of the department in which the Coast Guard is operating shall prepare the plans specified in paragraph (2) to adequately address contingencies arising from potential future aviation casualties or the planned or unplanned retirement of rotary wing airframes to avoid to the greatest extent practicable any substantial gap or diminishment in Coast Guard operational capabilities.

(2) ROTARY WING STRATEGIC PLANS.—

(A) ROTARY WING CONTINGENCY PLAN.—Not later than 1 year after the date of enactment of this Act, the Secretary of the department in which the Coast Guard is operating shall develop and submit to the Committee on Transportation and Infrastructure of the House of Representatives and the Committee on Commerce, Science, and Transportation of the Senate a contingency plan—

(i) to address the planned or unplanned losses of rotary wing airframes;

(ii) to reallocate resources as necessary to ensure the safety of the maritime public nationwide; and

(iii) to ensure the operational posture of Coast Guard units.

(B) ROTARY WING REPLACEMENT CAPITAL INVESTMENT PLAN.—

(i) IN GENERAL.—Not later than 2 years after the

date of enactment of this Act, the Secretary of the department in which the Coast Guard is operating shall develop and submit to the Committee on Transportation and Infrastructure of the House of Representatives and the Committee on Commerce, Science, and Transportation of the Senate a capital investment plan for the acquisition of new rotary wing airframes to replace the Coast Guard's legacy helicopters and fulfil all existing mission requirements.

(ii) REQUIREMENTS.—The plan developed under this subparagraph shall provide—

(I) a total estimated cost for completion;

(II) a timetable for completion of the acquisition project and phased in transition to new airframes; and

(III) projected annual funding levels for each fiscal year.

(c) TECHNICAL AND CONFORMING AMENDMENTS.—

(1) [14 U.S.C. 631] ANALYSIS FOR CHAPTER 17.—The analysis for chapter 17 of title 14, United States Code, is amended by inserting after the item relating to section 676 the following:

"676a. Air facility closures.".

(2) REPEAL OF PROHIBITION.—Section 225 of the Howard Coble Coast Guard and Maritime Transportation Act of 2014 (Public Law 113-281; 128 Stat. 3022) is amended—

(A) by striking subsection (b); and

(B) by striking "(a) In General.—".

SEC. 209. TECHNICAL CORRECTIONS TO TITLE 14, UNITED STATES CODE.

Title 14, United States Code, as amended by this Act, is further amended—

(1) [14 U.S.C. 1] in the analysis for part I, by striking the item relating to chapter 19 and inserting the following:

"**19.** Environmental Compliance and Restoration Program **690**";

(2) in section 46(a), by striking "subsection" and inserting "section";

(3) in section 47, in the section heading by striking "commandant" and inserting "Commandant";

(4) in section 93(f), by striking paragraph (2) and inserting the following:

"(2) LIMITATION.—The Commandant may lease submerged lands and tidelands under paragraph (1) only if—

"(A) the lease is for cash exclusively;

"(B) the lease amount is equal to the fair market value of the use of the leased submerged lands or tidelands for the period during which such lands are leased, as determined by the Commandant;

"(C) the lease does not provide authority to or commit the Coast Guard to use or support any improvements to such submerged lands and tidelands, or obtain goods and services from the lessee; and

"(D) proceeds from the lease are deposited in the Coast Guard Housing Fund established under section 687."

(5) **[14 U.S.C. 181]** in the analysis for chapter 9, by striking the item relating to section 199 and inserting the following:

"199. Marine safety curriculum.";

(6) in section 427(b)(2), by striking "this chapter" and inserting "chapter 61 of title 10";

(7) **[14 U.S.C. 561]** in the analysis for chapter 15 before the item relating to section 571, by striking the following:

"Sec."

(8) in section 581(5)(B), by striking "$300,000,0000," and inserting "$300,000,000,";

(9) in section 637(c)(3), in the matter preceding subparagraph (A) by inserting "it is" before "any";

(10) in section 641(d)(3), by striking "Guard, installation" and inserting "Guard installation";

(11) in section 691(c)(3), by striking "state" and inserting "State";

(12) **[14 U.S.C. 701]** in the analysis for chapter 21—

(A) by striking the item relating to section 709 and inserting the following:

"709. Reserve student aviation pilots; Reserve aviation pilots; appointments in commissioned grade.";

and

(B) by striking the item relating to section 740 and inserting the following:

"740. Failure of selection and removal from an active status.";

(13) in section 742(c), by striking "subsection" and inserting "subsections";

(14) in section 821(b)(1), by striking "Chapter 26" and inserting "Chapter 171"; and

(15) in section 823a(b)(1), by striking "Chapter 26" and inserting "Chapter 171".

SEC. 210. [14 U.S.C. 81 note] DISCONTINUANCE OF AN AID TO NAVIGATION.

(a) IN GENERAL.—Not later than 180 days after the date of the enactment of this Act, the Secretary of the department in which the Coast Guard is operating shall establish a process for the discontinuance of an aid to navigation (other than a seasonal or temporary aid) established, maintained, or operated by the Coast Guard.

(b) REQUIREMENT.—The process established under subsection (a) shall include procedures to notify the public of any discontinuance of an aid to navigation described in that subsection.

(c) CONSULTATION.—In establishing a process under subsection (a), the Secretary shall consult with and consider any recommendations of the Navigation Safety Advisory Council.

(d) NOTIFICATION.—Not later than 30 days after establishing a process under subsection (a), the Secretary shall notify the Committee on Transportation and Infrastructure of the House of Representatives and the Committee on Commerce, Science, and Transportation of the Senate of the process established.

SEC. 211. MISSION PERFORMANCE MEASURES.

Not later than 1 year after the date of the enactment of this Act, the Comptroller General of the United States shall submit to the Committee on Transportation and Infrastructure and the Committee on Homeland Security of the House of Representatives and the Committee on Commerce, Science, and Transportation of the Senate an assessment of the efficacy of the Coast Guard's Standard Operational Planning Process with respect to annual mission performance measures.

SEC. 212. [6 U.S.C. 194 note] COMMUNICATIONS.

(a) IN GENERAL.—If the Secretary of Homeland Security determines that there are at least two communications systems described under paragraph (1)(B) and certified under paragraph (2), the Secretary shall establish and carry out a pilot program across not less than three components of the Department of Homeland Security to assess the effectiveness of a communications system that—

(1) provides for—

(A) multiagency collaboration and interoperability; and

(B) wide-area, secure, and peer-invitation- and-acceptance-based multimedia communications;

(2) is certified by the Department of Defense Joint Interoperability Test Center; and

(3) is composed of commercially available, off-the-shelf technology.

(b) ASSESSMENT.—Not later than 6 months after the date on which the pilot program is completed, the Secretary shall submit to the Committee on Transportation and Infrastructure and the Committee on Homeland Security of the House of Representatives and the Committee on Commerce, Science, and Transportation and the Committee Homeland Security and Governmental Affairs of the Senate an assessment of the pilot program, including the impacts of the program with respect to interagency and Coast Guard response capabilities.

(c) STRATEGY.—The pilot program shall be consistent with the strategy required by the Department of Homeland Security Interoperable Communications Act (Public Law 114-29).

(d) TIMING.—The pilot program shall commence within 90 days after the date of the enactment of this Act or within 60 days after the completion of the strategy required by the Department of Homeland Security Interoperable Communications Act (Public Law 114-29), whichever is later.

SEC. 213. [14 U.S.C. 470 note] COAST GUARD GRADUATE MARITIME OPERATIONS EDUCATION.

Not later than 1 year after the date of the enactment of this Act, the Secretary of the department in which the Coast Guard is operating shall establish an education program, for members and employees of the Coast Guard, that—

(1) offers a master's degree in maritime operations;

(2) is relevant to the professional development of such members and employees;

(3) provides resident and distant education options, including the ability to utilize both options; and

(4) to the greatest extent practicable, is conducted using existing academic programs at an accredited public academic institution that—

(A) is located near a significant number of Coast Guard, maritime, and other Department of Homeland Security law enforcement personnel; and

(B) has an ability to simulate operations normally conducted at a command center.

SEC. 214. PROFESSIONAL DEVELOPMENT.

(a) MULTIRATER ASSESSMENT.—

(1) IN GENERAL.—Chapter 11 of title 14, United States Code, is amended by inserting after section 428 the following:

"SEC. 429. [14 U.S.C. 429] Multirater assessment of certain personnel

"(a) MULTIRATER ASSESSMENT OF CERTAIN PERSONNEL.—

"(1) IN GENERAL.—Commencing not later than one year after the date of the enactment of the Coast Guard Authorization Act of 2016, the Commandant of the Coast Guard shall develop and implement a plan to conduct every two years a multirater assessment for each of the following:

"(A) Each flag officer of the Coast Guard.

"(B) Each member of the Senior Executive Service of the Coast Guard.

"(C) Each officer of the Coast Guard nominated for promotion to the grade of flag officer.

"(2) POST-ASSESSMENT ELEMENTS.—Following an assessment of an individual pursuant to paragraph (1), the individual shall be provided appropriate post-assessment counseling and leadership coaching.

"(b) MULTIRATER ASSESSMENT DEFINED.—In this section, the term 'multirater assessment' means a review that seeks opinion from members senior to the reviewee and the peers and subordinates of the reviewee."

(2) [14 U.S.C. 211] CLERICAL AMENDMENT.—The analysis at the beginning of such chapter is amended by inserting after the item related to section 428 the following:

"429. Multirater assessment of certain personnel.".

(b) [14 U.S.C. 60] TRAINING COURSE ON WORKINGS OF CONGRESS.—

(1) IN GENERAL.—Chapter 3 of title 14, United States Code, is amended by adding at the end the following:

"SEC. 60. Training course on workings of Congress

"(a) IN GENERAL.—Not later than 180 days after the date of the enactment of the Coast Guard Authorization Act of 2016, the Commandant, in consultation with the Superintendent of the Coast Guard Academy and such other individuals and organizations as the Commandant considers appropriate, shall develop a training course on the workings of the Congress and offer that training course at least once each year.

"(b) COURSE SUBJECT MATTER.—The training course required by this section shall provide an overview and introduction to the Congress and the Federal legislative process, including—

"(1) the history and structure of the Congress and the committee systems of the House of Representatives and the Senate, including the functions and responsibilities of the Committee on Transportation and Infrastructure of the House of Representatives and the Committee on Commerce, Science, and Transportation of the Senate;

"(2) the documents produced by the Congress, including bills, resolutions, committee reports, and conference reports, and the purposes and functions of those documents;

"(3) the legislative processes and rules of the House

of Representatives and the Senate, including similarities and differences between the two processes and rules, including—

"(A) the congressional budget process;

"(B) the congressional authorization and appropriation processes;

"(C) the Senate advice and consent process for Presidential nominees;

"(D) the Senate advice and consent process for treaty ratification;

"(4) the roles of Members of Congress and congressional staff in the legislative process; and

"(5) the concept and underlying purposes of congressional oversight within our governance framework of separation of powers.

"(c) LECTURERS AND PANELISTS.—

"(1) OUTSIDE EXPERTS.—The Commandant shall ensure that not less than 60 percent of the lecturers, panelists, and other individuals providing education and instruction as part of the training course required by this section are experts on the Congress and the Federal legislative process who are not employed by the executive branch of the Federal Government.

"(2) AUTHORITY TO ACCEPT PRO BONO SERVICES.—In satisfying the requirement under paragraph (1), the Commandant shall seek, and may accept, educational and instructional services of lecturers, panelists, and other individuals and organizations provided to the Coast Guard on a pro bono basis.

"(d) COMPLETION OF REQUIRED TRAINING.—

"(1) CURRENT FLAG OFFICERS AND EMPLOYEES.—A Coast Guard flag officer appointed or assigned to a billet in the National Capital Region on the date of the enactment of this section, and a Coast Guard Senior Executive Service employee employed in the National Capital Region on the date of the enactment of this section, shall complete a training course that meets the requirements of this section within 60 days after the date on which the Commandant completes the development of the training course.

"(2) NEW FLAG OFFICERS AND EMPLOYEES.—A Coast Guard flag officer who is newly appointed or assigned to a billet in the National Capital Region, and a Coast Guard Senior Executive Service employee who is newly employed in the National Capital Region, shall complete a training course that meets the requirements of this section not later than 60 days after reporting for duty."

(2) **[14 U.S.C. 41]** CLERICAL AMENDMENT.—The analysis at the beginning of such chapter is amended by adding at the end the following:

"60. Training course on workings of Congress.".

(c) REPORT ON LEADERSHIP DEVELOPMENT.—

(1) IN GENERAL.—Not later than 180 days after the date of the enactment of this Act, the Commandant of the Coast Guard shall submit to the Committee on Commerce, Science, and Transportation of the Senate and the Committee on Transportation and Infrastructure of the House of Representatives a report on Coast Guard leadership development.

(2) CONTENTS.—The report shall include the following:

(A) An assessment of the feasibility of—

(i) all officers (other than officers covered by section 429(a) of title 14, United States Code, as amended by this section) completing a multirater assessment;

(ii) all members (other than officers covered by such section) in command positions completing a multirater assessment;

(iii) all enlisted members in a supervisory position completing a multirater assessment; and

(iv) members completing periodic multirater assessments.

(B) Such recommendations as the Commandant considers appropriate for the implementation or expansion of a multirater assessment in the personnel development programs of the Coast Guard.

(C) An overview of each of the current leadership

development courses of the Coast Guard, an assessment of the feasibility of the expansion of any such course, and a description of the resources, if any, required to expand such courses.

(D) An assessment on the state of leadership training in the Coast Guard, and recommendations on the implementation of a policy to prevent leadership that has adverse effects on subordinates, the organization, or mission performance, including—

(i) a description of methods that will be used by the Coast Guard to identify, monitor, and counsel individuals whose leadership may have adverse effects on subordinates, the organization, or mission performance;

(ii) the implementation of leadership recognition training to recognize such leadership in one's self and others;

(iii) the establishment of procedures for the administrative separation of leaders whose leadership may have adverse effects on subordinates, the organization, or mission performance; and

(iv) a description of the resources needed to implement this subsection.

SEC. 215. SENIOR ENLISTED MEMBER CONTINUATION BOARDS.

(a) IN GENERAL.—Section 357 of title 14, United States Code, is amended—

(1) by striking subsections (a) through (h) and subsection (j); and

(2) in subsection (i), by striking "(i)".

(b) CONFORMING AND CLERICAL AMENDMENTS.—

(1) HEADING AMENDMENT.—The heading of such section is amended to read as follows:

"SEC. 357. Retirement of enlisted members: increase in retired pay"

(2) [14 U.S.C. 211] CLERICAL AMENDMENT.—The analysis at the beginning of chapter 11 of such title is amended by striking the item relating to such section and inserting the

following:

"357. Retirement of enlisted members: increase in retired pay.".

SEC. 216. COAST GUARD MEMBER PAY.

(a) ANNUAL AUDIT OF PAY AND ALLOWANCES OF MEMBERS UNDERGOING PERMANENT CHANGE OF STATION.—

(1) IN GENERAL.—Chapter 13 of title 14, United States Code, is amended by adding at the end the following:

"SEC. 519. [14 U.S.C. 519] Annual audit of pay and allowances of members undergoing permanent change of station

"The Commandant shall conduct each calendar year an audit of member pay and allowances for the members who transferred to new units during such calendar year. The audit for a calendar year shall be completed by the end of the calendar year."

(2) [14 U.S.C. 461] CLERICAL AMENDMENT.—The analysis at the beginning of such chapter is amended by adding at the end the following:

"519. Annual audit of pay and allowances of members undergoing permanent change of station.".

(b) REPORT.—Not later than 180 days after the date of the enactment of this Act, the Commandant of the Coast Guard shall submit to the Committee on Commerce, Science, and Transportation of the Senate and the Committee on Transportation and Infrastructure of the House of Representatives a report on alternative methods for notifying members of the Coast Guard of their monthly earnings. The report shall include—

(1) an assessment of the feasibility of providing members a monthly notification of their earnings, categorized by pay and allowance type; and

(2) a description and assessment of mechanisms that may be used to provide members with notification of their earnings, categorized by pay and allowance type.[Section 217 was repealed by section 722(c) of Public Law 114-328.]

SEC. 218. PARTICIPATION OF THE COAST GUARD ACADEMY IN FEDERAL, STATE, OR OTHER EDUCATIONAL RESEARCH GRANTS.

Section 196 of title 14, United States Code, is amended—

(1) by inserting "(a) In General.—" before the first sentence; and

(2) by adding at the end the following:

"(b) QUALIFIED ORGANIZATIONS.—

"(1) IN GENERAL.—The Commandant of the Coast Guard may—

"(A) enter into a contract, cooperative agreement, lease, or licensing agreement with a qualified organization;

"(B) allow a qualified organization to use, at no cost, personal property of the Coast Guard; and

"(C) notwithstanding section 93, accept funds, supplies, and services from a qualified organization.

"(2) SOLE-SOURCE BASIS.—Notwithstanding chapter 65 of title 31 and chapter 137 of title 10, the Commandant may enter into a contract or cooperative agreement under paragraph (1)(A) on a sole-source basis.

"(3) MAINTAINING FAIRNESS, OBJECTIVITY, AND INTEGRITY.—The Commandant shall ensure that contributions under this subsection do not—

"(A) reflect unfavorably on the ability of the Coast Guard, any of its employees, or any member of the armed forces to carry out any responsibility or duty in a fair and objective manner; or

"(B) compromise the integrity or appearance of integrity of any program of the Coast Guard, or any individual involved in such a program.

"(4) LIMITATION.—For purposes of this subsection, employees or personnel of a qualified organization shall not be employees of the United States.

"(5) QUALIFIED ORGANIZATION DEFINED.—In this subsection the term 'qualified organization' means an organization—

"(A) described under section 501(c)(3) of the Internal Revenue Code of 1986 and exempt from taxation under section 501(a) of that Code; and

"(B) established by the Coast Guard Academy Alumni Association solely for the purpose of supporting academic research and applying for and administering Federal, State, or other educational research grants on behalf of the Coast Guard Academy."

SEC. 219. NATIONAL COAST GUARD MUSEUM.

Section 98(b) of title 14, United States Code, is amended—

(1) in paragraph (1), by striking "any appropriated Federal funds for" and insert "any funds appropriated to the Coast Guard on"; and

(2) in paragraph (2), by striking "artifacts." and inserting "artifacts, including the design, fabrication, and installation of exhibits or displays in which such artifacts are included.".

SEC. 220. INVESTIGATIONS.

(a) IN GENERAL.—Chapter 11 of title 14, United States Code, is further amended by adding at the end the following:

"SEC. 430. [14 U.S.C. 430] Investigations of flag officers and Senior Executive Service employees

"In conducting an investigation into an allegation of misconduct by a flag officer or member of the Senior Executive Service serving in the Coast Guard, the Inspector General of the Department of Homeland Security shall—

"(1) conduct the investigation in a manner consistent with Department of Defense policies for such an investigation; and

"(2) consult with the Inspector General of the Department of Defense."

(b) **[14 U.S.C. 211]** CLERICAL AMENDMENT.—The analysis at the beginning of such chapter is further amended by inserting after the item related to section 429 the following:

"430. Investigations of flag officers and Senior Executive Service employees.".

SEC. 221. [10 U.S.C. 1413a note] CLARIFICATION OF ELIGIBILITY OF MEMBERS OF THE COAST GUARD FOR COMBAT-RELATED SPECIAL COMPENSATION.

(a) CONSIDERATION OF ELIGIBILITY.—

(1) IN GENERAL.—Not later than 90 days after the date of the enactment of this Act, the Secretary of the department in which the Coast Guard is operating shall issue procedures and criteria to use in determining whether the disability of a member of the Coast Guard is a combat-related disability for purposes of the eligibility of such member for combat-related

special compensation under section 1413a of title 10, United States Code. Such procedures and criteria shall include the procedures and criteria prescribed by the Secretary of Defense pursuant to subsection (e)(2) of such section. Such procedures and criteria shall apply in determining whether the disability of a member of the Coast Guard is a combat-related disability for purposes of determining the eligibility of such member for combat-related special compensation under such section.

(2) DISABILITY FOR WHICH A DETERMINATION IS MADE.—For the purposes of this section, and in the case of a member of the Coast Guard, a disability under section 1413a(e)(2)(B) of title 10, United States Code, includes a disability incurred during aviation duty, diving duty, rescue swimmer or similar duty, hazardous service duty onboard a small vessel (such as duty as a surfman), or a duty in which chemical or other hazardous material exposure has occurred (such as during marine inspections or pollution response activities)—

(A) in the performance of duties for which special or incentive pay was paid pursuant to section 301, 301a, 304, 307, 334, or 351 of title 37, United States Code;

(B) in the performance of duties related to a statutory mission of the Coast Guard under section 888(a) of the Homeland Security Act of 2002 (6 U.S.C. 468(a)); or

(C) while engaged in a training exercise for the performance of a duty described in subparagraphs (A) and (B).

(b) APPLICABILITY OF PROCEDURES AND CRITERIA.—The procedures and criteria issued pursuant to subsection (a) shall apply to disabilities described in that subsection that are incurred on or after the effective date provided in section 636(a)(2) of the Bob Stump National Defense Authorization Act for Fiscal Year 2003 (Public Law 107-314; 116 Stat. 2574; 10 U.S.C. 1413a note).

(c) REAPPLICATION FOR COMPENSATION.—Any member of the Coast Guard who was denied combat-related special compensation under section 1413a of title 10, United States Code, during the period beginning on the effective date specified in subsection (b) and ending on the date of the issuance of the procedures and criteria required by subsection (a) may reapply for combat-related special compensation under such section on the basis of such procedures and criteria in accordance with such procedures as the Secretary of the department in which the Coast Guard is operating shall specify.

SEC. 222. LEAVE POLICIES FOR THE COAST GUARD.

(a) IN GENERAL.—Chapter 11 of title 14, United States Code, is further amended by inserting after section 430 the following:

"SEC. 431. [14 U.S.C. 431] Leave policies for the Coast Guard

"Not later than 1 year after the date on which the Secretary of the Navy promulgates a new rule, policy, or memorandum pursuant to section 704 of title 10, United States Code, with respect to leave associated with the birth or adoption of a child, the Secretary of the department in which the Coast Guard is operating shall promulgate a similar rule, policy, or memorandum that provides leave to officers and enlisted members of the Coast Guard that is equal in duration and compensation to that provided by the Secretary of the Navy."

(b) [14 U.S.C. 211] CLERICAL AMENDMENT.—The analysis at the beginning of such chapter is further amended by inserting after the item related to section 430 the following:

"431. Leave policies for the Coast Guard.".

TITLE III—SHIPPING AND NAVIGATION

SEC. 301. SURVIVAL CRAFT.

(a) IN GENERAL.—Section 3104 of title 46, United States Code, is amended to read as follows:

"SEC. 3104. Survival craft

"(a) REQUIREMENT TO EQUIP.—The Secretary shall require that a passenger vessel be equipped with survival craft that ensures that no part of an individual is immersed in water, if—

"(1) such vessel is built or undergoes a major conversion after January 1, 2016; and

"(2) operates in cold waters as determined by the Secretary.

"(b) HIGHER STANDARD OF SAFETY.—The Secretary may revise part 117 or part 180 of title 46, Code of Federal Regulations, as in effect before January 1, 2016, if such revision provides a higher standard of safety than is provided by the regulations in effect on or before the date of the enactment of the Coast Guard Authorization Act of 2016.

"(c) INNOVATIVE AND NOVEL DESIGNS.—The Secretary may, in lieu of the requirements set out in part 117 or part 180 of title

46, Code of Federal Regulations, as in effect on the date of the enactment of the Coast Guard Authorization Act of 2016, allow a passenger vessel to be equipped with a life-saving appliance or arrangement of an innovative or novel design that—

"(1) ensures no part of an individual is immersed in water; and

"(2) provides an equal or higher standard of safety than is provided by such requirements as in effect before such date of the enactment.

"(d) BUILT DEFINED.—In this section, the term 'built' has the meaning that term has under section 4503(e)."

(b) [46 U.S.C. 3104 note] REVIEW; REVISION OF REGULATIONS.—

(1) REVIEW.—Not later than December 31, 2016, the Secretary of the department in which the Coast Guard is operating shall submit to the Committee on Transportation and Infrastructure of the House of Representatives and the Committee on Commerce, Science, and Transportation of the Senate a review of—

(A) the number of casualties for individuals with disabilities, children, and the elderly as a result of immersion in water, reported to the Coast Guard over the preceding 30-year period, by vessel type and area of operation;

(B) the risks to individuals with disabilities, children, and the elderly as a result of immersion in water, by passenger vessel type and area of operation;

(C) the effect that carriage of survival craft that ensure that no part of an individual is immersed in water has on—

(i) passenger vessel safety, including stability and safe navigation;

(ii) improving the survivability of individuals, including individuals with disabilities, children, and the elderly; and

(iii) the costs, the incremental cost difference to vessel operators, and the cost effectiveness of requiring the carriage of such survival craft to address the risks to individuals with disabilities, children, and the elderly;

(D) the efficacy of alternative safety systems, devices, or measures in improving survivability of individuals with disabilities, children, and the elderly; and

(E) the number of small businesses and nonprofit vessel operators that would be affected by requiring the carriage of such survival craft on passenger vessels to address the risks to individuals with disabilities, children, and the elderly.

(2) SCOPE.—In conducting the review under paragraph (1), the Secretary shall include an examination of passenger vessel casualties that have occurred in the waters of other nations.

(3) UPDATES.—The Secretary shall update the review required under paragraph (1) every 5 years.

(4) REVISION.—Based on the review conducted under paragraph (1), including updates thereto, the Secretary shall revise regulations concerning the carriage of survival craft under section 3104(c) of title 46, United States Code.

(c) GAO STUDY.—

(1) IN GENERAL.—Not later than 5 years after the date of enactment of this Act, the Comptroller General of the United States shall complete and submit to the Committee on Transportation and Infrastructure of the House of Representatives and the Committee on Commerce, Science, and Transportation of the Senate a report to determine any adverse or positive changes in public safety after the implementation of the amendments and requirements under this section and section 3104 of title 46, United States Code.

(2) REQUIREMENTS.—In completing the report under paragraph (1), the Comptroller General shall examine—

(A) the number of casualties, by vessel type and area of operation, as the result of immersion in water reported to the Coast Guard for each of the 10 most recent fiscal years for which such data are available;

(B) data for each fiscal year on—

(i) vessel safety, including stability and safe navigation; and

(ii) survivability of individuals, including individuals with disabilities, children, and the elderly;

(C) the efficacy of alternative safety systems, devices, or measures; and

(D) any available data on the costs of the amendments and requirements under this section and section 3104 of title 46, United States Code.

SEC. 302. VESSEL REPLACEMENT.

(a) LOANS AND GUARANTEES.—Chapter 537 of title 46, United States Code, is amended—

(1) in section 53701—

(A) by redesignating paragraphs (8) through (14) as paragraphs (9) through (15), respectively; and

(B) by inserting after paragraph (7) the following:

"(8) HISTORICAL USES.—The term 'historical uses' includes—

"(A) refurbishing, repairing, rebuilding, or replacing equipment on a fishing vessel, without materially increasing harvesting capacity;

"(B) purchasing a used fishing vessel;

"(C) purchasing, constructing, expanding, or reconditioning a fishery facility;

"(D) refinancing existing debt;

"(E) reducing fishing capacity; and

"(F) making upgrades to a fishing vessel, including upgrades in technology, gear, or equipment, that improve—

"(i) collection and reporting of fishery-dependent data;

"(ii) bycatch reduction or avoidance;

"(iii) gear selectivity;

"(iv) adverse impacts caused by fishing gear; or

"(v) safety."

; and

(2) in section 53702(b), by adding at the end the following:

"(3) MINIMUM OBLIGATIONS AVAILABLE FOR HISTORIC

USES.—Of the direct loan obligations issued by the Secretary under this chapter, the Secretary shall make a minimum of $59,000,000 available each fiscal year for historic uses.

"(4) USE OF OBLIGATIONS IN LIMITED ACCESS FISHERIES.—In addition to the other eligible purposes and uses of direct loan obligations provided for in this chapter, the Secretary may issue direct loan obligations for the purpose of—

"(A) financing the construction or reconstruction of a fishing vessel in a fishery managed under a limited access system; or

"(B) financing the purchase of harvesting rights in a fishery that is federally managed under a limited access system."

(b) LIMITATION ON APPLICATION TO CERTAIN FISHING VESSELS OF PROHIBITION UNDER VESSEL CONSTRUCTION PROGRAM.—Section 302(b)(2) of the Fisheries Financing Act (title III of Public Law 104-297; 46 U.S.C. 53706 note) is amended—

(1) in the second sentence—

(A) by striking "or in" and inserting ", in"; and

(B) by inserting before the period the following: ", in fisheries that are under the jurisdiction of the North Pacific Fishery Management Council and managed under a fishery management plan issued under the Magnuson-Stevens Fishery Conservation and Management Act (16 U.S.C. 1801 et seq.), or in the Pacific whiting fishery that is under the jurisdiction of the Pacific Fishery Management Council and managed under a fishery management plan issued under that Act"; and

(2) by adding at the end the following: "Any fishing vessel operated in fisheries under the jurisdiction of the North Pacific Fishery Management Council and managed under a fishery management plan issued under the Magnuson-Stevens Fishery Conservation and Management Act (16 U.S.C. 1801 et seq.), or in the Pacific whiting fishery under the jurisdiction of the Pacific Fishery Management Council and managed under a fishery management plan issued under that Act, and that is replaced by a vessel that is constructed or rebuilt with a loan

or loan guarantee provided by the Federal Government may not be used to harvest fish in any fishery under the jurisdiction of any regional fishery management council, other than a fishery under the jurisdiction of the North Pacific Fishery Management Council or the Pacific Fishery Management Council.".

SEC. 303. MODEL YEARS FOR RECREATIONAL VESSELS.

(a) IN GENERAL.—Section 4302 of title 46, United States Code is amended by adding at the end the following:

"(e)(1) Under this section, a model year for recreational vessels and associated equipment shall, except as provided in paragraph (2)—

"(A) begin on June 1 of a year and end on July 31 of the following year; and

"(B) be designated by the year in which it ends.

"(2) Upon the request of a recreational vessel manufacturer to which this chapter applies, the Secretary may alter a model year for a model of recreational vessel of the manufacturer and associated equipment, by no more than 6 months from the model year described in paragraph (1)."

(b) [46 U.S.C. 4302 note] APPLICATION.—This section shall only apply with respect to recreational vessels and associated equipment constructed or manufactured, respectively, on or after the date of enactment of this Act.

SEC. 304. [46 U.S.C. 7302 note] MERCHANT MARINER CREDENTIAL EXPIRATION HARMONIZATION.

(a) IN GENERAL.—Except as provided in subsection (c) and not later than 1 year after the date of the enactment of this Act, the Secretary of the department in which the Coast Guard is operating shall establish a process to harmonize the expiration dates of merchant mariner credentials, mariner medical certificates, and radar observer endorsements for individuals applying to the Secretary for a new merchant mariner credential or for renewal of an existing merchant mariner credential.

(b) REQUIREMENTS.—The Secretary shall ensure that the process established under subsection (a)—

(1) does not require an individual to renew a merchant mariner credential earlier than the date on which the

individual's current credential expires; and

(2) results in harmonization of expiration dates for merchant mariner credentials, mariner medical certificates, and radar observer endorsements for all individuals by not later than 6 years after the date of the enactment of this Act.

(c) EXCEPTION.—The process established under subsection (a) does not apply to individuals—

(1) holding a merchant mariner credential with—

(A) an active Standards of Training, Certification, and Watchkeeping endorsement; or

(B) Federal first-class pilot endorsement; or

(2) who have been issued a time-restricted medical certificate.

SEC. 305. [33 U.S.C. 1231 note] SAFETY ZONES FOR PERMITTED MARINE EVENTS.

Not later than 6 months after the date of the enactment of this Act, the Secretary of the department in which the Coast Guard is operating shall establish and implement a process to—

(1) account for the number of safety zones established for permitted marine events;

(2) differentiate whether the event sponsor who requested a permit for such an event is—

(A) an individual;

(B) an organization; or

(C) a government entity; and

(3) account for Coast Guard resources utilized to enforce safety zones established for permitted marine events, including for—

(A) the number of Coast Guard or Coast Guard Auxiliary vessels used; and

(B) the number of Coast Guard or Coast Guard Auxiliary patrol hours required.

SEC. 306. TECHNICAL CORRECTIONS.

(a) TITLE 46.—Title 46, United States Code, is amended—

(1) in section 103, by striking "(33 U.S.C. 151)." and

inserting "(33 U.S.C. 151(b)).";

(2) in section 2118—

(A) in subsection (a), in the matter preceding paragraph (1), by striking "title," and inserting "subtitle,"; and

(B) in subsection (b), by striking "title" and inserting "subtitle";

(3) [46 U.S.C. 3501] in the analysis for chapter 35—

(A) by adding a period at the end of the item relating to section 3507; and

(B) by adding a period at the end of the item relating to section 3508;

(4) in section 3715(a)(2), by striking "; and" and inserting a semicolon;

(5) in section 4506, by striking "(a)";

(6) in section 8103(b)(1)(A)(iii), by striking "Academy." and inserting "Academy; and";

(7) in section 11113(c)(1)(A)(i), by striking "under this Act";

(8) [46 U.S.C. 70101] in the analysis for chapter 701—

(A) by adding a period at the end of the item relating to section 70107A;

(B) in the item relating to section 70112, by striking "security advisory committees." and inserting "Security Advisory Committees."; and

(C) in the item relating to section 70122, by striking "watch program." and inserting "Watch Program.";

(9) in section 70105(c)—

(A) in paragraph (1)(B)(xv)—

(i) by striking "18, popularly" and inserting "18 (popularly"; and

(ii) by striking "Act" and inserting "Act)"; and

(B) in paragraph (2), by striking "(D) paragraph" and inserting "(D) of paragraph";

(10) in section 70107—

(A) in subsection (b)(2), by striking "5121(j)(8))," and inserting "5196(j)(8)),"; and

(B) in subsection (m)(3)(C)(iii), by striking "that is" and inserting "that the applicant";

(11) in section 70122, in the section heading, by striking "watch program" and inserting "Watch Program"; and

(12) **[46 U.S.C. 70501]** in the analysis for chapter 705, by adding a period at the end of the item relating to section 70508.

(b) GENERAL BRIDGE STATUTES.—

(1) ACT OF MARCH 3, 1899.—The Act of March 3, 1899, popularly known as the Rivers and Harbors Appropriations Act of 1899, is amended—

(A) in section 9 (33 U.S.C. 401), by striking "Secretary of Transportation" each place it appears and inserting "Secretary of the department in which the Coast Guard is operating"; and

(B) in section 18 (33 U.S.C. 502), by striking "Secretary of Transportation" each place it appears and inserting "Secretary of the department in which the Coast Guard is operating".

(2) ACT OF MARCH 23, 1906.—The Act of March 23, 1906, popularly known as the Bridge Act of 1906, is amended—

(A) in the first section (33 U.S.C. 491), by striking "Secretary of Transportation" and inserting "Secretary of the department in which the Coast Guard is operating";

(B) in section 4 (33 U.S.C. 494), by striking "Secretary of Homeland Security" each place it appears and inserting "Secretary of the department in which the Coast Guard is operating"; and

(C) in section 5 (33 U.S.C. 495), by striking "Secretary of Transportation" each place it appears and inserting "Secretary of the department in which the Coast Guard is operating".

(3) ACT OF AUGUST 18, 1894.—Section 5 of the Act entitled "An Act making appropriations for the construction, repair, and preservation of certain public works on rivers and harbors, and for other purposes", approved August 18, 1894 (33 U.S.C. 499) is amended by striking "Secretary of Transportation" each place it appears and inserting "Secretary of the department in which the Coast Guard is operating".

(4) ACT OF JUNE 21, 1940.—The Act of June 21, 1940, popularly known as the Truman-Hobbs Act, is amended—

(A) in section 1 (33 U.S.C. 511), by striking "Secretary of Transportation" and inserting "Secretary of the department in which the Coast Guard is operating";

(B) in section 4 (33 U.S.C. 514), by striking "Secretary of Transportation" and inserting "Secretary of the department in which the Coast Guard is operating";

(C) in section 7 (33 U.S.C. 517), by striking "Secretary of Transportation" each place it appears and inserting "Secretary of the department in which the Coast Guard is operating"; and

(D) in section 13 (33 U.S.C. 523), by striking "Secretary of Transportation" and inserting "Secretary of the department in which the Coast Guard is operating".

(5) GENERAL BRIDGE ACT OF 1946.—The General Bridge Act of 1946 is amended—

(A) in section 502(b) (33 U.S.C. 525(b)), by striking "Secretary of Transportation" and inserting "Secretary of the department in which the Coast Guard is operating"; and

(B) in section 510 (33 U.S.C. 533), by striking "Secretary of Transportation" each place it appears and inserting "Secretary of the department in which the Coast Guard is operating".

(6) INTERNATIONAL BRIDGE ACT OF 1972.—The International Bridge Act of 1972 is amended—

(A) in section 5 (33 U.S.C. 535c), by striking "Secretary of Transportation" and inserting "Secretary of the department in which the Coast Guard is operating";

(B) in section 8 (33 U.S.C. 535e), by striking "Secretary of Transportation" each place it appears and inserting "Secretary of the department in which the Coast Guard is operating"; and

(C) by striking section 11 (33 U.S.C. 535h).

SEC. 307. RECOMMENDATIONS FOR IMPROVEMENTS OF MARINE CASUALTY REPORTING.

Not later than 180 days after the date of the enactment of this Act, the Commandant of the Coast Guard shall notify the Committee on Transportation and Infrastructure of the House of Representatives and the Committee on Commerce, Science, and Transportation of the Senate of the actions the Commandant will take to implement recommendations on improvements to the Coast Guard's marine casualty reporting requirements and procedures included in—

(1) the Department of Homeland Security Office of Inspector General report entitled "Marine Accident Reporting, Investigations, and Enforcement in the United States Coast Guard", released on May 23, 2013; and

(2) the Towing Safety Advisory Committee report entitled "Recommendations for Improvement of Marine Casualty Reporting", released on March 26, 2015.

SEC. 308. RECREATIONAL VESSEL ENGINE WEIGHTS.

Not later than 180 days after the date of the enactment of this Act, the Secretary of the department in which the Coast Guard is operating shall issue regulations amending table 4 to subpart H of part 183 of title 33, Code of Federal Regulations (relating to Weights (Pounds) of Outboard Motor and Related Equipment for Various Boat Horsepower Ratings) as appropriate to reflect "Standard 30-Outboard Engine and Related Equipment Weights" published by the American Boat and Yacht Council, as in effect on the date of the enactment of this Act.

SEC. 309. MERCHANT MARINER MEDICAL CERTIFICATION REFORM.

(a) IN GENERAL.—Chapter 75 of title 46, United States Code, is amended by adding at the end the following:

"SEC. 7509. [46 U.S.C. 7509] Medical certification by trusted agents

"(a) IN GENERAL.—Notwithstanding any other provision of law and pursuant to regulations prescribed by the Secretary, a trusted agent may issue a medical certificate to an individual who—

"(1) must hold such certificate to qualify for a license, certificate of registry, or merchant mariner's document, or endorsement thereto under this part; and

"(2) is qualified as to sight, hearing, and physical condition to perform the duties of such license, certificate, document, or endorsement, as determined by the trusted agent.

"(b) PROCESS FOR ISSUANCE OF CERTIFICATES BY SECRETARY.—A final rule implementing this section shall include a process for—

"(1) the Secretary of the department in which the Coast Guard is operating to issue medical certificates to mariners who submit applications for such certificates to the Secretary; and

"(2) a trusted agent to defer to the Secretary the issuance of a medical certificate.

"(c) TRUSTED AGENT DEFINED.—In this section the term 'trusted agent' means a medical practitioner certified by the Secretary to perform physical examinations of an individual for purposes of a license, certificate of registry, or merchant mariner's document under this part."

(b) [46 U.S.C. 7509 note] DEADLINE.—Not later than 5 years after the date of the enactment of this Act, the Secretary of the department in which the Coast Guard is operating shall issue a final rule implementing section 7509 of title 46, United States Code, as added by this section.

(c) CLERICAL AMENDMENT.—The analysis for such chapter is amended by adding at the end the following:

"7509. Medical certification by trusted agents.".

SEC. 310. ATLANTIC COAST PORT ACCESS ROUTE STUDY.

(a) ATLANTIC COAST PORT ACCESS ROUTE STUDY.—Not later than April 1, 2016, the Commandant of the Coast Guard shall conclude the Atlantic Coast Port Access Route Study and submit the results of such study to the Committee on Transportation and Infrastructure of the House of Representatives and the Committee on Commerce, Science, and Transportation of the Senate.

(b) NANTUCKET SOUND.—Not later than December 1, 2016, the Commandant of the Coast Guard shall complete and submit to the Committee on Transportation and Infrastructure of the House of Representatives and the Committee on Commerce, Science, and Transportation of the Senate a port access route study of Nantucket Sound using the standards and methodology of the Atlantic Coast Port Access Route Study, to determine whether the Coast Guard should revise existing regulations to improve navigation safety in Nantucket Sound due to factors such as increased vessel traffic, changing vessel traffic patterns, weather conditions, or navigational difficulty in the vicinity.

SEC. 311. [46 U.S.C. 12105 note] CERTIFICATES OF DOCUMENTATION FOR RECREATIONAL VESSELS.

Not later than one year after the date of the enactment of this Act, the Secretary of the department in which the Coast Guard is operating shall issue regulations that—

(1) make certificates of documentation for recreational vessels effective for 5 years; and

(2) require the owner of such a vessel—

(A) to notify the Coast Guard of each change in the information on which the issuance of the certificate of documentation is based, that occurs before the expiration of the certificate; and

(B) apply for a new certificate of documentation for such a vessel if there is any such change.

SEC. 312. [33 U.S.C. 1503 note] PROGRAM GUIDELINES.

Not later than 180 days after the date of the enactment this Act, the Secretary of Transportation shall—

(1) develop guidelines to implement the program authorized under section 304(a) of the Coast Guard and Maritime Transportation Act of 2006 (Public Law 109-241), including specific actions to ensure the future availability of able and credentialed United States licensed and unlicensed seafarers including—

(A) incentives to encourage partnership agreements with operators of foreign-flag vessels that carry liquified natural gas, that provide no less than one training billet per vessel for United States merchant mariners in order to meet minimum mandatory sea service requirements;

(B) development of appropriate training curricula for use by public and private maritime training institutions to meet all United States merchant mariner license, certification, and document laws and requirements under the International Convention on Standards of Training, Certification and Watchkeeping for Seafarers, 1978; and

(C) steps to promote greater outreach and awareness of additional job opportunities for sea service veterans of the

United States Armed Forces; and

(2) submit such guidelines to the Committee Transportation and Infrastructure of the House of Representatives and the Committee on Commerce, Science, and Transportation of the Senate.

SEC. 313. REPEALS.

(a) REPEALS, MERCHANT MARINE ACT, 1936.—Sections 601 through 606, 608 through 611, 613 through 616, 802, and 809 of the Merchant Marine Act, 1936 (46 U.S.C. 53101 note) are repealed.

(b) CONFORMING AMENDMENTS.—Chapter 575 of title 46, United States Code, is amended—

(1) in section 57501, by striking "titles V and VI" and inserting "title V"; and

(2) in section 57531(a), by striking "titles V and VI" and inserting "title V".

(c) TRANSFER FROM MERCHANT MARINE ACT, 1936.—

(1) IN GENERAL.—Section 801 of the Merchant Marine Act, 1936 (46 U.S.C. 53101 note) is—

(A) redesignated as section 57522 of title 46, United States Code, and transferred to appear after section 57521 of such title; and

(B) as so redesignated and transferred, is amended—

(i) by striking so much as precedes the first sentence and inserting the following:

"SEC. 57522. Books and records, balance sheets, and inspection and auditing"

(ii) by striking "the provision of title VI or VII of this Act" and inserting "this chapter"; and

(iii) by striking ": Provided, That" and all that follows through "Commission".

(2) [46 U.S.C. 57501] CLERICAL AMENDMENT.—The analysis for chapter 575, of title 46, United States Code, is amended by inserting after the item relating to section 57521 the following:

"57522. Books and records, balance sheets, and inspection and auditing.".

(d) REPEALS, TITLE 46, U.S.C.—Section 8103 of title 46, United States Code, is amended in subsections (c) and (d) by striking "or operating" each place it appears.

SEC. 314. MARITIME DRUG LAW ENFORCEMENT.

(a) PROHIBITIONS.—Section 70503(a) of title 46, United States Code, is amended to read as follows:

"(a) PROHIBITIONS.—While on board a covered vessel, an individual may not knowingly or intentionally—

"(1) manufacture or distribute, or possess with intent to manufacture or distribute, a controlled substance;

"(2) destroy (including jettisoning any item or scuttling, burning, or hastily cleaning a vessel), or attempt or conspire to destroy, property that is subject to forfeiture under section 511(a) of the Comprehensive Drug Abuse Prevention and Control Act of 1970 (21 U.S.C. 881(a)); or

"(3) conceal, or attempt or conspire to conceal, more than $100,000 in currency or other monetary instruments on the person of such individual or in any conveyance, article of luggage, merchandise, or other container, or compartment of or aboard the covered vessel if that vessel is outfitted for smuggling."

(b) COVERED VESSEL DEFINED.—Section 70503 of title 46, United States Code, is amended by adding at the end the following:

"(e) COVERED VESSEL DEFINED.—In this section the term 'covered vessel' means—

"(1) a vessel of the United States or a vessel subject to the jurisdiction of the United States; or

"(2) any other vessel if the individual is a citizen of the United States or a resident alien of the United States."

(c) PENALTIES.—Section 70506 of title 46, United States Code, is amended—

(1) in subsection (a), by striking "A person violating section 70503" and inserting "A person violating paragraph (1) of section 70503(a)"; and

(2) by adding at the end the following:

"(d) PENALTY.—A person violating paragraph (2) or (3) of section 70503(a) shall be fined in accordance with section 3571 of title 18, imprisoned not more than 15 years, or both."

(d) SEIZURE AND FORFEITURE.—Section 70507(a) of title 46,

United States Code, is amended by striking "section 70503" and inserting "section 70503 or 70508".

(e) CLERICAL AMENDMENTS.—

(1) The heading of section 70503 of title 46, United States Code, is amended to read as follows:

"SEC. 70503. Prohibited acts"

(2) [46 U.S.C. 70501] The analysis for chapter 705 of title 46, United States Code, is further amended by striking the item relating to section 70503 and inserting the following:

"70503. Prohibited acts.".

SEC. 315. EXAMINATIONS FOR MERCHANT MARINER CREDENTIALS.

(a) DISCLOSURE.—

(1) IN GENERAL.—Chapter 75 of title 46, United States Code, is further amended by adding at the end the following:

"SEC. 7510. [46 U.S.C. 7510] Examinations for merchant mariner credentials

"(a) DISCLOSURE NOT REQUIRED.—Notwithstanding any other provision of law, the Secretary is not required to disclose to the public—

"(1) a question from any examination for a merchant mariner credential;

"(2) the answer to such a question, including any correct or incorrect answer that may be presented with such question; and

"(3) any quality or characteristic of such a question, including—

"(A) the manner in which such question has been, is, or may be selected for an examination;

"(B) the frequency of such selection; and

"(C) the frequency that an examinee correctly or incorrectly answered such question.

"(b) EXCEPTION FOR CERTAIN QUESTIONS.—Notwithstanding subsection (a), the Secretary may, for the purpose of preparation by the general public for examinations required for merchant mariner credentials, release an examination question and answer that the Secretary has retired or is not presently on or part of an examination, or that the Secretary determines is appropriate for release.

"(c) EXAM REVIEW.—

"(1) IN GENERAL.—Not later than 90 days after the date of the enactment of the Coast Guard Authorization Act of 2016, and once every two years thereafter, the Commandant of the Coast Guard shall commission a working group to review new questions for inclusion in examinations required for merchant mariner credentials, composed of—

"(A) 1 subject matter expert from the Coast Guard;

"(B) representatives from training facilities and the maritime industry, of whom—

"(i) one-half shall be representatives from approved training facilities; and

"(ii) one-half shall be representatives from the appropriate maritime industry;

"(C) at least 1 representative from the Merchant Marine Personnel Advisory Committee;

"(D) at least 2 representatives from the State maritime academies, of whom one shall be a representative from the deck training track and one shall be a representative of the engine license track;

"(E) representatives from other Coast Guard Federal advisory committees, as appropriate, for the industry segment associated with the subject examinations;

"(F) at least 1 subject matter expert from the Maritime Administration; and

"(G) at least 1 human performance technology representative.

"(2) INCLUSION OF PERSONS KNOWLEDGEABLE ABOUT EXAMINATION TYPE.—The working group shall include representatives knowledgeable about the examination type under review.

"(3) LIMITATION.—The requirement to convene a working group under paragraph (1) does not apply unless there are new examination questions to review.

"(4) BASELINE REVIEW.—

"(A) IN GENERAL.—Within 1 year after the date of the enactment of the Coast Guard Authorization Act of 2016, the Secretary shall convene the working group to complete a baseline review of the Coast Guard's Merchant Mariner Credentialing Examination, including review of—

"(i) the accuracy of examination questions;

"(ii) the accuracy and availability of examination references;

"(iii) the length of merchant mariner examinations; and

"(iv) the use of standard technologies in administering, scoring, and analyzing the examinations.

"(B) PROGRESS REPORT.—The Coast Guard shall provide a progress report to the appropriate congressional committees on the review under this paragraph.

"(5) FULL MEMBERSHIP NOT REQUIRED.—The Coast Guard may convene the working group without all members present if any non-Coast-Guard representative is present.

"(6) NONDISCLOSURE AGREEMENT.—The Secretary shall require all members of the working group to sign a nondisclosure agreement with the Secretary.

"(7) TREATMENT OF MEMBERS AS FEDERAL EMPLOYEES.—A member of the working group who is not a Federal Government employee shall not be considered a Federal employee in the service or the employment of the Federal Government, except that such a member shall be considered a special government employee, as defined in section 202(a) of title 18 for purposes of sections 203, 205, 207, 208, and 209 of such title and shall be subject to any administrative standards of conduct applicable to an employee of the department in which the Coast Guard is operating.

"(8) FORMAL EXAM REVIEW.—The Secretary shall ensure that the Coast Guard Performance Technology

Center—

"(A) prioritizes the review of examinations required for merchant mariner credentials; and

"(B) not later than 3 years after the date of enactment of the Coast Guard Authorization Act of 2016, completes a formal review, including an appropriate analysis, of the topics and testing methodology employed by the National Maritime Center for merchant seamen licensing.

"(9) FACA.—The Federal Advisory Committee Act (5 U.S.C. App) shall not apply to any working group created under this section to review the Coast Guard's merchant mariner credentialing examinations.

"(d) MERCHANT MARINER CREDENTIAL DEFINED.—In this section, the term 'merchant mariner credential' means a merchant seaman license, certificate, or document that the Secretary is authorized to issue pursuant to this title."

(2) [46 U.S.C. 7501] CLERICAL AMENDMENT.—The analysis for such chapter is further amended by adding at the end the following:

"7510. Examinations for merchant mariner credentials.".

(b) EXAMINATIONS FOR MERCHANT MARINER CREDENTIALS.—

(1) IN GENERAL.—Chapter 71 of title 46, United States Code, is amended by adding at the end the following:

"SEC. 7116. [46 U.S.C. 7116] Examinations for merchant mariner credentials

"(a) REQUIREMENT FOR SAMPLE EXAMS.—The Secretary shall develop a sample merchant mariner credential examination and outline of merchant mariner examination topics on an annual basis.

"(b) PUBLIC AVAILABILITY.—Each sample examination and outline of topics developed under subsection (a) shall be readily available to the public.

"(c) MERCHANT MARINER CREDENTIAL DEFINED.—In this section, the term 'merchant mariner credential' has the meaning that term has in section 7510."

(2) [46 U.S.C. 7101] CLERICAL AMENDMENT.—The analysis for such chapter is amended by adding at the end the following:

"7116. Examinations for merchant mariner credentials.".

(c) [46 U.S.C. 7510 note] DISCLOSURE TO CONGRESS.—Nothing in this section may be construed to authorize the withholding of information from an appropriate inspector general, the Committee on Commerce, Science, and Transportation of the Senate, or the Committee on Transportation and Infrastructure of the House of Representatives.

SEC. 316. HIGHER VOLUME PORT AREA REGULATORY DEFINITION CHANGE.

(a) IN GENERAL.—Subsection (a) of section 710 of the Coast Guard Authorization Act of 2010 (Public Law 111-281; 124 Stat. 2986) is amended to read as follows:

"(a) HIGHER VOLUME PORTS.—Notwithstanding any other provision of law, the requirements of subparts D, F, and G of part 155 of title 33, Code of Federal Regulations, that apply to the higher volume port area for the Strait of Juan de Fuca at Port Angeles, Washington (including any water area within 50 nautical miles seaward), to and including Puget Sound, shall apply, in the same manner, and to the same extent, to the Strait of Juan de Fuca at Cape Flattery, Washington (including any water area within 50 nautical miles seaward), to and including Puget Sound."

(b) CONFORMING AMENDMENT.—Subsection (b) of such section is amended by striking "the modification of the higher volume port area definition required by subsection (a)." and inserting "higher volume port requirements made applicable under subsection (a).".

SEC. 317. RECOGNITION OF PORT SECURITY ASSESSMENTS CONDUCTED BY OTHER ENTITIES.

Section 70108 of title 46, United States Code, is amended by adding at the end the following:

"(f) RECOGNITION OF ASSESSMENT CONDUCTED BY OTHER ENTITIES.—

"(1) CERTIFICATION AND TREATMENT OF ASSESSMENTS.—For the purposes of this section and section 70109, the Secretary may treat an assessment that a foreign government (including, for the purposes of this subsection, an entity of or operating under the auspices of the European Union) or international organization has conducted as an assessment that the Secretary has conducted for the purposes of subsection (a), provided that the Secretary certifies that the foreign government or international organization has—

"(A) conducted the assessment in accordance with subsection (b); and

"(B) provided the Secretary with sufficient information pertaining to its assessment (including, but not limited to, information on the outcome of the assessment).

"(2) AUTHORIZATION TO ENTER INTO AN AGREEMENT.—For the purposes of this section and section 70109, the Secretary, in consultation with the Secretary of State, may enter into an agreement with a foreign government (including, for the purposes of this subsection, an entity of or operating under the auspices of the European Union) or international organization, under which parties to the agreement—

"(A) conduct an assessment, required under subsection (a);

"(B) share information pertaining to such assessment (including, but not limited to, information on the outcome of the assessment); or

"(C) both.

"(3) LIMITATIONS.—Nothing in this subsection shall be construed to—

"(A) require the Secretary to recognize an assessment that a foreign government or an international organization has conducted; or

"(B) limit the discretion or ability of the Secretary to conduct an assessment under this section.

"(4) NOTIFICATION TO CONGRESS.—Not later than 30 days before entering into an agreement or arrangement with a foreign government under paragraph (2), the Secretary shall notify the Committee on Homeland Security and the Committee on Transportation and Infrastructure of the House of Representatives and the Committee on Commerce, Science, and Transportation of the Senate of the proposed terms of such agreement or arrangement."

SEC. 318. FISHING VESSEL AND FISH TENDER VESSEL CERTIFICATION.

(a) ALTERNATIVE SAFETY COMPLIANCE PROGRAMS.—Section 4503 of title 46, United States Code, is amended—

(1) in subsection (a), by striking "this section" and inserting "this subsection";

(2) in subsection (b), by striking "This section" and inserting "Except as provided in subsection (d), subsection (a)";

(3) in subsection (c)—

(A) by striking "This section" and inserting "(1) Except as provided in paragraph (2), subsection (a)"; and

(B) by adding at the end the following:

"(2) Subsection (a) does not apply to a fishing vessel or fish tender vessel to which section 4502(b) of this title applies, if the vessel—

"(A) is at least 50 feet overall in length, and not more than 79 feet overall in length as listed on the vessel's certificate of documentation or certificate of number; and

"(B)(i) is built after the date of the enactment of the Coast Guard Authorization Act of 2016; and

"(ii) complies with—

"(I) the requirements described in subsection (e); or

"(II) the alternative requirements established by the Secretary under subsection (f)."

; and

(4) by redesignating subsection (e) as subsection (g), and inserting after subsection (d) the following:

"(e) The requirements referred to in subsection (c)(2)(B)(ii)(I) are the following:

"(1) The vessel is designed by an individual licensed by a State as a naval architect or marine engineer, and the design incorporates standards equivalent to those prescribed by a classification society to which the Secretary has delegated authority under section 3316 or another qualified organization approved by the Secretary for purposes of this paragraph.

"(2) Construction of the vessel is overseen and certified as being in accordance with its design by a marine surveyor of an organization accepted by the Secretary.

"(3) The vessel—

"(A) completes a stability test performed by a qualified individual;

"(B) has written stability and loading instructions from a qualified individual that are provided to the owner or operator; and

"(C) has an assigned loading mark.

"(4) The vessel is not substantially altered without the review and approval of an individual licensed by a State as a naval architect or marine engineer before the beginning of such substantial alteration.

"(5) The vessel undergoes a condition survey at least twice in 5 years, not to exceed 3 years between surveys, to the satisfaction of a marine surveyor of an organization accepted by the Secretary.

"(6) The vessel undergoes an out-of-water survey at least once every 5 years to the satisfaction of a certified marine surveyor of an organization accepted by the Secretary.

"(7) Once every 5 years and at the time of a substantial alteration to such vessel, compliance of the vessel with the requirements of paragraph (3) is reviewed and updated as necessary.

"(8) For the life of the vessel, the owner of the vessel maintains records to demonstrate compliance with this subsection and makes such records readily available for inspection by an official authorized to enforce this chapter.

"(f)(1) Not later than 10 years after the date of the enactment of the Coast Guard Authorization Act of 2016, the Secretary shall submit to the Committee on Transportation and Infrastructure of the House of Representatives and the Committee on Commerce, Science, and Transportation of the Senate a report that provides an analysis of the adequacy of the requirements under subsection (e) in maintaining the safety of the fishing vessels and fish tender vessels which are described in subsection (c)(2) and which comply with the requirements of subsection (e).

"(2) If the report required under this subsection includes a determination that the safety requirements under subsection (e) are not adequate or that additional safety measures are necessary, that the Secretary may establish an alternative safety compliance program for fishing vessels or fish tender vessels (or both) which are described in subsection (c)(2) and which comply with the requirements of subsection (e).

"(3) The alternative safety compliance program established under this subsection shall include requirements for—

"(A) vessel construction;

"(B) a vessel stability test;

"(C) vessel stability and loading instructions;

"(D) an assigned vessel loading mark;

"(E) a vessel condition survey at least twice in 5 years, not to exceed 3 years between surveys;

"(F) an out-of-water vessel survey at least once every 5 years;

"(G) maintenance of records to demonstrate compliance with the program, and the availability of such records for inspection; and

"(H) such other aspects of vessel safety as the Secretary considers appropriate."

(b) GAO REPORT ON COMMERCIAL FISHING VESSEL SAFETY.—

(1) IN GENERAL.—Not later than 12 months after the date of the enactment of this Act, the Comptroller General of the United States shall submit to the Committee on Transportation and Infrastructure of the House of Representatives and the Committee on Commerce, Science, and Transportation of the Senate a report on commercial fishing vessel safety. The report shall include—

(A) national and regional trends that can be identified with respect to rates of marine casualties, human injuries, and deaths aboard or involving fishing vessels greater than 79 feet in length that operate beyond the 3-nautical-mile demarcation line;

(B) a comparison of United States regulations for classification of fishing vessels to those established by other countries, including the vessel length at which such regulations apply;

(C) the additional costs imposed on vessel owners as a result of the requirement in section 4503(a) of title 46, United States Code, and how the those costs vary in relation to vessel size and from region to region;

(D) savings that result from the application of the requirement in section 4503(a) of title 46, United States Code, including reductions in insurance rates or reduction in the number of fishing vessels or fish tender vessels lost to major safety casualties, nationally and regionally;

(E) a national and regional comparison of the additional costs and safety benefits associated with fishing vessels or fish tender vessels that are built and maintained to class through a classification society to the additional costs and safety benefits associated with fishing vessels or fish tender vessels that are built to standards equivalent to classification society construction standards and maintained to standards equivalent to classification society standards with verification by independent surveyors; and

(F) the impact on the cost of production and availability of qualified shipyards, nationally and regionally, resulting from the application of the requirement in section 4503(a) of title 46, United States Code.

(2) CONSULTATION REQUIREMENT.—In preparing the report under paragraph (1), the Comptroller General shall—

(A) consult with owners and operators of fishing vessels or fish tender vessels, classification societies, shipyards, the National Institute for Occupational Safety and Health, the National Transportation Safety Board, the Coast Guard, academics, naval architects, and marine safety nongovernmental organizations; and

(B) obtain relevant data from the Coast Guard including data collected from enforcement actions, boardings, investigations of marine casualties, and serious marine incidents.

(3) TREATMENT OF DATA.—In preparing the report under paragraph (1), the Comptroller General shall—

(A) disaggregate data regionally for each of the regions managed by the regional fishery management councils established under section 302 of the Magnuson-Stevens Fisheries Conservation and Management Act (16 U.S.C. 1852), the Atlantic States Marine Fisheries Commission, the Pacific States Marine Fisheries Commission, and the Gulf States Marine Fisheries Commission; and

(B) include qualitative data on the types of fishing vessels or fish tender vessels included in the report.

SEC. 319. INTERAGENCY COORDINATING COMMITTEE ON OIL POLLUTION RESEARCH.

(a) IN GENERAL.—Section 7001(a)(3) of the Oil Pollution Act of 1990 (33 U.S.C. 2761(a)(3)) is amended—

(1) by striking "Minerals Management Service" and inserting "Bureau of Safety and Environmental Enforcement, the Bureau of Ocean Energy Management,"; and

(2) by inserting "the United States Arctic Research Commission," after "National Aeronautics and Space Administration,".

(b) TECHNICAL AMENDMENTS.—Section 7001 of the Oil Pollution Act of 1990 (33 U.S.C. 2761) is amended—

(1) in subsection (b)(2), in the matter preceding subparagraph (A), by striking "Department of Transportation" and inserting "department in which the Coast Guard is operating"; and

(2) in subsection (c)(8)(A), by striking "(1989)" and inserting "(2010)".

SEC. 320. INTERNATIONAL PORT AND FACILITY INSPECTION COORDINATION.

Section 825(a) of the Coast Guard Authorization Act of 2010 (6 U.S.C. 945 note; Public Law 111-281) is amended in the matter preceding paragraph (1)—

(1) by striking "the department in which the Coast Guard is operating" and inserting "Homeland Security"; and

(2) by striking "they are integrated and conducted by the

Coast Guard" and inserting "the assessments are coordinated between the Coast Guard and Customs and Border Protection".

TITLE IV—FEDERAL MARITIME COMMISSION

SEC. 401. AUTHORIZATION OF APPROPRIATIONS.

(a) IN GENERAL.—Chapter 3 of title 46, United States Code, is amended by adding at the end the following:

"SEC. 308. [46 U.S.C. 308] Authorization of appropriations

"There is authorized to be appropriated to the Federal Maritime Commission $24,700,000 for each of fiscal years 2016 and 2017 for the activities of the Commission authorized under this chapter and subtitle IV."

(b) [46 U.S.C. 301] CLERICAL AMENDMENT.—The analysis for chapter 3 of title 46, United States Code, is amended by adding at the end the following:

"308. Authorization of appropriations.".

SEC. 402. DUTIES OF THE CHAIRMAN.

Section 301(c)(3)(A) of title 46, United States Code, is amended—

(1) in clause (ii) by striking "units, but only after consultation with the other Commissioners;" and inserting "units (with such appointments subject to the approval of the Commission);";

(2) in clause (iv) by striking "and" at the end;

(3) in clause (v) by striking the period at the end and inserting "; and"; and

(4) by adding at the end the following:

"(vi) prepare and submit to the President and the Congress requests for appropriations for the Commission (with such requests subject to the approval of the Commission)."

SEC. 403. PROHIBITION ON AWARDS.

Section 307 of title 46, United States Code, is amended—

(1) by striking "The Federal Maritime Commission" and inserting the following:

"(a) IN GENERAL.—The Federal Maritime Commission"

; and

(2) by adding at the end the following:

"(b) PROHIBITION.—Notwithstanding subsection (a), the Federal Maritime Commission may not expend any funds appropriated or otherwise made available to it to a non-Federal entity to issue an award, prize, commendation, or other honor that is not related to the purposes set forth in section 40101."

TITLE V—CONVEYANCES

Subtitle A—Miscellaneous Conveyances

SEC. 501. CONVEYANCE OF COAST GUARD PROPERTY IN POINT REYES STATION, CALIFORNIA.

(a) CONVEYANCE.—

(1) IN GENERAL.—The Commandant of the Coast Guard shall convey to the County of Marin, California all right, title, and interest of the United States in and to the covered property—

(A) for fair market value, as provided in paragraph (2);

(B) subject to the conditions required by this section; and

(C) subject to any other term or condition that the Commandant considers appropriate and reasonable to protect the interests of the United States.

(2) FAIR MARKET VALUE.—The fair market value of the covered property shall be—

(A) determined by a real estate appraiser who has been selected by the County and is licensed to practice in California; and

(B) approved by the Commandant.

(3) PROCEEDS.—The Commandant shall deposit the proceeds from a conveyance under paragraph (1) in the Coast Guard Housing Fund established by section 687 of title 14, United States Code.

(b) CONDITION OF CONVEYANCE.—As a condition of any

conveyance of the covered property under this section, the Commandant shall require that all right, title, and interest in and to the covered property shall revert to the United States if the covered property or any part thereof ceases to be used for affordable housing, as defined by the County and the Commandant at the time of conveyance, or to provide a public benefit approved by the County.

(c) SURVEY.—The exact acreage and legal description of the covered property shall be determined by a survey satisfactory to the Commandant.

(d) RULES OF CONSTRUCTION.—Nothing in this section may be construed to affect or limit the application of or obligation to comply with any environmental law, including section 120(h) of the Comprehensive Environmental Response, Compensation, and Liability Act of 1980 (42 U.S.C. 9620(h)).

(e) COVERED PROPERTY DEFINED.—In this section, the term "covered property" means the approximately 32 acres of real property (including all improvements located on the property) that are—

(1) located in Point Reyes Station in the County of Marin, California;

(2) under the administrative control of the Coast Guard; and

(3) described as "Parcel A, Tract 1", "Parcel B, Tract 2", "Parcel C", and "Parcel D" in the Declaration of Taking (Civil No. C 71-1245 SC) filed June 28, 1971, in the United States District Court for the Northern District of California.

(f) EXPIRATION.—The authority to convey the covered property under this section shall expire on the date that is four years after the date of the enactment of this Act.

SEC. 502. CONVEYANCE OF COAST GUARD PROPERTY IN TOK, ALASKA.

(a) CONVEYANCE AUTHORIZED.—The Commandant of the Coast Guard may convey to the Tanana Chiefs' Conference all right, title, and interest of the United States in and to the covered property, upon payment to the United States of the fair market value of the covered property.

(b) SURVEY.—The exact acreage and legal description of the

covered property shall be determined by a survey satisfactory to the Commandant.

(c) FAIR MARKET VALUE.—The fair market value of the covered property shall be—

(1) determined by appraisal; and

(2) subject to the approval of the Commandant.

(d) COSTS OF CONVEYANCE.—The responsibility for all reasonable and necessary costs, including real estate transaction and environmental documentation costs, associated with a conveyance under this section shall be determined by the Commandant and the purchaser.

(e) ADDITIONAL TERMS AND CONDITIONS.—The Commandant may require such additional terms and conditions in connection with a conveyance under this section as the Commandant considers appropriate and reasonable to protect the interests of the United States.

(f) DEPOSIT OF PROCEEDS.—Any proceeds received by the United States from a conveyance under this section shall be deposited in the Coast Guard Housing Fund established under section 687 of title 14, United States Code.

(g) COVERED PROPERTY DEFINED.—

(1) IN GENERAL.—In this section, the term "covered property" means the approximately 3.25 acres of real property (including all improvements located on the property) that are—

(A) located in Tok, Alaska;

(B) under the administrative control of the Coast Guard; and

(C) described in paragraph (2).

(2) DESCRIPTION.—The property described in this paragraph is the following:

(A) Lots 11, 12 and 13, block "G", Second Addition to Hartsell Subdivision, Section 20, Township 18 North, Range 13 East, Copper River Meridian, Alaska as appears by Plat No. 72-39 filed in the Office of the Recorder for the Fairbanks Recording District of Alaska, bearing seal dated 25 September 1972, all containing approximately 1.25 acres and commonly knowggn as 2-PLEX - Jackie Circle, Units A and B.

(B) Beginning at a point being the SE corner of the SE ¼ of the SE ¼ Section 24, Township 18 North, Range 12 East, Copper River Meridian, Alaska; thence running westerly along the south line of said SE ¼ of the NE ¼ 260 feet; thence northerly parallel to the east line of said SE ¼ of the NE ¼ 335 feet; thence easterly parallel to the south line 260 feet; then south 335 feet along the east boundary of Section 24 to the point of beginning; all containing approximately 2.0 acres and commonly known as 4-PLEX - West "C" and Willow, Units A, B, C and D.

(h) EXPIRATION.—The authority to convey the covered property under this section shall expire on the date that is 4 years after the date of the enactment of this Act.

Subtitle B—Pribilof Islands

SEC. 521. [16 U.S.C. 1151 note] SHORT TITLE.

This subtitle may be cited as the "Pribilof Island Transition Completion Act of 2016".

SEC. 522. TRANSFER AND DISPOSITION OF PROPERTY.

(a) CONVEYANCE.—In partial settlement of land claims under the Alaska Native Claims Settlement Act (43 U.S.C. 1601 et seq.), and not later than 30 days after the date of enactment of the Pribilof Islands Transition Completion Amendments Act of 2016, the Secretary of Commerce shall, notwithstanding section 105(a) of the Pribilof Islands Transition Act (16 U.S.C. 1161 note; Public Law 106–562), convey to the Alaska Native Village Corporation for St. Paul Island all right, title, and interest of the United States in and to the following property, including improvements on such property:

(1) Lots 4, 5, and 6A, Block 18, Tract A, U.S. Survey 4943, Alaska, the plat of which was Officially Filed on January 20, 2004, aggregating 13,006 square feet (0.30 acres).

(2) T. 35 S., R. 131 W., Seward Meridian, Alaska, Tract 39, the plat of which was Officially Filed on May 14, 1986, containing 0.90 acres.

(b) AGREEMENT ON TRANSFER OF OTHER PROPERTY ON ST. PAUL ISLAND.—

(1) IN GENERAL.—In addition to the property transferred

under subsection (a), not later than 60 days after the date of the enactment of this Act, the Secretary of Commerce and the presiding officer of the Alaska native village corporation for St. Paul Island shall enter into an agreement to exchange of property on Tracts 50 and 38 on St. Paul Island and to finalize the recording of deeds, to reflect the boundaries and ownership of Tracts 50 and 38 as depicted on a survey of the National Oceanic and Atmospheric Administration, to be filed with the Office of the Recorder for the Department of Natural Resources for the State of Alaska.

(2) EASEMENTS.—The survey described in subsection (a) shall include respective easements granted to the Secretary and the Alaska native village corporation for the purpose of utilities, drainage, road access, and salt lagoon conservation.

(c) EASEMENT.—As part of the conveyance under subsection (a), the Secretary of Commerce, in cooperation with the Alaska Native Village Corporation for St. Paul Island, shall provide an easement to the Secretary of Transportation to maintain a non-directional beacon on the property described in subsection (a)(2).

SEC. 523. NOTICE OF CERTIFICATION.

Section 105 of the Pribilof Islands Transition Act (16 U.S.C. 1161 note; Public Law 106-562) is amended—

(1) in subsection (a)(1), by striking "The Secretary" and inserting "Notwithstanding paragraph (2) and effective beginning on the date the Secretary publishes the notice of certification required by subsection (b)(5), the Secretary";

(2) in subsection (b)—

(A) in paragraph (1)(A), by striking "section 205 of the Fur Seal Act of 1966 (16 U.S.C. 1165)" and inserting "section 205(a) of the Fur Seal Act of 1966 (16 U.S.C. 1165(a))"; and

(B) by adding at the end the following:

"(5) NOTICE OF CERTIFICATION.—The Secretary shall promptly publish and submit to the Committee on Natural Resources of the House of Representatives and the Committee on Commerce, Science, and Transportation of the Senate notice that the certification described in paragraph (2) has been made."

; and

(3) in subsection (c)—

(A) in the matter preceding paragraph (1), by striking "makes the certification described in subsection (b)(2)" and inserting "publishes the notice of certification required by subsection (b)(5)"; and

(B) in paragraph (1), by striking "Section 205" and inserting "Subsections (a), (b), (c), and (d) of section 205";

(4) by redesignating subsection (e) as subsection (g); and

(5) by inserting after subsection (d) the following:

"(e) NOTIFICATIONS.—

"(1) IN GENERAL.—Not later than 30 days after the Secretary makes a determination under subsection (f) that land on St. Paul Island, Alaska, not specified for transfer in the document entitled 'Transfer of Property on the Pribilof Islands: Descriptions, Terms and Conditions' or section 522 of the Pribilof Island Transition Completion Act of 2015 is in excess of the needs of the Secretary and the Federal Government, the Secretary shall notify the Alaska native village corporation for St. Paul Island of the determination.

"(2) ELECTION TO RECEIVE.—Not later than 60 days after the date receipt of the notification of the Secretary under subsection (a), the Alaska native village corporation for St. Paul Island shall notify the Secretary in writing whether the Alaska native village corporation elects to receive all right, title, and interest in the land or a portion of the land.

"(3) TRANSFER.—If the Alaska native village corporation provides notice under paragraph (2) that the Alaska native village corporation elects to receive all right, title and interest in the land or a portion of the land, the Secretary shall transfer all right, title, and interest in the land or portion to the Alaska native village corporation at no cost.

"(4) OTHER DISPOSITION.—If the Alaska native village corporation does not provide notice under paragraph (2) that the Alaska native village corporation elects to receive all right, title, and interest in the land or a portion of the land, the Secretary may dispose of the land in accordance with other applicable law.

"(f) DETERMINATION.—

"(1) IN GENERAL.—Not later than 2 years after the date of the enactment of this subsection and not less than once every 5 years thereafter, the Secretary shall determine whether property located on St. Paul Island and not transferred to the Natives of the Pribilof Islands is in excess of the smallest practicable tract enclosing land—

"(A) needed by the Secretary for the purposes of carrying out the Fur Seal Act of 1966 (16 U.S.C. 1151 et seq.);

"(B) in the case of land withdrawn by the Secretary on behalf of other Federal agencies, needed for carrying out the missions of those agencies for which land was withdrawn; or

"(C) actually used by the Federal Government in connection with the administration of any Federal installation on St. Paul Island.

"(2) REPORT OF DETERMINATION.—When a determination is made under subsection (a), the Secretary shall report the determination to—

"(A) the Committee on Natural Resources of the House of Representatives;

"(B) the Committee on Commerce, Science, and Transportation of the Senate; and

"(C) the Alaska native village corporation for St. Paul Island."

SEC. 524. TRANSFER, USE, AND DISPOSAL OF TRACT 43.

(a) TRANSFER.—Not later than 30 days after the date of the enactment of the Pribilof Islands Transition Completion Amendments Act of 2016, the Secretary of Commerce shall—

(1) terminate the license; and

(2) transfer tract 43 to the Secretary of the department in which the Coast Guard is operating.

(b) DETERMINATION, TRANSFER, AND CONVEYANCE.—

(1) IN GENERAL.—Not later than the end of the 90-day period beginning on the date of the transfer required under subsection (a)(2), the Secretary shall submit to the Committee on Transportation and Infrastructure of the House of Representatives and the Committee on Commerce, Science, and Transportation of the Senate a determination of—

(A) lands and improvements in tract 43 that are not necessary to carry out Coast Guard communications and search and rescue activities; and

(B) the smallest practicable tract enclosing lands and improvements in tract 43 that are necessary to carry out such communications and activities.

(2) SURVEYS, MAPS, DESCRIPTIONS, AND PLAN.—

(A) LANDS AND IMPROVEMENTS NOT NECESSARY TO COAST GUARD ACTIVITIES.—The determination under paragraph (1)(A) shall include a metes-and-bounds survey, map, and legal description of the lands and improvements to which the determination applies. Such survey, map, and legal description shall have the same force and effect as if included in this section, except that the Secretary may correct clerical and typographical errors in the survey, map, and legal description.

(B) LANDS AND IMPROVEMENTS NECESSARY TO COAST GUARD ACTIVITIES.—The determination under paragraph (1)(B) shall include with respect to the lands and improvements to which the determination applies—

(i) a metes-and-bounds survey, map, and legal description of such lands and improvements, which shall have the same force and effect as if included in this section, except that the Secretary may correct clerical and typographical errors in the survey, map, and legal description;

(ii) a description of Coast Guard actual use and occupancy of such lands and improvements intended to occur within 3 years after the date of the enactment of the Pribilof Islands Transition Completion Amendments Act of 2016; and

(iii) a plan to maintain existing facilities in useable condition, or demolish or replace those facilities, including a cost estimate for carrying out such plan.

(3) CONVEYANCE.—In partial settlement of land claims under the Alaska Native Claims Settlement Act (43 U.S.C. 1601 et seq.), and not later than 60 days after the submission of the determination under paragraph (1)(A), the Secretary shall convey to the Alaska Native Village Corporation for St. Paul Island all right, title, and interest of the United States in and to the land and improvements depicted on the metes-and-bounds survey, map, and legal description of the lands and improvements to which the determination under paragraph (1)(A) applies.

(4) FAILURE TO PROVIDE DETERMINATION.—If a determination under paragraph (1) is not provided within the period specified in that paragraph, in partial settlement of land claims under the Alaska Native Claims Settlement Act (43 U.S.C. 1601 et seq.) the Secretary shall, by not later than 30 days after the end of that period, convey all right, title, and interest of the United States in and to tract 43 to the Alaska Native Village Corporation for St. Paul Island.

(5) FAILURE TO IMPLEMENT USE AND OCCUPANCY.—If the use and occupancy described in paragraph (2)(B)(ii) have not been fully implemented within 5 years after the date of enactment of the Pribilof Islands Transition Completion Amendments Act of 2016, in partial settlement of land claims under the Alaska Native Claims Settlement Act (43 U.S.C. 1601 et seq.) the Secretary shall convey to the Alaska Native Village Corporation for St. Paul Island all right, title, and interest of the United States in and to such portions of the lands and improvements to which the determination under paragraph (1)(B) applies and for which such implementation has not occurred.

(c) FURTHER DETERMINATION AND CONVEYANCE.—

(1) IN GENERAL.—Not later than 5 years after the date of the enactment of the Pribilof Islands Transition Completion Amendments Act of 2016, and not less than once every 5 years thereafter, the Secretary shall—

(A) review the determination made under subsection (b)(1)(B); and

(B) determine if the lands and improvements to which the determination applies are in excess of the smallest practicable tract enclosing the lands and improvements needed to carry out Coast Guard missions.

(2) REPORT OF DETERMINATION.—When a determination is made under paragraph (1), the Secretary shall report the determination to—

(A) the Committee on Transportation and Infrastructure of the House of Representatives;

(B) the Committee on Commerce, Science, and Transportation of the Senate; and

(C) the Alaska Native Village Corporation for St. Paul Island.

(3) ELECTION TO RECEIVE.—Not later than 60 days after the date it receives a determination under paragraph (1), the Alaska Native Village Corporation for St. Paul Island shall notify the Secretary in writing whether the Alaska Native Village Corporation elects to receive all right, title, and interest of the United States in and to any lands and improvements or a portion of any lands and improvements determined to be in excess of those needed to carry out Coast Guard missions in partial settlement of land claims under the Alaska Native Claims Settlement Act (43 U.S.C. 1601 et seq.).

(4) CONVEYANCE.—If such Alaska Native Village Corporation provides notice under paragraph (3) that the Alaska Native Village Corporation elects to receive all right, title, and interest of the United States in and to any lands and improvements or a portion of any lands and improvements, in partial settlement of land claims under the Alaska Native Claims Settlement Act (43 U.S.C. 1601 et seq.) the Secretary shall convey all right, title, and interest of the United States in and to the lands and improvements or portion thereof to such Alaska Native Village Corporation.

(5) OTHER DISPOSAL.—If such Alaska Native Village Corporation does not provide notice under paragraph (3) that the Alaska Native Village Corporation elects to receive all right, title, and interest of the United States in and to any lands and improvements or a portion of any lands and improvements, the Secretary may dispose of the lands and improvements in

accordance with other applicable law.

(d) CERCLA NOT AFFECTED.—No transfer or conveyance of property under this section shall be construed to affect or limit the application of section 120(h) of the Comprehensive Environmental Response, Compensation, and Liability Act of 1980 (42 U.S.C. 9620(h)).

(e) REPORTS.—

(1) REMEDIATION OF CONTAMINATED SOIL.—Not later than 2 years after the date of the enactment of the Pribilof Islands Transition Completion Amendments Act of 2016 and not less than once every 2 years thereafter, the Secretary shall submit to the Committee on Transportation and Infrastructure of the House of Representatives and the Committee on Commerce, Science, and Transportation of the Senate a report on—

(A) efforts taken to remediate contaminated soils on tract 43 and tract 39; and

(B) a schedule for the completion of remediation of contaminated soils on tract 43 and tract 39.

(2) NUMBER OF COAST GUARD PERSONNEL WHO CARRIED OUT COAST GUARD MISSIONS.—On the 15th day of each April and October, the Commandant of the Coast Guard shall submit to the Committee on Transportation and Infrastructure of the House of Representatives and the Committee on Commerce, Science, and Transportation of the Senate a notice detailing the number of Coast Guard personnel who carried out Coast Guard missions on tract 43 during the previous six months and what Coast Guard missions were carried out by such personnel.

(f) REDUNDANT CAPABILITY.—

(1) RULE OF CONSTRUCTION.—Except as provided in paragraph (2), section 681 of title 14, United States Code, shall not be construed to prohibit any conveyance of lands or improvements under this subtitle or any actions that involve the dismantling or disposal of infrastructure that supported the former LORAN system that are associated with the conveyance of lands or improvements under this subtitle.

(2) REDUNDANT CAPABILITY.—If, within the 5-year period beginning on the date of the enactment of the Pribilof Islands Transition Completion Amendments Act of 2016, the Secretary determines that communication equipment, including towers,

antennae, and transmitters, on property conveyed in accordance with this subtitle is subsequently required to provide a positioning, navigation, and timing system to provide redundant capability in the event GPS signals are disrupted, the Secretary may—

(A) operate, maintain, keep, locate, inspect, repair, and replace such equipment; and

(B) in carrying out the activities described in subparagraph (A), enter, at any time, a facility without notice, to the extent that it is not possible to provide advance notice, for as long as such equipment is needed to provide such capability.

(g) FEDERAL USE.—In addition to entry under subsection (f)(2)(B), the Secretary may enter property conveyed in accordance with this subtitle for purposes of environmental compliance and remediation after providing advance notice to the property owner to the extent that it is possible to provide such notice.

(h) HIGH FREQUENCY COMMUNICATIONS.—

(1) RESTRICTION.—Except as provided in paragraph (2), on property contained within the boundaries of tract 43 as in effect on the date of enactment of the Pribilof Islands Transition Completion Amendments Act of 2016, no person may operate or maintain—

(A) radio frequency transmitting equipment that produces a signal that exceeds 5 microvolts per meter field intensity, other than such equipment that was in use on the site before the date of the enactment of such Act; or

(B) electric welding equipment, electric generating equipment, a diathermy machine, electric motors of any kind having greater than 5 horsepower, or any other machinery, engine, or equipment that causes any electromagnetic interference.

(2) EXCEPTION.—A person may engage in operations or maintenance otherwise prohibited by paragraph (1) with the concurrence of the Secretary.

(i) DEFINITIONS.—For purposes of this section:

(1) LICENSE.—The term "license" means the agreement dated January 9, 2006, entitled "License Agreement Between The Department of Homeland Security, United States Coast

Guard, and The Department of Commerce, National Oceanic and Atmospheric Administration".

(2) TRACT 39.—The term "tract 39" means T. 35 S., R. 131 W., Seward Meridian, Alaska, Tract 39, the plat of which was Officially Filed on May 14, 1986, containing 0.90 acres.

(3) TRACT 43.—The term "tract 43" means T. 35 S., R. 131 W., Seward Meridian, Alaska, Tract 43, the plat of which was Officially Filed on May 14, 1986, containing 84.88 acres, and any improvements on such tract.

(4) SECRETARY.—The term "Secretary" means the Secretary of the department in which the Coast Guard is operating.

Subtitle C—Conveyance of Coast Guard Property at Point Spencer, Alaska

SEC. 531. FINDINGS.

The Congress finds as follows:

(1) Major shipping traffic is increasing through the Bering Strait, the Bering and Chukchi Seas, and the Arctic Ocean, and will continue to increase whether or not development of the Outer Continental Shelf of the United States is undertaken in the future, and will increase further if such Outer Continental Shelf development is undertaken.

(2) There is a compelling national, State, Alaska Native, and private sector need for permanent infrastructure development and for a presence in the Arctic region of Alaska by appropriate agencies of the Federal Government, particularly in proximity to the Bering Strait, to support and facilitate search and rescue, shipping safety, economic development, oil spill prevention and response, protection of Alaska Native archaeological and cultural resources, port of refuge, arctic research, and maritime law enforcement on the Bering Sea, the Chukchi Sea, and the Arctic Ocean.

(3) The United States owns a parcel of land, known as Point Spencer, located between the Bering Strait and Port Clarence and adjacent to some of the best potential deepwater port sites on the coast of Alaska in the Arctic.

(4) Prudent and effective use of Point Spencer may be best achieved through marshaling the energy, resources, and leadership of the public and private sectors.

(5) It is in the national interest to develop infrastructure at Point Spencer that would aid the Coast Guard in performing its statutory duties and functions in the Arctic on a more permanent basis and to allow for public and private sector development of facilities and other infrastructure to support purposes that are of benefit to the United States.

SEC. 532. DEFINITIONS.

In this subtitle:

(1) ARCTIC.—The term "Arctic" has the meaning given that term in section 112 of the Arctic Research and Policy Act of 1984 (15 U.S.C. 4111).

(2) BSNC.—The term "BSNC" means the Bering Straits Native Corporation authorized under section 7 of the Alaska Native Claims Settlement Act (43 U.S.C. 1606).

(3) COUNCIL.—The term "Council" means the Port Coordination Council established under section 541.

(4) PLAN.—The term "Plan" means the Port Management Coordination Plan developed under section 541.

(5) POINT SPENCER.—The term "Point Spencer" means the land known as "Point Spencer" located in Townships 2, 3, and 4 South, Range 40 West, Kateel River Meridian, Alaska, between the Bering Strait and Port Clarence and withdrawn by Public Land Order 2650 (published in the Federal Register on April 12, 1962).

(6) SECRETARY.—Except as otherwise specifically provided, the term "Secretary" means the Secretary of the department in which the Coast Guard is operating.

(7) STATE.—The term "State" means the State of Alaska.

(8) TRACT.—The term "Tract" or "Tracts" means any of Tract 1, Tract 2, Tract 3, Tract 4, Tract 5, or Tract 6, as appropriate, or any portion of such Tract or Tracts.

(9) TRACTS 1, 2, 3, 4, 5, AND 6.—The terms "Tract 1", "Tract 2", "Tract 3", "Tract 4", "Tract 5", and "Tract 6" each mean the land generally depicted as Tract 1, Tract 2, Tract 3, Tract 4, Tract 5, or Tract 6, respectively, on the map entitled the "Point

Spencer Land Retention and Conveyance Map", dated January 2015, and on file with the Department of Homeland Security and the Department of the Interior.

SEC. 533. AUTHORITY TO CONVEY LAND IN POINT SPENCER.

(a) AUTHORITY TO CONVEY TRACTS 1, 3, AND 4.—Within 1 year after the Secretary notifies the Secretary of the Interior that the Coast Guard no longer needs to retain jurisdiction of Tract 1, Tract 3, or Tract 4 and subject to section 534, the Secretary of the Interior shall convey to BSNC or the State, subject to valid existing rights, all right, title, and interest of the United States in and to the surface and subsurface estates of that Tract in accordance with subsection (d).

(b) AUTHORITY TO CONVEY TRACTS 2 AND 5.—Within 1 year after the date of the enactment of this section and subject to section 534, the Secretary of the Interior shall convey, subject to valid existing rights, all right, title, and interest of the United States in and to the surface and subsurface estates of Tract 2 and Tract 5 in accordance with subsection (d).

(c) AUTHORITY TO TRANSFER TRACT 6.—Within one year after the date of the enactment of this Act and subject to sections 534 and 535, the Secretary of the Interior shall convey, subject to valid existing rights, all right, title, and interest of the United States in and to the surface and subsurface estates of Tract 6 in accordance with subsection (e).

(d) ORDER OF OFFER TO CONVEY TRACT 1, 2, 3, 4, OR 5.—

(1) DETERMINATION AND OFFER.—

(A) TRACT 1, 3, OR 4.—If the Secretary makes the determination under subsection (a) and subject to section 534, the Secretary of the Interior shall offer Tract 1, Tract 3, or Tract 4 for conveyance to BSNC under the Alaska Native Claims Settlement Act (43 U.S.C. 1601 et seq.).

(B) TRACT 2 AND 5.—Subject to section 534, the Secretary of the Interior shall offer Tract 2 and Tract 5 to BSNC under the Alaska Native Claims Settlement Act (43 U.S.C. 1601 et seq.).

(2) OFFER TO BSNC.—

(A) ACCEPTANCE BY BSNC.—If BSNC chooses to accept an offer of conveyance of a Tract under paragraph (1), the Secretary of the Interior shall consider such Tract as within BSNC's entitlement under section 14(h)(8) of the Alaska Native Claims Settlement Act (43 U.S.C. 1613(h)(8)) and shall convey such Tract to BSNC.

(B) DECLINE BY BSNC.—If BSNC declines to accept an offer of conveyance of a Tract under paragraph (1), the Secretary of the Interior shall offer such Tract for conveyance to the State under the Act of July 7, 1958 (commonly known as the "Alaska Statehood Act") (48 U.S.C. note prec. 21; Public Law 85-508).

(3) OFFER TO STATE.—

(A) ACCEPTANCE BY STATE.—If the State chooses to accept an offer of conveyance of a Tract under paragraph (2)(B), the Secretary of the Interior shall consider such Tract as within the State's entitlement under the Act of July 7, 1958 (commonly known as the "Alaska Statehood Act") (48 U.S.C. note prec. 21; Public Law 85-508) and shall convey such Tract to the State.

(B) DECLINE BY STATE.—If the State declines to accept an offer of conveyance of a Tract offered under paragraph (2)(B), such Tract shall be disposed of pursuant to applicable public land laws.

(e) ORDER OF OFFER TO CONVEY TRACT 6.—

(1) OFFER.—Subject to section 534, the Secretary of the Interior shall offer Tract 6 for conveyance to the State.

(2) OFFER TO STATE.—

(A) ACCEPTANCE BY STATE.—If the State chooses to accept an offer of conveyance of Tract 6 under paragraph (1), the Secretary of the Interior shall consider Tract 6 as within the State's entitlement under the Act of July 7, 1958 (commonly known as the "Alaska Statehood Act") (48 U.S.C. note prec. 21; Public Law 85-508) and shall convey Tract 6 to the State.

(B) DECLINE BY STATE.—If the State declines to accept an offer of conveyance of Tract 6 under paragraph (1), the Secretary of the Interior shall offer Tract 6 for conveyance to BSNC under the Alaska Native Claims Settlement Act (43 U.S.C. 1601 et seq.).

(3) OFFER TO BSNC.—

(A) ACCEPTANCE BY BSNC.—

(i) IN GENERAL.—Subject to clause (ii), if BSNC chooses to accept an offer of conveyance of Tract 6 under paragraph (2)(B), the Secretary of the Interior shall consider Tract 6 as within BSNC's entitlement under section 14(h)(8) of the Alaska Native Claims Settlement Act (43 U.S.C. 1613(h)(8)) and shall convey Tract 6 to BSNC.

(ii) LEASE BY THE STATE.—The conveyance of Tract 6 to BSNC shall be subject to BSNC negotiating a lease of Tract 6 to the State at no cost to the State, if the State requests such a lease.

(B) DECLINE BY BSNC.—If BSNC declines to accept an offer of conveyance of Tract 6 under paragraph (2)(B), the Secretary of the Interior shall dispose of Tract 6 pursuant to the applicable public land laws.

(f) REMEDIAL ACTIONS.—For purposes of the conveyances under this section, the remedial actions required under section 120(h) of the Comprehensive Environmental Response, Compensation, and Liability Act of 1980 (42 U.S.C. 9620(h)) may be completed by the United States Coast Guard after the date of such conveyance and a deed entered into for such conveyance shall include a clause granting the United States Coast Guard access to the property in any case in which remedial action or corrective action is found to be necessary after the date of such conveyance.

SEC. 534. [42 U.S.C. 9620 note] ENVIRONMENTAL COMPLIANCE, LIABILITY, AND MONITORING.

(a) ENVIRONMENTAL COMPLIANCE.—After the date on which the Secretary of the Interior conveys land under section 533 of this Act, nothing in this Act or any amendment made by this Act may be construed to affect or limit the application of or obligation to comply with any applicable environmental law, including section 120(h) of the Comprehensive Environmental Response, Compensation, and Liability Act of 1980 (42 U.S.C. 9620(h)), with respect to contaminants on such land prior to the date on which the land is conveyed.

(b) LIABILITY.—A person to which a conveyance is made under this subtitle shall hold the United States harmless from any liability with respect to activities carried out on or after the date of the conveyance of the real property conveyed. The United States shall remain responsible for any liability with respect to activities carried out before such date on the real property conveyed.

(c) MONITORING OF KNOWN CONTAMINATION.—

(1) IN GENERAL.—To the extent practicable and subject to paragraph (2), any contamination in a Tract to be conveyed to the State or BSNC under this subtitle that—

(A) is identified in writing prior to the conveyance; and

(B) does not pose an immediate or long-term risk to human health or the environment;

may be routinely monitored and managed by the State or BSNC, as applicable, through institutional controls.

(2) INSTITUTIONAL CONTROLS.—Institutional controls may be used if—

(A) the Administrator of the Environmental Protection Agency and the Governor of the State concur that such controls are protective of human health and the environment; and

(B) such controls are carried out in accordance with Federal and State law.

SEC. 535. EASEMENTS AND ACCESS.

(a) USE BY COAST GUARD.—The Secretary of the Interior shall make each conveyance of any relevant Tract under this subtitle subject to an easement granting the Coast Guard, at no cost to the Coast Guard—

(1) use of all existing and future landing pads, airstrips, runways, and taxiways that are located on such Tract; and

(2) the right to access such landing pads, airstrips, runways, and taxiways.

(b) USE BY STATE.—For any Tract conveyed to BSNC under this subtitle, BSNC shall provide to the State, if requested and pursuant to negotiated terms with the State, an easement granting to the State, at no cost to the State—

(1) use of all existing and future landing pads, airstrips, runways, and taxiways located on such Tract; and

(2) a right to access such landing pads, airstrips, runways, and taxiways.

(c) RIGHT OF ACCESS OR RIGHT OF WAY.—If the State requests a right of access or right of way for a road from the airstrip to the southern tip of Point Spencer, the location of such right of access or right of way shall be determined by the State, in consultation with the Secretary and BSNC, so that such right of access or right of way is compatible with other existing or planned infrastructure development at Point Spencer.

(d) ACCESS EASEMENT ACROSS TRACTS 2, 5, AND 6.—In conveyance documents to the State and BSNC under this subtitle, the Coast Guard shall retain an access easement across Tracts 2, 5, and 6 reasonably necessary to afford the Coast Guard with access to Tracts 1, 3, and 4 for its operations.

(e) ACCESS.—Not later than 30 days after the date of the enactment of this Act, the Coast Guard shall provide to the State and BSNC, access to Tracts for planning, design, and engineering related to remediation and use of and construction on those Tracts.

(f) PUBLIC ACCESS EASEMENTS.—No public access easements may be reserved to the United States under section 17(b) of the Alaska Native Claims Settlement Act (43 U.S.C. 1616(b)) with respect to the land conveyed under this subtitle.

SEC. 536. RELATIONSHIP TO PUBLIC LAND ORDER 2650.

(a) TRACTS NOT CONVEYED.—Any Tract that is not conveyed under this subtitle shall remain withdrawn pursuant to Public Land Order 2650 (published in the Federal Register on April 12, 1962).

(b) TRACTS CONVEYED.—For any Tract conveyed under this subtitle, Public Land Order 2650 shall automatically terminate upon issuance of a conveyance document issued pursuant to this subtitle for such Tract.

SEC. 537. ARCHEOLOGICAL AND CULTURAL RESOURCES.

Conveyance of any Tract under this subtitle shall not affect investigations, criminal jurisdiction, and responsibilities regarding theft or vandalism of archeological or cultural resources located in or on such Tract that took place prior to conveyance under this subtitle.

SEC. 538. MAPS AND LEGAL DESCRIPTIONS.

(a) PREPARATION OF MAPS AND LEGAL DESCRIPTIONS.—As soon

as practicable after the date of the enactment of this Act, the Secretary of the Interior in consultation with the Secretary shall prepare maps and legal descriptions of Tract 1, Tract 2, Tract 3, Tract 4, Tract 5, and Tract 6. In doing so, the Secretary of the Interior may use metes and bounds legal descriptions based upon the official survey plats of Point Spencer accepted by the Bureau of Land Management on December 6, 1978, and on information provided by the Secretary.

(b) SURVEY.—Not later than 5 years after the date of the enactment of this Act, the Secretary of the Interior shall survey Tracts conveyed under this subtitle and patent the Tracts in accordance with the official plats of survey.

(c) LEGAL EFFECT.—The maps and legal descriptions prepared under subsection (a) and the surveys prepared under subsection (b) shall have the same force and effect as if the maps and legal descriptions were included in this Act.

(d) CORRECTIONS.—The Secretary of the Interior may correct any clerical and typographical errors in the maps and legal descriptions prepared under subsection (a) and the surveys prepared under subsection (b).

(e) AVAILABILITY.—Copies of the maps and legal descriptions prepared under subsection (a) and the surveys prepared under subsection (b) shall be available for public inspection in the appropriate offices of—

(1) the Bureau of Land Management; and

(2) the Coast Guard.

SEC. 539. CHARGEABILITY FOR LAND CONVEYED.

(a) CONVEYANCES TO ALASKA.—The Secretary of the Interior shall charge any conveyance of land conveyed to the State of Alaska pursuant to this subtitle against the State's remaining entitlement under section 6(b) of the Act of July 7, 1958 (commonly known as the "Alaska Statehood Act"; Public Law 85-508: 72 Stat. 339).

(b) CONVEYANCES TO BSNC.—The Secretary of the Interior shall charge any conveyance of land conveyed to BSNC pursuant to this subtitle, against BSNC's remaining entitlement under section 14(h)(8) of the Alaska Native Claims Settlement Act (43 U.S.C. 1613(h)(8)).

SEC. 540. REDUNDANT CAPABILITY.

(a) IN GENERAL.—Except as provided in subsection (b), section 681 of title 14, United States Code, as amended by this Act, shall not be construed to prohibit any transfer or conveyance of lands under this subtitle or any actions that involve the dismantling or disposal of infrastructure that supported the former LORAN system that are associated with the transfer or conveyance of lands under this subtitle.

(b) CONTINUED ACCESS TO AND USE OF FACILITIES.—If the Secretary of the department in which the Coast Guard is operating determines, within the 5-year period beginning on the date of the enactment of this Act, that a facility on any of Tract 1, Tract 3, or Tract 4 that is transferred under this subtitle is subsequently required to provide a positioning, navigation, and timing system to provide redundant capability in the event GPS signals are disrupted, the Secretary may, for as long as such facility is needed to provide redundant capability—

(1) operate, maintain, keep, locate, inspect, repair, and replace such facility; and

(2) in carrying out the activities described in paragraph (1), enter, at any time, the facility without notice to the extent that it is not possible to provide advance notice.

SEC. 541. PORT COORDINATION COUNCIL FOR POINT SPENCER.

(a) ESTABLISHMENT.—There is established a Port Coordination Council for the Port of Point Spencer.

(b) MEMBERSHIP.—The Council shall consist of a representative appointed by each of the following:

(1) The State.

(2) BSNC (to serve as Council Chair).

(3) The Denali Commission.

(4) An oil spill removal organization that serves the area in which such Port is located.

(5) A salvage and marine firefighting organization that serves the area in which such Port is located. .

(c) DUTIES.—The duties of the Council are as follows:

(1) To develop a Port Management Coordination Plan to help coordinate infrastructure development and operations at

the Port of Point Spencer, that includes plans for—

(A) construction;

(B) funding eligibility; and

(C) land use planning and developmentat Point Spencer in support of the activities for which Congress finds a compelling need in section 531 of this subtitle.

(2) Update the Plan annually for the first 5 years after the date of the enactment of this Act and biennially thereafter.

(3) Facilitate coordination among members of the Council on the development and use of the land and coastline of Point Spencer, as such development and use relate to activities of the Council at the Port of Point Spencer.

(4) Assess the need, benefits, efficacy, and desirability of establishing in the future a port authority at Point Spencer under State law and act upon that assessment, as appropriate, including taking steps for the potential formation of such a port authority.

(d) PLAN.—In addition to the requirements under subsection (c)(1) to the greatest extent practicable, the Plan developed by the Council shall facilitate and support the statutory missions and duties of the Coast Guard and operations of the Coast Guard in the Arctic.

(e) COSTS.—Operations and management costs for airstrips, runways, and taxiways at Point Spencer shall be determined pursuant to provisions of the Plan, as negotiated by the Council.

TITLE VI—MISCELLANEOUS

SEC. 601. MODIFICATION OF REPORTS.

(a) DISTANT WATER TUNA FLEET.—Section 421(d) of the Coast Guard and Maritime Transportation Act of 2006 (46 U.S.C. 8103 note) is amended by striking "On March 1, 2007, and annually thereafter" and inserting "Not later than July 1 of each year".

(b) ANNUAL UPDATES ON LIMITS TO LIABILITY.—Section 603(c)(3) of the Coast Guard and Maritime Transportation Act of 2006 (33 U.S.C. 2704 note) is amended by striking "on an annual basis." and inserting "not later than January 30 of the year following each year in which occurs an oil discharge from a vessel or nonvessel source that results or is likely to result in removal costs and damages (as those terms are defined in section 1001 of the Oil Pollution Act of 1990 (33 U.S.C. 2701)) that exceed liability limits established under section 1004 of the Oil Pollution Act of 1990 (33 U.S.C. 2704).".

(c) REPORT.—Not later than 60 days after the date of the enactment of this Act, the Commandant of the Coast Guard shall submit to the Secretary of the department in which the Coast Guard is operating a report detailing the specifications and capabilities for interoperable communications the Commandant determines are necessary to allow the Coast Guard to successfully carry out its missions that require communications with other Federal agencies, State and local governments, and nongovernmental entities.

SEC. 602. SAFE VESSEL OPERATION IN THE GREAT LAKES.

The Howard Coble Coast Guard and Maritime Transportation Act of 2014 (Public Law 113-281) is amended—

(1) [16 U.S.C. 1431 note] in section 610, by—

(A) striking the section enumerator and heading and inserting the following:

"SEC. 610. SAFE VESSEL OPERATION IN THE GREAT LAKES"

(B) striking "existing boundaries and any future expanded boundaries of the Thunder Bay National Marine Sanctuary and Underwater Preserve" and inserting "boundaries of any national marine sanctuary that preserves shipwrecks or maritime heritage in the Great Lakes"; and

(C) inserting before the period at the end the following: ", unless the designation documents for such sanctuary do not allow taking up or discharging ballast water in such sanctuary"; and

(2) in the table of contents in section 2, by striking the item relating to such section and inserting the following:

"Sec. 610. Safe vessel operation in the Great Lakes."

SEC. 603. USE OF VESSEL SALE PROCEEDS.

(a) AUDIT.—The Comptroller General of the United States shall conduct an audit of funds credited in each fiscal year after fiscal year 2004 to the Vessel Operations Revolving Fund that are attributable to the sale of obsolete vessels in the National Defense Reserve Fleet that were scrapped or sold under sections 57102, 57103, and 57104 of title 46, United States Code, including—

(1) a complete accounting of all vessel sale proceeds attributable to the sale of obsolete vessels in the National Defense Reserve Fleet that were scrapped or sold under sections 57102, 57103, and 57104 of title 46, United States Code, in each fiscal year after fiscal year 2004;

(2) the annual apportionment of proceeds accounted for under paragraph (1) among the uses authorized under section 308704 of title 54, United States Code, in each fiscal year after fiscal year 2004, including—

(A) for National Maritime Heritage Grants, including a list of all annual National Maritime Heritage Grant grant and subgrant awards that identifies the respective grant and subgrant recipients and grant and subgrant amounts;

(B) for the preservation and presentation to the public of maritime heritage property of the Maritime Administration;

(C) to the United States Merchant Marine Academy and State maritime academies, including a list of annual awards; and

(D) for the acquisition, repair, reconditioning, or improvement of vessels in the National Defense Reserve Fleet; and

(3) an accounting of proceeds, if any, attributable to the sale of obsolete vessels in the National Defense Reserve Fleet that were scrapped or sold under sections 57102, 57103, and 57104 of title 46, United States Code, in each fiscal year after fiscal year 2004, that were expended for uses not authorized under section 308704 of title 54, United States Code.

(b) SUBMISSION TO CONGRESS.—Not later than 180 days after the date of the enactment this Act, the Comptroller General shall submit the audit conducted in subsection (a) to the Committee on Armed Services, the Committee on Natural Resources, and the Committee on Transportation and Infrastructure of the House of Representatives and the Committee on Commerce, Science, and Transportation of the Senate.

SEC. 604. NATIONAL ACADEMY OF SCIENCES COST ASSESSMENT.

(a) COST ASSESSMENT.—The Secretary of the department in which the Coast Guard is operating shall seek to enter into an arrangement with the National Academy of Sciences under which the Academy, by no later than 365 days after the date of the enactment of this Act, shall submit to the Committee on Transportation and Infrastructure and the Committee on Science, Space, and Technology of the House of Representatives and the Committee on Commerce, Science, and Transportation of the Senate an assessment of the costs incurred by the Federal Government to carry out polar icebreaking missions. The assessment shall—

(1) describe current and emerging requirements for the Coast Guard's polar icebreaking capabilities, taking into account the rapidly changing ice cover in the Arctic environment, national security considerations, and expanding commercial activities in the Arctic and Antarctic, including marine transportation, energy development, fishing, and tourism;

(2) identify potential design, procurement, leasing, service contracts, crewing, and technology options that could minimize life-cycle costs and optimize efficiency and reliability of Coast Guard polar icebreaker operations in the Arctic and Antarctic; and

(3) examine—

(A) Coast Guard estimates of the procurement and operating costs of a Polar icebreaker capable of carrying out Coast Guard maritime safety, national security, and stewardship responsibilities including—

(i) economies of scale that might be achieved for construction of multiple vessels; and

(ii) costs of renovating existing polar class icebreakers to operate for a period of no less than 10 years.

(B) the incremental cost to augment the design of such an icebreaker for multiuse capabilities for scientific missions;

(C) the potential to offset such incremental cost through cost-sharing agreements with other Federal departments and agencies; and

(D) United States polar icebreaking capability in comparison with that of other Arctic nations, and with nations that conduct research in the Arctic.

(b) INCLUDED COSTS.—For purposes of subsection (a), the assessment shall include costs incurred by the Federal Government for—

(1) the lease or operation and maintenance of the vessel or vessels concerned;

(2) disposal of such vessels at the end of the useful life of the vessels;

(3) retirement and other benefits for Federal employees who operate such vessels; and

(4) interest payments assumed to be incurred for Federal capital expenditures.

(c) ASSUMPTIONS.—For purposes of comparing the costs of such alternatives, the Academy shall assume that—

(1) each vessel under consideration is—

(A) capable of breaking out McMurdo Station and conducting Coast Guard missions in the Antarctic, and in the United States territory in the Arctic (as that term is defined in section 112 of the Arctic Research and Policy Act of 1984 (15 U.S.C. 4111)); and

(B) operated for a period of 30 years;

(2) the acquisition of services and the operation of each vessel begins on the same date; and

(3) the periods for conducting Coast Guard missions in the Arctic are of equal lengths.

(d) USE OF INFORMATION.—In formulating cost pursuant to subsection (a), the National Academy of Sciences may utilize information from other Coast Guard reports, assessments, or analyses regarding existing Coast Guard Polar class icebreakers or for the acquisition of a polar icebreaker for the Federal Government.

SEC. 605. COASTWISE ENDORSEMENTS.

(a) "ELETTRA III".—

(1) IN GENERAL.—Notwithstanding sections 12112 and 12132, of title 46, United States Code, and subject to paragraphs (2) and (3), the Secretary of the department in

which the Coast Guard is operating may issue a certificate of documentation with a coastwise endorsement for the vessel M/V Elettra III (United States official number 694607).

(2) LIMITATION ON OPERATION.—Coastwise trade authorized under a certificate of documentation issued under paragraph (1) shall be limited to the carriage of passengers and equipment in association with the operation of the vessel in the Puget Sound region to support marine and maritime science education.

(3) TERMINATION OF EFFECTIVENESS OF CERTIFICATE.—A certificate of documentation issued under paragraph (1) shall expire on the earlier of—

(A) the date of the sale of the vessel or the entity that owns the vessel;

(B) the date any repairs or alterations are made to the vessel outside of the United States; or

(C) the date the vessel is no longer operated as a vessel in the Puget Sound region to support the marine and maritime science education.

(b) "F/V RONDYS".—Notwithstanding section 12132 of title 46, United States Code, the Secretary of the department in which the Coast Guard is operating may issue a certificate of documentation with a coastwise endorsement for the F/V Rondys (O.N. 291085)

SEC. 606. INTERNATIONAL ICE PATROL.

(a) REQUIREMENT FOR REPORT.—Not later than 180 days after the date of the enactment of this Act, the Commandant of the Coast Guard shall submit to the Committee on Commerce, Science, and Transportation of the Senate and the Committee on Transportation and Infrastructure and the Committee on Science, Space, and Technology of the House of Representatives a report that describes the current operations to perform the International Ice Patrol mission and on alternatives for carrying out that mission, including satellite surveillance technology.

(b) ALTERNATIVES.—The report required by subsection (a) shall include whether an alternative—

(1) provides timely data on ice conditions with the highest possible resolution and accuracy;

(2) is able to operate in all weather conditions or any time

of day; and

(3) is more cost effective than the cost of current operations.

SEC. 607. ASSESSMENT OF OIL SPILL RESPONSE AND CLEANUP ACTIVITIES IN THE GREAT LAKES.

(a) ASSESSMENT.—The Commandant of the Coast Guard, in consultation with the Administrator of the National Oceanic and Atmospheric Administration and the head of any other agency the Commandant determines appropriate, shall conduct an assessment of the effectiveness of oil spill response activities specific to the Great Lakes. Such assessment shall include—

(1) an evaluation of new research into oil spill impacts in fresh water under a wide range of conditions; and

(2) an evaluation of oil spill prevention and clean up contingency plans, in order to improve understanding of oil spill impacts in the Great Lakes and foster innovative improvements to safety technologies and environmental protection systems.

(b) REPORT TO CONGRESS.—Not later than 2 years after the date of the enactment of this Act, the Commandant of the Coast Guard shall submit to the Congress a report on the results of the assessment required by subsection (a).

SEC. 608. REPORT ON STATUS OF TECHNOLOGY DETECTING PASSENGERS WHO HAVE FALLEN OVERBOARD.

Not later than 18 months after the date of the enactment of this Act, the Commandant of the Coast Guard shall submit a report to the Committee on Commerce, Science, and Transportation of the Senate and the Committee on Transportation and Infrastructure of the House of Representatives that—

(1) describes the status of technology for immediately detecting passengers who have fallen overboard;

(2) includes a recommendation to cruise lines on the feasibility of implementing technology that immediately detects passengers who have fallen overboard, factoring in cost and the risk of false positives;

(3) includes data collected from cruise lines on the status of the integration of the technology described in paragraph (2) on cruise ships, including—

(A) the number of cruise ships that have the technology

to capture images of passengers who have fallen overboard; and

(B) the number of cruise lines that have tested technology that can detect passengers who have fallen overboard; and

(4) includes information on any other available technologies that cruise ships could integrate to assist in facilitating the search and rescue of a passenger who has fallen overboard.

SEC. 609. VENUE.

Section 311(d) of the Magnuson-Stevens Fishery Conservation and Management Act (16 U.S.C. 1861(d)) is amended by striking the second sentence and inserting "In the case of Hawaii or any possession of the United States in the Pacific Ocean, the appropriate court is the United States District Court for the District of Hawaii, except that in the case of Guam and Wake Island, the appropriate court is the United States District Court for the District of Guam, and in the case of the Northern Mariana Islands, the appropriate court is the United States District Court for the District of the Northern Mariana Islands.".

SEC. 610. DISPOSITION OF INFRASTRUCTURE RELATED TO E-LORAN.

(a) DISPOSITION OF INFRASTRUCTURE.—

(1) IN GENERAL.—Chapter 17 of title 14, United States Code, is amended by adding at the end the following:

"SEC. 681. [14 U.S.C. 681] Disposition of infrastructure related to E-LORAN

"(a) IN GENERAL.—The Secretary may not carry out activities related to the dismantling or disposal of infrastructure comprising the LORAN-C system until the date on which the Secretary provides to the Committee on Transportation and Infrastructure and the Committee on Appropriations of the House of Representatives and the Committee on Commerce, Science, and Transportation and the Committee on Appropriations of the Senate notice of a determination by the Secretary that such infrastructure is not required to provide a positioning, navigation, and timing system to provide redundant capability in the event the Global

Positioning System signals are disrupted.

"(b) EXCEPTION.—Subsection (a) does not apply to activities necessary for the safety of human life.

"(c) DISPOSITION OF PROPERTY.—

"(1) IN GENERAL.—On any date after the notification is made under subsection (a), the Administrator of General Services, acting on behalf of the Secretary, may, notwithstanding any other provision of law, sell any real and personal property under the administrative control of the Coast Guard and used for the LORAN-C system, subject to such terms and conditions that the Secretary believes to be necessary to protect government interests and program requirements of the Coast Guard.

"(2) AVAILABILITY OF PROCEEDS.—

"(A) AVAILABILITY OF PROCEEDS.—The proceeds of such sales, less the costs of sale incurred by the General Services Administration, shall be deposited as offsetting collections into the Coast Guard 'Environmental Compliance and Restoration' account and, without further appropriation, shall be available until expended for—

"(i) environmental compliance and restoration purposes associated with the LORAN-C system;

"(ii) the costs of securing and maintaining equipment that may be used as a backup to the Global Positioning System or to meet any other Federal navigation requirement;

"(iii) the demolition of improvements on such real property; and

"(iv) the costs associated with the sale of such real and personal property, including due diligence requirements, necessary environmental remediation, and reimbursement of expenses incurred by the General Services Administration.

"(B) OTHER ENVIRONMENTAL COMPLIANCE AND RESTORATION ACTIVITIES.—After the completion of activities described in subparagraph (A), the unexpended balances of such proceeds shall be available for any other environmental compliance and restoration activities of the Coast Guard."

(2) CLERICAL AMENDMENT.—The analysis at the beginning of such chapter is amended by adding at the end the following:

"681. Disposition of infrastructure related to E-LORAN.".

(3) CONFORMING REPEALS.—

(A) Section 229 of the Howard Coble Coast Guard and Maritime Transportation Act of 2014 (Public Law 113- 281; 128 Stat. 3040), and the item relating to that section in section 2 of such Act, are repealed.

(B) Subsection 559(e) of the Department of Homeland Security Appropriations Act, 2010 (Public Law 111-83; 123 Stat. 2180) is repealed.

(b) AGREEMENTS TO DEVELOP BACKUP POSITIONING, NAVIGATION, AND TIMING SYSTEM.—Section 93(a) of title 14, United States Code, is amended by striking "and" after the semicolon at the end of paragraph (23), by striking the period at the end of paragraph (24) and inserting "; and", and by adding at the end the following the following:

"(25) enter into cooperative agreements, contracts, and other agreements with Federal entities and other public or private entities, including academic entities, to develop a positioning, navigation, and timing system to provide redundant capability in the event Global Positioning System signals are disrupted, which may consist of an enhanced LORAN system."

SEC. 611. PARKING.

Section 611(a) of the Howard Coble Coast Guard and Maritime Transportation Act of 2014 (Public Law 113-281; 128 Stat. 3064) is amended by adding at the end the following:

"(3) REIMBURSEMENT.—Through September 30, 2017, additional parking made available under paragraph (2) shall be made available at no cost to the Coast Guard or members and employees of the Coast Guard."

SEC. 612. INAPPLICABILITY OF LOAD LINE REQUIREMENTS TO CERTAIN UNITED STATES VESSELS TRAVELING IN THE GULF OF MEXICO.

Section 5102(b) of title 46, United States Code, is amended by adding at the end the following:

"(13) a vessel of the United States on a domestic voyage that is within the Gulf of Mexico and operating not more than 15 nautical miles seaward of the base line from which the territorial sea of the United States is measured between Crystal Bay, Florida and Hudson Creek, Florida."

JOHN S. McCAIN NATIONAL DEFENSE AUTHORIZATION ACT FOR FISCAL YEAR 2019

PUBLIC LAW 115-232

AS AMENDED THROUGH P.L. 118-159

John S. McCain National Defense Authorization Act for Fiscal Year 2019

[(Public Law 115–232)]

[As Amended Through P.L. 118–159, Enacted December 23, 2024]

AN ACT To authorize appropriations for fiscal year 2019 for military activities of the Department of Defense, for military construction, and for defense activities of the Department of Energy, to prescribe military personnel strengths for such fiscal year, and for other purposes.

Be it enacted by the Senate and House of Representatives of the United States of America in Congress assembled,

SECTION 1. SHORT TITLE.

(a) IN GENERAL.—This Act may be cited as the "John S. McCain National Defense Authorization Act for Fiscal Year 2019".

(b) REFERENCES.—Any reference in this or any other Act to the "National Defense Authorization Act for Fiscal Year 2019" shall be deemed to be a reference to the "John S. McCain National Defense Authorization Act for Fiscal Year 2019".

SEC. 2. ORGANIZATION OF ACT INTO DIVISIONS; TABLE OF CONTENTS.

(a) DIVISIONS.—This Act is organized into four divisions as follows:

(1) Division A—Department of Defense Authorizations.

(2) Division B—Military Construction Authorizations.

(3) Division C—Department of Energy National Security Authorizations and Other Authorizations.

(4) Division D—Funding Tables.

(b) TABLE OF CONTENTS.—The table of contents for this Act is as follows:

* * * * * * *

* * * * * * *

DIVISION C—DEPARTMENT OF ENERGY NATIONAL SECURITY AUTHORIZATIONS AND OTHER AUTHORIZATIONS

* * * * * * *

TITLE XXXV—MARITIME MATTERS

Subtitle A—Maritime Administration

SEC. 3501. AUTHORIZATION OF THE MARITIME ADMINISTRATION.

(a) IN GENERAL.—There are authorized to be appropriated to the Department of Transportation for fiscal year 2019, to be available without fiscal year limitation if so provided in appropriations Acts, for programs associated with maintaining the United States merchant marine, the following amounts:

(1) For expenses necessary for operations of the United States Merchant Marine Academy, $74,593,000, of which—

(A) $70,593,000 shall be for Academy operations; and

(B) $4,000,000 shall remain available until expended for capital asset management at the Academy.

(2) For expenses necessary to support the State maritime academies, $32,200,000, of which—

(A) $2,400,000 shall remain available until September 30, 2019, for the Student Incentive Program;

(B) $6,000,000 shall remain available until expended for direct payments to such academies;

(C) $22,000,000 shall remain available until expended for maintenance and repair of State maritime academy training vessels; and

(D) $1,800,000 shall remain available until expended for training ship fuel assistance.

(3) For expenses necessary to support the National Security Multi-Mission Vessel Program, $300,000,000, which shall remain available until expended.

(4) For expenses necessary to support Maritime Administration operations and programs, $60,442,000, of which $5,000,000 shall remain available until expended for port infrastructure development under section 50302 of title 46, United States Code.

(5) For expenses necessary to dispose of vessels in the National Defense Reserve Fleet, $5,000,000, which shall remain available until expended.

(6) For expenses necessary to maintain and preserve a United States flag merchant marine to serve the national security needs of the United States under chapter 531 of title 46, United States Code, $300,000,000.

(7) For expenses necessary for the loan guarantee program authorized under chapter 537 of title 46, United States Code, $33,000,000, of which—

(A) $30,000,000 may be used for the cost (as defined in section 502(5) of the Federal Credit Reform Act of 1990 (2 U.S.C. 661a(5))) of loan guarantees under the program; and

(B) $3,000,000 may be used for administrative expenses relating to loan guarantee commitments under the program.

(8) For expenses necessary to provide assistance to small shipyards and for maritime training programs under section 54101 of title 46, United States Code, $35,000,000.

(b) CAPITAL ASSET MANAGEMENT PROGRAM REPORT.—Not later than 180 days after the date of the enactment of this Act, the Maritime Administrator shall submit to the Committee on Commerce, Science, and Transportation of the Senate and the Committee on Armed Services and the Committee on Transportation and Infrastructure of the House of Representatives a report on the status of unexpended appropriations for capital asset management at the United States Merchant Marine Academy, and the plan for expending such appropriations.

SEC. 3502. [10 U.S.C. 2218 note] COMPLIANCE BY READY RESERVE FLEET VESSELS WITH SOLAS LIFEBOATS AND FIRE SUPPRESSION REQUIREMENTS.

The Secretary of Defense shall, consistent with section 2244a of title 10, United States Code, use authority under section 2218 of such title to make such modifications to Ready Reserve Fleet vessels as are necessary for such vessels to comply requirements for lifeboats and fire suppression under the International Convention for the Safety of Life at Sea by not later than October 1, 2021.

SEC. 3503. MARITIME ADMINISTRATION NATIONAL SECURITY MULTI-MISSION VESSEL PROGRAM.

Section 3505 of the National Defense Authorization Act for Fiscal Year 2017 (Public Law 114-328; 130 Stat. 2776) is amended by adding at the end the following:

"(h) LIMITATION ON USE OF FUNDS FOR USED VESSELS.—Amounts authorized by this or any other Act for use by the Maritime Administration to carry out this section may not be used for the procurement of any used vessel."

SEC. 3504. PERMANENT AUTHORITY OF SECRETARY OF TRANSPORTATION TO ISSUE VESSEL WAR RISK INSURANCE.

(a) IN GENERAL.—Section 53912 of title 46, United States Code, is repealed.

(b) [46 U.S.C. 53901] CLERICAL AMENDMENT.—The table of sections at the beginning of chapter 539 of title 46, United States Code,is amended by striking the item relating to section 53912.

SEC. 3505. USE OF STATE MARITIME ACADEMY TRAINING VESSELS.

Section 51504(g) of title 46, United States Code, is amended to read as follows:

"(g) VESSEL SHARING.—

"(1) IN GENERAL.—Not later than 90 days after the date of enactment of the National Defense Authorization Act for Fiscal Year 2019, the Secretary, acting through the Maritime Administrator, shall upon consultation with the maritime academies, and to the extent feasible with the consent of the maritime academies, implement a program of training vessel sharing, requiring maritime academies to share training vessel provided by the Secretary among maritime academies, as necessary to ensure that training needs of each academy are met.

"(2) PROGRAM OF VESSEL SHARING.—For purposes of this subsection, a program of vessel sharing shall include—

"(A) ways to maximize the available underway training available in the fleet of training vessels;

"(B) coordinating the dates and duration of training cruises with the academic calendars of maritime academies;

"(C) coordinating academic programs designed to be implemented aboard training vessels among maritime academies; and

"(D) identifying ways to minimize costs.

"(3) ADDITIONAL FUNDING.—Subject to the availability of appropriations, the Maritime Administrator may provide additional funding to State maritime academies during periods of limited training vessel capacity, for costs associated with training vessel sharing.

"(4) EVALUATION.—Not later than 30 days after the beginning of each fiscal year, the Secretary, acting through the Maritime Administrator, shall evaluate the vessel sharing program under this subsection to determine the optimal utilization of State maritime training vessels, and modify the program as necessary to improve utilization."

SEC. 3506. [46 U.S.C. 51301 note] CONCURRENT JURISDICTION.

Notwithstanding any other law, the Secretary of Transportation may relinquish, at the Secretary's discretion, to the State of New York, such measure of legislative jurisdiction over the lands constituting the United States Merchant Marine Academy in King's Point, New York, as is necessary to establish concurrent jurisdiction between the Federal Government and the State of New York. Such partial relinquishment of legislative jurisdiction shall be accomplished—

(1) by filing with the Governor of New York a notice of relinquishment to take effect upon acceptance thereof; or

(2) as the laws of that State may provide.

SEC. 3507. UNITED STATES MERCHANT MARINE ACADEMY POLICY ON SEXUAL HARASSMENT, DATING VIOLENCE, DOMESTIC VIOLENCE, SEXUAL ASSAULT, AND STALKING.

(a) POLICY ON SEXUAL HARASSMENT, DATING VIOLENCE, DOMESTIC VIOLENCE, SEXUAL ASSAULT, AND STALKING.—Section 51318 of title 46, United States Code, is amended—

(1) in subsection (a)(2)—

(A) in subparagraph (A), by inserting "and prevention" after "awareness";

(B) by redesignating subparagraph (B) as subparagraph (C), and subparagraphs (C) through (F) as subparagraphs (E) through (H), respectively;

(C) by inserting after subparagraph (A) the following:

"(B) procedures for documenting, tracking, and maintaining the data required to conduct the annual assessments to determine the effectiveness of the policies, procedures, and training program of the

Academy with respect to sexual harassment, dating violence, domestic violence, sexual assault, and stalking involving cadets or other Academy personnel, as required by subsection (c);"

; and

(D) by inserting after subparagraph (C), as redesignated by subparagraph (B), the following:

"(D) procedures for investigating sexual harassment, dating violence, domestic violence, sexual assault, or stalking involving a cadet or other Academy personnel to determine whether disciplinary action is necessary;"

(2) in subsection (b)(2)(A), by inserting "and other Academy personnel" after "cadets at the Academy"; and

(3) in subsection (d)—

(A) in paragraph (2)(A) by inserting ", including sexual harassment," after "sexual assaults, rapes, and other sexual offenses"; and

(B) in paragraph (4)(B), by striking "The Secretary" and inserting "Not later than January 15 of each year, the Secretary".

(b) [46 U.S.C. 51318 note] IMPLEMENTATION.—The Superintendent of the United States Merchant Marine Academy may implement the amendment to subsection (b)(2)(A) of section 51318 of title 46, United States Code, made by subsection (a)(2), by updating an existing plan issued pursuant to the National Defense Authorization Act for Fiscal Year 2018 (Public Law 115-91).

SEC. 3508. REPORT ON IMPLEMENTATION OF RECOMMENDATIONS FOR THE UNITED STATES MERCHANT MARINE ACADEMY SEXUAL ASSAULT PREVENTION AND RESPONSE PROGRAM.

Not later than April 1, 2019, the Maritime Administrator shall submit to the Committee on Commerce, Science, and Transportation of the Senate and the Committee on Armed Services and the Committee on Transportation and Infrastructure of the House of Representatives a report describing the progress of the Maritime Administration in implementing and closing each of the recommendations made in the Office of Inspector General's Report issued March 28, 2018 (ST-2018-039) identifying gaps in the United

States Merchant Marine Academy's Sexual Assault Prevention and Response Program.

SEC. 3509. REPORT ON THE APPLICATION OF THE UNIFORM CODE OF MILITARY JUSTICE TO THE UNITED STATES MERCHANT MARINE ACADEMY.

(a) REPORT.—Not later than 180 days after the date of the enactment of this Act, the Maritime Administrator shall submit a report to the Committee on Commerce, Science, and Transportation of the Senate and the Committee on Armed Services and the Committee on Transportation and Infrastructure of the House of Representatives on the impediments to the application of the Uniform Code of Military Justice at the United States Merchant Marine Academy.

(b) CONSULTATION.—The Maritime Administrator may, in preparing the report under subsection (a), consult with the Department of Defense, other Federal agencies, and non-Federal entities, as appropriate.

SEC. 3510. [46 U.S.C. 7502 note] ELECTRONIC RECORDS ON MARINER AVAILABILITY TO MEET NATIONAL SECURITY NEEDS.

The Secretary of the department in which the Coast Guard is operating shall ensure that electronic records maintained under section 7502 of title 46, United States Code, are able to be used by the Secretary of Transportation—

(1) to determine the potential availability of mariners credentialed under part E of subtitle II of title 46, United States Code, to meet national security sealift needs; and

(2) to receive information on the qualification of such mariners.

SEC. 3511. SMALL SHIPYARD GRANTS.

Section 54101(b) of title 46, United States Code, is amended—

(1) by redesignating paragraphs (2) and (3) as paragraphs (3) and (4), respectively;

(2) by inserting after paragraph (1) the following:

"(2) TIMING OF GRANT NOTICE.—The Administrator shall post a Notice of Funding Opportunity regarding grants awarded under this section not more than 15 days after the date of enactment of the appropriations Act for the fiscal year concerned."

; and

(3) in paragraph (4), as redesignated by paragraph (1), by striking "paragraph (2)" and inserting "paragraph (3)".

SEC. 3512. SEA YEAR ON CONTRACTED VESSELS.

Section 51307 of title 46, United States Code, is amended—

(1) by striking "The Secretary" and inserting the following:

"(a) IN GENERAL.—The Secretary"

(2) in paragraph (1) of subsection (a), by striking "owned or subsidized by" and inserting "owned, subsidized by, or contracted with"; and

(3) by adding at the end the following:

"(b) MARITIME SECURITY PROGRAM VESSELS.—The Secretary shall require an operator of a vessel participating in the Maritime Security Program under chapter 531 of this title to carry on each Maritime Security Program vessel 2 United States Merchant Marine Academy cadets, if available, on each voyage.

"(c) MILITARY SEALIFT COMMAND VESSELS.—

"(1) IN GENERAL.—Except as provided in paragraph (2), the Commander of the Military Sealift Command shall require an operator of a vessel in the United States Navy's Military Sealift Command to carry on each such vessel 2 United States Merchant Marine Academy cadets, if available, on each voyage, if the vessel—

"(A) is flagged in the United States; and

"(B) is rated at 10,000 gross tons or higher.

"(2) WAIVER.—The Commander of the Military Sealift Command may waive the requirement under paragraph (1) at any time if the Commander determines that carrying a cadet from the United States Merchant Marine Academy would place an undue burden on the vessel or the operator of the vessel.

"(d) DEFINITION OF OPERATOR.—In this section, the term 'operator' includes a government operator and a non-government operator.

"(e) SAVINGS CLAUSE.—Nothing in this section may be construed as affecting—

"(1) the discretion of the Secretary to determine whether to place a United States Merchant Marine Academy cadet on a vessel;

"(2) the authority of the Coast Guard regarding a vessel security plan approved under section 70103; or

"(3) the discretion of the master of the vessel to ensure the safety of all crew members."

SEC. 3513. GAO REPORT ON NATIONAL MARITIME STRATEGY.

(a) REPORT.—Not later than 12 months after the date of the enactment of this Act, the Comptroller General of the United States shall complete a study and submit to the Committee on Commerce, Science, and Transportation of the Senate, the Committee on Armed Services of the House of Representatives, and the Committee on Transportation and Infrastructure of the House of Representatives, a report on—

(1) the key challenges, if any, to ensuring that the United States marine transportation system and merchant marine are sufficient to support United States economic and defense needs, as articulated by the Maritime Administration, the Committee on the Marine Transportation System, and other stakeholders;

(2) the extent to which a national maritime strategy incorporates desirable characteristics of successful national strategies as identified by the Comptroller General, and any key obstacles (as identified by stakeholders) to successfully implementing such strategies; and

(3) the extent to which Federal efforts to establish a national maritime strategy are duplicative or fragmented, and if so, the impact on United States maritime policy for the future.

(b) DEADLINE.—Subsection (a) of section 603 of the Howard Coble Coast Guard and Maritime Transportation Act of 2014 (Public Law 113-281; 128 Stat. 3061) is amended by striking "Not later than 60 days after the date of the enactment of this Act" and inserting "Not later than 18 months after the date of the enactment of the John S. McCain National Defense Authorization Act for Fiscal Year 2019".

SEC. 3514. MULTI-YEAR CONTRACTS.

Section 3505 of the National Defense Authorization Act for Fiscal Year 2017 (Public Law 114-328; 130 Stat. 2776), as amended by section 3503 of this Act, is further amended by adding at the end the following:

"(i) CONTRACTING AUTHORITY NOT AFFECTED.—Nothing in this section may be construed to prohibit the entity responsible for contracting from entering into a multiple-year or block contract for the procurement of up to 6 new vessels and associated Government-furnished equipment, subject to the availability of appropriations."

SEC. 3515. MISCELLANEOUS.

(a) NONCOMMERCIAL VESSELS.—Section 3514(a) of the National Defense Authorization Act for Fiscal Year 2017 (Public Law 114-328; 46 U.S.C. 51318 note) is amended—

(1) by striking "Not later than" and inserting the following:

"(1) IN GENERAL.—Not later than"

; and

(2) by redesignating paragraphs (1) and (2) as subparagraphs (A) and (B), respectively, and adjusting the margins accordingly; and

(3) by adding at the end the following:

"(2) NONCOMMERCIAL VESSELS.—For the purposes of this section, vessels operated by any of the following entities shall not be considered commercial vessels:

"(A) Any entity or agency of the United States.

"(B) The government of a State or territory.

"(C) Any political subdivision of a State or territory.

"(D) Any other municipal organization."

(b) PASSENGER RECORDS.—Section 51322(c) of title 46, United States Code, is amended to read as follows:

"(c) MAINTENANCE OF SEXUAL ASSAULT TRAINING RECORDS.—The Maritime Administrator shall require the owner or operator of a commercial vessel, or the seafarer union for a commercial vessel, to maintain records of sexual assault training for any person required to have such training."

(c) NATIONAL OCEANIC AND ATMOSPHERIC ADMINISTRATION.—Section 3134 of title 40, United States Code, is amended by adding at the end the following:

"(c) NATIONAL OCEANIC AND ATMOSPHERIC ADMINISTRATION.—The Secretary of Commerce may waive this subchapter with respect to contracts for the construction, alteration, or repair of vessels, regardless of the terms of the contracts as to payment or title, when the contract is made under the Act entitled 'An Act to define the functions and duties of the Coast and Geodetic Survey, and for other purposes', approved August 6, 1947 (33 U.S.C. 883a et seq.)."

(d) ANNUAL PAYMENTS FOR MAINTENANCE AND SUPPORT.—Section 51505(b)(2) of title 46 is amended to read as follows:

"(2) MAXIMUM.—The amount under paragraph (1) may not be more than $25,000, unless the academy satisfies section 51506(b) of this title."

SEC. 3516. DEPARTMENT OF TRANSPORTATION INSPECTOR GENERAL REPORT ON TITLE XI PROGRAM.

Not later than 180 days after the date of enactment of this Act, the Department of Transportation Office of Inspector General shall—

(1) initiate an audit of the financial controls and protections included in the policies and procedures of the Department of Transportation for approving loan applications for the loan guarantee program authorized under chapter 537 of title 46, United States Code; and

(2) submit to the Committee on Commerce, Science, and Transportation of the Senate and the Committee on Armed Services and the Committee on Transportation and Infrastructure of the House of Representatives a report containing the results of that audit once the audit is completed.

Subtitle B—Coast Guard

SEC. 3521. ALIGNMENT WITH DEPARTMENT OF DEFENSE AND SEA SERVICES AUTHORITIES.

(a) PROHIBITING SEXUAL HARASSMENT; REPORT.—

(1) NOTIFICATION.—

(A) IN GENERAL.—The Commandant of the Coast Guard shall notify the Committee on Transportation and Infrastructure and the Committee on Homeland Security of the House of Representatives and the Committee on Commerce, Science, and Transportation of the Senate on August 26, 2018, if there is not in effect a general order or regulation prohibiting sexual harassment by members of the Coast Guard and clearly stating that a violation of such order or regulation is punishable in accordance with the Uniform Code of Military Justice.

(B) CONTENTS.—The notification required under subparagraph (A) shall include—

(i) details regarding the status of the drafting of such general order or regulation;

(ii) a projected implementation timeline for such general order or regulation; and

(iii) an explanation regarding any barriers to implementation.

(2) REPORT.—Section 217 of the Coast Guard Authorization Act of 2010 (Public Law 111-281; 14 U.S.C. 93 note) is amended—

(A) in subsection (a), by inserting "and incidents of sexual harassment" after "sexual assaults"; and

(B) in subsection (b)—

(i) in paragraph (1), by inserting "and incidents of sexual harassment" after "sexual assaults" each place it appears;

(ii) in paragraph (3), by inserting "and sexual harassment" after "sexual assault"; and

(iii) in paragraph (4), by inserting "and sexual harassment" after "sexual assault".

(b) ANNUAL PERFORMANCE REPORT.—

(1) IN GENERAL.—Chapter 29 of title 14, United States Code, is amended by adding at the end the following:

"SEC. 2905. [14 U.S.C. 2905] Annual performance repor

Not later than the date on which the President submits to Congress a budget pursuant to section 1105 of title 31, the Commandant of the Coast Guard shall make available on a public website and submit to the Committee on Transportation and Infrastructure of the House of Representatives and the Committee on Commerce, Science, and Transportation of the Senate an update on Coast Guard mission performance during the previous fiscal year."

(2) [14 U.S.C. 2901] CLERICAL AMENDMENT.—The analysis at the beginning of such chapter is amended by adding at the end the following:

"2905. Annual performance report."

SEC. 3522. PRELIMINARY DEVELOPMENT AND DEMONSTRATION.

Section 573 of title 14, United States Code, is amended—

(1) in subsection (b)(3), by—

(A) striking "require that safety concerns identified" and inserting "ensure that independent third parties and Government employees that identify safety concerns"; and

(B) striking "Coast Guard shall be communicated as" and inserting "Coast Guard communicate such concerns as";

(2) in subsection (b)(4), by striking "Any safety concerns that have been reported to the Chief Acquisition Officer for an acquisition program or project shall be reported by the Commandant" and inserting "The Commandant shall ensure that any safety concerns that have been communicated under paragraph (3) for an acquisition program or project are reported";

(3) in subsection (b)(5)—

(A) by striking the matter preceding subparagraph (A) and inserting the following:

"(5) ASSET ALREADY IN LOW, INITIAL, OR FULL-RATE PRODUCTION.—The Commandant shall ensure that if an independent third party or a Government employee identifies a safety concern with a capability or asset or any subsystems of a capability or asset not previously identified during operational test and evaluation of a capability or asset already in low, initial, or full-rate production—"

(B) in subparagraph (A), by inserting "the Commandant, through the Assistant Commandant for Capability, shall" before "notify"; and

(C) in subparagraph (B), by striking "notify the Chief Acquisition Officer and include in such notification" and inserting "the Deputy Commandant for Mission Support shall notify the Commandant and the Deputy Commandant for Operations of the safety concern within 50 days after the notification required under subparagraph (A), and include in such notification"; and

(4) in subsection (c)—

(A) in paragraph (2)(A), by striking "and that are delivered after the date of enactment of the Coast Guard Authorization Act of 2010"; and

(B) in paragraph (5), by striking "and delivered after the date of enactment of the Coast Guard Authorization Act of 2010".

SEC. 3523. CONTRACT TERMINATION.

(a) IN GENERAL.—Chapter 17 of title 14, United States Code, is amended by inserting after section 656 the following:

"SEC. 657. [14 U.S.C. 657] Contract terminatio

"(a) IN GENERAL.—

"(1) NOTIFICATION.—Before terminating a procurement or acquisition contract with a total value of more than $1,000,000, the Commandant of the Coast Guard shall notify each vendor under such contract and require the vendor to maintain all work product related to the contract until the earlier of—

"(A) not less than 1 year after the date of the notification; or

"(B) the date the Commandant notifies the vendor that maintenance of such work product is no longer required.

"(b) WORK PRODUCT DEFINED.—In this section the term 'work product'—

"(1) means tangible and intangible items and information produced or possessed as a result of a contract referred to in subsection (a); and

"(2) includes—

"(A) any completed end items;

"(B) any uncompleted end items; and

"(C) any property in the contractor's possession in which the United States Government has an interest.

"(c) PENALTY.—A vendor that fails to maintain work product as required under subsection (a) is liable to the United States for a civil penalty of not more than $25,000 for each day on which such work product is unavailable.

"(d) REPORT.—

"(1) IN GENERAL.—Except as provided in paragraph (2), not later than 45 days after the end of each fiscal year the Commandant of the Coast Guard shall provide to the Committee on Transportation and Infrastructure of the House of Representatives and the Committee on Commerce, Science, and Transportation of the Senate a report detailing—

"(A) all Coast Guard contracts with a total value of more than $1,000,000 that were terminated in the fiscal year;

"(B) all vendors who were notified under subsection (a)(1) in the fiscal year, and the date of such notification;

"(C) all criminal, administrative, and other investigations regarding any contract with a total value of more than $1,000,000 that were initiated by the Coast Guard in the fiscal year;

"(D) all criminal, administrative, and other investigations regarding contracts with a total value of more than $1,000,000 that were completed by the Coast Guard in the fiscal year; and

"(E) an estimate of costs incurred by the Coast Guard, including contract line items and termination costs, as a result of the requirements of this section.

"(2) LIMITATION.—The Commandant is not required to provide a report under paragraph (1) for any fiscal year for which there is no responsive information as described in subparagraphs (A) through (E) of paragraph (1)."

(b) [14 U.S.C. 631] CLERICAL AMENDMENT.—The analysis at the beginning of such chapter is amended by inserting after the item relating to section 656 the following:

"657. Contract termination."

SEC. 3524. REIMBURSEMENT FOR TRAVEL EXPENSES.

The text of section 518 of title 14, United States Codeis amended to read as follows:"In any case in which a covered beneficiary (as defined in section 1072(5) of title 10) resides on an island that is located in the 48 contiguous States and the District of Columbia and that lacks public access roads to the mainland, the Secretary shall reimburse the reasonable travel expenses of the covered beneficiary and, when accompaniment by an adult is necessary, for a parent or guardian of the covered beneficiary or another member of the covered beneficiary's family who is at least 21 years of age, if—

"(1) the covered beneficiary is referred by a primary care physician to a specialty care provider (as defined in section 1074i(b) of title 10) on the mainland who provides services less than 100 miles from the location where the beneficiary resides; or

"(2) the Coast Guard medical regional manager for the area in which such island is located determines that the covered beneficiary requires services of a primary care, specialty care, or dental provider and such a provider who is part of the network of providers of a TRICARE program (as that term is defined in section 1072(7) of title 10) does not practice on such island."

SEC. 3525. CAPITAL INVESTMENT PLAN.

Section 2902(a) of title 14, United States Code, is amended—

(1) by striking "On the date" and inserting "Not later than 60 days after the date";

(2) in paragraph (1)(D), by striking "and"; and

(3) by inserting after paragraph (1)(E) the following:

"(F) projected commissioning and decommissioning dates for each asset; and"

SEC. 3526. MAJOR ACQUISITION PROGRAM RISK ASSESSMENT.

(a) IN GENERAL.—Chapter 29 of title 14, United States Code, as amended by section 3521(b)(1) of this Act, is further amended by adding at the end the following:

"SEC. 2906. [14 U.S.C. 2906] Major acquisition program risk assessmen

"(a) IN GENERAL.—Not later than April 15 and October 15 of each year, the Commandant of the Coast Guard shall provide to the Committee on Transportation and Infrastructure of the House of Representatives and the Committee on Commerce, Science, and Transportation of the Senate a briefing regarding a current assessment of the risks associated with all current major acquisition programs, as that term is defined in section 2903(f).

"(b) ELEMENTS.—Each assessment under this subsection shall include, for each current major acquisition program, discussion of the following:

"(1) The top five current risks to such program.

"(2) Any failure of such program to demonstrate a key performance parameter or threshold during operational test and evaluation conducted during the 2 fiscal-year quarters preceding such assessment.

"(3) Whether there has been any decision in such 2 fiscal-year quarters to order full-rate production before all key performance parameters or thresholds are met.

"(4) Whether there has been any breach of major acquisition program cost (as defined by the Major Systems Acquisition Manual) in such 2 fiscal-year quarters.

"(5) Whether there has been any breach of major acquisition program schedule (as so defined) during such 2 fiscal-year quarters."

(b) [14 U.S.C. 2901] CLERICAL AMENDMENT.—The analysis at the beginning of such chapter is further amended by adding at the end the following:

"2906. Major acquisition program risk assessment."

(c) CONFORMING AMENDMENTS.—Section 2903 of title 14, United States Code, is amended—

(1) by striking subsection (f); and

(2) by redesignating subsection (g) as subsection (f).

SEC. 3527. MARINE SAFETY IMPLEMENTATION STATUS.

On the date on which the President submits to Congress a

budget for fiscal year 2020 under section 1105 of title 31, and on such date for each of the 2 subsequent years, the Commandant of the Coast Guard shall submit to the Committee on Transportation and Infrastructure of the House of Representatives and the Committee on Commerce, Science, and Transportation of the Senate a report on the status of implementation of each action outlined in the Commandant's final action memo dated December 19, 2017.

SEC. 3528. RETIREMENT OF VICE COMMANDANT.

(a) IN GENERAL.—Section 46 of title 14, United States Code, is amended—

(1) in the section heading, by inserting "or Vice Commandant" after "Commandant";

(2) by redesignating subsection (a) as subsection (a)(1);

(3) by adding at the end of subsection (a) the following:

"(2) A Vice Commandant who is not reappointed or appointed Commandant shall be retired with the grade of admiral at the expiration of the appointed term, except as provided in section 51(d)."

(4) in subsections (b) and (c), by inserting "or Vice Commandant" after "Commandant" each place it appears; and

(5) in subsection (c), by striking "his" and inserting "the officer's".

(b) CONFORMING AMENDMENT.—Section 51 of title 14, United States Code, is amended by striking "other than the Commandant," each place it appears and inserting "other than the Commandant or Vice Commandant,".

(c) [14 U.S.C. 41] CLERICAL AMENDMENT.—The analysis at the beginning of chapter 3 of title 14, United States Code, is amended by striking the item relating to section 46 and inserting the following:

"46. Retirement of Commandant or Vice Commandant."

SEC. 3529. LARGE RECREATIONAL VESSEL REGULATIONS.

(a) [46 U.S.C. 4302 note] IN GENERAL.—

(1) ISSUANCE.—The Secretary of the department in which the Coast Guard is operating shall issue large recreational vessel regulations applicable to any recreational vessel (as defined in section 2101 of title 46, United States Code) over 300

gross tons as measured under section 14502 of such title, or an alternate tonnage measured under section 14302 of such title as prescribed by the Secretary under section 14104 of such title, that does not carry any cargo or passengers for hire.

(2) SCOPE AND CONTENT OF REGULATIONS.—The regulations issued under this subsection—

(A) subject to subparagraph (B), shall be comparable to the code set forth in Merchant Shipping Notice 1851(M) (commonly referred to as the "Large Commercial Yacht Code (LY3)"), as published by the Maritime and Coastguard Agency of the United Kingdom on August 20, 2013, or an equivalent code, regulation, or standard that is acceptable to the Secretary; and

(B) shall require that, as part of the review of an application for documentation of a vessel that is subject to the regulations, the owner shall disclose to the Coast Guard—

(i) the identification and place of residence of such owner; and

(ii) if the owner is an entity described in paragraph (2), (3), or (4) of section 12103(b) of title 46, United States Code, the beneficial owners of such entity.

(3) DEADLINE.—The Secretary shall issue regulations required by paragraph (1) by not later than one year after the date of the enactment of this Act.

(4) INTERIM COMPLIANCE.—Until the effective date of regulations issued under paragraph (1), a recreational vessel described in paragraph (1) shall not be subject to inspection under section 3301(7) of title 46, United States Code, if the Secretary determines, as part of the review of the application for documentation submitted for the vessel by the owner of the vessel and other materials as considered necessary by the Secretary, that the vessel complies with the code set forth in Merchant Shipping Notice 1851(M) (commonly referred to as the "Large Commercial Yacht Code (LY3)"), as published by the Maritime and Coastguard Agency of the United Kingdom on August 20, 2013, or an equivalent code, regulation, or standard that is acceptable to the Secretary.

(5) DEFINITIONS.—

(A) BENEFICIAL OWNER.—In this subsection the term "beneficial owner"—

(i) means, with respect to an entity, each natural person who, directly or indirectly—

(I) exercises control over the entity through ownership interests, voting rights, agreements, or otherwise; or

(II) has an interest in or receives substantial economic benefits from the assets of the entity; and

(ii) does not include, with respect to an entity—

(I) a minor child;

(II) a person acting as a nominee, intermediary, custodian, or agent on behalf of another person;

(III) a person acting solely as an employee of the entity and whose control over or economic benefits from the entity derives solely from the employment status of the person;

(IV) a person whose only interest in the entity is through a right of inheritance, unless the person otherwise meets the definition of "beneficial owner" under this subparagraph; and

(V) a creditor of the entity, unless the creditor otherwise meets the requirements of "beneficial owner" under this subparagraph.

(B) OWNER.—In this subsection, other than in subparagraph (A) of this paragraph, the term "owner" means the person who is the eligible owner of the vessel for purposes of section 12103(b) of title 46, United States Code.

(b) CONFORMING AMENDMENT.—Section 3302 of title 46, United States Code, is amended by adding at the end the following:

"(n)(1) A seagoing motor vessel is not subject to inspection under section 3301(7) of this title if the vessel—

"(A) is a recreational vessel (as defined in section 2101 of this title) over 300 gross tons as measured under section 14502, or an alternate tonnage measured under section 14302 of this title as prescribed by the Secretary under section 14104 of this title;

"(B) does not carry any cargo or passengers for hire; and

"(C) is found by the Secretary to comply with large recreational vessel regulations issued by the Secretary.

"(2) This subsection shall apply only on and after the effective date of regulations referred to in paragraph (1)(C)."

Subtitle C—Coast Guard and Shipping Technical Corrections

CHAPTER 1—COAST GUARD

SEC. 3531. COMMANDANT DEFINED.

(a) IN GENERAL.—Chapter 1 of title 14, United States Code, is amended by adding at the end the following:

"SEC. 5. [14 U.S.C. 5] Commandant define

In this title, the term 'Commandant' means the Commandant of the Coast Guard."

(b) [14 U.S.C. 1] CLERICAL AMENDMENT.—The analysis for chapter 1 of title 14, United States Code, is amended by adding at the end the following:

"5. Commandant defined."

(c) CONFORMING AMENDMENTS.—Title 14, United States Code, is amended—

(1) in section 58(a) by striking "Commandant of the Coast Guard" and inserting "Commandant";

(2) in section 101 by striking "Commandant of the Coast Guard" and inserting "Commandant";

(3) in section 693 by striking "Commandant of the Coast Guard" and inserting "Commandant";

(4) in section 672a(a) by striking "Commandant of the Coast Guard" and inserting "Commandant";

(5) in section 678(a) by striking "Commandant of the Coast Guard" and inserting "Commandant";

(6) in section 561(a) by striking "Commandant of the Coast

Guard" and inserting "Commandant";

(7) in section 577(a) by striking "Commandant of the Coast Guard" and inserting "Commandant";

(8) in section 581—

(A) by striking paragraph (4); and

(B) by redesignating paragraphs (5) through (12) as paragraphs (4) through (11), respectively;

(9) in section 200(a) by striking "Commandant of the Coast Guard" and inserting "Commandant";

(10) in section 196(b)(1) by striking "Commandant of the Coast Guard" and inserting "Commandant";

(11) in section 199 by striking "Commandant of the Coast Guard" and inserting "Commandant";

(12) in section 429(a)(1) by striking "Commandant of the Coast Guard" and inserting "Commandant";

(13) in section 423(a)(2) by striking "Commandant of the Coast Guard" and inserting "Commandant";

(14) in section 2702(5) by striking "Commandant of the Coast Guard" and inserting "Commandant"; and

(15) in section 2902(a) by striking "Commandant of the Coast Guard" and inserting "Commandant".

SEC. 3532. TRAINING COURSE ON WORKINGS OF CONGRESS.

Section 60(d) of title 14, United States Code, is amended to read as follows:

"(d) COMPLETION OF REQUIRED TRAINING.—A Coast Guard flag officer who is newly appointed or assigned to a billet in the National Capital Region, and a Coast Guard Senior Executive Service employee who is newly employed in the National Capital Region, shall complete a training course that meets the requirements of this section not later than 60 days after reporting for duty."

SEC. 3533. MISCELLANEOUS.

(a) SECRETARY; GENERAL POWERS.—Section 92 of title 14, United States Code, is amended by redesignating subsections (f) through (i) as subsections (e) through (h), respectively.

(b) COMMANDANT; GENERAL POWERS.—Section 93(a)(21) of title 14, United States Code, is amended by striking "section 30305(a)" and inserting "section 30305(b)(7)".

(c) ENLISTED MEMBERS.—

(1) DEPARTMENT OF THE ARMY AND DEPARTMENT OF THE AIR FORCE.—Section 144(b) of title 14, United States Code, is amended by striking "enlisted men" each place it appears and inserting "enlisted members".

(2) NAVY DEPARTMENT.—Section 145(b) of title 14, United States Code, is amended by striking "enlisted men" each place it appears and inserting "enlisted members".

(3) PURCHASE OF COMMISSARY AND QUARTERMASTER SUPPLIES.—Section 4 of the Act of May 22, 1926 (44 Stat. 626, chapter 371; 33 U.S.C. 754a), is amended by striking "enlisted men" and inserting "enlisted members".

(d) ARCTIC MARITIME TRANSPORTATION.—Section 90(f) of title 14, United States Code, is amended by striking the question mark.

(e) LONG-TERM LEASE AUTHORITY FOR LIGHTHOUSE PROPERTY.—Section 672a(a) of title 14, United States Code, as amended by this Act, is further amended by striking "Section 321 of chapter 314 of the Act of June 30, 1932 (40 U.S.C. 303b)" and inserting "Section 1302 of title 40".

(f) REQUIRED CONTRACT TERMS.—Section 565 of title 14, United States Code, is amended—

(1) in subsection (a) by striking "awarded or issued by the Coast Guard after the date of enactment of the Coast Guard Authorization Act of 2010"; and

(2) in subsection (b)(1) by striking "after the date of enactment of the Coast Guard Authorization Act of 2010".

(g) ACQUISITION PROGRAM BASELINE BREACH.—Section 575(c) of title 14, United States Code, is amended by striking "certification, with a supporting explanation, that" and inserting "determination, with a supporting explanation, of whether".

(h) ENLISTMENTS; TERM, GRADE.—Section 351(a) of title 14, United States Code, is amended by inserting "the duration of their" before "minority".

(i) MEMBERS OF THE AUXILIARY; STATUS.—Section 823a(b)(9) of title 14, United States Code, is amended by striking "On or after January 1, 2001, section" and inserting "Section".

(j) USE OF MEMBER'S FACILITIES.—Section 826(b) of title 14,

United States Code, is amended by striking "section 154 of title 23, United States Code" and inserting "section 30102 of title 49".

(k) AVAILABILITY OF APPROPRIATIONS.—Section 830(b) of title 14, United States Code, is amended by striking "1954" and inserting "1986".

SEC. 3534. DEPARTMENT OF DEFENSE CONSULTATION.

Section 566 of title 14, United States Code, is amended—

(1) in subsection (b) by striking "enter into" and inserting "maintain"; and

(2) by striking subsection (d).

SEC. 3535. [14 U.S.C. 561] REPEAL.

Section 568 of title 14, United States Code, and the item relating to that section in the analysis for chapter 15 of that title, arerepealed.

SEC. 3536. MISSION NEED STATEMENT.

Section 569 of title 14, United States Code, is—

(1) amended in subsection (a)—

(A) by striking "for fiscal year 2016" and inserting "for fiscal year 2019"; and

(B) by striking ", on the date on which the President submits to Congress a budget for fiscal year 2019 under such section,".

SEC. 3537. CONTINUATION ON ACTIVE DUTY.

Section 290(a) of title 14, United States Code, is amended by striking "Officers, other than the Commandant, serving" and inserting "Officers serving".

SEC. 3538. SYSTEM ACQUISITION AUTHORIZATION.

(a) REQUIREMENT FOR PRIOR AUTHORIZATION OF APPROPRIATIONS.—Section 2701(2) of title 14, United States Code, is amended by striking "and aircraft" and inserting "aircraft, and systems".

(b) AUTHORIZATION OF APPROPRIATIONS.—Section 2702(2) of title 14, United States Code, is amended by striking "and aircraft" and inserting "aircraft, and systems".

SEC. 3539. INVENTORY OF REAL PROPERTY.

Section 679 of title 14, United States Code, is amended—

(1) in subsection (a) by striking "Not later than September 30, 2015, the Commandant shall establish" and inserting "The Commandant shall maintain"; and

(2) by striking subsection (b) and inserting the following:

"(b) UPDATES.—The Commandant shall update information on each unit of real property included in the inventory required under subsection (a) not later than 30 days after any change relating to the control of such property."

CHAPTER 2—MARITIME TRANSPORTATION

SEC. 3541. [10 U.S.C. 3541] DEFINITIONS.

(a) IN GENERAL.—

(1) Section 2101 of title 46, United States Code, is amended—

(A) by inserting after paragraph (4) the following:" ""( ) 'Commandant' means the Commandant of the Coast Guard."' "

(B) by striking the semicolon at the end of paragraph (14) and inserting a period; and

(C) by redesignating the paragraphs of such section in order as paragraphs (1) through (54), respectively.

(2) Section 3701 of title 46, United States Code, is amended by redesignating paragraphs (3) and (4) as paragraphs (2) and (3) respectively.

(b) CONFORMING AMENDMENTS.—

(1) Section 114(o)(3) of the Marine Mammal Protection Act of 1972 (16 U.S.C. 1383a(o)(3)) is amended—

(A) by striking "section 2101(11a)" and inserting "section 2101(12)"; and

(B) by striking "section 2101(11b)" and inserting "section 2101(13)"

(2) Section 3(3) of the Magnuson-Stevens Fishery Conservation and Management Act (16 U.S.C. 1802(3)), is amended by striking "section 2101(21a)" and inserting "section

2101(30)”

(3) Section 1992(d)(7) of title 18, United States Code, is amended by striking “section 2101(22)” and inserting “section 2101(31)”

(4) Section 12(c) of the Fishermen’s Protective Act of 1967 (22 U.S.C. 1980b(c)) is amended by striking “section 2101(11a)” and inserting “section 2101(12)”

(5) Section 311(a)(26)(D) of the Federal Water Pollution Control Act (33 U.S.C. 1321(a)(26)(D)) is amended by striking “section 2101(17a)” and inserting “section 2101(23)”

(6) Section 2113(3) of title 46, United States Code, is amended by striking “section 2101(42)(A)” and inserting “section 2101(51)(A)”

(7) Section 2116(d)(1) of title 46, United States Code, is amended by striking “Coast Guard Commandant” and inserting “Commandant”

(8) Section 3202(a)(1)(A) of title 46, United States Code, is amended by striking “section 2101(21)(A)” and inserting “section 2101(29)(A)”

(9) Section 3507 of title 46, United States Code, is amended—

(A) in subsection (k)(1), by striking “section 2101(22)” and inserting “section 2101(31)”; and

(B) by striking subsection (l) and inserting the following:

“(l) DEFINITION.—In this section and section 3508, the term “‘owner’” means the owner, charterer, managing operator, master, or other individual in charge of a vessel.”

(10) Section 4105 of title 46, United States Code, is amended—

(A) in subsection (b)(1), by striking “section 2101(42)” and inserting “section 2101(51)”; and

(B) in subsection (c), by striking “section 2101(42)(A)” and inserting “section 2101(51)(A)”

(11) Section 6101(i)(4) of title 46, United States Code, is amended by striking “of the Coast Guard”

(12) Section 7510(c)(1) of title 46, United States Code, is

amended by striking "Commandant of the Coast Guard" and inserting "Commandant"

(13) Section 7706(a) of title 46, United States Code, is amended by striking "of the Coast Guard"

(14) Section 8108(a)(1) of title 46, United States Code, is amended by striking "of the Coast Guard"

(15) Section 12119(a)(3) of title 46, United States Code, is amended by striking "section 2101(20)" and inserting "section 2101(26)"

(16) Section 80302(d) of title 46, United States Code, is amended by striking "of the Coast Guard" the first place it appears.

(17) Section 1101 of title 49, United States Code, is amended by striking "Section 2101(17a)" and inserting "Section 2101(23)"

SEC. 3542. AUTHORITY TO EXEMPT VESSELS.

(a) IN GENERAL.—Section 2113 of title 46, United States Code, is amended—

(1) by adding "and" after the semicolon at the end of paragraph (3); and

(2) by striking paragraphs (4) and (5) and inserting the following:

"(4) maintain different structural fire protection, manning, operating, and equipment requirements for vessels that satisfied requirements set forth in the Passenger Vessel Safety Act of 1993 (Public Law 103-206) before June 21, 1994."

(b) CONFORMING AMENDMENTS.—Section 3306(i) of title 46, United States Code, is amended by striking "section 2113(5)" and inserting "section 2113(4)".

SEC. 3543. PASSENGER VESSELS.

(a) PASSENGER VESSEL SECURITY AND SAFETY REQUIREMENTS.—Section 3507 of title 46, United States Code, is amended—

(1) by striking subsection (a)(3);

(2) in subsection (e)(2), by striking "services confidential"

and inserting "services as confidential"; and

(3) in subsection (i), by striking "Within 6 months after the date of enactment of the Cruise Vessel Security and Safety Act of 2010, the Secretary shall issue" and insert "The Secretary shall maintain".

(b) CRIME SCENE PRESERVATION TRAINING FOR PASSENGER VESSEL CREWMEMBERS.—Section 3508 of title 46, United States Code, is amended—

(1) in subsection (a), by striking "Within 1 year after the date of enactment of the Cruise Vessel Security and Safety Act of 2010, the" and inserting "The", and by striking "develop" and inserting "maintain";

(2) in subsection (c), by striking "Beginning 2 years after the standards are established under subsection (b), no" and inserting "No";

(3) by striking subsection (d) and redesignating subsections (e) and (f) as subsections (d) and (e), respectively; and

(4) in subsection (e), as redesignated by paragraph (3), by striking "subsection (e)" each place it appears and inserting "subsection (d)".

SEC. 3544. TANK VESSELS.

(a) TANK VESSEL CONSTRUCTION STANDARDS.—Section 3703a of title 46, United States Code, is amended—

(1) in subsection (b), by striking paragraph (3) and redesignating paragraphs (4), (5), and (6) as paragraphs (3), (4), and (5), respectively;

(2) in subsection (c)(2)—

(A) by striking "that is delivered" and inserting "that was delivered";

(B) by striking "that qualifies" and inserting "that qualified"; and

(C) by striking "after January 1, 2015,";

(3) in subsection (c)(3)—

(A) by striking "that is delivered" and inserting "that was delivered"; and

(B) by striking "that qualifies" and inserting "that

qualified";

(4) by striking subsection (c)(3)(A) and inserting the following:

"(A) in the case of a vessel of at least 5,000 gross tons but less than 15,000 gross tons as measured under section 14502, or an alternate tonnage measured under section 14302 as prescribed by the Secretary under section 14104, if the vessel is 25 years old or older and has a single hull, or is 30 years old or older and has a double bottom or double sides;"

(5) by striking subsection (c)(3)(B) and inserting the following:

"(B) in the case of a vessel of at least 15,000 gross tons but less than 30,000 gross tons as measured under section 14502, or an alternate tonnage measured under section 14302 as prescribed by the Secretary under section 14104, if the vessel is 25 years old or older and has a single hull, or is 30 years old or older and has a double bottom or double sides; and"

(6) by striking subsection (c)(3)(C) and inserting the following:

"(C) in the case of a vessel of at least 30,000 gross tons as measured under section 14502, or an alternate tonnage measured under section 14302 as prescribed by the Secretary under section 14104, if the vessel is 23 years old or older and has a single hull, or is 28 years old or older and has a double bottom or double sides."

; and

(7) in subsection (e)—

(A) in paragraph (1), by striking "and except as otherwise provided in paragraphs (2) and (3) of this subsection"; and

(B) by striking paragraph (2) and redesignating paragraph (3) as paragraph (2).

(b) CRUDE OIL TANKER MINIMUM STANDARDS.—Section 3705 of title 46, United States Code, is amended—

(1) in subsection (b)—

(A) by striking paragraph (2);

(B) by striking “(1)”; and

(C) by redesignating subparagraphs (A) and (B) as paragraphs (1) and (2), respectively; and

(2) in subsection (c), by striking “before January 2, 1986, or the date on which the tanker reaches 15 years of age, whichever is later”.

(c) PRODUCT CARRIER MINIMUM STANDARDS.—Section 3706(d) of title 46, United States Code, is amended by striking “before January 2, 1986, or the date on which it reaches 15 years of age, whichever is later”.

(d) DEFINITION.—Section 1001(32)(A) of the Oil Pollution Act of 1990 (33 U.S.C. 2701(32)(A)) is amended by striking “(other 132 STAT. 2326 than a vessel described in section 3703a(b)(3) of title 46, United States Code)”.

SEC. 3545. GROUNDS FOR DENIAL OR REVOCATION.

(a) DANGEROUS DRUGS AS GROUNDS FOR DENIAL.—Section 7503 of title 46, United States Code, is amended to read as follows:

“SEC. 7503. Dangerous drugs as grounds for denia

A license, certificate of registry, or merchant mariner’s document authorized to be issued under this part may be denied to an individual who—

“(1) within 10 years before applying for the license, certificate, or document, has been convicted of violating a dangerous drug law of the United States or of a State; or

“(2) when applying, has ever been a user of, or addicted to, a dangerous drug unless the individual provides satisfactory proof that the individual is cured.”

(b) DANGEROUS DRUGS AS GROUNDS FOR REVOCATION.—Section 7704 of title 46, United States Code, is amended by redesignating subsections (b) and (c) as subsections (a) and (b), respectively.

SEC. 3546. MISCELLANEOUS CORRECTIONS TO TITLE 46, U.S.C.

(a) Section 2110 of title 46, United States Code, is amended by striking subsection (k).

(b) Section 2116(c) of title 46, United States Code, is amended by striking “Beginning with fiscal year 2011 and each fiscal year thereafter, the” and inserting “The”.

(c) Section 3302(g)(2) of title 46, United States Code, is amended by striking "After December 31, 1988, this" and inserting "This".

(d) Section 6101(j) of title 46, United States Code, is amended by striking ", as soon as possible, and no later than January 1, 2005,".

(e) Section 7505 of title 46, United States Code, is amended by striking "section 206(b)(7) of the National Driver Register Act of 1982 (23 U.S.C. 401 note)" and inserting "section 30305(b)(7) of title 49".

(f) Section 7702(c)(1) of title 46, United States Code, is amended by striking "section 206(b)(4) of the National Driver Register Act of 1982 (23 U.S.C. 401 note)" and inserting "section 30305(b)(7) of title 49".

(g) Section 8106(f) of title 46, United States Code, is amended by striking paragraph (3) and inserting the following:

"(3) CONTINUING VIOLATIONS.—The maximum amount of a civil penalty for a violation under this subsection shall be $100,000."

(h) Section 8703 of title 46, United States Code, is amended by redesignating subsection (c) as subsection (b).

(i) Section 11113 of title 46, United States Code, is amended—

(1) in subsection (a)(4)(A) by striking "paragraph (2)" and inserting "paragraph (3)"; and

(2) in subsection (c)(2)(B)—

(A) by striking "section 2(9)(a)" and inserting "section 2(a)(9)(A)"; and

(B) by striking "33 U.S.C. 1901(9)(a)" and inserting "33 U.S.C. 1901(a)(9)(A)".

(j) Section 12113(d)(2)(C)(iii) of title 46, United States Code, is amended by striking "118 Stat. 2887)" and inserting "118 Stat. 2887))".

(k) Section 13107(c)(2) of title 46, United States Code, is amended by striking "On and after October 1, 2016, no" and inserting "No".

(l) Section 31322(a)(4)(B) of title 46, United States Code, is amended by striking "state" and inserting "State".

(m) Section 52101(d) of title 46, United States Code, is amended by striking "(50 App. U.S.C. 459(a))" and inserting "(50 U.S.C. 3808(a))".

(n) **[46 U.S.C. 53101]** The analysis for chapter 531 of title 46, United States Code, is amended by striking the item relating to section 53109:

(o) Section 53106(a)(1) of title 46, United States Code, is amended by striking subparagraphs (A), (B), (C), and (D), and by redesignating subparagraphs (E), (F), and (G) as subparagraphs (A), (B), and (C), respectively.

(p) Section 53111 of title 46, United States Code, is amended by striking paragraphs (1) through (4), and by redesignating paragraphs (5), (6), and (7) as paragraphs (1), (2), and (3), respectively.

(q) Section 53501 of title 46, United States Code, is amended—

(1) in paragraph (5)(A)(iii), by striking "transportation trade trade or" and inserting "transportation trade or";

(2) by redesignating paragraph (8) as paragraph (9);

(3) by striking the second paragraph (7) (relating to the definition of "United States foreign trade"); and

(4) by inserting after the first paragraph (7) the following:

"(8) UNITED STATES FOREIGN TRADE.—The term 'United States foreign trade' includes those areas in domestic trade in which a vessel built with a construction-differential subsidy is allowed to operate under the first sentence of section 506 of the Merchant Marine Act, 1936."

(r) Section 54101(f) of title 46, United States Code, is amended by striking paragraph (2) and inserting the following:

"(2) MINIMUM STANDARDS FOR PAYMENT OR REIMBURSEMENT.—Each application submitted under paragraph (1) shall include a comprehensive description of—

"(A) the need for the project;

"(B) the methodology for implementing the project; and

"(C) any existing programs or arrangements that can be used to supplement or leverage assistance under the program."

(s) Section 55305(d)(2)(D) of title 46, United States Code, is amended by striking "421(c)(1)" and inserting "1303(a)(1))".

(t) [46 U.S.C. 57501] The analysis for chapter 575 of title 46, United States Code, is amended in the item relating to section 57533 by adding a period at the end.

(u) Section 57532(d) of title 46, United States Code, is amended by striking "(50 App. U.S.C. 1291(a), (c), 1293(c), 1294)" and inserting "(50 U.S.C. 4701(a), (c), 4703(c), and 4704)".

(v) Section 60303(c) of title 46, United States Code, is amended in by striking "Subsection (a) section does" and inserting "Subsection (a) does".

SEC. 3547. MISCELLANEOUS CORRECTIONS TO OIL POLLUTION ACT OF 1990.

(a) Section 2 of the Oil Pollution Act of 1990 (33 U.S.C. 2701 note) is amended by—

(1) inserting after the item relating to section 5007 the following:

"Sec. 5008. North Pacific Marine Research Institute."

(2) striking the item relating to section 6003.

(b) Section 1003(d)(5) of the Oil Pollution Act of 1990 (33 U.S.C. 2703(d)(5)) is amended by inserting "section" before "1002(a)".

(c) Section 1004(d)(2)(C) of the Oil Pollution Act of 1990 (33 U.S.C. 2704(d)(2)(C)) is amended by striking "under this subparagraph (A)" and inserting "under subparagraph (A)".

(d) Section 4303 of the Oil Pollution Act of 1990 (33 U.S.C. 2716a) is amended—

(1) in subsection (a), by striking "subsection (c)(2)" and inserting "subsection (b)(2)"; and

(2) in subsection (b), by striking "this section 1016" and inserting "section 1016".

(e) Section 5002(l)(2) of the Oil Pollution Act of 1990 (33 U.S.C. 2732(l)(2)) is amended by striking "General Accounting Office" and inserting "Government Accountability Office".

SEC. 3548. MISCELLANEOUS CORRECTIONS.

(a) Section 1 of the Act of June 15, 1917 (chapter 30; 50 U.S.C. 191), is amended by striking "the Secretary of the Treasury" and inserting "the Secretary of the department in which the Coast Guard is operating".

(b) Section 5(b) of the Act entitled "An Act to regulate the construction of bridges over navigable waters", approved March 23, 1906, popularly known as the Bridge Act of 1906 (chapter 1130; 33 U.S.C. 495(b)), is amended by striking "$5,000 for a violation occurring in 2004; $10,000 for a violation occurring in 2005; $15,000 for a violation occurring in 2006; $20,000 for a violation occurring in 2007; and".

(c) Section 5(f) of the Act to Prevent Pollution from Ships (33 U.S.C. 1904(f)) is amended to read as follows:

"(f) SHIP CLEARANCE; REFUSAL OR REVOCATION.—If a ship is under a detention order under this section, the Secretary may refuse or revoke the clearance required by section 60105 of title 46, United States Code."

* * * * * * *

SAVE OUR SEAS ACT OF 2018

PUBLIC LAW 115-265
AS AMENDED THROUGH P.L. 117-58

Save Our Seas Act of 2018

[(Public Law 115–265)]

[As Amended Through P.L. 117–58, Enacted November 15, 2021]

AN ACT To reauthorize and amend the Marine Debris Act to promote international action to reduce marine debris, and for other purposes.

Be it enacted by the Senate and House of Representatives of the United States of America in Congress assembled,

SECTION 1. [46 U.S.C. 101 note] SHORT TITLE.

This Act may be cited as the "Save Our Seas Act of 2018".

TITLE I—MARINE DEBRIS

SEC. 101. NOAA MARINE DEBRIS PROGRAM.

Section 3 of the Marine Debris Act (33 U.S.C. 1952) is amended—

(1) in subsection (b)—

(A) in paragraph (4), by striking "; and" and inserting a semicolon;

(B) in paragraph (5)(C), by striking the period at the end and inserting a semicolon; and

(C) by adding at the end the following:

"(6) work to develop outreach and education strategies with other Federal agencies to address sources of marine debris;

"(7) except for discharges of marine debris from vessels, in consultation with the Department of State and other Federal agencies, promote international action, as appropriate, to reduce the incidence of marine debris, including providing technical assistance to expand waste management systems internationally; and

"(8) in the case of an event determined to be a severe marine debris event under subsection (c)—

"(A) assist in the cleanup and response required by the severe marine debris event; or

"(B) conduct such other activity as the Administrator determines is appropriate in response to the severe marine debris event."

(2) by redesignating subsection (c) as subsection (d);

(3) by inserting after subsection (b) the following:

"(c) SEVERE MARINE DEBRIS EVENTS.—At the discretion of the Administrator or at the request of the Governor of an affected State, the Administrator shall determine whether there is a severe marine debris event."

; and

(4) in subsection (d)(2), as redesignated—

(A) in subparagraph (A), by striking "subparagraph (B)" and inserting "subparagraphs (B) and (C)"; and

(B) by adding at the end the following:

"(C) SEVERE MARINE DEBRIS EVENTS.—Notwithstanding subparagraph (A), the Federal share of the cost of an activity carried out under a determination made under subsection (c) shall be—

"(i) 100 percent of the cost of the activity, for an activity funded wholly by funds made available by a person, including the government of a foreign country, to the Federal Government for the purpose of responding to a severe marine debris event; or

"(ii) 75 percent of the cost of the activity, for any activity other than an activity funded as described in clause (i)."

SEC. 102. SENSE OF CONGRESS ON INTERNATIONAL ENGAGEMENT TO RESPOND TO MARINE DEBRIS.

It is the sense of Congress that the President should—

(1) support research and development on systems and materials that reduce—

(A) derelict fishing gear; and

(B) the amount of solid waste that is generated from land-based sources and the amount of such waste that enters the marine environment;

(2) work with representatives of foreign countries that discharge the largest amounts of solid waste from land-based sources into the marine environment, to develop mechanisms to reduce such discharges;

(3) carry out studies to determine—

(A) the primary means of discharges referred to in paragraph (2);

(B) the manner in which waste management infrastructure can be most effective in preventing such discharges; and

(C) the long-term impacts of marine debris on the national economies of the countries with which work is undertaken under paragraph (2) and on the global economy, including the impacts of reducing the discharge of such debris;

(4) work with representatives of the countries with which work is undertaken in paragraph (2) to conclude one or more new international agreements that include provisions—

(A) to mitigate the discharge of land-based solid waste into the marine environment; and

(B) to provide technical assistance and investment in waste management infrastructure to reduce such discharges, if the President determines such assistance or investment is appropriate; and

(5) encourage the United States Trade Representative to consider the impact of discharges of land-based solid waste from the countries with which work is conducted under paragraph (2) in relevant future trade agreements.

SEC. 103. SENSE OF CONGRESS SUPPORTING GREAT LAKES LAND-BASED MARINE DEBRIS ACTION PLAN.

It is the sense of Congress that the Great Lakes Land-Based Marine Debris Action Plan (NOAA Technical Memorandum NOS-OR&R-49) is vital to the ongoing efforts to clean up the Great Lakes Region and getting rid of harmful debris, such as microplastics, abandoned vessels, and other forms of pollution that are threatening the survival of native marine animals and damaging the Great Lakes' recreation and tourism economy.

SEC. 104. MEMBERSHIP OF THE INTERAGENCY MARINE DEBRIS COORDINATING COMMITTEE.

Section 5(b) of the Marine Debris Act (33 U.S.C. 1954(b)) is amended—

(1) in paragraph (4), by striking "; and" and inserting a semicolon;

(2) by redesignating paragraph (5) as paragraph (7); and

(3) by inserting after paragraph (4) the following:

"(5) the Department of State;

"(6) the Department of the Interior; and"

SEC. 105. AUTHORIZATION OF APPROPRIATIONS.

Section 9 of the Marine Debris Act (33 U.S.C. 1958) is amended to read as follows:

"SEC. SEC. 9. AUTHORIZATION OF APPROPRIATIONS

"(a) IN GENERAL.—There is authorized to be appropriated to the Administrator $10,000,000 for each of fiscal years 2018 through 2022 for carrying out sections 3, 5, and 6, of which not more than 5 percent is authorized for each fiscal year for administrative costs.

"(b) AMOUNTS AUTHORIZED FOR COAST GUARD.—Of the amounts authorized for each fiscal year under section 2702(1) of title 14, United States Code, up to $2,000,000 is authorized for the Secretary of the department in which the Coast Guard is operating for use by the Commandant of the Coast Guard to carry out section 4 of this Act, of which not more than 5 percent is authorized for each fiscal year for administrative costs."

TITLE II—MARITIME SAFETY

SEC. 201. [46 U.S.C. 101 note] SHORT TITLE.

This title may be cited as the "Hamm Alert Maritime Safety Act of 2018".

SEC. 202. FINDINGS.

Congress finds the following:

(1) On September 29, 2015, the SS El Faro cargo vessel left Jacksonville, Florida bound for San Juan, Puerto Rico, carrying 391 shipping containers, 294 trailers and cars, and a crew of 33 people, including 28 Americans.

(2) On the morning of October 1, the El Faro sent its final communication reporting that the engines were disabled and the ship was listing, leaving the ship directly in the path of Hurricane Joaquin and resulting in the sinking of the vessel and the loss of all 33 lives.

(3) The National Transportation Safety Board and the Coast Guard made recommendations to address safety issues, such as improving weather information and training, improving planning and response to severe weather, reviewing the Coast Guard's program delegating vessel inspections to third-party organizations to assess the effectiveness of the program, and improving alerts and equipment on the vessels, among other recommendations.

(4) Safety issues are not limited to the El Faro. For 2017, over 21,000 deficiencies were issued to United States commercial vessels and more than 2,500 U.S. vessels were issued "no-sail" requirements.

(5) The maritime industry, particularly the men and women of the United States merchant marine, play a vital and important role to the national security and economy of our country, and a strong safety regime is necessary to ensure the vitality of the industry and the protection of current and future mariners, and to honor lost mariners.

SEC. 203. [46 U.S.C. 2101 note] DEFINITIONS.

In this title:

(1) COMMANDANT.—The term "Commandant" means the Commandant of the Coast Guard.

(2) RECOGNIZED ORGANIZATION.—The term "recognized organization" has the meaning given that term in section 2.45-1 of title 46, Code of Federal Regulations, as in effect on the date of the enactment of this Act.

(3) SECRETARY.—The term "Secretary" means the Secretary of the department in which the Coast Guard is operating.

SEC. 204. [46 U.S.C. 2116 note] DOMESTIC VESSEL COMPLIANCE.

(a) IN GENERAL.—Not later than 60 days after the date on which the President submits to the Congress a budget each year pursuant to section 1105 of title 31, United States Code, the Commandant shall publish on a publicly accessible Website information documenting domestic vessel compliance with the requirements of subtitle II of title 46, United States Code.

(b) CONTENT.—The information required under subsection (a) shall—

(1) include flag-State detention rates for each type of inspected vessel; and

(2) identify any recognized organization that inspected or surveyed a vessel that was later subject to a Coast Guard-issued control action attributable to a major nonconformity that the recognized organization failed to identify in such inspection or survey.

SEC. 205. [46 U.S.C. 3201 note] SAFETY MANAGEMENT SYSTEM.

(a) IN GENERAL.—The Comptroller General of the United States shall conduct an audit regarding the implementation and effectiveness of the Coast Guard's oversight and enforcement of safety management plans required under chapter 32 of title 46, United States Code.

(b) SCOPE.—The audit conducted under subsection (a) shall include an evaluation of—

(1) the effectiveness and implementation of safety management plans, including such plans for—

(A) a range of vessel types and sizes; and

(B) vessels that operate in a cross-section of regional operating areas; and

(2) the effectiveness and implementation of safety management plans in addressing the impact of heavy weather.

(c) REPORT.—Not later than 18 months after the date of enactment of this Act, the Comptroller General shall submit to the Committee on Commerce, Science, and Transportation of the Senate and the Committee on Transportation and Infrastructure of the House of Representatives a report detailing the results of the audit and providing recommendations related to such results, including ways to streamline and focus such plans on ship safety.

(d) MARINE SAFETY ALERT.—Not later than 60 days after the date the report is submitted under subsection (c), the Commandant shall publish a Marine Safety Alert providing notification of the completion of the report and including a link to the report on a publicly accessible website.

(e) ADDITIONAL ACTIONS.—

(1) IN GENERAL.—Upon completion of the report under subsection (c), the Commandant shall consider additional guidance or a rulemaking to address any deficiencies identified, and any additional actions recommended, in the report.

(2) REPORT.—Not later than 1 year after the date the report is submitted under subsection (c), the Commandant shall submit to the Committee on Commerce, Science, and Transportation of the Senate and the Committee on Transportation and Infrastructure of the House of Representatives a report on the actions the Commandant has taken to address any deficiencies identified, and any additional actions recommended, in the report submitted under subsection (c).

SEC. 206. EQUIPMENT REQUIREMENTS.

(a) REGULATIONS.—

(1) IN GENERAL.—Section 3306 of title 46, United States Code, is amended by adding at the end the following:

"(l)(1) The Secretary shall require that a freight vessel inspected under this chapter be outfitted with distress signaling and location technology for the higher of—

"(A) the minimum complement of officers and crew specified on the certificate of inspection for such vessel; or

"(B) the number of persons onboard the vessel; and

"(2) the requirement described in paragraph (1) shall not apply to vessels operating within the baseline from which the territorial sea of the United States is measured.

"(m)(1) The Secretary shall promulgate regulations

requiring companies to maintain records of all incremental weight changes made to freight vessels inspected under this chapter, and to track weight changes over time to facilitate rapid determination of the aggregate total.

"(2) Records maintained under paragraph (1) shall be stored, in paper or electronic form, onboard such vessels for not less than 3 years and shoreside for the life of the vessel."

(2) [46 U.S.C. 3306 note] DEADLINES.—The Secretary shall—

(A) begin implementing the requirement under section 3306(l) of title 46, United States Code, as amended by this subsection, by not later than 1 year after the date of the enactment of this Act; and

(B) promulgate the regulations required under section 3306(m) of title 46, United States Code, as amended by this subsection, by not later than 1 year after the date of the enactment of this Act.

(b) [46 U.S.C. 3306 note] ENGAGEMENT.—Not later than 1 year after the date of the enactment of this Act, the Commandant shall seek to enter into negotiations through the International Maritime Organization to amend regulation 25 of chapter II-1 of the International Convention for the Safety of Life at Sea to require a high-water alarm sensor in each cargo hold of a freight vessel (as that term is defined in section 2101 of title 46, United States Code), that connects with audible and visual alarms on the navigation bridge of the vessel.

SEC. 207. VOYAGE DATA RECORDER; ACCESS.

(a) IN GENERAL.—Chapter 63 of title 46, United States Code, is amended by adding at the end the following:

"SEC. §6309. [46 U.S.C. 6309] Voyage data recorder acces

"Notwithstanding any other provision of law, the Coast Guard shall have full, concurrent, and timely access to and ability to use voyage data recorder data and audio held by any Federal agency in all marine casualty investigations, regardless of which agency is the investigative lead."

(b) [46 U.S.C. 6301] CLERICAL AMENDMENT.—The analysis for such chapter is amended by adding at the end the following:

""6309. Voyage data recorder access.".

SEC. 208. VOYAGE DATA RECORDER; REQUIREMENTS.

(a) FLOAT-FREE AND BEACON REQUIREMENTS.—

(1) [46 U.S.C. 3306 note] IN GENERAL.—Not later than 1 year after the date of the enactment of this Act, the Commandant shall seek to enter into negotiations through the International Maritime Organization to amend regulation 20 of chapter V of the International Convention for the Safety of Life at Sea to require that all voyage data recorders are installed in a float-free arrangement and contain an integrated emergency position indicating radio beacon.

(2) PROGRESS UPDATE.—Not later than 3 years after the date of the enactment of this Act, the Commandant shall submit to the Committee on Commerce, Science, and Transportation of the Senate and the Committee on Transportation and Infrastructure of the House of Representatives an update on the progress of the engagement required under paragraph (1).

(b) COST-BENEFIT ANALYSIS.—Not later than 2 years after the date of the enactment of this Act, the Commandant shall submit to the Committee on Commerce, Science, and Transportation of the Senate and the Committee on Transportation and Infrastructure of the House of Representatives a cost-benefit analysis of requiring that voyage data recorders installed on commercial vessels documented under chapter 121 of title 46, United States Code, capture communications on the internal telephone systems of such vessels, including requiring the capture of both sides of all communications with the bridge onboard such vessels.

SEC. 209. [14 U.S.C. 88 note] SURVIVAL AND LOCATING EQUIPMENT.

Not later than 2 years after the date of the enactment of this Act, the Commandant shall, subject to the availability of appropriations, identify and procure equipment that will provide search-and-rescue units the ability to attach a radio or Automated Identification System strobe or beacon to an object that is not immediately retrievable.

SEC. 210. [14 U.S.C. 93 note] TRAINING OF COAST GUARD PERSONNEL.

(a) PROSPECTIVE SECTOR COMMANDER TRAINING.—Not later than 1 year after the date of the enactment of this Act, the Commandant shall implement an Officer in Charge, Marine Inspections segment to the sector commander indoctrination course for prospective sector commanders without a Coast Guard prevention ashore officer specialty code.

(b) STEAMSHIP INSPECTIONS.—Not later than 1 year after the date of the enactment of this Act, the Commandant shall implement steam plant inspection training for Coast Guard marine inspectors and, subject to availability, recognized organizations to which authority is delegated under section 3316 of title 46, United States Code.

(c) ADVANCED JOURNEYMAN INSPECTOR TRAINING.—

(1) IN GENERAL.—Not later than 2 years after the date of the enactment of this Act, the Commandant shall establish advanced training to provide instruction on the oversight of recognized organizations to which authority is delegated under section 3316 of title 46, United States Code, auditing responsibilities, and the inspection of unique vessel types.

(2) RECIPIENTS.—The Commandant shall—

(A) require that such training be completed by senior Coast Guard marine inspectors; and

(B) subject to availability of training capacity, make such training available to recognized organization surveyors authorized by the Coast Guard to conduct inspections.

(d) COAST GUARD INSPECTIONS STAFF; BRIEFING.—Not later than 1 year after the date of the enactment of this Act, the Commandant shall provide to the Committee on Commerce, Science, and Transportation of the Senate and the Committee on Transportation and Infrastructure of the House of Representatives a briefing detailing—

(1) the estimated time and funding necessary to triple the current size of the Coast Guard's traveling inspector staff; and

(2) other options available to the Coast Guard to enhance and maintain marine safety knowledge, including discussion of increased reliance on—

(A) civilian marine inspectors;

(B) experienced licensed mariners;

(C) retired members of the Coast Guard;

(D) arranging for Coast Guard inspectors to ride onboard commercial oceangoing vessels documented under chapter 121 of title 46, United States Code, to gain experience and insight; and

(E) extending tour-lengths for Coast Guard marine safety officers assigned to inspection billets.

(e) AUDITS; COAST GUARD ATTENDANCE AND PERFORMANCE.—Not later than 180 days after the date of the enactment of this Act, the Commandant shall—

(1) update Coast Guard policy to utilize risk analysis to target the attendance of Coast Guard personnel during external safety management certificate and document of compliance audits; and

(2) perform a quality assurance audit of recognized organization representation and performance regarding United States-flagged vessels.

SEC. 211. MAJOR MARINE CASUALTY PROPERTY DAMAGE THRESHOLD.

Section 6101(i)(3) of title 46, United States Code, is amended by striking "$500,000" and inserting "$2,000,000".

SEC. 212. REVIEWS, BRIEFINGS, REPORTS, AND TECHNICAL CORRECTIONS.

(a) MAJOR CONVERSION DETERMINATIONS.—

(1) REVIEW OF POLICIES AND PROCEDURES.—The Commandant shall conduct a review of policies and procedures for making and documenting major conversion determinations, including an examination of the deference given to precedent.

(2) BRIEFING.—Not later than 1 year after the date of the enactment of this Act, the Commandant shall provide to the Committee on Commerce, Science, and Transportation of the Senate and the Committee on Transportation and Infrastructure of the House of Representatives a briefing on the findings of the review required by paragraph (1).

(b) VENTILATORS, OPENINGS AND STABILITY STANDARDS.—

(1) REVIEW.—Not later than 1 year after the date of the

enactment of this Act, the Commandant shall complete a review of the effectiveness of United States regulations, international conventions, recognized organizations' class rules, and Coast Guard technical policy regarding—

(A) ventilators and other hull openings;

(B) fire dampers and other closures protecting openings normally open during operations;

(C) intact and damage stability standards under subchapter S of chapter I of title 46, Code of Federal Regulations; and

(D) lifesaving equipment for mariners, including survival suits and life jackets.

(2) BRIEFING.—Not later than 18 months after the date of the enactment of this Act, the Commandant shall provide to the Committee on Commerce, Science, and Transportation of the Senate and the Committee on Transportation and Infrastructure of the House of Representatives a briefing on the effectiveness of the regulations, international conventions, recognized organizations' class rules, and Coast Guard technical policy reviewed under paragraph (1).

(c) SELF-LOCATING DATUM MARKER BUOYS.—Not later than 6 months after the date of the enactment of this Act, the Commandant shall provide to the Committee on Commerce, Science, and Transportation of the Senate and the Committee on Transportation and Infrastructure of the House of Representatives a briefing on the reliability of self-locating datum marker buoys and other similar technology used during Coast Guard search-and-rescue operations. The briefing shall include a description of reasonable steps the Commandant could take to increase the reliability of such buoys, including the potential to leverage technology used by the Navy, and how protocols could be developed to conduct testing of such buoys before using them for operations.

(d) [45 U.S.C. 822 note] CORRECTION.—

(1) IN GENERAL.—Notwithstanding any other provision of law, the Secretary of Transportation, for purposes of section 22402 of title 49, United States Code (as in effect on the day before the amendments made by section 11607 of Public Law 114-94 (129 Stat. 1698) took effect)—

(A) not later than 30 days after the date of enactment

of this Act, and in consultation with the Director of the Office of Management and Budget, shall define the term "cohorts of loans";

(B) before the deadline described in paragraph (2), shall return to the original source, on a pro rata basis, the credit risk premiums paid for the loans in the cohort of loans, with interest accrued thereon, that were not used to mitigate losses; and

(C) shall not treat the repayment of a loan after the date of enactment of Public Law 114-94 as precluding, limiting, or negatively affecting the satisfaction of the obligation of its cohort prior to the enactment of Public Law 114-94.

(2) DEADLINE DESCRIBED.—The deadline described in this paragraph is—

(A) if all obligations attached to a cohort of loans have been satisfied, not later than 60 days after the date of enactment of this Act; and

(B) if all obligations attached to a cohort of loans have not been satisfied, not later than 60 days after the date on which all obligations attached to the cohort of loans are satisfied.

(e) OVERSIGHT PROGRAM; EFFECTIVENESS.—

(1) IN GENERAL.—Not later than 2 years after the date of the enactment of this Act, the Commandant shall commission an assessment of the effectiveness of the Coast Guard's oversight of recognized organizations and its impact on compliance by and safety of vessels inspected by such organizations.

(2) EXPERIENCE.—The assessment commissioned under paragraph (1) shall be conducted by a research organization with significant experience in maritime operations and marine safety.

(3) SUBMISSION TO CONGRESS.—Not later than 180 days after the date that the assessment required under paragraph (1) is completed, the Commandant shall submit to the Committee on Commerce, Science, and Transportation of the Senate and the Committee on Transportation and Infrastructure of the House of Representatives the results of

such assessment.

SEC. 213. [46 U.S.C. 3203 note] FLAG-STATE GUIDANCE AND SUPPLEMENTS.

(a) FREIGHT VESSELS; DAMAGE CONTROL INFORMATION.—Within 1 year after the date of the enactment of this Act, the Secretary shall issue flag-State guidance for all freight vessels documented under chapter 121 of title 46, United States Code, built before January 1, 1992, regarding the inclusion of comprehensive damage control information in safety management plans required under chapter 32 of title 46, United States Code.

(b) RECOGNIZED ORGANIZATIONS; UNITED STATES SUPPLEMENT.—The Commandant shall—

(1) work with recognized organizations to create a single United States Supplement to rules of such organizations for classification of vessels; and

(2) by not later than 1 year after the date of the enactment of this Act, provide to the Committee on Commerce, Science, and Transportation of the Senate and the Committee on Transportation and Infrastructure of the House of Representatives a briefing on whether it is necessary to revise part 8 of title 46, Code of Federal Regulations, to authorize only one United States Supplement to such rules.

SEC. 214. MARINE SAFETY STRATEGY.

Section 2116 of title 46, United States Code, is amended—

(1) in subsection (a), by striking "each year of an annual" and inserting "of a triennial";

(2) in subsection (b)—

(A) in the subsection heading, by striking "Annual" and inserting "Triennial"; and

(B) by striking "annual" each place it appears and inserting "triennial";

(3) in subsection (c)—

(A) by striking "fiscal year 2011 and each fiscal year" and inserting "fiscal year 2020 and triennially"; and

(B) by striking "annual plan" and inserting "triennial plan"; and

(4) in subsection (d)(2), by striking "annually" and inserting "triennially".

SEC. 215. RECOGNIZED ORGANIZATIONS; OVERSIGHT.

(a) IN GENERAL.—Section 3316 of title 46, United States Code, is amended by redesignating subsection (g) as subsection (h), and by inserting after subsection (f) the following:

"(g)(1) There shall be within the Coast Guard an office that conducts comprehensive and targeted oversight of all recognized organizations that act on behalf of the Coast Guard.

"(2) The staff of the office shall include subject matter experts, including inspectors, investigators, and auditors, who possess the capability and authority to audit all aspects of such recognized organizations.

"(3) In this subsection the term 'recognized organization' has the meaning given that term in section 2.45-1 of title 46, Code of Federal Regulations, as in effect on the date of the enactment of the Hamm Alert Maritime Safety Act of 2018."

(b) [46 U.S.C. 3316 note] DEADLINE FOR ESTABLISHMENT.—The Commandant of the Coast Guard shall establish the office required by the amendment made by subsection (a) by not later than 2 years after the date of the enactment of this Act.

SEC. 216. [46 U.S.C. 3201 note] TIMELY WEATHER FORECASTS AND HAZARD ADVISORIES FOR MERCHANT MARINERS.

Not later than 1 year after the date of enactment of this Act, the Commandant shall seek to enter into negotiations through the International Maritime Organization to amend the International Convention for the Safety of Life at Sea to require that vessels subject to the requirements of such Convention receive—

(1) timely synoptic and graphical chart weather forecasts; and

(2) where available, timely hazard advisories for merchant mariners, including broadcasts of tropical cyclone forecasts and advisories, intermediate public advisories, and tropical cyclone updates to mariners via appropriate technologies.

SEC. 217. [46 U.S.C. 3315 note] ANONYMOUS SAFETY ALERT SYSTEM.

(a) PILOT PROGRAM.—Not later than 1 year after the date of

enactment of this Act, the Commandant shall establish an anonymous safety alert pilot program.

(b) REQUIREMENTS.—The pilot program established under subsection (a) shall provide an anonymous reporting mechanism to allow crew members to communicate urgent and dire safety concerns directly and in a timely manner with the Coast Guard.

SEC. 218. MARINE SAFETY IMPLEMENTATION STATUS.

(a) IN GENERAL.—Not later than December 19 of 2018, and of each of the 2 subsequent years thereafter, the Commandant shall provide to the Committee on Commerce, Science, and Transportation of the Senate and the Committee on Transportation and Infrastructure of the House of Representatives a briefing on the status of implementation of each action outlined in the Commandant's final action memo dated December 19, 2017, regarding the sinking and loss of the vessel El Faro.

(b) REPORT.—Not later than 2 years after the date of enactment of this Act, the Department of Homeland Security Inspector General shall report to the Committee on Commerce, Science, and Transportation of the Senate and the Committee on Transportation and Infrastructure of the House of Representatives on the status of the Coast Guard's implementation of each action outlined in the Commandant's final action memo dated December 19, 2017, regarding the sinking and loss of the vessel El Faro.

SEC. 219. [46 U.S.C. 3316 note] DELEGATED AUTHORITIES.

(a) IN GENERAL.—Not later than 1 year after the date of the enactment of this Act, the Commandant shall review the authorities that have been delegated to recognized organizations for the alternative compliance program as described in subpart D of part 8 of title 46, Code of Federal Regulations, and, if necessary, revise or establish policies and procedures to ensure those delegated authorities are being conducted in a manner to ensure safe maritime transportation.

(b) BRIEFING.—Not later than 1 year after the date of the enactment of this Act, the Commandant shall provide to the Committee on Commerce, Science, and Transportation of the Senate and the Committee on Transportation and Infrastructure of the House of Representatives a briefing on the implementation of subsection (a).

TITLE III—CENTER OF EXPERTISE

SEC. 301. [14 U.S.C. 1 note] SHORT TITLE.

This title may be cited as the "Coast Guard Blue Technology Center of Expertise Act".

SEC. 302. [14 U.S.C. 58 note] COAST GUARD BLUE TECHNOLOGY CENTER OF EXPERTISE.

(a) ESTABLISHMENT.—Not later than 1 year after the date of the enactment of this Act and subject to the availability of appropriations, the Commandant may establish under section 58 of title 14, United States Code, a Blue Technology center of expertise.

(b) MISSIONS.—In addition to the missions listed in section 58(b) of title 14, United States Code, the Center may—

(1) promote awareness within the Coast Guard of the range and diversity of Blue Technologies and their potential to enhance Coast Guard mission readiness, operational performance, and regulation of such technologies;

(2) function as an interactive conduit to enable the sharing and dissemination of Blue Technology information between the Coast Guard and representatives from the private sector, academia, nonprofit organizations, and other Federal agencies;

(3) increase awareness among Blue Technology manufacturers, entrepreneurs, and vendors of Coast Guard acquisition policies, procedures, and business practices;

(4) provide technical support, coordination, and assistance to Coast Guard districts and the Coast Guard Research and Development Center, as appropriate; and

(5) subject to the requirements of the Coast Guard Academy, coordinate with the Academy to develop appropriate curricula regarding Blue Technology to be offered in professional courses of study to give Coast Guard cadets and officer candidates a greater background and understanding of Blue Technologies.

(c) BLUE TECHNOLOGY EXPOSITION; BRIEFING.—Not later than 6 months after the date of the enactment of this Act, the Commandant shall provide to the Committee on Transportation and Infrastructure of the House of Representatives and the Committee on Commerce, Science, and Transportation of the Senate a briefing on the costs and benefits of hosting a biennial Coast Guard Blue Technology exposition to further interactions between representatives from the private sector, academia, and nonprofit organizations, and the Coast Guard and examine emerging technologies and Coast Guard mission demands.

(d) DEFINITIONS.—In this section:

(1) CENTER.—The term "Center" means the Blue Technology center of expertise established under this section.

(2) COMMANDANT.—The term "Commandant" means the Commandant of the Coast Guard.

(3) BLUE TECHNOLOGY.—The term "Blue Technology" means any technology, system, or platform that—

(A) is designed for use or application above, on, or below the sea surface or that is otherwise applicable to Coast Guard operational needs, including such a technology, system, or platform that provides continuous or persistent coverage; and

(B) supports or facilitates—

(i) maritime domain awareness, including—

(I) surveillance and monitoring;

(II) observation, measurement, and modeling: or

(III) information technology and communications;

(ii) search and rescue;

(iii) emergency response;

(iv) maritime law enforcement;

(v) marine inspections and investigations; or

(vi) protection and conservation of the marine environment.

SAVE OUR SEAS 2.0 ACT

PUBLIC LAW 116-224

Save Our Seas 2.0 Act

[(Public Law 116–224)]

[This law has not been amended]

AN ACT To improve efforts to combat marine debris, and for other purposes.

Be it enacted by the Senate and House of Representatives of the United States of America in Congress assembled,

SECTION 1. SHORT TITLE; TABLE OF CONTENTS.

(a) [33 U.S.C. 4201 note] SHORT TITLE.—This Act may be cited as the "Save Our Seas 2.0 Act".

(b) TABLE OF CONTENTS.—The table of contents of this Act is as follows:

SEC. 2. [33 U.S.C. 4201 note] DEFINITIONS.

In this Act:

(1) CIRCULAR ECONOMY.—The term "circular economy" means an economy that uses a systems-focused approach and involves industrial processes and economic activities that—

(A) are restorative or regenerative by design;

(B) enable resources used in such processes and activities to maintain their highest values for as long as possible; and

(C) aim for the elimination of waste through the superior design of materials, products, and systems (including business models).

(2) EPA ADMINISTRATOR.—The term "EPA Administrator" means the Administrator of the Environmental Protection Agency.

(3) INDIAN TRIBE.—The term ""Indian Tribe" has the meaning given the term "Indian tribe" in section 4 of the Indian Self-Determination and Education Assistance Act (25 U.S.C. 5304), without regard to capitalization.

(4) INTERAGENCY MARINE DEBRIS COORDINATING COMMITTEE.—The term "Interagency Marine Debris Coordinating Committee" means the Interagency Marine Debris Coordinating Committee established under section 5 of the Marine Debris Act (33 U.S.C. 1954).

(5) MARINE DEBRIS.—The term "marine debris" has the meaning given that term in section 7 of the Marine Debris Act (33 U.S.C. 1956).

(6) MARINE DEBRIS EVENT.—The term "marine debris event" means an event or related events that affects or may imminently affect the United States involving—

(A) marine debris caused by a natural event, including a tsunami, flood, landslide, hurricane, or other natural source;

(B) distinct, nonrecurring marine debris, including derelict vessel groundings and container spills, that have immediate or long-term impacts on habitats with high ecological, economic, or human-use values; or

(C) marine debris caused by an intentional or grossly negligent act or acts that causes substantial economic or environmental harm.

(7) NON-FEDERAL FUNDS.—The term "non-Federal funds" means funds provided by—

(A) a State;

(B) an Indian Tribe;

(C) a territory of the United States;

(D) one or more units of local governments or Tribal organizations (as defined in section 4 of the Indian Self-Determination and Education Assistance Act (25 U.S.C. 5304));

(E) a foreign government;

(F) a private for-profit entity;

(G) a nonprofit organization; or

(H) a private individual.

(8) NONPROFIT ORGANIZATION.—The term "nonprofit organization" means an organization that is described in section 501(c) of the Internal Revenue Code of 1986 and exempt from tax under section 501(a) of such Code.

(9) POST-CONSUMER MATERIALS MANAGEMENT.—The term "post-consumer materials management" means the systems, operation, supervision, and long-term management of processes and equipment used for post-use material (including packaging, goods, products, and other materials), including—

(A) collection;

(B) transport;

(C) safe disposal of waste that cannot be recovered, reused, recycled, repaired, or refurbished; and

(D) systems and processes related to post-use materials that can be recovered, reused, recycled, repaired, or refurbished.

(10) STATE.—The term "State" means—

(A) a State;

(B) an Indian Tribe;

(C) the District of Columbia;

(D) a territory or possession of the United States; or

(E) any political subdivision of an entity described in subparagraphs (A) through (D).

(11) UNDER SECRETARY.—The term "Under Secretary" means the Under Secretary of Commerce for Oceans and Atmosphere and Administrator of the National Oceanic and

Atmospheric Administration.

TITLE I—COMBATING MARINE DEBRIS

Subtitle A—Amendments to the Marine Debris Act

SEC. 101. AMENDMENTS TO THE MARINE DEBRIS ACT.

The Marine Debris Act (33 U.S.C. 1951 et seq.) is amended—

(1) [33 U.S.C. 1951] in section 2 by striking "marine environment," and inserting "marine environment (including waters in the jurisdiction of the United States, the high seas, and waters in the jurisdiction of other countries),";

(2) [33 U.S.C. 1958] in section 9(a)—

(A) by striking "$10,000,000" and inserting "$15,000,000"; and

(B) by striking "5 percent" and inserting "7 percent"; and

(3) by adding at the end the following:

"SEC. 10. [33 U.S.C. 1959] PRIORITIZATION OF MARINE DEBRIS IN EXISTING INNOVATION AND ENTREPRENEURSHIP PROGRAMS

"In carrying out any relevant innovation and entrepreneurship programs that improve the innovation, effectiveness, and efficiency of the Marine Debris Program established under section 3 without undermining the purpose for which such program was established, the Secretary of Commerce, the Secretary of Energy, the Administrator of the Environmental Protection Agency, and the heads of other relevant Federal agencies, shall prioritize efforts to combat marine debris, including by—

"(1) increasing innovation in methods and the effectiveness of efforts to identify, determine sources of, assess, prevent, reduce, and remove marine debris; and

"(2) addressing the impacts of marine debris on—

"(A) the economy of the United States;

"(B) the marine environment; and

"(C) navigation safety. "

Subtitle B—Marine Debris Foundation

SEC. 111. [33 U.S.C. 4211] ESTABLISHMENT AND PURPOSES OF FOUNDATION.

(a) ESTABLISHMENT.—There is established the Marine Debris Foundation (in this title referred to as the "Foundation"). The Foundation is a charitable and nonprofit organization and is not an agency or establishment of the United States.

(b) PURPOSES.—The purposes of the Foundation are—

(1) to encourage, accept, and administer private gifts of property for the benefit of, or in connection with, the activities and services of the National Oceanic and Atmospheric Administration under the Marine Debris Program established under section 3 of the Marine Debris Act (33 U.S.C. 1952), and other relevant programs and agencies;

(2) to undertake and conduct such other activities as will augment efforts of the National Oceanic and Atmospheric Administration to assess, prevent, reduce, and remove marine debris and address the adverse impacts of marine debris on the economy of the United States, the marine environment, and navigation safety;

(3) to participate with, and otherwise assist, State, local, and Tribal governments, foreign governments, entities, and individuals in undertaking and conducting activities to assess, prevent, reduce, and remove marine debris and address the adverse impacts of marine debris and its root causes on the economy of the United States, the marine environment (including waters in the jurisdiction of the United States, the high seas, and waters in the jurisdiction of other countries), and navigation safety;

(4) subject to an agreement with the Secretary of Commerce, administer the Genius Prize for Save Our Seas Innovation as described in title II; and

(5) to support other Federal actions to reduce marine debris.

SEC. 112. [33 U.S.C. 4212] BOARD OF DIRECTORS OF THE

FOUNDATION.

(a) Establishment and Membership.—

(1) In general.—The Foundation shall have a governing Board of Directors (in this title referred to as the "Board"), which shall consist of the Under Secretary and 12 additional Directors appointed in accordance with subsection (b) from among individuals who are United States citizens.

(2) Representation of diverse points of view.—To the maximum extent practicable, the membership of the Board shall represent diverse points of view relating to the assessment, prevention, reduction, and removal of marine debris.

(3) Not federal employees.—Appointment as a Director of the Foundation shall not constitute employment by, or the holding of an office of, the United States for the purpose of any Federal law.

(b) Appointment and Terms.—

(1) Appointment.—Subject to paragraph (2), after consulting with the EPA Administrator, the Director of the United States Fish and Wildlife Service, the Assistant Secretary of State for the Bureau of Oceans and International Environmental and Scientific Affairs, and the Administrator of the United States Agency for International Development, and considering the recommendations submitted by the Board, the Under Secretary shall appoint 12 Directors who meet the criteria established by subsection (a), of whom—

(A) at least 4 shall be educated or experienced in the assessment, prevention, reduction, or removal of marine debris, which may include an individual with expertise in post-consumer materials management or a circular economy;

(B) at least 2 shall be educated or experienced in the assessment, prevention, reduction, or removal of marine debris outside the United States;

(C) at least 2 shall be educated or experienced in ocean and coastal resource conservation science or policy; and

(D) at least 2 shall be educated or experienced in international trade or foreign policy.

(2) TERMS.—

(A) IN GENERAL.—Any Director appointed after the initial appointments are made under subparagraph (B) (other than the Under Secretary), shall be appointed for a term of 6 years.

(B) INITIAL APPOINTMENTS TO NEW MEMBER POSITIONS.—Of the Directors appointed by the Under Secretary under paragraph (1), the Under Secretary shall appoint, not later than 180 days after the date of the enactment of this Act—

(i) 4 Directors for a term of 6 years;

(ii) 4 Directors for a term of 4 years; and

(iii) 4 Directors for a term of 2 years.

(3) VACANCIES.—

(A) IN GENERAL.—The Under Secretary shall fill a vacancy on the Board.

(B) TERM OF APPOINTMENTS TO FILL UNEXPIRED TERMS.—An individual appointed to fill a vacancy that occurs before the expiration of the term of a Director shall be appointed for the remainder of the term.

(4) REAPPOINTMENT.—An individual shall not serve more than 2 consecutive terms as a Director, excluding any term of less than 6 years.

(5) CONSULTATION BEFORE REMOVAL.—The Under Secretary may remove a Director from the Board only after consultation with the Assistant Secretary of State for the Bureau of Oceans and International Environmental and Scientific Affairs, the Director of the United States Fish and Wildlife Service, and the EPA Administrator.

(c) CHAIRMAN.—The Chairman shall be elected by the Board from its members for a 2-year term.

(d) QUORUM.—A majority of the current membership of the Board shall constitute a quorum for the transaction of business.

(e) MEETINGS.—The Board shall meet at the call of the Chairman at least once a year. If a Director misses 3 consecutive regularly scheduled meetings, that individual may be removed from the Board and that vacancy filled in accordance with subsection (b).

(f) REIMBURSEMENT OF EXPENSES.—Members of the Board shall

serve without pay, but may be reimbursed for the actual and necessary traveling and subsistence expenses incurred by them in the performance of the duties of the Foundation.

(g) GENERAL POWERS.—

(1) IN GENERAL.—The Board may complete the organization of the Foundation by—

(A) appointing officers and employees;

(B) adopting a constitution and bylaws consistent with the purposes of the Foundation and the provisions of this title; and

(C) undertaking of other such acts as may be necessary to carry out the provisions of this title.

(2) LIMITATIONS ON APPOINTMENT.—The following limitations apply with respect to the appointment of officers and employees of the Foundation:

(A) Officers and employees may not be appointed until the Foundation has sufficient funds to pay them for their service. Officers and employees of the Foundation shall be appointed without regard to the provisions of title 5, United States Code, governing appointments in the competitive service, and may be paid without regard to the provisions of chapter 51 and subchapter III of chapter 53 of such title relating to classification and General Schedule pay rates.

(B) The first officer or employee appointed by the Board shall be the Secretary of the Board who—

(i) shall serve, at the direction of the Board, as its chief operating officer; and

(ii) shall be knowledgeable and experienced in matters relating to the assessment, prevention, reduction, and removal of marine debris.

SEC. 113. [33 U.S.C. 4213] RIGHTS AND OBLIGATIONS OF THE FOUNDATION.

(a) IN GENERAL.—The Foundation—

(1) shall have perpetual succession;

(2) may conduct business throughout the several States, territories, and possessions of the United States and abroad; and

(3) shall at all times maintain a designated agent authorized to accept service of process for the Foundation.

(b) SERVICE OF PROCESS.—The serving of notice to, or service of process upon, the agent required under subsection (a)(3), or mailed to the business address of such agent, shall be deemed as service upon or notice to the Foundation.

(c) POWERS.—

(1) IN GENERAL.—To carry out its purposes under section 111, the Foundation shall have, in addition to the powers otherwise given it under this title, the usual powers of a corporation acting as a trustee in the District of Columbia, including the power—

(A) to accept, receive, solicit, hold, administer, and use any gift, devise, or bequest, either absolutely or in trust, of real or personal property or any income therefrom or other interest therein;

(B) to acquire by purchase or exchange any real or personal property or interest therein;

(C) to invest any funds provided to the Foundation by the Federal Government in obligations of the United States or in obligations or securities that are guaranteed or insured by the United States;

(D) to deposit any funds provided to the Foundation by the Federal Government into accounts that are insured by an agency or instrumentality of the United States;

(E) to make use of any interest or investment income that accrues as a consequence of actions taken under subparagraph (C) or (D) to carry out the purposes of the Foundation;

(F) to use Federal funds to make payments under cooperative agreements to provide substantial long-term benefits for the assessment, prevention, reduction, and removal of marine debris;

(G) unless otherwise required by the instrument of transfer, to sell, donate, lease, invest, reinvest, retain or otherwise dispose of any property or income therefrom;

(H) to borrow money and issue bonds, debentures, or other debt instruments;

(I) to sue and be sued, and complain and defend itself in any court of competent jurisdiction, except that the Directors of the Foundation shall not be personally liable, except for gross negligence;

(J) to enter into contracts or other arrangements with, or provide financial assistance to, public agencies and private organizations and persons and to make such payments as may be necessary to carry out its functions; and

(K) to do any and all acts necessary and proper to carry out the purposes of the Foundation.

(2) NON-FEDERAL CONTRIBUTIONS TO THE FUND.—A gift, devise, or bequest may be accepted by the Foundation without regard to whether the gift, devise, or bequest is encumbered, restricted, or subject to beneficial interests of private persons if any current or future interest in the gift, devise, or bequest is for the benefit of the Foundation.

(d) NOTICE TO MEMBERS OF CONGRESS.—The Foundation may not make a grant of Federal funds in an amount greater than $100,000 unless, by not later than 15 days before the grant is made, the Foundation provides notice of the grant to the Member of Congress for the congressional district in which the project to be funded with the grant will be carried out.

(e) COORDINATION OF INTERNATIONAL EFFORTS.—Any efforts of the Foundation carried out in a foreign country, and any grants provided to an individual or entity in a foreign country, shall be made only with the concurrence of the Secretary of State, in consultation, as appropriate, with the Administrator of the United States Agency for International Development.

(f) CONSULTATION WITH NOAA.—The Foundation shall consult with the Under Secretary during the planning of any restoration or remediation action using funds resulting from judgments or settlements relating to the damage to trust resources of the National Oceanic and Atmospheric Administration.

SEC. 114. [33 U.S.C. 4214 note] ADMINISTRATIVE SERVICES AND SUPPORT.

(a) PROVISION OF SERVICES.—The Under Secretary may provide personnel, facilities, and other administrative services to the

Foundation, including reimbursement of expenses, not to exceed the current Federal Government per diem rates, for a period of up to 5 years beginning on the date of the enactment of this Act.

(b) REIMBURSEMENT.—The Under Secretary shall require reimbursement from the Foundation for any administrative service provided under subsection (a). The Under Secretary shall deposit any reimbursement received under this subsection into the Treasury to the credit of the appropriations then current and chargeable for the cost of providing such services.

SEC. 115. [33 U.S.C. 4215] VOLUNTEER STATUS.

The Secretary of Commerce may accept, without regard to the civil service classification laws, rules, or regulations, the services of the Foundation, the Board, and the officers and employees of the Board, without compensation from the Department of Commerce, as volunteers in the performance of the functions authorized in this title.

SEC. 116. [33 U.S.C. 4216] REPORT REQUIREMENTS; PETITION OF ATTORNEY GENERAL FOR EQUITABLE RELIEF.

(a) REPORT.—The Foundation shall, as soon as practicable after the end of each fiscal year, transmit to the Committee on Commerce, Science, and Transportation of the Senate and the Committee on Natural Resources, the Committee on Transportation and Infrastructure, and the Committee on Energy and Commerce of the House of Representatives a report—

(1) describing the proceedings and activities of the Foundation during that fiscal year, including a full and complete statement of its receipts, expenditures, and investments; and

(2) including a detailed statement of the recipient, amount, and purpose of each grant made by the Foundation in the fiscal year.

(b) RELIEF WITH RESPECT TO CERTAIN FOUNDATION ACTS OR FAILURE TO ACT.—If the Foundation—

(1) engages in, or threatens to engage in, any act, practice, or policy that is inconsistent with its purposes set forth in section 111(b); or

(2) refuses, fails, or neglects to discharge its obligations under this title, or threatens to do so,

the Attorney General may petition in the United States District Court for the District of Columbia for such equitable relief as may be necessary or appropriate.

SEC. 117. [33 U.S.C. 4217] UNITED STATES RELEASE FROM LIABILITY.

The United States shall not be liable for any debts, defaults, acts, or omissions of the Foundation nor shall the full faith and credit of the United States extend to any obligation of the Foundation.

SEC. 118. [33 U.S.C. 4218] AUTHORIZATION OF APPROPRIATIONS.

(a) AUTHORIZATION OF APPROPRIATIONS.—

(1) IN GENERAL.—There are authorized to be appropriated to the Department of Commerce to carry out this title $10,000,000 for each of fiscal years 2021 through 2024.

(2) USE OF APPROPRIATED FUNDS.—Subject to paragraph (3), amounts made available under paragraph (1) shall be provided to the Foundation to match contributions (whether in currency, services, or property) made to the Foundation, or to a recipient of a grant provided by the Foundation, by private persons and State and local government agencies.

(3) PROHIBITION ON USE FOR ADMINISTRATIVE EXPENSES.—

(A) IN GENERAL.—Except as provided in subparagraph (B), no Federal funds made available under paragraph (1) may be used by the Foundation for administrative expenses of the Foundation, including for salaries, travel and transportation expenses, and other overhead expenses.

(B) EXCEPTION.—The Secretary may allow the use of Federal funds made available under paragraph (1) to pay for salaries during the 18-month period beginning on the date of the enactment of this Act.

(b) ADDITIONAL AUTHORIZATION.—

(1) IN GENERAL.—In addition to the amounts made available under subsection (a), the Foundation may accept Federal funds from a Federal agency under any other Federal law for use by the Foundation to further the assessment, prevention, reduction, and removal of marine debris in accordance with the requirements of this title.

(2) USE OF FUNDS ACCEPTED FROM FEDERAL AGENCIES.—Federal funds provided to the Foundation under paragraph (1) shall be used by the Foundation for matching, in whole or in part, contributions (whether in currency, services, or property) made to the Foundation by private persons and State and local government agencies.

(c) PROHIBITION ON USE OF GRANT AMOUNTS FOR LITIGATION AND LOBBYING EXPENSES.—Amounts provided as a grant by the Foundation shall not be used for—

(1) any expense related to litigation consistent with Federal-wide cost principles; or

(2) any activity the purpose of which is to influence legislation pending before Congress consistent with Federal-wide cost principles.

SEC. 119. [33 U.S.C. 4219] TERMINATION OF AUTHORITY.

The authority of the Foundation under this subtitle shall terminate on the date that is 10 years after the establishment of the Foundation, unless the Foundation is reauthorized by an Act of Congress.

Subtitle C—Genius Prize for Save Our Seas Innovations

SEC. 121. [33 U.S.C. 4231] DEFINITIONS.

In this subtitle:

(1) PRIZE COMPETITION.—The term "prize competition" means the competition for the award of the Genius Prize for Save Our Seas Innovations established under section 122.

(2) SECRETARY.—The term "Secretary" means the Secretary of Commerce.

SEC. 122. [33 U.S.C. 4232] GENIUS PRIZE FOR SAVE OUR SEAS INNOVATIONS.

(a) IN GENERAL.—

(1) IN GENERAL.—Not later than 1 year after the date of the enactment of this Act, the Secretary shall establish under section 24 of the Stevenson-Wydler Technology Innovation Act of 1980 (15 U.S.C. 3719) a prize competition—

(A) to encourage technological innovation with the potential to reduce plastic waste, and associated and potential pollution, and thereby prevent marine debris; and

(B) to award 1 or more prizes biennially for projects that advance human understanding and innovation in removing and preventing plastic waste, in one of the categories described in paragraph (2).

(2) CATEGORIES FOR PROJECTS.—The categories for projects are:

(A) Advancements in materials used in packaging and other products that, if such products enter the coastal or ocean environment, will fully degrade without harming the environment, wildlife, or human health.

(B) Innovations in production and packaging design that reduce the use of raw materials, increase recycled content, encourage reusability and recyclability, and promote a circular economy.

(C) Improvements in marine debris detection, monitoring, and cleanup technologies and processes.

(D) Improvements or improved strategies to increase solid waste collection, processing, sorting, recycling, or reuse.

(E) New designs or strategies to reduce overall packaging needs and promote reuse.

(b) DESIGNATION.—The prize competition established under subsection (a) shall be known as the "Genius Prize for Save Our Seas Innovations".

(c) PRIORITIZATION.—In selecting awards for the prize competition, priority shall be given to projects that—

(1) have a strategy, submitted with the application or proposal, to move the new technology, process, design, material, or other product supported by the prize to market-scale deployment;

(2) support the concept of a circular economy; and

(3) promote development of materials that—

(A) can fully degrade in the ocean without harming the environment, wildlife, or human health; and

(B) are to be used in fishing gear or other maritime

products that have an increased likelihood of entering the coastal or ocean environment as unintentional waste.

SEC. 123. [33 U.S.C. 4233] AGREEMENT WITH THE MARINE DEBRIS FOUNDATION.

(a) IN GENERAL.—The Secretary may offer to enter into an agreement, which may include a grant or cooperative agreement, under which the Marine Debris Foundation established under title I may administer the prize competition.

(b) REQUIREMENTS.—An agreement entered into under subsection (a) shall comply with the following requirements:

(1) DUTIES.—The Marine Debris Foundation shall—

(A) advertise the prize competition;

(B) solicit prize competition participants;

(C) administer funds relating to the prize competition;

(D) receive Federal and non-Federal funds—

(i) to administer the prize competition; and

(ii) to award a cash prize;

(E) carry out activities to generate contributions of non-Federal funds to offset, in whole or in part—

(i) the administrative costs of the prize competition; and

(ii) the costs of a cash prize;

(F) in the design and award of the prize, consult, as appropriate with experts from—

(i) Federal agencies with jurisdiction over the prevention of marine debris or the promotion of innovative materials;

(ii) State agencies with jurisdiction over the prevention of marine debris or the promotion of innovative materials;

(iii) State, regional, or local conservation or post-consumer materials management organizations, the mission of which relates to the prevention of marine debris or the promotion of innovative materials;

(iv) conservation groups, technology companies, research institutions, scientists (including those with expertise in marine environments) institutions of higher education, industry, or individual stakeholders with an interest in the prevention of marine debris or the promotion of innovative materials;

(v) experts in the area of standards development regarding the degradation, breakdown, or recycling of polymers; and

(vi) other relevant experts of the Board's choosing;

(G) in consultation with, and subject to final approval by, the Secretary, develop criteria for the selection of prize competition winners;

(H) provide advice and consultation to the Secretary on the selection of judges under section 124 based on criteria developed in consultation with, and subject to the final approval of, the Secretary;

(I) announce 1 or more annual winners of the prize competition;

(J) subject to paragraph (2), award 1 or more cash prizes biennially of not less than $100,000; and

(K) protect against unauthorized use or disclosure by the Marine Debris Foundation of any trade secret or confidential business information of a prize competition participant.

(2) ADDITIONAL CASH PRIZES.—The Marine Debris Foundation may award more than 1 cash prize in a year—

(A) if the initial cash prize referred to in paragraph (1)(J) and any additional cash prizes are awarded using only non-Federal funds; and

(B) consisting of an amount determined by the Under Secretary after the Secretary is notified by the Marine Debris Foundation that non-Federal funds are available for an additional cash prize.

(3) SOLICITATION OF FUNDS.—The Marine Debris Foundation—

(A) may request and accept Federal funds and non-Federal funds for a cash prize or administration of the prize competition;

(B) may accept a contribution for a cash prize in

exchange for the right to name the prize; and

(C) shall not give special consideration to any Federal agency or non-Federal entity in exchange for a donation for a cash prize awarded under this section.

SEC. 124. [33 U.S.C. 4234] JUDGES.

(a) APPOINTMENT.—The Secretary shall appoint not fewer than 3 judges who shall, except as provided in subsection (b), select the 1 or more annual winners of the prize competition.

(b) DETERMINATION BY THE SECRETARY.—The judges appointed under subsection (a) shall not select any annual winner of the prize competition if the Secretary makes a determination that, in any fiscal year, none of the technological advancements entered into the prize competition merits an award.

SEC. 125. [33 U.S.C. 4235] REPORT TO CONGRESS.

Not later than 60 days after the date on which a cash prize is awarded under this title, the Secretary shall post on a publicly available website a report on the prize competition that includes—

(1) if the Secretary has entered into an agreement under section 123, a statement by the Marine Debris Foundation that describes the activities carried out by the Marine Debris Foundation relating to the duties described in section 123; and

(2) a statement by 1 or more of the judges appointed under section 124 that explains the basis on which the winner of the cash prize was selected.

SEC. 126. [33 U.S.C. 4236] AUTHORIZATION OF APPROPRIATIONS.

Of the amounts authorized under section 118(a), the Secretary of Commerce shall use up to $1,000,000 to carry out this subtitle.

SEC. 127. [33 U.S.C. 4237] TERMINATION OF AUTHORITY.

The prize program will terminate after 5 prize competition cycles have been completed.

Subtitle D—Studies, Pilot Projects, and Reports

SEC. 131. REPORT ON OPPORTUNITIES FOR INNOVATIVE USES

OF PLASTIC WASTE.

Not later than 2 years after the date of enactment of this Act, the Interagency Marine Debris Coordinating Committee shall submit to Congress a report on innovative uses for plastic waste in consumer products.

SEC. 132. REPORT ON MICROFIBER POLLUTION.

Not later than 2 years after the date of the enactment of this Act, the Interagency Marine Debris Coordinating Committee shall submit to Congress a report on microfiber pollution that includes—

(1) a definition of microfiber;

(2) an assessment of the sources, prevalence, and causes of microfiber pollution;

(3) a recommendation for a standardized methodology to measure and estimate the prevalence of microfiber pollution;

(4) recommendations for reducing microfiber pollution; and

(5) a plan for how Federal agencies, in partnership with other stakeholders, can lead on opportunities to reduce microfiber pollution during the 5-year period beginning on such date of enactment.

SEC. 133. STUDY ON UNITED STATES PLASTIC POLLUTION DATA.

(a) IN GENERAL.—The Under Secretary, in consultation with the EPA Administrator and the Secretary of the Interior, shall seek to enter into an arrangement with the National Academies of Sciences, Engineering, and Medicine under which the National Academies will undertake a multifaceted study that includes the following:

(1) An evaluation of United States contributions to global ocean plastic waste, including types, sources, and geographic variations.

(2) An assessment of the prevalence of marine debris and mismanaged plastic waste in saltwater and freshwater United States navigable waterways and tributaries.

(3) An examination of the import and export of plastic waste to and from the United States, including the destinations of the exported plastic waste and the waste management infrastructure and environmental conditions of these locations.

(4) Potential means to reduce United States contributions

to global ocean plastic waste.

(b) REPORT.—Not later than 18 months after the date of the enactment of this Act, the Under Secretary shall submit to Congress a report on the study conducted under subsection (a) that includes—

(1) the findings of the National Academies;

(2) recommendations on knowledge gaps that warrant further scientific inquiry; and

(3) recommendations on the potential value of a national marine debris tracking and monitoring system and how such a system might be designed and implemented.

SEC. 134. STUDY ON MASS BALANCE METHODOLOGIES TO CERTIFY CIRCULAR POLYMERS.

(a) IN GENERAL.—The National Institute of Standards and Technology shall conduct a study of available mass balance methodologies that are or could be readily standardized to certify circular polymers.

(b) REPORT.—Not later than 1 year after the date of enactment of this Act, the Institute shall submit to Congress a report on the study conducted under subsection (a) that includes—

(1) an identification and assessment of existing mass balance methodologies, standards, and certification systems that are or may be applicable to supply chain sustainability of polymers, considering the full life cycle of the polymer, and including an examination of—

(A) the International Sustainability and Carbon Certification; and

(B) the Roundtable on Sustainable Biomaterials;

(2) an assessment of the environmental impacts of the full lifecycle of circular polymers, including impacts on climate change; and

(3) an assessment of any legal or regulatory barriers to developing a standard and certification system for circular polymers.

(c) DEFINITIONS.—In this section:

(1) CIRCULAR POLYMERS.—The term "circular polymers" means polymers that can be reused multiple times or converted into a new, higher-quality product.

(2) MASS BALANCE METHODOLOGY.—The term "mass balance methodology" means the method of chain of custody accounting designed to track the exact total amount of certain content in products or materials through the production system and to ensure an appropriate allocation of this content in the finished goods based on auditable bookkeeping.

SEC. 135. REPORT ON SOURCES AND IMPACTS OF DERELICT FISHING GEAR.

Not later than 2 years after the date of the enactment of this Act, the Under Secretary shall submit to Congress a report that includes—

(1) an analysis of the scale of fishing gear losses by domestic and foreign fisheries, including—

(A) how the amount of gear lost varies among—

(i) domestic and foreign fisheries;

(ii) types of fishing gear; and

(iii) methods of fishing;

(B) how lost fishing gear is transported by ocean currents; and

(C) common reasons fishing gear is lost;

(2) an evaluation of the ecological, human health, and maritime safety impacts of derelict fishing gear, and how those impacts vary across—

(A) types of fishing gear;

(B) materials used to construct fishing gear; and

(C) geographic location;

(3) recommendations on management measures—

(A) to prevent fishing gear losses; and

(B) to reduce the impacts of lost fishing gear;

(4) an assessment of the cost of implementing such management measures; and

(5) an assessment of the impact of fishing gear loss attributable to foreign countries.

SEC. 136. EXPANSION OF DERELICT VESSEL RECYCLING.

Not later than 1 year after the date of the enactment of this

Act, the Under Secretary and the EPA Administrator shall jointly conduct a study to determine the feasibility of developing a nationwide derelict vessel recycling program—

(1) using as a model the fiberglass boat recycling program from the pilot project in Rhode Island led by Rhode Island Sea Grant and its partners; and

(2) including, if possible, recycling of vessels made from materials other than fiberglass.

SEC. 137. [33 U.S.C. 4251] INCENTIVE FOR FISHERMEN TO COLLECT AND DISPOSE OF PLASTIC FOUND AT SEA.

(a) IN GENERAL.—The Under Secretary shall establish a pilot program to assess the feasibility and advisability of providing incentives, such as grants, to fishermen based in the United States who incidentally capture marine debris while at sea—

(1) to track or keep the debris on board; and

(2) to dispose of the debris properly on land.

(b) SUPPORT FOR COLLECTION AND REMOVAL OF DERELICT GEAR.—The Under Secretary shall encourage United States efforts, such as the Fishing for Energy net disposal program, that support—

(1) collection and removal of derelict fishing gear and other fishing waste;

(2) disposal or recycling of such gear and waste; and

(3) prevention of the loss of such gear.

TITLE II—ENHANCED GLOBAL ENGAGEMENT TO COMBAT MARINE DEBRIS

SEC. 201. [33 U.S.C. 4261] STATEMENT OF POLICY ON INTERNATIONAL COOPERATION TO COMBAT MARINE DEBRIS.

It is the policy of the United States to partner, consult, and coordinate with foreign governments (at the national and subnational levels), civil society, international organizations, international financial institutions, subnational coastal communities, commercial and recreational fishing industry leaders, and the private sector, in a concerted effort—

(1) to increase knowledge and raise awareness about—

(A) the linkages between the sources of plastic waste, mismanaged waste and post-consumer materials, and marine debris; and

(B) the upstream and downstream causes and effects of plastic waste, mismanaged waste and post-consumer materials, and marine debris on marine environments, marine wildlife, human health, and economic development;

(2) to support—

(A) strengthening systems for reducing the generation of plastic waste and recovering, managing, reusing, and recycling plastic waste, marine debris, and microfiber pollution in the world's oceans, emphasizing upstream post-consumer materials management solutions—

(i) to decrease plastic waste at its source; and

(ii) to prevent leakage of plastic waste into the environment;

(B) advancing the utilization and availability of safe and affordable reusable alternatives to disposable plastic products in commerce, to the extent practicable, and with consideration for the potential impacts of such alternatives, and other efforts to prevent marine debris;

(C) deployment of and access to advanced technologies to capture value from post-consumer materials and municipal solid waste streams through mechanical and other recycling systems;

(D) access to information on best practices in post-consumer materials management, options for post-consumer materials management systems financing, and options for participating in public-private partnerships; and

(E) implementation of management measures to reduce derelict fishing gear, the loss of fishing gear, and other sources of pollution generated from marine activities and to increase proper disposal and recycling of fishing gear; and

(3) to work cooperatively with international partners—

(A) on establishing—

(i) measurable targets for reducing marine debris,

lost fishing gear, and plastic waste from all sources; and

(ii) action plans to achieve those targets with a mechanism to provide regular reporting;

(B) to promote consumer education, awareness, and outreach to prevent marine debris;

(C) to reduce marine debris by improving advance planning for marine debris events and responses to such events; and

(D) to share best practices in post-consumer materials management systems to prevent the entry of plastic waste into the environment.

SEC. 202. [33 U.S.C. 4262] PRIORITIZATION OF EFFORTS AND ASSISTANCE TO COMBAT MARINE DEBRIS AND IMPROVE PLASTIC WASTE MANAGEMENT.

(a) IN GENERAL.—The Secretary of State shall, in coordination with the Administrator of the United States Agency for International Development, as appropriate, and the officials specified in subsection (b)—

(1) lead and coordinate efforts to implement the policy described in section 201; and

(2) develop strategies and implement programs that prioritize engagement and cooperation with foreign governments, subnational and local stakeholders, and the private sector to expedite efforts and assistance in foreign countries—

(A) to partner with, encourage, advise and facilitate national and subnational governments on the development and execution, where practicable, of national projects, programs and initiatives to—

(i) improve the capacity, security, and standards of operations of post-consumer materials management systems;

(ii) monitor and track how well post-consumer materials management systems are functioning nationwide, based on uniform and transparent standards developed in cooperation with municipal, industrial, and civil society stakeholders;

(iii) identify the operational challenges of post-consumer materials management systems and develop policy and programmatic solutions;

(iv) end intentional or unintentional incentives for municipalities, industries, and individuals to improperly dispose of plastic waste; and

(v) conduct outreach campaigns to raise public awareness of the importance of proper waste disposal and the reduction of plastic waste;

(B) to facilitate the involvement of municipalities and industries in improving solid waste reduction, collection, disposal, and reuse and recycling projects, programs, and initiatives;

(C) to partner with and provide technical assistance to investors, and national and local institutions, including private sector actors, to develop new business opportunities and solutions to specifically reduce plastic waste and expand solid waste and post-consumer materials management best practices in foreign countries by—

(i) maximizing the number of people and businesses, in both rural and urban communities, receiving reliable solid waste and post-consumer materials management services;

(ii) improving and expanding the capacity of foreign industries to responsibly employ post-consumer materials management practices;

(iii) improving and expanding the capacity and transparency of tracking mechanisms for marine debris to reduce the impacts on the marine environment;

(iv) eliminating incentives that undermine responsible post-consumer materials management practices and lead to improper waste disposal practices and leakage;

(v) building the capacity of countries—

(I) to reduce, monitor, regulate, and manage waste, post-consumer materials and plastic waste, and pollution appropriately and transparently, including imports of plastic waste from the United

States and other countries;

(II) to encourage private investment in post-consumer materials management and reduction; and

(III) to encourage private investment, grow opportunities, and develop markets for recyclable, reusable, and repurposed plastic waste and post-consumer materials, and products with high levels of recycled plastic content, at both national and local levels; and

(vi) promoting safe and affordable reusable alternatives to disposable plastic products, to the extent practicable; and

(D) to research, identify, and facilitate opportunities to promote collection and proper disposal of damaged or derelict fishing gear.

(b) OFFICIALS SPECIFIED.—The officials specified in this subsection are the following:

(1) The United States Trade Representative.

(2) The Under Secretary.

(3) The EPA Administrator.

(4) The Director of the Trade and Development Agency.

(5) The President and the Board of Directors of the Overseas Private Investment Corporation or the Chief Executive Officer and the Board of Directors of the United States International Development Finance Corporation, as appropriate.

(6) The Chief Executive Officer and the Board of Directors of the Millennium Challenge Corporation.

(7) The Commandant of the Coast Guard, with respect to pollution from ships.

(8) The heads of such other agencies as the Secretary of State considers appropriate.

(c) PRIORITIZATION.—In carrying out subsection (a), the officials specified in subsection (b) shall prioritize assistance to countries with, and regional organizations in regions with—

(1) rapidly developing economies; and

(2) rivers and coastal areas that are the most severe sources of marine debris, as identified by the best available science.

(d) EFFECTIVENESS MEASUREMENT.—In prioritizing and expediting efforts and assistance under this section, the officials specified in subsection (b) shall use clear, accountable, and metric-based targets to measure the effectiveness of guarantees and assistance in achieving the policy described in section 201.

(e) RULE OF CONSTRUCTION.—Nothing in this section may be construed to authorize the modification of or the imposition of limits on the portfolios of any agency or institution led by an official specified in subsection (b).

SEC. 203. [33 U.S.C. 4263] UNITED STATES LEADERSHIP IN INTERNATIONAL FORA.

In implementing the policy described in section 201, the President shall direct the United States representatives to appropriate international bodies and conferences (including the United Nations Environment Programme, the Association of Southeast Asian Nations, the Asia Pacific Economic Cooperation, the Group of 7, the Group of 20, the Organization for Economic Co-Operation and Development (OECD), and the Our Ocean Conference) to use the voice, vote, and influence of the United States, consistent with the broad foreign policy goals of the United States, to advocate that each such body—

(1) commit to significantly increasing efforts to promote investment in well-designed post-consumer materials management and plastic waste elimination and mitigation projects and services that increase access to safe post-consumer materials management and mitigation services, in partnership with the private sector and consistent with the constraints of other countries;

(2) address the post-consumer materials management needs of individuals and communities where access to municipal post-consumer materials management services is historically impractical or cost-prohibitive;

(3) enhance coordination with the private sector—

(A) to increase access to solid waste and post-consumer materials management services;

(B) to utilize safe and affordable alternatives to disposable plastic products, to the extent practicable;

(C) to encourage and incentivize the use of recycled content; and

(D) to grow economic opportunities and develop markets for recyclable, compostable, reusable, and repurposed plastic waste materials and post-consumer materials and other efforts that support the circular economy;

(4) provide technical assistance to foreign regulatory authorities and governments to remove unnecessary barriers to investment in otherwise commercially-viable projects related to—

(A) post-consumer materials management;

(B) the use of safe and affordable alternatives to disposable plastic products; or

(C) beneficial reuse of solid waste, plastic waste, post-consumer materials, plastic products, and refuse;

(5) use clear, accountable, and metric-based targets to measure the effectiveness of such projects; and

(6) engage international partners in an existing multilateral forum (or, if necessary, establish through an international agreement a new multilateral forum) to improve global cooperation on—

(A) creating tangible metrics for evaluating efforts to reduce plastic waste and marine debris;

(B) developing and implementing best practices at the national and subnational levels of foreign countries, particularly countries with little to no solid waste or post-consumer materials management systems, facilities, or policies in place for—

(i) collecting, disposing, recycling, and reusing plastic waste and post-consumer materials, including building capacity for improving post-consumer materials management; and

(ii) integrating alternatives to disposable plastic products, to the extent practicable;

(C) encouraging the development of standards and

practices, and increasing recycled content percentage requirements for disposable plastic products;

(D) integrating tracking and monitoring systems into post-consumer materials management systems;

(E) fostering research to improve scientific understanding of—

(i) how microfibers and microplastics may affect marine ecosystems, human health and safety, and maritime activities;

(ii) changes in the amount and regional concentrations of plastic waste in the ocean, based on scientific modeling and forecasting;

(iii) the role rivers, streams, and other inland waterways play in serving as conduits for mismanaged waste traveling from land to the ocean;

(iv) effective means to eliminate present and future leakages of plastic waste into the environment; and

(v) other related areas of research the United States representatives deem necessary;

(F) encouraging the World Bank and other international finance organizations to prioritize efforts to reduce plastic waste and combat marine debris;

(G) collaborating on technological advances in post-consumer materials management and recycled plastics;

(H) growing economic opportunities and developing markets for recyclable, compostable, reusable, and repurposed plastic waste and post-consumer materials and other efforts that support the circular economy; and

(I) advising foreign countries, at both the national and subnational levels, on the development and execution of regulatory policies, services, including recycling and reuse of plastic, and laws pertaining to reducing the creation and the collection and safe management of—

(i) solid waste;

(ii) post-consumer materials;

(iii) plastic waste; and

(iv) marine debris.

SEC. 204. [33 U.S.C. 4264] ENHANCING INTERNATIONAL OUTREACH AND PARTNERSHIP OF UNITED STATES AGENCIES INVOLVED IN MARINE DEBRIS ACTIVITIES.

(a) FINDINGS.—Congress recognizes the success of the marine debris program of the National Oceanic and Atmospheric Administration and the Trash-Free Waters program of the Environmental Protection Agency.

(b) AUTHORIZATION OF EFFORTS TO BUILD FOREIGN PARTNERSHIPS.—The Under Secretary and the EPA Administrator shall work with the Secretary of State and the Administrator of the United States Agency for International Development to build partnerships, as appropriate, with the governments of foreign countries and to support international efforts to combat marine debris.

SEC. 205. NEGOTIATION OF NEW INTERNATIONAL AGREEMENTS.

Not later than 1 year after the date of the enactment of this Act, the Secretary of State shall submit to Congress a report—

(1) assessing the potential for negotiating new international agreements or creating a new international forum to reduce land-based sources of marine debris and derelict fishing gear, consistent with section 203;

(2) describing the provisions that could be included in such agreements; and

(3) assessing potential parties to such agreements.

SEC. 206. [33 U.S.C. 4265] CONSIDERATION OF MARINE DEBRIS IN NEGOTIATING INTERNATIONAL AGREEMENTS.

In negotiating any relevant international agreement with any country or countries after the date of the enactment of this Act, the President shall, as appropriate—

(1) consider the impact of land-based sources of plastic waste and other solid waste from that country on the marine and aquatic environment; and

(2) ensure that the agreement strengthens efforts to eliminate land-based sources of plastic waste and other solid waste from that country that impact the marine and aquatic environment.

TITLE III—IMPROVING DOMESTIC INFRASTRUCTURE TO PREVENT MARINE DEBRIS

SEC. 301. [33 U.S.C. 4281] STRATEGY FOR IMPROVING POST-CONSUMER MATERIALS MANAGEMENT AND WATER MANAGEMENT.

(a) IN GENERAL.—Not later than 1 year after the date of enactment of this Act, the EPA Administrator shall, in consultation with stakeholders, develop a strategy to improve post-consumer materials management and infrastructure for the purpose of reducing plastic waste and other post-consumer materials in waterways and oceans.

(b) RELEASE.—On development of the strategy under subsection (a), the EPA Administrator shall—

(1) distribute the strategy to States; and

(2) make the strategy publicly available, including for use by—

(A) for-profit private entities involved in post-consumer materials management; and

(B) other nongovernmental entities.

SEC. 302. [33 U.S.C. 4282] GRANT PROGRAMS.

(a) POST-CONSUMER MATERIALS MANAGEMENT INFRASTRUCTURE GRANT PROGRAM.—

(1) IN GENERAL.—The EPA Administrator may provide grants to States to implement the strategy developed under section 301(a) and—

(A) to support improvements to local post-consumer materials management, including municipal recycling programs; and

(B) to assist local waste management authorities in making improvements to local waste management systems.

(2) APPLICATIONS.—To be eligible to receive a grant under paragraph (1), the applicant State shall submit to the EPA Administrator an application at such time, in such manner, and containing such information as the EPA Administrator may require.

(3) CONTENTS OF APPLICATIONS.—In developing application requirements, the EPA Administrator shall consider requesting that a State applicant provide—

(A) a description of—

(i) the project or projects to be carried out using grant funds; and

(ii) how the project or projects would result in the generation of less plastic waste;

(B) a description of how the funds will support disadvantaged communities; and

(C) an explanation of any limitations, such as flow control measures, that restrict access to reusable or recyclable materials.

(4) REPORT TO CONGRESS.—Not later than January 1, 2023, the EPA Administrator shall submit to the Committee on Environment and Public Works of the Senate and the Committee on Transportation and Infrastructure and the Committee on Energy and Commerce of the House of Representatives a report that includes—

(A) a description of the activities carried out under this subsection;

(B) estimates as to how much plastic waste was prevented from entering the oceans and other waterways as a result of activities funded pursuant to this subsection; and

(C) a recommendation on the utility of evolving the grant program into a new waste management State revolving fund.

(b) DRINKING WATER INFRASTRUCTURE GRANTS.—

(1) IN GENERAL.—The EPA Administrator may provide competitive grants to units of local government, Indian Tribes, and public water systems (as defined in section 1401 of the Safe Drinking Water Act (42 U.S.C. 300f)) to support improvements in reducing and removing plastic waste and post-consumer materials, including microplastics and microfibers, from drinking water or sources of drinking water, including planning, design, construction, technical assistance, and planning support for operational adjustments.

(2) APPLICATIONS.—To be eligible to receive a grant under paragraph (1), an applicant shall submit to the EPA Administrator an application at such time, in such manner, and containing such information as the EPA Administrator may require.

(c) WASTEWATER INFRASTRUCTURE GRANTS.—

(1) IN GENERAL.—The EPA Administrator may provide grants to municipalities (as defined in section 502 of the Federal Water Pollution Control Act (33 U.S.C. 1362)) or Indian Tribes that own and operate treatment works (as such term is defined in section 212 of such Act (33 U.S.C. 1292)) for the construction of improvements to reduce and remove plastic waste and post-consumer materials, including microplastics and microfibers, from wastewater.

(2) APPLICATIONS.—To be eligible to receive a grant under paragraph (1), an applicant shall submit to the EPA Administrator an application at such time, in such manner, and containing such information as the EPA Administrator may require.

(d) TRASH-FREE WATERS GRANTS.—

(1) IN GENERAL.—The EPA Administrator may provide grants to units of local government, Indian Tribes, and nonprofit organizations—

(A) to support projects to reduce the quantity of solid waste in bodies of water by reducing the quantity of waste at the source, including through anti-litter initiatives;

(B) to enforce local post-consumer materials management ordinances;

(C) to implement State or local policies relating to solid waste;

(D) to capture post-consumer materials at stormwater inlets, at stormwater outfalls, or in bodies of water;

(E) to provide education and outreach about post-consumer materials movement and reduction; and

(F) to monitor or model flows of post-consumer materials, including monitoring or modeling a reduction in trash as a result of the implementation of best management practices for the reduction of plastic waste and other post-consumer materials in sources of drinking water.

(2) APPLICATIONS.—To be eligible to receive a grant under paragraph (1), an applicant shall submit to the EPA Administrator an application at such time, in such manner, and containing such information as the EPA Administrator may require.

(e) APPLICABILITY OF FEDERAL LAW.—

(1) IN GENERAL.—The EPA Administrator shall ensure that all laborers and mechanics employed on projects funded directly, or assisted in whole or in part, by a grant established by this section shall be paid wages at rates not less than those prevailing on projects of a character similar in the locality as determined by the Secretary of Labor in accordance with subchapter IV of chapter 31 of part A of subtitle II of title 40, United States Code.

(2) AUTHORITY.—With respect to the labor standards specified in paragraph (1), the Secretary of Labor shall have the authority and functions set forth in Reorganization Plan Numbered 14 of 1950 (64 Stat. 1267; 5 U.S.C. App.) and section 3145 of title 40, United States Code.

(3) REQUIREMENTS.—The requirements of section 608 of the Federal Water Pollution Control Act (33 U.S.C. 1388) shall apply to the construction of a project carried out, in whole or in part, with assistance made available under this section in the same manner as the requirements of such section apply with respect to funds made available pursuant to title VI of such Act.

(f) LIMITATION ON USE OF FUNDS.—A grant under this section may not be used (directly or indirectly) as a source of payment (in whole or in part) of, or security for, an obligation the interest on which is excluded from gross income under section 103 of the Internal Revenue Code of 1986.

(g) AUTHORIZATION OF APPROPRIATIONS.—There are authorized to be appropriated—

(1) for the program described subsection (a), $55,000,000 for each of fiscal years 2021 through 2025; and

(2) for each of the programs described subsections (b), (c), and (d), $10,000,000 for each of fiscal years 2021 through 2025.

SEC. 303. STUDY ON REPURPOSING PLASTIC WASTE IN INFRASTRUCTURE.

(a) IN GENERAL.—The Secretary of Transportation (referred to in this section as the "Secretary") and the EPA Administrator shall jointly enter into an arrangement with the National Academies of Sciences, Engineering, and Medicine under which the National Academies will—

(1) conduct a study on the uses of plastic waste in infrastructure; and

(2) as part of the study under paragraph (1)—

(A) identify domestic and international examples of—

(i) the use of plastic waste materials described in that paragraph;

(ii) infrastructure projects in which the use of plastic waste has been applied; and

(iii) projects in which the use of plastic waste has been incorporated into or with other infrastructure materials;

(B) assess—

(i) the effectiveness and utility of the uses of plastic waste described in that paragraph;

(ii) the extent to which plastic waste materials are consistent with recognized specifications for infrastructure construction and other recognized standards;

(iii) relevant impacts of plastic waste materials compared to non-waste plastic materials;

(iv) the health, safety, and environmental impacts of—

(I) plastic waste on humans and animals; and

(II) the increased use of plastic waste for infrastructure;

(v) the ability of plastic waste infrastructure to withstand natural disasters, extreme weather events, and other hazards; and

(vi) plastic waste in infrastructure through an economic analysis; and

(C) make recommendations with respect to what standards or matters may need to be addressed with respect to ensuring human and animal health and safety from the use of plastic waste in infrastructure.

(b) REPORT REQUIRED.—Not later than 2 years after the date of enactment of this Act and subject to the availability of appropriations, the Secretary and the EPA Administrator shall submit to Congress a report on the study conducted under subsection (a).

SEC. 304. STUDY ON EFFECTS OF MICROPLASTICS IN FOOD SUPPLIES AND SOURCES OF DRINKING WATER.

(a) IN GENERAL.—The EPA Administrator, in consultation with the Under Secretary, shall seek to enter into an arrangement with the National Academies of Sciences, Engineering, and Medicine under which the National Academies will conduct a human health and environmental risk assessment on microplastics, including microfibers, in food supplies and sources of drinking water.

(b) REPORT REQUIRED.—Not later than 2 years after the date of enactment of this Act, the EPA Administrator shall submit to Congress a report on the study conducted under subsection (a) that includes—

(1) a science-based definition of "microplastics" that can be adopted in federally supported monitoring and future assessments supported or conducted by a Federal agency;

(2) recommendations for standardized monitoring, testing, and other necessary protocols relating to microplastics;

(3) an assessment of—

(A) the extent to which microplastics are present in the food supplies and sources of drinking water; and

(B) the type, source, prevalence, and risk of microplastics in the food supplies and sources of drinking water, including—

(i) an identification of the most significant sources of those microplastics; and

(ii) a review of the best available science to determine any potential hazards of microplastics in the food supplies and sources of drinking water; and

(4) a measurement of—

(A) the quantity of environmental chemicals that adsorb to microplastics; and

(B) the quantity described in subparagraph (A) that would be available for human exposure through food supplies or sources of drinking water.

SEC. 305. REPORT ON ELIMINATING BARRIERS TO INCREASE THE COLLECTION OF RECYCLABLE MATERIALS.

Not later than 1 year after the date of enactment of this Act, the EPA Administrator shall submit to Congress a report describing—

(1) the economic, educational, technological, resource availability, legal, or other barriers to increasing the collection, processing, and use of recyclable materials; and

(2) recommendations to overcome the barriers described under paragraph (1).

SEC. 306. REPORT ON ECONOMIC INCENTIVES TO SPUR DEVELOPMENT OF NEW END-USE MARKETS FOR RECYCLED PLASTICS.

Not later than 1 year after the date of enactment of this Act, the EPA Administrator shall submit to Congress a report describing the most efficient and effective economic incentives to spur the development of additional new end-use markets for recycled plastics, including plastic film, including the use of increased recycled content by manufacturers in the production of plastic goods and packaging.

SEC. 307. REPORT ON MINIMIZING THE CREATION OF NEW PLASTIC WASTE.

(a) IN GENERAL.—The EPA Administrator, in coordination with the Interagency Marine Debris Coordinating Committee and the National Institute of Standards and Technology, shall conduct a study on minimizing the creation of new plastic waste.

(b) REPORT.—Not later than 2 years after the date of enactment of this Act, the EPA Administrator shall submit to Congress a report on the study conducted under subsection (a) that includes—

(1) an estimate of the current and projected United States production and consumption of plastics, by type of plastic, including consumer food products;

(2) an estimate of the environmental effects and impacts of plastic production and use in relation to other materials;

(3) an estimate of current and projected future recycling rates of plastics, by type of plastic;

(4) an assessment of opportunities to minimize the creation of new plastic waste, including consumer food products, by reducing, recycling, reusing, refilling, refurbishing, or capturing plastic that would otherwise be part of a waste stream; and

(5) an assessment of what post-consumer recycled content standards for plastic are technologically and economically feasible, and the impact of the standards on recycling rates.

MARITIME SECURITY IMPROVEMENT ACT OF 2018
DIVISION J OF THE FAA REAUTHORIZATION ACT OF 2018

PUBLIC LAW 115-254

AS AMENDED THROUGH P.L. 118-63

FRANK LOBIONDO COAST GUARD AUTHORIZATION ACT OF 2018

PUBLIC LAW 115-254
AS AMENDED THROUGH P.L. 118-63

Frank LoBiondo Coast Guard Authorization Act of 2018

[(Public Law 115–282)]

[As Amended Through P.L. 117–263, Enacted December 23, 2022]

AN ACT To authorize appropriations for the Coast Guard, and for other purposes.

Be it enacted by the Senate and House of Representatives of the United States of America in Congress assembled,

SECTION 1. SHORT TITLE.

This Act may be cited as the "Frank LoBiondo Coast Guard Authorization Act of 2018".

SEC. 2. TABLE OF CONTENTS.

The table of contents of this Act is as follows:

TITLE I—REORGANIZATION OF TITLE

14, UNITED STATES CODE

SEC. 101. [14 U.S.C. 1] INITIAL MATTER.

Title 14, United States Code,is amended by striking the title designation, the title heading, and the table of parts at the beginning and inserting the following:

"TITLE 14—COAST GUARD

"Subtitle

"Sec.

"I. Establishment, Powers, Duties, and Administration

"II. Personnel

"III. Coast Guard Reserve and Auxiliary

"IV. Coast Guard Authorizations and Reports to Congress"

SEC. 102. [14 U.S.C. 1] SUBTITLE I.

Part I of title 14, United States Code,is amended by striking the part designation, the part heading, and the table of chapters at the beginning and inserting the following:

"Subtitle I—Establishment, Powers, Duties, and Administration

"Chap.

"Sec.	
"1.	Establishment and Duties
"3.	Composition and Organization
"5.	Functions and Powers
"7.	Cooperation
"9.	Administration
"11.	Acquisitions "

SEC. 103. CHAPTER 1.

(a) [14 U.S.C. 1] Initial Matter.—Chapter 1 of title 14, United States Code, is amended by striking the chapter designation, the chapter heading, and the table of sections at the beginning and inserting the following:

"CHAPTER 1—ESTABLISHMENT AND DUTIES

"Sec.
"101. Establishment of Coast Guard.
"102. Primary duties.
"103. Department in which the Coast Guard operates.
"104. Removing restrictions.
"105. Secretary defined.
"106. Commandant defined."

(b) REDESIGNATIONS AND TRANSFERS.—

(1) REQUIREMENT.—The sections of title 14, United States Code, identified in the table provided in paragraph (2) are amended—

(A) by redesignating the sections as described in the table; and

(B) by transferring the sections, as necessary, so that the sections appear after the table of sections for chapter 1 of such title (as added by subsection (a)), in the order in which the sections are presented in the table.

(2) TABLE.—The table referred to in paragraph (1) is the following:

Title 14 section number before redesignationSection heading (provided for identification purposes only-not amended)Title 14 section number after redesignation

1Establishment of Coast Guard1012Primary duties1023Department in which the Coast Guard operates103652Removing restrictions1044Secretary defined1055Commandant defined106

SEC. 104. CHAPTER 3.

(a) [14 U.S.C. 41] INITIAL MATTER.—Chapter 3 of title 14, United States Code, is amended by striking the chapter designation, the chapter heading, and the table of sections at the beginning and inserting the following:

"CHAPTER 3—COMPOSITION AND ORGANIZATION

"Sec.
"301. Grades and ratings.

"302.	Commandant; appointment.
"303.	Retirement of Commandant or Vice Commandant.
"304.	Vice Commandant; appointment.
"305.	Vice admirals.
"306.	Retirement.
"307.	Vice admirals and admiral, continuity of grade.
"308.	Chief Acquisition Officer.
"309.	Office of the Coast Guard Reserve; Director.
"310.	Chief of Staff to President: appointment.
"311.	Captains of the port.
"312.	Prevention and response workforces.
"313.	Centers of expertise for Coast Guard prevention and response.
"314.	Marine industry training program.
"315.	Training course on workings of Congress.
"316.	National Coast Guard Museum.
"317.	United States Coast Guard Band; composition; director.
"318.	Environmental Compliance and Restoration Program."

(b) REDESIGNATIONS AND TRANSFERS.—

(1) REQUIREMENT.—The sections of title 14, United States Code, identified in the table provided in paragraph (2) are amended—

(A) by redesignating the sections as described in the table; and

(B) by transferring the sections, as necessary, so that the sections appear after the table of sections for chapter 3 of such title (as added by subsection (a)), in the order in which the sections are presented in the table.

(2) TABLE.—The table referred to in paragraph (1) is the following:

Title 14 section number before redesignationSection heading (provided for identification purposes only-not amended)Title 14 section number after redesignation

41Grades and ratings30144Commandant; appointment30246Retirement of Commandant or Vice Commandant30347Vice Commandant; appointment30450Vice admirals30551Retirement30652Vice admirals and admiral, continuity of grade30756Chief Acquisition Officer30853Office of the Coast Guard Reserve; Director30954Chief of Staff to President: appointment31057Prevention and response workforces31258Centers of expertise for Coast Guard prevention and response31359Marine industry training program31460Training course on workings of Congress31598National Coast Guard Museum316336United States Coast Guard Band; composition; director317

(c) ADDITIONAL CHANGES.—

(1) IN GENERAL.—Chapter 3 of title 14, United States Code, is further amended—

(A) by inserting after section 310 (as so redesignated and transferred under subsection (b)) the following:

"SEC. § 311. [14 U.S.C. 311] Captains of the por

"Any officer, including any petty officer, may be designated by the Commandant as captain of the port or ports or adjacent high seas or waters over which the United States has jurisdiction, as the Commandant deems necessary to facilitate execution of Coast Guard duties."

; and

(B) by inserting after section 317 (as so redesignated and transferred under subsection (b)) the following:

"SEC. § 318. [14 U.S.C. 318] Environmental Compliance and Restoration Progra

"(a) DEFINITIONS.—For the purposes of this section—

"(1) 'environment', 'facility', 'person', 'release', 'removal', 'remedial', and 'response' have the same meaning they have in section 101 of the Comprehensive Environmental Response, Compensation, and Liability Act (42 U.S.C. 9601);

"(2) 'hazardous substance' has the same meaning it has in section 101 of the Comprehensive Environmental Response, Compensation, and Liability Act (42 U.S.C. 9601), except that it also includes the meaning given 'oil' in section 311 of the Federal Water Pollution Control Act (33 U.S.C. 1321); and

"(3) 'pollutant' has the same meaning it has in section 502 of the Federal Water Pollution Control Act (33 U.S.C. 1362).

"(b) PROGRAM.—

"(1) The Secretary shall carry out a program of environmental compliance and restoration at current and former Coast Guard facilities.

"(2) Program goals include:

"(A) Identifying, investigating, and cleaning up contamination from hazardous substances and pollutants.

"(B) Correcting other environmental damage that poses an imminent and substantial danger to the public health or welfare or to the environment.

"(C) Demolishing and removing unsafe buildings and structures, including buildings and structures at former Coast Guard facilities.

"(D) Preventing contamination from hazardous substances and pollutants at current Coast Guard facilities.

"(3)(A) The Secretary shall respond to releases of hazardous substances and pollutants—

"(i) at each Coast Guard facility the United States owns, leases, or otherwise possesses;

"(ii) at each Coast Guard facility the United States owned, leased, or otherwise possessed when the actions leading to contamination from hazardous substances or pollutants occurred; and

"(iii) on each vessel the Coast Guard owns or operates.

"(B) Subparagraph (A) of this paragraph does not apply to a removal or remedial action when a potentially responsible person responds under section 122 of the Comprehensive Environmental Response, Compensation, and Liability Act (42 U.S.C. 9622).

"(C) The Secretary shall pay a fee or charge imposed by a State authority for permit services for disposing of hazardous substances or pollutants from Coast Guard facilities to the same extent that nongovernmental entities are required to pay for permit services. This subparagraph does not apply to a payment that is the responsibility of a lessee, contractor, or other private person.

"(4) The Secretary may agree with another Federal agency for that agency to assist in carrying out the Secretary's responsibilities under this section. The Secretary may enter into contracts, cooperative agreements, and grant agreements with State and local governments to assist in carrying out the Secretary's responsibilities under this section. Services that may be obtained under this paragraph include identifying, investigating, and cleaning up off-site contamination that may have resulted from the release of a hazardous substance or pollutant at a Coast Guard facility.

"(5) Section 119 of the Comprehensive Environmental Response, Compensation, and Liability Act (42 U.S.C. 9619) applies to response action contractors that carry out response actions under this section. The Coast Guard shall indemnify response action contractors to the extent that adequate insurance is not generally available at a fair price at the time the contractor enters into the contract to cover the contractor's reasonable, potential, long-term liability.

"(c) AMOUNTS RECOVERED FOR RESPONSE ACTIONS.—

"(1) All sums appropriated to carry out the Coast Guard's environmental compliance and restoration functions under this section or another law shall be credited or transferred to an appropriate Coast Guard account, as determined by the Commandant and remain available until expended.

"(2) Funds may be obligated or expended from such account to carry out the Coast Guard's environmental compliance and restoration functions under this section or another law.

"(3) In proposing the budget for any fiscal year under section 1105 of title 31, the President shall set forth separately the amount requested for the Coast Guard's environmental compliance and restoration activities under this section or another law.

"(4) Amounts recovered under section 107 of the Comprehensive Environmental Response, Compensation, and Liability Act (42 U.S.C. 9607) for the Secretary's response actions at current and former Coast Guard facilities shall be credited to an appropriate Coast Guard account, as determined by the Commandant.

"(d) ANNUAL LIST OF PROJECTS TO CONGRESS.—The Commandant shall submit to the Committee on Transportation and Infrastructure of the House of Representatives and the Committee on Commerce, Science, and Transportation of the Senate a prioritized list of projects eligible for environmental compliance and restoration funding for each fiscal year concurrent with the President's budget submission for that fiscal year."

(2) CONFORMING REPEALS.—Sections 634, 690, 691, 692, and 693 of title 14, United States Code, are repealed.

SEC. 105. CHAPTER 5.

(a) [14 U.S.C. 81] INITIAL MATTER.—Chapter 5 of title 14, United States Code, is amended by striking the chapter designation, the chapter heading, and the table of sections at the beginning and inserting the following:

"CHAPTER 5—FUNCTIONS AND POWERS

" subchapter i— general powers

"Sec.
"501. Secretary; general powers.
"502. Delegation of powers by the Secretary.
"503. Regulations.
"504. Commandant; general powers.
"505. Functions and powers vested in the Commandant.
"506. Prospective payment of funds necessary to provide medical care.
"507. Appointment of judges.

" subchapter ii— life saving and law enforcement authorities

"521. Saving life and property.
"522. Law enforcement.
"523. Enforcement authority.
"524. Enforcement of coastwise trade laws.
"525. Special agents of the Coast Guard Investigative Service law enforcement authority.
"526. Stopping vessels; indemnity for firing at or into vessel.
"527. Safety of naval vessels.
"528. Protecting against unmanned aircraft.

" subchapter iii— aids to navigation

"541. Aids to navigation authorized.

"542.	Unauthorized aids to maritime navigation; penalty.
"543.	Interference with aids to navigation; penalty.
"544.	Aids to maritime navigation; penalty.
"545.	Marking of obstructions.
"546.	Deposit of damage payments.
"547.	Rewards for apprehension of persons interfering with aids to navigation.
" subchapter iv—	miscellaneous
"561.	Icebreaking in polar regions.
"562.	Appeals and waivers.
"563.	Notification of certain determinations."

(b) REDESIGNATIONS AND TRANSFERS.—

(1) REQUIREMENT.—The sections of title 14, United States Code, identified in the table provided in paragraph (2) are amended—

(A) by redesignating the sections as described in the table; and

(B) by transferring the sections, as necessary, so that the sections appear after the table of sections for chapter 5 of such title (as added by subsection (a)), in the order in which the sections are presented in the table.

(2) TABLE.—The table referred to in paragraph (1) is the following:

Title 14 section number before redesignationSection heading (provided for identification purposes only-not amended)Title 14 section number after redesignation

92Secretary; general powers501631Delegation of powers by the Secretary502633Regulations50393Commandant; general powers504632Functions and powers vested in the Commandant505520Prospective payment of funds necessary to provide medical care506153Appointment of judges50788Saving life and property52189Law enforcement52299Enforcement authority523100Enforcement of coastwise trade laws52495Special agents of the Coast Guard Investigative Service law enforcement authority525637Stopping vessels; indemnity for firing at or into vessel52691Safety of naval vessels527104Protecting against unmanned aircraft52881Aids to navigation authorized54183Unauthorized aids to maritime navigation; penalty54284Interference with aids to navigation; penalty54385Aids to maritime navigation; penalty54486Marking of obstructions545642Deposit of damage payments546643Rewards for apprehension of persons interfering with aids to navigation54787Icebreaking in polar regions561101Appeals and waivers562103Notification of certain determinations563

(c) ADDITIONAL CHANGES.—Chapter 5 of title 14, United States Code, is further amended—

(1) by inserting before section 501 (as so redesignated and transferred under subsection (b)) the following:

SUBCHAPTER "SUBCHAPTER I—GENERAL POWERS""

(2) by inserting before section 521 (as so redesignated and transferred under subsection (b)) the following:

SUBCHAPTER "SUBCHAPTER II—LIFE SAVING AND LAW ENFORCEMENT AUTHORITIES""

(3) by inserting before section 541 (as so redesignated and transferred under subsection (b)) the following:and

SUBCHAPTER "SUBCHAPTER III—AIDS TO NAVIGATION""

(4) by inserting before section 561 (as so redesignated and transferred under subsection (b)) the following:

SUBCHAPTER "SUBCHAPTER IV—MISCELLANEOUS""

SEC. 106. CHAPTER 7.

(a) [14 U.S.C. 141] INITIAL MATTER.—Chapter 7 of title 14, United States Code, is amended by striking the chapter designation, the chapter heading, and the table of sections at the beginning and inserting the following:

"CHAPTER 7—COOPERATION

"Sec.

"701.	Cooperation with other agencies, States, territories, and political subdivisions.
"702.	State Department.
"703.	Treasury Department.
"704.	Department of the Army and Department of the Air Force.
"705.	Navy Department.
"706.	United States Postal Service.
"707.	Department of Commerce.
"708.	Department of Health and Human Services.
"709.	Maritime instruction.

"710.	Assistance to foreign governments and maritime authorities.
"711.	Coast Guard officers as attachés to missions.
"712.	Contracts with Government-owned establishments for work and material.
"713.	Nonappropriated fund instrumentalities: contracts with other agencies and instrumentalities to provide or obtain goods and services.
"714.	Arctic maritime domain awareness.
"715.	Oceanographic research.
"716.	Arctic maritime transportation.
"717.	Agreements."

(b) REDESIGNATIONS AND TRANSFERS.—

(1) REQUIREMENT.—The sections of title 14, United States Code, identified in the table provided in paragraph (2) are amended—

(A) by redesignating the sections as described in the table; and

(B) by transferring the sections, as necessary, so that the sections appear after the table of sections for chapter 7 of such title (as added by subsection (a)), in the order in which the sections are presented in the table.

(2) TABLE.—The table referred to in paragraph (1) is the following:

Title 14 section number before redesignationSection heading (provided for identification purposes only-not amended)Title 14 section number after redesignation

141Cooperation with other agencies, States, territories, and political subdivisions701142State Department702143Treasury Department703144Department of the Army and Department of the Air Force704145Navy Department705146United States Postal Service706147Department of Commerce707147aDepartment of Health and Human Services708148Maritime instruction709149Assistance to foreign governments and maritime authorities710150Coast Guard officers as attachés to missions711151Contracts with Government-owned establishments for work and material712152Nonappropriated fund instrumentalities: contracts with other agencies and instrumentalities to provide or obtain goods and services713154Arctic maritime domain awareness71494Oceanographic research71590Arctic maritime transportation716102Agreements717

SEC. 107. CHAPTER 9.

(a) [14 U.S.C. 181] INITIAL MATTER.—Chapter 9 of title 14, United States Code, is amended by striking the chapter designation, the chapter heading, and the table of sections at the beginning and inserting the following:

"CHAPTER 9—ADMINISTRATION

" subchapter i— real and personal property

" subchapter ii— miscellaneous

(b) REDESIGNATIONS AND TRANSFERS.—

(1) REQUIREMENT.—The sections of title 14, United States Code, identified in the table provided in paragraph (2) are amended—

(A) by redesignating the sections as described in the table; and

(B) by transferring the sections, as necessary, so that the sections appear after the table of sections for chapter 9 of such title (as added by subsection (a)), in the order in which the sections are presented in the table.

(2) TABLE.—The table referred to in paragraph (1) is the following:

Title 14 section number before redesignationSection heading (provided for identification purposes only-not amended)Title 14 section number after redesignation

641Disposal of certain material901653Employment of draftsmen and engineers902656Use of certain appropriated funds903666Local hire904670Procurement authority for family housing905671Air Station Cape Cod Improvements906672Long-term lease of special purpose facilities907672aLong-term lease authority for lighthouse property908674Small boat station rescue capability909675Small boat station closures910676Search and rescue center standards911676aAir facility closures912677Turnkey selection procedures913681Disposition of infrastructure related to E-LORAN914635Oaths required for boards931636Administration of oaths932638Coast Guard ensigns and pennants933639Penalty for unauthorized use of words "Coast Guard"934640Coast Guard band recordings for commercial sale935645Confidentiality of medical quality assurance records; qualified immunity for participants936646Admiralty claims against the United States937647Claims for damage to property of the United States938648Accounting for industrial work939649Supplies and equipment from stock940650Coast Guard Supply Fund941654Public and commercial vessels and other watercraft; sale of fuel, supplies, and services942655Arms and ammunition; immunity from taxation943658Confidential investigative expenses944659Assistance to film producers945664User fees946667Vessel construction bonding requirements947668Contracts for medical care for retirees, dependents, and survivors: alternative delivery of health care948669Telephone installation and charges949673Designation, powers, and accountability of deputy disbursing officials950678Aircraft accident investigations951

(c) ADDITIONAL CHANGES.—Chapter 9 of title 14, United States Code, is further amended—

(1) by inserting before section 901 (as so redesignated and transferred under subsection (b)) the following:and

SUBCHAPTER "SUBCHAPTER I—REAL AND PERSONAL PROPERTY""

(2) by inserting before section 931 (as so redesignated and transferred under subsection (b)) the following:

SUBCHAPTER "SUBCHAPTER II—MISCELLANEOUS""

SEC. 108. CHAPTER 11.

(a) [14 U.S.C. 211] INITIAL MATTER.—Chapter 11 of title 14, United States Code, is amended by striking the chapter designation, the chapter heading, and the table of sections at the beginning and inserting the following:

"CHAPTER 11—ACQUISITIONS

" subchapter i— general provisions

"Sec.

"1101.	Acquisition directorate.
"1102.	Improvements in Coast Guard acquisition management.
"1103.	Role of Vice Commandant in major acquisition programs.
"1104.	Recognition of Coast Guard personnel for excellence in acquisition.
"1105.	Prohibition on use of lead systems integrators.
"1106.	Required contract terms.
"1107.	Extension of major acquisition program contracts.
"1108.	Department of Defense consultation.
"1109.	Undefinitized contractual actions.
"1110.	Mission need statement.

" subchapter ii— improved acquisition process and procedures

"1131.	Identification of major system acquisitions.
"1132.	Acquisition.
"1133.	Preliminary development and demonstration.
"1134.	Acquisition, production, deployment, and support.
"1135.	Acquisition program baseline breach.
"1136.	Acquisition approval authority.

" subchapter iii— procurement

"1151.	Restriction on construction of vessels in foreign shipyards.
"1152.	Advance procurement funding.
"1153.	Prohibition on overhaul, repair, and maintenance of Coast Guard vessels in foreign shipyards.
"1154.	Procurement of buoy chain.
"1155.	Contract termination.

" subchapter iv— definitions

"1171. Definitions."

(b) REDESIGNATIONS AND TRANSFERS.—

(1) REQUIREMENT.—The sections of title 14, United States Code, identified in the table provided in paragraph (2) are amended—

(A) by redesignating the sections as described in the table; and

(B) by transferring the sections, as necessary, so that the sections appear after the table of sections for chapter 11 of such title (as added by subsection (a)), in the order in which the sections are presented in the table.

(2) TABLE.—The table referred to in paragraph (1) is the following:

Title 14 section number before redesignationSection heading (provided for identification purposes only-not amended)Title 14 section number after redesignation

561Acquisition directorate1101562Improvements in Coast Guard acquisition management1102578Role of Vice Commandant in major acquisition programs1103563Recognition of Coast Guard personnel for excellence in acquisition1104564Prohibition on use of lead systems integrators1105565Required contract terms1106579Extension of major acquisition program contracts1107566Department of Defense consultation1108567Undefinitized contractual actions1109569Mission need statement1110571Identification of major system acquisitions1131572Acquisition1132573Preliminary development and demonstration1133574Acquisition, production, deployment, and support1134575Acquisition program baseline breach1135576Acquisition approval authority1136665Restriction on construction of vessels in foreign shipyards1151577Advance procurement funding115296Prohibition on overhaul, repair, and maintenance of Coast Guard vessels in foreign shipyards115397Procurement of buoy chain1154657Contract termination1155581Definitions1171

(c) ADDITIONAL CHANGES.—Chapter 11 of title 14, United States Code, is further amended—

(1) [14 U.S.C. 211] by striking all subdivision designations and headings in such chapter, except for—

(A) the chapter designation and heading added by subsection (a);

(B) the subchapter designations and headings added by this subsection; and

(C) any designation or heading of a section or a subdivision of a section;

(2) by inserting before section 1101 (as so redesignated and

transferred under subsection (b)) the following:

SUBCHAPTER "SUBCHAPTER I—GENERAL PROVISIONS""

(3) by inserting before section 1131 (as so redesignated and transferred under subsection (b)) the following:

SUBCHAPTER "SUBCHAPTER II—IMPROVED ACQUISITION PROCESS AND PROCEDURES""

(4) by inserting before section 1151 (as so redesignated and transferred under subsection (b)) the following:and

SUBCHAPTER "SUBCHAPTER III—PROCUREMENT""

(5) by inserting before section 1171 (as so redesignated and transferred under subsection (b)) the following:

SUBCHAPTER "SUBCHAPTER IV—DEFINITIONS""

SEC. 109. SUBTITLE II.

(a) INITIAL MATTER.—Title 14, United States Code, is further amended by inserting after chapter 11 (as amended by section 108) the following:

"Subtitle II—Personnel

"Chap.

"Sec.	
"19.	Coast Guard Academy
"21.	Personnel; Officers
"23.	Personnel; Enlisted
"25.	Personnel; General Provisions
"27.	Pay, Allowances, Awards, and Other Rights and Benefits
"29.	Coast Guard Family Support, Child Care, and Housing "

(b) RESERVED CHAPTER NUMBERS.—

(1) [14 U.S.C. 461] CHAPTER 13.—Chapter 13 of title 14, United States Code, is amended by striking the chapter designation, the chapter heading, and the table of sections at the beginning.

(2) CHAPTER 14.—Chapter 14 of title 14, United States Code, is amended—

(A) [14 U.S.C. 531] by striking the chapter designation, the chapter heading, and the table of sections at the beginning; and

(B) [14 U.S.C. 531] by striking the subchapter designation and the subchapter heading for each of the subchapters of such chapter.

(3) CHAPTER 15.—Chapter 15 of title 14, United States Code, is amended—

(A) [14 U.S.C. 561] by striking the chapter designation, the chapter heading, and the table of sections at the beginning; and

(B) [14 U.S.C. 561] by striking the subchapter designation and the subchapter heading for each of the subchapters of such chapter.

(4) [14 U.S.C. 631] CHAPTER 17.—Chapter 17 of title 14, United States Code, is amendedby striking the chapter designation, the chapter heading, and the table of sections at the beginning.

(5) [14 U.S.C. 680] CHAPTER 18.—Chapter 18 of title 14, United States Code, is amendedby striking the chapter designation, the chapter heading, and the table of sections at the beginning.

SEC. 110. CHAPTER 19.

(a) [14 U.S.C. 690] INITIAL MATTER.—Chapter 19 of title 14, United States Code, is amendedby striking the chapter designation, the chapter heading, and the table of sections at the beginning and inserting the following:

"CHAPTER 19—COAST GUARD ACADEMY

" subchapter i— administration

"Sec.	
"1901.	Administration of Academy.
"1902.	Policy on sexual harassment and sexual violence.
"1903.	Annual Board of Visitors.
"1904.	Participation in Federal, State, or other educational research grants.

" subchapter ii— cadets

"1921.	Corps of Cadets authorized strength.
"1922.	Appointments.
"1923.	Admission of foreign nationals for instruction; restrictions; conditions.
"1924.	Conduct.
"1925.	Agreement.
"1926.	Cadet applicants; preappointment travel to Academy.
"1927.	Cadets; initial clothing allowance.
"1928.	Cadets; degree of bachelor of science.
"1929.	Cadets; appointment as ensign.
"1930.	Cadets: charges and fees for attendance; limitation.

" subchapter iii— faculty

"1941.	Civilian teaching staff.
"1942.	Permanent commissioned teaching staff; composition.
"1943.	Appointment of permanent commissioned teaching staff.
"1944.	Grade of permanent commissioned teaching staff.
"1945.	Retirement of permanent commissioned teaching staff.
"1946.	Credit for service as member of civilian teaching staff.
"1947.	Assignment of personnel as instructors.
"1948.	Marine safety curriculum."

(b) REDESIGNATIONS AND TRANSFERS.—

(1) REQUIREMENT.—The sections of title 14, United States Code, identified in the table provided in paragraph (2) are amended—

(A) by redesignating the sections as described in the table; and

(B) by transferring the sections, as necessary, so that the sections appear after the table of sections for chapter 19 of such title (as added by subsection (a)), in the order in which the sections are presented in the table.

(2) TABLE.—The table referred to in paragraph (1) is the following:

Title 14 section number before redesignationSection heading (provided for identification purposes only-not amended)Title 14 section number after redesignation

181Administration of Academy1901200Policy on sexual harassment and sexual violence1902194Annual Board of Visitors1903196Participation in Federal, State, or other educational research grants1904195Admission of foreign nationals for instruction; restrictions; conditions1923181aCadet applicants; preappointment travel to Academy1926183Cadets; initial clothing allowance1927184Cadets; degree of bachelor of science1928185Cadets; appointment as ensign1929197Cadets: charges and fees for attendance; limitation1930186Civilian teaching staff1941187Permanent commissioned teaching staff; composition1942188Appointment of permanent commissioned teaching staff1943189Grade of permanent commissioned teaching staff1944190Retirement of permanent commissioned teaching staff1945191Credit for service as member of civilian teaching staff1946192Assignment of personnel as instructors1947199Marine safety curriculum1948

(c) ADDITIONAL CHANGES.—

(1) IN GENERAL.—Chapter 19 of title 14, United States Code, is further amended—

(A) by inserting before section 1901 (as so redesignated and transferred under subsection (b)) the following:

SUBCHAPTER "SUBCHAPTER I—ADMINISTRATION""

(B) by inserting before section 1923 (as so redesignated and transferred under subsection (b)) the following:

SUBCHAPTER "SUBCHAPTER II—CADETS

"SEC. § 1921. [14 U.S.C. 1921] Corps of Cadets authorized strengt

"The number of cadets appointed annually to the Academy shall be as determined by the Secretary but the number appointed in any one year shall not exceed six hundred.

"SEC. § 1922. [14 U.S.C. 1922] Appointment

"Appointments to cadetships shall be made under regulations prescribed by the Secretary, who shall determine age limits, methods of selection of applicants, term of service as a cadet before graduation, and all other matters affecting such appointments. In the administration of this section, the Secretary shall take such action as may be necessary and appropriate to insure that female individuals shall be eligible for appointment and admission to the Coast Guard Academy, and that the relevant standards required for appointment, admission, training, graduation, and commissioning of female individuals shall be the same as those required for male individuals, except for those minimum essential adjustments in such standards required because of physiological differences between male and female individuals."

(C) by inserting before section 1926 (as so redesignated and transferred under subsection (b)) the following:

"SEC. § 1924. [14 U.S.C. 1924] Conduc

"The Secretary may summarily dismiss from the Coast Guard any cadet who, during his cadetship, is found unsatisfactory in either studies or conduct, or may be deemed not adapted for a career in the Coast Guard. Cadets shall be subject to rules governing discipline prescribed by the Commandant.

"SEC. § 1925. [14 U.S.C. 1925] Agreemen

"(a) Each cadet shall sign an agreement with respect to the cadet's length of service in the Coast Guard. The agreement shall provide that the cadet agrees to the following:

"(1) That the cadet will complete the course of instruction at the Coast Guard Academy.

"(2) That upon graduation from the Coast Guard Academy the cadet—

"(A) will accept an appointment, if tendered, as a commissioned officer of the Coast Guard; and

"(B) will serve on active duty for at least five years immediately after such appointment.

"(3) That if an appointment described in paragraph (2) is not tendered or if the cadet is permitted to resign as a regular officer before the completion of the commissioned service obligation of the cadet, the cadet—

"(A) will accept an appointment as a

commissioned officer in the Coast Guard Reserve; and

"(B) will remain in that reserve component until completion of the commissioned service obligation of the cadet.

"(b)(1) The Secretary may transfer to the Coast Guard Reserve, and may order to active duty for such period of time as the Secretary prescribes (but not to exceed four years), a cadet who breaches an agreement under subsection (a). The period of time for which a cadet is ordered to active duty under this paragraph may be determined without regard to section 651(a) of title 10.

"(2) A cadet who is transferred to the Coast Guard Reserve under paragraph (1) shall be transferred in an appropriate enlisted grade or rating, as determined by the Secretary.

"(3) For the purposes of paragraph (1), a cadet shall be considered to have breached an agreement under subsection (a) if the cadet is separated from the Coast Guard Academy under circumstances which the Secretary determines constitute a breach by the cadet of the cadet's agreement to complete the course of instruction at the Coast Guard Academy and accept an appointment as a commissioned officer upon graduation from the Coast Guard Academy.

"(c) The Secretary shall prescribe regulations to carry out this section. Those regulations shall include—

"(1) standards for determining what constitutes, for the purpose of subsection (b), a breach of an agreement under subsection (a);

"(2) procedures for determining whether such a breach has occurred; and

"(3) standards for determining the period of time for which a person may be ordered to serve on active duty under subsection (b).

"(d) In this section, 'commissioned service obligation', with respect to an officer who is a graduate of the Academy, means the period beginning on the date of the officer's appointment as a commissioned officer and ending on the sixth anniversary of such appointment or, at the discretion of the Secretary, any later date up to the eighth anniversary of such appointment.

"(e)(1) This section does not apply to a cadet who is not a citizen or national of the United States.

"(2) In the case of a cadet who is a minor and who has parents or a guardian, the cadet may sign the agreement required by subsection (a) only with the consent of the parent or guardian.

"(f) A cadet or former cadet who does not fulfill the terms of the obligation to serve as specified under section (a), or the alternative obligation imposed under subsection (b), shall be subject to the repayment provisions of section 303a(e) of title 37."

; and

(D) by inserting before section 1941 (as so redesignated and transferred under subsection (b)) the following:

SUBCHAPTER "SUBCHAPTER III—FACULTY""

(2) Conforming repeal.—Section 182 of title 14, United States Code, is repealed.

SEC. 111. [14 U.S.C. 701] PART II.

Part II of title 14, United States Code,is amended by striking the part designation, the part heading, and the table of chapters at the beginning.

SEC. 112. CHAPTER 21.

(a) [14 U.S.C. 701] Initial Matter.—Chapter 21 of title 14, United States Code,is amended by striking the chapter designation, the chapter heading, and the table of sections at the beginning and inserting the following:

"CHAPTER 21—PERSONNEL; OFFICERS

" subchapter i— appointment and promotion

"Sec.

"2101.	Original appointment of permanent commissioned officers.
"2102.	Active duty promotion list.
"2103.	Number and distribution of commissioned officers on active duty promotion list.
"2104.	Appointment of temporary officers.
"2105.	Rank of warrant officers.
"2106.	Selection boards; convening of boards.
"2107.	Selection boards; composition of boards.
"2108.	Selection boards; notice of convening; communication with board.
"2109.	Selection boards; oath of members.
"2110.	Number of officers to be selected for promotion.
"2111.	Promotion zones.
"2112.	Promotion year; defined.
"2113.	Eligibility of officers for consideration for promotion.
"2114.	United States Deputy Marshals in Alaska.
"2115.	Selection boards; information to be furnished boards.
"2116.	Officers to be recommended for promotion.
"2117.	Selection boards; reports.
"2118.	Selection boards; submission of reports.
"2119.	Failure of selection for promotion.
"2120.	Special selection boards; correction of errors.
"2121.	Promotions; appointments.
"2122.	Removal of officer from list of selectees for promotion.
"2123.	Promotions; acceptance; oath of office.
"2124.	Promotions; pay and allowances.
"2125.	Wartime temporary service promotions.
"2126.	Promotion of officers not included on active duty promotion list.
"2127.	Recall to active duty during war or national emergency.
"2128.	Recall to active duty with consent of officer.
"2129.	Aviation cadets; appointment as Reserve officers.

" subchapter ii—	discharges; retirements; revocation of commissions; separation for cause

"2141.	Revocation of commissions during first five years of commissioned service.
"2142.	Regular lieutenants (junior grade); separation for failure of selection for promotion.
"2143.	Regular lieutenants; separation for failure of selection for

	promotion; continuation.
"2144.	Regular Coast Guard; officers serving under temporary appointments.
"2145.	Regular lieutenant commanders and commanders; retirement for failure of selection for promotion.
"2146.	Discharge in lieu of retirement; separation pay.
"2147.	Regular warrant officers: separation pay.
"2148.	Separation for failure of selection for promotion or continuation; time of.
"2149.	Regular captains; retirement.
"2150.	Captains; continuation on active duty; involuntary retirement.
"2151.	Rear admirals and rear admirals (lower half); continuation on active duty; involuntary retirement.
"2152.	Voluntary retirement after twenty years' service.
"2153.	Voluntary retirement after thirty years' service.
"2154.	Compulsory retirement.
"2155.	Retirement for physical disability after selection for promotion; grade in which retired.
"2156.	Deferment of retirement or separation for medical reasons.
"2157.	Flag officers.
"2158.	Review of records of officers.
"2159.	Boards of inquiry.
"2160.	Boards of review.
"2161.	Composition of boards.
"2162.	Rights and procedures.
"2163.	Removal of officer from active duty; action by Secretary.
"2164.	Officers considered for removal; retirement or discharge; separation benefits.
"2165.	Relief of retired officer promoted while on active duty.
" subchapter iii—	general provisions
"2181.	Physical fitness of officers.
"2182.	Multirater assessment of certain personnel."

(b) REDESIGNATIONS AND TRANSFERS.—

(1) REQUIREMENT.—The sections of title 14, United States Code, identified in the table provided in paragraph (2) are amended—

(A) by redesignating the sections as described in the table; and

(B) by transferring the sections, as necessary, so that the sections appear after the table of sections for chapter 21 of such title (as added by subsection (a)), in the order in which the sections are presented in the table.

(2) TABLE.—The table referred to in paragraph (1) is the following:

Title 14 section number before redesignationSection heading (provided for identification purposes only-not amended)Title 14 section number after redesignation

211Original appointment of permanent commissioned officers210141aActive duty promotion list210242Number and distribution of commissioned officers on active duty promotion list2103214Appointment of temporary officers2104215Rank of warrant officers2105251Selection boards; convening of boards2106252Selection boards; composition of boards2107253Selection boards; notice of convening; communication with board2108254Selection boards; oath of members2109255Number of officers to be selected for promotion2110256Promotion zones2111256aPromotion year; defined2112257Eligibility of officers for consideration for promotion2113258Selection boards; information to be furnished boards2115259Officers to be recommended for promotion2116260Selection boards; reports2117261Selection boards; submission of reports2118262Failure of selection for promotion2119263Special selection boards; correction of errors2120271Promotions; appointments2121272Removal of officer from list of selectees for promotion2122273Promotions; acceptance; oath of office2123274Promotions; pay and allowances2124275Wartime temporary service promotions2125276Promotion of officers not included on active duty promotion list2126331Recall to active duty during war or national emergency2127332Recall to active duty with consent of officer2128373Aviation cadets; appointment as Reserve officers2129281Revocation of commissions during first five years of commissioned service2141282Regular lieutenants (junior grade); separation for failure of selection for promotion2142283Regular lieutenants; separation for failure of selection for promotion; continuation2143284Regular Coast Guard; officers serving under temporary appointments2144285Regular lieutenant commanders and commanders; retirement for failure of selection for promotion2145286Discharge in lieu of retirement; separation pay2146286aRegular warrant officers: separation pay2147287Separation for failure of selection for promotion or continuation; time of2148288Regular captains; retirement2149289Captains; continuation on active duty; involuntary retirement2150290Rear admirals and rear admirals (lower half); continuation on active duty; involuntary retirement2151291Voluntary retirement after twenty years' service2152292Voluntary retirement after thirty years' service2153293Compulsory retirement2154294Retirement for physical disability after selection for promotion; grade in which retired2155295Deferment of retirement or separation for medical reasons2156296Flag officers2157321Review of records of officers2158322Boards of inquiry2159323Boards of review2160324Composition of boards2161325Rights and procedures2162326Removal of officer from active duty; action by Secretary2163327Officers considered for removal; retirement or discharge; separation benefits2164333Relief of retired officer promoted while on active duty2165335Physical fitness of officers2181429Multirater assessment of certain personnel2182

(c) ADDITIONAL CHANGES.—Chapter 21 of title 14, United States Code, is further amended—

(1) [14 U.S.C. 701] by striking all subchapter designations and headings in such chapter, except for the subchapter designations and headings added by this subsection;

(2) by inserting before section 2101 (as so redesignated and transferred under subsection (b)) the following:

SUBCHAPTER "SUBCHAPTER I—APPOINTMENT AND PROMOTION""

(3) by inserting before section 2115 (as so redesignated and

transferred under subsection (b)) the following:

"SEC. §2114. [14 U.S.C. 2114] United States Deputy Marshals in Alask

"Commissioned officers may be appointed as United States Deputy Marshals in Alaska."

(4) by inserting before section 2141 (as so redesignated and transferred under subsection (b)) the following:and

SUBCHAPTER "SUBCHAPTER II—DISCHARGES; RETIREMENTS; REVOCATION OF COMMISSIONS; SEPARATION FOR CAUSE""

(5) by inserting before section 2181 (as so redesignated and transferred under subsection (b)) the following:

SUBCHAPTER "SUBCHAPTER III—GENERAL PROVISIONS""

SEC. 113. CHAPTER 23.

(a) **[14 U.S.C. 821]** INITIAL MATTER.—Chapter 23 of title 14, United States Code,is amended by striking the chapter designation, the chapter heading, and the table of sections at the beginning and inserting the following:

"CHAPTER 23—PERSONNEL; ENLISTED

"Sec.	
"2301.	Recruiting campaigns.
"2302.	Enlistments; term, grade.
"2303.	Promotion.
"2304.	Compulsory retirement at age of sixty-two.
"2305.	Voluntary retirement after thirty years' service.
"2306.	Voluntary retirement after twenty years' service.
"2307.	Retirement of enlisted members: increase in retired pay.
"2308.	Recall to active duty during war or national emergency.
"2309.	Recall to active duty with consent of member.
"2310.	Relief of retired enlisted member

	promoted while on active duty.
"2311.	Retirement in cases where higher grade or rating has been held.
"2312.	Extension of enlistments.
"2313.	Retention beyond term of enlistment in case of disability.
"2314.	Detention beyond term of enlistment.
"2315.	Inclusion of certain conditions in enlistment contract.
"2316.	Discharge within three months before expiration of enlistment.
"2317.	Aviation cadets; procurement; transfer.
"2318.	Aviation cadets; benefits.
"2319.	Critical skill training bonus."

(b) REDESIGNATIONS AND TRANSFERS.—

(1) REQUIREMENT.—The sections of title 14, United States Code, identified in the table provided in paragraph (2) are amended—

(A) by redesignating the sections as described in the table; and

(B) by transferring the sections, as necessary, so that the sections appear after the table of sections for chapter 23 of such title (as added by subsection (a)), in the order in which the sections are presented in the table.

(2) TABLE.—The table referred to in paragraph (1) is the following:

Title 14 section number before redesignationSection heading (provided for identification purposes only-not amended)Title 14 section number after redesignation

350Recruiting campaigns2301351Enlistments; term, grade2302352Promotion2303353Compulsory retirement at age of sixty-two2304354Voluntary retirement after thirty years' service2305355Voluntary retirement after twenty years' service2306357Retirement of enlisted members: increase in retired pay2307359Recall to active duty during war or national emergency2308360Recall to active duty with consent of member2309361Relief of retired enlisted member promoted while on active duty2310362Retirement in cases where higher grade or rating has been held2311365Extension of enlistments2312366Retention beyond term of enlistment in case of disability2313367Detention beyond term of enlistment2314369Inclusion of certain conditions in enlistment contract2315370Discharge within three months before expiration of enlistment2316371Aviation cadets; procurement; transfer2317372Aviation cadets; benefits2318374Critical skill training bonus2319

SEC. 114. CHAPTER 25.

(a) [14 U.S.C. 891] INITIAL MATTER.—Chapter 25 of title 14, United States Code, is amendedby striking the chapter designation, the chapter heading, and the table of sections at the beginning and inserting the following:

"CHAPTER 25—PERSONNEL; GENERAL PROVISIONS

(b) REDESIGNATIONS AND TRANSFERS.—

(1) REQUIREMENT.—The sections of title 14, United States Code, identified in the table provided in paragraph (2) are amended—

(A) by redesignating the sections as described in the table; and

(B) by transferring the sections, as necessary, so that the sections appear after the table of sections for chapter 25 of such title (as added by subsection (a)), in the order in which the sections are presented in the table.

(2) TABLE.—The table referred to in paragraph (1) is the following:

Title 14 section number before redesignationSection heading (provided for identification purposes only-not amended)Title 14 section number after redesignation

334Grade on retirement2501421Retirement2502422Status of recalled personnel2503423Computation of retired pay2504424Limitations on retirement and retired pay2505424aSuspension of payment of retired pay of members who are absent from the United States to avoid prosecution2506425Board for Correction of Military Records deadline2507426Emergency leave retention authority2508427Prohibition of certain involuntary administrative separations2509428Sea service letters2510430Investigations of flag officers and Senior Executive Service employees2511431Leave policies for the Coast Guard2512467Computation of length of service2513432Personnel of former Lighthouse Service2531

(c) ADDITIONAL CHANGES.—Chapter 25 of title 14, United States Code, is further amended—

(1) by inserting before section 2501 (as so redesignated and transferred under subsection (b)) the following:and

SUBCHAPTER "SUBCHAPTER I—GENERAL PROVISIONS""

(2) by inserting before section 2531 (as so redesignated and transferred under subsection (b)) the following:

SUBCHAPTER "SUBCHAPTER II—LIGHTHOUSE SERVICE""

SEC. 115. [14 U.S.C. 2701] PART III.

Part III of title 14, United States Code, is amended by striking the part designation, the part heading, and the table of chapters at the beginning.

SEC. 116. CHAPTER 27.

(a) [14 U.S.C. 2701] INITIAL MATTER.—Chapter 27 of title 14, United States Code,is amended by striking the chapter designation, the chapter heading, and the table of sections at the beginning and inserting the following:

"CHAPTER 27—PAY, ALLOWANCES, AWARDS, AND OTHER RIGHTS AND BENEFITS

" subchapter i— personnel rights and benefits

"Sec.	
"2701.	Procurement of personnel.
"2702.	Training.
"2703.	Contingent expenses.
"2704.	Equipment to prevent accidents.
"2705.	Clothing at time of discharge for good of service.
"2706.	Right to wear uniform.
"2707.	Protection of uniform.
"2708.	Clothing for officers and enlisted personnel.
"2709.	Procurement and sale of stores to members and civilian employees.
"2710.	Disposition of effects of decedents.
"2711.	Deserters; payment of expenses incident to apprehension and delivery; penalties.
"2712.	Payment for the apprehension of stragglers.

" subchapter ii—	awards
"2731.	Delegation of powers to make awards; rules and regulations.
"2732.	Medal of honor.
"2733.	Medal of honor: duplicate medal.
"2734.	Medal of honor: presentation of Medal of Honor Flag.
"2735.	Coast Guard cross.
"2736.	Distinguished service medal.
"2737.	Silver star medal.
"2738.	Distinguished flying cross.
"2739.	Coast Guard medal.
"2740.	Insignia for additional awards.
"2741.	Time limit on award; report concerning deed.
"2742.	Honorable subsequent service as condition to award.
"2743.	Posthumous awards.
"2744.	Life-saving medals.
"2745.	Replacement of medals.
"2746.	Award of other medals.
"2747.	Awards and insignia for excellence in service or conduct.
"2748.	Presentation of United States flag upon retirement.

" subchapter iii—	payments
"2761.	Persons discharged as result of court-martial; allowances to.
"2762.	Shore patrol duty; payment of expenses.
"2763.	Compensatory absence from duty for military personnel at isolated duty stations.
"2764.	Monetary allowance for transportation of household effects.
"2765.	Retroactive payment of pay and allowances delayed by administrative error or oversight.
"2766.	Travel card management.
"2767.	Reimbursement for medical-related travel expenses for

(b) REDESIGNATIONS AND TRANSFERS.—

(1) REQUIREMENT.—The sections of title 14, United States Code, identified in the table provided in paragraph (2) are amended—

(A) by redesignating the sections as described in the table; and

(B) by transferring the sections, as necessary, so that the sections appear after the table of sections for chapter 27 of such title (as added by subsection (a)), in the order in which the sections are presented in the table.

(2) TABLE.—The table referred to in paragraph (1) is the following:

Title 14 section number before redesignationSection heading (provided for identification purposes only-not amended)Title 14 section number after redesignation

468Procurement of personnel2701469Training2702476Contingent expenses2703477Equipment to prevent accidents2704482Clothing at time of discharge for good of service2705483Right to wear uniform2706484Protection of uniform2707485Clothing for officers and enlisted personnel2708487Procurement and sale of stores to members and civilian employees2709507Disposition of effects of decedents2710508Deserters; payment of expenses incident to apprehension and delivery; penalties2711644Payment for the apprehension of stragglers2712499Delegation of powers to make awards; rules and regulations2731491Medal of honor2732504Medal of honor: duplicate medal2733505Medal of honor: presentation of Medal of Honor Flag2734491aCoast Guard cross2735492Distinguished service medal2736492aSilver star medal2737492bDistinguished flying cross2738493Coast Guard medal2739494Insignia for additional awards2740496Time limit on award; report concerning deed2741497Honorable subsequent service as condition to award2742498Posthumous awards2743500Life-saving medals2744501Replacement of medals2745502Award of other medals2746503Awards and insignia for excellence in service or conduct2747516Presentation of United States flag upon retirement2748509Persons discharged as result of court-martial; allowances to2761510Shore patrol duty; payment of expenses2762511Compensatory absence from duty for military personnel at isolated duty stations2763512Monetary allowance for

Title 14 section number before redesignationSection heading (provided for identification purposes only-not amended)Title 14 section number after redesignation

transportation of household effects2764513Retroactive payment of pay and allowances delayed by administrative error or oversight2765517Travel card management2766518Reimbursement for medical-related travel expenses for certain persons residing on islands in the continental United States2767519Annual audit of pay and allowances of members undergoing permanent change of station2768461Remission of indebtedness2769470Special instruction at universities2770471Attendance at professional meetings2771472Education loan repayment program2772478Rations or commutation therefor in money2773479Sales of ration supplies to messes2774480Flight rations2775481Payments at time of discharge for good of service2776486Clothing for destitute shipwrecked persons2777488Advancement of public funds to personnel2778660Transportation to and from certain places of employment2779

(c) ADDITIONAL CHANGES.—Chapter 27 of title 14, United States Code, is further amended—

(1) by inserting before section 2701 (as so redesignated and transferred under subsection (b)) the following:

SUBCHAPTER "SUBCHAPTER I—PERSONNEL RIGHTS AND BENEFITS""

(2) by inserting before section 2731 (as so redesignated and transferred under subsection (b)) the following:and

SUBCHAPTER "SUBCHAPTER II—AWARDS""

(3) by inserting before section 2761 (as so redesignated and transferred under subsection (b)) the following:

SUBCHAPTER "SUBCHAPTER III—PAYMENTS""

SEC. 117. CHAPTER 29.

(a) [14 U.S.C. 2901] INITIAL MATTER.—Chapter 29 of title 14, United States Code, is amended by striking the chapter designation, the chapter heading, and the table of sections at the beginning and inserting the following:

"CHAPTER 29—COAST GUARD FAMILY SUPPORT, CHILD CARE, AND HOUSING

" subchapter i— coast guard families

"Sec.	
"2901.	Work-life policies and programs.
"2902.	Surveys of Coast Guard families.
"2903.	Reimbursement for adoption expenses.
"2904.	Education and training opportunities for Coast Guard spouses.
"2905.	Youth sponsorship initiatives.
"2906.	Dependent school children.

" subchapter ii— coast guard child care

"2921.	Definitions.
"2922.	Child development services.
"2923.	Child development center standards and inspections.
"2924.	Child development center employees.
"2925.	Parent partnerships with child development centers.

" subchapter iii— housing

"2941.	Definitions.
"2942.	General authority.
"2943.	Leasing and hiring of quarters; rental of inadequate housing.
"2944.	Retired service members and dependents serving on advisory committees.
"2945.	Conveyance of real property.
"2946.	Coast Guard Housing Fund.
"2947.	Reports."

(b) REDESIGNATIONS AND TRANSFERS.—

(1) REQUIREMENT.—The sections of title 14, United States Code, identified in the table provided in paragraph (2) are amended—

(A) by redesignating the sections as described in the table; and

(B) by transferring the sections, as necessary, so that the sections appear after the table of sections for chapter 29 of such title (as added by subsection (a)), in the order in which the sections are presented in the table.

(2) TABLE.—The table referred to in paragraph (1) is the following:

Title 14 section number before redesignationSection heading (provided for identification purposes only-not amended)Title 14 section number after redesignation

531Work-life policies and programs2901532Surveys of Coast Guard families2902541Reimbursement for adoption expenses2903542Education and training

Title 14 section number before redesignationSection heading (provided for identification purposes only-not amended)Title 14 section number after redesignation

opportunities for Coast Guard spouses2904543Youth sponsorship initiatives2905544Dependent school children2906551Definitions2921552Child development services2922553Child development center standards and inspections2923554Child development center employees2924555Parent partnerships with child development centers2925680Definitions2941681General authority2942475Leasing and hiring of quarters; rental of inadequate housing2943680Retired service members and dependents serving on advisory committees2944685Conveyance of real property2945687Coast Guard Housing Fund2946688Reports2947

(c) ADDITIONAL CHANGES.—Chapter 29 of title 14, United States Code, is further amended—

(1) by inserting before section 2901 (as so redesignated and transferred under subsection (b)) the following:

SUBCHAPTER "SUBCHAPTER I—COAST GUARD FAMILIES""

(2) by inserting before section 2921 (as so redesignated and transferred under subsection (b)) the following:and

SUBCHAPTER "SUBCHAPTER II—COAST GUARD CHILD CARE""

(3) by inserting before section 2941 (as so redesignated and transferred under subsection (b)) the following:

SUBCHAPTER "SUBCHAPTER III—HOUSING""

SEC. 118. SUBTITLE III AND CHAPTER 37.

(a) INITIAL MATTER.—Title 14, United States Code, is further amended by adding after chapter 29 (as amended by section 117) the following:

"Subtitle III—Coast Guard Reserve and Auxiliary

"Chap.

"Sec.

"37.	Coast Guard Reserve
"39.	Coast Guard Auxiliary
"41.	General Provisions for Coast Guard Reserve and Auxiliary

"CHAPTER 1—COAST GUARD RESERVE

" subchapter i— administration

"Sec.	
"3701.	Organization.
"3702.	Authorized strength.
"3703.	Coast Guard Reserve Boards.
"3704.	Grades and ratings; military authority.
"3705.	Benefits.
"3706.	Temporary members of the Reserve; eligibility and compensation.
"3707.	Temporary members of the Reserve; disability or death benefits.
"3708.	Temporary members of the Reserve; certificate of honorable service.
"3709.	Reserve student aviation pilots; Reserve aviation pilots; appointments in commissioned grade.
"3710.	Reserve student pre-commissioning assistance program.
"3711.	Appointment or wartime promotion; retention of grade upon release from active duty.
"3712.	Exclusiveness of service.
"3713.	Active duty for emergency augmentation of regular forces.
"3714.	Enlistment of members engaged in schooling.

" subchapter ii— personnel

"3731.	Definitions.
"3732.	Applicability of this subchapter.
"3733.	Suspension of this subchapter in time of war or national emergency.
"3734.	Effect of this subchapter on retirement and retired pay.
"3735.	Authorized number of officers.
"3736.	Precedence.
"3737.	Running mates.
"3738.	Constructive credit upon initial appointment.
"3739.	Promotion of Reserve officers on active duty.
"3740.	Promotion; recommendations of selection boards.
"3741.	Selection boards; appointment.
"3742.	Establishment of promotion zones under running mate system.

"3743.	Eligibility for promotion.
"3744.	Recommendation for promotion of an officer previously removed from an active status.
"3745.	Qualifications for promotion.
"3746.	Promotion; acceptance; oath of office.
"3747.	Date of rank upon promotion; entitlement to pay.
"3748.	Type of promotion; temporary.
"3749.	Effect of removal by the President or failure of consent of the Senate.
"3750.	Failure of selection for promotion.
"3751.	Failure of selection and removal from an active status.
"3752.	Retention boards; removal from an active status to provide a flow of promotion.
"3753.	Maximum ages for retention in an active status.
"3754.	Rear admiral and rear admiral (lower half); maximum service in grade.
"3755.	Appointment of a former Navy or Coast Guard officer.
"3756.	Grade on entry upon active duty.
"3757.	Recall of a retired officer; grade upon release.".”

(b) REDESIGNATIONS AND TRANSFERS.—

(1) REQUIREMENT.—The sections of title 14, United States Code, identified in the table provided in paragraph (2) are amended—

(A) by redesignating the sections as described in the table; and

(B) by transferring the sections, as necessary, so that the sections appear after the table of sections for chapter 37 of such title (as added by subsection (a)), in the order in which the sections are presented in the table.

(2) TABLE.—The table referred to in paragraph (1) is the following:

Title 14 section number before redesignationSection heading (provided for identification purposes only-not amended)Title 14 section number after redesignation

701Organization3701702Authorized strength3702703Coast Guard Reserve Boards3703704Grades and ratings; military authority3704705Benefits3705706Temporary members of the Reserve; eligibility and compensation3706707Temporary members of the Reserve; disability or death benefits3707708Temporary members of the Reserve; certificate of honorable service3708709Reserve student aviation pilots; Reserve aviation pilots; appointments in commissioned grade3709709aReserve student pre-commissioning assistance program3710710Appointment or wartime promotion; retention of grade upon release from active duty3711711Exclusiveness of service3712712Active duty for emergency augmentation of regular forces3713713Enlistment of members engaged in schooling3714720Definitions3731721Applicability of this subchapter3732722Suspension of this subchapter in time of war or national emergency3733723Effect of this subchapter on retirement and retired pay3734724Authorized number of officers3735725Precedence3736726Running mates3737727Constructive credit upon initial

Title 14 section number before redesignationSection heading (provided for identification purposes only-not amended)Title 14 section number after redesignation

appointment3738728Promotion of Reserve officers on active duty3739729Promotion; recommendations of selection boards3740730Selection boards; appointment3741731Establishment of promotion zones under running mate system3742732Eligibility for promotion3743733Recommendation for promotion of an officer previously removed from an active status3744734Qualifications for promotion3745735Promotion; acceptance; oath of office3746736Date of rank upon promotion; entitlement to pay3747737Type of promotion; temporary3748738Effect of removal by the President or failure of consent of the Senate3749739Failure of selection for promotion3750740Failure of selection and removal from an active status3751741Retention boards; removal from an active status to provide a flow of promotion3752742Maximum ages for retention in an active status3753743Rear admiral and rear admiral (lower half); maximum service in grade3754744Appointment of a former Navy or Coast Guard officer3755745Grade on entry upon active duty3756746Recall of a retired officer; grade upon release3757

(c) ADDITIONAL CHANGES.—Chapter 37 of title 14, United States Code, is further amended—

(1) by inserting before section 3701 (as so redesignated and transferred under subsection (b)) the following:and

SUBCHAPTER "SUBCHAPTER I—ADMINISTRATION""

(2) by inserting before section 3731 (as so redesignated and transferred under subsection (b)) the following:

SUBCHAPTER "SUBCHAPTER II—PERSONNEL""

SEC. 119. CHAPTER 39.

(a) INITIAL MATTER.—Title 14, United States Code, is further amended by adding after chapter 37 (as added by section 118) the following:

"CHAPTER 39—COAST GUARD AUXILIARY

"Sec.

"3906.	Membership in other organizations.
"3907.	Use of member's facilities.
"3908.	Vessel deemed public vessel.
"3909.	Aircraft deemed public aircraft.
"3910.	Radio station deemed government station.
"3911.	Availability of appropriations.
"3912.	Assignment and performance of duties.
"3913.	Injury or death in line of duty."

(b) REDESIGNATIONS AND TRANSFERS.—

(1) REQUIREMENT.—The sections of title 14, United States Code, identified in the table provided in paragraph (2) are amended—

(A) by redesignating the sections as described in the table; and

(B) by transferring the sections, as necessary, so that the sections appear after the table of sections for chapter 39 of such title (as added by subsection (a)), in the order in which the sections are presented in the table.

(2) TABLE.—The table referred to in paragraph (1) is the following:

Title 14 section number before redesignationSection heading (provided for identification purposes only-not amended)Title 14 section number after redesignation

821Administration of the Coast Guard Auxiliary3901822Purpose of the Coast Guard Auxiliary3902823Eligibility; enrollments3903823aMembers of the Auxiliary; status3904824Disenrollment3905825Membership in other organizations3906826Use of member's facilities3907827Vessel deemed public vessel3908828Aircraft deemed public aircraft3909829Radio station deemed government station3910830Availability of appropriations3911831Assignment and performance of duties3912832Injury or death in line of duty3913

SEC. 120. CHAPTER 41.

(a) INITIAL MATTER.—Title 14, United States Code, is further amended by adding after chapter 39 (as added by section 119) the following:

"CHAPTER 41—GENERAL PROVISIONS FOR COAST GUARD RESERVE AND AUXILIARY

"Sec.	
"4101.	Flags; pennants; uniforms and insignia.
"4102.	Penalty.

(b) REDESIGNATIONS AND TRANSFERS.—

(1) REQUIREMENT.—The sections of title 14, United States Code, identified in the table provided in paragraph (2) are amended—

(A) by redesignating the sections as described in the table; and

(B) by transferring the sections, as necessary, so that the sections appear after the table of sections for chapter 41 of such title (as added by subsection (a)), in the order in which the sections are presented in the table.

(2) TABLE.—The table referred to in paragraph (1) is the following:

Title 14 section number before redesignationSection heading (provided for identification purposes only-not amended)Title 14 section number after redesignation

891Flags; pennants; uniforms and insignia4101892Penalty4102893Limitation on rights of members of the Auxiliary and temporary members of the Reserve4103894Availability of facilities and appropriations4104

SEC. 121. SUBTITLE IV AND CHAPTER 49.

(a) INITIAL MATTER.—Title 14, United States Code, is further amended by adding after chapter 41 (as added by section 120) the following:

"Subtitle IV—Coast Guard Authorizations and Reports to Congress

"CHAPTER 49—AUTHORIZATIONS

(b) REDESIGNATIONS AND TRANSFERS.—

(1) REQUIREMENT.—The sections of title 14, United States Code, identified in the table provided in paragraph (2) are amended—

(A) by redesignating the sections as described in the table; and

(B) by transferring the sections, as necessary, so that the sections appear after the table of sections for chapter 49 of such title (as added by subsection (a)), in the order in which the sections are presented in the table.

(2) TABLE.—The table referred to in paragraph (1) is the following:

Title 14 section number before redesignationSection heading (provided for identification purposes only-not amended)Title 14 section number after redesignation

2701Requirement for prior authorization of appropriations49012702Authorization of appropriations49022703Authorization of personnel end strengths49032704Authorized levels of military strength and training4904

SEC. 122. CHAPTER 51.

(a) INITIAL MATTER.—Title 14, United States Code, is further amended by adding after chapter 49 (as added by section 121) the following:

"CHAPTER 51—REPORTS

(b) REDESIGNATIONS AND TRANSFERS.—

(1) REQUIREMENT.—The sections of title 14, United States Code, identified in the table provided in paragraph (2) are amended—

(A) by redesignating the sections as described in the table; and

(B) by transferring the sections, as necessary, so that the sections appear after the table of sections for chapter 51 of such title (as added by subsection (a)), in the order in which the sections are presented in the table.

(2) TABLE.—The table referred to in paragraph (1) is the following:

Title 14 section number before redesignationSection heading (provided for identification purposes only-not amended)Title 14 section number after redesignation

2901Transmission of annual Coast Guard authorization request51012902Capital investment plan51022903Major acquisitions51032904Manpower requirements plan5104679Inventory of real property51052905Annual performance report51062906Major acquisition risk assessment5107

SEC. 123. REFERENCES.

(a) [14 U.S.C. 101 note] DEFINITIONS.—In this section, the following definitions apply:

(1) REDESIGNATED SECTION.—The term "redesignated section" means a section of title 14, United States Code, that is redesignated by this title, as that section is so redesignated.

(2) SOURCE SECTION.—The term "source section" means a section of title 14, United States Code, that is redesignated by this title, as that section was in effect before the redesignation.

(b) REFERENCE TO SOURCE SECTION.—

(1) [14 U.S.C. 101 note] TREATMENT OF REFERENCE.—A reference to a source section, including a reference in a regulation, order, or other law, is deemed to refer to the corresponding redesignated section.

(2) [49 U.S.C. 303-305] TITLE 14.—In title 14, United States Code, each reference in the text of such title to a source section is amended by striking such reference and inserting a reference to the appropriate, as determined using the tables located in this title, redesignated section.

(c) OTHER CONFORMING AMENDMENTS.—

(1) REFERENCE TO SECTION 182.—Section 1923(c) of title 14, United States Code, as so redesignated by this title, is further amended by striking "section 182" and inserting "section 1922".

(2) REFERENCES TO CHAPTER 11.—Title 14, United States Code, is further amended—

(A) in section 2146(d), as so redesignated by this title, by striking "chapter 11 of this title" and inserting "this chapter"; and

(B) in section 3739, as so redesignated by this title, by striking "chapter 11" each place that it appears and inserting "chapter 21".

(3) REFERENCE TO CHAPTER 13.—Section 3705(b) of title 14, United States Code, as so redesignated by this title, is further amended by striking "chapter 13" and inserting "chapter 27".

(4) REFERENCE TO CHAPTER 15.—Section 308(b)(3) of title 14, United States Code, as so redesignated by this title, is further amended by striking "chapter 15" and inserting "chapter 11".

(5) REFERENCES TO CHAPTER 19.—Title 14, United States Code, is further amended—

(A) in section 4901(4), as so redesignated by this title, by striking "chapter 19" and inserting "section 318"; and

(B) in section 4902(4), as so redesignated by this title, by striking "chapter 19" and inserting "section 318".

(6) REFERENCE TO CHAPTER 23.—Section 701(a) of title 14, United States Code, as so redesignated by this title, is further amended by striking "chapter 23" and inserting "chapter 39".

SEC. 124. [14 U.S.C. 101 note] RULE OF CONSTRUCTION.

This title, including the amendments made by this title, is intended only to reorganize title 14, United States Code, and may not be construed to alter—

(1) the effect of a provision of title 14, United States Code, including any authority or requirement therein;

(2) a department or agency interpretation with respect to title 14, United States Code; or

(3) a judicial interpretation with respect to title 14, United States Code.

TITLE II—AUTHORIZATIONS

SEC. 201. AMENDMENTS TO TITLE 14, UNITED STATES CODE, AS AMENDED BY TITLE I OF THIS ACT.

Except as otherwise expressly provided, whenever in this title an amendment or repeal is expressed in terms of an amendment to, or a repeal of, a section or other provision of title 14, United States Code, the reference shall be considered to be made to title 14, United States Code, as amended by title I of this Act.

SEC. 202. AUTHORIZATIONS OF APPROPRIATIONS.

(a) IN GENERAL.—Section 4902 of title 14, United States Code, is amended to read as follows:

"SEC. § 4902. Authorizations of appropriation

"(a) FISCAL YEAR 2018.—Funds are authorized to be appropriated for fiscal year 2018 for necessary expenses of the Coast Guard as follows:

"(1) For the operation and maintenance of the Coast Guard, not otherwise provided for, $7,210,313,000 for fiscal year 2018.

"(2) For the acquisition, construction, renovation, and improvement of aids to navigation, shore facilities, vessels, aircraft, and systems, including equipment related thereto, and for maintenance, rehabilitation, lease, and operation of facilities and equipment, $2,694,745,000 for fiscal year 2018.

"(3) For the Coast Guard Reserve program, including operations and maintenance of the program, personnel and training costs, equipment, and services, $114,875,000 for fiscal year 2018.

"(4) For the environmental compliance and restoration functions of the Coast Guard under chapter 3 of this title, $13,397,000 for fiscal year 2018.

"(5) To the Commandant for research, development, test, and evaluation of technologies, materials, and human factors directly related to improving the performance of the Coast Guard's mission with respect to search and rescue, aids to navigation, marine safety, marine environmental protection, enforcement of laws and treaties, ice operations, oceanographic research, and defense readiness, and for maintenance, rehabilitation, lease, and operation of facilities and equipment,

$29,141,000 for fiscal year 2018.

"(b) FISCAL YEAR 2019.—Funds are authorized to be appropriated for fiscal year 2019 for necessary expenses of the Coast Guard as follows:

"(1)(A) For the operation and maintenance of the Coast Guard, not otherwise provided for, $7,914,195,000 for fiscal year 2019.

"(B) Of the amount authorized under subparagraph (A)—

"(i) $16,701,000 shall be for environmental compliance and restoration; and

"(ii) $199,360,000 shall be for the Coast Guard's Medicare-eligible retiree health care fund contribution to the Department of Defense.

"(2) For the procurement, construction, renovation, and improvement of aids to navigation, shore facilities, vessels, aircraft, and systems, including equipment related thereto, and for maintenance, rehabilitation, lease, and operation of facilities and equipment, $2,694,745,000 for fiscal year 2019.

"(3) To the Commandant for research, development, test, and evaluation of technologies, materials, and human factors directly related to improving the performance of the Coast Guard's mission with respect to search and rescue, aids to navigation, marine safety, marine environmental protection, enforcement of laws and treaties, ice operations, oceanographic research, and defense readiness, and for maintenance, rehabilitation, lease, and operation of facilities and equipment, $29,141,000 for fiscal year 2019."

(b) [14 U.S.C. 4902 note] REPEAL.—On October 1, 2018—

(1) section 4902(a) of title 14, United States Code, as amended by subsection (a), shall be repealed; and

(2) subsection 4902(b) of title 14, United States Code, as amended by subsection (a), shall be amended by striking "(b) Fiscal Year 2019.—".

SEC. 203. AUTHORIZED LEVELS OF MILITARY STRENGTH AND TRAINING.

Section 4904 of title 14, United States Code, is amended—

(1) in subsection (a), by striking "for each of fiscal years 2016 and 2017" and inserting "for fiscal year 2018 and 44,500 for fiscal year 2019"; and

(2) in subsection (b), by striking "fiscal years 2016 and 2017" and inserting "fiscal years 2018 and 2019".

SEC. 204. AUTHORIZATION OF AMOUNTS FOR FAST RESPONSE CUTTERS.

(a) IN GENERAL.—Of the amounts authorized under section 4902 of title 14, United States Code, as amended by this Act, for each of fiscal years 2018 and 2019 up to $167,500,000 is authorized for the acquisition of 3 Fast Response Cutters.

(b) TREATMENT OF ACQUIRED CUTTERS.—Any cutters acquired pursuant to subsection (a) shall be in addition to the 58 cutters approved under the existing acquisition baseline.

SEC. 205. AUTHORIZATION OF AMOUNTS FOR SHORESIDE INFRASTRUCTURE.

Of the amounts authorized under section 4902 of title 14, United States Code, as amended by this Act, for each of fiscal years 2018 and 2019 up to $167,500,000 is authorized for the Secretary of the department in which the Coast Guard is operating to fund the acquisition, construction, rebuilding, or improvement of Coast Guard shoreside infrastructure and facilities necessary to support Coast Guard operations and readiness.

SEC. 206. AUTHORIZATION OF AMOUNTS FOR AIRCRAFT IMPROVEMENTS.

Of the amounts authorized under section 4902 of title 14, United States Code, as amended by this Act, for each of fiscal years 2018 and 2019 up to $3,500,000 is authorized for the Secretary of the department in which the Coast Guard is operating to fund analysis and program development for improvements to or the replacement of rotary-wing aircraft.

TITLE III—COAST GUARD

SEC. 301. AMENDMENTS TO TITLE 14, UNITED STATES CODE, AS AMENDED BY TITLE I OF THIS ACT.

Except as otherwise expressly provided, whenever in this title an amendment or repeal is expressed in terms of an amendment to, or a repeal of, a section or other provision of title 14, United States Code, the reference shall be considered to be made to title 14, United States Code, as amended by title I of this Act.

SEC. 302. PRIMARY DUTIES.

Section 102(7) of title 14, United States Code, is amended to read as follows:

"(7) maintain a state of readiness to assist in the defense of the United States, including when functioning as a specialized service in the Navy pursuant to section 103."

SEC. 303. NATIONAL COAST GUARD MUSEUM.

Section 316 of title 14, United States Code, is amended to read as follows:

"SEC. § 316. National Coast Guard Museu

"(a) ESTABLISHMENT.—The Commandant may establish a National Coast Guard Museum, on lands which will be federally owned and administered by the Coast Guard, and are located in New London, Connecticut, at, or in close proximity to, the Coast Guard Academy.

"(b) LIMITATION ON EXPENDITURES.—

"(1) The Secretary shall not expend any funds appropriated to the Coast Guard on the construction of any museum established under this section.

"(2) The Secretary shall fund the National Coast Guard Museum with nonappropriated and non-Federal funds to the maximum extent practicable. The priority use of Federal funds should be to preserve and protect historic Coast Guard artifacts, including the design, fabrication, and installation of exhibits or displays in which such artifacts are included.

"(3) The Secretary may expend funds appropriated to the Coast Guard on the engineering and design of a National Coast Guard Museum.

"(c) FUNDING PLAN.—Before the date on which the Commandant establishes a National Coast Guard Museum under subsection (a), the Commandant shall provide to the Committee on Commerce, Science, and Transportation of the Senate and the Committee on Transportation and Infrastructure of the House of Representatives a plan for constructing, operating, and maintaining such a museum, including—

"(1) estimated planning, engineering, design, construction, operation, and maintenance costs;

"(2) the extent to which appropriated, nonappropriated, and non-Federal funds will be used for such purposes, including the extent to which there is any shortfall in funding for engineering, design, or construction; and

"(3) a certification by the Inspector General of the department in which the Coast Guard is operating that the estimates provided pursuant to paragraphs (1) and (2) are reasonable and realistic.

"(d) AUTHORITY.—The Commandant may not establish a National Coast Guard museum except as set forth in this section."

SEC. 304. UNMANNED AIRCRAFT.

(a) LAND-BASED UNMANNED AIRCRAFT SYSTEM PROGRAM.—Chapter 3 of title 14, United States Code, is amended by adding at the end the following:

"SEC. §319. [14 U.S.C. 319] Land-based unmanned aircraft system progra

"(a) IN GENERAL.—Subject to the availability of appropriations, the Secretary shall establish a land-based unmanned aircraft system program under the control of the Commandant.

"(b) UNMANNED AIRCRAFT SYSTEM DEFINED.—In this section, the term 'unmanned aircraft system' has the meaning given that term in section 331 of the FAA Modernization and Reform Act of 2012 (49 U.S.C. 40101 note)."

(b) LIMITATION ON UNMANNED AIRCRAFT SYSTEMS.—Chapter 11 of title 14, United States Code, is amended by inserting after section 1155 the following:

"SEC. §1156. [14 U.S.C. 1156] Limitation on unmanned aircraft system

"(a) IN GENERAL.—During any fiscal year for which funds are appropriated for the design or construction of an Offshore Patrol Cutter, the Commandant—

"(1) may not award a contract for design of an unmanned aircraft system for use by the Coast Guard; and

"(2) may lease, acquire, or acquire the services of an unmanned aircraft system only if such system—

"(A) has been part of a program of record of, procured by, or used by a Federal entity (or funds for research, development, test, and evaluation have been received from a Federal entity with regard to such system) before the date on which the Commandant leases, acquires, or acquires the services of the system; and

"(B) is leased, acquired, or utilized by the Commandant through an agreement with a Federal entity, unless such an agreement is not practicable or would be less cost-effective than an independent contract action by the Coast Guard.

"(b) SMALL UNMANNED AIRCRAFT EXEMPTION.—Subsection (a)(2) does not apply to small unmanned aircraft.

"(c) DEFINITIONS.—In this section, the terms 'small unmanned aircraft' and 'unmanned aircraft system' have the meanings given those terms in section 331 of the FAA Modernization and Reform Act of 2012 (49 U.S.C. 40101 note)."

(c) CLERICAL AMENDMENTS.—

(1) **[14 U.S.C. 301]** CHAPTER 3.—The analysis for chapter 3 of title 14, United States Code, is amended by adding at the end the following:

"319. Land-based unmanned aircraft system program."

(2) **[14 U.S.C. 1101]** CHAPTER 11.—The analysis for chapter 11 of title 14, United States Code, is amended by inserting after the item relating to section 1155 the following:

"1156. Limitation on unmanned aircraft systems."

(d) CONFORMING AMENDMENT.—Subsection (c) of section 1105 of title 14, United States Code, is repealed.

SEC. 305. COAST GUARD HEALTH-CARE PROFESSIONALS; LICENSURE PORTABILITY.

(a) IN GENERAL.—Chapter 5 of title 14, United States Code, is amended by inserting after section 507 the following:

"SEC. §508. [14 U.S.C. 508] Coast Guard health-care professionals; licensure portabilit

"(a) IN GENERAL.—Notwithstanding any other provision of law regarding the licensure of health-care providers, a health-care professional described in subsection (b) may practice the health profession or professions of the health-care professional at any location in any State, the District of Columbia, or a Commonwealth, territory, or possession of the United States, regardless of where such health-care professional or the patient is located, if the practice is within the scope of the authorized Federal duties of such health-care professional.

"(b) DESCRIBED INDIVIDUALS.—A health-care professional described in this subsection is an individual—

"(1) who is—

"(A) a member of the Coast Guard;

"(B) a civilian employee of the Coast Guard;

"(C) a member of the Public Health Service who is assigned to the Coast Guard; or

"(D) any other health-care professional credentialed and privileged at a Federal health-care institution or location specially designated by the Secretary; and

"(2) who—

"(A) has a current license to practice medicine, osteopathic medicine, dentistry, or another health profession; and

"(B) is performing authorized duties for the Coast Guard.

"(c) DEFINITIONS.—In this section, the terms 'license' and 'health-care professional' have the meanings given those terms in section 1094(e) of title 10."

(b) [14 U.S.C. 501] CLERICAL AMENDMENT.—The analysis for chapter 5 of title 14, United States Code,is amended by inserting after the item relating to section 507 the following:

"508.	Coast Guard health-care professionals; licensure portability."

(c) [14 U.S.C. 504 note] ELECTRONIC HEALTH RECORDS.—

(1) SYSTEM.—The Commandant of the Coast Guard is authorized to procure for the Coast Guard an electronic health record system that—

(A) has been competitively awarded by the Department of Defense; and

(B) ensures full integration with the Department of Defense electronic health record systems.

(2) SUPPORT SERVICES.—

(A) IN GENERAL.—The Commandant is authorized to procure support services for the electronic health record system procured under paragraph (1) necessary to ensure full integration with the Department of Defense electronic health record systems.

(B) SCOPE.—Support services procured pursuant to this paragraph may include services for the following:

(i) System integration support.

(ii) Hosting support.

(iii) Training, testing, technical, and data migration support.

(iv) Hardware support.

(v) Any other support the Commandant considers appropriate.

(3) AUTHORIZED PROCUREMENT ACTIONS.—The Commandant is authorized to procure an electronic health record system under this subsection through the following:

(A) A task order under the Department of Defense electronic health record contract.

(B) A sole source contract award.

(C) An agreement made pursuant to sections 1535 and 1536 of title 31, United States Code.

(D) A contract or other procurement vehicle otherwise authorized.

(4) COMPETITION IN CONTRACTING; EXEMPTION.—Procurement of an electronic health record system and support services pursuant to this subsection shall be exempt from the competition requirements of section 2304 of title 10, United States Code.

SEC. 306. TRAINING; EMERGENCY RESPONSE PROVIDERS.

(a) IN GENERAL.—Chapter 7 of title 14, United States Code, is amended by adding at the end the following:

"SEC. § 718. [14 U.S.C. 718] Training; emergency response provider

"(a) IN GENERAL.—The Commandant may, on a reimbursable or a non-reimbursable basis, make a training available to emergency response providers whenever the Commandant determines that—

"(1) a member of the Coast Guard, who is scheduled to participate in such training, is unable or unavailable to participate in such training;

"(2) no other member of the Coast Guard, who is assigned to the unit to which the member of the Coast Guard who is unable or unavailable to participate in such training is assigned, is able or available to participate in such training; and

"(3) such training, if made available to such emergency response providers, would further the goal of interoperability among Federal agencies, non-Federal governmental agencies, or both.

"(b) EMERGENCY RESPONSE PROVIDERS DEFINED.—In this section, the term 'emergency response providers' has the meaning given that term in section 2 of the Homeland Security Act of 2002 (6 U.S.C. 101).

"(c) TREATMENT OF REIMBURSEMENT.—Any reimbursements for a training that the Coast Guard receives under this section shall be credited to the appropriation used to pay the costs for such training.

"(d) STATUS; LIMITATION ON LIABILITY.—

"(1) STATUS.—Any individual to whom, as an emergency response provider, training is made available under this section, who is not otherwise a Federal employee, shall not, because of that training, be considered a Federal employee for any purpose (including the purposes of chapter 81 of title 5 (relating to compensation for injury) and sections 2671 through 2680 of title 28 (relating to tort claims)).

"(2) LIMITATION ON LIABILITY.—The United States shall not be liable for actions taken by an individual in the course of training made available under this section."

(b) [14 U.S.C. 701] CLERICAL AMENDMENT.—The analysis for chapter 7 of title 14, United States Code, is amended by adding at the end the following:

"718. Training; emergency response providers."

SEC. 307. INCENTIVE CONTRACTS FOR COAST GUARD YARD AND INDUSTRIAL ESTABLISHMENTS.

Section 939 of title 14, United States Code, is amended—

(1) by inserting before "The Secretary may" the following: "(a) In General.—";

(2) in subsection (a), as so designated by paragraph (1) of this section, by striking the period at the end of the last sentence and inserting "or in accordance with subsection (b)."; and

(3) by adding at the end the following:

"(b) INCENTIVE CONTRACTS.—

"(1) The parties to an order for industrial work to be performed by the Coast Guard Yard or a Coast Guard industrial establishment designated under subsection (a) may enter into an order or a cost-plus-incentive-fee order in accordance with this subsection.

"(2) If such parties enter into such an order or a cost-plus-incentive-fee order, an agreed-upon amount of any adjustment described in subsection (a) may be distributed as an incentive to the wage-grade industrial employees who complete the order.

"(3) Before entering into such an order or cost-plus-incentive-fee order such parties must agree that the wage-grade employees of the Coast Guard Yard or Coast Guard industrial establishment will take action to improve the delivery schedule or technical performance agreed to in the order for industrial work to which such parties initially agreed.

"(4) Notwithstanding any other provision of law, if the industrial workforce of the Coast Guard Yard or Coast Guard industrial establishment satisfies the performance target established in such an order or cost-plus-incentive-fee order—

"(A) the adjustment to be made pursuant to subsection (a) shall be reduced by an agreed-upon amount and distributed to such wage-grade industrial employees; and

"(B) the remainder of the adjustment shall be credited to the appropriation for such order current at that time."

SEC. 308. CONFIDENTIAL INVESTIGATIVE EXPENSES.

Section 944 of title 14, United States Code, is amended by striking "$45,000" and inserting "$250,000".

SEC. 309. REGULAR CAPTAINS; RETIREMENT.

Section 2149(a) of title 14, United States Code, is amended—

(1) by striking "zone is" and inserting "zone, or from being placed at the top of the list of selectees promulgated by the Secretary under section 2121(a) of this title, is"; and

(2) by striking the period at the end and inserting "or placed at the top of the list of selectees, as applicable.".

SEC. 310. CONVERSION, ALTERATION, AND REPAIR PROJECTS.

(a) IN GENERAL.—Chapter 9 of title 14, United States Code, as amended by this Act, is further amended by inserting after section 951 the following:

"SEC. §952. [14 U.S.C. 952] Construction of Coast Guard vessels and assignment of vessel project

"The assignment of Coast Guard vessel conversion, alteration, and repair projects shall be based on economic and military considerations and may not be restricted by a requirement that certain parts of Coast Guard shipwork be assigned to a particular type of shipyard or geographical area or by a similar requirement."

(b) [14 U.S.C. 901] CLERICAL AMENDMENT.—The analysis for chapter 9 of title 14, United States Code, is amended by inserting after the item relating to section 951 the following:

"952. Construction of Coast Guard vessels and assignment of vessel projects."

SEC. 311. CONTRACTING FOR MAJOR ACQUISITIONS PROGRAMS.

(a) GENERAL ACQUISITION AUTHORITY.—Section 501(d) of title 14, United States Code, is amended by inserting "aircraft, and systems," after "vessels,".

(b) CONTRACTING AUTHORITY.—Chapter 11 of title 14, United States Code, as amended by this Act, is further amended by inserting after section 1136 the following:

"SEC. §1137. [14 U.S.C. 1137] Contracting for major acquisitions

program

"(a) IN GENERAL.—In carrying out authorities provided to the Secretary to design, construct, accept, or otherwise acquire assets and systems under section 501(d), the Secretary, acting through the Commandant or the head of an integrated program office established for a major acquisition program, may enter into contracts for a major acquisition program.

"(b) AUTHORIZED METHODS.—Contracts entered into under subsection (a)—

"(1) may be block buy contracts;

"(2) may be incrementally funded;

"(3) may include combined purchases, also known as economic order quantity purchases, of—

"(A) materials and components; and

"(B) long lead time materials; and

"(4) as provided in section 2306b of title 10, may be multiyear contracts.

"(c) SUBJECT TO APPROPRIATIONS.—Any contract entered into under subsection (a) shall provide that any obligation of the United States to make a payment under the contract is subject to the availability of amounts specifically provided in advance for that purpose in subsequent appropriations Acts."

(c) [14 U.S.C. 1101] CLERICAL AMENDMENT.—The analysis for chapter 11 of title 14, United States Code, as amended by this Act, is further amended by inserting after the item relating to section 1136 the following:

"1137. Contracting for major acquisitions programs."

(d) CONFORMING AMENDMENTS.—The following provisions are repealed:

(1) [14 U.S.C. 577 note] Section 223 of the Howard Coble Coast Guard and Maritime Transportation Act of 2014 (14 U.S.C. 1152 note), and the item relating to that section in the table of contents in section 2 of such Act.

(2) [14 U.S.C. 573] Section 221(a) of the Coast Guard and Maritime Transportation Act of 2012 (14 U.S.C. 1133 note).

(3) [14 U.S.C. 87] Section 207(a) of the Coast Guard Authorization Act of 2016 (14 U.S.C. 561 note).

(e) [14 U.S.C. 1137 note] INTERNAL REGULATIONS AND POLICY.—Not later than 180 days after the date of enactment of this Act, the Secretary of the department in which the Coast Guard is operating shall establish the internal regulations and policies necessary to exercise the authorities provided under this section, including the amendments made in this section.

(f) [14 U.S.C. 1133 note] MULTIYEAR CONTRACTS.—The Secretary of the department in which the Coast Guard is operating is authorized to enter into a multiyear contract for the procurement of a tenth, eleventh, and twelfth National Security Cutter and associated government-furnished equipment.

SEC. 312. OFFICER PROMOTION ZONES.

Section 2111(a) of title 14, United States Code, is amended by striking "six-tenths." and inserting "one-half.".

SEC. 313. CROSS REFERENCE.

Section 2129(a) of title 14, United States Code, is amended by inserting "designated under section 2317" after "cadet".

SEC. 314. COMMISSIONED SERVICE RETIREMENT.

For Coast Guard officers who retire in fiscal year 2018 or 2019, the President may reduce the period of active commissioned service required under section 2152 of title 14, United States Code, to a period of not less than 8 years.

SEC. 315. LEAVE FOR BIRTH OR ADOPTION OF CHILD.

(a) POLICY.—Section 2512 of title 14, United States Code, is amended—

(1) by striking "Not later than 1 year" and inserting the following:

"(a) IN GENERAL.—Except as provided in subsection (b), not later than 1 year"

; and

(2) by adding at the end the following:

"(b) LEAVE ASSOCIATED WITH BIRTH OR ADOPTION OF CHILD.—Notwithstanding subsection (a), sections 701 and 704 of title 10, or any other provision of law, all officers and enlisted members of the Coast Guard shall be authorized leave associated with the birth or adoption of a child during the

1-year period immediately following such birth or adoption and, at the discretion of the Commanding Officer, such officer or enlisted member shall be permitted—

"(1) to take such leave in increments; and

"(2) to use flexible work schedules (pursuant to a program established by the Secretary in accordance with chapter 61 of title 5)."

(b) [14 U.S.C. 2512 note] FLEXIBLE WORK SCHEDULES.—Not later than 180 days after the date of enactment of this Act, the Secretary of the department in which the Coast Guard is operating shall ensure that a flexible work schedule program under chapter 61 of title 5, United States Code, is in place for officers and enlisted members of the Coast Guard.

SEC. 316. [14 U.S.C. 2701] CLOTHING AT TIME OF DISCHARGE.

Section 2705 of title 14, United States Code, and the item relating to that section in the analysis for chapter 27 of that title, are repealed.

SEC. 317. UNFUNDED PRIORITIES LIST.

(a) IN GENERAL.—Section 5102 of title 14, United States Code, is amended—

(1) by striking subsection (a) and inserting the following:

"(a) IN GENERAL.—Not later than 60 days after the date on which the President submits to Congress a budget pursuant to section 1105 of title 31, the Commandant shall submit to the Committee on Transportation and Infrastructure of the House of Representatives and the Committee on Commerce, Science, and Transportation of the Senate a capital investment plan for the Coast Guard that identifies for each capital asset for which appropriations are proposed in that budget—

"(1) the proposed appropriations included in the budget;

"(2) the total estimated cost of completion based on the proposed appropriations included in the budget;

"(3) projected funding levels for each fiscal year for the next 5 fiscal years or until project completion, whichever is earlier;

"(4) an estimated completion date based on the

proposed appropriations included in the budget;

"(5) an acquisition program baseline, as applicable; and

"(6) projected commissioning and decommissioning dates for each asset."

; and

(2) by striking subsection (c) and inserting the following:

"(c) DEFINITIONS.—In this section, the term 'new capital asset' means—

"(1) an acquisition program that does not have an approved acquisition program baseline; or

"(2) the acquisition of a capital asset in excess of the number included in the approved acquisition program baseline."

(b) UNFUNDED PRIORITIES.—Chapter 51 of title 14, United States Code, is amended by adding at the end the following:

"SEC. § 5108. [14 U.S.C. 5108] Unfunded priorities lis

"(a) IN GENERAL.—Not later than 60 days after the date on which the President submits to Congress a budget pursuant to section 1105 of title 31, the Commandant shall submit to the Committee on Transportation and Infrastructure of the House of Representatives and the Committee on Commerce, Science, and Transportation of the Senate a list of each unfunded priority for the Coast Guard.

"(b) PRIORITIZATION.—The list required under subsection (a) shall present the unfunded priorities in order from the highest priority to the lowest, as determined by the Commandant.

"(c) UNFUNDED PRIORITY DEFINED.—In this section, the term 'unfunded priority' means a program or mission requirement that—

"(1) has not been selected for funding in the applicable proposed budget;

"(2) is necessary to fulfill a requirement associated with an operational need; and

"(3) the Commandant would have recommended for inclusion in the applicable proposed budget had additional resources been available or had the requirement emerged before the budget was submitted."

(c) [14 U.S.C. 510] CLERICAL AMENDMENT.—The analysis for chapter 51 of title 14, United States Code, is amended by adding at the end the following:

"5108. Unfunded priorities list."

SEC. 318. SAFETY OF VESSELS OF THE ARMED FORCES.

(a) IN GENERAL.—Section 527 of title 14, United States Code, is amended—

(1) in the heading, by striking "naval vessels" and inserting "vessels of the Armed Forces";

(2) in subsection (a), by striking "United States naval vessel" and inserting "vessel of the Armed Forces";

(3) in subsection (b)—

(A) by striking "senior naval officer present in command" and inserting "senior officer present in command"; and

(B) by striking "United States naval vessel" and inserting "vessel of the Armed Forces"; and

(4) by adding at the end the following:

"(e) For purposes of this title, the term 'vessel of the Armed Forces' means—

"(1) any vessel owned or operated by the Department of Defense or the Coast Guard, other than a time- or voyage-chartered vessel; and

"(2) any vessel owned and operated by the Department of Transportation that is designated by the Secretary of the department in which the Coast Guard is operating as a vessel equivalent to a vessel described in paragraph (1)."

(b) [14 U.S.C. 501] CLERICAL AMENDMENT.—The analysis for chapter 5 of title 14, United States Code, is further amended by striking the item relating to section 527 and inserting the following:

"527. Safety of vessels of the Armed Forces."

(c) CONFORMING AMENDMENTS.—Section 2510(a)(1) of title 14, United States Code, is amended—

(1) by striking "armed forces" and inserting "Armed Forces"; and

(2) by striking "section 101(a) of title 10" and inserting "section 527(e)".

SEC. 319. AIR FACILITIES.

Section 912 of title 14, United States Code, is amended—

(1) by striking subsection (a);

(2) by redesignating subsections (b) and (c) as subsections (a) and (b), respectively;

(3) in subsection (a) as redesignated—

(A) by amending paragraph (3) to read as follows:

"(3) PUBLIC NOTICE AND COMMENT.—

"(A) IN GENERAL.—Prior to closing an air facility, the Secretary shall provide opportunities for public comment, including the convening of public meetings in communities in the area of responsibility of the air facility with regard to the proposed closure or cessation of operations at the air facility.

"(B) PUBLIC MEETINGS.—Prior to convening a public meeting under subparagraph (A), the Secretary shall notify each congressional office representing any portion of the area of responsibility of the air station that is the subject to such public meeting of the schedule and location of such public meeting."

(B) in paragraph (4)—

(i) in the matter preceding subparagraph (A) by striking "2015" and inserting "2017"; and

(ii) by amending subparagraph (A) to read as follows:

"(A) submit to the Congress a proposal for such closure, cessation, or reduction in operations along with the budget of the President submitted to Congress under section 1105(a) of title 31 that includes—

"(i) a discussion of the determination made by the Secretary pursuant to paragraph (2); and "(ii) a report summarizing the public comments received by the Secretary under paragraph (3)"

; and

(C) by adding at the end the following:

"(5) CONGRESSIONAL REVIEW.—The Secretary may not close, cease operations, or significantly reduce personnel and use of a Coast Guard air facility for which a written notice is provided under paragraph (4)(A) until a period of 18 months beginning on the date on which such notice is provided has elapsed."

TITLE IV—PORTS AND WATERWAYS SAFETY

SEC. 401. CODIFICATION OF PORTS AND WATERWAYS SAFETY ACT.

(a) CODIFICATION.—Subtitle VII of title 46, United States Code, is amended by inserting before chapter 701 the following:

"CHAPTER 700—PORTS AND WATERWAYS SAFETY

SUBCHAPTER "SUBCHAPTER I—VESSEL OPERATIONS

"SEC. § 70001. [46 U.S.C. 70001] Vessel traffic service

"(a) Subject to the requirements of section 70004, the Secretary—

"(1) in any port or place under the jurisdiction of the United States, in the navigable waters of the United States, or in any area covered by an international agreement negotiated pursuant to section 70005, may construct, operate, maintain, improve, or expand vessel traffic services, that consist of measures for controlling or supervising vessel traffic or for protecting navigation and the marine environment and that may include one or more of reporting and operating requirements, surveillance and communications systems, routing systems, and fairways;

"(2) shall require appropriate vessels that operate in an area of a vessel traffic service to utilize or comply with that service;

"(3)(A) may require vessels to install and use specified navigation equipment, communications equipment, electronic relative motion analyzer equipment, or any electronic or other device necessary to comply with a vessel traffic service or that is necessary in the interests of vessel safety.

"(B) Notwithstanding subparagraph (A), the Secretary shall not require fishing vessels under 300 gross tons as measured under section 14502, or an alternate tonnage measured under section 14302 as prescribed by the Secretary under section 14104, or recreational vessels 65 feet or less to possess or use the equipment or devices required by this subsection solely under the authority of this chapter;

"(4) may control vessel traffic in areas subject to the

jurisdiction of the United States that the Secretary determines to be hazardous, or under conditions of reduced visibility, adverse weather, vessel congestion, or other hazardous circumstances, by—

"(A) specifying times of entry, movement, or departure;

"(B) establishing vessel traffic routing schemes;

"(C) establishing vessel size, speed, or draft limitations and vessel operating conditions; and

"(D) restricting operation, in any hazardous area or under hazardous conditions, to vessels that have particular operating characteristics or capabilities that the Secretary considers necessary for safe operation under the circumstances;

"(5) may require the receipt of prearrival messages from any vessel, destined for a port or place subject to the jurisdiction of the United States, in sufficient time to permit advance vessel traffic planning before port entry, which shall include any information that is not already a matter of record and that the Secretary determines necessary for the control of the vessel and the safety of the port or the marine environment; and

"(6) may prohibit the use on vessels of electronic or other devices that interfere with communication and navigation equipment, except that such authority shall not apply to electronic or other devices certified to transmit in the maritime services by the Federal Communications Commission and used within the frequency bands 157.1875-157.4375 MHz and 161.7875-162.0375 MHz.

"(b) COOPERATIVE AGREEMENTS.—

"(1) IN GENERAL.—The Secretary may enter into cooperative agreements with public or private agencies, authorities, associations, institutions, corporations, organizations, or other persons to carry out the functions under subsection (a)(1).

"(2) LIMITATION.—

"(A) A nongovernmental entity may not under this subsection carry out an inherently governmental function.

"(B) As used in this paragraph, the term 'inherently governmental function' means any activity that is so intimately related to the public interest as to mandate performance by an officer or employee of the Federal Government, including an activity that requires either the exercise of discretion in applying the authority of the Government or the use of judgment in making a decision for the Government.

"(c) LIMITATION OF LIABILITY FOR COAST GUARD VESSEL TRAFFIC SERVICE PILOTS AND NON-FEDERAL VESSEL TRAFFIC SERVICE OPERATORS.—

"(1) COAST GUARD VESSEL TRAFFIC SERVICE PILOTS.—Any pilot, acting in the course and scope of his or her duties while at a Coast Guard Vessel Traffic Service, who provides information, advice, or communication assistance while under the supervision of a Coast Guard officer, member, or employee shall not be liable for damages caused by or related to such assistance unless the acts or omissions of such pilot constitute gross negligence or willful misconduct.

"(2) NON-FEDERAL VESSEL TRAFFIC SERVICE OPERATORS.—An entity operating a non-Federal vessel traffic information service or advisory service pursuant to a duly executed written agreement with the Coast Guard, and any pilot acting on behalf of such entity, is not liable for damages caused by or related to information, advice, or communication assistance provided by such entity or pilot while so operating or acting unless the acts or omissions of such entity or pilot constitute gross negligence or willful misconduct.

"SEC. § 70002. [46 U.S.C. 70002] Special power

"The Secretary may order any vessel, in a port or place subject to the jurisdiction of the United States or in the navigable waters of the United States, to operate or anchor in a manner the Secretary directs if—

"(1) the Secretary has reasonable cause to believe such vessel does not comply with any regulation issued under section 70034 or any other applicable law or treaty;

"(2) the Secretary determines such vessel does not satisfy the conditions for port entry set forth in section 70021 of this title; or

"(3) by reason of weather, visibility, sea conditions, port congestion, other hazardous circumstances, or the condition of such vessel, the Secretary is satisfied such direction is justified in the interest of safety.

"SEC. § 70003. [46 U.S.C. 70003] Port access route

"(a) AUTHORITY TO DESIGNATE.—Except as provided in subsection (b) and subject to the requirements of subsection (c), in order to provide safe access routes for the movement of vessel traffic proceeding to or from ports or places subject to the jurisdiction of the United States, the Secretary shall designate necessary fairways and traffic separation schemes for vessels operating in the territorial sea of the United States and in high seas approaches, outside the territorial sea, to such ports or places. Such a designation shall recognize, within the designated area, the paramount right of navigation over all other uses.

"(b) LIMITATION.—

"(1) IN GENERAL.—No designation may be made by the Secretary under this section if—

"(A) the Secretary determines such a designation, as implemented, would deprive any person of the effective exercise of a right granted by a lease or permit executed or issued under other applicable provisions of law; and

"(B) such right has become vested before the time of publication of the notice required by paragraph (1) of subsection (c).

"(2) CONSULTATION REQUIRED.—The Secretary shall make the determination under paragraph (1)(A) after consultation with the head of the agency responsible for executing the lease or issuing the permit.

"(c) CONSIDERATION OF OTHER USES.—Before making a designation under subsection (a), and in accordance with the requirements of section 70004, the Secretary shall—

"(1) undertake a study of the potential traffic density and the need for safe access routes for vessels in any area for which fairways or traffic separation schemes are proposed or that may otherwise be considered and publish notice of such undertaking in the Federal Register;

"(2) in consultation with the Secretary of State, the Secretary of the Interior, the Secretary of Commerce, the Secretary of the Army, and the Governors of affected States, as their responsibilities may require, take into account all other uses of the area under consideration, including, as appropriate, the exploration for, or exploitation of, oil, gas, or other mineral resources, the construction or operation of deepwater ports or other structures on or above the seabed or subsoil of the submerged lands or the Outer Continental Shelf of the United States, the establishment or operation of marine or estuarine sanctuaries, and activities involving recreational or commercial fishing; and

"(3) to the extent practicable, reconcile the need for safe access routes with the needs of all other reasonable uses of the area involved.

"(d) STUDY.—In carrying out the Secretary's responsibilities under subsection (c), the Secretary shall—

"(1) proceed expeditiously to complete any study undertaken; and

"(2) after completion of such a study, promptly—

"(A) issue a notice of proposed rulemaking for the designation contemplated; or

"(B) publish in the Federal Register a notice that no designation is contemplated as a result of the study and the reason for such determination.

"(e) IMPLEMENTATION OF DESIGNATION.—In connection with a designation made under this section, the Secretary—

"(1) shall issue reasonable rules and regulations governing the use of such designated areas, including rules and regulations regarding the applicability of rules 9 and 10 of the International Regulations for Preventing Collisions at Sea, 1972, relating to narrow channels and traffic separation schemes, respectively, in waters where such regulations apply;

"(2) to the extent that the Secretary finds reasonable and necessary to effectuate the purposes of the designation, make the use of designated fairways and traffic separation schemes mandatory for specific types and sizes of vessels, foreign and domestic, operating in the territorial sea of the United States and for specific types and sizes of vessels of the United States operating on the high seas beyond the territorial sea of the United States;

"(3) may, from time to time, as necessary, adjust the

location or limits of designated fairways or traffic separation schemes in order to accommodate the needs of other uses that cannot be reasonably accommodated otherwise, except that such an adjustment may not, in the judgment of the Secretary, unacceptably adversely affect the purpose for which the existing designation was made and the need for which continues; and

"(4) shall, through appropriate channels—

"(A) notify cognizant international organizations of any designation, or adjustment thereof; and

"(B) take action to seek the cooperation of foreign States in making it mandatory for vessels under their control to use, to the same extent as required by the Secretary for vessels of the United States, any fairway or traffic separation scheme designated under this section in any area of the high seas.

"SEC. § 70004. [46 U.S.C. 70004] Considerations by Secretar

"In carrying out the duties of the Secretary under sections 70001, 70002, and 70003, the Secretary shall—

"(1) take into account all relevant factors concerning navigation and vessel safety, protection of the marine environment, and the safety and security of United States ports and waterways, including—

"(A) the scope and degree of the risk or hazard involved;

"(B) vessel traffic characteristics and trends, including traffic volume, the sizes and types of vessels involved, potential interference with the flow of commercial traffic, the presence of any unusual cargoes, and other similar factors;

"(C) port and waterway configurations and variations in local conditions of geography, climate, and other similar factors;

"(D) the need for granting exemptions for the installation and use of equipment or devices for use with vessel traffic services for certain classes of small vessels, such as self-propelled fishing vessels and recreational vessels;

"(E) the proximity of fishing grounds, oil and gas drilling and production operations, or any other potential or actual conflicting activity;

"(F) environmental factors;

"(G) economic impact and effects;

"(H) existing vessel traffic services; and

"(I) local practices and customs, including voluntary arrangements and agreements within the maritime community; and

"(2) at the earliest possible time, consult with and receive and consider the views of representatives of the maritime community, ports and harbor authorities or associations, environmental groups, and other persons who may be affected by the proposed actions.

"SEC. § 70005. [46 U.S.C. 70005] International agreement

"(a) TRANSMITTAL OF REGULATIONS.—The Secretary shall transmit, via the Secretary of State, to appropriate international bodies or forums, any regulations issued under this subchapter, for consideration as international standards.

"(b) AGREEMENTS.—The President is authorized and encouraged to—

"(1) enter into negotiations and conclude and execute agreements with neighboring nations, to establish compatible vessel standards and vessel traffic services, and to establish, operate, and maintain international vessel traffic services, in areas and under circumstances of mutual concern; and

"(2) enter into negotiations, through appropriate international bodies, and conclude and execute agreements to establish vessel traffic services in appropriate areas of the high seas.

"(c) OPERATIONS.—The Secretary, pursuant to any agreement negotiated under subsection (b) that is binding upon the United States in accordance with constitutional requirements, may—

"(1) require vessels operating in an area of a vessel traffic service to utilize or to comply with the vessel traffic service, including the carrying or installation of equipment and devices as necessary for the use of the service; and

"(2) waive, by order or regulation, the application of any United States law or regulation concerning the design, construction, operation, equipment, personnel qualifications, and manning standards for vessels operating in waters over which the United States exercises jurisdiction if such vessel is not en route to or from a United States port or place, and if vessels en route to or from a United States port or place are accorded equivalent waivers of laws and regulations of the neighboring nation, when operating in waters over which that nation exercises jurisdiction.

"(d) SHIP REPORTING SYSTEMS.—The Secretary, in cooperation with the International Maritime Organization, may implement and enforce two mandatory ship reporting systems, consistent with international law, with respect to vessels subject to such reporting systems entering the following areas of the Atlantic Ocean:

"(1) Cape Cod Bay, Massachusetts Bay, and Great South Channel (in the area generally bounded by a line starting from a point on Cape Ann, Massachusetts at 42 deg. 39′ N., 70 deg. 37′ W; then northeast to 42 deg. 45′ N., 70 deg. 13′ W; then southeast to 42 deg. 10′ N., 68 deg. 31′ W, then south to 41 deg. 00′ N., 68 deg. 31′ W; then west to 41 deg. 00′ N., 69 deg. 17′ W; then northeast to 42 deg. 05′ N., 70 deg. 02′ W, then west to 42 deg. 04′ N., 70 deg. 10′ W; and then along the Massachusetts shoreline of Cape Cod Bay and Massachusetts Bay back to the point on Cape Ann at 42 deg. 39′ N., 70 deg. 37′ W).

"(2) In the coastal waters of the Southeastern United States within about 25 nm along a 90 nm stretch of the Atlantic seaboard (in an area generally extending from the shoreline east to longitude 80 deg. 51.6′ W with the southern and northern boundary at latitudes 30 deg. 00′ N., 31 deg. 27′ N., respectively).

SUBCHAPTER "SUBCHAPTER II—PORTS AND WATERWAYS SAFETY

"SEC. § 70011. [46 U.S.C. 70011] Waterfront safet

"(a) IN GENERAL.—The Secretary may take such action as is necessary to—

"(1) prevent damage to, or the destruction of, any bridge

or other structure on or in the navigable waters of the United States, or any land structure or shore area immediately adjacent to such waters; and

"(2) protect the navigable waters and the resources therein from harm resulting from vessel or structure damage, destruction, or loss.

"(b) ACTIONS AUTHORIZED.—Actions authorized by subsection (a) include—

"(1) establishing procedures, measures, and standards for the handling, loading, unloading, storage, stowage, and movement on a structure (including the emergency removal, control, and disposition) of explosives or other dangerous articles and substances, including oil or hazardous material as those terms are defined in section 2101;

"(2) prescribing minimum safety equipment requirements for a structure to assure adequate protection from fire, explosion, natural disaster, and other serious accidents or casualties;

"(3) establishing water or waterfront safety zones, or other measures, for limited, controlled, or conditional access and activity when necessary for the protection of any vessel, structure, waters, or shore area; and

"(4) establishing procedures for examination to assure compliance with the requirements prescribed under this section.

"(c) STATE LAW.—Nothing in this section, with respect to structures, prohibits a State or political subdivision thereof from prescribing higher safety equipment requirements or safety standards than those that may be prescribed by regulations under this section.

"SEC. § 70012. [46 U.S.C. 70012] Navigational hazard

"(a) REPORTING PROCEDURE.—The Secretary shall establish a program to encourage fishermen and other vessel operators to report potential or existing navigational hazards involving pipelines to the Secretary through Coast Guard field offices.

"(b) SECRETARY'S RESPONSE.—

"(1) NOTIFICATION BY THE OPERATOR OF A PIPELINE.—Upon notification by the operator of a pipeline of a hazard to navigation with respect to that pipeline, the Secretary shall immediately notify Coast Guard headquarters, the Pipeline and Hazardous Materials Safety Administration, other affected Federal and State agencies, and vessel owners and operators in the pipeline's vicinity.

"(2) NOTIFICATION BY OTHER PERSONS.—Upon notification by any other person of a hazard or potential hazard to navigation with respect to a pipeline, the Secretary shall promptly determine whether a hazard exists, and if so shall immediately notify Coast Guard headquarters, the Pipeline and Hazardous Materials Safety Administration, other affected Federal and State agencies, vessel owners and operators in the pipeline's vicinity, and the owner and operator of the pipeline.

"(c) PIPELINE DEFINED.—For purposes of this section, the term 'pipeline' has the meaning given the term 'pipeline facility' in section 60101(a)(18) of title 49.

"SEC. § 70013. [46 U.S.C. 70013] Requirement to notify Coast Guard of release of objects into the navigable waters of the United State

"(a) REQUIREMENT.—As soon as a person has knowledge of any release from a vessel or facility into the navigable waters of the United States of any object that creates an obstruction prohibited under section 10 of the Act of March 3, 1899, popularly known as the Rivers and Harbors Appropriations Act of 1899 (33 U.S.C. 403), such person shall notify the Secretary and the Secretary of the Army of such release.

"(b) RESTRICTION ON USE OF NOTIFICATION.—Any notification provided by an individual in accordance with subsection (a) may not be used against such individual in any criminal case, except a prosecution for perjury or for giving a false statement.

SUBCHAPTER "SUBCHAPTER III—CONDITION FOR ENTRY INTO PORTS IN THE UNITED STATES

"SEC. § 70021. [46 U.S.C. 70021] Conditions for entry to ports in the United State

"(a) IN GENERAL.—No vessel that is subject to chapter 37 shall operate in the navigable waters of the United States or transfer cargo or residue in any port or place under the jurisdiction of the United States, if such vessel—

"(1) has a history of accidents, pollution incidents, or serious repair problems that, as determined by the Secretary, creates reason to believe that such vessel may be unsafe or may create a threat to the marine environment;

"(2) fails to comply with any applicable regulation issued under section 70034, chapter 37, or any other applicable law or treaty;

"(3) discharges oil or hazardous material in violation of any law of the United States or in a manner or quantities inconsistent with any treaty to which the United States is a party;

"(4) does not comply with any applicable vessel traffic service requirements;

"(5) is manned by one or more officers who are licensed by a certificating State that the Secretary has determined, pursuant to section 9101 of title 46, does not have standards for licensing and certification of seafarers that are comparable to or more stringent than United States standards or international standards that are accepted by the United States;

"(6) is not manned in compliance with manning levels as determined by the Secretary to be necessary to insure the safe navigation of the vessel; or

"(7) while underway, does not have at least one licensed deck officer on the navigation bridge who is capable of clearly understanding English.

"(b) EXCEPTIONS.—

"(1) IN GENERAL.—The Secretary may allow provisional entry of a vessel that is not in compliance with subsection (a), if the owner or operator of such vessel proves, to the satisfaction of the Secretary, that such vessel is not unsafe or a threat to the marine environment, and if such entry is necessary for the safety of the vessel or persons aboard.

"(2) PROVISIONS NOT APPLICABLE.—Paragraphs (1), (2), (3), and (4) of subsection (a) of this section shall not apply to a vessel allowed provisional entry under paragraph (1) if the owner or operator of such vessel proves, to the satisfaction of the Secretary, that such vessel is no longer unsafe or a threat to the marine environment, and is no longer in violation of any applicable law, treaty, regulation, or condition, as appropriate.

SUBCHAPTER "SUBCHAPTER IV—DEFINITIONS, REGULATIONS, ENFORCEMENT, INVESTIGATORY POWERS, APPLICABILITY

"SEC. § 70031. [46 U.S.C. 70031] Definition

"As used in subchapters A through C and this subchapter, unless the context otherwise requires:

"(1) The term 'marine environment' means—

"(A) the navigable waters of the United States and the land and resources therein and thereunder;

"(B) the waters and fishery resources of any area over which the United States asserts exclusive fishery management authority;

"(C) the seabed and subsoil of the Outer Continental Shelf of the United States, the resources thereof, and the waters superjacent thereto; and

"(D) the recreational, economic, and scenic values of such waters and resources.

"(2) The term 'Secretary' means the Secretary of the department in which the Coast Guard is operating, except that such term means the Secretary of Transportation with respect to the application of this chapter to the Saint Lawrence Seaway.

"(3) The term 'navigable waters of the United States' includes all waters of the territorial sea of the United States as described in Presidential Proclamation No. 5928 of December 27, 1988.

"SEC. § 70032. [46 U.S.C. 70032] Saint Lawrence Seawa

"The authority granted to the Secretary under sections 70001, 70002, 70003, 70004, and 70011 may not be delegated with respect to the Saint Lawrence Seaway to any agency other than the Saint Lawrence Seaway Development Corporation. Any other authority granted the Secretary under subchapters A through C and this subchapter shall be delegated by the Secretary to the Saint Lawrence Seaway Development Corporation to the extent the Secretary determines such delegation is necessary for the proper operation of the Saint Lawrence Seaway.

"SEC. § 70033. [46 U.S.C. 70033] Limitation on application to foreign vessel

"Except pursuant to international treaty, convention, or agreement, to which the United States is a party, subchapters A through C and this subchapter shall not apply to any foreign vessel that is not destined for, or departing from, a port or place subject to the jurisdiction of the United States and that is in—

"(1) innocent passage through the territorial sea of the United States; or

"(2) transit through the navigable waters of the United States that form a part of an international strait.

"SEC. § 70034. [46 U.S.C. 70034] Regulation

"(a) IN GENERAL.—In accordance with section 553 of title 5, the Secretary shall issue, and may from time to time amend or repeal, regulations necessary to implement subchapters A through C and this subchapter.

"(b) CONSULTATION.—In the exercise of the regulatory authority under subchapters A through C and this subchapter, the Secretary shall consult with, and receive and consider the views of all interested persons, including—

"(1) interested Federal departments and agencies;

"(2) officials of State and local governments;

"(3) representatives of the maritime community;

"(4) representatives of port and harbor authorities or associations;

"(5) representatives of environmental groups;

"(6) any other interested persons who are knowledgeable or experienced in dealing with problems involving vessel safety, port and waterways safety, and protection of the marine environment; and

"(7) advisory committees consisting of all interested segments of the public when the establishment of such committees is considered necessary because the issues involved are highly complex or controversial.

"SEC. § 70035. [46 U.S.C. 70035] Investigatory power

"(a) SECRETARY.—The Secretary may investigate any incident, accident, or act involving the loss or destruction of, or damage to, any structure subject to subchapters A through C and this subchapter, or that affects or may affect the safety or environmental quality of the ports, harbors, or navigable waters of the United States.

"(b) POWERS.—In an investigation under this section, the Secretary may issue subpoenas to require the attendance of witnesses and the production of documents or other evidence relating to such incident, accident, or act. If any person refuses to obey a subpoena, the Secretary may request the Attorney General to invoke the aid of the appropriate district court of the United States to compel compliance with the subpoena. Any district court of the United States may, in the case of refusal to obey a subpoena, issue an order requiring compliance with the subpoena, and failure to obey the order may be punished by the court as contempt. Witnesses may be paid fees for travel and attendance at rates not exceeding those allowed in a district court of the United States.

"SEC. § 70036. [46 U.S.C. 70036] Enforcemen

"(a) CIVIL PENALTY.—

"(1) IN GENERAL.—Any person who is found by the Secretary, after notice and an opportunity for a hearing, to have violated subchapters A through C or this subchapter or a regulation issued under subchapters A through C or this subchapter shall be liable to the United States for a civil penalty, not to exceed $25,000 for each violation. Each day of a continuing violation shall constitute a separate violation. The amount of such civil penalty shall be assessed by the Secretary, or the Secretary's designee, by written notice. In determining the amount of such penalty, the Secretary shall take into account the nature, circumstances, extent, and gravity of the prohibited acts committed and, with respect to the violator, the degree of culpability, any history of prior offenses, ability to pay, and such other matters as justice may require.

"(2) COMPROMISE, MODIFICATION, OR REMISSION.—The Secretary may compromise, modify, or remit, with or without conditions, any civil penalty that is subject to imposition or that has been imposed under this section.

"(3) FAILURE TO PAY PENALTY.—If any person fails to pay

an assessment of a civil penalty after it has become final, the Secretary may refer the matter to the Attorney General of the United States, for collection in any appropriate district court of the United States.

"(b) CRIMINAL PENALTY.—

"(1) CLASS D FELONY.—Any person who willfully and knowingly violates subchapters A through C or this subchapter or any regulation issued thereunder commits a class D felony.

"(2) CLASS C FELONY.—Any person who, in the willful and knowing violation of subchapters A through C or this subchapter or of any regulation issued thereunder, uses a dangerous weapon, or engages in conduct that causes bodily injury or fear of imminent bodily injury to any officer authorized to enforce the provisions of such a subchapter or the regulations issued under such subchapter, commits a class C felony.

"(c) IN REM LIABILITY.—Any vessel that is used in violation of subchapters A, B, or C or this subchapter, or any regulations issued under such subchapter, shall be liable in rem for any civil penalty assessed pursuant to subsection (a) and may be proceeded against in the United States district court for any district in which such vessel may be found.

"(d) INJUNCTION.—The United States district courts shall have jurisdiction to restrain violations of subchapter A, B, or C or this subchapter or of regulations issued under such subchapter, for cause shown.

"(e) DENIAL OF ENTRY.—Except as provided in section 70021, the Secretary may, subject to recognized principles of international law, deny entry by any vessel that is not in compliance with subchapter A, B, or C or this subchapter or the regulations issued under such subchapter—

"(1) into the navigable waters of the United States; or

"(2) to any port or place under the jurisdiction of the United States.

"(f) WITHHOLDING OF CLEARANCE.—

"(1) IN GENERAL.—If any owner, operator, or individual in charge of a vessel is liable for a penalty or fine under this section, or if reasonable cause exists to believe that the owner, operator, or individual in charge may be subject to a penalty or fine under this section, the Secretary of the Treasury, upon the request of the Secretary, shall with respect to such vessel refuse or revoke any clearance required by section 60105 of title 46.

"(2) GRANTING CLEARANCE REFUSED OR REVOKED.—Clearance refused or revoked under this subsection may be granted upon filing of a bond or other surety satisfactory to the Secretary."

(b) [46 U.S.C. 70001] CLERICAL AMENDMENT.—The analysis at the beginning of such subtitleis amended by inserting before the item relating to chapter 701 the following:

"700. Ports and Waterways Safety"

SEC. 402. CONFORMING AMENDMENTS.

(a) ELECTRONIC CHARTS.—

(1) TRANSFER OF PROVISION.—Section 4A of the Ports and Waterways Safety Act (33 U.S.C. 1223a)—

(A) is redesignated as section 3105 of title 46, United States Code, and transferred to appear after section 3104 of that title; and

(B) is amended by striking subsection (b) and inserting the following:

"(b) LIMITATION ON APPLICATION.—Except pursuant to an international treaty, convention, or agreement, to which the United States is a party, this section shall not apply to any foreign vessel that is not destined for, or departing from, a port or place subject to the jurisdiction of the United States and that is in—

"(1) innocent passage through the territorial sea of the United States; or

"(2) transit through the navigable waters of the United States that form a part of an international strait."

(2) [46 U.S.C. 3101] CLERICAL AMENDMENT.—The analysis at the beginning of chapter 31 of such titleis amended by adding at the end the following:

"3105. Electronic charts."

(b) PORT, HARBOR, AND COASTAL FACILITY SECURITY.—

(1) TRANSFER OF PROVISIONS.—So much of section 7 of the Ports and Waterways Safety Act (33 U.S.C. 1226) as precedes subsection (c) of that section is redesignated as section 70116 of title 46, United States Code, and transferred to section 70116 of that title.

(2) DEFINITIONS, ADMINISTRATION, AND ENFORCEMENT.—Section 70116 of title 46, United States Code, as amended by paragraph (1) of this subsection, is amended by adding at the end the following:

"(c) DEFINITIONS, ADMINISTRATION, AND ENFORCEMENT.—This section shall be treated as part of chapter 700 for purposes of sections 70031, 70032, 70034, 70035, and 70036."

(3) [46 U.S.C. 70101] CLERICAL AMENDMENT.—The analysis at the beginning of chapter 701 of such titleis amended by striking the item relating to section 70116 and inserting the following:

"70116. Port, harbor, and coastal facility security."

(c) NONDISCLOSURE OF PORT SECURITY PLANS.—Subsection (c) of section 7 of the Ports and Waterways Safety Act (33 U.S.C. 1226), as so designated before the application of subsection (b)(1) of this section—

(1) is redesignated as subsection (f) of section 70103 of title 46, United States Code, and transferred so as to appear after subsection (e) of such section; and

(2) is amended by striking "this Act" and inserting "this chapter".

(d) [46 U.S.C. 2301] REPEAL.—Section 2307 of title 46, United States Code, and the item relating to that section in the analysis at the beginning of chapter 23 of that title, are repealed.

(e) REPEAL.—The Ports and Waterways Safety Act (33 U.S.C. 1221-1231, 1232-1232b), as amended by this Act, is repealed.

SEC. 403. [46 U.S.C. 101 note] TRANSITIONAL AND SAVINGS PROVISIONS.

(a) DEFINITIONS.—In this section:

(1) SOURCE PROVISION.—The term "source provision" means a provision of law that is replaced by a title 46 provision

under this title.

(2) TITLE 46 PROVISION.—The term “title 46 provision” means a provision of title 46, United States Code, that is enacted by section 402.

(b) CUTOFF DATE.—The title 46 provisions replace certain provisions of law enacted before the date of the enactment of this Act. If a law enacted after that date amends or repeals a source provision, that law is deemed to amend or repeal, as the case may be, the corresponding title 46 provision. If a law enacted after that date is otherwise inconsistent with a title 46 provision or a provision of this title, that law supersedes the title 46 provision or provision of this title to the extent of the inconsistency.

(c) ORIGINAL DATE OF ENACTMENT UNCHANGED.—For purposes of determining whether one provision of law supersedes another based on enactment later in time, a title 46 provision is deemed to have been enacted on the date of enactment of the source provision that the title 46 provision replaces.

(d) REFERENCES TO TITLE 46 PROVISIONS.—A reference to a title 46 provision, including a reference in a regulation, order, or other law, is deemed to refer to the corresponding source provision.

(e) REFERENCES TO SOURCE PROVISIONS.—A reference to a source provision, including a reference in a regulation, order, or other law, is deemed to refer to the corresponding title 46 provision.

(f) REGULATIONS, ORDERS, AND OTHER ADMINISTRATIVE ACTIONS.—A regulation, order, or other administrative action in effect under a source provision continues in effect under the corresponding title 46 provision.

(g) ACTIONS TAKEN AND OFFENSES COMMITTED.—An action taken or an offense committed under a source provision is deemed to have been taken or committed under the corresponding title 46 provision.

SEC. 404. [46 U.S.C. 101 note] RULE OF CONSTRUCTION.

This title, including the amendments made by this title, is intended only to transfer provisions of the Ports and Waterways Safety Act to title 46, United States Code, and may not be construed to alter—

(1) the effect of a provision of the Ports and Waterways Safety Act, including any authority or requirement therein;

(2) a department or agency interpretation with respect to the Ports and Waterways Safety Act; or

(3) a judicial interpretation with respect to the Ports and Waterways Safety Act.

SEC. 405. ADVISORY COMMITTEE: REPEAL.

Section 18 of the Coast Guard Authorization Act of 1991 (Public Law 102-241; 105 Stat. 2213) is repealed.

SEC. 406. REGATTAS AND MARINE PARADES.

(a) IN GENERAL.—Chapter 700 of title 46, United States Code, as established by section 401 of this Act, is amended by adding at the end the following:

SUBCHAPTER "SUBCHAPTER V—REGATTAS AND MARINE PARADES

"SEC. § 70041. [46 U.S.C. 70041] Regattas and marine parade

"(a) IN GENERAL.—The Commandant of the Coast Guard may issue regulations to promote the safety of life on navigable waters during regattas or marine parades.

"(b) DETAIL AND USE OF VESSELS.—To enforce regulations issued under this section—

"(1) the Commandant may detail any public vessel in the service of the Coast Guard and make use of any private vessel tendered gratuitously for that purpose; and

"(2) upon the request of the Commandant, the head of any other Federal department or agency may enforce the regulations by means of any public vessel of such department and any private vessel tendered gratuitously for that purpose.

"(c) TRANSFER OF AUTHORITY.—The authority of the Commandant under this section may be transferred by the President for any special occasion to the head of another Federal department or agency whenever in the President's judgment such transfer is desirable.

"(d) PENALTIES.—

"(1) IN GENERAL.—For any violation of regulations issued pursuant to this section the following penalties shall be incurred:

"(A) A licensed officer shall be liable to suspension or revocation of license in the manner prescribed by law for incompetency or misconduct.

"(B) Any person in charge of the navigation of a vessel other than a licensed officer shall be liable to a penalty of $5,000.

"(C) The owner of a vessel (including any corporate officer of a corporation owning the vessel) actually on board shall be liable to a penalty of $5,000, unless the violation of regulations occurred without the owner's knowledge.

"(D) Any other person shall be liable to a penalty of $2,500.

"(2) MITIGATION OR REMISSION.—The Commandant may mitigate or remit any penalty provided for in this subsection in the manner prescribed by law for the mitigation or remission of penalties for violation of the navigation laws."

(b) [46 U.S.C. 700001] CLERICAL AMENDMENT.—The analysis for chapter 700 of title 46, United States Code, as established by section 401 of this Act,is amended by adding at the end the following:

"subchapter e— regattas and marine parades

"70041. Regattas and marine parades."

(c) REPEAL.—The Act of April 28, 1908 (35 Stat. 69, chapter 151; 33 U.S.C. 1233 et seq.), is repealed.

SEC. 407. REGULATION OF VESSELS IN TERRITORIAL WATERS OF UNITED STATES.

(a) ESTABLISHMENT OF SUBCHAPTER F.—Chapter 700 of title 46, United States Code, as established by section 401 of this Act, is amended by adding at the end the following:

SUBCHAPTER "SUBCHAPTER VI—REGULATION OF VESSELS IN TERRITORIAL WATERS OF UNITED STATES

"SEC. § 70054. [46 U.S.C. 70054] Definition

"In this subchapter:

"(1) UNITED STATES.—The term 'United States' includes all territory and waters, continental or insular, subject to the jurisdiction of the United States.

"(2) TERRITORIAL WATERS.—The term 'territorial waters of the United States' includes all waters of the territorial sea of the United States as described in Presidential Proclamation 5928 of December 27, 1988."

(b) REGULATION OF ANCHORAGE AND MOVEMENT OF VESSELS DURING NATIONAL EMERGENCY.—Section 1 of title II of the Act of June 15, 1917 (40 Stat. 220, chapter 30; 50 U.S.C. 191), is amended—

(1) by striking the section designation and all that follows before "by proclamation" and inserting the following:

"SEC. § 70051. [46 U.S.C. 70051] Regulation of anchorage and movement of vessels during national emergenc

"Whenever the President"

(2) by striking "of the Treasury";

(3) by striking "of the department in which the Coast Guard is operating";

(4) by striking "this title" and inserting "this subchapter"; and

(5) by transferring the section so that the section appears before section 70054 of title 46, United States Code (as added by subsection (a) of this section).

(c) SEIZURE AND FORFEITURE OF VESSEL; FINE AND IMPRISONMENT.—Section 2 of title II of the Act of June 15, 1917 (40 Stat. 220, chapter 30; 50 U.S.C. 192), is amended—

(1) by striking the section designation and all that follows before "agent," and inserting the following:

"SEC. § 70052. [46 U.S.C. 70052] Seizure and forfeiture of vessel; fine and imprisonmen

"(a) IN GENERAL.—If any owner,"

(2) by striking "this title" each place it appears and inserting "this subchapter"; and

(3) by transferring the section so that the section appears after section 70051 of title 46, United States Code (as transferred by subsection (b) of this section).

(d) ENFORCEMENT PROVISIONS.—Section 4 of title II of the Act of June 15, 1917 (40 Stat. 220, chapter 30; 50 U.S.C. 194), is amended—

(1) by striking all before "may employ" and inserting the following:

"SEC. § 70053. [46 U.S.C. 70053] Enforcement provision

"The President"

(2) by striking "the purpose of this title" and inserting "this subchapter"; and

(3) by transferring the section so that the section appears after section 70052 of title 46, United States Code (as transferred by subsection (c) of this section).

(e) [46 U.S.C. 70001] CLERICAL AMENDMENT.—The analysis for chapter 700 of title 46, United States Code, as established by section 401 of this Act, is amended by adding at the end the following:

" subchapter f— regulation of vessels in territorial waters of united states

"70051.	Regulation of anchorage and movement of vessels during national emergency.
"70052.	Seizure and forfeiture of vessel; fine and imprisonment.
"70053.	Enforcement provisions.
"70054.	Definitions."

TITLE V—MARITIME TRANSPORTATION SAFETY

SEC. 501. CONSISTENCY IN MARINE INSPECTIONS.

(a) IN GENERAL.—Section 3305 of title 46, United States Code, is amended by adding at the end the following:

"(d)(1) The Commandant of the Coast Guard shall ensure that Officers in Charge, Marine Inspections consistently interpret regulations and standards under this subtitle and chapter 700 to avoid disruption and undue expense to industry.

"(2)(A) Subject to subparagraph (B), in the event of a disagreement regarding the condition of a vessel or the interpretation of a regulation or standard referred to in subsection (a) between a local Officer in Charge, Marine Inspection conducting an inspection of the vessel and the Officer in Charge, Marine Inspection that issued the most recent certificate of inspection for the vessel, such Officers shall seek to resolve such disagreement.

"(B) If a disagreement described in subparagraph (A) involves vessel design or plan review, the Coast Guard marine safety center shall be included in all efforts to resolve such disagreement.

"(C) If a disagreement described in subparagraph (A) or (B) cannot be resolved, the local Officer in Charge, Marine Inspection shall submit to the Commandant of the Coast Guard, through the cognizant Coast Guard district commander, a request for a final agency determination of the matter in disagreement.

"(3) The Commandant of the Coast Guard shall—

"(A) provide to each person affected by a decision or action by an Officer in Charge, Marine Inspection or by the Coast Guard marine safety center all information necessary for such person to exercise any right to appeal such decision or action; and

"(B) if such an appeal is filed, process such appeal under parts 1 through 4 of title 46, Code of Federal Regulations, as in effect on the date of enactment of the Coast Guard Authorization Act of 2017.

"(4) In this section, the term 'Officer in Charge, Marine Inspection' means any person from the civilian or military branch of the Coast Guard who—

"(A) is designated as such by the Commandant; and

"(B) under the superintendence and direction of the cognizant Coast Guard district commander, is in charge of an inspection zone for the performance of duties with respect to the inspections under, and enforcement and administration of, subtitle II, chapter 700, and regulations under such laws."

(b) REPORT ON MARINE INSPECTOR TRAINING.—Not later than 1 year after the date of the enactment of this Act, the Commandant of the Coast Guard shall submit to the Committee on Commerce, Science, and Transportation of the Senate and the Committee on Transportation and Infrastructure of the House of Representatives a report on the training, experience, and qualifications required for assignment as a marine inspector under section 312 of title 14,

United States Code, including—

(1) a description of any continuing education requirement, including a specific list of the required courses;

(2) a description of the training, including a specific list of the included courses, offered to a journeyman or an advanced journeyman marine inspector to advance inspection expertise;

(3) a description of any training that was offered in the 15-year period before the date of the enactment of this Act, but is no longer required or offered, including a specific list of the included courses, including the senior marine inspector course and any plan review courses;

(4) a justification for why a course described in paragraph (3) is no longer required or offered; and

(5) a list of the course content the Commandant considers necessary to promote consistency among marine inspectors in an environment of increasingly complex vessels and vessel systems.

SEC. 502. UNINSPECTED PASSENGER VESSELS IN ST. LOUIS COUNTY, MINNESOTA.

Section 4105 of title 46, United States Code, amended—

(1) by redesignating subsection (c) as subsection (d); and

(2) by inserting after subsection (b) the following:

"(c) In applying this title with respect to an uninspected vessel of less than 25 feet overall in length that carries passengers on Crane Lake or waters contiguous to such lake in St. Louis County, Minnesota, the Secretary shall substitute '12 passengers' for '6 passengers' each place it appears in section 2101(51)."

SEC. 503. ENGINE CUT-OFF SWITCH REQUIREMENTS.

(a) IN GENERAL.—Chapter 43 of title 46, United States Code, is amended by adding at the end the following:

"SEC. §4312. [46 U.S.C. 4312] Engine cut-off switche

"(a) INSTALLATION REQUIREMENT.—A manufacturer, distributor, or dealer that installs propulsion machinery and associated starting controls on a covered recreational vessel shall equip such vessel with an engine cut-off switch and engine cut-off switch link that meet American Boat and Yacht Council Standard

A-33, as in effect on the date of the enactment of the Coast Guard Authorization Act of 2017.

"(b) EDUCATION ON CUT-OFF SWITCHES.—The Commandant of the Coast Guard, through the National Boating Safety Advisory Committee established under section 15105, may initiate a boating safety program on the use and benefits of cut-off switches for recreational vessels.

"(c) AVAILABILITY OF STANDARD FOR INSPECTION.—

"(1) IN GENERAL.—Not later than 90 days after the date of the enactment of this section, the Commandant shall transmit American Boat and Yacht Council Standard A-33, as in effect on the date of enactment of the Coast Guard Authorization Act of 2017, to—

"(A) the Committee on Transportation and Infrastructure of the House of Representatives;

"(B) the Committee on Commerce, Science, and Transportation of the Senate; and

"(C) the Coast Guard Office of Design and Engineering Standards; and

"(D) the National Archives and Records Administration.

"(2) AVAILABILITY.—The standard submitted under paragraph (1) shall be kept on file and available for public inspection at such Coast Guard office and the National Archives and Records Administration.

"(d) DEFINITIONS.—In this section:

"(1) COVERED RECREATIONAL VESSEL.—The term 'covered recreational vessel' means a recreational vessel that is—

"(A) less than 26 feet overall in length; and

"(B) capable of developing 115 pounds or more of static thrust.

"(2) DEALER.—The term 'dealer' means any person who is engaged in the sale and distribution of recreational vessels or associated equipment to purchasers whom the seller in good faith believes to be purchasing any such vessel or associated equipment for purposes other than resale.

"(3) DISTRIBUTOR.—The term 'distributor' means any person engaged in the sale and distribution of recreational vessels and associated equipment for the purposes of resale.

"(4) MANUFACTURER.—The term 'equipment manufacturer' means any person engaged in the manufacture, construction, or assembly of recreational vessels or associated equipment, or the importation of recreational vessels into the United States for subsequent sale.

"(5) PROPULSION MACHINERY.—The term 'propulsion machinery' means a self-contained propulsion system, and includes, but is not limited to, inboard engines, outboard motors, and sterndrive engines.

"(6) STATIC THRUST.—The term 'static thrust' means the forward or backwards thrust developed by propulsion machinery while stationary."

(b) **[46 U.S.C. 4301]** CLERICAL AMENDMENT.—The analysis at the beginning of such chapter is amended by adding at the end the following:

"4312. Engine cut-off switches."

(c) **[46 U.S.C. 4312 note]** EFFECTIVE DATE.—Section 4312 of title 46, United States Code, as amended by this section, shall take effect one year after the date of the enactment of this Act.

SEC. 504. EXCEPTION FROM SURVIVAL CRAFT REQUIREMENTS.

Section 4502(b) of title 46, United States Code, is amended—

(1) in paragraph (2)(B), by striking "a survival craft" and inserting "subject to paragraph (3), a survival craft";

(2) by adding at the end the following:

"(3) Except for a nonapplicable vessel, an auxiliary craft shall satisfy the equipment requirement under paragraph (2)(B) if such craft is—

"(A) necessary for normal fishing operations;

"(B) readily accessible during an emergency; and

"(C) capable, in accordance with the Coast Guard capacity rating, when applicable, of safely holding all individuals on board the vessel to which the craft functions as an auxiliary."

; and

(3) by adding at the end the following:

"(k) For the purposes of this section, the term 'auxiliary craft' means a vessel that is carried onboard a fishing vessel and is normally used to support fishing operations."

SEC. 505. SAFETY STANDARDS.

Section 4502(f) of title 46, United States Code, is amended by striking paragraphs (2) and (3) and inserting the following:

"(2) shall examine at dockside a vessel described in subsection (b) at least once every 5 years, but may require an exam at dockside every 2 years for certain vessels described in subsection (b) if requested by the owner or operator; and

"(3) shall issue a certificate of compliance to a vessel meeting the requirements of this chapter and satisfying the requirements in paragraph (2)."

SEC. 506. FISHING SAFETY GRANTS.

Section 4502 of title 46, United States Code, is amended—

(1) in subsections (i) and (j), by striking "Secretary" each place it appears and inserting "Secretary of Health and Human Services";

(2) in subsection (i)(2), as amended by paragraph (1), by inserting ", in consultation with and based on criteria established by the Commandant of the Coast Guard" after "Health and Human Services";

(3) in subsection (i)(3), by striking "75" and inserting "50";

(4) in subsection (i)(4), by striking "$3,000,000 for each of fiscal years 2015 through 2017" and inserting "$3,000,000 for each of fiscal years 2018 through 2019";

(5) in subsection (j)(2), as amended by paragraph (1), by inserting ", in consultation with and based on criteria established by the Commandant of the Coast Guard," after "Health and Human Services";

(6) in subsection (j)(3), by striking "75" and inserting "50"; and

(7) in subsection (j)(4), by striking "$3,000,000 for each fiscal years 2015 through 2017" and inserting "$3,000,000 for each of fiscal years 2018 through 2019".

SEC. 507. FISHING, FISH TENDER, AND FISH PROCESSING VESSEL

CERTIFICATION.

(a) NONAPPLICATION.—Section 4503(c)(2)(A) of title 46, United States Code, is amended by striking “79” and inserting “180”.

(b) DETERMINING WHEN KEEL IS LAID.—Section 4503(f) of title 46, United States Code, as redesignated by section 508 of this Act, is further amended to read as follows:

“(f)(1) For purposes of this section and section 4503a, the term ‘built’ means, with respect to a vessel, that the vessel’s construction has reached any of the following stages:

“(A) The vessel’s keel is laid.

“(B) Construction identifiable with the vessel has begun and assembly of that vessel has commenced comprising of at least 50 metric tons or one percent of the estimated mass of all structural material, whichever is less.

“(2) In the case of a vessel greater than 79 feet overall in length, for purposes of paragraph (1)(A) a keel is deemed to be laid when a marine surveyor affirms that a structure adequate for serving as a keel for such vessel is in place and identified for use in the construction of such vessel.”

SEC. 508. DEADLINE FOR COMPLIANCE WITH ALTERNATE SAFETY COMPLIANCE PROGRAM.

(a) [46 U.S.C. 4503a] IN GENERAL.—Section 4503(d) of title 46, United States Code, is redesignated as section 4503a and transferred to appear after section 4503 of such title.

(b) FISHING, FISH TENDER, AND FISH PROCESSING VESSEL CERTIFICATION.—Section 4503 of title 46, United States Code, is amended—

(1) by redesignating subsections (e), (f), and (g) as subsections (d), (e), and (f), respectively;

(2) in subsection (b), by striking “subsection (d)” and inserting “section 4503a”;

(3) in subsection (c)(2)(B)(ii)(I), by striking “subsection (e)” and inserting “subsection (d)”;

(4) in subsection (c)(2)(B)(ii)(II), by striking “subsection (f)” and inserting “subsection (e)”;

(5) in subsection (e)(1), as amended by paragraph (1) of this subsection, by striking “subsection (e)” each place it appears

and inserting "subsection (d)"; and

(6) in subsection (e)(2), as amended by paragraph (1) of this subsection, by striking "subsection (e)" each place it appears and inserting "subsection (d)";

(c) ALTERNATE SAFETY COMPLIANCE PROGRAM.—Section 4503a of title 46, United States Code, as redesignated and transferred by subsection (a) of this section, is amended—

(1) by redesignating paragraphs (1), (2), (3), (4), and (5) as subsections (a), (b), (c), (d), and (e), respectively;

(2) by inserting before subsection (a), as so redesignated, the following:

"SEC. § 4503a. Alternate safety compliance program"

(3) in subsection (a), as redesignated by paragraph (1) of this subsection, by striking "After January 1, 2020," and all that follows through "the Secretary, if" and inserting "Subject to subsection (c), beginning on the date that is 3 years after the date that the Secretary prescribes an alternate safety compliance program, a fishing vessel, fish processing vessel, or fish tender vessel to which section 4502(b) of this title applies shall comply with such an alternate safety compliance program, if";

(4) in subsection (a), as so redesignated, by redesignating subparagraphs (A), (B), and (C) as paragraphs (1), (2), and (3), respectively;

(5) in subsection (b), as so redesignated, by striking "establishes standards for an alternate safety compliance program, shall comply with such an alternative safety compliance program that is developed in cooperation with the commercial fishing industry and prescribed by the Secretary" and inserting "prescribes an alternate safety compliance program under subsection (a), shall comply with such an alternate safety compliance program";

(6) by amending subsection (c), as so redesignated, to read as follows:

"(c) For purposes of subsection (a), a separate alternate safety compliance program may be developed for a specific region or specific fishery."

(7) in subsection (d), as so redesignated—

(A) by striking "paragraph (1)" and inserting "subsection (a)"; and

(B) by striking "that paragraph" each place it appears and inserting "that subsection";

(8) in subsection (e), as so redesignated, by—

(A) inserting "is not eligible to participate in an alternative safety compliance program prescribed under subsection (a) and" after "July 1, 2012"; and

(B) redesignating subparagraphs (A) and (B) as paragraphs (1) and (2), respectively;

(9) by adding at the end the following:

"(f) For the purposes of this section, the term 'built' has the meaning given that term in section 4503(f)."

(d) [46 U.S.C. 4501] CLERICAL AMENDMENT.—The analysis at the beginning of chapter 45 of such titleis amended by inserting after the item relating to section 4503 the following

"4503a. Alternate safety compliance program."

(e) CONFORMING AMENDMENT.—Section 3104 of title 46, United States Code, is amended by striking "section 4503(e)" and inserting "section 4503(d)".

(f) [46 U.S.C. 4503 note] FINAL RULE.—Not later than 1 year after the date of enactment of this Act, the Secretary of the department in which the Coast Guard is operating shall issue a final rule implementing the requirements enumerated in section 4503(d) of title 46, as amended by subsection (b)(1) of this section.

(g) ALTERNATE SAFETY COMPLIANCE PROGRAM STATUS REPORT.—

(1) IN GENERAL.—Not later than January 1, 2020, the Secretary of the department in which the Coast Guard is operating shall submit to the Committee on Transportation and Infrastructure of the House of Representatives and the Committee on Commerce, Science, and Transportation of the Senate a report on the status of the development of the alternate safety compliance program directed by section 4503a of title 46, United States Code, as redesignated by subsection (c).

(2) CONTENTS.—The report required under paragraph (1)

shall include discussion of—

(A) steps taken in the rulemaking process to establish the alternate safety compliance program;

(B) communication and collaboration between the Coast Guard, the department in which the Coast Guard is operating, and the commercial fishing vessel industry regarding the development of the alternate safety compliance program;

(C) consideration given to developing alternate safety compliance programs for specific regions and fisheries, as authorized in section 4503a(c) of such title, as redesignated by subsection (c);

(D) any identified legislative changes necessary to implement an effective alternate safety compliance program; and

(E) the timeline and planned actions that will be taken to implement regulations necessary to fully establish an alternate safety compliance program before January 1, 2020.

SEC. 509. TERMINATION OF UNSAFE OPERATIONS; TECHNICAL CORRECTION.

Section 4505(2) of title 46, United States Code, is amended—

(1) by striking "4503(1)" and inserting "4503(a)(2)"; and

(2) by inserting before the period the following: ", except that this paragraph shall not apply with respect to a vessel to which section 4503a applies".

SEC. 510. TECHNICAL CORRECTIONS: LICENSES, CERTIFICATES OF REGISTRY, AND MERCHANT MARINER DOCUMENTS.

Title 46, United States Code, is amended—

(1) in section 7106(b), by striking "merchant mariner's document," and inserting "license,";

(2) in section 7107(b), by striking "merchant mariner's document," and inserting "certificate of registry,";

(3) in section 7507(b)(1), by striking "licenses or certificates of registry" and inserting "merchant mariner documents"; and

(4) in section 7507(b)(2) by striking "merchant mariner's document." and inserting "license or certificate of registry.".

SEC. 511. CLARIFICATION OF LOGBOOK ENTRIES.

(a) IN GENERAL.—Section 11304 of title 46, United States Code, is amended—

(1) in subsection (a), by striking "an official logbook, which" and inserting "a logbook, which may be in any form, including electronic, and"; and

(2) in subsection (b), by amending paragraph (3) to read as follows:

"(3) Each illness of, and injury to, a seaman of the vessel, the nature of the illness or injury, and the medical treatment provided for the injury or illness."

(b) TECHNICAL AMENDMENT.—Section 11304(b) is amended by striking "log book" and inserting "logbook".

SEC. 512. CERTIFICATES OF DOCUMENTATION FOR RECREATIONAL VESSELS.

Section 12105 of title 46, United States Code, is amended by adding at the end the following:

"(e) EFFECTIVE PERIOD.—

"(1) IN GENERAL.—Except as provided in paragraphs (2) and (3), a certificate of documentation issued under this part is valid for a 1-year period and may be renewed for additional 1-year periods.

"(2) RECREATIONAL VESSELS.—

"(A) IN GENERAL.—A certificate of documentation for a recreational vessel and the renewal of such a certificate shall be effective for a 5-year period.

"(B) PHASE-IN PERIOD.—During the period beginning January 1, 2019, and ending December 31, 2021, the owner or operator of a recreational vessel may choose a period of effectiveness of between 1 and 5 years for such a certificate of documentation for such vessel or the renewal thereof.

"(C) FEES.—

"(i) REQUIREMENT.—The Secretary shall assess and collect a fee—

"(I) for the issuance of a certificate of documentation for a recreational vessel that is equivalent to the fee established for the issuance of a certificate of documentation under section 2110; and

"(II) for the renewal of a certificate of documentation for a recreational vessel that is equivalent to the number of years of effectiveness of the certificate of documentation multiplied by the fee established for the renewal of a certificate of documentation under section 2110.

"(ii) TREATMENT.—Fees collected under this subsection—

"(I) shall be credited to the account from which the costs of such issuance or renewal were paid; and

"(II) may remain available until expended.

"(3) NOTICE OF CHANGE IN INFORMATION.—

"(A) REQUIREMENT.—The owner of a vessel shall notify the Coast Guard of each change in the information on which the issuance of the certificate of documentation for the vessel is based that occurs before the expiration of the certificate under this subsection, by not later than 30 days after such change.

"(B) TERMINATION OF CERTIFICATE.—The certificate of documentation for a vessel shall terminate upon the expiration of such 30-day period if the owner has not notified the Coast Guard of such change before the end of such period.

"(4) STATE AND LOCAL AUTHORITY TO REMOVE ABANDONED AND DERELICT VESSELS.—Nothing in this section shall be construed to limit the authority of a State or local authority from taking action to remove an abandoned or derelict vessel."

SEC. 513. NUMBERING FOR UNDOCUMENTED BARGES.

Section 12301(b) of title 46, United States Code, is amended—

(1) by striking "shall" and inserting "may"; and

(2) by inserting "of" after "barge".

SEC. 514. BACKUP NATIONAL TIMING SYSTEM.

(a) [49 U.S.C. 101 note] SHORT TITLE.—This section may be cited as the "National Timing Resilience and Security Act of 2018".

(b) IN GENERAL.—Chapter 3 of title 49, United States Code, is amended by adding at the end the following:

"SEC. § 312. [49 U.S.C. 312] Alternative timing syste

"(a) IN GENERAL.—Subject to the availability of appropriations, the Secretary of Transportation shall provide for the establishment, sustainment, and operation of a land-based, resilient, and reliable alternative timing system—

"(1) to reduce critical dependencies and provide a complement to and backup for the timing component of the Global Positioning System (referred to in this section as 'GPS'); and

"(2) to ensure the availability of uncorrupted and non-degraded timing signals for military and civilian users in the event that GPS timing signals are corrupted, degraded, unreliable, or otherwise unavailable.

"(b) ESTABLISHMENT OF REQUIREMENTS.—

"(1) IN GENERAL.—Not later than 180 days after the date of enactment of the National Timing Resilience and Security Act of 2018, the Secretary of Transportation shall establish requirements for the procurement of the system required by subsection (a) as a complement to and backup for the timing component of GPS in accordance with the timing requirements study required by section 1618 of the National Defense Authorization Act for Fiscal Year 2017 (Public Law 114-328; 130 Stat. 2595).

"(2) REQUIREMENTS.—The Secretary of Transportation shall ensure, to the maximum extent practicable, that the system established under subsection (a) will—

"(A) be wireless;

"(B) be terrestrial;

"(C) provide wide-area coverage;

"(D) be synchronized with coordinated universal time;

"(E) be resilient and extremely difficult to disrupt or degrade;

"(F) be able to penetrate underground and inside buildings;

"(G) be capable of deployment to remote locations;

"(H) be developed, constructed, and operated incorporating applicable private sector expertise;

"(I) work in concert with and complement any other similar positioning, navigation, and timing systems, including enhanced long-range navigation systems and Nationwide Differential GPS systems;

"(J) be available for use by Federal and non-Federal government agencies for public purposes at no net cost to the Federal Government within 10 years of initiation of operation;

"(K) be capable of adaptation and expansion to provide position and navigation capabilities;

"(L) incorporate the recommendations from any GPS back-up demonstration program initiated and completed by the Secretary, in coordination with other Federal agencies, before the date specified in subsection (c)(1); and

"(M) incorporate such other elements as the Secretary considers appropriate.

"(c) IMPLEMENTATION PLAN.—

"(1) PLAN REQUIRED.—Not later than 180 days after the date of enactment of the National Timing Resilience and Security Act of 2018, the Secretary of Transportation shall submit to the Committee on Commerce, Science, and Transportation of the Senate and the Committee on Transportation and Infrastructure of the House of Representatives a report setting forth the following:

"(A) A plan to develop, construct, and operate the system required by subsection (a).

"(B) A description and assessment of the advantages of a system to provide a follow-on complementary and backup positioning and navigation capability to the timing component of GPS.

"(2) DEADLINE FOR COMMENCEMENT OF OPERATION.—The system required by subsection (a) shall be in operation by not later than 2 years after the date of enactment of the National Timing Resilience and Security Act of 2018.

"(3) MINIMUM DURATION OF OPERATIONAL CAPABILITY.—The system required by subsection (a) shall be designed to be fully operational for not less than 20 years.

"(d) LORAN FACILITIES.—

"(1) IN GENERAL.—If the Secretary of Transportation determines that any LORAN infrastructure, including the underlying real property and any spectrum associated with LORAN, in the possession of the Coast Guard is required by the Department of Transportation for the purpose of establishing the system required by subsection (a), the Commandant shall transfer such property, spectrum, and equipment to the Secretary.

"(2) CERCLA NOT AFFECTED.—This subsection shall not be construed to limit the application of or otherwise affect section 120(h) of the Comprehensive Environmental Response, Compensation, and Liability Act of 1980 (42 U.S.C. 9620(h)) with respect to the Federal Government facilities described in paragraph (1).

"(e) COOPERATIVE AGREEMENT.—

"(1) IN GENERAL.—The Secretary of Transportation may enter into a cooperative agreement (as that term is described in section 6305 of title 31) with an entity upon such terms and conditions as the Secretary of Transportation determines will fulfill the purpose and requirements of this section and be in the public interest.

"(2) REQUIREMENTS.—The cooperative agreement under paragraph (1) shall, at a minimum, require the Secretary of Transportation to—

"(A) authorize the entity to sell timing and other services to commercial and non-commercial third parties, subject to any national security requirements determined by the Secretary, in consultation with the Secretary of Defense;

"(B) require the entity to develop, construct, and operate at private expense the backup timing system in accordance with this section;

"(C) allow the entity to make any investments in technologies necessary over the life of such agreement to meet future requirements for advanced timing resilience and technologies;

"(D) require the entity to share 25 percent of the gross

proceeds received by the entity from the sale of timing services to third parties with the Secretary for at least 10 years after the date upon which the Secretary enters into the cooperative agreement;

"(E) require the entity—

"(i) to assume all financial risk for the completion and operational capability of the system, after the Secretary provides any LORAN facilities necessary for the system under subsection (d), if required for the alternative timing system; and

"(ii) to furnish performance and payment bonds in connection with the system in a reasonable amount as determined by the Secretary; and

"(F) require the entity to make any investments in technologies necessary over the life of the agreement to meet future requirements for advanced timing resiliency.

"(3) COMPETITION REQUIRED.—The Secretary shall use competitive procedures similar to those authorized under section 2667 of title 10 in selecting an entity to enter into a cooperative agreement pursuant to this subsection.

"(4) AUTHORIZATION TO PURCHASE SERVICES.—The Secretary may not purchase timing system services from the entity for use by the Department of Transportation or for provision to other Federal and non-Federal governmental agencies until the system achieves operational status, and then only if the necessary funds for such purchases are provided for in subsequent yearly appropriations acts made available to the Secretary for each and every year in which such purchases are made.

"(5) DETERMINATION REQUIREMENT.—The Secretary may not enter into a cooperative agreement under this subsection unless the Secretary determines that the cooperative agreement is in the best financial interest of the Federal Government. The Secretary shall notify the Committee on Committee on Commerce, Science, and Transportation of the Senate and the Committee on Transportation and Infrastructure of the House of Representatives of such determination not later than 30 days after the date of the determination.

"(6) DEFINITION.—In this subsection the term 'entity' means a non-Federal entity with the demonstrated technical expertise and requisite administrative and financial resources to meet any terms and conditions established by the Secretary for purposes of this subsection."

(c) [49 U.S.C. 301] TABLE OF CONTENTS.—The table of contents for chapter 3 of title 49, United States Code, is amended by adding at the end the following:

"312. Alternative timing system."

SEC. 515. SCIENTIFIC PERSONNEL.

Section 2101(41) of title 46, United States Code, is amended—

(1) by inserting "(A) Subject to subparagraph (B)," before the text; and

(2) by adding at the end the following:

"(B)(i) Such term includes an individual who is on board an oceanographic research vessel only to—

"(I) engage in scientific research;

"(II) instruct in oceanography or limnology; or

"(III) receive instruction in oceanography or limnology.

"(ii) For purposes of clause (i), the age of an individual may not be considered in determining whether the individual is described in such clause."

SEC. 516. TRANSPARENCY.

(a) [46 U.S.C. 12101 note] IN GENERAL.—The Commandant of the Coast Guard shall publish any letter of determination issued by the Coast Guard National Vessel Documentation Center after the date of the enactment of this Act on the National Vessel Documentation Center website not later than 30 days after the date of issuance of such letter of determination.

(b) AUDIT.—

(1) IN GENERAL.—The Comptroller General of the United States shall conduct an audit, the results of which shall be made publicly available, of—

(A) the method or process by which the Coast Guard National Vessel Documentation Center develops policy for and documents compliance with the requirements of section 67.97 of title 46, Code of Federal Regulations, for the purpose of issuing endorsements under section 12112 and 12113 of title 46, United States Code;

(B) the coordination between the Coast Guard and U.S. Customs and Border Protection with respect to the enforcement of such requirements; and

(C) the extent to which the Secretary of the department in which the Coast Guard is operating and the Secretary of Transportation, through the Maritime Administration, have published and disseminated information to promote compliance with applicable vessel construction requirements.

(2) REPORT.—Not later than 90 days after the audit under paragraph (1) is complete, the Comptroller General of the United States shall submit to the Committee on Commerce, Science, and Transportation of the Senate and the Committee on Transportation and Infrastructure of the House of Representatives a report regarding the results of and recommendations made pursuant to such audit.

(c) OUTLINE.—Not later than 180 days after the date of the submission of the Comptroller General of the United States report required under subsection (b), the Commandant of the Coast Guard shall submit to the Committee on Commerce, Science, and Transportation of the Senate and the Committee on Transportation and Infrastructure of the House of Representatives an outline of plans—

(1) to enhance the transparency of the documentation process, and communications with the maritime industry regarding such process over the next 5 years; and

(2) to implement the recommendations made by the Comptroller General of the United States in the report required under subsection (b)(2).

TITLE VI—ADVISORY COMMITTEES

SEC. 601. NATIONAL MARITIME TRANSPORTATION ADVISORY COMMITTEES.

(a) IN GENERAL.—Subtitle II of title 46, United States Code, is amended by adding at the end the following:

"PART K—NATIONAL MARITIME TRANSPORTATION ADVISORY COMMITTEES

"CHAPTER 151—NATIONAL MARITIME TRANSPORTATION ADVISORY COMMITTEES

"SEC. § 15101. [46 U.S.C. 15101] National Chemical Transportation Safety Advisory Committe

"(a) ESTABLISHMENT.—There is established a National Chemical Transportation Safety Advisory Committee (in this section referred to as the 'Committee').

"(b) FUNCTION.—The Committee shall advise the Secretary on matters relating to the safe and secure marine transportation of hazardous materials.

"(c) MEMBERSHIP.—

"(1) IN GENERAL.—The Committee shall consist of not more than 25 members appointed by the Secretary in accordance with this section and section 15109 of this chapter.

"(2) EXPERTISE.—Each member of the Committee shall have particular expertise, knowledge, and experience in matters relating to the function of the Committee.

"(3) REPRESENTATION.—Each member of the Committee shall represent 1 of the following:

"(A) Chemical manufacturing entities.

"(B) Entities related to marine handling or transportation of chemicals.

"(C) Vessel design and construction entities.

"(D) Marine safety or security entities.

"(E) Marine environmental protection entities.

"(4) DISTRIBUTION.—The Secretary shall, based on the needs of the Coast Guard, determine the number of members of the Committee who represent each entity specified in paragraph (3). Neither this paragraph nor any other provision of law shall be construed to require an equal distribution of members representing each entity specified in paragraph (3).

"SEC. § 15102. [46 U.S.C. 15102] National Commercial Fishing Safety Advisory Committe

"(a) ESTABLISHMENT.—There is established a National Commercial Fishing Safety Advisory Committee (in this section referred to as the 'Committee').

"(b) FUNCTION.—The Committee shall—

"(1) advise the Secretary on matters relating to the safe operation of vessels to which chapter 45 of this title applies, including the matters of—

"(A) navigation safety;

"(B) safety equipment and procedures;

"(C) marine insurance;

"(D) vessel design, construction, maintenance, and operation; and

"(E) personnel qualifications and training; and

"(2) review regulations proposed under chapter 45 of this title (during preparation of the regulations).

"(c) MEMBERSHIP.—

"(1) IN GENERAL.—The Committee shall consist of 18 members appointed by the Secretary in accordance with this section and section 15109 of this chapter.

"(2) EXPERTISE.—Each member of the Committee shall

have particular expertise, knowledge, and experience in matters relating to the function of the Committee.

"(3) REPRESENTATION.—Members of the Committee shall be appointed as follows:

"(A) 10 members shall represent the commercial fishing industry and—

"(i) as a group, shall together reflect a regional and representational balance; and

"(ii) as individuals, shall each have experience—

"(I) in the operation of vessels to which chapter 45 of this title applies; or

"(II) as a crew member or processing line worker on a fish processing vessel.

"(B) 1 member shall represent naval architects and marine engineers.

"(C) 1 member shall represent manufacturers of equipment for vessels to which chapter 45 of this title applies.

"(D) 1 member shall represent education and training professionals related to fishing vessel, fish processing vessel, and fish tender vessel safety and personnel qualifications.

"(E) 1 member shall represent underwriters that insure vessels to which chapter 45 of this title applies.

"(F) 1 member shall represent owners of vessels to which chapter 45 of this title applies.

"(G) 3 members shall represent the general public and, to the extent possible, shall include—

"(i) an independent expert or consultant in maritime safety;

"(ii) a marine surveyor who provides services to vessels to which chapter 45 of this title applies; and

"(iii) a person familiar with issues affecting fishing communities and the families of fishermen.

"SEC. § 15103. [46 U.S.C. 15103] National Merchant Marine Personnel Advisory Committe

"(a) ESTABLISHMENT.—There is established a National Merchant Marine Personnel Advisory Committee (in this section referred to as the 'Committee').

"(b) FUNCTION.—The Committee shall advise the Secretary on matters relating to personnel in the United States merchant marine, including the training, qualifications, certification, documentation, and fitness of mariners.

"(c) MEMBERSHIP.—

"(1) IN GENERAL.—The Committee shall consist of 19 members appointed by the Secretary in accordance with this section and section 15109 of this chapter.

"(2) EXPERTISE.—Each member of the Committee shall have particular expertise, knowledge, and experience in matters relating to the function of the Committee.

"(3) REPRESENTATION.—Members of the Committee shall be appointed as follows:

"(A) 9 members shall represent mariners and, of the 9—

"(i) each shall—

"(I) be a citizen of the United States; and

"(II) hold an active license or certificate issued under chapter 71 of this title or a merchant mariner document issued under chapter 73 of this title;

"(ii) 3 shall be deck officers who represent merchant marine deck officers and, of the 3—

"(I) 2 shall be licensed for oceans any gross tons;

"(II) 1 shall be licensed for inland river route with a limited or unlimited tonnage;

"(III) 2 shall have a master's license or a master of towing vessels license;

"(IV) 1 shall have significant tanker experience; and

"(V) to the extent practicable—

"(aa) 1 shall represent labor; and

"(bb) 1 shall represent management;

"(iii) 3 shall be engineering officers who represent merchant marine engineering officers and, of the 3—

"(I) 2 shall be licensed as chief engineer any horsepower;

"(II) 1 shall be licensed as either a limited chief engineer or a designated duty engineer; and

"(III) to the extent practicable—

"(aa) 1 shall represent labor; and

"(bb) 1 shall represent management;

"(iv) 2 shall be unlicensed seamen who represent merchant marine unlicensed seaman and, of the 2—

"(I) 1 shall represent able-bodied seamen; and

"(II) 1 shall represent qualified members of the engine department; and

"(v) 1 shall be a pilot who represents merchant marine pilots.

"(B) 6 members shall represent marine educators and, of the 6—

"(i) 3 shall be marine educators who represent maritime academies and, of the 3—

"(I) 2 shall represent State maritime academies (and are jointly recommended by such academies); and

"(II) 1 shall represent either State maritime academies or the United States Merchant Marine Academy; and

"(ii) 3 shall be marine educators who represent other maritime training institutions and, of the 3, 1 shall represent the small vessel industry.

"(C) 2 members shall represent shipping companies employed in ship operation management.

"(D) 2 members shall represent the general public.

"SEC. § 15104. [46 U.S.C. 15104] National Merchant Mariner Medical Advisory Committe

"(a) ESTABLISHMENT.—There is established a National Merchant Mariner Medical Advisory Committee (in this section referred to as the 'Committee').

"(b) FUNCTION.—The Committee shall advise the Secretary on matters relating to—

"(1) medical certification determinations for the issuance of licenses, certification of registry, and merchant mariners' documents with respect to merchant mariners;

"(2) medical standards and guidelines for the physical qualifications of operators of commercial vessels;

"(3) medical examiner education; and

"(4) medical research.

"(c) MEMBERSHIP.—

"(1) IN GENERAL.—The Committee shall consist of 14 members appointed by the Secretary in accordance with this section and section 15109 of this chapter.

"(2) EXPERTISE.—Each member of the Committee shall have particular expertise, knowledge, and experience in matters relating to the function of the Committee.

"(3) REPRESENTATION.—Members of the Committee shall be appointed as follows:

"(A) 9 shall represent health-care professionals and have particular expertise, knowledge, and experience regarding the medical examinations of merchant mariners or occupational medicine.

"(B) 5 shall represent professional mariners and have particular expertise, knowledge, and experience in occupational requirements for mariners.

"SEC. § 15105. [46 U.S.C. 15105] National Boating Safety Advisory Committe

"(a) ESTABLISHMENT.—There is established a National Boating Safety Advisory Committee (in this section referred to as the 'Committee').

"(b) FUNCTION.—The Committee shall advise the Secretary on matters relating to national boating safety.

"(c) MEMBERSHIP.—

"(1) IN GENERAL.—The Committee shall consist of 21 members appointed by the Secretary in accordance with this section and section 15109 of this chapter.

"(2) EXPERTISE.—Each member of the Committee shall have particular expertise, knowledge, and experience in matters relating to the function of the Committee.

"(3) REPRESENTATION.—Members of the Committee shall be appointed as follows:

"(A) 7 members shall represent State officials responsible for State boating safety programs.

"(B) 7 members shall represent recreational vessel and associated equipment manufacturers.

"(C) 7 members shall represent the general public or national recreational boating organizations and, of the 7, at least 5 shall represent national recreational boating organizations.

"SEC. § 15106. [46 U.S.C. 15106] National Offshore Safety Advisory Committe

"(a) ESTABLISHMENT.—There is established a National Offshore Safety Advisory Committee (in this section referred to as the 'Committee').

"(b) FUNCTION.—The Committee shall advise the Secretary on matters relating to activities directly involved with, or in support of, the exploration of offshore mineral and energy resources, to the extent that such matters are within the jurisdiction of the Coast Guard.

"(c) MEMBERSHIP.—

"(1) IN GENERAL.—The Committee shall consist of 15 members appointed by the Secretary in accordance with this section and section 15109 of this chapter.

"(2) EXPERTISE.—Each member of the Committee shall have particular expertise, knowledge, and experience in matters relating to the function of the Committee.

"(3) REPRESENTATION.—Members of the Committee shall be appointed as follows:

"(A) 2 members shall represent entities engaged in the production of petroleum.

"(B) 2 members shall represent entities engaged in offshore drilling.

"(C) 2 members shall represent entities engaged in the support, by offshore supply vessels or other vessels, of offshore mineral and oil operations, including geophysical services.

"(D) 1 member shall represent entities engaged in the construction of offshore exploration and recovery facilities.

"(E) 1 member shall represent entities engaged in diving services related to offshore construction, inspection, and maintenance.

"(F) 1 member shall represent entities engaged in safety and training services related to offshore exploration and construction.

"(G) 1 member shall represent entities engaged in pipelaying services related to offshore construction.

"(H) 2 members shall represent individuals employed in offshore operations and, of the 2, 1 shall have recent practical experience on a vessel or offshore unit involved in the offshore mineral and energy industry.

"(I) 1 member shall represent national environmental entities.

"(J) 1 member shall represent deepwater ports.

"(K) 1 member shall represent the general public (but not a specific environmental group).

"SEC. § 15107. [46 U.S.C. 15107] National Navigation Safety Advisory Committe

"(a) ESTABLISHMENT.—There is established a National Navigation Safety Advisory Committee (in this section referred to as the 'Committee').

"(b) FUNCTION.—The Committee shall advise the Secretary on matters relating to maritime collisions, rammings, and groundings, Inland Rules of the Road, International Rules of the Road, navigation regulations and equipment, routing measures, marine information, and aids to navigation systems.

"(c) MEMBERSHIP.—

"(1) IN GENERAL.—The Committee shall consist of not more than 21 members appointed by the Secretary in accordance with this section and section 15109 of this chapter.

"(2) EXPERTISE.—Each member of the Committee shall have particular expertise, knowledge, and experience in matters relating to the function of the Committee.

"(3) REPRESENTATION.—Each member of the Committee shall represent 1 of the following:

"(A) Commercial vessel owners or operators.

"(B) Professional mariners.

"(C) Recreational boaters.

"(D) The recreational boating industry.

"(E) State agencies responsible for vessel or port safety.

"(F) The Maritime Law Association.

"(4) DISTRIBUTION.—The Secretary shall, based on the needs of the Coast Guard, determine the number of members of the Committee who represent each entity specified in paragraph (3). Neither this paragraph nor any other provision of law shall be construed to require an equal distribution of members representing each entity specified in paragraph (3).

"SEC. § 15108. [46 U.S.C. 15108] National Towing Safety Advisory Committe

"(a) ESTABLISHMENT.—There is established a National Towing Safety Advisory Committee (in this section referred to as the 'Committee').

"(b) FUNCTION.—The Committee shall advise the Secretary on matters relating to shallow-draft inland navigation, coastal waterway navigation, and towing safety.

"(c) MEMBERSHIP.—

"(1) IN GENERAL.—The Committee shall consist of 18 members appointed by the Secretary in accordance with this section and section 15109 of this chapter.

"(2) EXPERTISE.—Each member of the Committee shall have particular expertise, knowledge, and experience in matters relating to the function of the Committee.

"(3) REPRESENTATION.—Members of the Committee shall be appointed as follows:

"(A) 7 members shall represent the barge and towing industry, reflecting a regional geographic balance.

"(B) 1 member shall represent the offshore mineral and oil supply vessel industry.

"(C) 1 member shall represent masters and pilots of towing vessels who hold active licenses and have experience on the Western Rivers and the Gulf Intracoastal Waterway.

"(D) 1 member shall represent masters of towing vessels in offshore service who hold active licenses.

"(E) 1 member shall represent masters of active ship-docking or harbor towing vessels.

"(F) 1 member shall represent licensed and unlicensed towing vessel engineers with formal training and experience.

"(G) 2 members shall represent port districts, authorities, or terminal operators.

"(H) 2 members shall represent shippers and, of the 2, 1 shall be engaged in the shipment of oil or hazardous materials by barge.

"(I) 2 members shall represent the general public.

"SEC. § 15109. [46 U.S.C. 15109] Administratio

"(a) MEETINGS.—Each committee established under this chapter shall, at least once each year, meet at the call of the Secretary or a majority of the members of the committee.

"(b) EMPLOYEE STATUS.—A member of a committee established under this chapter shall not be considered an employee of the Federal Government by reason of service on such committee, except for the purposes of the following:

"(1) Chapter 81 of title 5.

"(2) Chapter 171 of title 28 and any other Federal law relating to tort liability.

"(c) COMPENSATION.—Notwithstanding subsection (b), a member of a committee established under this chapter, when actually engaged in the performance of the duties of such committee, may—

"(1) receive compensation at a rate established by the Secretary, not to exceed the maximum daily rate payable under section 5376 of title 5; or

"(2) if not compensated in accordance with paragraph (1)—

"(A) be reimbursed for actual and reasonable expenses incurred in the performance of such duties; or

"(B) be allowed travel expenses, including per diem in lieu of subsistence, as authorized by section 5703 of title 5.

"(d) ACCEPTANCE OF VOLUNTEER SERVICES.—A member of a committee established under this chapter may serve on such committee on a voluntary basis without pay without regard to section 1342 of title 31 or any other law.

"(e) STATUS OF MEMBERS.—

"(1) IN GENERAL.—Except as provided in paragraph (2), with respect to a member of a committee established under this chapter whom the Secretary appoints to represent an entity or group—

"(A) the member is authorized to represent the interests of the applicable entity or group; and

"(B) requirements under Federal law that would interfere with such representation and that apply to a special Government employee (as defined in section 202(a) of title 18), including requirements relating to employee conduct, political activities, ethics, conflicts of interest, and corruption, do not apply to the member.

"(2) EXCEPTION.—Notwithstanding subsection (b), a member of a committee established under this chapter shall be treated as a special Government employee for purposes of the committee service of the member if—

"(A) the Secretary appointed the member to represent the general public; or

"(B) the member, without regard to service on the committee, is a special Government employee.

"(f) SERVICE ON COMMITTEE.—

"(1) SOLICITATION OF NOMINATIONS.—Before appointing an individual as a member of a committee established under this chapter, the Secretary shall publish, in the Federal Register, a timely notice soliciting nominations for membership on such committee.

"(2) APPOINTMENTS.—

"(A) IN GENERAL.—After considering nominations

received pursuant to a notice published under paragraph (1), the Secretary may, as necessary, appoint a member to the applicable committee established under this chapter.

"(B) PROHIBITION.—The Secretary shall not seek, consider, or otherwise use information concerning the political affiliation of a nominee in making an appointment to any committee established under this chapter.

"(3) SERVICE AT PLEASURE OF THE SECRETARY.—

"(A) IN GENERAL.—Each member of a committee established under this chapter shall serve at the pleasure of the Secretary.

"(B) EXCEPTION.—Notwithstanding subparagraph (A), a member of the committee established under section 15102 may only be removed prior to the end of the term of that member for just cause.

"(4) SECURITY BACKGROUND EXAMINATIONS.—The Secretary may require an individual to have passed an appropriate security background examination before appointment to a committee established under this chapter.

"(5) PROHIBITION.—

"(A) IN GENERAL.—Except as provided in subparagraph (B), a Federal employee may not be appointed as a member of a committee established under this chapter.

"(B) SPECIAL RULE FOR NATIONAL MERCHANT MARINE PERSONNEL ADVISORY COMMITTEE.—The Secretary may appoint a Federal employee to serve as a member of the National Merchant Marine Personnel Advisory Committee to represent the interests of the United States Merchant Marine Academy and, notwithstanding paragraphs (1) and (2), may do so without soliciting, receiving, or considering nominations for such appointment.

"(6) TERMS.—

"(A) IN GENERAL.—The term of each member of a committee established under this chapter shall expire on December 31 of the third full year after the effective date of the appointment.

"(B) CONTINUED SERVICE AFTER TERM.—When the term

of a member of a committee established under this chapter ends, the member, for a period not to exceed 1 year, may continue to serve as a member until a successor is appointed.

"(7) VACANCIES.—A vacancy on a committee established under this chapter shall be filled in the same manner as the original appointment.

"(8) SPECIAL RULE FOR REAPPOINTMENTS.—Notwithstanding paragraphs (1) and (2), the Secretary may reappoint a member of a committee established under this chapter for any term, other than the first term of the member, without soliciting, receiving, or considering nominations for such appointment.

"(g) STAFF SERVICES.—The Secretary shall furnish to each committee established under this chapter any staff and services considered by the Secretary to be necessary for the conduct of the committee's functions.

"(h) CHAIRMAN; VICE CHAIRMAN.—

"(1) IN GENERAL.—Each committee established under this chapter shall elect a Chairman and Vice Chairman from among the committee's members.

"(2) VICE CHAIRMAN ACTING AS CHAIRMAN.—The Vice Chairman shall act as Chairman in the absence or incapacity of, or in the event of a vacancy in the office of, the Chairman.

"(i) SUBCOMMITTEES AND WORKING GROUPS.—

"(1) IN GENERAL.—The Chairman of a committee established under this chapter may establish and disestablish subcommittees and working groups for any purpose consistent with the function of the committee.

"(2) PARTICIPANTS.—Subject to conditions imposed by the Chairman, members of a committee established under this chapter and additional persons drawn from entities or groups designated by this chapter to be represented on the committee or the general public may be assigned to subcommittees and working groups established under paragraph (1).

"(3) CHAIR.—Only committee members may chair subcommittees and working groups established under paragraph (1).

"(j) CONSULTATION, ADVICE, REPORTS, AND RECOMMENDATIONS.—

"(1) CONSULTATION.—

"(A) IN GENERAL.—Before taking any significant action, the Secretary shall consult with, and consider the information, advice, and recommendations of, a committee established under this chapter if the function of the committee is to advise the Secretary on matters related to the significant action.

"(B) INCLUSION.—For purposes of this paragraph, regulations proposed under chapter 45 of this title are significant actions.

"(2) ADVICE, REPORTS, AND RECOMMENDATIONS.—Each committee established under this chapter shall submit, in writing, to the Secretary its advice, reports, and recommendations, in a form and at a frequency determined appropriate by the committee.

"(3) EXPLANATION OF ACTIONS TAKEN.—Not later than 60 days after the date on which the Secretary receives recommendations from a committee under paragraph (2), the Secretary shall—

"(A) publish the recommendations on a website accessible at no charge to the public;

"(B) if the recommendations are from the committee established under section 15102, establish a mechanism for the submission of public comments on the recommendations; and

"(C) respond, in writing, to the committee regarding the recommendations, including by providing an explanation of actions taken regarding the recommendations.

"(4) SUBMISSION TO CONGRESS.—

"(A) IN GENERAL.—The Secretary shall submit to the Committee on Transportation and Infrastructure of the House of Representatives and the Committee on Commerce, Science, and Transportation of the Senate the advice, reports, and recommendations received from committees under paragraph (2).

"(B) ADDITIONAL SUBMISSION.—With respect to a committee established under section 70112 and to which this section applies, the Secretary shall submit the advice, reports, and recommendations received from the committee under paragraph (2) to the Committee on Homeland Security of the House of Representatives in addition to the committees specified in subparagraph (A).

"(k) OBSERVERS.—Any Federal agency with matters under such agency's administrative jurisdiction related to the function of a committee established under this chapter may designate a representative to—

"(1) attend any meeting of such committee; and

"(2) participate as an observer at meetings of such committee that relate to such a matter.

"(l) TERMINATION.—Each committee established under this chapter shall terminate on September 30, 2027."

(b) CLERICAL AMENDMENT.—The analysis for subtitle II of title 46, United States Code, is amended by inserting after the item relating to chapter 147 the following:

"Part K-National Maritime Transportation Advisory Committees

"151. National Maritime Transportation Advisory Committees"

(c) CONFORMING AMENDMENTS.—

(1) [46 U.S.C. 4501] COMMERCIAL FISHING SAFETY ADVISORY COMMITTEE.—Section 4508 of title 46, United States Code, and the item relating to that section in the analysis for chapter 45 of that title, are repealed.

(2) [46 U.S.C. 7101] MERCHANT MARINER MEDICAL ADVISORY COMMITTEE.—Section 7115 of title 46, United States Code, and the item relating to that section in the analysis for chapter 71 of that title, arerepealed.

(3) MERCHANT MARINE PERSONNEL ADVISORY COMMITTEE.—

(A) [46 U.S.C. 8101] REPEAL.—Section 8108 of title 46, United States Code, and the item relating to that section in the analysis for chapter 81 of that title, are repealed.

(B) CONFORMING AMENDMENT.—Section 7510(c)(1)(C) of title 46, United States Code, is amended by inserting "National" before "Merchant Marine".

(4) NATIONAL BOATING SAFETY ADVISORY COUNCIL.—

(A) [46 U.S.C. 13101] REPEAL.—Section 13110 of title 46, United States Code, and the item relating to that section in the analysis for chapter 131 of that title, are repealed.

(B) CONFORMING AMENDMENTS.—

(i) REGULATIONS.—Section 4302(c)(4) of title 46, United States Code, is amended by striking "Council established under section 13110 of this title" and inserting "Committee established under section 15105 of this title".

(ii) REPAIR AND REPLACEMENT OF DEFECTS.—Section 4310(f) of title 46, United States Code, is amended by striking "Advisory Council" and inserting "Advisory Committee".

(5) NAVIGATION SAFETY ADVISORY COUNCIL.—Section 5 of the Inland Navigational Rules Act of 1980 (33 U.S.C. 2073) is repealed.

(6) TOWING SAFETY ADVISORY COMMITTEE.—

(A) REPEAL.—Public Law 96-380 (33 U.S.C. 1231a) is repealed.

(B) CONFORMING AMENDMENTS.—

(i) REDUCTION OF OIL SPILLS FROM SINGLE HULL NON-SELF-PROPELLED TANK VESSELS.—Section 3719 of title 46, United States Code, is amended by inserting "National" before "Towing Safety".

(ii) SAFETY EQUIPMENT.—Section 4102(f)(1) of title 46, United States Code, is amended by inserting "National" before "Towing Safety".

(d) [46 U.S.C. 15101 note] TREATMENT OF EXISTING COUNCILS AND COMMITTEES.—Notwithstanding any other provision of law—

(1) an advisory council or committee substantially similar to an advisory committee established under chapter 151 of title 46, United States Code, as added by this Act, and that was in force or in effect on the day before the date of enactment of this section, including a council or committee the authority for which was repealed under subsection (c), may remain in force or in effect for a period of 2 years from the date of enactment of

this section, including that the charter, membership, and other aspects of the council or committee may remain in force or in effect; and

(2) during the 2-year period referenced in paragraph (1)—

(A) requirements relating to the applicable advisory committee established under chapter 151 of title 46, United States Code, shall be treated as satisfied by the substantially similar advisory council or committee; and

(B) the enactment of this section, including the amendments made in this section, shall not be the basis—

(i) to deem, find, or declare such council or committee, including the charter, membership, and other aspects thereof, void, not in force, or not in effect;

(ii) to suspend the activities of such council or committee; or

(iii) to bar the members of such council or committee from meeting.

SEC. 602. MARITIME SECURITY ADVISORY COMMITTEES.

(a) IN GENERAL.—Section 70112 of title 46, United States Code, is amended to read as follows:

"SEC. § 70112. Maritime Security Advisory Committee

"(a) NATIONAL MARITIME SECURITY ADVISORY COMMITTEE.—

"(1) ESTABLISHMENT.—There is established a National Maritime Security Advisory Committee (in this subsection referred to as the 'Committee').

"(2) FUNCTION.—The Committee shall advise the Secretary on matters relating to national maritime security, including on enhancing the sharing of information related to cybersecurity risks that may cause a transportation security incident, between relevant Federal agencies and—

"(A) State, local, and tribal governments;

"(B) relevant public safety and emergency response agencies;

"(C) relevant law enforcement and security organizations;

"(D) maritime industry;

"(E) port owners and operators; and

"(F) terminal owners and operators.

"(3) MEMBERSHIP.—

"(A) IN GENERAL.—The Committee shall consist of at least 8 members, but not more than 21 members, appointed by the Secretary in accordance with this subsection and section 15109 of this title.

"(B) EXPERTISE.—Each member of the Committee shall have particular expertise, knowledge, and experience in matters relating to the function of the Committee.

"(C) REPRESENTATION.—Each of the following shall be represented by at least 1 member of the Committee:

"(i) Port authorities.

"(ii) Facilities owners and operators.

"(iii) Terminal owners and operators.

"(iv) Vessel owners and operators.

"(v) Maritime labor organizations.

"(vi) The academic community.

"(vii) State and local governments.

"(viii) The maritime industry.

"(D) DISTRIBUTION.—If the Committee consists of at least 8 members who, together, satisfy the minimum representation requirements of subparagraph (C), the Secretary shall, based on the needs of the Coast Guard, determine the number of additional members of the Committee who represent each entity specified in that subparagraph. Neither this subparagraph nor any other provision of law shall be construed to require an equal distribution of members representing each entity specified in subparagraph (C).

"(4) ADMINISTRATION.—For purposes of section 15109 of this title, the Committee shall be treated as a committee established under chapter 151 of such title.

"(b) AREA MARITIME SECURITY ADVISORY COMMITTEES.—

"(1) IN GENERAL.—

"(A) ESTABLISHMENT.—The Secretary may—

"(i) establish an Area Maritime Security Advisory Committee for any port area of the United States; and

"(ii) request such a committee to review the proposed Area Maritime Transportation Security Plan developed under section 70103(b) and make recommendations to the Secretary that the committee considers appropriate.

"(B) ADDITIONAL FUNCTIONS AND MEETINGS.—A committee established under this subsection for an area—

"(i) may advise, consult with, report to, and make recommendations to the Secretary on matters relating to maritime security in that area;

"(ii) may make available to the Congress recommendations that the committee makes to the Secretary; and

"(iii) shall meet at the call of—

"(I) the Secretary, who shall call such a meeting at least once during each calendar year; or

"(II) a majority of the committee.

"(2) MEMBERSHIP.—

"(A) IN GENERAL.—Each committee established under this subsection shall consist of at least 7 members appointed by the Secretary, each of whom has at least 5 years practical experience in maritime security operations.

"(B) TERMS.—The term of each member of a committee established under this subsection shall be for a period of not more than 5 years, specified by the Secretary.

"(C) NOTICE.—Before appointing an individual to a position on a committee established under this subsection, the Secretary shall publish a notice in the Federal Register soliciting nominations for membership on the committee.

"(D) BACKGROUND EXAMINATIONS.—The Secretary may require an individual to have passed an appropriate security background examination before appointment to a committee established under this subsection.

"(E) REPRESENTATION.—Each committee established under this subsection shall be composed of individuals who represent the interests of the port industry, terminal operators, port labor organizations, and other users of the port areas.

"(3) CHAIRPERSON AND VICE CHAIRPERSON.—

"(A) IN GENERAL.—Each committee established under this subsection shall elect 1 of the committee's members as the Chairperson and 1 of the committee's members as the Vice Chairperson.

"(B) VICE CHAIRPERSON ACTING AS CHAIRPERSON.—The Vice Chairperson shall act as Chairperson in the absence or incapacity of the Chairperson, or in the event of a vacancy in the office of the Chairperson.

"(4) OBSERVERS.—

"(A) IN GENERAL.—The Secretary shall, and the head of any other interested Federal agency may, designate a representative to participate as an observer with a committee established under this subsection.

"(B) ROLE.—The Secretary's designated representative to a committee established under this subsection shall act as the executive secretary of the committee and shall perform the duties set forth in section 10(c) of the Federal Advisory Committee Act (5 U.S.C. App.).

"(5) CONSIDERATION OF VIEWS.—The Secretary shall consider the information, advice, and recommendations of each committee established under this subsection in formulating policy regarding matters affecting maritime security.

"(6) COMPENSATION AND EXPENSES.—

"(A) IN GENERAL.—A member of a committee established under this subsection, when attending meetings of the committee or when otherwise engaged in the business of the committee, is entitled to receive—

"(i) compensation at a rate fixed by the Secretary, not exceeding the daily equivalent of the current rate of basic pay in effect for GS-15 of the General Schedule under section 5332 of title 5 including travel time; and

"(ii) travel or transportation expenses under section 5703 of title 5.

"(B) STATUS.—A member of a committee established

under this subsection shall not be considered to be an officer or employee of the United States for any purpose based on the receipt of any payment under this paragraph.

"(7) FACA.—The Federal Advisory Committee Act (5 U.S.C. App.) does not apply to a committee established under this subsection."

(b) [46 U.S.C. 70112 note] TREATMENT OF EXISTING COMMITTEE.—Notwithstanding any other provision of law—

(1) an advisory committee substantially similar to the National Maritime Security Advisory Committee established under section 70112(a) of title 46, United States Code, as amended by this section, and that was in force or in effect on the day before the date of enactment of this section, may remain in force or in effect for a period of 2 years from the date of enactment of this section, including that the charter, membership, and other aspects of the committee may remain in force or in effect; and

(2) during the 2-year period referenced in paragraph (1)—

(A) requirements relating to the National Maritime Security Advisory Committee established under section 70112(a) of title 46, United States Code, as amended by this section, shall be treated as satisfied by the substantially similar advisory committee; and

(B) the enactment of this section, including the amendments made in this section, shall not be the basis—

(i) to deem, find, or declare such committee, including the charter, membership, and other aspects thereof, void, not in force, or not in effect;

(ii) to suspend the activities of such committee; or

(iii) to bar the members of such committee from meeting.

TITLE VII—FEDERAL MARITIME COMMISSION

SEC. 701. SHORT TITLE.

This title may be cited as the "Federal Maritime Commission Authorization Act of 2017".

SEC. 702. AUTHORIZATION OF APPROPRIATIONS.

Section 308 of title 46, United States Code, is amended by striking "$24,700,000 for each of fiscal years 2016 and 2017" and inserting "$28,012,310 for fiscal year 2018 and $28,544,543 for fiscal year 2019".

SEC. 703. REPORTING ON IMPACT OF ALLIANCES ON COMPETITION.

Section 306 of title 46, United States Code, is amended—

(1) in subsection (b)—

(A) in paragraph (4), by striking "; and" and inserting a semicolon;

(B) in paragraph (5), by striking the period at the end and inserting "; and"; and

(C) by adding at the end the following:

"(6) an analysis of the impacts on competition for the purchase of certain covered services by alliances of ocean common carriers acting pursuant to an agreement under this part between or among ocean common carriers, including a summary of actions, including corrective actions, taken by the Commission to promote such competition."

; and

(2) by adding at the end the following:

"(c) DEFINITION OF CERTAIN COVERED SERVICES.—In this section, the term 'certain covered services' has the meaning given the term in section 40102."

SEC. 704. DEFINITION OF CERTAIN COVERED SERVICES.

Section 40102 of title 46, United States Code, is amended—

(1) by redesignating paragraphs (5) through (25) as paragraphs (6) through (26), respectively; and

(2) by inserting after paragraph (4), the following:

"(5) CERTAIN COVERED SERVICES.—For purposes of sections 41105 and 41307, the term 'certain covered services' means, with respect to a vessel—

"(A) the berthing or bunkering of the vessel;

"(B) the loading or unloading of cargo to or from

the vessel to or from a point on a wharf or terminal;

"(C) the positioning, removal, or replacement of buoys related to the movement of the vessel; and

"(D) with respect to injunctive relief under section 41307, towing vessel services provided to such a vessel."

SEC. 705. REPORTS FILED WITH THE COMMISSION.

Section 40104(a) of title 46, United States Code, is amended to read as follows:

"(a) REPORTS.—

"(1) IN GENERAL.—The Federal Maritime Commission may require a common carrier or marine terminal operator, or an officer, receiver, trustee, lessee, agent, or employee of the common carrier or marine terminal operator to file with the Commission a periodical or special report, an account, record, rate, or charge, or a memorandum of facts and transactions related to the business of the common carrier or marine terminal operator, as applicable.

"(2) REQUIREMENTS.—Any report, account, record, rate, charge, or memorandum required to be filed under paragraph (1) shall—

"(A) be made under oath if the Commission requires; and

"(B) be filed in the form and within the time prescribed by the Commission.

"(3) LIMITATION.—The Commission shall—

"(A) limit the scope of any filing ordered under this section to fulfill the objective of the order; and

"(B) provide a reasonable period of time for respondents to respond based upon their capabilities and the scope of the order."

SEC. 706. PUBLIC PARTICIPATION.

(a) NOTICE OF FILING.—Section 40304(a) of title 46, United States Code, is amended to read as follows:

"(a) NOTICE OF FILING.—Not later than 7 days after the date an agreement is filed, the Federal Maritime Commission shall—

"(1) transmit a notice of the filing to the Federal Register for publication; and

"(2) request interested persons to submit relevant information and documents."

(b) REQUEST FOR INFORMATION AND DOCUMENTS.—Section 40304(d) of title 46, United States Code, is amended by striking "section" and inserting "part".

(c) [46 U.S.C. 40304 note] SAVING CLAUSE.—Nothing in this section, or the amendments made by this section, may be construed—

(1) to prevent the Federal Maritime Commission from requesting from a person, at any time, any additional information or documents the Commission considers necessary to carry out chapter 403 of title 46, United States Code;

(2) to prescribe a specific deadline for the submission of relevant information and documents in response to a request under section 40304(a)(2) of title 46, United States Code; or

(3) to limit the authority of the Commission to request information under section 40304(d) of title 46, United States Code.

SEC. 707. OCEAN TRANSPORTATION INTERMEDIARIES.

(a) LICENSE REQUIREMENT.—Section 40901(a) of title 46, United States Code, is amended by inserting "advertise, hold oneself out, or" after "may not".

(b) APPLICABILITY.—Section 40901 of title 46, United States Code, is amended by adding at the end the following:

"(c) APPLICABILITY.—Subsection (a) and section 40902 do not apply to a person that performs ocean transportation intermediary services on behalf of an ocean transportation intermediary for which it is a disclosed agent."

(c) FINANCIAL RESPONSIBILITY.—Section 40902(a) of title 46, United States Code, is amended by inserting "advertise, hold oneself out, or" after "may not".

SEC. 708. COMMON CARRIERS.

(a) Section 41104 of title 46, United States Code, is amended—

(1) in the matter preceding paragraph (1), by inserting "(a)

In General.—" before "A common carrier";

(2) in subsection (a), as designated—

(A) by amending paragraph (11) to read as follows:

"(11) knowingly and willfully accept cargo from or transport cargo for the account of a non-vessel-operating common carrier that does not have a tariff as required by section 40501 of this title, or an ocean transportation intermediary that does not have a bond, insurance, or other surety as required by section 40902 of this title;"

(B) in paragraph (12), by striking the period at the end and inserting "; or"; and

(C) by adding at the end the following:

"(13) continue to participate simultaneously in a rate discussion agreement and an agreement to share vessels, in the same trade, if the interplay of the authorities exercised by the specified agreements is likely, by a reduction in competition, to produce an unreasonable reduction in transportation service or an unreasonable increase in transportation cost."

; and

(3) by adding at the end the following:

"(b) RULE OF CONSTRUCTION.—Notwithstanding any other provision of law, there is no private right of action to enforce the prohibition under subsection (a)(13).

"(c) AGREEMENT VIOLATION.—Participants in an agreement found by the Commission to violate subsection (a)(13) shall have 90 days from the date of such Commission finding to withdraw from the agreement as necessary to comply with that subsection."

(b) [46 U.S.C. 41104 note] APPLICATION.—Section 41104(a)(13) of title 46, United States Code, as amended, shall apply to any agreement filed or with an effective date before, on, or after the date of enactment of this Act.

SEC. 709. NEGOTIATIONS.

(a) CONCERTED ACTION.—Section 41105 of title 46, United States Code, is amended—

(1) by redesignating paragraphs (5) through (8) as paragraphs (7) through (10), respectively; and

(2) by inserting after paragraph (4) the following:

"(5) negotiate with a tug or towing vessel service provider on any matter relating to rates or services provided within the United States by those tugs or towing vessels;

"(6) with respect to a vessel operated by an ocean common carrier within the United States, negotiate for the purchase of certain covered services, unless the negotiations and any resulting agreements are not in violation of the antitrust laws and are consistent with the purposes of this part, except that this paragraph does not prohibit the setting and publishing of a joint through rate by a conference, joint venture, or association of ocean common carriers;"

(b) AUTHORITY.—Chapter 411 of title 46, United States Code, is amended—

(1) by inserting after section 41105 the following:

"SEC. §41105A. [46 U.S.C. 41105A] Authorit

"Nothing in section 41105, as amended by the Federal Maritime Commission Authorization Act of 2017, shall be construed to limit the authority of the Department of Justice regarding antitrust matters."

; and

(2) **[46 U.S.C. 41101]** in the analysis at the beginning of chapter 411, by inserting after the item relating to section 41105 the following:

"41105A. Authority."

(c) EXEMPTION.—Section 40307(b)(1) of title 46, United States Code, is amended by inserting "tug operators," after "motor carriers,".

SEC. 710. INJUNCTIVE RELIEF SOUGHT BY THE COMMISSION.

(a) IN GENERAL.—Section 41307(b) of title 46, United States Codeis amended—

(1) in paragraph (1) by inserting "or to substantially lessen competition in the purchasing of certain covered services" after

"transportation cost"; and

(2) by adding at the end the following:

"(4) COMPETITION FACTORS.—In making a determination under this subsection regarding whether an agreement is likely to substantially lessen competition in the purchasing of certain covered services, the Commission may consider any relevant competition factors in affected markets, including, without limitation, the competitive effect of agreements other than the agreement under review."

(b) [46 U.S.C. 41307 note] APPLICATION.—Section 41307(b) of title 46, United States Code, as amended, shall apply to any agreement filed or with an effective date before, on, or after the date of enactment of this Act.

SEC. 711. DISCUSSIONS.

(a) IN GENERAL.—Section 303 of title 46, United States Code, is amended to read as follows:

"SEC. § 303. Meeting

"(a) IN GENERAL.—The Federal Maritime Commission shall be deemed to be an agency for purposes of section 552b of title 5.

"(b) RECORD.—The Commission, through its secretary, shall keep a record of its meetings and the votes taken on any action, order, contract, or financial transaction of the Commission.

"(c) NONPUBLIC COLLABORATIVE DISCUSSIONS.—

"(1) IN GENERAL.—Notwithstanding section 552b of title 5, a majority of the Commissioners may hold a meeting that is not open to public observation to discuss official agency business if—

"(A) no formal or informal vote or other official agency action is taken at the meeting;

"(B) each individual present at the meeting is a Commissioner or an employee of the Commission;

"(C) at least 1 Commissioner from each political party is present at the meeting, if applicable; and

"(D) the General Counsel of the Commission is present at the meeting.

"(2) DISCLOSURE OF NONPUBLIC COLLABORATIVE

DISCUSSIONS.—Except as provided under paragraph (3), not later than 2 business days after the conclusion of a meeting under paragraph (1), the Commission shall make available to the public, in a place easily accessible to the public—

"(A) a list of the individuals present at the meeting; and

"(B) a summary of the matters discussed at the meeting, except for any matters the Commission properly determines may be withheld from the public under section 552b(c) of title 5.

"(3) EXCEPTION.—If the Commission properly determines matters may be withheld from the public under section 555b(c) of title 5, the Commission shall provide a summary with as much general information as possible on those matters withheld from the public.

"(4) ONGOING PROCEEDINGS.—If a meeting under paragraph (1) directly relates to an ongoing proceeding before the Commission, the Commission shall make the disclosure under paragraph (2) on the date of the final Commission decision.

"(5) PRESERVATION OF OPEN MEETINGS REQUIREMENTS FOR AGENCY ACTION.—Nothing in this subsection may be construed to limit the applicability of section 552b of title 5 with respect to a meeting of the Commissioners other than that described in this subsection.

"(6) STATUTORY CONSTRUCTION.—Nothing in this subsection may be construed—

"(A) to limit the applicability of section 552b of title 5 with respect to any information which is proposed to be withheld from the public under paragraph (2)(B) of this subsection; or

"(B) to authorize the Commission to withhold from any individual any record that is accessible to that individual under section 552a of title 5."

(b) **[46 U.S.C. 301]** TABLE OF CONTENTS.—The analysis at the beginning of chapter 3 of title 46, United States Code,is amended by amending the item relating to section 303 to read as follows:

"303. Meetings."

SEC. 712. [46 U.S.C. 305 note] TRANSPARENCY.

(a) IN GENERAL.—Beginning not later than 60 days after the date of enactment of this Act, the Federal Maritime Commission shall submit to the Committee on Commerce, Science, and Transportation of the Senate and the Committee on Transportation and Infrastructure of the House of Representatives biannual reports that describe the Commission's progress toward addressing the issues raised in each unfinished regulatory proceeding, regardless of whether the proceeding is subject to a statutory or regulatory deadline.

(b) FORMAT OF REPORTS.—Each report under subsection (a) shall, among other things, clearly identify for each unfinished regulatory proceeding—

(1) the popular title;

(2) the current stage of the proceeding;

(3) an abstract of the proceeding;

(4) what prompted the action in question;

(5) any applicable statutory, regulatory, or judicial deadline;

(6) the associated docket number;

(7) the date the rulemaking was initiated;

(8) a date for the next action; and

(9) if a date for next action identified in the previous report is not met, the reason for the delay.

SEC. 713. STUDY OF BANKRUPTCY PREPARATION AND RESPONSE.

(a) STUDY.—The Comptroller General of the United States shall conduct a study that examines the immediate aftermath of a major ocean carrier bankruptcy and its impact through the supply chain. The study shall consider any financial mechanisms that could be used to mitigate the impact of any future bankruptcy events on the supply chain.

(b) REPORT.—No later than 1 year after the date of enactment of this Act, the Comptroller General of the United States shall submit to the Committee on Commerce, Science, and Transportation of the Senate and the Committee on Transportation and Infrastructure of the House of Representatives a report containing the findings, conclusions, and recommendations, if any, from the study required under subsection (a).

SEC. 714. [46 U.S.C. 40102 note] AGREEMENTS UNAFFECTED.

Nothing in this Act may be construed—

(1) to limit or amend the definition of "agreement" in section 40102(1) of title 46, United States Code, with respect to the exclusion of maritime labor agreements; or

(2) to apply to a maritime labor agreement (as defined in section 40102(15) of that title).

TITLE VIII—MISCELLANEOUS

SEC. 801. REPEAL OF OBSOLETE REPORTING REQUIREMENT.

Subsection (h) of section 888 of the Homeland Security Act of 2002 (6 U.S.C. 468) is repealed.

SEC. 802. CORRECTIONS TO PROVISIONS ENACTED BY COAST GUARD AUTHORIZATION ACTS.

Section 604(b) of the Howard Coble Coast Guard and Maritime Transportation Act of 2014 (Public Law 113-281; 128 Stat. 3061) is amended by inserting "and fishery endorsement" after "endorsement".

SEC. 803. [14 U.S.C. 2101 note] OFFICER EVALUATION REPORT.

(a) IN GENERAL.—Not later than 3 years after the date of the enactment of this Act, the Commandant of the Coast Guard shall reduce lieutenant junior grade evaluation reports to the same length as an ensign or place lieutenant junior grade evaluations on an annual schedule.

(b) SURVEYS.—Not later than 1 year after the date of the enactment of this Act, the Commandant of the Coast Guard shall conduct surveys of—

(1) outgoing promotion board members and assignment officers to determine, at a minimum—

(A) which sections of the officer evaluation report were most useful;

(B) which sections of the officer evaluation report were least useful;

(C) how to better reflect high performers; and

(D) any recommendations for improving the officer evaluation report; and

(2) at least 10 percent of the officers from each grade of officers from O1 to O6 to determine how much time each member of the rating chain spends on that member's portion of the officer evaluation report.

(c) REVISIONS.—

(1) IN GENERAL.—Not later than 4 years after the date of the completion of the surveys required by subsection (b), the Commandant of the Coast Guard shall revise the officer evaluation report, and provide corresponding directions, taking into account the requirements under paragraph (2).

(2) REQUIREMENTS.—In revising the officer evaluation report under paragraph (1), the Commandant shall—

(A) consider the findings of the surveys under subsection (b);

(B) improve administrative efficiency;

(C) reduce and streamline performance dimensions and narrative text;

(D) eliminate redundancy with the officer specialty management system and any other record information systems that are used during the officer assignment or promotion process;

(E) provide for fairness and equity for Coast Guard officers with regard to promotion boards, selection panels, and the assignment process; and

(F) ensure officer evaluation responsibilities can be accomplished within normal working hours—

(i) to minimize any impact to officer duties; and

(ii) to eliminate any need for an officer to take liberty or leave for administrative purposes.

(d) REPORT.—

(1) IN GENERAL.—Not later than 545 days after the date of the enactment of this Act, the Commandant of the Coast Guard shall submit to the Committee on Commerce, Science, and Transportation of the Senate and the Committee on

Transportation and Infrastructure of the House of Representatives a report on the findings of the surveys under subsection (b).

(2) FORMAT.—The report under paragraph (1) shall be formatted by each rank, type of board, and position, as applicable.

SEC. 804. [14 U.S.C. 1102 note] EXTENSION OF AUTHORITY.

Section 404 of the Coast Guard Authorization Act of 2010 (Public Law 111-281; 124 Stat. 2950)is amended—

(1) in subsection (a), in the text preceding paragraph (1), by striking "sections 3304, 5333, and 5753" and inserting "section 3304"; and

(2) by striking subsection (b), and redesignating subsection (c) as subsection (b).

SEC. 805. COAST GUARD ROTC PROGRAM.

Not later than 1 year after the date of enactment of this Act, the Commandant of the Coast Guard shall submit to the Committee on Commerce, Science, and Transportation of the Senate and the Committee on Transportation and Infrastructure of the House of Representatives a report on the costs and benefits of creating a Coast Guard Reserve Officers' Training Corps Program based on the other Armed Forces programs.

SEC. 806. [14 U.S.C. 522 note] CURRENCY DETECTION CANINE TEAM PROGRAM.

(a) DEFINITIONS.—In this section:

(1) CANINE CURRENCY DETECTION TEAM.—The term "canine currency detection team" means a canine and a canine handler that are trained to detect currency.

(2) SECRETARY.—The term "Secretary" means the Secretary of the department in which the Coast Guard is operating.

(b) ESTABLISHMENT.—Not later than 1 year after the date of enactment of this Act, the Secretary shall establish a program to allow the use of canine currency detection teams for purposes of Coast Guard maritime law enforcement, including underway vessel boardings.

(c) OPERATION.—The Secretary may cooperate with, or enter

into an agreement with, the head of another Federal agency to meet the requirements under subsection (b).

SEC. 807. [14 U.S.C. 313 note] CENTER OF EXPERTISE FOR GREAT LAKES OIL SPILL SEARCH AND RESPONSE.

(a) IN GENERAL.—Not later than 1 year after the date of enactment of this Act, the Commandant of the Coast Guard shall establish a Center of Expertise for Great Lakes Oil Spill Preparedness and Response (referred to in this section as the "Center of Expertise") in accordance with section 313 of title 14, United States Code, as amended by this Act.

(b) LOCATION.—The Center of Expertise shall be located in close proximity to—

(1) critical crude oil transportation infrastructure on and connecting the Great Lakes, such as submerged pipelines and high-traffic navigation locks; and

(2) an institution of higher education with adequate aquatic research laboratory facilities and capabilities and expertise in Great Lakes aquatic ecology, environmental chemistry, fish and wildlife, and water resources.

(c) FUNCTIONS.—The Center of Expertise shall—

(1) monitor and assess, on an ongoing basis, the current state of knowledge regarding freshwater oil spill response technologies and the behavior and effects of oil spills in the Great Lakes;

(2) identify any significant gaps in Great Lakes oil spill research, including an assessment of major scientific or technological deficiencies in responses to past spills in the Great Lakes and other freshwater bodies, and seek to fill those gaps;

(3) conduct research, development, testing, and evaluation for freshwater oil spill response equipment, technologies, and techniques to mitigate and respond to oil spills in the Great Lakes;

(4) educate and train Federal, State, and local first responders located in Coast Guard District 9 in—

(A) the incident command system structure;

(B) Great Lakes oil spill response techniques and

strategies; and

(C) public affairs; and

(5) work with academic and private sector response training centers to develop and standardize maritime oil spill response training and techniques for use on the Great Lakes.

(d) DEFINITION.—In this section, the term "Great Lakes" means—

(1) Lake Ontario;

(2) Lake Erie;

(3) Lake Huron (including Lake St. Clair);

(4) Lake Michigan;

(5) Lake Superior; and

(6) the connecting channels (including the following rivers and tributaries of such rivers: Saint Mary's River, Saint Clair River, Detroit River, Niagara River, Illinois River, Chicago River, Fox River, Grand River, St. Joseph River, St. Louis River, Menominee River, Muskegon River, Kalamazoo River, and Saint Lawrence River to the Canadian border).

SEC. 808. PUBLIC SAFETY ANSWERING POINTS AND MARITIME SEARCH AND RESCUE COORDINATION.

Not later than 180 days after the date of the enactment of this Act—

(1) the Secretary of the department in which the Coast Guard is operating acting through the Commandant of the Coast Guard shall review Coast Guard policies and procedures for public safety answering points and search-and-rescue coordination with State and local law enforcement entities in order to—

(A) further minimize the possibility of maritime 911 calls being improperly routed; and

(B) assure the Coast Guard is able to effectively carry out the Coast Guard's maritime search and rescue mission; and

(2) the Commandant shall—

(A) formulate a national maritime public safety answering points policy; and

(B) submit a report to the Congress on such assessment and policy, which shall include an update to the report submitted in accordance with section 233 of the Howard Coble Coast Guard and Maritime Transportation Act of 2014.

SEC. 809. SHIP SHOAL LIGHTHOUSE TRANSFER: REPEAL.

Effective January 1, 2021, section 27 of the Coast Guard Authorization Act of 1991 (Public Law 102-241; 105 Stat. 2218) is repealed.

SEC. 810. LAND EXCHANGE, AYAKULIK ISLAND, ALASKA.

(a) LAND EXCHANGE; AYAKULIK ISLAND, ALASKA.—If the owner of Ayakulik Island, Alaska, offers to exchange the Island for the Tract—

(1) within 10 days after receiving such offer, the Secretary shall provide notice of the offer to the Commandant;

(2) within 90 days after receiving the notice under paragraph (1), the Commandant shall develop and transmit to the Secretary proposed operational restrictions on commercial activity conducted on the Tract, including the right of the Commandant to—

(A) order the immediate termination, for a period of up to 72 hours, of any activity occurring on or from the Tract that violates or threatens to violate one or more of such restrictions; or

(B) commence a civil action for appropriate relief, including a permanent or temporary injunction enjoining the activity that violates or threatens to violate such restrictions;

(3) within 90 days after receiving the proposed operational restrictions from the Commandant, the Secretary shall transmit such restrictions to the owner of Ayakulik Island; and

(4) within 30 days after transmitting the proposed operational restrictions to the owner of Ayakulik Island, and if the owner agrees to such restrictions, the Secretary shall convey all right, title, and interest of the United States in and to the Tract to the owner, subject to an easement granted to the Commandant to enforce such restrictions, in exchange for all right, title, and interest of such owner in and to Ayakulik

Island.

(b) BOUNDARY REVISIONS.—The Secretary may make technical and conforming revisions to the boundaries of the Tract before the date of the exchange.

(c) PUBLIC LAND ORDER.—Effective on the date of an exchange under subsection (a), Public Land Order 5550 shall have no force or effect with respect to submerged lands that are part of the Tract.

(d) FAILURE TO TIMELY RESPOND TO NOTICE.—If the Commandant does not transmit proposed operational restrictions to the Secretary in accordance within subsection (a)(2), the Secretary shall convey all right, title, and interest of the United States in and to the Tract to the owner of Ayakulik Island in exchange for all right, title, and interest of such owner in and to Ayakulik Island.

(e) CERCLA NOT AFFECTED.—This section and an exchange under this section shall not be construed to limit the application of or otherwise affect section 120(h) of the Comprehensive Environmental Response, Compensation, and Liability Act of 1980 (42 U.S.C. 9620(h)).

(f) DEFINITIONS.—In this section:

(1) COMMANDANT.—The term "Commandant" means the Secretary of the department in which the Coast Guard is operating, acting through the Commandant of the Coast Guard.

(2) SECRETARY.—The term "Secretary" means the Secretary of the Interior.

(3) TRACT.—The term "Tract" means the land (including submerged land) depicted as "PROPOSED PROPERTY EXCHANGE AREA" on the survey titled "PROPOSED PROPERTY EXCHANGE PARCEL" and dated 3/22/17.

SEC. 811. USE OF TRACT 43.

Section 524(e)(2) of the Pribilof Island Transition Completion Act of 2016 (Public Law 114-120), as amended by section 3533 of the Pribilof Island Transition Completion Amendments Act of 2016 (subtitle B of title XXXV of Public Law 114-328), is amended by—

(1) striking "each month" and inserting "each April and October"; and

(2) striking "previous month" and inserting "previous six months".

SEC. 812. COAST GUARD MARITIME DOMAIN AWARENESS.

(a) IN GENERAL.—The Secretary of the department in which the Coast Guard is operating shall seek to enter into an arrangement with the National Academy of Sciences not later than 60 days after the date of the enactment of this Act under which the Academy shall prepare an assessment of available unmanned, autonomous, or remotely controlled maritime domain awareness technologies for use by the Coast Guard.

(b) ASSESSMENT.—The assessment shall—

(1) describe the potential limitations of current and emerging unmanned technologies used in the maritime domain for—

(A) ocean observation;

(B) vessel monitoring and identification;

(C) weather observation;

(D) to the extent practicable for consideration by the Academy, intelligence gathering, surveillance, and reconnaissance; and

(E) communications;

(2) examine how technologies described in paragraph (1) can help prioritize Federal investment by examining;

(A) affordability, including acquisition, operations, and maintenance;

(B) reliability;

(C) versatility;

(D) efficiency; and

(E) estimated service life and persistence of effort; and

(3) analyze whether the use of new and emerging maritime domain awareness technologies can be used to—

(A) carry out Coast Guard missions at lower costs;

(B) expand the scope and range of Coast Guard maritime domain awareness;

(C) allow the Coast Guard to more efficiently and effectively allocate Coast Guard vessels, aircraft, and personnel; and

(D) identify adjustments that would be necessary in

Coast Guard policies, procedures, and protocols to incorporate unmanned technologies to enhance efficiency.

(c) REPORT TO CONGRESS.—Not later than 1 year after entering into an arrangement with the Secretary under subsection (a), the National Academy of Sciences shall submit the assessment prepared under this section to the Committees on Transportation and Infrastructure and Homeland Security of the House of Representatives and the Committee on Commerce, Science, and Transportation of the Senate.

(d) USE OF INFORMATION.—In formulating costs pursuant to subsection (b), the National Academy of Sciences may utilize information from other Coast Guard reports, assessments, or analyses regarding existing Coast Guard manpower requirements or other reports, assessments, or analyses for the acquisition of unmanned, autonomous, or remotely controlled technologies by the Federal Government.

SEC. 813. MONITORING.

(a) IN GENERAL.—The Secretary of the department in which the Coast Guard is operating shall conduct a 1-year pilot program to determine the impact of persistent use of different types of surveillance systems on illegal maritime activities, including illegal, unreported, and unregulated fishing, in the Western Pacific region.

(b) REQUIREMENTS.—The pilot program shall—

(1) consider the use of light aircraft-based detection systems that can identify potential illegal activity from high altitudes and produce enforcement-quality evidence at low altitudes; and

(2) be directed at detecting and deterring illegal maritime activities, including illegal, unreported, and unregulated fishing, and enhancing maritime domain awareness.

SEC. 814. REIMBURSEMENTS FOR NON-FEDERAL CONSTRUCTION COSTS OF CERTAIN AIDS TO NAVIGATION.

(a) IN GENERAL.—Subject to the availability of amounts specifically provided in advance in subsequent appropriations Acts and in accordance with this section, the Commandant of the Coast Guard may reimburse a non-Federal entity for costs incurred by the entity for a covered project.

(b) CONDITIONS.—The Commandant may not provide reimbursement under subsection (a) with respect to a covered project unless—

(1) the need for the project is a result of the completion of construction with respect to a federally authorized navigation channel;

(2) the Commandant determines, through an appropriate navigation safety analysis, that the project is necessary to ensure safe marine transportation;

(3) the Commandant approves the design of the project to ensure that it meets all applicable Coast Guard aids-to-navigation standards and requirements;

(4) the non-Federal entity agrees to transfer the project upon completion to the Coast Guard for operation and maintenance by the Coast Guard as a Federal aid to navigation;

(5) the non-Federal entity carries out the project in accordance with the same laws and regulations that would apply to the Coast Guard if the Coast Guard carried out the project, including obtaining all permits required for the project under Federal and State law; and

(6) the Commandant determines that the project satisfies such additional requirements as may be established by the Commandant.

(c) LIMITATIONS.—Reimbursements under subsection (a) may not exceed the following:

(1) For a single covered project, $5,000,000.

(2) For all covered projects in a single fiscal year, $5,000,000.

(d) EXPIRATION.—The authority granted under this section shall expire on the date that is 4 years after the date of enactment of this section.

(e) COVERED PROJECT DEFINED.—In this section, the term "covered project" means a project carried out—

(1) by a non-Federal entity to construct and establish an aid to navigation that facilitates safe and efficient marine transportation on a Federal navigation project authorized by title I of the Water Resources Development Act of 2007 (Public Law 110-114); and

(2) in an area that was affected by Hurricane Harvey.

SEC. 815. [14 U.S.C. 946 note] TOWING SAFETY MANAGEMENT SYSTEM FEES.

(a) REVIEW.—The Commandant of the Coast Guard shall—

(1) review and compare the costs to the Government of—

(A) towing vessel inspections performed by the Coast Guard; and

(B) such inspections performed by a third party; and

(2) based on such review and comparison, determine whether the costs to the Government of such inspections performed by a third party are different than the costs to the Government of such inspections performed by the Coast Guard.

(b) REVISION OF FEES.—If the Commandant determines under subsection (a) that the costs to the Government of such inspections performed by a third party are different than the costs to the Government of such inspections performed by the Coast Guard, then the Commandant shall revise the fee assessed by the Coast Guard for such inspections as necessary to conform to the requirements under section 9701 of title 31, United States Code, that such fee be based on the cost to the Government of such inspections and accurately reflect such costs.

SEC. 816. OIL SPILL DISBURSEMENTS AUDITING AND REPORT.

Section 1012 of the Oil Pollution Act of 1990 (33 U.S.C. 2712) is amended—

(1) by repealing subsection (g);

(2) in subsection (l)(1), by striking "Within one year after the date of enactment of the Coast Guard Authorization Act of 2010, and annually thereafter," and inserting "Each year, on the date on which the President submits to Congress a budget under section 1105 of title 31, United States Code,"; and

(3) by amending subsection (l)(2) to read as follows:

"(2) CONTENTS.—The report shall include—

"(A) a list of each incident that—

"(i) occurred in the preceding fiscal year; and

"(ii) resulted in disbursements from the Fund, for removal costs and damages, totaling $500,000 or more;

"(B) a list of each incident that—

"(i) occurred in the fiscal year preceding the preceding fiscal year; and

"(ii) resulted in disbursements from the Fund, for removal costs and damages, totaling $500,000 or more; and

"(C) an accounting of any amounts reimbursed to the Fund in the preceding fiscal year that were recovered from a responsible party for an incident that resulted in disbursements from the Fund, for removal costs and damages, totaling $500,000 or more."

SEC. 817. FLEET REQUIREMENTS ASSESSMENT AND STRATEGY.

(a) REPORT.—Not later than 1 year after the date of enactment of this Act, the Secretary of the department in which the Coast Guard is operating, in consultation with interested Federal and non-Federal stakeholders, shall submit to the Committee on Commerce, Science, and Transportation of the Senate and the Committee on Transportation and Infrastructure of the House of Representatives a report including—

(1) an assessment of Coast Guard at-sea operational fleet requirements to support its statutory missions established in the Homeland Security Act of 2002 (6 U.S.C. 101 et seq.); and

(2) a strategic plan for meeting the requirements identified under paragraph (1).

(b) CONTENTS.—The report under subsection (a) shall include—

(1) an assessment of—

(A) the extent to which the Coast Guard at-sea operational fleet requirements referred to in subsection (a)(1) are currently being met;

(B) the Coast Guard's current fleet, its operational lifespan, and how the anticipated changes in the age and distribution of vessels in the fleet will impact the ability to meet at-sea operational requirements;

(C) fleet operations and recommended improvements to minimize costs and extend operational vessel life spans; and

(D) the number of Fast Response Cutters, Offshore Patrol Cutters, and National Security Cutters needed to meet at-sea operational requirements as compared to planned acquisitions under the current programs of record;

(2) an analysis of—

(A) how the Coast Guard at-sea operational fleet requirements are currently met, including the use of the Coast Guard's current cutter fleet, agreements with partners, chartered vessels, and unmanned vehicle technology; and

(B) whether existing and planned cutter programs of record (including the Fast Response Cutter, Offshore Patrol Cutter, and National Security Cutter) will enable the Coast Guard to meet at-sea operational requirements; and

(3) a description of—

(A) planned manned and unmanned vessel acquisition; and

(B) how such acquisitions will change the extent to which the Coast Guard at-sea operational requirements are met.

(c) CONSULTATION AND TRANSPARENCY.—

(1) CONSULTATION.—In consulting with the Federal and non-Federal stakeholders under subsection (a), the Secretary of the department in which the Coast Guard is operating shall—

(A) provide the stakeholders with opportunities for input—

(i) prior to initially drafting the report, including the assessment and strategic plan; and

(ii) not later than 3 months prior to finalizing the report, including the assessment and strategic plan, for submission; and

(B) document the input and its disposition in the report.

(2) TRANSPARENCY.—All input provided under paragraph (1) shall be made available to the public.

(d) ENSURING MARITIME COVERAGE.—In order to meet Coast Guard mission requirements for search and rescue, ports, waterways, and coastal security, and maritime environmental response during recapitalization of Coast Guard vessels, the Coast Guard shall ensure continuity of the coverage, to the maximum extent practicable, in the locations that may lose assets.

SEC. 818. [14 U.S.C. 1133 note] NATIONAL SECURITY CUTTER.

(a) STANDARD METHOD FOR TRACKING.—The Commandant of the Coast Guard may not certify an eighth National Security Cutter as Ready for Operations before the date on which the Commandant provides to the Committee on Transportation and Infrastructure of the House of Representatives and the Committee on Commerce, Science, and Transportation of the Senate—

(1) a notification of a new standard method for tracking operational employment of Coast Guard major cutters that does not include time during which such a cutter is away from its homeport for maintenance or repair; and

(2) a report analyzing cost and performance for different approaches to achieving varied levels of operational employment using the standard method required by paragraph (1) that, at a minimum—

(A) compares over a 30-year period the average annualized baseline cost and performances for a certified National Security Cutter that operated for 185 days away from homeport or an equivalent alternative measure of operational tempo—

(i) against the cost of a 15 percent increase in days away from homeport or an equivalent alternative measure of operational tempo for a National Security Cutter; and

(ii) against the cost of the acquisition and operation of an additional National Security Cutter; and

(B) examines the optimal level of operational employment of National Security Cutters to balance National Security Cutter cost and mission performance.

(b) CONFORMING AMENDMENTS.—

(1) [14 U.S.C. 573 note] Section 221(b) of the Coast Guard and Maritime Transportation Act of 2012 (126 Stat. 1560) is repealed.

(2) [14 U.S.C. 504 note] Section 204(c)(1) of the Coast Guard Authorization Act of 2016 (130 Stat. 35) is repealed.

SEC. 819. ACQUISITION PLAN FOR INLAND WATERWAY AND RIVER TENDERS AND BAY-CLASS ICEBREAKERS.

(a) ACQUISITION PLAN.—Not later than 270 days after the date of the enactment of this Act, the Commandant of the Coast Guard shall submit to the Committee on Commerce, Science, and Transportation of the Senate and the Committee on Transportation and Infrastructure of the House of Representatives a plan to replace or extend the life of the Coast Guard fleet of inland waterway and river tenders, and the Bay-class icebreakers.

(b) CONTENTS.—The plan under subsection (a) shall include—

(1) an analysis of the work required to extend the life of vessels described in subsection (a);

(2) recommendations for which, if any, such vessels it is cost effective to undertake a ship-life extension or enhanced maintenance program;

(3) an analysis of the aids to navigation program to determine if advances in navigation technology may reduce the needs for physical aids to navigation;

(4) recommendations for changes to physical aids to navigation and the distribution of such aids that reduce the need for the acquisition of vessels to replace the vessels described in subsection (a);

(5) a schedule for the acquisition of vessels to replace the vessels described in subsection (a), including the date on which the first vessel will be delivered;

(6) the date such acquisition will be complete;

(7) a description of the order and location of replacement vessels;

(8) an estimate of the cost per vessel and of the total cost of the acquisition program of record; and

(9) an analysis of whether existing vessels can be used.

SEC. 820. GREAT LAKES ICEBREAKER ACQUISITION.

(a) ICEBREAKING ON THE GREAT LAKES.—For fiscal year 2019, the Commandant of the Coast Guard may use funds made available pursuant to section 4902 of title 14, United States Code, as amended by this Act, for the construction of an icebreaker that is at least as capable as the Coast Guard Cutter *Mackinaw* to enhance icebreaking capacity on the Great Lakes.

(b) ACQUISITION PLAN.—Not later than 45 days after the date of enactment of this Act, the Commandant shall submit a plan to the Committee on Commerce, Science, and Transportation of the Senate and the Committee on Transportation and Infrastructure of the House of Representatives for acquiring an icebreaker described in subsections (a) and (b). Such plan shall include—

(1) the details and schedule of the acquisition activities to be completed; and

(2) a description of how the funding for Coast Guard acquisition, construction, and improvements that was appropriated under the Consolidated Appropriations Act, 2017 (Public Law 115-31) and the Consolidated Appropriations Act, 2018 (Public Law 115–141) will be allocated to support the acquisition activities referred to in paragraph (1).

[Section 821 was repealed by section 8111(c)(4) of Public Law 116–283.]

SEC. 822. STRATEGIC ASSETS IN THE ARCTIC.

(a) DEFINITION OF ARCTIC.—In this section, the term "Arctic" has the meaning given the term in section 112 of the Arctic Research and Policy Act of 1984 (15 U.S.C. 4111).

(b) SENSE OF CONGRESS.—It is the sense of Congress that—

(1) the Arctic continues to grow in significance to both the national security interests and the economic prosperity of the United States; and

(2) the Coast Guard must ensure it is positioned to respond to any accident, incident, or threat with appropriate assets.

(c) REPORT.—Not later than 1 year after the date of enactment of this Act, the Commandant of the Coast Guard, in consultation with the Secretary of Defense and taking into consideration the Department of Defense 2016 Arctic Strategy, shall submit to the Committee on Commerce, Science, and Transportation of the Senate and the Committee on Transportation and Infrastructure of the House of Representatives a report on the progress toward implementing the strategic objectives described in the United

States Coast Guard Arctic Strategy dated May 2013.

(d) CONTENTS.—The report under subsection (c) shall include—

(1) a description of the Coast Guard's progress toward each strategic objective identified in the United States Coast Guard Arctic Strategy dated May 2013;

(2) an assessment of the assets and infrastructure necessary to meet the strategic objectives identified in the United States Coast Guard Arctic Strategy dated May 2013 based on factors such as—

(A) response time;

(B) coverage area;

(C) endurance on scene;

(D) presence; and

(E) deterrence;

(3) an analysis of the sufficiency of the distribution of National Security Cutters, Offshore Patrol Cutters, and Fast Response Cutters both stationed in various Alaskan ports and in other locations to meet the strategic objectives identified in the United States Coast Guard Arctic Strategy, dated May 2013;

(4) plans to provide communications throughout the entire Coastal Western Alaska Captain of the Port zone to improve waterway safety and mitigate close calls, collisions, and other dangerous interactions between the shipping industry and subsistence hunters;

(5) plans to prevent marine casualties, when possible, by ensuring vessels avoid environmentally sensitive areas and permanent security zones;

(6) an explanation of—

(A) whether it is feasible to establish a vessel traffic service, using existing resources or otherwise; and

(B) whether an Arctic Response Center of Expertise is necessary to address the gaps in experience, skills, equipment, resources, training, and doctrine to prepare, respond to, and recover spilled oil in the Arctic; and

(7) an assessment of whether sufficient agreements are in place to ensure the Coast Guard is receiving the information it

needs to carry out its responsibilities.

SEC. 823. [33 U.S.C. 1321 note] ARCTIC PLANNING CRITERIA.

(a) ALTERNATIVE PLANNING CRITERIA.—

(1) IN GENERAL.—For purposes of the Oil Pollution Act of 1990 (33 U.S.C. 2701 et seq.), the Commandant of the Coast Guard may approve a vessel response plan under section 311 of the Federal Water Pollution Control Act (33 U.S.C. 1321) for a vessel operating in any area covered by the Captain of the Port Zone (as established by the Commandant) that includes the Arctic, if the Commandant verifies that—

(A) equipment required to be available for response under the plan has been tested and proven capable of operating in the environmental conditions expected in the area in which it is intended to be operated; and

(B) the operators of such equipment have conducted training on the equipment within the area covered by such Captain of the Port Zone.

(2) POST-APPROVAL REQUIREMENTS.—In approving a vessel response plan under paragraph (1), the Commandant shall—

(A) require that the oil spill removal organization identified in the vessel response plan conduct regular exercises and drills using the response resources identified in the plan in the area covered by the Captain of the Port Zone that includes the Arctic; and

(B) allow such oil spill removal organization to take credit for a response to an actual spill or release in the area covered by such Captain of the Port Zone, instead of conducting an exercise or drill required under subparagraph (A), if the oil spill removal organization—

(i) documents which exercise or drill requirements were met during the response; and

(ii) submits a request for credit to, and receives approval from, the Commandant.

(b) REPORT.—

(1) IN GENERAL.—Not later than 120 days after the date of enactment of this Act, the Commandant of the Coast Guard shall submit to the Committee on Commerce, Science, and

Transportation of the Senate and the Committee on Transportation and Infrastructure of the House of Representatives a report on the oil spill prevention and response capabilities for the area covered by the Captain of the Port Zone (as established by the Commandant) that includes the Arctic.

(2) CONTENTS.—The report submitted under paragraph (1) shall include the following:

(A) A description of equipment and assets available for response under the vessel response plans approved for vessels operating in the area covered by the Captain of the Port Zone, including details on any providers of such equipment and assets.

(B) A description of the location of such equipment and assets, including an estimate of the time to deploy the equipment and assets.

(C) A determination of how effectively such equipment and assets are distributed throughout the area covered by the Captain of the Port Zone.

(D) A statement regarding whether the ability to maintain and deploy such equipment and assets is taken into account when measuring the equipment and assets available throughout the area covered by the Captain of the Port Zone.

(E) A validation of the port assessment visit process and response resource inventory for response under the vessel response plans approved for vessels operating in the area covered by the Captain of the Port Zone.

(F) A determination of the compliance rate with Federal vessel response plan regulations in the area covered by the Captain of the Port Zone during the previous 3 years.

(G) A description of the resources needed throughout the area covered by the Captain of the Port Zone to conduct port assessments, exercises, response plan reviews, and spill responses.

(c) DEFINITION OF ARCTIC.—In this section, the term "Arctic" has the meaning given the term under section 112 of the Arctic Research and Policy Act of 1984 (15 U.S.C. 4111).

SEC. 824. VESSEL RESPONSE PLAN AUDIT.

(a) IN GENERAL.—Not later than 1 year after the date of enactment of this Act, the Comptroller General of the United States shall complete and submit to the Committee on Commerce, Science, and Transportation of the Senate and the Committee on Transportation and Infrastructure of the House of Representatives a comprehensive review of the processes and resources used by the Coast Guard to implement vessel response plan requirements under section 311 of the Federal Water Pollution Control Act (33 U.S.C. 1321).

(b) REQUIRED ELEMENTS OF REVIEW.—The review required under subsection (a) shall, at a minimum, include—

(1) a study, or an audit if appropriate, of the processes the Coast Guard uses—

(A) to approve the vessel response plans referred to in subsection (a);

(B) to approve alternate planning criteria used in lieu of National Planning Criteria in approving such plans;

(C) to verify compliance with such plans; and

(D) to act in the event of a failure to comply with the requirements of such plans;

(2) an examination of all Federal and State agency resources used by the Coast Guard in carrying out the processes identified under paragraph (1), including—

(A) the current staffing model and organization;

(B) data, software, simulators, systems, or other technology, including those pertaining to weather, oil spill trajectory modeling, and risk management;

(C) the total amount of time per fiscal year expended by Coast Guard personnel to approve and verify compliance with vessel response plans; and

(D) the average amount of time expended by the Coast Guard for approval of, and verification of compliance with, a single vessel response plan;

(3) an analysis of how, including by what means or methods, the processes identified under paragraph (1)—

(A) ensure compliance with applicable law;

(B) are implemented by the Coast Guard, including at the district and sector levels;

(C) are informed by public comment and engagement with States, Indian Tribes, and other regional stakeholders;

(D) ensure availability and adequate operational capability and capacity of required assets and equipment, including in cases in which contractual obligations may limit the availability of such assets and equipment for response;

(E) provide for adequate asset and equipment mobilization time requirements, particularly with respect to—

(i) calculation and establishment of such requirements;

(ii) verifying compliance with such requirements; and

(iii) factoring in weather, including specific regional adverse weather as defined in section 155.1020 of title 33, Code of Federal Regulations, in calculating, establishing, and verifying compliance with such requirements;

(F) ensure response plan updates and vessel compliance when changes occur in response planning criteria, asset and equipment mobilization times, or regional response needs, such as trends in transportation of high gravity oils or changes in vessel traffic volume; and

(G) enable effective action by the Coast Guard in the event of a failure to comply with response plan requirements;

(4) a determination regarding whether asset and equipment mobilization time requirements under approved vessel response plans can be met by the vessels to which they apply; and

(5) recommendations for improving the processes identified under paragraph (1), including recommendations regarding the sufficiency of Coast Guard resources dedicated to those processes.

SEC. 825. WATERS DEEMED NOT NAVIGABLE WATERS OF THE UNITED STATES FOR CERTAIN PURPOSES.

For purposes of the application of subtitle II of title 46, United States Code, to the Volunteer (Hull Number CCA4108), the Illinois and Michigan Canal is deemed to not be navigable waters of the United States.

SEC. 826. [46 U.S.C. 12114 note] DOCUMENTATION OF RECREATIONAL VESSELS.

Coast Guard personnel performing nonrecreational vessel documentation functions under subchapter II of chapter 121 of title 46, United States Code, may perform recreational vessel documentation under section 12114 of such title in any fiscal year in which—

(1) funds available for Coast Guard operating expenses may not be used for expenses incurred for recreational vessel documentation;

(2) fees collected from owners of yachts and credited to such use are insufficient to pay expenses of recreational vessel documentation; and

(3) there is a backlog of applications for recreational vessel documentation.

SEC. 827. [46 U.S.C. 4302 note] EQUIPMENT REQUIREMENTS; EXEMPTION FROM THROWABLE PERSONAL FLOTATION DEVICES REQUIREMENT.

Not later than one year after the date of enactment of this Act, the Secretary of the department in which the Coast Guard is operating shall—

(1) prescribe regulations in part 160 of title 46, Code of Federal Regulations, that treat a marine throw bag, as that term is commonly used in the commercial whitewater rafting industry, as a type of lifesaving equipment; and

(2) revise section 175.17 of title 33, Code of Federal Regulations, to exempt rafts that are 16 feet or more overall in length from the requirement to carry an additional throwable personal flotation device when such a marine throw bag is onboard and accessible.

SEC. 828. [46 U.S.C. 4302 note] VISUAL DISTRESS SIGNALS AND

ALTERNATIVE USE.

(a) IN GENERAL.—The Secretary of the department in which the Coast Guard is operating shall develop a performance standard for the alternative use and possession of visual distress alerting and locating signals as mandated by carriage requirements for recreational boats in subpart C of part 175 of title 33, Code of Federal Regulations.

(b) REGULATIONS.—Not later than 180 days after the performance standard for alternative use and possession of visual distress alerting and locating signals is finalized, the Secretary shall revise part 175 of title 33, Code of Federal Regulations, to allow for carriage of such alternative signal devices.

SEC. 829. [46 U.S.C. 7302] RADAR REFRESHER TRAINING.

Not later than 60 days after the date of enactment of this Act, the Secretary of the department in which the Coast Guard is operating shall prescribe a final rule eliminating the requirement that a mariner actively using the mariner's credential complete an approved refresher or recertification course to maintain a radar observer endorsement. This rulemaking shall be exempt from chapters 5 and 6 of title 5, United States Code, and Executive Orders 12866 and 13563.

SEC. 830. [46 U.S.C. 4502 note] COMMERCIAL FISHING VESSEL SAFETY NATIONAL COMMUNICATIONS PLAN.

(a) REQUIREMENT FOR PLAN.—Not later than 1 year after the date of enactment of this Act, the Secretary of the department in which the Coast Guard is operating shall develop and submit to the Committee on Commerce, Science, and Transportation of the Senate and the Committee on Transportation and Infrastructure of the House of Representatives a national communications plan for the purposes of—

(1) disseminating information to the commercial fishing vessel industry;

(2) conducting outreach with the commercial fishing vessel industry;

(3) facilitating interaction with the commercial fishing vessel industry; and

(4) releasing information collected under section 15102 of title 46, United States Code, as added by this Act, to the

commercial fishing vessel industry.

(b) CONTENT.—The plan required by subsection (a), and each annual update, shall—

(1) identify staff, resources, and systems available to the Secretary to ensure the widest dissemination of information to the commercial fishing vessel industry;

(2) include a means to document all communication and outreach conducted with the commercial fishing vessel industry; and

(3) include a mechanism to measure effectiveness of such plan.

(c) IMPLEMENTATION.—Not later than one year after submission of the initial plan, the Secretary of the department in which the Coast Guard is operating shall implement the plan and shall at a minimum—

(1) leverage Coast Guard staff, resources, and systems available;

(2) monitor implementation nationwide to ensure adherence to plan contents;

(3) allow each Captain of the Port to adopt the most effective strategy and means to communicate with commercial fishing vessel industry in that Captain of the Port Zone;

(4) document communication and outreach; and

(5) solicit feedback from the commercial fishing vessel industry.

(d) REPORT AND UPDATES.—The Secretary of the department in which the Coast Guard is operating shall—

(1) submit to the Committee on Commerce, Science, and Transportation of the Senate and the Committee on Transportation and Infrastructure of the House of Representatives a report on the effectiveness of the plan to date and any updates to ensure maximum impact of the plan one year after the date of enactment of this Act, and every 4 years thereafter; and

(2) include in such report input from individual Captains of the Port and any feedback received from the commercial fishing vessel industry.

SEC. 831. ATLANTIC COAST PORT ACCESS ROUTE STUDY RECOMMENDATIONS.

Not later than 30 days after the date of the enactment of the Act, the Commandant of the Coast Guard shall notify the Committee on Transportation and Infrastructure of the House of Representatives and the Committee on Commerce, Science, and Transportation of the Senate of action taken to carry out the recommendations contained in the final report issued by the Atlantic Coast Port Access Route Study (ACPARS) workgroup for which notice of availability was published March 14, 2016 (81 Fed. Reg. 13307).

SEC. 832. DRAWBRIDGES.

Section 5 of the Act entitled "An Act making appropriations for the construction, repair, and preservation of certain public works on rivers and harbors, and for other purposes", approved August 18, 1894 (33 U.S.C. 499), is amended by adding at the end the following:

"(d) TEMPORARY CHANGES TO DRAWBRIDGE OPERATING SCHEDULES.—Notwithstanding section 553 of title 5, United States Code, whenever a temporary change to the operating schedule of a drawbridge, lasting 180 days or less—

"(1) is approved—

"(A) the Secretary of the department in which the Coast Guard is operating shall—

"(i) issue a deviation approval letter to the bridge owner; and

"(ii) announce the temporary change in—

"(I) the Local Notice to Mariners;

"(II) a broadcast notice to mariners and through radio stations; or

"(III) such other local media as the Secretary considers appropriate; and

"(B) the bridge owner, except a railroad bridge owner, shall notify—

"(i) the public by publishing notice of the temporary change in a newspaper of general circulation published in the place where the bridge is located;

"(ii) the department, agency, or office of transportation with jurisdiction over the roadway that abuts the approaches to the bridge; and

"(iii) the law enforcement organization with jurisdiction over the roadway that abuts the approaches to the bridge; or

"(2) is denied, the Secretary of the department in which the Coast Guard is operating shall—

"(A) not later than 10 days after the date of receipt of the request, provide the bridge owner in writing the reasons for the denial, including any supporting data and evidence used to make the determination; and

"(B) provide the bridge owner a reasonable opportunity to address each reason for the denial and resubmit the request.

"(e) DRAWBRIDGE MOVEMENTS.—The Secretary of the department in which the Coast Guard is operating—

"(1) shall require a drawbridge operator to record each movement of the drawbridge in a logbook;

"(2) may inspect the logbook to ensure drawbridge movement is in accordance with the posted operating schedule;

"(3) shall review whether deviations from the posted operating schedule are impairing vehicular and pedestrian traffic; and

"(4) may determine if the operating schedule should be adjusted for efficiency of maritime or vehicular and pedestrian traffic.

"(f) REQUIREMENTS.—

"(1) LOGBOOKS.—An operator of a drawbridge built across a navigable river or other water of the United States—

"(A) that opens the draw of such bridge for the passage of a vessel, shall record in a logbook—

"(i) the bridge identification and date of each opening;

"(ii) the bridge tender or operator for each opening;

"(iii) each time it is opened for navigation;

"(iv) each time it is closed for navigation;

"(v) the number and direction of vessels passing through during each opening;

"(vi) the types of vessels passing through during each opening;

"(vii) an estimated or known size (height, length, and beam) of the largest vessel passing through during each opening;

"(viii) for each vessel, the vessel name and registration number if easily observable; and

"(ix) all maintenance openings, malfunctions, or other comments; and

"(B) that remains open to navigation but closes to allow for trains to cross, shall record in a logbook—

"(i) the bridge identification and date of each opening and closing;

"(ii) the bridge tender or operator;

"(iii) each time it is opened to navigation;

"(iv) each time it is closed to navigation; and

"(v) all maintenance openings, closings, malfunctions, or other comments.

"(2) MAINTENANCE OF LOGBOOKS.—A drawbridge operator shall maintain logbooks required under paragraph (1) for not less than 5 years.

"(3) SUBMISSION OF LOGBOOKS.—At the request of the Secretary of the department in which the Coast Guard is operating, a drawbridge operator shall submit to the Secretary the logbook required under paragraph (1) as the Secretary considers necessary to carry out this section.

"(4) EXEMPTION.—The requirements under paragraph (1) shall be exempt from sections 3501 to 3521 of title 44, United States Code."

SEC. 833. WAIVER.

Section 8902 of title 46, United States Code, shall not apply to the chain ferry DIANE (United States official number CG002692) when such vessel is operating on the Kalamazoo River in Saugatuck, Michigan.

SEC. 834. FIRE-RETARDANT MATERIALS.

Section 3503 of title 46, United States Code, is amended to read as follows:

"SEC. § 3503. Fire-retardant material

"(a)(1) A passenger vessel of the United States having berth or stateroom accommodations for at least 50 passengers shall be granted a certificate of inspection only if—

"(A) the vessel is constructed of fire-retardant materials; and

"(B) the vessel—

"(i) is operating engines, boilers, main electrical distribution panels, fuel tanks, oil tanks, and generators that meet current Coast Guard regulations; and

"(ii) is operating boilers and main electrical generators that are contained within noncombustible enclosures equipped with fire suppression systems.

"(2) Before December 1, 2028, this subsection does not apply to any vessel in operation before January 1, 1968, and operating only within the Boundary Line.

"(b)(1) The owner or managing operator of an exempted vessel described in subsection (a)(2) shall—

"(A) notify in writing prospective passengers, prior to purchase, and each crew member that the vessel does not comply with applicable fire safety standards due primarily to the wooden construction of passenger berthing areas;

"(B) display in clearly legible font prominently throughout the vessel, including in each state room the following: 'THIS VESSEL FAILS TO COMPLY WITH SAFETY RULES AND REGULATIONS OF THE U.S. COAST GUARD.';

"(C) acquire prior to the vessel entering service, and maintain, liability insurance in an amount to be prescribed by the Federal Maritime Commission;

"(D) make annual structural alteration to not less than 10 percent of the areas of the vessel that are not constructed of fire retardant materials;

"(E) prioritize alterations in galleys, engineering areas of the vessel, including all spaces and compartments containing, or adjacent to spaces and compartments containing, engines, boilers, main electrical distribution panels, fuel tanks, oil tanks, and generators;

"(F) ensure, to the satisfaction of the Secretary, that the combustible fire-load has been reduced pursuant to subparagraph (D) during each annual inspection for certification;

"(G) ensure the vessel has multiple forms of egress off the vessel's bow and stern;

"(H) provide advance notice to the Coast Guard regarding the structural alterations made pursuant to subparagraph (D) and comply with any noncombustible material requirements prescribed by the Coast Guard;

"(I) annually notify all ports of call and State emergency management offices of jurisdiction that the vessel does not comply with the requirement under subsection (a)(1);

"(J) provide crewmembers manning such vessel shipboard training that—

"(i) is specialized for exempted vessels;

"(ii) exceeds requirements related to standards for firefighting training under chapter I of title 46, Code of Federal Regulations, as in effect on October 1, 2017; and

"(iii) is approved by the Coast Guard; and

"(K) to the extent practicable, take all steps to retain previously trained crew knowledgeable of such vessel or to hire crew trained in operations aboard exempted vessels.

"(2) The owner or managing operator of an exempted vessel described in subsection (a)(2) may not disclaim liability to a passenger or crew member of such vessel for death, injury, or any other loss caused by fire due to the negligence of the owner or managing operator.

"(3) The Secretary shall—

"(A) conduct an annual audit and inspection of each exempted vessel described in subsection (a)(2);

"(B) in implementing subparagraph (b)(1)(F), consider, to the extent practicable, the goal of preservation of the historic integrity of such vessel in areas carrying or accessible to passengers or generally visible to the public; and

"(C) prescribe regulations to carry out this section, including to prescribe the manner in which prospective passengers are to be notified under paragraph (1)(A).

"(4) The penalties provided in section 3504(c) of this title shall apply to a violation of this subsection.

"(c) In addition to otherwise applicable penalties, the Secretary may immediately withdraw a certificate of inspection for an exempted vessel described in subsection (a)(2) that does not comply with any requirement under subsection (b)."

SEC. 835. VESSEL WAIVER.

(a) IN GENERAL.—Upon the date of enactment of this Act and notwithstanding sections 12112(a)(2)(A) and 12113(a)(2) of title 46, United States Code, the Secretary shall issue a certificate of documentation with coastwise and fishery endorsements to the certificated vessel.

(b) REPLACEMENT VESSEL.—The certificated vessel shall qualify as a replacement vessel for the vessel "AMERICA NO.1" (United States official number 610654) and not be precluded from operating as an Amendment 80 replacement vessel under the provisions of part 679 of title 50, Code of Federal Regulations.

(c) COAST GUARD REVIEW AND DETERMINATION.—

(1) REVIEW.—Not later than 30 days after the date of enactment of this Act, the Secretary shall conduct a review of the use of certain foreign fabricated steel components in the hull or superstructure of the certificated vessel.

(2) DETERMINATION.—Based on the review conducted under paragraph (1), the Secretary shall determine whether the shipyard that constructed the certificated vessel or the purchaser of the certificated vessel knew before such components were procured or installed that the use of such components would violate requirements under sections 12112(a)(2)(A) and 12113(a)(2) of title 46, United States Code.

(3) REVOCATION.—If the Secretary determines under paragraph (2) that the shipyard that constructed the certificated vessel or the purchaser of the certificated vessel knew before such components were procured or installed that the use of such components would violate requirements under sections 12112(a)(2)(A) and 12113(a)(2) of title 46, United

States Code, the Secretary shall immediately revoke the certificate of documentation issued under subsection (a).

(4) USE OF DOCUMENTS.—In conducting the review required under paragraph (1), the Secretary may request and review any information, correspondence, or documents related to the construction of the certificated vessel, including from the shipyard that constructed the certificated vessel and the purchaser of the certificated vessel.

(d) TERMINATION.—If the contract for purchase of the certificated vessel that is in effect on the date of enactment of this Act is terminated, the purchasing party to that contract shall be prohibited from entering into a subsequent contract or agreement for purchase of such vessel.

(e) DEFINITIONS.—In this section:

(1) CERTIFICATED VESSEL.—The term "certificated vessel" means the vessel America's Finest (United States official number 1276760).

(2) SECRETARY.—The term "Secretary" means the Secretary of the department in which the Coast Guard is operating, acting through the Commandant of the Coast Guard.

SEC. 836. TEMPORARY LIMITATIONS.

(a) LIMITATIONS.—

(1) IN GENERAL.—Upon the Coast Guard issuing a certificate of documentation with coastwise and fishery endorsements for the vessel "AMERICA'S FINEST" (United States official number 1276760) and during any period such certificate is in effect, and subject to subsection (b), the total amount of groundfish harvested with respect to subparagraph (A) or the total amount of deliveries processed from other vessels with respect to subparagraph (B) by the vessels described in paragraph (2) shall not collectively exceed—

(A) the percentage of the harvest available in any Gulf of Alaska groundfish fisheries (other than fisheries subject to a limited access privilege program created by the North Pacific Fishery Management Council) that is equivalent to the total harvest by the vessels described in paragraph (2) in those fisheries in the calendar years that a vessel described in paragraph (2) had harvest from 2012 through

2017 relative to the total allowable catch available to such vessels in the calendar years 2012 through 2017; or

(B) the percentage of processing of deliveries from other vessels in any Bering Sea, Aleutian Islands, and Gulf of Alaska groundfish fisheries (including fisheries subject to a limited access privilege program created by the North Pacific Fishery Management Council, or community development quotas as described in section 305(i) of the Magnuson-Stevens Fishery Conservation and Management Act (16 U.S.C. 1855(i))) that is equivalent to the total processing of such deliveries by the vessels described in paragraph (2) in those fisheries in the calendar years 2012 through 2017 relative to the total allowable catch available in the calendar years 2012 through 2017.

(2) APPLICABLE VESSELS.—The limitations described in paragraph (1) shall apply, in the aggregate, to—

(A) the vessel AMERICA'S FINEST (United States official number 1276760);

(B) the vessel US INTREPID (United States official number 604439);

(C) the vessel AMERICAN NO. 1 (United States official number 610654);

(D) any replacement of a vessel described in subparagraph (A), (B), or (C); and

(E) any vessel assigned license number LLG3217 under the license limitation program under part 679 of title 50, Code of Federal Regulations.

(b) EXPIRATION.—The limitations described in subsection (a) shall apply to a groundfish species in Bering Sea, Aleutian Islands, and Gulf of Alaska only until the earlier of—

(1) the end of the 6-year period beginning on the date of enactment of this Act; or

(2) the date on which the Secretary of Commerce issues a final rule, based on recommendations developed by the North Pacific Fishery Management Council consistent with the Magnuson-Stevens Fishery Conservation and Management Act (16 U.S.C. 1801 et seq.), that limits processing deliveries of that groundfish species from other vessels in any Bering Sea, Aleutian Islands, and Gulf of Alaska groundfish fisheries that

are not subject to conservation and management measures under section 206 of the American Fisheries Act (16 U.S.C. 1851 note).

(c) EXISTING AUTHORITY.—Except for the measures required by this section, nothing in this title shall be construed to limit the authority of the North Pacific Fishery Management Council or the Secretary of Commerce under the Magnuson-Stevens Fishery Conservation and Management Act (16 U.S.C. 1801 et seq.).

SEC. 837. [16 U.S.C. 668dd note] TRANSFER OF COAST GUARD PROPERTY IN JUPITER ISLAND, FLORIDA, FOR INCLUSION IN HOBE SOUND NATIONAL WILDLIFE REFUGE.

(a) TRANSFER.—Administrative jurisdiction over the property described in subsection (b) is transferred to the Secretary of the Interior.

(b) PROPERTY DESCRIBED.—The property described in this subsection is real property administered by the Coast Guard in the Town of Jupiter Island, Florida, comprising Parcel #35-38-42-004-000-02590-6 (Bon Air Beach lots 259 and 260 located at 83 North Beach Road) and Parcel #35-38-42-004-000-02610-2 (Bon Air Beach lots 261 to 267), including any improvements thereon that are not authorized or required by another provision of law to be conveyed to another person.

(c) ADMINISTRATION.—The property described in subsection (b) is included in Hobe Sound National Wildlife Refuge, and shall be administered by the Secretary of the Interior acting through the United States Fish and Wildlife Service.

SEC. 838. EMERGENCY RESPONSE.

Not later than 90 days after the date of enactment of this Act, the Commandant of the Coast Guard shall request the National Offshore Safety Advisory Committee to examine whether there are unnecessary regulatory barriers to the use of small passenger vessels, crewboats, and offshore supply vessels in disaster response and provide recommendations, as appropriate, to reduce such barriers.

SEC. 839. DRAWBRIDGES CONSULTATION.

(a) CONSULTATION.—In addition and subsequent to any rulemaking conducted under section 117.8 of title 33, Code of

Federal Regulations, related to permanent changes to drawbridge openings that result from Amtrak service between New Orleans, Louisiana and Orlando, Florida, the Commandant shall consult with owners or operators of rail lines used for Amtrak passenger service between New Orleans, Louisiana and Orlando, Florida and affected waterway users on changes to drawbridge operating schedules necessary to facilitate the On Time Performance of passenger trains. These changes to schedules shall not impact Coast Guard response times to operational missions.

(b) TIMING.—Consultation in subsection (a) shall occur after commencement of Amtrak passenger service on the rail lines between New Orleans, Louisiana and Orlando, Florida at the following intervals:

(1) Not less than 3 months following the commencement of Amtrak passenger service.

(2) Not less than 6 months following the commencement of Amtrak passenger service.

(c) REPORT.—If after conducting the consultations required by subsection (b)(2), the Commandant finds that permanent changes to drawbridge operations are necessary to mitigate delays in the movement of trains described in subsection (a) and that those changes do not unreasonably obstruct the navigability of the affected waterways, then the Commandant shall submit those findings to the Committee on Commerce, Science, and Transportation of the Senate and the Committee on Transportation and Infrastructure of the House of Representatives.

TITLE IX—VESSEL INCIDENTAL DISCHARGE ACT

SEC. 901. [33 U.S.C. 1251 note] SHORT TITLE.

This title may be cited as the "Vessel Incidental Discharge Act of 2018".

SEC. 902. [33 U.S.C. 1322 note] PURPOSES; FINDINGS.

(a) PURPOSES.—The purposes of this title are—

(1) to provide for the establishment of uniform, environmentally sound standards and requirements for the management of discharges incidental to the normal operation

of a vessel;

(2) to charge the Environmental Protection Agency with primary responsibility for establishing standards relating to the discharge of pollutants from vessels;

(3) to charge the Coast Guard with primary responsibility for prescribing, administering, and enforcing regulations, consistent with the discharge standards established by the Environmental Protection Agency, for the design, construction, installation, and operation of the equipment and management practices required onboard vessels; and

(4) to preserve the flexibility of States, political subdivisions, and certain regions with respect to the administration and enforcement of standards relating to the discharge of pollutants from vessels engaged in maritime commerce and transportation.

(b) FINDINGS.—Congress finds that—

(1) the Environmental Protection Agency is the principal Federal authority charged under the Federal Water Pollution Control Act (33 U.S.C. 1251 et seq.) with regulating through the issuance of permits for the discharge of pollutants into the navigable waters of the United States;

(2) the Coast Guard is the principal Federal authority charged with administering, enforcing, and prescribing regulations relating to the discharge of pollutants from vessels; and

(3) during the period of 1973 to 2010—

(A) the Environmental Protection Agency promulgated regulations exempting certain discharges incidental to the normal operation of vessels from otherwise applicable permitting requirements of the Federal Water Pollution Control Act (33 U.S.C. 1251 et seq.); and

(B) Congress enacted laws on numerous occasions governing the regulation of discharges incidental to the normal operation of vessels, including—

(i) the Act to Prevent Pollution from Ships (33 U.S.C. 1901 et seq.);

(ii) the Nonindigenous Aquatic Nuisance Prevention and Control Act of 1990 (16 U.S.C. 4701 et seq.);

(iii) the National Invasive Species Act of 1996 (16 U.S.C. 4701 note; Public Law 104-332);

(iv) section 415 of the Coast Guard Authorization Act of 1998 (Public Law 105-383; 112 Stat. 3434) and section 623 of the Coast Guard and Maritime Transportation Act of 2004 (33 U.S.C. 1901 note; Public Law 108-293), which established interim and permanent requirements, respectively, for the regulation of vessel discharges of certain bulk cargo residue;

(v) title XIV of division B of Appendix D of the Consolidated Appropriations Act, 2001 (Public Law 106-554; 114 Stat. 2763A-315), which prohibited or limited certain vessel discharges in certain areas of Alaska;

(vi) section 204 of the Maritime Transportation Security Act of 2002 (33 U.S.C. 1902a), which established requirements for the regulation of vessel discharges of agricultural cargo residue material in the form of hold washings; and

(vii) title X of the Coast Guard Authorization Act of 2010 (33 U.S.C. 3801 et seq.), which provided for the implementation of the International Convention on the Control of Harmful Anti-Fouling Systems on Ships, 2001.

SEC. 903. STANDARDS FOR DISCHARGES INCIDENTAL TO NORMAL OPERATION OF VESSELS.

(a) UNIFORM NATIONAL STANDARDS.—

(1) IN GENERAL.—Section 312 of the Federal Water Pollution Control Act (33 U.S.C. 1322) is amended by adding at the end the following:

"(p) UNIFORM NATIONAL STANDARDS FOR DISCHARGES INCIDENTAL TO NORMAL OPERATION OF VESSELS.—

"(1) DEFINITIONS.—In this subsection:

"(A) AQUATIC NUISANCE SPECIES.—The term 'aquatic nuisance species' means a nonindigenous species that threatens—

"(i) the diversity or abundance of a native species;

"(ii) the ecological stability of—

"(I) waters of the United States; or

"(II) waters of the contiguous zone; or

"(iii) a commercial, agricultural, aquacultural, or recreational activity that is dependent on—

"(I) waters of the United States; or

"(II) waters of the contiguous zone.

"(B) BALLAST WATER.—

"(i) IN GENERAL.—The term 'ballast water' means any water, suspended matter, and other materials taken onboard a vessel—

"(I) to control or maintain trim, draught, stability, or stresses of the vessel, regardless of the means by which any such water or suspended matter is carried; or

"(II) during the cleaning, maintenance, or other operation of a ballast tank or ballast water management system of the vessel.

"(ii) EXCLUSION.—The term 'ballast water' does not include any substance that is added to the water described in clause (i) that is directly related to the operation of a properly functioning ballast water management system.

"(C) BALLAST WATER DISCHARGE STANDARD.—The term 'ballast water discharge standard' means—

"(i) the numerical ballast water discharge standard established by section 151.1511 or 151.2030 of title 33, Code of Federal Regulations (or successor regulations); or

"(ii) if a standard referred to in clause (i) is superseded by a numerical standard of performance under this subsection, that superseding standard.

"(D) BALLAST WATER EXCHANGE.—The term 'ballast water exchange' means the replacement of water in a ballast water tank using 1 of the following methods:

"(i) Flow-through exchange, in which ballast water is flushed out by pumping in midocean water at the bottom of the tank if practicable, and continuously overflowing the tank from the top, until 3 full volumes of water have been changed to minimize the number of original organisms remaining in the tank.

"(ii) Empty and refill exchange, in which ballast water taken on in ports, estuarine waters, or territorial waters is pumped out until the pump loses suction, after which the ballast tank is refilled with midocean water.

"(E) BALLAST WATER MANAGEMENT SYSTEM.—The term 'ballast water management system' means any marine pollution control device (including all ballast water treatment equipment, ballast tanks, pipes, pumps, and all associated control and monitoring equipment) that processes ballast water—

"(i) to kill, render nonviable, or remove organisms; or

"(ii) to avoid the uptake or discharge of organisms.

"(F) BEST AVAILABLE TECHNOLOGY ECONOMICALLY ACHIEVABLE.—The term 'best available technology economically achievable' means—

"(i) best available technology economically achievable (within the meaning of section 301(b)(2)(A));

"(ii) best available technology (within the meaning of section 304(b)(2)(B)); and

"(iii) best available technology, as determined in accordance with section 125.3(d)(3) of title 40, Code of Federal Regulations (or successor regulations).

"(G) BEST CONVENTIONAL POLLUTANT CONTROL TECHNOLOGY.—The term 'best conventional pollutant control technology' means—

"(i) best conventional pollutant control technology (within the meaning of section 301(b)(2)(E));

"(ii) best conventional pollutant control technology (within the meaning of section 304(b)(4)); and

"(iii) best conventional pollutant control technology, as determined in accordance with section 125.3(d)(2) of title 40, Code of Federal Regulations (or successor regulations).

"(H) BEST MANAGEMENT PRACTICE.—

"(i) IN GENERAL.—The term 'best management practice' means a schedule of activities, prohibitions of practices, maintenance procedures, and other management practices to prevent or reduce the pollution of—

"(I) the waters of the United States; or

"(II) the waters of the contiguous zone.

"(ii) INCLUSIONS.—The term 'best management practice' includes any treatment requirement, operating procedure, or practice to control—

"(I) vessel runoff;

"(II) spillage or leaks;

"(III) sludge or waste disposal; or

"(IV) drainage from raw material storage.

"(I) BEST PRACTICABLE CONTROL TECHNOLOGY CURRENTLY AVAILABLE.—The term 'best practicable control technology currently available' means—

"(i) best practicable control technology currently available (within the meaning of section 301(b)(1)(A));

"(ii) best practicable control technology currently available (within the meaning of section 304(b)(1)); and

"(iii) best practicable control technology currently available, as determined in accordance with section 125.3(d)(1) of title 40, Code of Federal Regulations (or successor regulations).

"(J) CAPTAIN OF THE PORT ZONE.—The term 'Captain of the Port Zone' means a Captain of the Port Zone established by the Secretary pursuant to sections 92, 93, and 633 of title 14, United States Code.

"(K) EMPTY BALLAST TANK.—The term 'empty ballast tank' means a tank that—

"(i) has previously held ballast water that has been drained to the limit of the functional or operational capabilities of the tank (such as loss of suction);

"(ii) is recorded as empty on a vessel log; and

"(iii) contains unpumpable residual ballast water and sediment.

"(L) GREAT LAKES COMMISSION.—The term 'Great Lakes Commission' means the Great Lakes Commission established by article IV A of the Great Lakes Compact to which Congress granted consent in the Act of July 24, 1968 (Public Law 90-419; 82 Stat. 414).

"(M) GREAT LAKES STATE.—The term 'Great Lakes State' means any of the States of—

"(i) Illinois;

"(ii) Indiana;

"(iii) Michigan;

"(iv) Minnesota;

"(v) New York;

"(vi) Ohio;

"(vii) Pennsylvania; and

"(viii) Wisconsin.

"(N) GREAT LAKES SYSTEM.—The term 'Great Lakes System' has the meaning given the term in section 118(a)(3).

"(O) INTERNAL WATERS.—The term 'internal waters' has the meaning given the term in section 2.24 of title 33, Code of Federal Regulations (or a successor regulation).

"(P) MARINE POLLUTION CONTROL DEVICE.—The term 'marine pollution control device' means any equipment or management practice (or combination of equipment and a management practice), for installation or use onboard a vessel, that is—

"(i) designed to receive, retain, treat, control, or discharge a discharge incidental to the normal operation of a vessel; and

"(ii) determined by the Administrator and the Secretary to be the most effective equipment or management practice (or combination of equipment and a management practice) to reduce the environmental impacts of the discharge, consistent with the factors for consideration described in paragraphs (4) and (5).

"(Q) NONINDIGENOUS SPECIES.—The term 'nonindigenous species' means an organism of a species that enters an ecosystem beyond the historic range of the species.

"(R) ORGANISM.—The term 'organism' includes—

"(i) an animal, including fish and fish eggs and larvae;

"(ii) a plant;

"(iii) a pathogen;

"(iv) a microbe;

"(v) a virus;

"(vi) a prokaryote (including any archean or bacterium);

"(vii) a fungus; and

"(viii) a protist.

"(S) PACIFIC REGION.—

"(i) IN GENERAL.—The term 'Pacific Region' means any Federal or State water—

"(I) adjacent to the State of Alaska, California, Hawaii, Oregon, or Washington; and

"(II) extending from shore.

"(ii) INCLUSION.—The term 'Pacific Region' includes the entire exclusive economic zone (as defined in section 1001 of the Oil Pollution Act of 1990 (33 U.S.C. 2701)) adjacent to each State described in clause (i)(I).

"(T) PORT OR PLACE OF DESTINATION.—The term 'port or place of destination' means a port or place to which a vessel is bound to anchor or moor.

"(U) RENDER NONVIABLE.—The term 'render nonviable', with respect to an organism in ballast water, means the action of a ballast water management system that renders the organism permanently incapable of reproduction following treatment.

"(V) SALTWATER FLUSH.—

"(i) IN GENERAL.—The term 'saltwater flush' means—

"(I)(aa) the addition of as much midocean water into each empty ballast tank of a vessel as is safe for the vessel and crew; and

"(bb) the mixing of the flushwater with residual ballast water and sediment through the motion of the vessel; and

"(II) the discharge of that mixed water, such that the resultant residual water remaining in the tank—

"(aa) has the highest salinity possible; and

"(bb) is at least 30 parts per thousand.

"(ii) MULTIPLE SEQUENCES.—For purposes of clause (i), a saltwater flush may require more than 1 fill-mix-empty sequence, particularly if only small quantities of water can be safely taken onboard a vessel at 1 time.

"(W) SECRETARY.—The term 'Secretary' means the Secretary of the department in which the Coast Guard is operating.

"(X) SMALL VESSEL GENERAL PERMIT.—The term 'Small Vessel General Permit' means the permit that is the subject of the notice of final permit issuance entitled 'Final National Pollutant Discharge Elimination System (NPDES) Small Vessel General Permit for Discharges Incidental to the Normal Operation of Vessels Less Than 79 Feet' (79 Fed. Reg. 53702 (September 10, 2014)).

"(Y) SMALL VESSEL OR FISHING VESSEL.—The term 'small vessel or fishing vessel' means a vessel that is—

"(i) less than 79 feet in length; or

"(ii) a fishing vessel, fish processing vessel, or fish tender vessel (as those terms are defined in section 2101 of title 46, United States Code), regardless of the length of the vessel.

"(Z) VESSEL GENERAL PERMIT.—The term 'Vessel General Permit' means the permit that is the subject of the notice of final permit issuance entitled 'Final National Pollutant Discharge Elimination System (NPDES) General Permit for Discharges Incidental to the Normal Operation of a Vessel' (78 Fed. Reg. 21938 (April 12, 2013)).

"(2) APPLICABILITY.—

"(A) IN GENERAL.—Except as provided in subparagraph (B), this subsection applies to—

"(i) any discharge incidental to the normal operation of a vessel; and

"(ii) any discharge incidental to the normal operation of a vessel (such as most graywater) that is commingled with sewage, subject to the conditions that—

"(I) nothing in this subsection prevents a State from regulating sewage discharges; and

"(II) any such commingled discharge shall comply with all applicable requirements of—

"(aa) this subsection; and

"(bb) any law applicable to discharges

of sewage.

"(B) EXCLUSION.—This subsection does not apply to any discharge incidental to the normal operation of a vessel—

"(i) from—

"(I) a vessel of the Armed Forces subject to subsection (n);

"(II) a recreational vessel subject to subsection (o);

"(III) a small vessel or fishing vessel, except that this subsection shall apply to any discharge of ballast water from a small vessel or fishing vessel; or

"(IV) a floating craft that is permanently moored to a pier, including a 'floating' casino, hotel, restaurant, or bar;

"(ii) of ballast water from a vessel—

"(I) that continuously takes on and discharges ballast water in a flow-through system, if the Administrator determines that system cannot materially contribute to the spread or introduction of an aquatic nuisance species into waters of the United States;

"(II) in the National Defense Reserve Fleet that is scheduled for disposal, if the vessel does not have an operable ballast water management system;

"(III) that discharges ballast water consisting solely of water taken onboard from a public or commercial source that, at the time the water is taken onboard, meets the applicable requirements or permit requirements of the Safe Drinking Water Act (42 U.S.C. 300f et seq.);

"(IV) that carries all permanent ballast water in sealed tanks that are not subject to discharge; or

"(V) that only discharges ballast water

into a reception facility; or

"(iii) that results from, or contains material derived from, an activity other than the normal operation of the vessel, such as material resulting from an industrial or manufacturing process onboard the vessel.

"(3) CONTINUATION IN EFFECT OF EXISTING REQUIREMENTS.—

"(A) VESSEL GENERAL PERMIT.—Notwithstanding the expiration date of the Vessel General Permit or any other provision of law, all provisions of the Vessel General Permit shall remain in force and effect, and shall not be modified, until the applicable date described in subparagraph (C).

"(B) NONINDIGENOUS AQUATIC NUISANCE PREVENTION AND CONTROL ACT REGULATIONS.—Notwithstanding section 903(a)(2)(A) of the Vessel Incidental Discharge Act of 2018, all regulations promulgated by the Secretary pursuant to section 1101 of the Nonindigenous Aquatic Nuisance Prevention and Control Act of 1990 (16 U.S.C. 4711) (as in effect on the day before the date of enactment of this subsection), including the regulations contained in subparts C and D of part 151 of title 33, Code of Federal Regulations, and subpart 162.060 of part 162 of title 46, Code of Federal Regulations (as in effect on the day before that date of enactment), shall remain in force and effect until the applicable date described in subparagraph (C).

"(C) REPEAL ON EXISTENCE OF FINAL, EFFECTIVE, AND ENFORCEABLE REQUIREMENTS.—Effective beginning on the date on which the requirements promulgated by the Secretary under subparagraphs (A), (B), and (C) of paragraph (5) with respect to every discharge incidental to the normal operation of a vessel that is subject to regulation under this subsection are final, effective, and enforceable, the requirements of the Vessel General Permit and the regulations described in subparagraph (B) shall have no force or effect.

"(4) NATIONAL STANDARDS OF PERFORMANCE FOR MARINE POLLUTION CONTROL DEVICES AND WATER QUALITY ORDERS.—

"(A) ESTABLISHMENT.—

"(i) IN GENERAL.—Not later than 2 years after the date of enactment of this subsection, the Administrator, in concurrence with the Secretary (subject to clause (ii)), and in consultation with interested Governors (subject to clause (iii)), shall promulgate Federal standards of performance for marine pollution control devices for each type of discharge incidental to the normal operation of a vessel that is subject to regulation under this subsection.

"(ii) CONCURRENCE WITH SECRETARY.—

"(I) REQUEST.—The Administrator shall submit to the Secretary a request for written concurrence with respect to a proposed standard of performance under clause (i).

"(II) EFFECT OF FAILURE TO CONCUR.—A failure by the Secretary to concur with the Administrator under clause (i) by the date that is 60 days after the date on which the Administrator submits a request for concurrence under subclause (I) shall not prevent the Administrator from promulgating the relevant standard of performance in accordance with the deadline under clause (i), subject to the condition that the Administrator shall include in the administrative record of the promulgation—

"(aa) documentation of the request submitted under subclause (I); and

"(bb) the response of the Administrator to any written objections received from the Secretary relating to the proposed standard of performance during the 60-day period beginning on the date of submission of the request.

"(iii) CONSULTATION WITH GOVERNORS.—

"(I) IN GENERAL.—The Administrator, in promulgating a standard of performance under clause (i), shall develop the standard of performance—

"(aa) in consultation with interested Governors; and

"(bb) in accordance with the deadlines under that clause.

"(II) PROCESS.—The Administrator shall develop a process for soliciting input from interested Governors, including information sharing relevant to such process, to allow interested Governors to inform the development of standards of performance under clause (i).

"(III) OBJECTION BY GOVERNORS.—

"(aa) SUBMISSION.—An interested Governor that objects to a proposed standard of performance under clause (i) may submit to the Administrator in writing a detailed objection to the proposed standard of performance, describing the scientific, technical, or operational factors that form the basis of the objection.

"(bb) RESPONSE.—Before finalizing a standard of performance under clause (i) that is subject to an objection under item (aa) from 1 or more interested Governors, the Administrator shall provide a written response to each interested Governor that submitted an objection under that item that details the scientific, technical, or operational factors that form the basis for that standard of performance.

"(cc) JUDICIAL REVIEW.—A response of the Administrator under item (bb) shall not be subject to judicial review.

"(iv) PROCEDURE.—The Administrator shall promulgate the standards of performance under this subparagraph in accordance with—

"(I) this paragraph; and

"(II) section 553 of title 5, United States Code.

"(B) STRINGENCY.—

"(i) IN GENERAL.—Subject to clause (iii), the standards of performance promulgated under this paragraph shall require—

"(I) with respect to conventional pollutants, toxic pollutants, and nonconventional pollutants (including aquatic nuisance species), the application of the best practicable control technology currently available;

"(II) with respect to conventional pollutants, the application of the best conventional pollutant control technology; and

"(III) with respect to toxic pollutants and nonconventional pollutants (including aquatic nuisance species), the application of the best available technology economically achievable for categories and classes of vessels, which shall result in reasonable progress toward the national goal of eliminating discharges of all pollutants.

"(ii) BEST MANAGEMENT PRACTICES.—The Administrator shall require the use of best management practices to control or abate any discharge incidental to the normal operation of a vessel if—

"(I) numeric standards of performance are infeasible under clause (i); or

"(II) the best management practices are reasonably necessary—

"(aa) to achieve the standards of

performance; or

"(bb) to carry out the purpose and intent of this subsection.

"(iii) MINIMUM REQUIREMENTS.—Subject to subparagraph (D)(ii)(II), the combination of any equipment or best management practice comprising a marine pollution control device shall not be less stringent than the following provisions of the Vessel General Permit:

"(I) All requirements contained in parts 2.1 and 2.2 (relating to effluent limits and related requirements), including with respect to waters subject to Federal protection, in whole or in part, for conservation purposes.

"(II) All requirements contained in part 5 (relating to vessel class-specific requirements) that concern effluent limits and authorized discharges (within the meaning of that part), including with respect to waters subject to Federal protection, in whole or in part, for conservation purposes.

"(C) CLASSES, TYPES, AND SIZES OF VESSELS.—The standards promulgated under this paragraph may distinguish—

"(i) among classes, types, and sizes of vessels; and

"(ii) between new vessels and existing vessels.

"(D) REVIEW AND REVISION.—

"(i) IN GENERAL.—Not less frequently than once every 5 years, the Administrator, in consultation with the Secretary, shall—

"(I) review the standards of performance in effect under this paragraph; and

"(II) if appropriate, revise those standards of performance—

"(aa) in accordance with subparagraphs (A) through (C); and

"(bb) as necessary to establish

requirements for any discharge that is subject to regulation under this subsection.

"(ii) MAINTAINING PROTECTIVENESS.—

"(I) IN GENERAL.—Except as provided in subclause (II), the Administrator shall not revise a standard of performance under this subsection to be less stringent than an applicable existing requirement.

"(II) EXCEPTIONS.—The Administrator may revise a standard of performance to be less stringent than an applicable existing requirement—

"(aa) if information becomes available that—

"(AA) was not reasonably available when the Administrator promulgated the initial standard of performance or comparable requirement of the Vessel General Permit, as applicable (including the subsequent scarcity or unavailability of materials used to control the relevant discharge); and

"(BB) would have justified the application of a less-stringent standard of performance at the time of promulgation; or

"(bb) if the Administrator determines that a material technical mistake or misinterpretation of law occurred when promulgating the existing standard of performance or comparable requirement of the Vessel General Permit, as applicable.

"(E) BEST MANAGEMENT PRACTICES FOR AQUATIC NUISANCE SPECIES EMERGENCIES AND FURTHER PROTECTION OF WATER QUALITY.—

"(i) IN GENERAL.—Notwithstanding any other

provision of this subsection, the Administrator, in concurrence with the Secretary (subject to clause (ii)), and in consultation with States, may require, by order, the use of an emergency best management practice for any region or category of vessels in any case in which the Administrator determines that such a best management practice—

"(I) is necessary to reduce the reasonably foreseeable risk of introduction or establishment of an aquatic nuisance species; or

"(II) will mitigate the adverse effects of a discharge that contributes to a violation of a water quality requirement under section 303, other than a requirement based on the presence of an aquatic nuisance species.

"(ii) CONCURRENCE WITH SECRETARY.—

"(I) REQUEST.—The Administrator shall submit to the Secretary a request for written concurrence with respect to an order under clause (i).

"(II) EFFECT OF FAILURE TO CONCUR.—A failure by the Secretary to concur with the Administrator under clause (i) by the date that is 60 days after the date on which the Administrator submits a request for concurrence under subclause (I) shall not prevent the Administrator from issuing the relevant order, subject to the condition that the Administrator shall include in the administrative record of the issuance—

"(aa) documentation of the request submitted under subclause (I); and

"(bb) the response of the Administrator to any written objections received from the Secretary relating to the proposed order during the 60-day period beginning on the date of submission of the request.

"(iii) DURATION.—An order issued by the Administrator under clause (i) shall expire not later than the date that is 4 years after the date of issuance.

"(iv) EXTENSIONS.—The Administrator may reissue an order under clause (i) for such subsequent periods of not longer than 4 years as the Administrator determines to be appropriate.

"(5) IMPLEMENTATION, COMPLIANCE, AND ENFORCEMENT REQUIREMENTS.—

"(A) ESTABLISHMENT.—

"(i) IN GENERAL.—As soon as practicable, but not later than 2 years, after the date on which the Administrator promulgates any new or revised standard of performance under paragraph (4) with respect to a discharge, the Secretary, in consultation with States, shall promulgate the regulations required under this paragraph with respect to that discharge.

"(ii) MINIMUM REQUIREMENTS.—Subject to subparagraph (C)(ii)(II), the regulations promulgated under this paragraph shall not be less stringent with respect to ensuring, monitoring, and enforcing compliance than—

"(I) the requirements contained in part 3 of the Vessel General Permit (relating to corrective actions);

"(II) the requirements contained in part 4 of the Vessel General Permit (relating to inspections, monitoring, reporting, and recordkeeping), including with respect to waters subject to Federal protection, in whole or in part, for conservation purposes;

"(III) the requirements contained in part 5 of the Vessel General Permit (relating to vessel class-specific requirements) regarding monitoring, inspection, and educational and training requirements (within the meaning of that part), including with respect to waters subject to Federal protection, in whole or in part, for conservation purposes; and

"(IV) any comparable, existing requirements promulgated under the Nonindigenous Aquatic Nuisance Prevention and Control Act of 1990 (16 U.S.C. 4701 et seq.) (including section 1101 of that Act (16 U.S.C. 4711) (as in effect on the day before the date of enactment of this subsection)) applicable to that discharge.

"(iii) COORDINATION WITH STATES.—The Secretary, in coordination with the Governors of the States, shall develop, publish, and periodically update inspection, monitoring, data management, and enforcement procedures for the enforcement by States of Federal standards and requirements under this subsection.

"(iv) EFFECTIVE DATE.—In determining the effective date of a regulation promulgated under this paragraph, the Secretary shall take into consideration the period of time necessary—

"(I) to communicate to affected persons the applicability of the regulation; and

"(II) for affected persons reasonably to comply with the regulation.

"(v) PROCEDURE.—The Secretary shall promulgate the regulations under this subparagraph in accordance with—

"(I) this paragraph; and

"(II) section 553 of title 5, United States Code.

"(B) IMPLEMENTATION REGULATIONS FOR MARINE POLLUTION CONTROL DEVICES.—The Secretary shall promulgate such regulations governing the design, construction, testing, approval, installation, and use of marine pollution control devices as are necessary to ensure compliance with the standards of performance promulgated under paragraph (4).

"(C) COMPLIANCE ASSURANCE.—

"(i) IN GENERAL.—The Secretary shall promulgate requirements (including requirements for vessel owners and operators with respect to inspections, monitoring, reporting, sampling, and recordkeeping) to ensure, monitor, and enforce compliance with—

"(I) the standards of performance promulgated by the Administrator under paragraph (4); and

"(II) the implementation regulations promulgated by the Secretary under subparagraph (B).

"(ii) MAINTAINING PROTECTIVENESS.—

"(I) IN GENERAL.—Except as provided in subclause (II), the Secretary shall not revise a requirement under this subparagraph or subparagraph (B) to be less stringent with respect to ensuring, monitoring, or enforcing compliance than an applicable existing requirement.

"(II) EXCEPTIONS.—The Secretary may revise a requirement under this subparagraph or subparagraph (B) to be less stringent than an applicable existing requirement—

"(aa) in accordance with this subparagraph or subparagraph (B), as applicable;

"(bb) if information becomes available that—

"(AA) the Administrator determines was not reasonably available when the Administrator promulgated the existing requirement of the Vessel General Permit, or that the Secretary determines was not reasonably available when the Secretary promulgated the existing requirement under the Nonindigenous Aquatic Nuisance Prevention and Control Act of 1990 (16 U.S.C. 4701 et seq.) or the applicable existing requirement under this subparagraph, as applicable (including subsequent scarcity or unavailability of materials used to control the relevant discharge); and

"(BB) would have justified the application of a less-stringent requirement at the time of promulgation; or

"(cc) if the Administrator determines that a material technical mistake or misinterpretation of law occurred when promulgating an existing requirement of the Vessel General Permit, or if the Secretary determines that a material mistake or misinterpretation of law occurred when promulgating an existing requirement under the Nonindigenous Aquatic Nuisance Prevention and Control Act of 1990 (16 U.S.C. 4701 et seq.) or this subsection.

"(D) DATA AVAILABILITY.—Beginning not later than 1 year after the date of enactment of this subsection, the Secretary shall provide to the Governor of a State, on request by the Governor, access to Automated Identification System arrival data for inbound vessels to specific ports or places of destination in the State.

"(6) ADDITIONAL PROVISIONS REGARDING BALLAST WATER.—

"(A) IN GENERAL.—In addition to the other applicable requirements of this subsection, the requirements of this paragraph shall apply with respect to any discharge incidental to the normal operation of a vessel that is a discharge of ballast water.

"(B) EMPTY BALLAST TANKS.—

"(i) REQUIREMENTS.—Except as provided in clause (ii), the owner or operator of a vessel with empty ballast tanks bound for a port or place of destination subject to the jurisdiction of the United States shall, prior to arriving at that port or place of destination, conduct a ballast water exchange or saltwater flush—

"(I) not less than 200 nautical miles from any shore for a voyage originating outside the United States or Canadian exclusive economic zone; or

"(II) not less than 50 nautical miles from any shore for a voyage originating within the United States or Canadian exclusive economic zone.

"(ii) EXCEPTIONS.—Clause (i) shall not apply—

"(I) if the unpumpable residual waters and sediments of an empty ballast tank were subject to treatment, in compliance with applicable requirements, through a type-approved ballast water management system approved by the Secretary;

"(II) except as otherwise required under this subsection, if the unpumpable residual waters and sediments of an empty ballast tank were sourced within—

"(aa) the same port or place of destination; or

"(bb) contiguous portions of a single Captain of the Port Zone;

"(III) if complying with an applicable requirement of clause (i)—

"(aa) would compromise the safety of the vessel; or

"(bb) is otherwise prohibited by any Federal, Canadian, or international law (including regulations) pertaining to vessel safety;

"(IV) if design limitations of the vessel prevent a ballast water exchange or saltwater flush from being conducted in accordance with clause (i); or

"(V) if the vessel is operating exclusively within the internal waters of the United States or Canada.

"(C) PERIOD OF USE OF INSTALLED BALLAST WATER MANAGEMENT SYSTEMS.—

"(i) IN GENERAL.—Except as provided in clause (ii), a vessel shall be deemed to be in compliance with a standard of performance for a marine pollution control device that is a ballast water management system if the ballast water management system—

"(I) is maintained in proper working condition, as determined by the Secretary;

"(II) is maintained and used in accordance with manufacturer specifications;

"(III) continues to meet the ballast water discharge standard applicable to the vessel at the time of installation, as determined by the Secretary; and

"(IV) has in effect a valid type-approval certificate issued by the Secretary.

"(ii) LIMITATION.—Clause (i) shall cease to apply with respect to any vessel on, as applicable—

"(I) the expiration of the service life, as determined by the Secretary, of—

"(aa) the ballast water management system; or

"(bb) the vessel;

"(II) the completion of a major conversion (as defined in section 2101 of title 46, United States Code) of the vessel; or

"(III) a determination by the Secretary that there are other type-approved systems for the vessel or category of vessels, with respect to the use of which the environmental, health, and economic benefits would exceed the costs.

"(D) REVIEW OF BALLAST WATER MANAGEMENT SYSTEM TYPE-APPROVAL TESTING METHODS.—

"(i) DEFINITION OF LIVE; LIVING.—Notwithstanding any other provision of law (including regulations), for purposes of section 151.1511 of title 33, and part 162 of title 46, Code of Federal Regulations (or successor regulations), the terms 'live' and 'living' shall not—

"(I) include an organism that has been rendered nonviable; or

"(II) preclude the consideration of any method of measuring the concentration of organisms in ballast water that are capable of reproduction.

"(ii) DRAFT POLICY.—Not later than 180 days after the date of enactment of this subsection, the Secretary, in coordination with the Administrator, shall publish a draft policy letter, based on the best available science, describing type-approval testing methods and protocols for ballast water management systems, if any, that—

"(I) render nonviable organisms in ballast water; and

"(II) may be used in addition to the methods established under subpart 162.060 of title 46, Code of Federal Regulations (or successor regulations)—

"(aa) to measure the concentration of organisms in ballast water that are capable of reproduction;

"(bb) to certify the performance of each ballast water management system under this subsection; and "(cc) to certify laboratories to evaluate applicable treatment technologies.

"(iii) PUBLIC COMMENT.—The Secretary shall provide a period of not more than 60 days for public comment regarding the draft policy letter published under clause (ii).

"(iv) FINAL POLICY.—

"(I) IN GENERAL.—Not later than 1 year after the date of enactment of this subsection, the Secretary, in coordination with the Administrator, shall publish a final policy letter describing type-approval testing methods, if any, for ballast water management systems that render nonviable organisms in ballast water.

"(II) METHOD OF EVALUATION.—The ballast water management systems under subclause (I) shall be evaluated by measuring the concentration of organisms in ballast water that are capable of reproduction based on the best available science that may be used in addition to the methods established under subpart 162.060 of title 46, Code of Federal Regulations (or successor regulations).

"(III) REVISIONS.—The Secretary shall revise the final policy letter under subclause (I) in any case in which the Secretary, in coordination with the Administrator, determines that additional testing methods are capable of measuring the concentration of organisms in ballast water that have not been rendered nonviable.

"(v) FACTORS FOR CONSIDERATION.—In developing a policy letter under this subparagraph, the Secretary, in coordination with the Administrator—

"(I) shall take into consideration a testing method that uses organism grow-out and most probable number statistical analysis to determine the concentration of organisms in ballast water that are capable of reproduction; and

"(II) shall not take into consideration a testing method that relies on a staining method that measures the concentration of—

"(aa) organisms greater than or equal to 10 micrometers; and

"(bb) organisms less than or equal to 50 micrometers.

"(E) INTERGOVERNMENTAL RESPONSE FRAMEWORK.—

"(i) IN GENERAL.—The Secretary, in consultation with the Administrator and acting in coordination with, or through, the Aquatic Nuisance Species Task Force established by section 1201(a) of the Nonindigenous Aquatic Nuisance Prevention and Control Act of 1990 (16 U.S.C. 4721(a)), shall establish a framework for Federal and intergovernmental response to aquatic nuisance species risks from discharges from vessels subject to ballast water and incidental discharge compliance requirements under this subsection, including the introduction, spread, and establishment of aquatic nuisance species populations.

"(ii) BALLAST DISCHARGE RISK RESPONSE.—The Administrator, in coordination with the Secretary and taking into consideration information from the National Ballast Information Clearinghouse developed under section 1102(f) of the Nonindigenous Aquatic Nuisance Prevention and Control Act of 1990 (16 U.S.C. 4712(f)), shall establish a risk assessment and response framework using ballast water discharge data and aquatic nuisance species monitoring data for the purposes of—

"(I) identifying and tracking populations

of aquatic invasive species;

"(II) evaluating the risk of any aquatic nuisance species population tracked under subclause (I) establishing and spreading in waters of the United States or waters of the contiguous zone; and

"(III) establishing emergency best management practices that may be deployed rapidly, in a local or regional manner, to respond to emerging aquatic nuisance species threats.

"(7) PETITIONS BY GOVERNORS FOR REVIEW.—

"(A) IN GENERAL.—The Governor of a State (or a designee) may submit to the Administrator or the Secretary a petition—

"(i) to issue an order under paragraph (4)(E); or

"(ii) to review any standard of performance, regulation, or policy promulgated under paragraph (4), (5), or (6), respectively, if there exists new information that could reasonably result in a change to—

"(I) the standard of performance, regulation, or policy; or

"(II) a determination on which the standard of performance, regulation, or policy was based.

"(B) INCLUSION.—A petition under subparagraph (A) shall include a description of any applicable scientific or technical information that forms the basis of the petition.

"(C) DETERMINATION.—

"(i) TIMING.—The Administrator or the Secretary, as applicable, shall grant or deny—

"(I) a petition under subparagraph (A)(i) by not later than the date that is 180 days after the date on which the petition is submitted; and

"(II) a petition under subparagraph (A)(ii) by not later than the date that is 1 year after the date on which the petition is submitted.

"(ii) EFFECT OF GRANT.—If the Administrator or the Secretary determines under clause (i) to grant a petition—

"(I) in the case of a petition under subparagraph (A)(i), the Administrator shall immediately issue the relevant order under paragraph (4)(E); or

"(II) in the case of a petition under subparagraph (A)(ii), the Administrator or Secretary shall publish in the Federal Register, by not later than 30 days after the date of that determination, a notice of proposed rulemaking to revise the relevant standard, requirement, regulation, or policy under paragraph (4), (5), or (6), as applicable.

"(iii) NOTICE OF DENIAL.—If the Administrator or the Secretary determines under clause (i) to deny a petition, the Administrator or Secretary shall publish in the Federal Register, by not later than 30 days after the date of that determination, a detailed explanation of the scientific, technical, or operational factors that form the basis of the determination.

"(iv) REVIEW.—A determination by the Administrator or the Secretary under clause (i) to deny a petition shall be—

"(I) considered to be a final agency action; and

"(II) subject to judicial review in accordance with section 509, subject to clause (v).

"(v) EXCEPTIONS.—

"(I) VENUE.—Notwithstanding section 509(b), a petition for review of a determination by the Administrator or the Secretary under clause (i) to deny a petition submitted by the Governor of a State under subparagraph (A) may be filed in any United States district court of competent jurisdiction.

"(II) DEADLINE FOR FILING.—Notwithstanding section 509(b), a petition for review of a determination by the Administrator or the Secretary under clause (i) shall be filed by not later than 180 days after the date on which the justification for the determination is published in the Federal Register under clause (iii).

"(8) PROHIBITION.—

"(A) IN GENERAL.—It shall be unlawful for any person to violate—

"(i) a provision of the Vessel General Permit in force and effect under paragraph (3)(A);

"(ii) a regulation promulgated pursuant to section 1101 of the Nonindigenous Aquatic Nuisance Prevention and Control Act of 1990 (16 U.S.C. 4711) (as in effect on the day before the date of enactment of this subsection) in force and effect under paragraph (3)(B); or

"(iii) an applicable requirement or regulation under this subsection.

"(B) COMPLIANCE WITH REGULATIONS.—Effective beginning on the effective date of a regulation promulgated under paragraph (4), (5), (6), or (10), as applicable, it shall be unlawful for the owner or operator of a vessel subject to the regulation—

"(i) to discharge any discharge incidental to the normal operation of the vessel into waters of the United States or waters of the contiguous zone, except in compliance with the regulation; or

"(ii) to operate in waters of the United States or waters of the contiguous zone, if the vessel is not equipped with a required marine pollution control device that complies with the requirements established under this subsection, unless—

"(I) the owner or operator of the vessel

denotes in an entry in the official logbook of the vessel that the equipment was not operational; and

"(II) either—

"(aa) the applicable discharge was avoided; or

"(bb) an alternate compliance option approved by the Secretary as meeting the applicable standard was employed.

"(C) AFFIRMATIVE DEFENSE.—No person shall be found to be in violation of this paragraph if—

"(i) the violation was in the interest of ensuring the safety of life at sea, as determined by the Secretary; and

"(ii) the applicable emergency circumstance was not the result of negligence or malfeasance on the part of—

"(I) the owner or operator of the vessel;

"(II) the master of the vessel; or

"(III) the person in charge of the vessel.

"(D) TREATMENT.—Each day of continuing violation of an applicable requirement of this subsection shall constitute a separate offense.

"(E) IN REM LIABILITY.—A vessel operated in violation of this subsection is liable in rem for any civil penalty assessed for the violation.

"(F) REVOCATION OF CLEARANCE.—The Secretary shall withhold or revoke the clearance of a vessel required under section 60105 of title 46, United States Code, if the owner or operator of the vessel is in violation of this subsection.

"(9) EFFECT ON OTHER LAWS.—

"(A) STATE AUTHORITY.—

"(i) IN GENERAL.—Except as provided in clauses (ii) through (v) and paragraph (10), effective beginning on the date on which the requirements promulgated by the Secretary under subparagraphs (A), (B), and (C) of paragraph (5) with respect to every discharge incidental to the normal operation of a vessel that is subject to regulation under this subsection are final, effective, and enforceable, no State, political subdivision of a State, or interstate agency may adopt or enforce any law, regulation, or other requirement of the State, political subdivision, or interstate agency with respect to any such discharge.

"(ii) IDENTICAL OR LESSER STATE LAWS.—Clause (i) shall not apply to any law, regulation, or other requirement of a State, political subdivision of a State, or interstate agency in effect on or after the date of enactment of this subsection—

"(I) that is identical to a Federal requirement under this subsection applicable to the relevant discharge; or

"(II) compliance with which would be achieved concurrently in achieving compliance with a Federal requirement under this subsection applicable to the relevant discharge.

"(iii) STATE ENFORCEMENT OF FEDERAL REQUIREMENTS.—A State may enforce any standard of performance or other Federal requirement of this subsection in accordance with subsection (k) or other applicable Federal authority.

"(iv) EXCEPTION FOR CERTAIN FEES.—

"(I) IN GENERAL.—Subject to subclauses (II) and (III), a State that assesses any fee pursuant to any State or Federal law relating to the regulation of a discharge incidental to the normal operation of a vessel before the date of enactment of this subsection may assess or retain a fee to cover the costs of administration, inspection, monitoring, and enforcement activities by the State to achieve compliance with the applicable requirements of this subsection.

"(II) MAXIMUM AMOUNT.—

"(aa) IN GENERAL.—Except as provided in item (bb), a State may assess a fee for activities under this clause equal to not more than $1,000 against the owner or operator of a vessel that—

"(AA) has operated outside of that State; and

"(BB) arrives at a port or place of destination in the State (excluding movement entirely within a single port or place of destination).

"(bb) VESSELS ENGAGED IN COASTWISE TRADE.—A State may assess against the owner or operator of a vessel registered in accordance with applicable Federal law and lawfully engaged in the coastwise trade not more than $5,000 in fees under this clause per vessel during a calendar year.

"(III) ADJUSTMENT FOR INFLATION.—

"(aa) IN GENERAL.—A State may adjust the amount of a fee authorized under this clause not more frequently than once every 5 years to reflect the percentage by which the Consumer Price Index for All Urban Consumers published by the Department of Labor for the month of October immediately preceding the date of adjustment exceeds the Consumer Price Index for All Urban Consumers published by the Department of Labor for the month of October that immediately precedes the date that is 5 years before the date of adjustment.

"(bb) EFFECT OF SUBCLAUSE.—Nothing in this subclause

prevents a State from adjusting a fee in effect before the date of enactment of this subsection to the applicable maximum amount under subclause (II).

"(cc) APPLICABILITY.—This subclause applies only to increases in fees to amounts greater than the applicable maximum amount under subclause (II).

"(v) ALASKA GRAYWATER.—Clause (i) shall not apply with respect to any discharge of graywater (as defined in section 1414 of the Consolidated Appropriations Act, 2001 (Public Law 106-554; 114 Stat. 2763A-323)) from a passenger vessel (as defined in section 2101 of title 46, United States Code) in the State of Alaska (including all waters in the Alexander Archipelago) carrying 50 or more passengers.

"(vi) PRESERVATION OF AUTHORITY.—Nothing in this subsection preempts any State law, public initiative, referendum, regulation, requirement, or other State action, except as expressly provided in this subsection.

"(B) ESTABLISHED REGIMES.—Except as expressly provided in this subsection, nothing in this subsection affects the applicability to a vessel of any other provision of Federal law, including—

"(i) this section;

"(ii) section 311;

"(iii) the Act to Prevent Pollution from Ships (33 U.S.C. 1901 et seq.); and

"(iv) title X of the Coast Guard Authorization Act of 2010 (33 U.S.C. 3801 et seq.).

"(C) PERMITTING.—Effective beginning on the date of enactment of this subsection—

"(i) the Small Vessel General Permit is repealed; and

"(ii) the Administrator, or a State in the case of a permit program approved under section 402, shall not require, or in any way modify, a permit under that section for—

"(I) any discharge that is subject to regulation under this subsection;

"(II) any discharge incidental to the normal operation of a vessel from a small vessel or fishing vessel, regardless of whether that discharge is subject to regulation under this subsection; or

"(III) any discharge described in paragraph (2)(B)(ii).

"(D) NO EFFECT ON CIVIL OR CRIMINAL ACTIONS.—Nothing in this subsection, or any standard, regulation, or requirement established under this subsection, modifies or otherwise affects, preempts, or displaces—

"(i) any cause of action; or

"(ii) any provision of Federal or State law establishing a remedy for civil relief or criminal penalty.

"(E) NO EFFECT ON CERTAIN SECRETARIAL AUTHORITY.—Nothing in this subsection affects the authority of the Secretary of Commerce or the Secretary of the Interior to administer any land or waters under the administrative control of the Secretary of Commerce or the Secretary of the Interior, respectively.

"(F) NO LIMITATION ON STATE INSPECTION AUTHORITY.—Nothing in this subsection limits the authority of a State to inspect a vessel pursuant to paragraph (5)(A)(iii) in order to monitor compliance with an applicable requirement of this section.

"(10) ADDITIONAL REGIONAL REQUIREMENTS.—

"(A) MINIMUM GREAT LAKES SYSTEM REQUIREMENTS.—

"(i) IN GENERAL.—Except as provided in clause (ii), the owner or operator of a vessel entering the St. Lawrence Seaway through the mouth of the St. Lawrence River shall conduct a complete ballast water exchange or saltwater flush—

"(I) not less than 200 nautical miles from any shore for a voyage originating outside the United States or Canadian exclusive economic zone; or

"(II) not less than 50 nautical miles from any shore for a voyage originating within the United States or Canadian exclusive economic zone.

"(ii) EXCEPTIONS.—Clause (i) shall not apply to a vessel if—

"(I) complying with an applicable requirement of clause (i)—

"(aa) would compromise the safety of the vessel; or

"(bb) is otherwise prohibited by any Federal, Canadian, or international law (including regulations) pertaining to vessel safety;

"(II) design limitations of the vessel prevent a ballast water exchange from being conducted in accordance with an applicable requirement of clause (i);

"(III) the vessel—

"(aa) is certified by the Secretary as having no residual ballast water or sediments onboard; or

"(bb) retains all ballast water while in waters subject to the requirement; or

"(IV) empty ballast tanks on the vessel are sealed and certified by the Secretary in a manner that ensures that—

"(aa) no discharge or uptake occurs; and

"(bb) any subsequent discharge of ballast water is subject to the requirement.

"(B) ENHANCED GREAT LAKES SYSTEM REQUIREMENTS.—

"(i) PETITIONS BY GOVERNORS FOR PROPOSED ENHANCED STANDARDS AND REQUIREMENTS.—

"(I) IN GENERAL.—The Governor of a Great Lakes State (or a State employee designee) may submit a petition in accordance with subclause (II) to propose that other Governors of Great Lakes States endorse an enhanced standard of performance or other requirement with respect to any discharge that—

"(aa) is subject to regulation under this subsection; and

"(bb) occurs within the Great Lakes System.

"(II) SUBMISSION.—A Governor shall submit a petition under subclause (I), in writing, to—

"(aa) the Executive Director of the Great Lakes Commission, in such manner as may be prescribed by the Great Lakes Commission;

"(bb) the Governor of each other Great Lakes State; and

"(cc) the Director of the Great Lakes National Program Office established by section 118(b).

"(III) PRELIMINARY ASSESSMENT BY GREAT LAKES COMMISSION.—

"(aa) IN GENERAL.—After the date of receipt of a petition under subclause (II)(aa), the Great Lakes Commission (acting through the Great Lakes Panel on Aquatic Nuisance Species, to the maximum extent practicable) may develop a preliminary assessment regarding each enhanced standard of performance or other requirement described in the petition.

"(bb) PROVISIONS.—The preliminary assessment developed by the Great Lakes Commission under item (aa)—

"(AA) may be developed in consultation with relevant experts and stakeholders;

"(BB) may be narrative in nature;

"(CC) may include the preliminary views, if any, of the Great Lakes Commission on the propriety of the proposed enhanced standard of performance or other requirement;

"(DD) shall be submitted, in writing, to the Governor of each Great Lakes State and the Director of the Great Lakes National Program Office and published on the internet website of the Great Lakes National Program Office; and

"(EE) except as provided in clause (iii), shall not be taken into consideration, or provide a basis for review, by the Administrator or the Secretary for purposes of that clause.

"(ii) PROPOSED ENHANCED STANDARDS AND REQUIREMENTS.—

"(I) PUBLICATION IN FEDERAL REGISTER.—

"(aa) REQUEST BY GOVERNOR.—Not earlier than the date that is 90 days after the date on which the Executive Director of the Great Lakes Commission receives from a Governor of a Great Lakes State a petition under clause (i)(II)(aa), the Governor may request the Director of the

Great Lakes National Program Office to publish, for a period requested by the Governor of not less than 30 days, and the Director shall so publish, in the Federal Register for public comment—

"(AA) a copy of the petition; and

"(BB) if applicable as of the date of publication, any preliminary assessment of the Great Lakes Commission developed under clause (i)(III) relating to the petition.

"(bb) REVIEW OF PUBLIC COMMENTS.—On receipt of a written request of a Governor of a Great Lakes State, the Director of the Great Lakes National Program Office shall make available all public comments received in response to the notice under item (aa).

"(cc) NO RESPONSE REQUIRED.—Notwithstanding any other provision of law, a Governor of a Great Lakes State or the Director of the Great Lakes National Program Office shall not be required to provide a response to any comment received in response to the publication of a petition or preliminary assessment under item (aa).

"(dd) PURPOSE.—Any public comments received in response to the publication of a petition or preliminary assessment under item (aa) shall be used solely for the purpose of providing information and feedback to the Governor of each Great Lakes State regarding the decision to endorse the proposed standard or requirement.

"(ee) EFFECT OF PETITION.—A proposed standard or requirement developed under subclause (II) may differ from the proposed standard or requirement described in a petition published under item (aa).

"(II) COORDINATION TO DEVELOP PROPOSED STANDARD OR REQUIREMENT.—After the expiration of the public comment period for the petition under subclause (I), any interested Governor of a Great Lakes State may work in coordination with the Great Lakes Commission to develop a proposed standard of performance or other requirement applicable to a discharge referred to in the petition.

"(III) REQUIREMENTS.—A proposed standard of performance or other requirement under subclause (II)—

"(aa) shall be developed—

"(AA) in consultation with representatives from the Federal and provincial governments of Canada;

"(BB) after notice and opportunity for public comment on the petition published under subclause (I); and

"(CC) taking into consideration the preliminary assessment, if any, of the Great Lakes Commission under clause (i)(III);

"(bb) shall be specifically endorsed in writing by—

"(AA) the Governor of each Great Lakes State, if the proposed standard or requirement would impose any additional equipment requirement on a vessel; or

"(BB) not fewer than 5 Governors of Great Lakes States, if the proposed standard or requirement would not impose any additional equipment requirement on a vessel; and "(cc) in the case of a proposed requirement to prohibit 1 or more types of discharge regulated under this subsection, whether treated or not treated, into waters within the Great Lakes System, shall not apply outside the waters of the Great Lakes States of the Governors endorsing the proposed requirement under item (bb).

"(iii) PROMULGATION BY ADMINISTRATOR AND SECRETARY.—

"(I) SUBMISSION.—

"(aa) IN GENERAL.—The Governors endorsing a proposed standard or requirement under clause (ii)(III)(bb) may jointly submit to the Administrator and the Secretary for approval each proposed standard of performance or other requirement developed and endorsed pursuant to clause (ii).

"(bb) INCLUSION.—Each submission under item (aa) shall include an explanation regarding why the applicable standard of performance or other requirement is—

"(AA) at least as stringent as a comparable standard of performance or other requirement under this subsection;

"(BB) in accordance with maritime safety; and

"(CC) in accordance with applicable maritime and navigation laws and regulations.

"(cc) WITHDRAWAL.—

"(AA) IN GENERAL.—The Governor of any Great Lakes State that endorses a proposed standard or requirement under clause (ii)(III)(bb) may withdraw the endorsement by not later than the date that is 90 days after the date on which the Administrator and the Secretary receive the proposed standard or requirement.

"(BB) EFFECT ON FEDERAL REVIEW.—If, after the withdrawal of an endorsement under subitem (AA), the proposed standard or requirement does not have the applicable number of endorsements under clause (ii)(III)(bb), the Administrator and the Secretary shall terminate the review under this clause.

"(dd) DISSENTING OPINIONS.—The Governor of a Great Lakes State that does not endorse a proposed standard or requirement under clause (ii)(III)(bb) may submit to the Administrator and the Secretary any dissenting opinions of the Governor.

"(II) JOINT NOTICE.—On receipt of a proposed standard of performance or other requirement under subclause (I), the Administrator and the Secretary shall publish in the Federal Register a joint notice that, at minimum—

"(aa) states that the proposed standard or requirement is publicly available; and

"(bb) provides an opportunity for public comment regarding the proposed standard or requirement during the 90-day period beginning on the date of receipt by the Administrator and the Secretary of the proposed standard or requirement.

"(III) REVIEW.—

"(aa) IN GENERAL.—As soon as practicable after the date of publication of a joint notice under subclause (II)—

"(AA) the Administrator shall commence a review of each proposed standard of performance or other requirement covered by the notice to determine whether that standard or requirement is at least as stringent as comparable standards and requirements under this subsection; and

"(BB) the Secretary shall commence a review of each proposed standard of performance or other requirement covered by the notice to determine whether that standard or requirement is in accordance with maritime safety and applicable maritime and navigation laws and regulations.

"(bb) CONSULTATION.—In carrying out item (aa), the Administrator and the Secretary—

"(AA) shall consult with the Governor of each Great Lakes State and representatives from the Federal and provincial governments of Canada;

"(BB) shall take into consideration any relevant data or public comments received under subclause (II)(bb); and

"(CC) shall not take into consideration any preliminary assessment by the Great Lakes Commission under clause (i)(III), or any dissenting opinion under subclause (I)(dd), except to the extent that such an assessment or opinion is relevant to the criteria for the applicable determination under item (aa).

"(IV) APPROVAL OR DISAPPROVAL.—Not later than 180 days after the date of receipt of each proposed standard of performance or other requirement under subclause (I), the Administrator and the Secretary shall—

"(aa) determine, as applicable, whether each proposed standard or other requirement satisfies the criteria under subclause (III)(aa);

"(bb) approve each proposed standard or other requirement, unless the Administrator or the Secretary, as applicable, determines under item (aa) that the proposed standard or other requirement does not satisfy the criteria under subclause (III)(aa); and

"(cc) submit to the Governor of each Great Lakes State, and publish in the Federal Register, a notice of the determination under item (aa).

"(V) ACTION ON DISAPPROVAL.—

"(aa) RATIONALE AND RECOMMENDATIONS.—If the Administrator and the Secretary disapprove a proposed standard of performance or other requirement under subclause (IV)(bb), the notices under subclause (IV)(cc) shall include—

"(AA) a description of the reasons why the standard or requirement is, as applicable, less stringent than a comparable standard or requirement under this subsection, inconsistent with maritime safety, or inconsistent with applicable maritime and navigation laws and regulations; and

"(BB) any recommendations regarding changes the Governors of the Great Lakes States could make to conform the disapproved portion of the standard or requirement to the requirements of this subparagraph.

"(bb) REVIEW.—Disapproval of a proposed standard or requirement by the Administrator and the Secretary under this subparagraph shall be considered to be a final agency action subject to judicial review under section 509.

"(VI) ACTION ON APPROVAL.—On approval by the Administrator and the Secretary of a proposed standard of performance or other requirement under subclause (IV)(bb)—

"(aa) the Administrator shall establish, by regulation, the proposed standard or requirement within the Great Lakes System in lieu of any comparable standard or other requirement promulgated under paragraph (4); and

"(bb) the Secretary shall establish, by regulation, any requirements necessary to implement, ensure compliance with, and enforce the standard or requirement under item (aa), or to apply the proposed requirement, within the Great Lakes System in lieu of any comparable requirement promulgated under paragraph (5).

"(VII) NO JUDICIAL REVIEW FOR CERTAIN ACTIONS.—An action or inaction of a Governor of a Great Lakes State or the Great Lakes Commission under this subparagraph shall not be subject to judicial review.

"(VIII) GREAT LAKES COMPACT.—Nothing in this subsection limits, alters, or amends the Great Lakes Compact to which Congress granted consent in the Act of July 24, 1968

(Public Law 90-419; 82 Stat. 414).

"(IX) AUTHORIZATION OF APPROPRIATIONS.—There is authorized to be appropriated to the Great Lakes Commission $5,000,000, to be available until expended.

"(C) MINIMUM PACIFIC REGION REQUIREMENTS.—

"(i) DEFINITION OF COMMERCIAL VESSEL.—In this subparagraph, the term 'commercial vessel' means a vessel operating between—

"(I) 2 ports or places of destination within the Pacific Region; or

"(II) a port or place of destination within the Pacific Region and a port or place of destination on the Pacific Coast of Canada or Mexico north of parallel 20 degrees north latitude, inclusive of the Gulf of California.

"(ii) BALLAST WATER EXCHANGE.—

"(I) IN GENERAL.—Except as provided in subclause (II) and clause (iv), the owner or operator of a commercial vessel shall conduct a complete ballast water exchange in waters more than 50 nautical miles from shore.

"(II) EXEMPTIONS.—Subclause (I) shall not apply to a commercial vessel—

"(aa) using, in compliance with applicable requirements, a type-approved ballast water management system approved by the Secretary; or

"(bb) voyaging—

"(AA) between or to a port or place of destination in the State of Washington, if the ballast water to be discharged from the commercial vessel originated solely from waters located between the parallel 46 degrees north latitude, including the internal waters of the Columbia River, and the internal waters of

Canada south of parallel 50 degrees north latitude, including the waters of the Strait of Georgia and the Strait of Juan de Fuca;

"(BB) between ports or places of destination in the State of Oregon, if the ballast water to be discharged from the commercial vessel originated solely from waters located between the parallel 40 degrees north latitude and the parallel 50 degrees north latitude;

"(CC) between ports or places of destination in the State of California within the San Francisco Bay area east of the Golden Gate Bridge, including the Port of Stockton and the Port of Sacramento, if the ballast water to be discharged from the commercial vessel originated solely from ports or places within that area;

"(DD) between the Port of Los Angeles, the Port of Long Beach, and the El Segundo offshore marine oil terminal, if the ballast water to be discharged from the commercial vessel originated solely from the Port of Los Angeles, the Port of Long Beach, or the El Segundo offshore marine oil terminal;

"(EE) between a port or place of destination in the State of Alaska within a single Captain of the Port Zone;

"(FF) between ports or places of destination in different counties of the State of Hawaii, if the vessel may conduct a complete ballast water exchange in waters that are more than 10 nautical miles from shore and at least 200 meters deep; or

"(GG) between ports or places of destination within the same county of the State of Hawaii, if the vessel does not transit outside State marine waters during the voyage.

"(iii) LOW-SALINITY BALLAST WATER.—

"(I) IN GENERAL.—Except as provided in subclause (II) and clause (iv), the owner or operator of a commercial vessel that transports ballast water sourced from waters with a measured salinity of less than 18 parts per thousand and voyages to a Pacific Region port or place of destination with a measured salinity of less than 18 parts per thousand shall conduct a complete ballast water exchange—

"(aa) not less than 50 nautical miles from shore, if the ballast water was sourced from a Pacific Region port or place of destination; or

"(bb) more than 200 nautical miles from shore, if the ballast water was not sourced from a Pacific Region port or place of destination.

"(II) EXCEPTION.—Subclause (I) shall not apply to a commercial vessel voyaging to a port or place of destination in the Pacific Region that is using, in compliance with applicable requirements, a type-approved ballast water management system approved by the Secretary to achieve standards of performance of—

"(aa) less than 1 organism per 10 cubic meters, if that organism—

"(AA) is living, or has not been rendered nonviable; and

"(BB) is 50 or more micrometers in minimum dimension;

"(bb) less than 1 organism per 10 milliliters, if that organism—

"(AA) is living, or has not been rendered nonviable; and

"(BB) is more than 10, but less than 50, micrometers in minimum dimension;

"(cc) concentrations of indicator microbes that are less than—

"(AA) 1 colony-forming unit of toxicogenic Vibrio cholera (serotypes O1 and O139) per 100 milliliters or less than 1 colony-forming unit of that microbe per gram of wet weight of zoological samples;

"(BB) 126 colony-forming units of escherichia coli per 100 milliliters; and

"(CC) 33 colony-forming units of intestinal enterococci per 100 milliliters; and

"(dd) concentrations of such additional indicator microbes and viruses as may be specified in the standards of performance established by the Administrator under paragraph (4).

"(iv) GENERAL EXCEPTIONS.—The requirements of clauses (ii) and (iii) shall not apply to a commercial vessel if—

"(I) complying with the requirement would compromise the safety of the commercial vessel;

"(II) design limitations of the commercial vessel prevent a ballast water exchange from being conducted in accordance with clause (ii) or (iii), as applicable;

"(III) the commercial vessel—

"(aa) is certified by the Secretary as

having no residual ballast water or sediments onboard; or

"(bb) retains all ballast water while in waters subject to those requirements; or

"(IV) empty ballast tanks on the commercial vessel are sealed and certified by the Secretary in a manner that ensures that—

"(aa) no discharge or uptake occurs; and

"(bb) any subsequent discharge of ballast water is subject to those requirements.

"(D) ESTABLISHMENT OF STATE NO-DISCHARGE ZONES.—

"(i) STATE PROHIBITION.—Subject to clause (ii), after the effective date of regulations promulgated by the Secretary under paragraph (5), if any State determines that the protection and enhancement of the quality of some or all of the waters within the State require greater environmental protection, the State may prohibit 1 or more types of discharge regulated under this subsection, whether treated or not treated, into such waters.

"(ii) APPLICABILITY.—A prohibition by a State under clause (i) shall not apply until the date on which the Administrator makes the applicable determinations described in clause (iii).

"(iii) PROHIBITION BY ADMINISTRATOR.—

"(I) DETERMINATION.—On application of a State, the Administrator, in concurrence with the Secretary (subject to subclause (II)), shall, by regulation, prohibit the discharge from a vessel of 1 or more discharges subject to regulation under this subsection, whether treated or not treated, into the waters covered by the application if the Administrator determines that—

"(aa) prohibition of the discharge

would protect and enhance the quality of the specified waters within the State;

"(bb) adequate facilities for the safe and sanitary removal and treatment of the discharge are reasonably available for the water and all vessels to which the prohibition would apply;

"(cc) the discharge can be safely collected and stored until a vessel reaches a discharge facility or other location; and

"(dd) in the case of an application for the prohibition of discharges of ballast water in a port (or in any other location where cargo, passengers, or fuel are loaded and unloaded)—

"(AA) the adequate facilities described in item (bb) are reasonably available for commercial vessels, after considering, at a minimum, water depth, dock size, pumpout facility capacity and flow rate, availability of year-round operations, proximity to navigation routes, and the ratio of pumpout facilities to the population and discharge capacity of commercial vessels operating in those waters; and

"(BB) the prohibition will not unreasonably interfere with the safe loading and unloading of cargo, passengers, or fuel.

"(II) CONCURRENCE WITH SECRETARY.—

"(aa) REQUEST.—The Administrator shall submit to the Secretary a request for written concurrence with respect to a prohibition under subclause (I).

"(bb) EFFECT OF FAILURE TO CONCUR.—A failure by the Secretary to concur with the Administrator under subclause (I) by the date that is 60 days after the date on which the Administrator submits a request for concurrence under item (aa) shall not prevent the Administrator from prohibiting the relevant discharge in accordance with subclause (III), subject to the condition that the Administrator shall include in the administrative record of the promulgation—

"(AA) documentation of the request submitted under item (aa); and

"(BB) the response of the Administrator to any written objections received from the Secretary relating to the proposed standard of performance during the 60-day period beginning on the date of submission of the request.

"(III) TIMING.—The Administrator shall approve or disapprove an application submitted under subclause (I) by not later than 90 days after the date on which the application is submitted to the Administrator.

"(E) MAINTENANCE IN EFFECT OF MORE-STRINGENT STANDARDS.—In any case in which a requirement established under this paragraph is more stringent or environmentally protective than a comparable requirement established under paragraph (4), (5), or (6), the more-stringent or more-protective requirement shall control."

(2) REPEALS.—

(A) [16 U.S.C. 4711 note] IN GENERAL.—Effective beginning on the date of enactment of this Act, the following provisions of law are repealed:

(i) Section 1101 of the Nonindigenous Aquatic Nuisance Prevention and Control Act of 1990 (16 U.S.C. 4711).

(ii) Public Law 110-299 (33 U.S.C. 1342 note).

(B) CONFORMING AMENDMENTS.—Section 1102 of the Nonindigenous Aquatic Nuisance Prevention and Control Act of 1990 (16 U.S.C. 4712) is amended—

(i) in subsection (c)(1), by inserting "(as in effect on the day before the date of enactment of the Vessel Incidental Discharge Act of 2018)" after "section 1101(b)"; and

(ii) in subsection (f)(1)(B), by inserting "(as in effect on the day before the date of enactment of the Vessel Incidental Discharge Act of 2018)" after "section 1101(c)".

(b) REGULATIONS FOR USE OF MARINE POLLUTION CONTROL DEVICES.—Section 312 of the Federal Water Pollution Control Act (33 U.S.C. 1322) is amended—

(1) by striking the section designation and heading and all that follows through "For the purpose of" in subsection (a) and inserting the following:

"SEC. SEC. 312. MARINE SANITATION DEVICES; DISCHARGES INCIDENTAL TO THE NORMAL OPERATION OF VESSELS

"(a) DEFINITIONS.—In"

(2) in subsection (a)—

(A) in paragraph (7), by striking "devices or of vessels" and inserting "devices, marine pollution control device equipment, or vessels"; and

(B) in paragraph (13), in the matter preceding subparagraph (A), by inserting ", except as provided in subsection (p)," after "means";

(3) in subsection (g)—

(A) by inserting "or marine pollution control device equipment" after "marine sanitation device" each place it appears;

(B) in paragraph (1)—

(i) by inserting "or equipment" after "such device"; and

(ii) by inserting "or equipment" after "test device"; and

(C) in paragraph (2)—

(i) by inserting "or equipment" after "the device" each place it appears; and

(ii) in the fourth sentence, by inserting "or equipment" after "device" each place it appears; and

(4) in subsection (h)—

(A) in paragraph (1), by inserting "and marine pollution control device equipment" after "marine sanitation device";

(B) in paragraph (2), by inserting "or any certified marine pollution control device equipment or element of design of such equipment" after "such device";

(C) by redesignating paragraphs (1) through (4) as subparagraphs (A) through (D), respectively, and indenting the subparagraphs appropriately;

(D) by striking "(h) After" and inserting the following:

"(h) SALE AND RESALE OF PROPERLY EQUIPPED VESSELS; OPERABILITY OF CERTIFIED MARINE SANITATION DEVICES.—

"(1) IN GENERAL.—Subject to paragraph (2), after"

; and

(E) by adding at the end the following:

"(2) EFFECT OF SUBSECTION.—Nothing in this subsection requires certification of a marine pollution control device for use on any vessel of the Armed Forces."

(c) ENFORCEMENT AUTHORITY.—

(1) IN GENERAL.—Section 312(k) of the Federal Water Pollution Control Act (33 U.S.C. 1322(k)) is amended—

(A) by striking the second sentence and inserting the following:

"(3) STATES.—

"(A) IN GENERAL.—This section may be enforced by a State or political subdivision of a State (including the attorney general of a State), including by filing a civil action in an appropriate Federal district court to enforce any violation of subsection (p).

"(B) JURISDICTION.—The appropriate Federal district court shall have jurisdiction with respect to a civil action filed pursuant to subparagraph (A), without regard to the amount in controversy or the citizenship of the parties—

"(i) to enforce the requirements of this section; and

"(ii) to apply appropriate civil penalties under this section or section 309(d), as appropriate."

(B) by striking "(k) The provisions of this" and inserting the following:

"(k) ENFORCEMENT AUTHORITY.—

"(1) ADMINISTRATOR.—This section shall be enforced by the Administrator, to the extent provided in section 309.

"(2) SECRETARY.—

"(A) IN GENERAL.—This"

; and

(C) in paragraph (2) (as so designated)—

(i) in subparagraph (A), by striking "operating and he may utilize by agreement" and inserting "operating, who may use, by agreement"; and

(ii) by adding at the end the following:

"(B) INSPECTIONS.—For purposes of ensuring compliance with this section, the Secretary—

"(i) may carry out an inspection (including the taking of ballast water samples) of any vessel at any time; and

"(ii) shall—

"(I) establish procedures for—

"(aa) reporting violations of this section; and

"(bb) accumulating evidence regarding those violations; and

"(II) use appropriate and practicable measures of detection and environmental monitoring of vessels.

"(C) DETENTION.—The Secretary may detain a vessel if the Secretary—

"(i) has reasonable cause to believe that the vessel—

"(I) has failed to comply with an applicable requirement of this section; or

"(II) is being operated in violation of such a requirement; and

"(ii) the Secretary provides to the owner or operator of the vessel a notice of the intent to detain."

(2) PRESERVATION OF FEDERAL ENFORCEMENT AUTHORITY.—Section 309 of the Federal Water Pollution Control Act (33 U.S.C. 1319) is amended—

(A) in subsection (a)(3), by striking "318" and inserting "312(p), 318";

(B) in subsection (c), by striking "318" each place it appears and inserting "312(p), 318";

(C) in subsection (d), in the first sentence—

(i) by striking "318" and inserting "312(p), 318,"; and

(ii) by striking "State,," and inserting "State,"; and

(D) in subsection (g)(1)(A), by striking "318" and inserting "312(p), 318".

(3) PRESERVATION OF PUBLIC ENFORCEMENT AUTHORITY.—Section 505(f) of the Federal Water Pollution Control Act (33 U.S.C. 1365(f)) is amended by striking "(5) certification" and all that follows through the period at the end and inserting the following: "(5) a standard of performance or requirement under section 312(p); (6) a certification under section 401; (7) a permit or condition of a permit issued under section 402 that is in effect under this Act (including a requirement applicable by reason of section 313); or (8) a regulation under section 405(d).".

(4) REVIEW.—Section 509(b) of the Federal Water Pollution

Control Act (33 U.S.C. 1369(b)) is amended by adding at the end the following:

"(4) DISCHARGES INCIDENTAL TO NORMAL OPERATION OF VESSELS.—

"(A) IN GENERAL.—Except as provided in subparagraph (B), any interested person may file a petition for review of a final agency action under section 312(p) of the Administrator or the Secretary of the department in which the Coast Guard is operating in accordance with the requirements of this subsection.

"(B) VENUE EXCEPTION.—Subject to section 312(p)(7)(C)(v), a petition for review of a final agency action under section 312(p) of the Administrator or the Secretary of the department in which the Coast Guard is operating may be filed only in the United States Court of Appeals for the District of Columbia Circuit."

(d) LOGBOOK REQUIREMENTS.—Section 11301(b) of title 46, United States Code, is amended by adding at the end the following:

"(13) when a vessel fails to carry out ballast water management requirements as applicable and pursuant to regulations promulgated by the Secretary, including when the vessel fails to carry out ballast water management requirements due to an allowed safety exemption, a statement regarding the failure to comply and the circumstances under which the failure occurred, made immediately after the failure, when practicable to do so."

(e) QUAGGA MUSSEL.—Section 42(a)(1) of title 18, United States Code, is amended, in the first sentence, by inserting "of the quagga mussel of the species Dreissena rostriformis or Dreissena bugensis;" after "Dreissena polymorpha;".

(f) **[16 U.S.C. 4729]** COASTAL AQUATIC INVASIVE SPECIES MITIGATION GRANT PROGRAM AND MITIGATION FUND.—

(1) DEFINITIONS.—In this subsection:

(A) COASTAL ZONE.—The term "coastal zone" has the meaning given the term in section 304 of the Coastal Zone Management Act of 1972 (16 U.S.C. 1453).

(B) ELIGIBLE ENTITY.—The term "eligible entity" means—

(i) a State;

(ii) a unit of local government;

(iii) an Indian Tribe;

(iv) a nongovernmental organization; and

(v) an institution of higher education.

(C) EXCLUSIVE ECONOMIC ZONE.—The term "Exclusive Economic Zone" means the Exclusive Economic Zone of the United States, as established by Presidential Proclamation 5030, dated March 10, 1983 (16 U.S.C. 1453 note).

(D) FOUNDATION.—The term "Foundation" means the National Fish and Wildlife Foundation established by section 2(a) of the National Fish and Wildlife Foundation Establishment Act (16 U.S.C. 3701(a)).

(E) FUND.—The term "Fund" means the Coastal Aquatic Invasive Species Mitigation Fund established by paragraph (3)(A).

(F) PROGRAM.—The term "Program" means the Coastal Aquatic Invasive Species Mitigation Grant Program established under paragraph (2)(A).

(G) SECRETARY.—The term "Secretary" means the Secretary of Commerce.

(2) GRANT PROGRAM.—

(A) ESTABLISHMENT.—The Secretary and the Foundation shall establish a program, to be known as the "Coastal Aquatic Invasive Species Mitigation Grant Program", under which the Secretary and the Foundation shall award grants to eligible entities in accordance with this paragraph.

(B) PURPOSES.—The purposes of the Program are—

(i) to improve the understanding, prevention, and mitigation of, and response to, aquatic invasive species in—

(I) the coastal zone; and

(II) the Exclusive Economic Zone;

(ii) to support the prevention and mitigation of impacts from aquatic invasive species in the coastal zone; and

(iii) to support the restoration of Pacific Island habitats, marine, estuarine, and Great Lakes environments in the coastal zone and the Exclusive Economic Zone that are impacted by aquatic invasive species.

(C) USE OF GRANTS.—

(i) IN GENERAL.—A grant awarded under the Program shall be used for an activity to carry out the purposes of the Program, including an activity—

(I) to develop and implement procedures and programs, including permissible State ballast water inspection programs, to prevent, detect, control, mitigate, and rapidly or progressively eradicate aquatic invasive species in the coastal zone or the Exclusive Economic Zone, particularly in areas with high numbers of established aquatic invasive species;

(II) to restore habitat impacted by an aquatic invasive species;

(III) to develop new shipboard and land-based ballast water treatment system technologies and performance standards to prevent the introduction of aquatic invasive species;

(IV) to develop mitigation measures to protect natural and cultural living resources, including shellfish, from the impacts of aquatic invasive species; or

(V) to develop mitigation measures to protect infrastructure, such as hydroelectric infrastructure, from aquatic invasive species.

(ii) PROHIBITION ON FUNDING LITIGATION.—A grant awarded under the Program may not be used to fund litigation in any matter.

(D) ADMINISTRATION.—Not later than 90 days after the date of enactment of this Act, the Foundation, in consultation with the Secretary, shall establish the following:

(i) Application and review procedures for awarding grants under the Program.

(ii) Approval procedures for awarding grants under the Program, including a requirement for consultation with—

(I) the Secretary of the Interior; and

(II) the Administrator.

(iii) Performance accountability and monitoring measures for activities funded by a grant awarded under the Program.

(iv) Procedures and methods to ensure accurate accounting and appropriate administration of grants awarded under the Program, including standards of recordkeeping.

(E) MATCHING REQUIREMENT.—Each eligible entity that receives a grant under the Program shall provide, in cash or through in-kind contributions from non-Federal sources, matching funds to carry out the activities funded by the grant in an amount equal to not less than 25 percent of the cost of the activities.

(F) FUNDING.—The Secretary and the Foundation are authorized to use the amounts available in the Fund to award grants under the Program.

(3) MITIGATION FUND.—

(A) ESTABLISHMENT.—There is established in the Treasury of the United States a trust fund, to be known as the "Coastal Aquatic Invasive Species Mitigation Fund", consisting of such amounts as are appropriated or credited to the Fund in accordance with this paragraph or section 9602 of the Internal Revenue Code of 1986.

(B) TRANSFERS TO FUND.—

(i) APPROPRIATION.—There is authorized to be appropriated from the Treasury to the Fund, for each fiscal year, an amount equal to the amount of penalties assessed for violations of subsection (p) of section 312 of the Federal Water Pollution Control Act (33 U.S.C. 1322) during the preceding fiscal year.

(ii) ADDITIONAL AUTHORIZATION.—In addition to the amounts transferred to the Fund under clause (i), there is authorized to be appropriated to the Fund

$5,000,000 for each fiscal year.

(C) USE OF FUND.—Subject to appropriations, the amounts in the Fund shall be available to the Secretary and the Foundation to award grants under the Program.

(g) [16 U.S.C. 4730] GREAT LAKES AND LAKE CHAMPLAIN INVASIVE SPECIES PROGRAM.—

(1) DEFINITIONS.—In this subsection:

(A) ADMINISTRATOR.—The term "Administrator" means the Administrator of the Environmental Protection Agency.

(B) AQUATIC NUISANCE SPECIES.—The term "aquatic nuisance species" has the meaning given that term in subsection (p)(1) of section 312 of the Federal Water Pollution Control Act (33 U.S.C. 1322).

(C) DIRECTOR.—The term "Director" means the Director of the Great Lakes National Program Office established by section 118(b) of the Federal Water Pollution Control Act (33 U.S.C. 1268(b)).

(D) GREAT LAKES AND LAKE CHAMPLAIN SYSTEMS.—The term "Great Lakes and Lake Champlain Systems" includes—

(i) Lake Champlain; and

(ii) all bodies of water (including wetlands) within—

(I) the Great Lakes System (as defined in section 118(a)(3) of the Federal Water Pollution Control Act (33 U.S.C. 1268(a)(3))); or

(II) the Lake Champlain drainage basin (as defined in section 120(g) of the Federal Water Pollution Control Act (33 U.S.C. 1270(g))).

(E) PROGRAM.—The term "Program" means the Great Lakes and Lake Champlain Invasive Species Program established under paragraph (2)(A).

(2) ESTABLISHMENT OF PROGRAM.—

(A) IN GENERAL.—The Administrator shall establish within the Great Lakes National Program Office a program, to be known as the "Great Lakes and Lake Champlain Invasive Species Program"—

(i) in collaboration with—

(I) the Director of the United States Fish and Wildlife Service;

(II) the Administrator of the National Oceanic and Atmospheric Administration;

(III) the Director of the United States Geological Survey; and

(IV) the Secretary of the department in which the Coast Guard is operating; and

(ii) in consultation with—

(I) the head of Great Lakes Aquatic Nonindigenous Species Information System of the National Oceanic and Atmospheric Administration; and

(II) the head of Great Lakes Environmental Research Laboratory of the National Oceanic and Atmospheric Administration.

(B) PURPOSES.—The purposes of the Program shall be—

(i) to monitor for the introduction and spread of aquatic nuisance species into or within the Great Lakes and Lake Champlain Systems;

(ii) to detect newly introduced aquatic nuisance species prior to the establishment of the aquatic nuisance species in the Great Lakes and Lake Champlain Systems;

(iii) to inform, and assist with, management and response actions to prevent or stop the establishment or spread of an aquatic nuisance species;

(iv) to establish a watch list of candidate aquatic nuisance species that may be introduced or spread, and that may survive and establish, within the Great Lakes and Lake Champlain Systems;

(v) to monitor vectors likely to be contributing to the introduction or spread of aquatic nuisance species, including ballast water operations;

(vi) to work collaboratively with the Federal, State, local, and Tribal agencies to develop criteria for prioritizing and distributing monitoring efforts;

(vii) to develop, achieve type approval for, and pilot shipboard or land-based ballast water management systems installed on, or available for use by, commercial vessels operating solely within the Great Lakes and Lake Champlain Systems to prevent the spread of aquatic nuisance species populations within the Great Lakes and Lake Champlain Systems; and

(viii) to facilitate meaningful Federal and State implementation of the regulatory framework in this subsection, including monitoring, shipboard education, inspection, and compliance conducted by States.

(3) METHODOLOGY.—The Program shall seek—

(A) to build on—

(i) existing aquatic nuisance species monitoring efforts; and

(ii) efforts to develop criteria for prioritizing and distributing monitoring efforts, geographically and among taxa, in the Great Lakes and Lake Champlain Systems;

(B) to advance early detection and monitoring, and capacity to control the establishment and spread, of aquatic nuisance species within the Great Lakes and Lake Champlain Systems;

(C) to identify opportunities to interdict the introduction and spread of aquatic nuisance species through sound science and technological advancements;

(D) to assess the risk of aquatic nuisance species introduction and spread via the range of vectors active within the Great Lakes and Lake Champlain Systems;

(E) to advance the development of type-approved ballast water management system (as defined in subsection (p)(1) of section 312 of the Federal Water Pollution Control Act (33 U.S.C. 1322) equipment for commercial, non-seagoing vessels that operate solely within the Great Lakes System (as defined in section 118(a)(3) of the Federal Water Pollution Control Act (33 U.S.C. 1268(a)(3)));

(F) to immediately make available to the public information regarding—

(i) the detection of new aquatic nuisance species within the Great Lakes and Lake Champlain Systems; or

(ii) the spread of aquatic nuisance species within the Great Lakes and Lake Champlain Systems;

(G) to annually submit to appropriate individuals and entities in each affected region a report describing the findings and activities of the Program;

(H) to identify roles and responsibilities of Federal agencies in aquatic nuisance species monitoring and response; and

(I) to provide resource assistance to States implementing State-level programs to enter into partnerships with Federal agencies in enforcing the requirements under subsection (p) of section 312 of the Federal Water Pollution Control Act (33 U.S.C. 1322).

(4) COLLABORATION.—In carrying out and developing the Program, the Director shall collaborate with—

(A) applicable Federal, State, local, and Tribal agencies; and

(B) such other research entities or stakeholders as the Director determines to be appropriate.

(5) DATA AVAILABILITY.—The Director shall—

(A) make the data collected under the Program available on a publicly accessible internet website, including in an annual summary report; and

(B) in coordination with the entities identified under paragraph (4), develop communication and notification protocols for the purpose of communicating the range of aquatic nuisance species and any identification of a new aquatic nuisance species introduced to the Great Lakes and Lake Champlain Systems.

(6) REPORT TO CONGRESS.—

(A) IN GENERAL.—Not later than December 31, 2019, the Director shall submit to Congress a report summarizing the outcomes of activities carried out under the Program.

(B) CONTENTS.—The report under subparagraph (A) shall include—

(i) a description of activities carried out under the Program, including an explanation of how those activities help to achieve the purposes described in paragraph (2)(B);

(ii) an analysis of Federal, State, and local efforts to enhance multidisciplinary approaches to achieve the purposes described in paragraph (2)(B);

(iii) recommendations relating to activities that would contribute to achievement of the purposes described in paragraph (2)(B); and

(iv) recommendations to improve the efficiency and effectiveness of the Program.

(7) AUTHORIZATION OF APPROPRIATIONS.—There is authorized to be appropriated to carry out the Program $50,000,000 for each of fiscal years 2019 through 2023.

(h) TECHNICAL AND CONFORMING AMENDMENTS.—

(1) Section 1102(f) of the Nonindigenous Aquatic Nuisance Prevention and Control Act of 1990 (16 U.S.C. 4712(f)) is amended by striking paragraph (2) and inserting the following:

"(2) BALLAST WATER REPORTING REQUIREMENTS.—

"(A) IN GENERAL.—The owner or operator of a vessel subject to this title shall submit to the National Ballast Information Clearinghouse, by not later than 6 hours after the arrival of the vessel at a United States port or place of destination, the ballast water management report form approved by the Office of Management and Budget numbered OMB 1625-0069 (or a successor form), unless the vessel is operating exclusively on a voyage between ports or places within contiguous portions of a single Captain of the Port Zone.

"(B) MULTIPLE DISCHARGES.—The owner or operator of a vessel subject to this title may submit a single report under subparagraph (A) for multiple ballast water discharges within a single port or place of destination during the same voyage.

"(C) ADVANCE REPORT TO STATES.—A State may require the owner or operator of a vessel subject to this title to submit directly to the State, or to an appropriate regional forum, a ballast water management report form—

"(i) not later than 24 hours prior to arrival at a United States port or place of destination in the State, if the voyage of the vessel is anticipated to exceed 24 hours; or

"(ii) before departing the port or place of departure, if the voyage of the vessel to the United States port or place of destination is not anticipated to exceed 24 hours.

"(3) VESSEL REPORTING DATA.—

"(A) DISSEMINATION TO STATES.—On receipt of a ballast water management report under paragraph (2), the National Ballast Information Clearinghouse shall—

"(i) in the case of a form submitted electronically, immediately disseminate the report to interested States; or

"(ii) in the case of a form submitted by means other than electronically, disseminate the report to interested States as soon as practicable.

"(B) AVAILABILITY TO PUBLIC.—Not later than 30 days after the date of receipt of a ballast water management report under paragraph (2), the National Ballast Information Clearinghouse shall make the data in the report fully and readily available to the public in a searchable and fully retrievable electronic format.

"(4) REPORT.—

"(A) IN GENERAL.—Not later than July 1, 2019, and annually thereafter, the Secretary shall prepare and submit a report in accordance with this paragraph.

"(B) CONTENTS.—Each report under this

paragraph shall synthesize and analyze the data described in paragraph (1) for the preceding 2-year period to evaluate nationwide status and trends relating to—

"(i) ballast water delivery and management; and

"(ii) invasions of aquatic nuisance species resulting from ballast water.

"(C) DEVELOPMENT.—The Secretary shall prepare each report under this paragraph in consultation and cooperation with—

"(i) the Task Force; and

"(ii) the Smithsonian Institution (acting through the Smithsonian Environmental Research Center).

"(D) SUBMISSION.—The Secretary shall—

"(i) submit each report under this paragraph to—

"(I) the Task Force;

"(II) the Committee on Commerce, Science, and Transportation of the Senate; and

"(III) the Committee on Transportation and Infrastructure of the House of Representatives; and

"(ii) make each report available to the public.

"(5) WORKING GROUP.—Not later than 1 year after the date of enactment of this paragraph, the Secretary shall establish a working group, including members from the National Ballast Information Clearinghouse and States with ballast water management programs, to establish a process for compiling and readily sharing Federal and State commercial vessel reporting and enforcement data regarding compliance with this Act."

(2) Section 1205 of the Nonindigenous Aquatic Nuisance Prevention and Control Act of 1990 (16 U.S.C. 4725) is amended—

(A) in the third sentence, by striking "Compliance" and

inserting the following:

"(c) EFFECT OF COMPLIANCE.—Compliance"

(B) in the second sentence, by striking "Nothing" and inserting the following:

"(b) EFFECT OF TITLE.—

"(1) IN GENERAL.—Except as provided in paragraph (2), nothing"

(C) in the first sentence, by striking "All actions" and inserting the following:

"(a) CONSISTENCY WITH ENVIRONMENTAL LAWS.—All actions"

; and

(D) in subsection (b) (as so designated), by adding at the end the following:

"(2) EXCEPTION.—Any discharge incidental to the normal operation of a vessel, including any discharge of ballast water (as those terms are defined in subsections (a) and (p)(1) of section 312 of the Federal Water Pollution Control Act (33 U.S.C. 1322)), shall be regulated in accordance with that section."

TITLE X—HYDROGRAPHIC SERVICES AND OTHER MATTERS

SEC. 1001. REAUTHORIZATION OF HYDROGRAPHIC SERVICES IMPROVEMENT ACT OF 1998.

(a) REAUTHORIZATIONS.—Section 306 of the Hydrographic Services Improvement Act of 1998 (33 U.S.C. 892d) is amended—

(1) in the matter before paragraph (1), by striking "There are" and inserting the following:

"(a) IN GENERAL.—There are"

(2) in subsection (a) (as designated by paragraph (1))—

(A) in paragraph (1), by striking "surveys—" and all that follows through the end of the paragraph and inserting "surveys, $70,814,000 for each of fiscal years 2019 through 2023.";

(B) in paragraph (2), by striking "vessels—" and all

that follows through the end of the paragraph and inserting "vessels, $25,000,000 for each of fiscal years 2019 through 2023.";

(C) in paragraph (3), by striking "Administration—" and all that follows through the end of the paragraph and inserting "Administration, $29,932,000 for each of fiscal years 2019 through 2023.";

(D) in paragraph (4), by striking "title—" and all that follows through the end of the paragraph and inserting "title, $26,800,000 for each of fiscal years 2019 through 2023."; and

(E) in paragraph (5), by striking "title—" and all that follows through the end of the paragraph and inserting "title, $30,564,000 for each of fiscal years 2019 through 2023."; and

(3) by adding at the end the following:

"(b) ARCTIC PROGRAMS.—Of the amount authorized by this section for each fiscal year—

"(1) $10,000,000 is authorized for use in the Arctic—

"(A) to acquire hydrographic data;

"(B) to provide hydrographic services;

"(C) to conduct coastal change analyses necessary to ensure safe navigation;

"(D) to improve the management of coastal change; and

"(E) to reduce risks of harm to subsistence and coastal communities associated with increased international maritime traffic; and

"(2) $2,000,000 is authorized for use to acquire hydrographic data and provide hydrographic services in the Arctic necessary to delineate the United States extended Continental Shelf."

(b) LIMITATION ON ADMINISTRATIVE EXPENSES FOR SURVEYS.—Section 306 of such Act (33 U.S.C. 892d) is further amended by adding at the end the following:

"(c) LIMITATION ON ADMINISTRATIVE EXPENSES FOR SURVEYS.—Of amounts authorized by this section for each fiscal year for contract hydrographic surveys, not more than 5 percent is authorized for administrative costs associated with contract management."

SEC. 1002. [33 U.S.C. 892 note] SYSTEM FOR TRACKING AND REPORTING ALL-INCLUSIVE COST OF HYDROGRAPHIC SURVEYS.

(a) IN GENERAL.—Not later than 1 year after the date of the enactment of this Act, the Secretary of Commerce shall—

(1) develop and implement a system to track and report the full cost to the Department of Commerce of hydrographic data collection, including costs relating to vessel acquisition, vessel repair, and administration of contracts to procure data;

(2) evaluate measures for comparing cost per unit effort in addition to measures of cost per nautical square mile; and

(3) submit to the Committee on Commerce, Science, and Transportation of the Senate and the Committee on Natural Resources of the House of Representatives a report on which additional measures for comparing cost per unit effort the Secretary intends to use and the rationale for such use.

(b) DEVELOPMENT OF STRATEGY FOR INCREASED CONTRACTING WITH NONGOVERNMENTAL ENTITIES FOR HYDROGRAPHIC DATA COLLECTION.—Not later than 180 days after the date on which the Secretary completes the activities required by subsection (a), the Secretary shall develop a strategy for how the National Oceanic and Atmospheric Administration will increase contracting with nongovernmental entities for hydrographic data collection in a manner that is consistent with the requirements of the Ocean and Coastal Mapping Integration Act (Public Law 111-11; 33 U.S.C. 3501 et seq.).

SEC. 1003. HOMEPORT OF CERTAIN RESEARCH VESSELS.

(a) ACCEPTANCE OF FUNDS AUTHORIZED.—The Secretary of Commerce may accept non-Federal funds for the purpose of the construction of a new port facility, including obtaining such cost estimates, designs, and permits as may be necessary to facilitate the homeporting of the R/V FAIRWEATHER in accordance with title II of the Departments of Commerce, Justice, and State, the Judiciary, and Related Agencies Appropriations Act, 2002 (Public Law 107-77; 115 Stat. 775) at a location that during such homeporting shall be under the administrative jurisdiction of the Under Secretary of Commerce for Oceans and Atmosphere.

(b) STRATEGIC PLAN REQUIRED.—Not later than 180 days after the date of the enactment of this Act, the Secretary shall develop and submit to the Committee on Commerce, Science, and Transportation of the Senate and the Committee on Natural Resources of the House of Representatives a strategic plan for implementing subsection (a).

(c) ACCEPTANCE OF FUNDS AUTHORIZED.—The Secretary may accept non-Federal funds for the purpose of the construction of a new port facility, including obtaining such cost estimates, designs, and permits as may be necessary to facilitate the homeporting of a new, existing, or reactivated research vessel in the city of St. Petersburg, Florida, at a location that during such homeporting shall be under the administrative jurisdiction of the Under Secretary of Commerce for Oceans and Atmosphere.

(d) STRATEGIC PLAN REQUIRED.—Not later than 180 days after the date of the enactment of this Act, the Secretary shall develop and submit to Congress a strategic plan for construction or acquisition of the facilities needed to allow for an oceanographic research vessel to be homeported in St. Petersburg, Florida. The strategic plan shall include an estimate of funding needed to construct such facilities.

www.ingramcontent.com/pod-product-compliance
Lightning Source LLC
Chambersburg PA
CBHW070046030426
42335CB00016B/1811
9781962978118